America's Foreign Policy in a Changing World

America's Foreign Policy in a Changing World

Frederick H. Hartmann

Robert L. Wendzel

■ HarperCollinsCollegePublishers

The views expressed in this book are entirely the authors' own. They do not necessarily reflect the official opinion of the Department of the Navy or the Department of the Air Force. Nor do they necessarily reflect the views of the Naval War College or the Air University, Air War College.

Acquisitions Editor: Maria Hartwell
Project Coordination and Text Design: Proof Positive/Farrowlyne Associates, Inc.
Cover Design: Kay Petronio
Production Manager: Kewal Sharma
Compositor: Black Dot Graphics
Printer and Binder: Malloy Lithographing, Inc.
Cover Printer: Malloy Lithographing, Inc.

America's Foreign Policy in a Changing World, First Edition

Copyright © 1994 by HarperCollins College Publishers

Library of Congress Cataloging-in-Publication Data

Hartmann, Frederick H.
    America's foreign policy in a changing world / Frederick H. Hartmann, Robert L. Wendzel.
        p.   cm.
    Includes index.
    ISBN 0-673-46874-7 (paperback)—ISBN 0-673-99247-0
    1. United States—Foreign relations—20th century.   2. United States—Foreign relations—Decision making.   I. Wendzel, Robert L., 1938– .   II. Title.
E744.H37 1994   93-21387
327.73--dc20   CIP

93 94 95 96 9 8 7 6 5 4 3 2 1

To Our Wives—
Reggie and Karen

Contents

Boxes

Maps

Diagrams

Preface

The study of American foreign policy can be approached from a number of perspectives. In *America's Foreign Policy in a Changing World,* we start from the proposition that policymaking always comes down to choices between opposing alternatives. Instead of focusing only on how policy is *made,* we also examine the actual content of policy and the effects that have stemmed from those choices. For not just how policy is made is important, but whether America prospers or suffers as a result. To assess the validity of U.S. assumptions and choices, we use a set of four cardinal principles. These four principles provide a pragmatic basis for understanding and judging what is decided. They shed light both on the making of foreign policy and on the nature of the international system to which policy is addressed. The four principles are *counterbalancing national interests, third-party influences, past-future linkages* and *conservation of enemies.*

Throughout *America's Foreign Policy in a Changing World,* our primary objective has been to use this simple and effective set of theoretical propositions as a strong organizational focus. Without such a guide, students will retain very little knowledge. With such propositions, however, the student is equipped with a way not only to understand the past and the present but also to use what he or she has learned as the future unfolds. The educational theory in this book has been class tested for years, and it works.

The experience of writing a dozen and more books and teaching hundreds of students over the years has taught us that professors and students need certain things in a textbook. We have already named one—a simple and usable theoretical framework. But a *clear and concise style* is just as important. So is the provision of enough *historical background* so that students gain a sense of perspective. Neither the world nor U.S. foreign policy began just a little while ago, and what we deal with now reflects what began some time before.

To these three objectives we have added a fourth: to *describe the international context* within which U.S. decisions have been made. Understanding the international relations environment is essential to avoid shallowness, especially the easily acquired idea that American policy is simply the result of some analysis in Washington influenced predominantly (or, even worse, exclusively) by internal political and/or bureaucratic concerns. The environment outside the United States plays an equal part in determining the range of feasible choice.

Our fifth objective has been to give a *balanced treatment of American foreign policy,* avoiding polemics. We have been more interested in showing cause and effect than making value judgments. At the time when a people are trying to decide hard problems, the choices between alternatives rarely appear simple, as some of the heated debates over policy show. The important point to grasp is that, no matter how far afield opposing arguments go when decisions have to be made, the decisions themselves always involve choosing between alternatives that move the United States toward or away from commitment or involvement. But we have not avoided making our own views known, once we have done justice to the arguments on either side of the issue.

Acknowledgements

We are both very appreciative of the painstaking and useful reviews of the manuscript by Professors Lynn Miller of Temple University, Herbert K. Tillema of the University of Missouri, and Timothy Lomperis of Duke University. They will see that we have made use of their suggestions and profited from their comments. We also want to thank Maria Hartwell, acquisitions editor at Harper-Collins, for guiding us through the preliminaries of publication, and to Gail Savage of Proof Positive/Farrowlyne Associates, Inc., who has taken us through production with good humor, excellent advice, and thorough attention to detail. Authors write books, but it takes all of the above to make a good one.

Frederick H. Hartmann
Robert L. Wendzel

About the Authors

Frederick H. Hartmann, Alfred Thayer Mahan Professor Emeritus at the U.S. Naval War College, Newport, Rhode Island, is a specialist in international relations, foreign policy, and national security affairs. He has taught at a number of institutions, including Princeton, Brown, Florida, Wheaton, Texas Tech, and the University of California, Berkeley. He has also held research appointments at the University of Bonn (Fulbright grant) and at the Hoover Institution, Stanford. Most recently he was visiting professor at Middle Eastern Technical University in Turkey. His dozen or so books include *The Conservation of Enemies, Germany Between East and West, World in Crisis, Defending America's Security* (coauthored with Robert L. Wendzel), *The U.S. Navy in the 1980s,* and *The Relations of Nations.*

Robert L. Wendzel is the educational advisor at the U.S. Air War College, Air University, Maxwell Air Force Base, Alabama. A frequent lecturer on national security matters and foreign policy, Wendzel has written four textbooks— *International Relations: A Policymaker Focus, International Politics: Policymakers and Policymaking, To Preserve the Republic: United States Foreign Policy* (with Frederick Hartmann), and *Defending America's Security* (with Hartmann), now in its second edition. Wendzel formerly was a professor of political science at the University of Maine and in 1987 was a member of the Council of Foreign Relations Study Group on Military Power Projection.

The strength of a political philosophy lies in the questions it does not have to answer. A nation's foreign policy, like its political philosophy, rests on faith and on assumptions—beliefs about the world, about the intentions of others, and about power and security—that are no more demonstrable than any other set of beliefs. One may attack the policy or argue its implausibilities, but as long as its proponents can hold the faith of the flock, the ideas remain unassailable. Once the keepers of the gate feel compelled to answer challenges, the days of the policy's eminence are numbered.

Thus runs the story of the containment doctrine, unassailable from 1947 to 1968, then suddenly vulnerable and on the defensive.

Leslie H. Gelb, *with Richard K. Betts*
The Irony of Vietnam: The System Worked
p. 181

America's
Foreign Policy in a
Changing World

Introduction

An Orientation to American Foreign Policy

All of us come to a new subject with ideas and images in our heads. This is especially true if the subject is one frequently discussed in the media, where information and misinformation can often appear side by side. Even when the information is correct it is often out of focus, its perspective all wrong. After all, facts and events do not carry their own self-evident meaning with them, neatly printed on a card. Either the reporter adds the interpretation, or we do. And those who have never served in any policy position in the U.S. government are the more easily led to interpretations that have subtle or obvious defects. That adds up to a situation where it is as important for a student to understand what is *not* true as to understand what *is* true about all the things one believes one already knows. Even more important, since no subject can be learned in a true sense without having an intellectual framework on which to hang the various facts, the perspective by which we approach such a study becomes critical.

1

Many contemporary political science analyses speak of independent and dependent variables, meaning essentially causes and effects. But in a world in which nation-states interact with international institutions such as a World Bank and a United Nations, it is extremely difficult to decide what is a cause and what is an effect in foreign policy. Even with a relatively focused interaction, with the United States arrayed against the Soviet Union in a Cold War, it is not easy—especially now that the Cold War is over and emotions have subsided—to explain why they spent many, many billions of dollars for defense against one another. A whole series of American presidents said it was because communism was an expansive and threatening ideology. The Soviets, though, argued that the Cold War stemmed from capitalism's innate hostility to communism. Psychologists tell us that the mirror-image effect is highly pertinent here: Each party is projecting onto the other its own feelings and fears. Each accuses the other of the same sins. What creates this sense of enmity?

Again, if the United States uses force to bring an end to Saddam Hussein's invasion of Kuwait, what caused the initial move by Saddam or the U.S. response? (Saddam would claim that *his* move was itself a response to other and prior causes). What was cause and what was effect when Hussein claims that Kuwait was really a province of Iraq, unjustifiably given separate status? Trying to decide on a first cause here takes us quickly back through the centuries. And, does it really affect the Israeli-Arab argument over Palestine, for example, if we know the first cause and the first effect? We are in a tangled net when we deal in this way with foreign policy. By contrast, it is usually clear how each of the nations involved saw the problem and its implications. It is usually clear what each actor considered to be its major alternatives. We probably can trace why each made the decision it did initially, rejecting one alternative and choosing another. In that rather limited and rather immediate sense, we can trace cause and effect.

Contemplating cause and effect is intriguing; examining the alternatives in an actual decision is more useful. Accordingly, we shall concentrate on the approaches taken to foreign policy issues, the kinds of alternatives considered, the justifications and arguments offered in defense of each alternative, and the results of those decisions.

This kind of approach uses generalizations that have proved useful and relevant in practice to analysts of foreign policy. It falls essentially into the realm of what James Rosenau called "pre-theory." He meant propositions that appear to be valid but have not yet been scientifically verified. (Actually, since history repeats itself only in a certain sense, it will probably never be possible to get really "scientific" about foreign policy.) As we proceed, though, bear in mind that *any* attempt to organize data is always in some degree a distortion from the real universe.

Every decision in foreign policy involves choosing between alternatives. But to make such a choice requires some assumptions about where each alternative will lead. These assumptions, so critical in the decision-making process, are distilled out of the national historical and sociological experience of a nation. That experience, telling them what is likely to come of a given choice, is usually expressed in a form of verbal shorthand, a few words summing up a whole series of complicated and interrelated thoughts. In American foreign policy such *shorthand formulas* or *guidelines* have played an enormously important role, especially "containment" and the "domino theory."

It is clear where such formulas and guidelines come from. Less evident is whether they give rise to correct predictions about the consequences that will follow once a choice of alternative is made. We shall look closely at how well the formulas Americans used depicted the problems faced at particular times, given the realities of the international system. In turn, to describe the realities of that international system, we shall define and use throughout this book four cardinal principles. These principles, as a "pre-theory," explain what is central to effective foreign policymaking, given the way the international system functions.

It should be apparent why some knowledge of America's background experience as a nation is necessary. The nation has a past, and that past influences the present. Knowing what Americans have done in the past and how Americans have tended to react to problems gives clues about what they will do now, allowing of course for the changing nature of problems.

The kind of shorthand formulas a people evolve to encapsulate more complicated reactions to ongoing events is one of the more distinctive offshoots of nationalism. Every nation in its view of the outside universe sees many events in the same general perspective, if only because they share a common planet. But they also evolve national-particular views, and these views play a very important role.

The kind of governmental institutions Americans created are also important to understand. These institutions differentiate the conduct of American foreign policy from that of other major nations in important respects. An example is the division of powers between the states and the federal government. Some years ago, when President Pompidou of France toured the United States, he was shocked by the extent to which police protection for foreign dignitaries in American cities was in the hands of (sometimes inefficient) local police forces. (Most foreign major powers have a national police force that is used for this purpose.) A second example is the separation of powers in the federal government itself, where the Senate has a separate and important voice in confirming the acceptability of a treaty negotiated on behalf of the U.S. president. In many other countries, that would simply not be possible. Soviet leaders, for instance, usually assumed that when one of our presidents told them that Congress would have to be consulted, he was really just stalling. Given these special ways of conducting official business in the United States as compared to many nations abroad, we must know something about how the American government actually functions and especially where that is unusual.

In considering the governmental "machinery" as it affects foreign policy, it is of limited utility to study only its formal structure. We must also see it in action, for much that happens will otherwise come as a surprise. The Gilbert and Sullivan line in "The Mikado" overstates it: "Things are seldom what they seem." Yet things are *often* not quite what they seem. Anyone who has ever worked at a policy level in the federal government knows that organization charts and formal structures mean only so much. The real power and decision-making may and often does occur outside those charts and is in the hands of people with quite innocent-sounding titles (or even no formal titles at all). During President Franklin Roosevelt's administrations, Harry Hopkins actually lived for some years in the family quarters in the White House. He was sent abroad as the eyes and ears of a polio-paralyzed president, to negotiate with Churchill and Stalin during World War II, even though Hopkins had little in the way of a title and held no formal position in the U.S. government at all. But everyone knew he had the ear of the president and that Roosevelt had enormous respect for Hopkins' recommendations.

On one occasion, Dean Acheson, one of our most urbane secretaries of state in modern times (in Truman's administration) said he had just been discussing the "machinery of government" with a prominent U.S. senator. "And do you know," said Acheson, "he really thinks it *is* machinery." Such an assumption, which implies that the role of personality counts far less than the formal powers that an office confers, would lead anyone far astray from the truth. Of the secretaries of state since World War II, only a few (Marshall, Acheson, Kissinger, and Baker in particular) stand out as exercising power in any creative sense. But in every such case, these secretaries were effective because they also kept the confidence of the president who appointed them.

Like anything else inside or outside government, the possession and exercise of power is partly a matter of intellect, partly a question of the vantage point occupied, partly a question of "old boy's network," and so on. Formal machinery plays a much more limited role than the beginning student might assume. Consider someone like Les Aspin, who in 1992 was the chairman of the House Armed Services Committee. Aspin was exercising enormous power in the U.S. government because he was a man with definite ideas and a forceful personality, while occupying a decision seat on the U.S. defense budget at a time when the most alluring "honey-pot" within Congress's domain was the about-to-be-reduced defense budget. Everyone had plans for spending the "peace dividend." And Aspin was in a position to hand out the perks on the one hand and to take away privilege on the other. His position also made him a natural candidate to be President Clinton's defense secretary.

Congress varies in its interest in foreign policy. So does the American public. Anyone who doubts this should compare March 1991, and the end of the Gulf War, with March 1992, when joblessness was high and foreign policy on the most remote of back burners. When there is no crisis, Congress, although it has become more assertive since Vietnam, still tends to let the president lead and decide—until or unless his leadership becomes quite controversial. Public opinion equally stays placid and permissive about foreign policy unless there is reason not to. That changes abruptly if the initial tolerance customarily accorded to presidential commitments (or lack of commitments, as in the years before World War II) seems to be working out very poorly. At that point the breakdown of a popular consensus launches a great debate (as occurred with the Vietnam War). So the process of making foreign policy decisions sometimes is highly presidential and sometimes includes lots of other elements in the American scene.

Thus the way in which American public opinion affects American foreign policy is very easily misunderstood. Walter Lippmann, a very much respected "pundit" in the middle of this century, once wrote a book on public opinion in which he made many sage comments. Lippmann was not under the illusion that public opinion was a thing in itself, something tangible—except in one sense. Public opinion can wield overwhelming force when it approaches unanimity. But that is because everyone is already converted. This is no play on words. It is very important to understand the distinction between thinking of public opinion as influencing inert legislators, toting up letters for and against, and the real life of those legislators. In real life the representative or senator has some very definite opinions on almost anything his or her constituents bother to write about. That does not mean the congressman will not take note of which way the mail is running. Nor does it mean that the congressman will necessarily vote according to the trend in the mail. But a successful politician making a career in Congress usually largely shares the feelings and attitudes of the opinion-forming, actively voting groups back home. That is why the congressman was elected in the first place. The exception occurs, of course, with highly emotional domestic issues like abortion, but only *if* the congressman's supporters largely split into two camps.[1]

Public opinion on foreign policy issues initially tends to support executive action, as does the Congress. (It may be hard to believe now, but there were very few voices heard against President Johnson's decision to commit the United States to an outright combat role in Vietnam in 1965.) It is only when policies encounter major difficulties or call for major commitments that serious divisions in opinion can occur and spark national debate. At that point, those in Congress who have to vote one way or the other will encounter lots of pressure from constituents who have become polarized into two opposing camps. No wonder the Congress in such circumstances is so long and so ineffective at bringing pressure on the president. And while the Congress, too, tends then to become polarized, an opposite trend tends to occur in the White House. There, those who oppose the president's policy or want it modified soon find themselves squeezed out. That tendency, too, by lessening the common ground between White House and Capitol Hill, complicates the problem of finding a way out of the difficulty. We shall see how all of this works out when we examine the Vietnam War.

In Part One of this book we begin with a case study of the Gulf War of 1991. In that foreign policy commitment, only a few crosscurrents showed up, particularly because it was a short and largely successful war. The value of an early discussion of this case study is that it shows something else of significance about foreign policy in a crisis: the intricate relationships between the problems the president faces abroad in coordinating an allied effort, and those he faces at home in juggling congressional sentiment, popular reaction, and media tone.

That chapter is followed by one introducing the terminology and concepts used consistently throughout this book. Part One, designed to provide a framework for the analysis of foreign policy, concludes with a succinct look at the formative experiences that shaped the American outlook before the United States became a major actor in its own right on the world stage.

Part Two examines the formulation and implementation of foreign policy from two standpoints: the intellectual element governing American attitudes and perceptions of problems, and the organizational element as it affects coordination across the government. Included is a discussion of the strategic and social uniqueness of the American historical experience and the effects of that experience on the American national character and outlook. Part Two also describes and analyzes America's rudimentary pre–World War II decision-making machinery, assesses decision making during World War II, and examines the steps taken toward more effective coordinating mechanisms after 1945.

Part Three shows how Washington functions to decide foreign policy issues, beginning with an overview of the relations between the White House and the Congress on Capitol Hill. That is followed by an analysis of the relationship between policymaking and the bureaucracy, including both the key departments and the National Security Council. Part Three concludes with an examination of the public context of foreign policy making, assessing the role and influence of public opinion, the mass media, and interest groups.

Part Four analyzes actual U.S. policy in the period of the Cold War, roughly from 1945 to 1991. Four major policy problems confronted successive presidents, from Truman through Bush. These four problems were not always equally urgent, but the first priority always was to provide worldwide deterrence against Soviet pressures and threats. Much of the time, that focus was on Europe. The second major problem, which to some extent overlaps the first, was the goal of ensuring a minimum stability in areas of great strategic interest to the United States, such as the Middle East with its oil. The third problem was centered on providing an adequate defense against threats, and the corollary of that problem—curbing an uncontrolled arms race, especially in strategic weapons. The fourth major problem concerned how to contribute to and encourage an environment in which economic, legal, and ecological issues could be resolved in ways that simultaneously advanced American interests as well as those of the world outside.

Although these major problems were the prime focus of U.S. policy for many decades, they preoccupied different presidents in different ways. As will become clear, Kennedy's name will forever be associated with the highly dramatic Cuban missile crisis (as well as with a connected threat to Berlin), just as Lyndon Johnson's name remains linked to the Vietnam War because he initiated the U.S. combat involvement there, while Richard Nixon is remembered above all for the "China card," which accompanied American disengagement from Vietnam. For readers who want to follow the specific development for any one of these major policy problems as such, each is clearly marked with subheadings in the text.

Part Five focuses on present and future foreign policy problems of the United States, highlighting eight major "decision areas." Most of these decision areas are geographical, though some are functional. Each is clearly marked in the text. But, unlike Part Four, where the four major problems are treated as they unfolded chronologically, here the chapters themselves take up the decision areas sequentially: occasionally two of them appear in a single chapter. For each major decision area, the problem is described as well as the issues it presents. This is accompanied by an analysis of the alternatives available for decision and, usually, a recommendation.

Unlike the years before World War I, or even before World War II, when U.S. policy involvements were so much more modest and confined, these policy issues today span a much greater range. As always, they include important issues of security (for mistakes there can have deadly consequences and make any progress with other problems irrelevant). The decline of the Soviet Union as a threat and the end of the Cold War have not ushered in a time when nations can shed the burden of military readiness. At the same time, the decrease in the international tension level changes great power relations. Japan, for example, is less reliant on U.S. deterrent power at the very time that conflicts over the two countries' trade policies are increasing. And the increase in regional conflicts and buildup of arms in many areas continues. So does terrorism.

All the recent changes have not made the problems that U.S. foreign policy confronts less difficult. The problems facing the country are much broader and far more extensive than merely security issues and many require international cooperation—broad issues such as dealing with the hole in the ozone layer, agreeing on uses of outer space, assisting the technical revolution in communications, rationalizing and improving the use of ocean fisheries in a world beginning to encounter limited food supplies, preventing and cleaning up ocean pollution, handling the refugee problem as millions flee their former homeland and create ethnic tensions in the process. These problems are all priority items today for U.S. foreign policy, along with the older security concerns.

We shall also examine the economic and financial institutions that America helped create to both expand world trade and increase its own ability to export. In that context, we shall look at the efforts of the United States to control its ballooning budget deficits as these affect trade and the value of the dollar as a trading unit. We shall look at oil and oil dependence, both for the United States and its allies. In a time of worldwide economic recession and decreasing military tension, these problems all bulk large. There are critical links here between the American political scene, U.S. foreign policy, and international circumstances.

To sum up, the book starts out with a framework of analysis and a clarification of terminology. It then looks at U.S. pre–World War II experiences and the way they affected American attitudes toward foreign policy problems. By 1945 the shift of the United States to a global role required changes in how the government functioned, and this focus concludes the second part. Then Part Three examines how the government in Washington functions to decide foreign policy issues. Part Four focuses on the evolution of the Cold War and the four major problems that dominated this almost half century. The book concludes in Part Five with an examination of the problems and issues in eight major decision areas that the United States will confront in the time ahead.

Notes

1. One of the authors was interviewing Senator John Warner of Virginia when Warner was about to cast a deciding vote on one of the most controversial Supreme Court nominations in recent years—that of Judge Robert Bork. Warner knew perfectly well that his vote would draw flak, and his secretaries were carefully screening which calls he would take over the telephone. Some he answered and others, not.

Part I

The Framework

Foreign Policy Decisions

A Beginning

American foreign policy, like that of any important nation, involves many hundreds of items and thousands of decisions, even in just one month's time. Both items and decisions are of varying importance. The most critical ones filter to the top, which means the White House. Of all the decisions made at that level, those few that seriously involve the potential or actual use of armed force are the most fateful ones. Such decisions about the use of force in the service of foreign policy are universally described as involving *vital interests,* meaning that their achievement or protection are so important that, if it is necessary, they are worth fighting for. Beginning with a recent example of this most important kind of foreign policy decision will focus attention on many of the relationships and considerations that will be elaborated in the chapters which follow.

The Persian Gulf Crisis I: Serious Involvement, or Not

On August 2, 1990, Iraq invaded its small neighbor Kuwait, quickly over-running it. That action, far away from American shores, immediately became the focus of intense scrutiny and analysis in Washington. American officials pondered on how to react. In this case, as with all serious foreign policy problems, the government faced a host of decisions. The first one was the most crucial. Would the United States become seriously involved, or not? Would it count itself in or out insofar as contesting or reversing Saddam Hussein's move was concerned? The choice between these two alternatives was stark and unavoidable. That choice would govern the lesser choices that would follow logically once the basic thrust was decided. Only if the United States opted in would questions of modalities or of how to succeed arise.

When assessing a threat situation prior to deciding on the best response, military leaders normally examine two factors: capabilities and intentions. There was no question that in terms of military capabilities, Iraq's military strength far exceeded that of the two countries many thought were next on its list of victims, Saudi Arabia and the United Arab Emirates. If Saddam intended to go further and conquer those countries and if no external forces intervened, he would be quickly successful.

But while the capability equation was quite clear, Saddam's intentions were not. There were three basic interpretations. First was the view that this was just the first step in an extended campaign of aggression. Saddam was seen as a kind of modern day Hitler. This view believed he also intended to attack Saudi Arabia, and eventually planned to control the entire Gulf and its oil. Such a strategy would enable him to control 70 percent of the world's known oil reserves. He then could dictate world oil prices, moving them up and down at whim, offering oil at below cost to his friends, and at extravagant prices to his enemies. Or, he could shut down the pipeline altogether now and again. Given his chemical weapon and embryonic nuclear capability, he could plow the enormous revenues into vastly greater military strength. At some point he would seek to eliminate Israel and dominate the entire Middle East. If he was not opposed, and opposed quickly—and successfully—further aggression inevitably would occur. This was the majority American view.

A second view was that Saddam's objectives were really quite limited and had already been achieved. He wanted to incorporate Kuwait into Iraq and "restore" Iraq to its rightful sovereignty over its "nineteenth province." And, he needed Kuwait's oil resources to remedy some of the economic problems Iraq had developed in its long war (1980–1988) with Iran. With the invasion, he already was in a position to achieve these goals and planned to go no further.

A third view was that while Saddam would have *liked* to have gone further, he had *no intention* of doing so. Iraq had a very unfavorable geopolitical situation. It had major potential adversaries, Syria and Iran, on both flanks. It had a strong potential enemy in Turkey to the north. And the Israelis, who were unlikely to permit a major expansion, were just over the horizon. Saddam well knew (in this view) that a major regional aggression on his part would provoke a countercoalition of forces that would be superior to his. Thus, he would stay where he was.

Because the administration held the first view, the initial objective that logically followed was to deter any further aggression. But there were other objectives also: to liberate Kuwait and to destroy Iraq's capability to continue as a significant regional military threat.

On August 7, President Bush, with Iraqi troops moving toward the Saudi frontier and with Saudi consent, ordered American land, sea, and air forces to Saudi Arabia to take up defensive positions. (Within six weeks that force had grown to almost a quarter-million.) On August 12, Bush ordered American forces to block all oil exports from Iraq and block all imports, except for some food shipments. Parallel to these moves, the United States pressed the U.N. for economic sanctions against Iraq, finding widespread support in that body. The first U.N. resolution in a series of them was passed on August 7. Bush, in his usual "reach out and touch someone" style, spent much time on the telephone, successfully coordinating policy with leaders around the world.

On August 24, U.S. reservists were put on alert, and 7,500 National Guard and reservists were called to active duty. In September, with world oil prices fluctuating wildly, Bush put five million barrels of oil from U.S. reserves on the market to discourage price increases that, already reaching a ten-year high, could trigger drastic inflation. To keep Congress informed of his thinking, on September 5 he met with thirty or so members of Congress at the White House.[1] On November 8, Bush ordered the American military buildup in the Persian Gulf area to increase to about 430,000. On November 29, the U.N. Security Council, by a 12–2 vote, authorized the use of military force unless the Iraqi forces withdrew from Kuwait by January 15, 1991.

Once the Security Council deadline passed, America would have to decide whether to actually use force or not. Although the affirmative vote in the U.N. to *permit* the use of force did not commit the United States to actually using force itself, political and ethical issues were now involved, as well as matters of credibility. There was also the constitutional question of the presidential authority to order troops into places where they might be engaged in fighting as against the congressional authority to declare war.[2] In a manner typical of presidents, President Bush believed he had the necessary authority as commander-in-chief to order U.S. forces into a deliberate attack on Iraqi forces. On December 4, however, Democrats in Congress voted 177–37 to request Bush to refrain from any military action against Iraq without prior approval of Congress, unless to "protect American lives from imminent endangerment." As the go–no-go decision time approached, the Congress had to stand up and be counted, Republicans as well as Democrats: Should the United States wait to see if sanctions would do the job, or should it use the force now assembled on the Kuwaiti frontier? War or peace?

Nowhere was the issue encapsulated more effectively than in the almost simultaneous comments of one present and one former secretary of defense, one in formal testimony, the other editorially. Appearing before the Senate Armed Services Committee in December 1990, Secretary of Defense Dick Cheney expressed skepticism that the U.N. sanctions against Iraq would work—at least, that they would work in time. Cheney's assessment was both hard-line and stark. He thought that Saddam Hussein's "brutality to his own people" and his complete control over the Iraqi economy would allow him to survive the effects of economic sanctions for one or even two years. He added, "There's no guarantee, given five years, that sanctions might force him out of Kuwait. Delay, I think, entails certain costs." Cheney had in mind the treatment of American hostages while the United States waited, plus the probable dissolution of the allied coalition against Saddam as time went on. Cheney thought that while America temporized, Saddam would "become an even better armed and more threatening regional superpower." Cheney's position was clear: "It is far better for us to deal with him now. . . ." (Senator Sam Nunn, chairman of the committee, asked Cheney how we would ever know if the sanctions would have worked if the United States went to war before it found out.)[3]

Caspar W. Weinberger, the preceding secretary of defense, weighed in with an article in *The New York Times*. He thought there should be no real confusion over why President Bush had sent troops to the Persian Gulf. "We are there to prevent a particularly brutal aggression that, if successful, would have badly crippled a large part of the world and left us subject to continual blackmail by one of the world's most miserable leaders." He added: "To say we are in the gulf only because of oil is to trivialize the great role we are playing." What America was really doing, though, was "protecting the world from continual blackmail and relieving it of the incalculable cost of clawing Hussein out of [these areas and thus] achieving complementary goals: preventing aggression from succeeding and from undermining the quality of life Americans and millions of others enjoy." However, Weinberger believed that none of this meant that the United States should resort to combat now. "I believe the economic sanctions, enforced by a tight air-and-sea blockade and supported by some 21 other countries . . . are succeeding. It will bring Iraq to its knees" if the United States was patient and persevered.[4]

When the whole Congress took up the issue, in literal form the resolutions voted up on did not exclude a vote now for sanctions and a later vote for force, if sanctions did not work. But in fact, it was "fish or cut bait" time. And Congress knew it. Each house of Congress responded to two alternative resolutions. The first of these, known in the Senate as the Mitchell-Nunn resolution and in the House as the Hamilton-Gephart resolution, emphasized the continued use of sanctions. (The House version left off a final paragraph that was included in the Senate version, to the effect that they did not rule out the use of force at a later time.) Both houses voted against.

The other resolution authorized the use of military force. It was introduced in the House by Stephen J. Solarz, Democrat, and Robert H. Michel, Republican; in the Senate by Bob Dole and John Warner, both Republicans. It was approved in the Senate, 52–47 (with 42 Republicans joined by 10 Democrats), and in the House by 250–183 (with 164 Republicans and 86 Democrats voting for and 179 Democrats, 3 Republicans, and 1 independent voting against).

The text of the resolution reads as follows:

> The President is authorized . . . to use United States Armed Forces pursuant to United Nations Security Council Resolution 678. . . .
>
> Before exercising [this] authority, the President shall make available to the Speaker of the House of Representatives and the President pro tempore of the Senate his determination that:
>
> (a) The United States has used all appropriate diplomatic and other peaceful means to obtain compliance . . . and
>
> (b) That those efforts have not been and would not be successful in obtaining such compliance.

The U.N. deadline expired at midnight, Eastern Standard Time, January 15. The weather being right, President Bush ordered the attack to begin on January 16.

President Bush, on television that evening, explained why he had acted and what he expected to achieve. After recounting failed efforts at a peaceful solution, he said: "We are determined to knock out Saddam Hussein's nuclear bomb potential. We will also destroy his chemical weapons facilities. Much of Saddam's artillery and tanks will be destroyed." He added: "Our objectives are clear. Saddam Hussein's forces will leave Kuwait. The legitimate government of Kuwait will be restored. . . ." As to sanctions, while they had had some effect, Bush had concluded that "they showed no sign of accomplishing their objective . . . and we and our allies concluded that sanctions alone would not force Saddam from Kuwait." Bush went on:

> While the world waited Saddam Hussein systematically raped, pillaged and plundered a tiny nation—no threat to his own. . . . And while the world waited, while the world talked peace and withdrawal Saddam Hussein dug in and moved massive forces into Kuwait. While the world waited, while Saddam stalled, more damage was being done to the fragile economies of the Third World, the emerging democracies of Eastern Europe, to the entire world, including to our own economy.[5]

A short but intense public debate followed. Some quickly broke out American flags, holding rallies in support of the troops. On Martin Luther King day some groups tried to draw a line between supporting the troops and supporting the war—a position rather difficult to sustain. Some student demonstrations also tended to oppose an American commitment. Most interesting of all, many who had been against the war in Vietnam assumed that this was Act II in the same American play, complete with the same problems and inevitable failure. They saw no strategic difference between the two areas. In front of the White House, other protesters appeared with banners with slogans like "NO BLOOD FOR OIL." The implication was that the war's purpose would be to protect U.S. supplies of imported gasoline so that Americans would not have to cut back on the use of their cars. This last reaction reduced a complicated policy question to one oversimplified issue, one that in particular ignored the strategic aspects of the problem and left unexplored the probable consequences of inaction.

President Bush had concentrated his own arguments on the moral aspect (aggression must not go unpunished, a large nation had invaded a small one and was brutally despoiling it). He spoke of the American action as the beginning of a new world order in which the weak would no longer be prey to the strong, implying that this one action by the United States would have a lasting effect on future world history.

Persian Gulf Crisis II: War and Aftermath

Since the administration believed economics would not work and diplomacy was out, force was necessary.[6] On January 16, 1991 the bombing began.[7] Utilizing a well thought out strategic air campaign plan, extraordinarily effective air strikes were launched against Iraq's command and control capabilities, key productive assets (especially electricity), and the nation's infrastructure.[8] Before the first week was over more than 8,000 missions had been flown. Led by the precision bombing of advanced weapons such as the F-117 Stealth Fighter, the battlefield soon was cut off and Hussein's communications abilities destroyed. Hussein was "blind, deaf, and dumb," unable to know what was going on or command and control his forces. By mid-February many of his units in occupied Kuwait, *literally* were hardly able to subsist. Needless to say, their combat capability was minimal.

In mid-February as an allied ground assault appeared increasingly imminent, Hussein offered to withdraw. But he coupled his offer to ten conditions, including a settlement of the Palestine question, a demand that the U.N. abrogate 11 of its 12 resolutions on Kuwait, and the cancellation of all sanctions. The United States and its Allies decided to reject his offer out of hand. On February 18 Mikhail Gorbachev proposed a Soviet peace plan. But that, too, was rejected. It failed to hold Iraq responsible for reparations and provided for a two-day pause between cease-fire and withdrawal. This would have allowed resupply to Iraqi forces and permitted Saddam's armor and artillery to escape.

On February 24, at 4:00 A.M. Iraqi time, the ground offensive, what Saddam had said would be the "mother of all battles," began. General Norman Schwarzkopf, Command in Chief of the U.S. Central Command, for months had concentrated his troops in positions across from the Iraqis dug-in on the Kuwaiti-Saudi border. But on February 23 (U.S. time) a massive lightning shift to the west was completed (soon dubbed both the "Hail Mary" or "left hook"). A gigantic encirclement operation followed. Because of the intensive air campaign, the Iraqis did not discover these movements until much too late. (Nor could they have communicated or coordinated their efforts even if they had.) Simultaneously, enough allied air and ground forces attacked frontally to hold

the Iraqis in position, while an enormous logistics resupply effort to the encircling forces occurred.

By Monday and Tuesday the encircling maneuver in the west was well advanced. Soon the Iraqis in Kuwait were entirely cut off and unable to fight effectively. By Wednesday night the war was over. The ground offensive had taken
exactly one hundred hours from start to finish. On March 2 the U.N. Security
Council, by a vote of 11 of the 15 members (with India, China, and Yemen abstaining, and Cuba against) passed a new resolution designed to convert the temporary cease-fire into a permanent end to hostilities. Iraq was required to rescind
its annexation of Kuwait, return all POWs and abducted Kuwaitis, accept lia-
bility under international law for all it had done, and help rebuild Kuwait.

The decisive action of the United States, Bush's skill at holding an amaz-
ingly diverse coalition together, his ability to keep Israel on the sidelines (even
with the Scud missile attacks against it), his prudent decision to choose a clear
and firm military objective and allow the military the freedom to achieve it—all
this contributed to an overwhelming allied victory at a cost of less than 150
Americans killed in action, with total Allied dead less than 200.

As always, though, there were alternatives to the course chosen. One alternative argued against the lead role played by the United States, especially before hostilities had begun. But Bush subscribed fully to the traditional American
view that the United States had to be the leader in maintaining the peace. The
situation had presented both an obligation and an opportunity. And there is little doubt that without the decisive and early lead role by the United States the
political/economic coalition and the successful diplomatic maneuvers at the U.N.
probably would not have happened. Saddam might even have held on to Kuwait.
Even if war would have occurred, it *certainly* would have gone differently.

Another key decision for the president was when and how to terminate
hostilities. In the aftermath, Bush was heavily criticized for not having "finished
the job." Saddam Hussein was still in power in Baghdad. As U.N. inspection
teams, despite Iraqi noncooperation, discovered the startling dimensions of the
Iraqi nuclear effort, these criticisms redoubled. Bush was also under pressure
from another direction. The sanctions were kept in effect. Although Iraq was
permitted to sell some oil and use it for purchases that would relieve civilian suffering inside Iraq, women and children there were in obvious distress. Humanitarian groups were protesting, both in America and elsewhere. Yet the sanctions
were a vital part of Bush's program to keep the pressure on Saddam.

Was Bush's decision not to take over all of Iraq wise? Consider the alternative. Since we know which he chose, let us consider what he might have done
instead. Suppose U.S. forces had taken over Iraq much as the allies did in Germany in 1945. America would have found itself responsible in the most direct
sense for the well-being of the population at the time when the industrial and
communications infrastructure of the country had been destroyed. The United
States would be in occupation of a country in an area of the world with much
anti-Western sentiment built-in. America would have had to maintain a very
substantial armed force there, probably for a number of years. There was no

democratic successor waiting in the wings, and prolonged occupation would increase anti-American (anti-foreign) sentiment in the region. The demands on the overstrained national budget would have been severe. The picture is not an attractive one.

It is clear that many of the critics did not really take these factors into account, or at least did not give them much weight. That is to say, with the negative side of the alternative actually chosen so clearly apparent, they ignore or downplay the negative side of the "shelved" alternative, supposing that the positive side (getting rid of Saddam) is really all that counts.[9] Yet, as this book will consistently argue, every set of alternatives has *four* values, two on *each* side. To ignore any of the four is unwise.

The Differences Between America's Wars

It is true, whether we like it or not, that decisions concerning the possibility or actuality of war are the most critical in foreign policy, for a simple reason: War is a game of hazard in which all can be lost. Deciding that something is worth fighting for (that it is a *vital interest*) exceeds in importance everything else that the government does. We should not be surprised, therefore, that any competent analysis of American foreign policy must have a good deal in it about conflict as well as cooperation with other states.

If we focus on three wars the United States has fought *since* World War II, we are struck by the variety of results. Korea (1950–53) ended in what many people considered a stalemate, a draw. Vietnam, the American part of which ended in 1973, finished as a definite defeat. The Persian Gulf War was a triumph as a military operation. The contrast is especially startling between Vietnam and the Persian Gulf. Although even today there is no consensus in the United States as to what went wrong in Vietnam, very few Americans consider that much went right with it. But the end of the Persian Gulf War was greeted by a kind of euphoria. President Bush announced that the Vietnam syndrome had been laid to rest. Yet the official rationales for U.S. intervention and participation in these two disputes had a disturbing similarity. In both Americans were "resisting aggression." In both Americans were insisting on "the rule of law." In both Americans stood for "the freedom of people to choose their own form of government free from outside coercion." What then accounted for the difference in results?

Besides the obvious difference in geographical area for the two conflicts, one in the Far East, one in the Middle East, it made a great deal of difference that in the case of Vietnam the United States was defending a government still functioning in the areas where war was being waged. In the Persian Gulf operation, Kuwait had already been subjugated and its government was in exile in Saudi Arabia. The circumstances in the Gulf War therefore made for a much simpler problem in two respects: There was no complicated chain of command in which American forces were subject to a foreign authority, at least for liaison purposes, in the actual theater of operations. And the enemy forces were much more clearly defined in the Persian Gulf. Vietnam had many elements of a civil war, even if the United States officially termed it the result of North Vietnamese aggression. In the Persian Gulf, the enemy was the Iraqi army and the whole affair could follow much more conventional military operational lines. There was even a "front line" on the Kuwait-Saudi border rather than the murky situation in Vietnam, where the allegiance of any village nominally in a secured area could not be relied upon. In the Vietnam case, especially since the war went on so long, troops—and, especially, officers—were rotated. That meant that the forces in the field were often under inexperienced guidance. Not so in the Persian Gulf.

Perhaps the feature that military analysts would point to as critical (in a negative sense) was that in the Vietnam conflict, the president routinely picked bombing targets, and the war was fought with savage bombing followed by pauses, in an on-and-off manner. In the Gulf, the military commanders were given the green light to do the job in the most efficient way open to them (and they operated very effectively).

None of these observations go, though, to the "big picture"—the contrast in the strategic framework in which the two conflicts were fought. For Vietnam was fought on China's southern flank. That raised the ever-present possibility that China might intervene, perhaps along with the Soviet Union. That would turn what in Pentagon jargon was officially a "1/2 war" (a "minor" war) into something very major indeed. In the Persian Gulf case, both superpowers were in agreement that Iraq must surrender its conquest, and China did not oppose.

But even that does not get to the heart of things. There were two serious problems with the Vietnam War, as we shall see in more detail later. First, the Vietnam conflict inhibited the development of the Sino-Soviet split by imposing prudence on China, given China's concern about the possibility of war with America. Since for several decades America had perceived itself as confronted by a "Communist bloc," that split would be very beneficial. Second, the Vietnam War was fought in an area of the world of little importance in any geopolitical or strategic sense. Observe how indifferent the United States is today to the fact that the Vietnamese Communists control the entire country. Contrast this with the significance of the Persian Gulf, where a great part of the oil reserves of the whole world are concentrated. Add to that the fact that in geopolitical terms the Middle East has been for at least the last four thousand years perhaps the most strategic (and most fought-over) area in the whole world. It is the communication and transportation link between three continents. The majority of the great empires in our historical memory arose and flourished there. Three of the great world religions had their birth there. Who could write off the Middle East as of little concern to the United States?

Of the conflicts in both areas, one could say that the rule of law was in question, that aggression must not prosper. But of only one of these situations could one say that its outcome might well affect the global balance of power and the future and well-being of countless people around the globe. In the Vietnam case, moral (or moralizing) slogans accompanied the American effort, but they could not turn that area into one really worthy of the shedding of much American blood. What determines the viability of that cost is how the future will unfold, given such an American sacrifice or without such a sacrifice.

Any decision for or against serious involvement has to be made with incomplete knowledge and many assumptions that may turn out to be either true or false. But these ambiguities, built into every major decision, although they may justify pity for mistakes, will not lessen the penalties if mistakes are made when peering into the future's crystal ball. Without accurate estimates, foreign policy stumbles from one problem to the next. Estimating the future accurately, on the other hand, allows a nation to pursue a prudent, successful, and cost-effective foreign policy. The ability to peer into the future and make sound judgments about where alternative courses of action will lead is the most critical component of a successful foreign policy.

There Is More to It

We have started with an example which shows a president in a situation where his ability to act is largest. If we leave the analysis at that point, we can make two mistakes: we can give the impression that deciding whether or not to go to war is about all there really is to foreign policy, or that such decisions have occurred very rarely in the American experience. Take the second point first. In the half century between 1941 and 1991 alone, the United States fought four wars (or six, if we count Grenada and Panama). For at least fifteen out of fifty of these years, U.S. troops were in combat. That is 30 percent or more of the total time. That image does not fit the one Americans have that says war is an aberration and Americans are a very peace-loving people. Peace-loving Americans may be, but they are also warlike when aroused or when the occasion seems to warrant it.

But foreign policy is not just about wars—it involves all official relations with other nations. It covers a very broad gamut indeed, much of it centered upon adjusting and coordinating American affairs with foreign nations to the mutual benefit of all. In this context, the president's role, while still very important, has to be seen in a somewhat different perspective.

This perspective leads to our other point. If we took the Persian Gulf War as is, without further discussion, we would severely overstate both the president's powers in general and the degree of consensus prevalent over many foreign policy issues.

What we learned in our first school years is still true. The United States has a system of checks and balances, plus a division and sharing of powers. The Founding Fathers, having successfully resisted what they denounced as the arbitrary rule of London over the colonies, were determined to create a government that would not develop the same features. Being neo-classicists in the Greek tradition—Washington, D.C. is full of pseudo-Grecian temples—they set out to achieve the Greek ideal of "moderation in all things." No one caught that point of view more accurately than James Madison, in Number 51 of *The Federalist Papers*.

Ambition must be made to counteract ambition. . . . It may be a reflection on human nature, that such devices should be necessary to control the abuses of government. But what is government itself, but the greatest of all reflections on human nature? If men were angels, no government would be necessary. If angels were to govern men, neither external nor internal controls on government would be necessary.[10]

The Founding Fathers were steadfast in their conviction, to quote Lord Acton's famous maxim, that "power corrupts, and absolute power corrupts absolutely." For an executive there would be neither what one president not too long ago called "an imperiled presidency" nor what critics charged when Richard Nixon was in the White House—that we had an "Imperial presidency." As a goal, the Founding Fathers set out to establish a governmental system that could not operate effectively without a great deal of consensus, a system in which no one of the three branches of government would be supreme. Rather, each would be preeminent in its own area: Congress with money and legislation, the Supreme Court with interpreting laws and settling disputes, and the President as Commander-in-Chief and principal director for foreign affairs.[11] Each branch would be preeminent, not supreme.

In the years since the American experiment in government began, many well-informed observers of the American political system have pointed out that most presidents are more comfortable with foreign policy than with domestic issues. The events that preceded the Gulf War illustrate the main reason why this is so. In foreign affairs the president can much more effectively shape policy, while the Congress normally reacts to his initiatives rather than itself trying to steer the ship of state.[12] The president's powers are even more substantial in his role as commander-in-chief. We saw that on his own say-so he moved a half-million men to Saudi Arabia. Just the symbolism of that move had a powerful impact on public opinion and, as we said above, if Congress opposes, it will cut off funds only as a last resort. Instead, it will pass a resolution which states its opposition and which is, in effect, an appeal for popular support against the president. In fact, even to speak of Congress having "its" view means that hundreds of members of that body have been able to agree on a single statement. That is not easy, whatever the subject.

What you see, of course, depends in large part on where you are standing. The view from Capitol Hill and the halls of Congress is not the same as the view from the White House or its Rose Garden. Many presidents in their memoirs have argued that they have very limited powers, in any sphere. They have said that the president mainly must persuade if he wants to be able to lead. He can't just order things done. Harry Truman, for instance, thought that when Dwight Eisenhower, with his military background, arrived at the White House and began to issue orders, he would be astonished at how little would happen. (Eisenhower did not prove quite so naive.)

Many Americans, knowing that the Constitution proclaims the president as commander-in-chief, overestimate presidential powers. They do not fully appreciate how the roles and powers of Congress (and sometimes the courts) limit what the president can do. Professional military officers are particularly so inclined. We see some of this in the Iran-Contra case. Because President Reagan wanted to assist the Contras in Nicaragua, his national security adviser (who was an admiral) and a member of his staff (the well-known Lieutenant Colonel Oliver North) felt that they should diligently seek to implement his wishes, even though the Congress had prohibited certain kinds of assistance. On the other hand, Admiral Tom Moorer, former chairman of the Joint Chiefs, in speaking about fears current in 1973–74 that Nixon would try a military coup rather than resign, scoffed. He said he picked up a newspaper whose headlines read "Nixon to order 82nd Airborne to Washington to capture Congress." "As if," said Moorer, "Erlichman [Nixon's right-hand man] could pick up a phone and call the general down there" and simply tell him to move. "It takes 25 messages at least to get the 82nd Airborne going—the airplanes are out in Kentucky and some of their forces are out in the field, and so on. So it's ridiculous, you know, because the first thing that general would do is pick up the phone and call the Chairman of the Joint Chiefs of Staff and say, 'What the hell is going on here?' "[13]

Moorer's statement is a good image of the other side of the picture.

What about public opinion? Does the president listen? People writing letters to the White House receive back canned acknowledgments of their interest, with a few paragraphs reiterating the president's position. Should they conclude that he is not really interested and that he goes on doing whatever he wants to? While it has long been recognized that the public often is not very interested in foreign policy matters and may not hold a single coherent view, it also is clear that when a president takes strong action his stock rises (even if he is unsuccessful).[14] He knows, too, that the public can set boundaries or, as in Vietnam, can even compel a policy change. It is no accident that the White House staff dotes on public opinion polls. (We know that Lyndon Johnson actually kept three television sets side by side in his office, each one tuned to the news programs of the major networks.)

So, where is the center of gravity in these rather conflicting statements and approaches?

One important thing to remember is that domestic politics and foreign policy politics are two quite different things. When the president gives his annual State of the Union address to Congress, he lists many things in the domestic area that he would like to see happen. Rarely are many of these actually enacted into law, especially if the opposition party controls either or both houses of Congress. President Bush, on his birthday in 1991, complained that Congress had failed to enact his two most urgent legislative proposals within the hundred-day deadline he had set.

It can be quite different with foreign affairs, especially since the president *on his own* can set so many things into motion and put the Congress on a spot where infinite delay in tackling the problem is not feasible because doing so would expose the country to obvious dangers or difficulties. President Kennedy, early in his term, once said that the difference for a president between being defeated in domestic affairs or defeated in foreign affairs was substantial: "The big difference is between a bill being defeated and the country being wiped out."[15]

A More Balanced View

Probably the main source of confusion in understanding the policymaking process comes simply from looking at our government too mechanically. It is "divided" into three branches, yes. And the different and shared powers, responsibilities, and opportunities inherent in the system are important. But what often receives inadequate emphasis is the fact that the people in all three branches are Americans, with an American set of values and attitudes. With the trauma of Vietnam and the divisions that have wracked the United States in recent years still fresh in everyone's mind, it is easy to overlook the extent to which Americans do share common approaches to problems, regardless of whether they want different solutions. The common attitudes or approaches do not mean that every American will view any event abroad in identical terms, but they do provide a common frame of reference through which events will be judged. The desired goals tend to be common, even when the means to reach them remain controversial. To argue that this is not so is to reject the most fundamental effects of American nationalism.

If events like Kuwait or Pearl Harbor require an almost immediate choice of alternatives, non-crisis foreign policy decisions can be made with greater leisure, in a sequence of iterations as the problem unfolds. Yet the greater leisure disguises the fact that here, too, the ultimate, decisive question is whether to do it or not. The United States may ponder whether to give aid to Latin American nations, and, if so, whether it should be in the form of U.S. government guaranteed loans or more Peace Corps experts. Perhaps it would be best to dispatch agricultural experts to assist. Or would it be still better to offer increased training to the police forces there, to help stamp out corruption? Perhaps all of it ought to be done?

But this whole range of alternatives still has an underlying and implicit question that is fundamental: does the United States wish to get involved in any serious action in Latin America now at all? The answer has to be yes or no. It may be delayed by tentatively trying out steps easy to abandon later, but the very fact of acting ultimately makes answering this question inescapable. If this fact is not obvious at the outset, it will become so. Think of the situation like a funnel: what is poured into it ultimately has to pass through its narrow outlet. The difference between this kind of "progressive" situation and one in which a full-blown crisis occurs abroad at 4 A.M. is that in the second case the narrowness of the American choices tends to become apparent more quickly—we start out right at the outlet at the bottom of the funnel. The United States can either turn aside or be involved. In cases such as the Cuban missile crisis, which we shall examine later, the officials see the threat in common terms and the choices quickly focus on a subordinate question: what means can government use to effect the chosen alternative? The most important foreign affairs problems, in short, demand a choice on commitment, followed by a choice of modalities.

Although we have spoken of common American attitudes, there is not, of course, just one prevailing American attitude. Foreign policy debates therefore often take the form of arguments over which prevailing attitude is correct. We shall see this in Chapter 2, with the famous American flyer, Colonel Lindbergh, arguing for "going it alone" while President Roosevelt argued the wisdom instead of "lending our neighbor our garden hose" to put out the fire of Nazi aggression. If Americans want both peace and security, which abstract attitude provides better guidance in a specific case? Americans can want both peace and security as abstractly desirable conditions, but when an event like Saddam Hussein's invasion of Kuwait takes place, they find they have to choose one or the other.

As a general rule, the degree of popular consensus is linked to the starkness of the event, like a Pearl Harbor attack. Presidents acting in such cases can count on the response. They will be supported. Where the situation is more debatable, but the president feels strongly about it he can still *initiate* an action. And he will probably find himself supported, at least initially, because the American public wants the president to be decisive. Over the longer run, though, he needs continued backing from both the Congress and the general population and whether he gets it depends on the quality of the judgment he made. Because the members of the House of Representatives are elected for only two-year terms, they are forever running for reelection even as they take their seats the first day in Congress. As we pointed out earlier, we can be quite sure that Congress—especially the lower house—will be a fairly accurate indicator in microcosm of the range of feelings and views and hopes and fears of the general public at any moment in time.

The president, in his role as initiator of foreign policy and supplemented by his authority as commander-in-chief, has enormous potential power. That power will grow or decline as the American people react to the unfolding of the events which follow his decisions and his actions.

In addition to the constraints imposed by the domestic context and the nature of the American political system, a second major factor affecting the success of the president's policy is how well the policy fits with the reactions of other nations. If President Bush's decisions had not been acceptable, for example, to many nations of the Middle East, very little could have been done about Saddam Hussein, even if the United States was ready to use military force.

Consequently, the president can initiate; he will get support if his decision fits American attitudes, and he will need continued congressional and public backing as events unfold. To accomplish this, his initiative must be showing some plausible signs of being able to succeed. And to succeed, his initiative must take into account the interests and reactions of other nations, given the particular circumstances. Therefore—and this is the real point—a student of foreign affairs has to free himself or herself from a merely mechanical approach to American government, with a bureaucratic emphasis largely confined to what America decides to do. To understand American foreign affairs, we must look much more widely at both U.S. and foreign behavior, especially looking critically at how American attitudes have developed over the decades of national experience. We must also look at where these attitudes depart from the universal and are specifically or nationally-particular American. For that will influence what happens to U.S. policy once it is set in motion.

Leslie H. Gelb, writing in *The New York Times,* speaks to certain national-particular American attitudes toward foreign policy questions.

> Americans transform every success and every failure in foreign affairs into a policy doctrine and a political cudgel. We refuse to rest until we possess one lens through which to view the world and one answer for all challenges. We are forever brushing off small but important lessons in the quest for great and single truths.
>
> Ours is a short and tumultuous history of taking large unique events—the fall of Eastern Europe and China to Communism, the Korean War, the Cuban missile crisis and Vietnam—and elevating their purported lessons into policy dogmas, be they Truman Doctrines, Kennedy Corollaries or Vietnam Syndromes.[16]

Granted that this tendency is multiplied and exaggerated in the United States because the media love to simplify and give tags to events, what Gelb says needs pondering. We could add to his list the domino theory, which played so great a role in taking us into the Vietnam War.

Gelb correctly describes the contemporary period, as we shall see. But it was not always so, and all of the policy dogmas he names date from after World War II, from after 1945. He raises a significant issue, one to which we shall return in Part Two. The rest of Part One will be concerned with concepts and terminology essential to an informed discussion of foreign policy and its interaction with the world of states outside our frontiers, followed by a succinct review of the major foreign policy developments from President Washington to the outbreak of World War II.

Notes

1. Bush and his inner circle also met with key congressmen and senators on several occasions. See Bob Woodward, *The Commanders* (New York: Simon & Schuster, 1991), Ch. 19ff. Certain details in the Woodward book are inaccurate: General Colin Powell did not differ with President Bush on halting the fighting, for example. But there seems little doubt that Woodward has captured their essence and general tenor.

2. Since about the middle of the Vietnam War, this has been a very controversial issue. In 1973 Congress passed a "War Powers Resolution" over President Nixon's veto. It deals directly with the introduction of United States forces "into hostilities, or into situations where imminent involvement in hostilities is clearly indicated . . ." It specifies certain presidential-congressional powers, obligations, relationships, and procedures in that connection. But it was not utilized here in the Gulf War situation. We discuss the Resolution further in Chapter 6.

3. Nunn's comment raises a fundamental question, which we shall consider in some depth in Chapter 2: the dilemma of deciding *now* without knowing what the consequences will be.

4. Weinberger is not opposing a *later* use of force. Several other well-respected authori-

ties advocated patience, including Admiral William J. Crowe, the immediate predecessor of General Colin Powell as Chairman of the Joint Chiefs of Staff.

5. *The New York Times,* January 17, 1991.

6. For a thoughtful and quite different view not only of sanctions but of American policy generally—including its objectives, the use of force, and relations with Israel—see Robert W. Tucker and David C. Hendrickson, *The Imperial Temptation: The New World Order and America's Purpose* (New York: Council on Foreign Relations Press, 1992), Chs. 5–14.

7. One of the best accounts of the military features of the Gulf War is Norman Friedman, *Desert Victory: The War for Kuwait* (Annapolis, MD: Naval Institute Press, 1991). His appendices alone are over a hundred pages long, listing such items as air units involved, naval forces used, Scud attacks, and so on.

8. "With roughly 1% of the bombs dropped in 11 years in Vietnam, allied air assets shut down Iraq's gasoline production, electricity, transportation, communications, ability to produce offensive weapons, and ability to defend against air attack," in "Global Change, Global Reach, and Global Power." An address of Secretary of the Air Force Donald B. Rice at the Air Force/Tufts University Conference on Aerospace Challenges and Missions in the 1990s, Cambridge, MA, April 3, 1991, p. 4.

9. Of course, a few of the critiques were quite thoughtful. Tucker and Hendrickson, *The Imperial Temptation,* cited earlier, is one of the better ones.

10. Alexander Hamilton, James Madison, and John Jay, *The Federalist or the New Constitution* (Avon, CT: Heritage Press, 1945), pp. 347–348.

11. The Constitution does not actually *say* the president is in charge of foreign affairs. It says that he holds "the executive Power" (Article II, Section 1), that he is "Commander in Chief" (Section 2, 1), that he can "make treaties, provided two thirds of the Senators present concur," and can "nominate ambassadors" (Section 2,2).

12. This remains true, if to a lesser extent than at some other eras in American history, despite the increased assertiveness of Congress in the last two decades or so. We discuss that increased assertiveness in Chapter 6.

13. Quote from a taped interview with one of the authors, Washington, D.C., June 3, 1986. For the context in which Moorer is giving his views, see Frederick H. Hartmann, *Naval Renaissance: The U.S. Navy in the 1980s* (Annapolis, MD: Naval Institute Press, 1990), p. 219.

14. After the 1961 Bay of Pigs debacle, President Kennedy's popularity actually increased. In 1972 with domestic dissent strong and the American troop withdrawal from Vietnam well underway, nearly 60 percent of the people supported President Nixon's sudden mining of Haiphong Harbor.

15. Theodore C. Sorensen, *Kennedy* (New York: Harper & Row, 1965), p. 509.

16. Leslie Gelb's comments in March, 1991, were made as the media were generalizing about the results of the Persian Gulf War.

2

Foreign Policy and National Interests

A small and weak nation like the United States in 1789 has one advantage over the great and powerful one it became: it does not have to agonize over whether to send a half-million troops half way around the world to fight a war. It does not have a half-million troops, it cannot transport or supply them at such a distance, and it would not choose to do so because the problems immediately around its frontier are bound to take priority. George Washington never considered sending troops to Vietnam—or to the Persian Gulf. He had more pressing concerns on his doorstep.

Whether the small and weak nation has simpler foreign policy decisions to make is less clear. They may be very complex, indeed. Did President Thomas Jefferson face a simpler problem than President George Bush almost two hundred years later, when Saddam Hussein invaded Kuwait? Jefferson had to reverse all of his prejudices and principles when he was offered the entire Louisiana Territory. He had started out wanting to settle the southern frontier issues and instead was offered by France an area as big again as his new nation. He wanted a Federal government with limited powers and he ended by having one exercising greatly expanded controls in a greatly expanded area. The Congress, which had appropriated $2 million, found itself confronted with $15 million to pay.[1] Although the United States took the plunge, it was not an easy decision. But at least the issue was clear-cut: expand and remove a foreign threat on the Western frontier, or continue to be closely surrounded in a relatively small territory.

The difference between decisions of weak and strong states is not, then, necessarily one of simplicity versus complexity. The difference is in the *scope*. The more powerful state moves always on a larger stage, and its actions impinge on a greater number of other nations. When the United States became a great or super power, able to send a half-million troops half way around the world, it had to consider the reactions of dozens of other states. Jefferson had to think primarily only of Spain, Britain, and France, whereas President Bush, in Operation Desert Shield, followed by Operation Desert Storm, had to juggle Israel and the Arab states, the United Nations, world opinion, the policies of the NATO allies, and the attitudes of the Soviet Union, among other things.

Nor can we say that weak nations are always insecure and strong nations secure. That depends upon the tension level in the world (about which more, later) and upon the policies that other nations, especially neighbors, decide to follow. Over the years the United States passed from a situation of having great power neighbors on every frontier to one in which the great powers were not only far removed, territorially, but also were preoccupied. But that increase in security allowed the United States to become less sensitive to strategic concerns in its foreign policy. And because Americans were more secure they also had fewer important foreign policy issues to decide—at least until the coming of World War I.

Foreign Policy Decisions and Past-Future Linkages

Every day the United States, as all nations, deals with hundreds or thousands of foreign policy matters spanning a whole gamut of subjects from trade to diplomacy to the ozone layer. These matters vary enormously in their importance and scope, and in the attention devoted to them. All require decisions of one sort or another, and within America's fragmented government system myriads of individuals will play some role in designing or implementing what are deemed to be the appropriate policies. The president has an enormous bureaucracy to help him deal with these everyday, routine concerns that constitute so much of his policy agenda.

But for the most important issues, things are different. Decisions on these matters, which involve a fundamental choice of *direction* or *commitment,* are not made by the bureaucracy. They are made by the first echelon—the president and key senior advisers.

We must not see such decisions too simply: it may not be clearly apparent at the time of a first decision in what becomes a series of decisions that a new direction has indeed been chosen or that a new commitment has been made. Getting involved may come one step at a time, creating the presumption that it is still feasible to reverse course. This is, in fact, how the United States approached its Vietnam venture. Sending a few advisers was the first step, committing U.S. troops to combat was the last. Eisenhower, who made the first decision, certainly would not have agreed that it led inexorably to the last decision, made by Johnson. But one thing tends to lead to the next, in foreign affairs as elsewhere. Decisions like Eisenhower's in fact lead policy in a radically new direction or influence the spectrum of opposition that the nation faces from outside its boundaries. But there is no bold print on any decision document to point that out.

When the immediate issue for the nation is war or peace, ambiguities disappear. But most decisions are not made in such a stark atmosphere, even on important questions. Usually a decision document setting forth choices presents quite a few "options." They can cover a whole spectrum of choices arranged in an ascending or descending series of steps leading toward or away from a commitment. However, this spectrum is also largely window dressing. If the issue is important, the choice always boils down either to becoming more involved or less involved. Those are always the real alternatives. The other options are "tweaking" at the margins. As we saw in Chapter 1, President Bush made an *important* decision in determining what size armed force he would assign to the Middle East as tensions grew over Saddam Hussein's invasion of Kuwait. But he made a *vital* decision when he concluded that it would take the use of force to expel Saddam and Bush ordered the attack to be prepared.

Some choices have fairly predictable consequences, others do not. Jefferson and the Congress of his time were in no doubt about how their decision would create very different futures for the infant American republic. Bush and his Congress, especially contemplating the use of force whose results always contain an element of chance, could legitimately worry the ramifications of their choices much further, because any major American intervention in the troubled Middle East had unforseeable consequences.

In this respect, things have not changed since at least the fifth century before Christ. Herodotus, commonly called the "father of history," wrote about how the decision was taken by the Greeks to oppose the Persian invasion of Europe: "If we submit to the Persians . . . there is little doubt what misery must then ensue: but if we fight and win, then this city [Athens] may well grow to preeminence amongst all the cities of Greece." But the ten commanders who had to decide the issue were not agreed: ". . . half of us are for a battle, half against it. If we refuse to fight [there is] little doubt that the result will be bitter dissension [among the Greek cities]; our purpose will be shaken, and we shall submit to Persia. But if we fight before the rot can show itself in any of us, then, if God gives us fair play, we cannot only fight but win." So they gave Callimachus, the War Archon, a deciding vote. Tiny Greece then humbled mighty Persia.[2]

So the most critical foreign policy decisions tend to be choices between fundamentally divergent alternatives. What policymakers actually do in making these choices is envision the consequences they would expect to result from each alternative, if chosen. The word "envision" here is very important.

If we think about decisions we make in our own lives, we realize that we go through the same process. What we are really doing parallels national decision-making. We project (or "envision") presumed consequences that will probably follow from doing one thing or the other. Either individually or the nation as a whole, we draw upon our past experience, gather what facts we can (some of them of doubtful reliability), and either make the plunge or remain uncomfortably indecisive. In our minds is a continuum linking past, present, and future.

It follows logically that if the experience of two nations is different, or if they consider a different set of facts or presumed facts to be significant, they will be making their decision from contrasting perspectives. In terms of international relations principles, their **past-future linkages** will give them separate perspectives so that even the same problem (as judged by an outside observer) will not appear to be, or in fact be, the same to both. In the old story about the glass half full of water, it is specified that the liquid *was* water; otherwise the optimists and the pessimists would have had *two* things to argue about. Foreign policy decisions will be made by projecting likely consequences and that projection will carry the stamp of the history of the nation making it. Past-future linkages is the first of four cardinal principles of international relations we shall come across in this chapter.

Foreign policy decisions, even when they involve fairly clear-cut alternatives, are hardly ever made in democratic nations like the United States without a great deal of controversy and soul-searching. True, there are a few events, dramatic in their impact, where no debate is needed. In such cases as the Japanese attack at Pearl Harbor in December 1941, two alternative courses of action were open, but only one had any real chance of being adopted. In terms of logic, the United States could have reacted by *not* declaring war in response, but anyone with the slightest knowledge of the American mood and temperament would have known that only one choice would be seriously considered.

The very nature of such rare but dramatic events, which tend to telegraph ahead their own likely response, obscures the nature of the more usual type of important foreign policy decisions. For almost always, at least at the time, each of the alternatives seems to have merit. That is why foreign policy debates occur. If the answer was always obvious, there would be little need for discussion.

This is a difficult point to take in, although very important to understand. Looking back on developments, and knowing how they turned out, we fail to allow for *the atmosphere of confusion and uncertainty which surrounded the issue at the time*. The best way to see this is to look at some of the American debates. We have already discussed the Persian Gulf War. Even more illuminating is the debate in the 1930s, as World War II hovered on the horizon.

Before Pearl Harbor: Isolationists vs. Interventionists

President Franklin D. Roosevelt once made a famous speech, the theme of which was "I Hate War." (He went on to say that his wife, Eleanor, hated war, and the rest of his family, too. Wags added his dog, etc.). But in late 1937, as he saw Europe's increasing instability in the wake of Germany's deliberate and serious violations of the Versailles Treaty by introducing conscription and reoccupying the Rhineland,[3] plus the Italian attack on Ethiopia, Roosevelt argued for "quarantining the aggressors" through the cooperation of the other great powers.[4] He later lobbied hard and successfully for the repeal of the arms sales restrictions in the neutrality acts that Congress had passed to insulate the United States from any temptation to again become involved in Europe's quarrels. But he was dealing with an American public and a U.S. Congress far from convinced that they should lay aside that neutrality and play an active role.

Samuel Eliot Morison comments on this period in American history: "Had any pollster been looking for one idea on which the vast majority of the American people agreed . . . it would have been that if Europe were so wicked or stupid as to start another war, America would resolutely stay out."[5] So when a popular figure like Colonel Charles A. Lindbergh spoke out before Pearl Harbor on behalf of the America First Committee, the leading group opposing American intervention, he could be assured of a large and sympathetic audience. Lindbergh argued that America First stood not for isolation but independence, that America had "divided our own people by this dabbling in Europe's wars."[6] He was speaking in April 1941, by which time Congress had just passed the Lend-Lease Act of March 11, 1941.[7] Lend-Lease allowed President Roosevelt vast powers "to sell, transfer title to, exchange, lease, lend, or otherwise dispose of" all kinds of defense articles with few restrictions. This Lend-Lease Act was already a major step away from isolationism, or "go it alone" unilateralism. It was America's most important response to Hitler's defeat of France in June 1940, and Britain's forced evacuation from the continent at Dunkirk. To Lindbergh, this response was "dabbling," especially unwarranted since "No one can make us fight abroad unless we ourselves are willing to do so. No one will attempt to fight us here if we arm ourselves as a great nation should be armed." The polarities in this argument are clearly set out in the slogans of the day. (Box 2.1)

Earlier, Lindbergh had said: "I ask you to look at the map of Europe today and see if you can suggest any way in which we could win this war if we entered it. Suppose we had a large army in America, trained and equipped. Where would we send it to fight? The campaigns of the war show only too clearly how difficult it is to force a landing . . . on a hostile coast." Earlier in this speech, Lindbergh had argued that England and France had no reasonable chance of winning against Hitler and that "it is now obvious that England is losing the war." Any support America gave the British would be wasted and tend to draw the United

---

| Box 2.1 | **Debating the National Interest** |

Stay Out of Europe's Wars!	Help the Allies Now!
pro argument	*pro argument*
• U.S. doesn't need to fight	• It is amoral to stay neutral on Hitler
• American people would be divided	• U.S. would soon be outflanked
• No practical military way to intervene anyhow	• U.S. would fight later anyhow— but alone
• England and France can't win	
con argument	*con argument*
• If U.S. does have to fight, it will be all alone	• Any support given is a complete loss if Allies lose

---

States in. Lindbergh also said that 80 percent of the American people agreed with him, over 100 million people.[8]

Note what Lindbergh was saying. He claimed that there was no reason why America should intervene, that if it did it would be wasted effort because there was no way to really use U.S. armed forces effectively, besides which, America's allies were already defeated. Anyhow, if the United States armed enough, Hitler could not attack America in its own territory, in "Fortress America," as Lindbergh supporters liked to label it.

Lindbergh thought his alternative of staying neutral would save the United States from an unnecessary war as well as keep the United States from linking its destiny to already-defeated allies. The major disadvantage of such a choice, which Lindbergh dismissed, was that Hitler might later bring the war to the Americas.

Today we know that much of what Lindbergh said was quite wrong. American forces *did* land on the hostile coast of Normandy, and England was not defeated. Hitler was. That was an outcome that would not have happened without American intervention. But how about the reverse, if Hitler had won? Can we visualize how it would have been to be in a world in which Hitler stood astride Europe (with Japan holding the Far East), liquidating "inferior" peoples, and having a good part of the significant resources of the world at his disposal? How long then would American peace or security have lasted? But these things which we know with fair certainty today were still arguable then.

Notice, too, the important role that projections of anticipated consequences play in the argument of the America Firsters, as they do also in the arguments of those, like ex-Secretary of State Stimson, who opposed them.

Stimson, as early as October 1937, was writing in *The New York Times* that U.S. neutrality legislation had attempted "to impose a dead level of neutral conduct . . . between right and wrong, between an aggressor and its victim. . . . It won't work. Such a policy of amoral drift . . . will not save us from entanglement. It will even make entanglement more certain."[9]

Stimson, and increasingly Roosevelt, thought that the alternative of aiding the allies would make what they considered America's inevitable involvement less costly, because the United States and its European allies shared that involvement. The major disadvantage of such a choice was, admittedly, acting upon the assumption that peace and security had become mutually exclusive.

Stimson's forecast contrasts with Lindbergh's, and Stimson was much more nearly right, but part of his argument implies that those who do not do the moral thing pay dearly for it in the end. Here Stimson is arguing in the traditional American idiom. But he also asks Americans to consider the practical strategic consequences that would follow Hitler's victory. The first result, he wrote, "would be the prompt appearance of imitation Nazi regimes in a half-dozen Latin American nations, forced to be on the winning side, begging favors, clamoring for admission to the Axis [the Fascist grouping, a quasi-alliance]. What shall we do then? Make war . . . ? Or shall we sit tight while the area of Nazi influence draws ever closer . . . ?"[10]

Lindbergh, who at the beginning of his talk said he would confine himself to the practical side of the problem, thought that it sufficed for American security if the Nazis were not able easily to attack the United States in its own territory. He did not really appreciate the fact that even in the Western Hemisphere the United States would be in a pressured and untenable position, regardless of any immediate and direct attack.

Counterbalancing National Interests

The most basic issue in this pre–World War II debate was whether for the sake of its security the United States should intervene in the war in Europe. The confusion and uncertainty were apparent. Each side proposed a policy quite opposed to that of the other, but each argued with equal sincerity. Both Stimson and Lindbergh, both the isolationist America Firsters and the interventionist Committee to Defend America by Aiding the Allies, were confident that their particular policy would benefit the United States and their opponents' policy would harm it. They were each arguing for their version of the *national interest* (or national interests) of the United States.

This term, **national interest** (see Box 2.2), whether in the singular or in the plural, has a long history. It goes back at least to the time of the Romans and quite possibly earlier. But despite its antiquity, it is often the source of confusion, primarily because it is used in two quite different senses. The first use, as in the pre–World War II debates, pits two opposed views against one another, each claiming to be in the nation's interest. Obviously, both cannot be the right course

Box 2.2	**Key Terms**
Balance of power	A venerable term in international relations. Usually used in one of two ways. First, to describe a system or process in which when any party threatens to become dominant, other parties (sooner or later) ally together to restrain or defeat the threatener. Second, the term sometimes is used simply to describe the actual distribution of power.
Domino Theory	The idea that if an aggression occurs, parties must be willing to use their power immediately to halt the aggressor; that otherwise the aggressed-upon actor will become more and more demoralized and be tempted to quit, and neighboring parties soon will lose the will to resist and will fall "like a row of dominoes."
National interest(s)	Used as a singular or plural term. Used in foreign policy debates to describe what a particular group thinks should be sought or protected in foreign policy. Also used historically and universally among governments to refer to particular elements in their foreign policy which they set value on and seek to achieve or protect.
Strategic sensitivity	To be strategically sensitive means to understand how any set of circumstances, patterns, or events does one or both of two things: changes the general tension level in the world, and/or increases or decreases the threat to a nation's vital interests.
Power problem	Refers to the possibility of attack by one party against another. Originates in the fact that the world outside the national frontiers is divided into separate sovereign states who each possess some armed force and can decide to use it. We can speak, therefore, of a universal condition for all states, and we can refer to the specific power problem faced by a given state with given neighbors and/or enemies.
Threat estimates	A military term used universally to describe an estimate of danger stemming from the potential use of force by an enemy or opponent. Threat analysis often consists of two elements: capability and intention.

to benefit the nation. One alternative is wrong. Nevertheless the claim is made. Just as in a presidential election, where each candidate tries to persuade the public that his election will be best for the nation, each side in the debate stresses the value of its alternative for the nation's future.

The second use of the term *national interest,* though, is to describe aspects of a policy settled upon, *after* the debate is over. In this usage we say that Congress passed the Lend-Lease Act because it was in the national interest of the United States. Here, in the second usage, the term refers to an accepted thing, something being implemented in the policy. Now, even at this point there is no guarantee that the policy *will* work out well. That still depends on the reactions of other nations in the time ahead. But in this second use we know that the proposition is being implemented, for better or for worse. The argument for and against it has been terminated by a decision.

Since in neither usage can we assert confidently that we are in fact serving the national interest, some critics have proposed that the term be abolished as imprecise and misleading. But it is difficult to find less ambiguous terms for what is inherently an ambiguous process. And since nations use that terminology we are better off using it too.

We can see now also how serious choices in foreign policy come down to two alternatives. Stimson actually ended his argument by saying: "We have only two alternatives. We can surrender or we can do our part in holding the line." The critical foreign policy choice is one of direction, of involvement, of momentum, but it is a choice that is rarely clear-cut at the time. If it were, there would be no debate. And since the very fact that a debate is needed shows that the two alternatives appear to carry relatively equal weight, each tending to run counter to and balance the other, we shall name these pairs of alternatives, **counterbalancing national interests.**

This term, *counterbalancing national interests* (See Box 2.3), will recur throughout these pages. We shall use it in two ways. First, to describe, as here, how foreign policy alternatives are examined in the United States. The second use is in connection with the whole system of nation-states. For what is true for America is true also elsewhere: A fundamental precondition to any important change in foreign policy is the prior examination of alternatives. When we use the term the first way, we shall be more concerned with the internal debate; using it the second way, we shall be looking in a much wider context, where the change of one nation triggers other changes elsewhere. Counterbalancing national interests is therefore a highly important theoretical construct. It is the second of four cardinal principles. Remember, though, that while the foreign policy decision process in this sense is uniform from nation to nation, each nation has its own ideas about what facts and projections seem pertinent to its decision.

One other important point needs to be made about counterbalancing national interests. As we saw in the debate over America's neutrality in the 1930s, when there were two alternatives, equal justice is rarely done to the negative side of the argument. Nor is the advocate of one alternative merely reversing the argument made by the other side. (The "pro" side of one does not equate to the "con" side of the other, either in the stress put on it or even in its formulation.) The rival advocates tend to argue past one another rather than rebutting their opponent's points because the alternatives are not based upon the same assumptions. So each proponent projects a different world as the "bottom line." This is clear enough from the summary of the debate points in Box 2.1.

Later on when we analyze the Vietnam War debate, we shall see the same mismatch of the "pro" of one argument to the "con" of the other. The main reason advocated by those who wanted to intervene and fight on was that otherwise the domino effect would occur: By failing to stop a first aggression, the next

---

Box 2.3	**Cardinal Principles**

Past-future linkages	All parties' decisions about the present and future are influenced by their perceptions of the past, especially their assumptions and projections about pluses and minuses and where in the future the choice of one alternative rather than another will lead.
Counterbalancing national interests	Refers to an important aspect of choice in decision. Explains that the two major alternatives in important but controversial foreign policy choices often seem, as decision time approaches, of fairly equal value, and each to some extent tends to run counter to and balance the other. Also explains that all alternatives have both pluses and minuses, and potential changes in the international system often can be understood by examining the advantages and disadvantages of what a state has not yet chosen to do, but might.
Third-party influences	No relationship between two parties in international relations is ever wholly bilateral. There are always "third" (other) parties who are affected by anything two parties do with one another, and each is affected in a different way. Moreover, any party's decision or policy may originate out of or be shaped by concern about "third" parties.
Conservation of enemies	Indicates that, to some extent, the enmity a nation faces is a variable, something that can be controlled or modified, increased or reduced. Refers specifically to making decisions which keep the number of enemies to no more than are inescapable.

---

victims, more vulnerable now, would topple over "like a row of falling dominoes." Their "pro" was itself a kind of negative argument. But one main reason advocated by those who wanted to avoid or discontinue the war (apart from war-weariness) was that it prevented a rapprochement with Communist China—something not even recognized as a possibility by the domino theory advocates.

From this observation comes another: that any analysis of foreign policy alternatives should not only pay close attention to the arguments of *each* side but also particular attention to the negative aspects that are glossed over.

Guidelines to the National Interest

We argued above that a nation's experience shapes its attitudes toward problems and therefore also its sense of reality, its understanding of cause and effect. It's experience shapes which alternatives are seriously considered. Consequently, a guideline or formula that appeals to one nation may not seem useful to another. Moreover, any guideline at best can only represent a compressed statement of a useful truth.

Many years ago, the United States diplomatic service used a number code called the "Gray code," to save on the costs of sending diplomatic cables. For example, "I have the honor, Your Excellency, to inform you that . . ." might have been 73, while "In reference to your note . . ." became 16. One veteran diplomat, at his retirement banquet, had his audience in stitches as he gave his entire speech in the number code so well known by everyone in the room. A foreign policy debate is like that number code: it compresses the essentials, providing a shorthand sense of direction or statement of what is at stake.

Debates over the national interest tend to reflect the Gray code, as both sides use stereotyped and simplified ideas. The very names of the opposing groups in the 1930s illustrates that: America First and the Committee to Defend America by Aiding the Allies. Roosevelt won his greatest congressional support for Lend-Lease by saying simply that if your neighbor's house is on fire you don't stop to ask who owns the hose. Notice how "neighbor" here conveys the thrust of a much more complicated analysis. In this case, our "neighbor"—England—was 3,000 miles away.

Only strong powers will have this kind of debate. A weak power cannot send forces half way around the world. It does not have the ability, it does not feel the need, and protecting its own security at home has an obviously higher priority. Nothing would be more foolish than to send armed forces far away only to find an enemy right at home taking advantage of your defenselessness. But what of the great or super power like the United States that could do this? Is the greater scope of its policy merely a trap for the unwary, its greater freedom to take action merely an invitation to squander resources? If the arguments on both sides will inevitably be couched in simplified terms, can we find ways to spot the misleading ones?

We can see from the 1930s how the issue is debated; but can it be brought into clearer focus? Are there more certain guidelines for establishing whether one alternative is *really* in the national interest, especially when the decision involves commitment in a larger arena than a nation's immediate vicinity? Are there guidelines, conversely, that are bound to get us into trouble? Is there no rule of thumb that directs us to the proper counterbalancing interest? These are all questions that are both very difficult and very important to answer correctly. When America chose to fight the Vietnam War, it turned out rather badly. But when America opposed Saddam Hussein's conquest of Kuwait, it turned out rather well. Yet the rationales for America's decision to use force were strikingly similar in both cases.

A guideline that played an important role in both cases, one much favored by American presidents after World War II, is the already-mentioned **domino theory.** That domino theory was named by Dwight D. Eisenhower, but the idea it represents is much older. In a news conference on April 7, 1954, Eisenhower used the term to describe what would happen if the Communist aggression in Indochina were allowed to succeed. Then the rest of the potential victims would quickly lose heart, thus eroding any effective opposition. He said: "You have a row of dominoes set up, you knock over the first one, and what will happen to the last one is that it will go over very quickly. So you have a beginning of a disintegration that would have the most profound influences."[11] And President Kennedy, asked whether he thought that guideline made sense, responded, "I believe it. I believe it."[12]

With the pre–World War II debate fresh in our minds we can easily see that the domino theory is a simplified shorthand version of what some saw as the lessons of the history of Europe between 1933, when Hitler came to power, and 1939, when World War II broke out with the allied side in terrible disarray. Dominoes *did* fall after Hitler was not initially stopped, as when Germany annexed Austria in March 1938, and followed by swallowing Czechoslovakia. And some nations, like Italy, in 1934 an opponent of Hitler,[13] became his ally. Russia, too, though vehemently opposed to fascism, nonetheless decided to make a deal, and in the 1939 Nazi-Soviet Pact the two nations agreed to divide Poland between them. Only Britain and France still stood in the way of Hitler dominating Europe.

It is this same sequence of events that Harry Truman had in mind when he ordered U.S. forces to the protection of South Korea in the wake of North Korea's aggression in 1950.

Truman records his reaction in his memoirs.

> In my generation, this was not the first occasion when the strong had attacked the weak. I recalled some earlier instances: Manchuria, Ethiopia, Austria. I remembered how each time that the democracies failed to act it had encouraged the aggressors to keep going ahead. Communism was acting in Korea just as Hitler, Mussolini, and the Japanese had acted ten, fifteen, and twenty years earlier. I felt certain that if South Korea was allowed to fall Communist leaders would be emboldened to override nations closer to our own shores [and] no small nation would have the courage to resist threats and aggression by stronger Communist neighbors. If this was allowed to go unchallenged it would mean a third world war, just as similar incidents had brought on the second world war.[14]

Stimson, too, had very much this sequence in mind when he opposed Lindbergh.

Leaving aside for the moment whether the domino theory, looked at in more detail, is correct, we can see that like the Gray code it serves as a form of shorthand. Instead of a long argument, the rationale is presented in only two words: domino effect. That describes and projects a whole process that will occur if no action is taken to thwart an aggression. As a guideline, it provides a "shorthand analysis" of all that is at stake in the decision to be made, and prescribes the appropriate choice of alternative.

Secretary of State Dean Rusk, testifying before the Senate Committee on Foreign Relations on February 18, 1966, obviously was embracing this same set of ideas and this same assumed sequence when he explained why the Johnson Administration had decided to involve the United States in Vietnam.

> South Vietnam is a long way from the United States, and the issues posed may seem remote from our daily experience and our immediate interests. . . . Why are we in Vietnam? . . . [B]ecause the issues there are deeply intertwined with our

security. . . . [W]hat we are seeking to achieve in South Vietnam is part of a process . . . of preventing the expansion and extension of Communist domination by the use of force against the weaker nations on the perimeter of Communist power.[15]

And the U.S. Joint Chiefs of Staff, in a policy statement as early as January 27, 1962, made a very specific argument to that same effect.

It is recognized that the military and political effort of Communist China in South Vietnam . . . is part of a major campaign to extend Communist control beyond the periphery of the Sino-Soviet bloc and overseas to both island and continental areas in the Free World. . . . It is, in fact, a planned phase in the Communist time-table for world domination.[16]

Eisenhower gave the name to the domino theory in the 1950s. In the 1960s, as these last two quotations show, this guideline was increasingly linked to a second guideline, which explained Communist moves as a deliberate and Moscow-coordinated plan to achieve world domination. Actually, the proposition that the Communists intended to force the capitalist world into an armed struggle for supremacy was already current in the 1950s, but its focus then was on *Soviet* aggression. By the 1960s the theory had moved full-fledged to a world setting in which the Soviets were seen as orchestrating Communist aggressive moves anywhere the opportunity offered. Since the domino theory was still accepted as a policy guideline, coupling it now to the Communist bloc aggression theory added up to advice that any *Communist* aggression anywhere in the world, unless stopped at the first instance, would create a follow-on domino effect. Coupling both theories as guidelines virtually eliminated any serious consideration of where the aggression had occurred and why, or who had initiated it. The nominal aggressor might be a minor Communist power and the aggression might be in an area that, apart from these two theories, would have no significance in world affairs. But these things did not matter.

Coupling these theories as guidelines led President Johnson intellectually to the Vietnam War.

Too Simple Guidelines Create Problems

The adoption of these two guidelines underlined the lack of strategic sensitivity in the United States, even after the experience of two world wars in modern times. For each had serious faults.

The problem with the domino-theory type of thinking in Truman's version is that it is mere speculation that the success of Japan's seizure of Manchuria led to Mussolini's aggression against Ethiopia, which in turn triggered Hitler's conquests in Europe. It is true that the disarray of the great powers in doing anything serious about any of these moves in the 1930s encouraged others, but the actual facts in all of these situations included many complexities glossed over by the simplistic assertion that one thing simply led to or caused another.

Begin with the Manchurian case. The Japanese takeover began in 1931. But after World War I, Japan had actual treaty rights with China to maintain

Japanese armed forces in Manchuria, where they guarded a railway line. Although the Japanese fabricated the actual incident that started their takeover, they did have a legal right to be there. A League of Nations commission of inquiry established to investigate the incident quite properly pointed this out, saying that it was not "a simple case of the violation of the frontier of one country by the armed forces of a neighboring country." In Manchuria there were "many features without an exact parallel in other parts of the world."

The commission's report explained that both China and Japan "claim to have rights and interests, only some of which are clearly defined by international law," that Manchuria, "although legally an integral part of China, had a sufficiently autonomous character to carry on direct negotiations with Japan. . . ." It added that Japan, by treaty, also exercised "the rights of jurisdiction over all her subjects in Manchuria and maintains consular police throughout the country."[17] Given that Japan's reputation up to that point in the League's history was very good, and given that these complications existed, there was little disposition at the time to simply brand Japan as an aggressor.

Now consider Italy. Mussolini may have been heartened by events in Asia. But he had long had in mind revenging Italy's ignominious rout by Ethiopian forces at Aduwa in 1896. His intended prize, Ethiopia, along with Liberia, were the only remaining non-colonial territories in the whole of Africa. Since the British and the French owned colonies adjacent to Ethiopia they could hardly be supposed to think it extraordinary if Italy did the same. Indeed, if after commencing the assault in 1935, Mussolini had not been so arrogant in defying the League, there would probably have been no move against him in the form of sanctions by the world organization.[18] England and France were much more interested in retaining good relations with Italy, which had already frustrated Hitler's first attempt to take over Austria by sending troops to the Brenner Pass the year before. In short, Italy had much better reasons to think it could attack with impunity than the example of Japan in Manchuria, half a world away.[19]

As to Adolf Hitler needing encouragement to commit aggression, the very idea is farfetched. He well understood why Britain and France were not enthusiastic about confronting Italy with sanctions. He profited by the ambiguity of their interests, but there can be little question that he would have proceeded with his program anyhow. He came to power with promises that Germany would be restored to its proper status in power.

The weaknesses of the theory of a single, inherently aggressive, Communist bloc controlled and directed by the Soviets were more difficult to show before the open Sino-Soviet split in the 1960s. Still, the evidence was already available that Moscow only exerted clear control where the Red Army was an occupying force. As early as the dissolution of the Communist world organization, the Comintern, in 1943 there was evidence that Communist nations and Communist parties outside the Soviet Union were not automatically subservient to Soviet wishes. The announcement of the disbanding of the Comintern referred specifically to the "deep differences in the historic paths of development of various countries, differences in their character and even contradictions in their social orders, differences in the level and the tempo of their economic and political development [that] conditioned different problems affecting the working class of the various countries."[20] Even in this short quotation, note that "different" or "differences" is used four times. Heavy hand of Moscow—lift off!

In the Korean War, when the United States assumed that Stalin had given the order to North Korea to attack South Korea, Nikita Khrushchev's memoirs state clearly that it was the North Korean leader, Kim Il-sung, who took the initiative. Khrushchev writes: "I must stress that the war wasn't Stalin's idea, but Kim Il-sung's. Kim was the initiator. Stalin, of course, didn't try to dissuade him." And, just before this quotation: Kim "told Stalin he was absolutely certain of success. I remember Stalin had his doubts. He was worried that the Americans would jump in. . . ."[21]

So, as a guideline for U.S. foreign policy, the assumption of a unified Communist bloc also was too simple and in need of serious qualification.

These ideas have one feature in common. If they are accepted as guidelines to U.S. commitments, they take the place of serious strategic analysis. They guide on the basis of categories of events, regardless of situational specifics. They appeal to the American temperament precisely because they provide what is assumed to be universally valid guidance for action any time, any place. If you truly believe in the domino theory, you know that every aggression everywhere must be opposed, and if it is a Communist nation which commits it you also know that it is the whole Communist world, led by Moscow, which is behind it. But believing in either or both of these theories as *sufficient* guidelines to U.S. policy simply is inadequate in terms of strategic analysis.

Although the domino theory or effect was overstated or overvalued by American presidents after World War II, it did describe correctly what might be called the first, disintegrating phase of a power equilibrium, or **balance of power.** When an aggressor first begins to be successful, initial opposition can crumble as the potential victims hasten to make their peace. We have also already pointed out how the onward march of Saddam Hussein would have had extremely serious consequences for the United States. With him controlling much of the world's oil resources, one could have predicted that many of the weaker or weak-willed among the nations of the world would have tried to come to terms with him.

But the domino theory, by concentrating on the *first* phase of a disintegrating balance of power leaves unsaid what typically happens in the *second* phase. For then, those nations who are still able to fight back and who see the inevitable if they do not, normally band together in a desperate or at least determined effort to bring the aggressor's march forward to a halt. This is what finally happened to Adolf Hitler, after his impressive beginning. It also happened to Napoleon Bonaparte in an early time and to Saddam Hussein in a later time.

The domino theory is also an incomplete and too simple portrayal of a much more complex reality, not just from the point of view of cause and effect. It also tends to elevate the *fact* of an aggression to the determining element, rather than where it happens and who is involved in that event as either victim or aggressor. The fact that the domino theory, with these evident defects, had a serious hold on American official thinking about foreign policy for decades after

World War II—and who is to say that it has no grip on American thinking now?—shows that the United States drifted into habits which add up to strategic insensitivity.

The Importance of Strategic Sensitivity

Particularly in the changed world of apparently reduced threat, once the Soviet Union fell apart, one may wonder why this emphasis on **strategic sensitivity** or insensitivity. There is certainly far more to foreign policy than this. True. The point here is that strategic sensitivity is the part of foreign policy where a nation, if it does not know what it is doing, may encounter disaster.

To be strategically sensitive means to be aware of how to avoid disaster. It means understanding how any given set of circumstances or external events does one or both of two things: changes the *tension level* in the world, or increases (decreases) the threat to (U.S.) *vital interests*.

Actions that lead to a high tension level increase the likelihood of general war. So strategic sensitivity means knowing just what developments in world affairs cause general war to become more likely or less likely, and it means knowing which interests under what circumstances at what cost deserve defending by force. Strategic sensitivity for both categories rests upon an adequate understanding of the nature of international relations, just as strategic insensitivity indicates either a lack of knowledge or incorrect assumptions (guidelines) about how the world system operates.

The International System

The term "international system," applied to the world outside America's frontiers, is in one important sense a misnomer. Systems consist of parts linked in some logical fashion, the parts interacting with each other in some regular and predictable fashion. In some areas, nation-states, as the primary parts in the international system,[22] do behave in regular patterns—they observe standardized rules of international law, exchange and treat diplomats according to customary usages, issue visas, attend international conferences to regulate global pollution, and many other things. But sometimes they do not act predictably. Where the important exception to the usual concept of "a system" occurs is that all of the behavior is *voluntary*, and at any time any one of these nation-states can and will behave in a totally aberrant way. Iran did just that in President Carter's time, when it held American diplomats hostage after violating the sanctity of the American Embassy in Tehran. What keeps aberrant behavior from occurring much more frequently is the prospect of reprisal. Privileges are reciprocal: raid someone's embassy, and your own embassies become fair game. Shoot prisoners-of-war or mistreat them, and your own nationals are likely to encounter something of the same. Fail to adhere to treaties you have freely negotiated, and other nations will quit making treaties with you.

The most curious feature about the world as a whole to which U.S. foreign policy is addressed is that there is no world government. There is no central agency to make the rules (like the Congress), settle disputes (like the courts), or enforce rules and agreements once they are made (like the executive branch). Every inhabited territory on the face of the globe has an organized authority over it, whether that authority is a savage dictatorship or one responsible to a democratic people. Every territory has its own authority, but the world as a whole has none. There is the United Nations, of course. But essentially the United Nations is a large-scale diplomatic conference that reflects the interests of its members. For instance, when the Security Council considered what to do about the Kurdish refugees in northern Iraq in 1991, no one could guarantee that all the members would act together. Each has its own vote, and in the case of the permanent members of the Security Council, they also have the veto. That veto is the symbol of this very point—apart from being compelled by superior force, no nation will agree to any policy or program unless it wishes to do so and sees benefit in so doing. The world of states is *decentralized* in terms of decision-making, the ultimate power of decision resting in the various national capitals.[23]

In making such decisions, these states cannot escape their consequences. But they nevertheless can make decisions, wise or unwise, including a decision to attack another state. This creates what we shall call a **power problem** for every nation, because any nation may be the victim of attack by one or more other nations. Also, from a system point of view (i.e., looking at the multilateral effects of this universal vulnerability), it creates the balance of power, which we earlier called a power equilibrium. What historically is known by the name *balance of power* is really an attempt to sum up system behavior in a world of sovereign states. In such a world, each country depends in the first instance on its own military power. But two or more states who feel the same threat (i.e., who share a more or less common power problem) will see advantages in making an alliance. That, in turn, is likely to cause the opposing or, let us say, the threatening state to look around for alliances of its own. In doing so it will turn to the enemies or opponents of any of the members of the first group to make alliances. Thus rival alliance systems tend to come into existence and produce a rough equilibrium. If the alliance groups are both *very* evenly matched and provocative in their policies, the tension level will rise because each group will then tend either to look for reinforcements among uncommitted powers or else try to wean away members of the opposing group. Either maneuver tends to raise the tension level and produce what we have elsewhere called the first phase of a disintegrating balance of power. But it is well to remember that this progression of events is not inevitable. The balance of power may resist becoming rigid for many decades at a time.

This decentralized situation (and its corollaries in terms of alliances and tension) has not always prevailed, at least for what was called the "known," or civilized world—a term which the Western world applied to Europe and the Middle East when the Far East was too far away to be in real contact, Africa south of the Sahara was largely unexplored, and the Americas unknown. In the days of the Roman Empire, the Romans governed this entire "civilized" world—essentially the Mediterranean Sea and the adjacent land areas. At its greatest extent, this world included Britain and much of the Middle East. Throughout this area a uniform system of laws was enforced. Even in pre-Christian times, the road system laid out by the Romans was so good that it was no serious trouble to move from one area to the other. (Not until the eighteenth century were the roads that good again.) These roads were policed by the Romans as well, and hostels and changes of horses were available for easy and safe transit. So, in a serious sense, there was "one world," as far as it went.

Later, in the Christian era, a quasi-universal authority was exercised by the pope. Determined popes were able to exercise real power, over Europe in particular, but as far as the faith had spread. For example, in the period following 1095, Pope Urban I enforced the "Truce of God" on warring parties. There could be no fighting from Wednesday evening to Monday morning, for the entire forty days of Lent, and for Advent and all other holy days (of which there were many). In the twelfth century, when the Truce was most effective, scarcely one fourth of the year was left for fighting. But the Protestant Reformation, which began in 1517, changed all that, and the Thirty Years War (1618–48) intensified the breakdown of universal authority. The change is readily seen in England, when in 1534 King Henry VIII took the title of Supreme Head on Earth of the Church of England. Secular and spiritual power were then in the hands of one man, but only to the borders of his territory. No longer was there a single person or a universal symbol of authority that *all* Christendom would respect and obey.

Actually, it was the unparalleled chaos in the relations of the sovereign states in this period in history that led them to begin to institutionalize some of their dealings with one another. International law took a great step forward under the influence of Hugo Grotius, who published his great work, *De jure belli ac pacis* (On the Law of War and Peace) in 1625. Diplomacy, initially designed to facilitate relations between sovereign states, was still bedeviled by the lack of agreed procedures, especially as to precedence. Who should sign a treaty first? When several or all ambassadors were invited to an audience, which one should enter before which others? These were not trivial issues because the ambassador represented the monarch and therefore the prestige of his nation. When Louis XIV said, "L'Etat, c'est moi" ("I am the state"), he was saying no more or less than the truth. Louis was France just as Henry was England, and the usage of many decades was to call them that: "England says this," "France says that." Not until 1815 were diplomatic ranks standardized. By that time, too, nation-states had solved the difficult problem of who should sign a multilateral treaty first. It was decided that each nation would sign its own copy first, and that they should sign in alphabetical order in the French language.

This kind of thing may seem trivial, but disputes over such matters caused unnecessary friction and sometimes even wars. What the institutionalization of international law and diplomacy did, followed later by the establishment of international organizations of many kinds, was to remove some of that friction that is inherent in the relations of completely independent states who nonetheless have to deal with one another. Wars after that were, one might say, more deliberate and less accidental.

The Power Problem and Threat Analysis

But after as well as before the institutionalization described above, war was common in the international system. There was then and is now no guarantee from one day to another that somewhere one state will not launch an attack upon another. Nor can any state feel its territory or interests are immune from this threat, regardless of its armaments and preparations for war. States tend to arm against specific threats. Since the threatening power naturally is threatened in its turn by such a response, defense efforts often turn into arms races.[24] More powerful states tend to have more powerful enemies, but there are no reliable generalizations one can make about the source of threats. They can come to a superpower like the United States from a small nation like Libya, which fires off a missile at a U.S. plane. An Argentina may attack Great Britain in the form of the Falkland Islands assault. A great power may be drawn into a war simply because the other great powers are at war and the consequences of merely staying neutral (assuming that is permitted) are too enormous to make that a feasible option.

The international tension level can and does fluctuate, waning or waxing in intensity. But because each sovereign state controls some military power and can decide to use it, no nation is ever completely relieved of a potential power problem. The likelihood of attack and the identity and seriousness of the threat can vary, but some potential for an attack is always there.

In practice, a state can be virtually immune from any realistic threat for a period of time or even for decades. That happened to the United States, but that happy situation also came to an end at the time of World War I. More than one state has made the tragic mistake of assuming it need not worry, only to find itself attacked. And when an attack comes as a surprise, there is no time for a lengthy and expensive rearmament program; the war has to be fought with the stocks on hand and the forces available.

The military, who are professionally charged with the defense of the nation, as in the United States, do **threat estimates.** These focus not so much on the whole international situation in which the power problem takes shape, but on a narrower comparison of their own forces and equipment to that of the potential enemy. As noted in Chapter 1, American threat analysis for several years has been made in terms of two components: capability and intention.[25] Capability means just what it says: military power in all its forms. The technical term is "order of battle"—a listing of units, their equipment, and their deployment. If intelligence data is accurate, so will be the estimate of the enemy's capability. The second component used by the Pentagon, "intentions," is a psychological or political appraisal as to whether the enemy is *likely* to attack at any foreseen time.

Although threat appraisal in the United States has two components, it tends to put great stress on only one—capability, the "hard" data—and much less stress on the "soft" data of intentions. After all, as one former chairman of the U.S. Joint Chiefs of Staff remarked, intentions can change rather rapidly. And this is true if we think of intentions as depending primarily on what a nation's leaders decide they would *like* to do, apart from whether they feel it is safe or expedient to do so. But if we think of intentions as being determined through an analysis of the risks such an attack will likely entail, the assessment will necessarily lead to a much more far-reaching appraisal of the international environment. Looking at national intentions outside an international context can result in a rather superficial appraisal of why and when intentions can change, especially if the assessment ignores the *circumstances* that influence any such change.

Any would-be attacker nation will take the measure of the armed forces of its enemy. Apart from its victim's ability and readiness to defend itself, the greatest restraint other than domestic considerations on a would-be attacker is concern over what will happen at its own flanks and rear once it becomes tied down frontally with its victim. In more systematic terms, behind any bilateral antagonism lies the shadow of potential third-party involvements. Japan, convinced in 1940 that war with the United States had become necessary, could not attack the United States with an uncommitted Soviet Union in the background. Hitler's attack on the Soviets, combined with Japan's military occupation of China, changed all that. The result, six months after Hitler's move, was Japan's attack on Pearl Harbor. That attack, tragically for America, achieved surprise. It should not have, if Americans had realized how Germany's assault on Russia had changed the strategic opportunities for Japan.

Third-Party Influences and Conservation of Enemies

The power problem of a nation stems from the whole of the system rather than from a simple bilateral relationship. It is quite understandable that a military will appraise a "threat" primarily in bilateral, capability terms. But a foreign policy specialist must think in power problem terms and be especially sensitive to how intentions fluctuate with moves by third states. While it is appropriate for the military to focus on the threat, it would be unpardonable for the government as a whole to react to its power problem as though it consisted only or even primarily of a military component, especially a bilateral military component.

Any state confronted with the possibility of attack has therefore three useful responses that it can make: to arm itself, to acquire allies, and to cultivate third parties in positions on the antagonist's flanks or at its back. Thus diplomacy supplements military power. Where military power focuses on *containing* or *countering* the perceived threat, foreign policy decisions on strategic issues are directed at *changing* or *reducing* the threat.

The simplest illustration of the use of this third principle of international relations, called **third-party influences,** is the "China card."[26] President Nixon, although a dedicated hard-liner on Communists, from the beginning of his presidency in 1969 saw the strategic value of terminating the hostile relationship with China that had prevailed ever since "our side" lost the Chinese civil war in 1949. In policy terms, Nixon reevaluated the shelved alternative of a friendlier policy and saw great advantage in a change that could reduce the hostile Communist bloc by detaching the Chinese.

The question was, were the Chinese detachable? To express the point in terms of counterbalancing national interest (our first international relations principle), did the Chinese see advantage in shifting to friendlier relations with the United States? For a variety of reasons that will become clearer as we go on, the answer was yes. So the United States played the China card (and the Chinese played the American card), and system relations were transformed. The effect was to reduce the threat and shrink the dimensions of the U.S. power problem while increasing Soviet strategic concerns. In terms of principles, again, by shortening America's list of enemies, Nixon was implementing our fourth principle of international relations—the prudential principle. We call it the **conservation** (or limiting) of **enemies** (or enmity).

Note that to accomplish such a conservation there must be mutual advantage to, in this case, China and the United States. Later we shall see why China, frustrated by the Soviet threat to its interests despite a common Communist bond, was eager for a change from a situation where it had no liberty to maneuver. Having done so, China could not be taken for granted any longer by the Soviets.

In his memoirs, Nixon tells how Soviet leader Brezhnev, visiting the United States for a summit meeting in June 1973, showed his concern over the change. The Soviets, wrote Nixon, were "apparently still worried that we were contemplating some secret military arrangement . . . with the Chinese."[27] Both China and America profited by this Soviet unease because it made Soviet policy toward both of them much more careful. Employing the conservation of enemies principle in this manner is an excellent example of strategic sensitivity in dealing with one's power problem.

Summing Up

Foreign policy is the name we give to decisions and follow-on actions that address the outside world. That world is a dangerous one, for it contains many sovereign states that, because they can make their own decisions, can decide to cause all kinds of trouble to America, up to and including armed attack, alone or in combination. Because Americans, like the people of every other state, live in the context of a power problem, foreign policy, although it must address economic, social, environmental, and a host of other issues, must above all else be strategically sensitive. That is, it must be sensitive to the implications of changes in the system and in the policies of other states as they affect U.S. vital interests and the tension level. This is especially true if the tension level is already high and if fear more than cooperation keynotes the relations of nations. When strategic issues are at stake, although it is important and necessary for the military to concentrate in the first instance on the capability of any opponent or set of opponents that might attack, it would be totally unwise for a foreign policy to be so restrictive in its scope. That is why we have begun to relate the making of American foreign policy to the functioning of the international system, by pointing to fundamental (cardinal) principles that provide some strategic direction for policy in the context of how that system operates.

Since the problems of U.S. foreign policy, so far as their strategic features go, will henceforth be addressed through the analytical principles and concepts discussed in this chapter, we shall restate them here before turning to the U.S. foreign policy record before World War II.

The first point is that foreign policy decisions involve alternatives that, in a fundamental sense, come in pairs. These sets of alternatives, which compose what we called counterbalancing national interests, can be seen from a dual perspective. For any single nation the alternatives represent possible (but contrasting) policy contents. For the system as a whole, though, they can be seen as providing the way in which single states, by changing their minds about which alternative is preferable, can alter the strategic environment. Both perspectives have to be borne in mind, even if we are primarily concerned with the foreign policy of a single state such as the United States. Not only will U.S. changes make a difference; the changes others make actually force a reappraisal of what America is already doing to see whether in the altered external environment, the United States, too, needs to change.

It follows logically from this multilateral dimension of policy decisions that every such decision made by any major "player" will have two effects. One is to increase or decrease the enmity focused on any particular player. The other is to raise or lower the tension level (the likelihood of war) in the whole system. Such effects are inescapable, whatever the intentions of those who make the decisions that cause them. Thus it is critical to keep this dimension of foreign policy choices always in mind.

The second point is to keep in mind the dual usage of the term "national interests": as alternatives each claimed to be in the nation's interest, or as (presumably beneficial) aspects of a policy already settled upon. In foreign policy debates, counterbalancing national interest alternatives are each advanced by their advocates with the goal and hope claim that their claims will be accepted as in the national interest, and that they will then be incorporated into policy. The merit of such contending claims will be determined in a democratic nation like the United States through a public debate if the issue stirs the public. Any nation making such judgments will rely on its own past experience, seeing the future as an extension of that past and linking the two together. This phenomenon of past-future linkages applies universally to all states but its specific content will vary from state to state. Although the process is universal, the results will be nation-particular.

Such debates do not occur about minor issues, of course. They take place when the choice of alternatives is centered on whether to become involved or not involved in potentially dangerous action, or on whether to adopt a radically new policy or continue essentially as before. Usually each side uses analytical short-cuts (which we called guidelines) to argue its case. Such guidelines, because they can be both very effective in deciding the debate and very misleading, need to be examined very critically. The road to Vietnam was paved with too simple guidelines and half-baked strategic notions.

Once the debate climaxes, one alternative is chosen and the other shelved, at least for the time being. But the fact that a decision is made is, of course, no guarantee that the decision will lead to the expected outcome.

The third point to remember is that the military will look at any set of alternatives through a more limited and specific prism than the government authorities or, for that matter, the population at large. Since it is concerned about the potential use of force that could follow from any foreign policy decision, it looks very specifically at the order of battle (the forces) available for any likely threat. There is a clear difference here in point of view between the political and military authorities, and it is built-in. The military, for good and sufficient reasons, focus bilaterally—U.S. forces against the enemy's—while the political authorities, if they are tending properly to their business, are thinking and acting with the multilateral dimension of their decisions very much in mind. (The military can be counted on for their way of looking at problems; less assured is that political authorities will indeed look at the whole picture when they decide on policy.) But even if a nation's unilateral choice (e.g. by the United States) is made in the context of a bilateral relationship (say toward Iraq), its consequences will be shaped heavily by the multilateral environment in which it is implemented.

The fourth point applies to the cardinal principles. We have seen that they play an important role both in foreign policy and in international relations. In judging any particular foreign policy decision by the United States, it is well to form the early habit of taking all four principles into account when judging the merits of the decision and the effects on the international system. All four principles will always be closely interrelated, from both perspectives. *Counterbalancing national interests* may be the most obvious and useful point of departure in making these judgments. When a fundamental change in the system originates with a decision by any major nation to substitute the previously shelved alternative in its policy, it can have a significant effect on the distribution of enmity in the system. But changes of this sort, like the "China card" example we gave, although they change the bilateral relations of two parties, are typically made out of mutual concern about a third state. Thus *third-party influences* are much involved.

As was also evident in the China card example, the *past-future linkages* for both states who contemplate a "card" must be compatible with the projected shift in foreign policy—in this particular case it could build upon a long history of sympathetic relations between the United States and China prior to the Communist takeover in 1949. Indeed, even though often overlooked in the 1960s, the predominant historical relationship of the United States and China was friendly if not cordial, while the relations of China and Russia, temporarily friendly in the 1950s, were mostly hostile and noncooperative in any longer historical sense. Finally, when these kinds of shifts are made, often both participants do so with the deliberate intention of reducing the list of enemies or potential antagonists, thus achieving the *conservation of enemies.*

From the beginning of recorded history, some nations have been more sensitive to these kinds of considerations than others. Thucydides, describing events twenty-three hundred years ago, spoke of imprudent policy, tracing it to *hubris,* the Greek term for arrogance or excessive pride. Napoleon Bonaparte and Adolf Hitler each in their time showed the same contempt for prudence. Ultimately they led their nations to a strategic defeat and disaster that was unnecessary if they had been willing to quit earlier. Ironically, in each case, their enemies were willing to accept their gains until quite late, provided they would be content with what they already had. But for Napoleon and for Hitler, their ambitions—and the foreign policies that reflected that ambition—had no bounds.

As we have said repeatedly, foreign policy is more than simply strategic decisions. But strategic insensitivity is the quickest way that foreign policy can lead to a disaster. That the United States has demonstrated such insensitivity at times in its policy is quite clear. That will be pointed out in the chapters which follow.

Notes

1. The figures given in standard references do not always agree because, although the total paid was $15 million, it represented $11,250,000 outright, plus U.S. assumption of $3,750,000 more in claims against France. It is astonishing, given the Revolutionary War debt to boot, that we had no remaining federal debt by 1836.

2. Herodotus, *The Histories,* trans. by Aubrey de Selicourt (London: Penguin Books, 1954), p. 428.

3. The Rhineland is that portion of Germany between the Rhine River and the French border. Its demilitarization had been a significant protection for France against German invasion.

4. The outbreak of the Sino-Japanese War in the summer of 1937 also was an important factor in his decision.

5. Samuel Eliot Morison, *The Oxford History of the American People* (New York: Oxford University Press, 1965), pp. 987–88.

6. The whole text is printed in *The New York Times,* April 24, 1941; see also Ruhl J. Bartlett, ed., *The Record of American Diplomacy* (New York: Knopf, 1948), pp. 612–16.

7. Under Lend-Lease, although the Soviets were later to belittle the American contribution to their war effort, the United States sent the Soviets over 400,000 motor vehicles and 13,300 planes.

8. See footnote 6.

9. Stimson's letter is reprinted in Bartlett, *The Record of American Diplomacy,* pp. 580–84.

10. Bartlett, pp. 580–84.

11. Dwight D. Eisenhower, news conference, April 7, 1954, *Public Papers of the Presidents: Dwight D. Eisenhower, 1954* (Washington, DC: U.S. Government Printing Office, 1960), p. 383.

12. Kennedy sent overt military advisers to South Vietnam. As early as 1954, Eisenhower approved a "Saigon Military Mission," which was to "enter into Vietnam quietly and assist . . . in unconventional warfare." *Pentagon Papers, New York Times* edition (New York: Quadrangle Books, 1975), p. 55.

13. When the Nazis attempted a *putsch* in Austria in 1934, Mussolini moved four divisions to the Brenner Pass. Hitler quickly backed down and the *putsch* failed.

14. Harry S. Truman, *Memoirs,* vol. 2, *Years of Trial and Hope* (Garden City, NY: Doubleday, 1956), pp. 332–33.

15. Dean Rusk, "The United States Commitment in Vietnam: Fundamental Issues." Testimony before the U.S. Senate Committee on Foreign Relations, February 18, 1966. Department of State *Bulletin,* March 7, 1966. Department of State Publication 8054.

16. *Pentagon Papers* (Gravel edition), vol. 2, p. 664.

17. [Lytton] Commission of Inquiry, League of Nations, Political Publications, 1932, VII, 12, pp. 126–27.

18. Even when they were imposed the decision was made with much reluctance.

19. On June 18, 1935, a British fact-finding commission reported to the British government: "There are no vital British interests in Abyssinia [Ethiopia] or adjoining countries such as to necessitate British resistance to an Italian conquest of Abyssinia." This statement became available to Mussolini by espionage almost immediately.

20. The text is in *The New York Times,* May 23, 1943.

21. Strobe Talbott, ed., *Khruschev Remembers* (Boston: Little, Brown, 1970), pp. 368–70. Although there is room for different views of the Stalin-Kim relationship, it is quite clear that Kim was not controlled and directed by Stalin and that North Korea was not the Soviet proxy the administration assumed it was.

22. There are a host of nonstate actors also, from general international organizations (U.N.) to regional organizations (EC) to national liberation organizations (PLO) to multinational corporations (ITT). Nonstate actors vary in all kinds of ways, including importance, and we discuss them later as appropriate. They all have one feature in common, though (despite repeated predictions by observers to the contrary): they rarely are critical to the outcome of problems seriously affecting vital national interests. That is why we largely exclude them in our overview discussion of the "system," except for our brief reference to the U.N. They will receive their due later.

23. With the end of the Cold War the United Nations began to play a larger role in international peacekeeping, and there was much optimism about its future. But it was able to act more effectively only because its members now were more in agreement than before. If that changed, "the U.N." would suddenly be "less capable" again!

24. While the decline of the Cold War brought about arms reductions by the nations

(and their successors) who had been its main actors, nations in the Middle East, whose primary threats were each other, continued to arm. Indeed, some such as Iran and Syria, increased their efforts.

25. See the United States Department of Defense, Joint Chiefs of Staff, *Dictionary of Military and Associated Terms.* JCS Publication 1, September 3, 1974, and later revisions.

26. Discussed in Chapter 12.

27. Richard M. Nixon, *RN: The Memoirs of Richard Nixon* (New York: Warner Books, 1978), pp. 426–27.

3

A Nation in Search
of a Proper Role

Following the disintegration of the Soviet empire, the Pentagon in 1992 was searching the horizon for enemies. But in 1789 potential enemies surrounded the United States. Until after the American Civil War of 1861–65, the U.S. foreign policy problem was focused on keeping threats to American security at a safe distance. After the 1870s, as American power increased and the threat of foreign intervention decreased, the problem was focused on where to draw the geographical and political line of U.S. involvement on the world scene.

Drawn substantially into Asian affairs after the Spanish-American War of 1898, through acquisition of the Philippines, in 1917 America reluctantly intervened in Europe in World War I. Then the United States returned to what is often called an isolationist mode, although the policy between 1919 and 1939 is better described as *unilateralist*. America would make no commitments. When

Hitler brought on World War II, the United States ultimately found itself again drawn into Europe's affairs. And when Japan attacked Pearl Harbor in December 1941, the involvement became worldwide. It was to remain so for a half-century of Cold War confrontation with the Soviet Union.

The history of the period between 1789 and 1945, the end of World War II, shows the United States seeking a proper role for its foreign policy, making some mistakes but on the whole choosing wisely from its alternatives. In this chapter we shall summarize the major policy choices in this period of 156 years. That history is necessary if we are to understand how these choices and their results shaped the attitudes with which Americans began their later superpower role.

Three Long-Range Trends

From its beginning in 1789 until the end of the Civil War, United States foreign policy was characterized by three long-range trends or themes. First, there was a drive for continental supremacy, a drive that included enlarging the American domain and eliminating European holdings in what is now the continental United States. Second, there was a closely related concern for hemispheric security symbolized by the Monroe Doctrine—a concern for limiting or eliminating European interests in the New World. Third, there was the studied avoidance of substantive commitments in either Europe or Asia.

When the American colonies successfully defied Britain and achieved their independence, they had behind them almost two hundred years of previous experience. Because they were British colonies, they had regularly participated in the American branch of Europe's perennial wars. And both that fact of participation and the recurrence of European wars strongly influenced the attitude of the Founding Fathers to strategic questions.

The strong connection between war in Europe and war in the Americas is clear from Box 3.1 (p. 54).

George Washington, inaugurated as president on April 30, 1789, had himself taken part in the last of these wars, as well as having led the American armies in the Revolution. He was well aware that the United States, although free, was a weak, debt-ridden, almost friendless nation. It had one ally, France, without which it could not have won independence, but France had acted out of hatred for Britain, rather than love of America; its continued aid and support were uncertain at best. And France was soon caught up in revolution and decades of war in Europe. Spain and the Dutch Republic, who had joined the war on England in 1779 and 1780 for their own reasons, certainly could not be counted on. Spain soon shifted sides.

Years later, Jules Jusserand, French ambassador to the United States from 1902 to 1925, quipped that America was blessed in terms of its frontiers: a weak neighbor to the north, a weak neighbor to the south, fish to the east, fish to the west. But the situation that confronted America in its early years was much more

Box 3.1	**Wars in Europe, in America**

In Europe	In America
War of the League of Augsburg (1688–97)	King William's War (1689–97)
War of the Spanish Succession (1701–13)	Queen Anne's War (1702–13)
War of the Austrian Succession (1740–48)	King George's War (1744–48)
Seven Years' War (1756–63)	French and Indian War (1754–63)

difficult. It had the British to the north (in Canada), the Spanish to the south (in Florida, Mexico, and Central and South America), the French and British both to the southeast (in the Indies), and to the west, the French (dominating the Mississippi). Even further west were the Spanish (in areas like southern California and New Mexico), the Russians (in northern California and up into Alaska), and the British again (in the Oregon Territory). The United States had as immediate or near neighbors *all* the great powers of the world except for Austria. The United States had no reliable friends, and it had more potential enemies than it could handle.

Despite these unfavorable strategic circumstances, over a period of seven or so decades American frontiers were successfully expanded and the European presence drastically reduced. But it certainly was not easy. Even early on there were conflicts, from an undeclared war at sea with France between 1798 and 1800, to the War of 1812 with Britain (and the simultaneous struggle with Spain over West Florida).

In these early years, as was so true later, there were vigorous debates over policy. The primary topic turned on prioritizing threats: would it benefit America most to support the British or the French in their continuing struggles? The alternatives were clear enough, for what would benefit the one would weaken the other, and America would have to live with the result. Such fundamental decisions were not devoid of ethical and emotional complications. But when push came to shove, it was the most basic and hardheaded considerations of American national interest that won out. Indeed, the early period of America's national existence has often and correctly been called one of *realism*. Policymakers knew the infant republic was weak, friendless, and surrounded by the territories of Europe's great powers. The fact that independence was achieved in a time of extraordinary turbulence in international affairs, just before the long years of great power wars during the French Revolution and under Napoleon, increased those risks. America's power problem was clear. The most vital national interest of all, national survival, was at risk. The United States had to minimize the enmity it confronted, avoid unnecessary self-sought involvements, parry any aggressive initiatives from abroad, and avoid all-out confrontations with major nations until, with the passage of time, its power increased.

Jefferson's acquisition of the Louisiana Territory (April 30, 1803) is a good example of realism. Jefferson, an advocate of a modest role for the federal government, purchased the area and doubled the size of the republic, with the new half under federal control. He knew the opportunity was too good to miss.[1]

In just sixty-four years, as the drive for continental supremacy went on, the United States expanded from coast to coast, adding the area west of Lake Superior in 1818, Florida in 1819, the Maine boundary and Lake of the Woods area in 1842, Texas in 1845, Oregon in 1846, California and the Mexican cession in 1848, and the Gadsden Purchase in 1853. This expansion had the additional merit that it removed foreign troops from all of these territories.

During this period United States foreign policy was focused on problems close to home, whose implications were well understood. The first of a number of foreign policy "doctrines" was announced by President Monroe (December 2, 1823). British Foreign Secretary Canning had suggested a joint warning against any European intervention in the Western Hemisphere that was to restore Spain's newly independent colonies to Spain's rule. Monroe decided to proceed unilaterally, instead, but confident that the new doctrine would, in fact, have the support of the British whose fleet could block any naval expeditions to the New World.[2] The Monroe Doctrine had three main points: Europe to keep "hands off" the New World, no new colonization, and American noninvolvement in European affairs. This was another example of realism. The doctrine addressed a clear American interest: to expand continentally while seeking the elimination of effective European power bases in the Americas. It addressed both ends of the problem, claiming a special role for the United States, and denying it for Europe's powers. And although Britain still held Canada, in time separatist sentiments could be expected to develop there, too.

As European possessions in the Americas disappeared and the United States expanded, America broke out of its "containment." Only once after the Monroe Doctrine did a European power attempt military conquest in the Western Hemisphere. During the Civil War, France backed Maximilian of Austria to become emperor of Mexico. With the war over and the American army ready to intervene, France withdrew support and Maximilian was executed.

There were also occasions on which very poor decisions were narrowly avoided. The War of 1812, although a draw, was almost a disaster—the British occupied Washington and burned the White House. Yet the United States, because French interference with U.S. shipping had been almost as irritating as that of the British, came close to taking on both great powers simultaneously. The U.S. Senate vote that rejected war with France was only 18 to 14! Again, with trouble with Mexico brewing, President Polk, losing patience with the British over the division of the Oregon Territory, in December 1845 boldly claimed all of Oregon.[3] With this problem at a crisis, on January 13, 1846, Polk also ordered General Taylor to advance his troops up to the Rio Grande, into territory disputed with Mexico. A two-front war loomed, had not the British compromised on Oregon.[4]

The Civil War, although a time of maximum danger for the United States because the British flirted with recognizing the Confederacy, was handled very carefully by President Lincoln, who well understood the virtue of "conserving enemies."

The record shows that during this early period the United States generally made prudent and realistic choices between alternatives, that its sense of priorities was sound, and that its occasional temptations to overstep were either resisted or the consequences escaped. By the late 1860s, the United States was largely invulnerable militarily within its own frontiers, it had extended to continental dimensions, and it was free of any serious foreign threats. Consequently, American energies could be focused internally on economic growth and development. Total farm acreage, 493 million by 1865, by 1890 reached 839 million. In 1870, the U.S. percentage of world manufacturing production already was 23.3. Only Britain's share was greater: 31.8 percent. Germany's was a mere 13.2, France's was 10.3, Russia's was 3.7.[5]

An Expanding Role

This great economic expansion was not at first paralleled by equal activity in foreign policy. Yet some significant changes were underway, changes that implied a new and larger American role. Between the late 1860s and through the 1880s, the United States began to reach out to the Pacific. Commodore Matthew Perry "opened" Japan to the West in 1854. In 1867 Midway was taken. That same year Alaska was bought from Russia. In 1887 the United States gained the exclusive right to a naval base at Pearl Harbor. Then in 1889, the United States joined Germany and Britain in making Samoa a tripartite protectorate.

Latin America also came in for U.S. attention. The 1850 Clayton-Bulwer Treaty with Great Britain stipulated that neither party would act alone in owning or fortifying any future canal built through Central America. The United States also began to intervene in Latin American disputes and revolutions (as in Haiti, Brazil, and Nicaragua).[6]

Another harbinger of change was the gradual expansion of the U.S. Navy. In 1883, Congress voted money for three light cruisers and a dispatch vessel. By that decade's end, Congress had added other cruisers and authorized two large armored cruisers (or small battleships), *Maine* and *Texas.*[7] Coastal fortifications were strengthened and military education institutions such as the Naval War College (1884) were established. The Naval Act of 1890 added three seagoing (but coastline) battleships.

There was no public clamor for playing a larger role—not as yet. It was almost as if the United States somehow got ready to play that role before the conscious decision was made.

United States relations with Great Britain continued to be the most important of all, throughout the nineteenth century. By 1895, when America intervened in a boundary dispute between Venezuela and British Guiana, the British had little relish for a third conflict. British relations with France and Russia were poor, and the new German Empire had embarked upon building a high-seas fleet that could have no other purpose than contesting British rule of the seas. Given an abundance of potential enemies, the British swallowed their pride when U.S. Secretary of State Olney sent them a "diplomatic" note boasting that "Today the United States is practically sovereign on this continent, and its fiat is law upon the subjects" it chooses. The outcome of Britain's prudence and desire to "conserve" enemies, and America's boisterousness, was arbitration of the frontier.

A festering sore off the American coast was Spanish Cuba. Not only did Americans want the Spanish out, but they also wanted an end to the harsh and continuing suppression of every effort by Cuban nationalists to win freedom. Fanned by the so-called "yellow journals" of the day (we would call them "tabloids"), popular anger grew intense in America in 1897–98. When the battleship *Maine* blew up mysteriously in Havana Harbor in February 1898, the pressures on President McKinley became almost overwhelming. In March, Congress voted for war preparations, and in April McKinley decided to request authority to intervene with force. Congress declared war on April 19. "Remember the *Maine*!" became the battle cry.

The war began over Cuba, but ended with the Philippines. In America's first two-ocean war, the United States defeated the Spanish in Cuba, occupied Puerto Rico, and won a second battle off Manila with the Spanish Far Eastern forces.

The Spanish-American War was a watershed in several respects.[8] Hawaii was annexed to ensure reinforcement for the fleet in the Philippines, the United States took over the Philippines as an American possession, and America embarked on a global role. The decision on the Philippines was not taken easily.[9] As McKinley pondered his alternatives, he began from the point of view that it would be unwise, for several reasons, including geopolitical ones, to let the islands fall into foreign hands. (Germany and Japan were both strongly interested, as was England.) Commercial considerations were also involved; the China market beckoned. Public opinion made a simple withdrawal infeasible. There was also a strong religious aspect. McKinley later told his fellow Methodists how he decided the issue. He said he had thought of taking only Manila, or perhaps the island of Luzon at first.

> I walked the floor of the White House night after night until midnight . . . I went down on my knees and prayed Almighty God for light and guidance. And one night late it came to me . . . (1) that we could not give them back to Spain—that would be cowardly and dishonorable; (2) that we could not turn them over to . . . our commercial rivals [since] that would be bad business and discreditable; (3) that we could not leave them to themselves [since] they would soon have anarchy and misrule [so] (4) that there was nothing left for us to do but to take them all, and to educate the Filipinos, and uplift and civilize and Christianize them, and by

God's grace do the very best we could by them, as our fellowmen for whom Christ also died.[10]

McKinley saw four options, but they really reduced, as the most important decisions always do, to two: withdraw or stay and be involved.

In early 1899 the Filipinos rose in revolt against their new American masters. It took 70,000 troops until 1902 to suppress the uprising. It showed there were more ramifications to the Filipino situation than McKinley had realized.[11] Rarely do wars produce entirely predictable results.

Toward Increasing Global Awareness (1899–1914)

The decision to take the Philippines was a true watershed, then. It showed a growing interest in Asia. It showed a willingness to use force. It showed an ability to use force far from American shores, marking as it did the first deployment of substantial U.S. military forces far from the continental United States.

The growing interest in Asia was also reflected in U.S. policies toward China and Japan. Once Japan, flexing its new military muscles, defeated China in 1894–95, most of the great powers rushed to take advantage of China's revealed weakness. They demanded and got lease-holds and "spheres of interest" up and down the Chinese coast. The most immediate American reaction was to avoid being shut out. In the "Open Door" note of 1899, Washington demanded equal treatment in the British, German, and Russian spheres, especially for harbor access and railroad use.

As the century closed, Chinese resentment against these "foreign devils" sparked the Boxer uprising. Soon the foreign legations were besieged in Beijing, and an international rescue force had to be dispatched to their relief. That force, which included 2,500 U.S. troops, marked another landmark. It was the first American force to land on the Asian mainland—where so many would follow in later years.

China's disintegration brought a new "Open Door" note in which Secretary Hay demanded "equal and impartial trade" with China (a later generation would say, a "level playing field"). Hay added that U.S. policy was "to seek a solution [that would] preserve 'China' as a territorial and administrative entity."[12] The great powers paid little attention to the note but, since they could not agree on how to divide China up further, the question remained moot. The *concepts* in these notes, though, remained central to U.S. foreign policy, even if they avoided any substantive commitments.

Japan, as a rising and ambitious power, was to prove the greatest threat to China. After its centuries of isolation, once Perry opened Japan, the Japanese went full bore for modernization. After its victory over China it ended Chinese influence in Korea and acquired Taiwan and the Pescadores. In 1904–05 Japan defeated Tsarist Russia in a new war, much to the surprise of many. President

Teddy Roosevelt mediated the peace settlement, the terms of which reflected Japanese military success. In 1905, the Taft-Katsura memorandum signified America's willingness to allow Japan a free hand in Korea, in return for giving up any ambitions regarding the Philippines. This was a first attempt to draw a line between Japanese and American Pacific interests. (Japan subsequently annexed Korea.)

In 1908 a new U.S.-Japanese agreement, the Root-Takahira arrangement, accepted the "existing status quo" in the Pacific and accepted the Open Door principle for China. But in 1911, Russia and Japan nevertheless agreed on dividing up Manchuria into spheres, regardless of American desires. By the time World War I began, it was obvious that Japan and the United States would each play major roles in Asia. Whether they would do so and be able to take each other's interests into account and adjust to each other peacefully was a question for the future.

By century's end, the U.S. role in Central America and in the Caribbean had also grown. Few doubted that the United States was intent on dominating this area. In 1901, for example, Congress passed the Platt Amendment. This gave the United States the "right" to intervene in Cuba's domestic and foreign affairs. In 1903, the U.S. Navy established the Guantanamo Bay naval base on land leased from Cuba in perpetuity. Cuba had become an American protectorate. In 1902, when Britain and Germany seized Venezuelan gunboats in a dispute over debt, and when the Germans then later bombarded a Venezuelan village, President Teddy Roosevelt took strong action. His annual message to Congress in 1904, recognizing the provocation that South American debt defaults represented, interposed the United States between the debt-collectors and those who owed. Roosevelt said that "the Monroe Doctrine may force the United States, however reluctantly, in flagrant cases . . . to the exercise of an international police power."[13] This "Roosevelt Corollary" to the Monroe Doctrine was repeated in his message of 1905, almost word for word. It was the stepping stone to armed U.S. intervention in the Dominican Republic in 1905, and in Cuba in 1906.

A second illustration of increased U.S. activism to the south was over a Central American canal. England, pressed by the United States, agreed to set aside the Clayton-Bulwer Treaty and instead allow America the right to unilaterally fortify any such canal. At the time of the agreement, this second Hay-Pauncefort Treaty remained hypothetical, though, because of the inconvenient fact that the United States did not possess any Central American territory. In 1903, with the approval (and thinly disguised assistance) of the Roosevelt Administration, Panamanians rose up in revolt and declared their independence from Colombia (which had spurned U.S. offers). The day *before* the revolt, President Roosevelt ordered the U.S. Navy to maintain "free and uninterrupted transit" across the Isthmus. A canal treaty was quickly negotiated with the new state, guaranteeing Panama's independence and giving the United States "sovereign" rights in a ten mile wide canal zone.[14]

Intervention in the Caribbean continued with U.S. troops sent to Cuba in 1898–1902, 1906–09, and 1912. Marines were used to restore order in the

Dominican Republic in 1912 and again in 1916.[15] Marines sent to Nicaragua in 1912 were not fully withdrawn until 1933. Marines also were sent to Haiti.

Mexico, too, was involved in tensions with the United States. Over 50,000 Americans lived there; about a billion American dollars were invested there. Incidents at Vera Cruz spurred President Wilson on April 20, 1914, to ask for congressional authority to intervene, and soon more violence occurred at Vera Cruz. With Mexican central authority a revolving door, General Pancho Villa carried on his own campaign, massacring eighteen American mining engineers at Santa Ysabel in January, 1916. When Villa crossed the frontier and sacked Columbus, New Mexico, General Pershing was ordered to cross into Mexico to pursue Villa with some 12,000 American troops.[16]

On the Eve of War

This was the situation, and this was the foreign policy record of the United States on the eve of World War I. Despite the American foray into the Pacific, despite the interventions to the south, there was no public consensus for a larger and truly global role. Attention was primarily focused inward—on economic expansion. The traditional enemy or opponent of the United States was Britain, with whom Americans had fought two wars and narrowly avoided two or three other return engagements. When Britain was at war elsewhere, America was normally much freer from threat, because only Britain had the naval forces to pose even a credible danger. It was to take several years of World War I before two great psychological changes would occur in the American people. First, they would cast off their long-maintained conviction that America should stay out of Europe's affairs. Second, they would recognize that a British defeat could actually be very adverse to fundamental American national interests.

Before World War I, Americans had not spent much time thinking about the nature of the international political system and the major developments in that system between 1815 and 1914, developments that had contributed so much to their security. That they had lived through a nineteenth century characterized by very unusual strategic features in the international system was not appreciated. For when World War I did come, it was at the end of a hundred years of general peace in which all wars had been local. These many decades without general war, of course, greatly contrasted with American experience in the seventeenth and eighteenth centuries. As Box 3.1 showed, wars then were frequent.

The prime cause of this unusual American freedom from danger was that the major European nations, who were the key actors in the global balance of power, were preoccupied elsewhere, This was a time of very significant changes in Europe. Between 1848 and 1871, Italy and Germany, which had remained fragmented into the nineteenth century, were being unified. That not only changed great power relationships, but it was accompanied by a series of limited wars that focused their attention at home.

Germany's role in the long international peace was key. Otto von Bismarck (the first prime minister of Prussia and later the "Iron Chancellor" of the unified, imperial Germany) could easily have caused a dangerous increase in the tension level. But Bismarck's adroit diplomatic maneuvering allowed him to fight one opponent at a time, avoiding the general war that the far-reaching changes in Europe could so easily have ignited. His most important move (after defeating France in 1871) was isolating the revenge-minded French by exploiting the counterbalancing interests of Russia and Austria so that both powers needed German support—an excellent example of the conservation of enemies. With a unified Germany by 1871 as the premier power on the Continent, Bismarck made every effort to keep Europe at peace. He encouraged France to look abroad for colonies and, in fact, from 1871 until the end of the century, the great powers carved out huge new empires in militarily weak Africa and Asia.

It was the stabilized European situation that permitted this new drive for colonies. What inspired it, though, was a general belief that colonies in an industrial age were a great economic asset as sources of raw materials and as a market. This drive for colonies accompanied an enormous expansion in world trade which, from a mere $4 billion in 1850, rose by 1913 to $40.4 billion. Colonies were sources of raw materials as well as secondary markets for manufactures.

The drive for colonies brought Britain and France into competition while encouraging Franco-German cooperation against Britain. But in 1890, when Bismarck was retired by the young and aggressive Kaiser Wilhelm, things began to change. France was feeling threatened, and counterbalancing interests led as always in two different directions. The fruit of this policy review came in 1904 with the Anglo-French Entente. This was not an alliance, but it was a *quid pro quo* agreement that settled the colonial arguments between France and Britain.

Great Britain welcomed the change, especially since the Kaiser was building a high-seas fleet that could only be directed against it. Similarly, in 1907, for much the same reasons that motivated France, Russia entered into a similar arrangement with Britain. The Anglo-Russian Entente ended the perennial colonial disputes that for decades had threatened to bring England and Russia to war, but the agreement also eliminated the counterbalancing interests that had kept Europe from lining up into two distinct camps. Soon Germany, Austria, and an ambivalent Italy were in one formal alliance, while Britain, France, and Russia were informally aligned in another.

The results of all these developments on the United States hardly needs underlining. It should be quite clear why Britain, now well embarked on the conservation of its enemies, in the 1890s had decided to forego the luxury of war with its sometimes obstreperous American "cousin" over British Guiana's frontiers with Venezuela.

Already after 1904, and even more so after 1905, the elimination of counterbalancing interest considerations from Europe's power politics brought on a steady increase in the tension level, triggering a series of major crises. The sixth—and last—in the series began on June 28, 1914, when Archduke Franz Ferdinand of Austria was assassinated by a Serbian nationalist. On July 28

Austria declared war on Serbia, and Russia mobilized in response. Germany, whose war plans depended on defeating France in the west before the Russians could move, felt compelled to act. On August 1 Germany declared war on Russia. Russia's allies, Britain and France, responded. World War I had begun.

World War I

When World War I broke out, the United States declared its neutrality. After all, it was a "European" quarrel. Besides, many Americans had emigrated from the nations now at war and taking sides would divide the nation. Finally, what would America gain by participation? So when Wilson urged Americans to be "impartial in thought as well as in action," it did not seem unwise.

Events were to make Americans change their minds, but only gradually. A primary cause was the institution of rival blockades by the Germans and the British, which threatened America's right to the freedom of the seas. But the blockades were not enforced in the same way by both belligerents. Where the British forced American vessels with supposed war materials to sail into British harbors to be condemned for a price, the Germans, using submarines, sank ships. (With their surface ships swept off the seas by the British navy, the Germans had to use U-boats to continue the struggle at all. These submarines, with fragile hulls and little space aboard for prisoners, could not simply surface for prolonged "discussions" with merchant ships.)

When the Germans decided to sink enemy ships on sight in the war zone, the United States responded with a sharp warning in February 1915. Then the British steamship *Lusitania* was sunk, with a loss of 1,198 lives, including 128 Americans.[17] American public opinion now began a decided shift against Germany.[18] Not wanting to bring America into the war, the Germans halted unrestricted submarine warfare, concentrating on freighters rather than liners. But as German U-boats increased in number and were increasingly effective, the Germans in January 1917 resumed unrestricted submarine warfare. With 74 submarines in August 1916, and an expected total of 103 by February 1917, the Germans felt confident they could finish England by mid-1917.[19] With the United States army at less than 150,000 men, backed by a slightly larger number of National Guardsmen, Germany did not believe that America could field significant forces in Europe before Germany had achieved its victory.

Quickly following this event came another. In March the "Zimmerman note," a German proposal to Mexico to enter the war and recover Texas, Arizona, and New Mexico, was intercepted and deciphered by the British. On April 1, 1917, President Wilson asked Congress for a declaration of war, and on April 4 the Senate agreed, 82–6, and the House on April 6, by 373–50.

President Wilson's war message was filled with abstract moralisms. The German submarine warfare was a "warfare against mankind." The United States had "no quarrel with the German people," only with the "little groups of ambitious men" who used "their fellow men as pawns and tools." The world had to "be made safe for democracy." There was little sign that Wilson understood the complex series of events that had first saved the United States from unwanted war in the nineteenth century and that later had made war inevitable.

One could argue that beneath the rhetoric there was some semblance of strategic thinking. The reaction to the belligerents was not equal, in part because their offenses against American interests were not equal. The Zimmerman note and unrestricted submarine warfare were real and tangible concerns. Stripped of the garments of moral universalism that Americans by this time used to discuss political issues, Wilson was recognizably talking about an opponent who was a real and tangible threat to concrete American interests.

Germany's bet, of course, was wrong. With the battlefield warfare almost stalemated, the influx of much larger numbers of American troops than the Germans had anticipated made all the difference. For an extremely low cost in lives (48,909 battlefield dead and 112,432 from all causes, plus 230,074 wounded) and a direct war expenditure of only about $22 billion, the United States added the final blow, restored the balance of power, and won a prime seat at the peace conference.[20]

Interlude (1918–35)

The 1918–35 period represented an interlude in America's erratic movement toward an increasingly major world role. These years began with America considering a proposal by Wilson to keep the United States as a major actor in world affairs; it ended with the United States mired in its isolationism as war clouds gathered again in Europe.

The slogan on the American victory medals from World War I (*THE GREAT WAR FOR CIVILIZATION*) catches rather well Wilson's approach. Noting only the "down" side of the balance of power (the series of crises between 1905 and 1914), Wilson wanted to replace that balance of power with something better. It apparently did not occur to him to wonder much why no one had done that in the preceding several thousand years of international relations. Wilson's idea was to guarantee every nation's existing territorial integrity through a League of Nations that would provide a collective security from all, to all.

Wilson explained his idea for a League of Nations to the U.S. Senate on January 22, 1917:

> I am proposing that all nations henceforth avoid entangling alliances which would draw them into competition of power, catch them in a net of intrigue and selfish rivalry, and disturb their own affairs with influences intruded from without. [A very American view!] There is no entangling alliance in a concert of power. When all unite to act in the common interest and with the same purpose, all act in the common interest and are free to live their own lives under a common protection.[21]

On January 8, 1918, Wilson announced a Fourteen Point program to provide what he considered a just peace, one that would include "open covenants of peace, openly arrived at, freedom of the seas, reduction of arms, and territorial adjustments to correct old wrongs." His fourteenth point was the League of Nations itself.[22] Germany, worn out, accepted the program. But the Versailles peace settlement that followed, although Wilson participated, was an unmitigated disaster, providing copious incentives to a new war as soon as possible—which proved to be 1939.

Hitler was later to correctly label the Versailles Treaty as a *diktat,* a dictated peace. The Germans were essentially forced to sign an Allied draft, their protests brushed aside. The treaty included a clause saddling Germany with the guilt of having caused the war (which was partly true), imposed huge and open-ended reparations that would cripple Germany's economy, took German territories in Europe and abroad, forced German disarmament, and provided a "Polish Corridor" between East Prussia and the main body of Germany (in order to allow Polish access to the "free port" of Danzig on the Baltic).

In the other settlements that ended the war, Russia, which had undergone a Communist Revolution, was stripped of even more territories, while Austria-Hungary was literally dismantled into a group of small weak states. Two great powers despoiled, and one dismantled! It is hard to imagine a weaker basis for a lasting peace.[23] Built in was the likelihood that one day Germany and Russia would reach out together to absorb the small weak states scattered between them.

The United States rejected the Versailles Treaty, including membership in the League, but not because of the defects mentioned above. The treaty might have been approved if Wilson had agreed to reservations that would have made the League's decisions only recommendations until the Senate approved. But for America to be required to act through the decisions of other nations proved too much.[24] Summing up the new mood in the United States, President Warren Harding, Wilson's successor, outlined a quite different role for the United States: "We seek no part in directing the destinies of the world."[25]

America did not mean thereby not to protect its own interests as it unilaterally interpreted them. It did not, as is so often said, "retreat into isolationism." What it did was "to go it alone," to act *unilaterally.*[26] H.G. Wells was quite accurate when he said of American policy in the 1930s, "Every time Europe looks across the Atlantic to see the American eagle, it observed only the rear end of an ostrich."[27] But that ostrich's head was pointed toward Japan.

McKinley's decision at the end of the Spanish-American War to take the Philippines had led logically to a concern for security in the Far Pacific. Japan, which had used World War I as an excuse to take Germany's Pacific islands (the Marianas, the Carolines, and the Marshalls), had also forced Germany out of China's Shantung province. Japan's Twenty-One Demands of January 8, 1915, had already showed Japan's ambition to turn China into a protectorate. But the United States, although increasingly anxious about Japanese expansionism, was in no mood to use force to protect what it saw as its interests. These years, accordingly, were marked by a series of Japanese moves and American protest notes. In fact, the United States took the lead in negotiating a naval arms agreement which prevented the United States from intervening effectively in force in the Western Pacific.

The Washington Naval Conference of 1921 produced a series of treaties designed to stabilize the status quo in the Pacific. The one on naval armaments established a ratio for capital ships (meaning battleships and battle cruisers) based on tonnage. The 525,000 for the United States and Britain shaded off to 315,000 tons for Japan (and 175,000 for Italy and for France). Aircraft carrier tonnage was also set: 135,000 for the United States and Britain, 81,000 for Japan (60,000 each for Italy and France). That provided in both cases a ratio of 5:5:3 for the first three nations. Additionally, these three powers were to maintain the status quo "with regard to fortifications and naval bases" in the Pacific, except for the Japanese home islands, Hawaii for the United States, and Singapore for Britain.

These provisions meant that, given the technological conditions of the day, when long range air power was still in its infancy and missiles were still in the future, neither Japan nor America could in principle fight each other in the other's home waters, assuming reasonable vigilance. Without full-scale repair and staging facilities nearer to each other, even the larger forces of the United States—even if all concentrated in the Pacific—would not be superior to Japan's in Japanese home waters. Because each of the three nations had naval superiority in its own corner of the Pacific Ocean area, the agreement went far to assuring each party against effective attack.[28]

In these treaties the United States exchanged military inferiority in the Western Pacific for a Japanese promise to behave. Contrary to later views clouded by the Pearl Harbor attack, the Japanese in fact did behave for several years. When Japan refused to extend the naval treaty, denouncing it effective December 31, 1936, it was within its rights. But America did not strengthen its Philippine bases in any significant way. Nor, between 1922 and 1930, did the United States even build much in naval categories *not* restricted. The disconnection between announced policy for the Far East and the American willingness to take realistic steps to back that policy, grew.

In the 1930s the trend continued. In September, 1931, an incident took place in Manchuria that the Japanese used as a pretext for the occupation of the whole province. In the Stimson Doctrine the United States said it would not "admit the legality of any situation de facto" that purported to end its established legal treaty rights.[29] The League Commission of Inquiry, looking into this Mukden incident, concluded that the situation in China was ambiguous, since Japan had a right by treaty to maintain troops in Manchuria to protect the Japanese-controlled South Manchurian railway. Secretary of State Cordell Hull, discussing the possibility of the League instituting an arms embargo against Japan, dismissed an embargo as ineffective. Nor would the United States join such an action "unless we had secured substantial guarantees from the governments of all of the great powers which would ensure us against the effect of any retaliatory measures which the Japanese might undertake." This was surely a far cry for the United States from acting like a great power! Please protect us, indeed. Hull went on to say that America would act only "with a due and prudent regard for American interests and in particular for our *paramount interest of remaining free from any entanglements* which would involve this country *in a foreign war*." [Italics added.][30]

Was this really America's "paramount interest"—remaining "free" from "entanglements"? When the United States later found itself at war with Japan, was that war then, since the United States was part of it, no longer "foreign" (and therefore acceptable)? The U.S. Far Eastern policy was making less and less sense. If America really cared what happened there, it was approaching the situation in a curiously ineffective fashion—assuming as the United States was that mere words could change events where other nations were prepared to use naked force.

The second area of American policy activity in the 1920s and 1930s was Latin America. There, because no other great power could say nay, the United States dominated, although at the cost of being cordially disliked. Franklin D. Roosevelt, with his "good neighbor" policy, first announced on March 4, 1933, began to change this.[31] By August 1936, the United States had abrogated the Platt Amendment and withdrawn the marines from Haiti. In 1936 the American republics signed a consultative agreement in the event of war. U.S. policy for Latin America showed a realistic appreciation of Latin interests and problems, coupled with an imaginative approach to hemispheric cooperation that would stand the United States in good stead very shortly.

U.S. foreign policy in this period is a mixed record, beginning with Wilsonian idealism, continuing with verbal opposition to Japan unaccompanied by any willingness to go beyond words, and ending with a very sensible change of policy toward U.S. neighbors to the south. That the United States was far from free of the delusion that words *were* policy, even without commitments, is showed best for the whole period by the Senate debate over the Kellogg-Briand Pact. Concluded in 1928, it purported to "outlaw" war. Senator William E. Borah of Idaho stoutly maintained that the pact contained no obligation, expressed or implied, that was binding on the United States. Senator Hiram Johnson of California challenged Borah, who reaffirmed his judgment: "Exactly. In other words, when the treaty is broken the United States is absolutely free. It is just as free to choose its course as if the treaty had never been written. . . ."[32] Rather than ridicule the idea of a meaningless treaty, Senator Claude Swanson of Virginia called it "a noble gesture . . . and as such I shall support it. . . ."[33] The treaty was quickly approved and ratified. But words and gestures do not a peaceful world make.

The Great Depression

By the mid-1930s the United States had another potent reason for recoiling from commitments. It was mired in the Great Depression. Severe economic problems at home reinforced the determination not to become involved in "another mistake." It is important to bear in mind that in 1932, when the American voters rejected Herbert Hoover's do-nothing approach to the depression and elected Franklin D. Roosevelt (FDR), Germany was already caught up in its own political crisis and was only months from installing Adolf Hitler to solve German problems.

It is not easy to bring alive the depths of despair that accompanied the Great Depression and that also aborted any slight temptation by the United States to become involved far from its own frontiers. The generations since the 1930s hear about the Great Depression much as, until AIDS came along, they heard about the Great Plague. Nothing like that depression has ever happened to them, only recessions, which have usually had the happy feature of ending with a fine upward sweep in GNP. So it takes a little effort to realize what happened, how World War I veterans, unable to find work and uncushioned by any unemployment and social security system, camped out on the Washington Mall to demand help, how ordinary people were homeless and unemployed in numbers that make anything since pale into insignificance, how people around the world were ready to try almost anything. That "anything" included the New Deal in the United States and the Hitler movement in Germany.

In the last analysis, the Versailles Treaty provisions, themselves the product of hate engendered by the enormously destructive war, were responsible for much of this misery. For among other things, World War I destroyed Europe's economic mechanisms that had previously brought prosperity.

Enormous war costs were paid for only very little out of current taxes. War bonds raised funds; national debts increased; money was turned out by the printing presses and in the process necessarily changed value.[34] For example, French francs in circulation at the end of 1913 were 5,713,000,000. At the end of 1919, the total was 37,274,000,000.[35] When, at the end of World War I, Germany was saddled with impossible reparations costs, they helped to drag down even the more healthy economies of the world.[36] American short-term funds poured into Germany to be paid out by German banks to the allies as reparations; the allies used these funds to pay off America's war loans to them; and these funds then were loaned back by American banks to Germany as short-term funds.[37] The whole unstable international system began its collapse with the Great Stock Market Crash in the United States in October 1929. In America that collapse caused the "margin" to be called in, creating shortages in short-term funds.[38] With systems built on credit contracting enormously and in some places inflation rampant, the shortage spread to Europe. In 1931 the collapse of the great European bank in Vienna, the Credit Anstalt, signaled the beginning of worldwide depression.

The 1930s was a dismal decade. Widespread unemployment everywhere; money devaluations; strikes; Hitler.

What had kept the monetary aspects of the international economy going was the gold standard. The major currencies of the world, prior to the Depression, were all exchangeable for gold. The common standard gave them assured values in terms of each other. If conditions in one country made its price level cheaper, it would export more as demand rose abroad for the cheaper goods.

Foreign countries, paying for these goods with gold (or reserves of convertible currencies, which was the same thing) would thereby tend to raise the price level in the exporting country (i.e., more money in circulation would drive prices up). Higher prices at home would attract more imports from abroad to take advantage of it; higher costs at home (because of higher prices) would make it harder to export; and therefore gold would soon be exported to pay for the excessive imports. This "natural equilibrium," as economists at the time described it, worked fairly well as predicted, so long as trade remained free and the nations used the gold standard. But neither of these conditions were to be true after World War I.

Tariffs had been steadily rising since 1879. The average increase for sixteen leading industrial nations between 1913 and 1925 was a third. Even the British put on a 33 1/3 duty on certain items after 1921. The Hawley-Smoot Tariff of 1930 in the United States raised the general *ad valorem* level to 41.5 percent.[39] As other nations retaliated, American exports, which had been $2.62 billion in early 1929, fell to $0.84 billion in early 1932. In the same period, the new tariffs exacerbated the downturn, and imports into the United States decreased by 62.1 percent. Similar things were happening worldwide.

Now add the problem of converting currencies. In the spring of 1931, most currencies were on what was called a "gold exchange" basis (meaning usually pegged to the British pound, itself convertible). In September 1931, Britain was forced to leave the gold standard. By 1936 not a state in the world had its currency on a freely convertible gold basis. Nations now began to depreciate their currencies, most of them between 30 and 40 percent. On January 31, 1934, President Roosevelt set the American dollar's value at a little less than 60 percent of its former gold value. He later made that 50 percent.

Even without high tariffs, currency manipulations meant a deathblow to much international trade. How could one contract for goods when the price of currencies changed drastically overnight? It got much worse, with import quotas and blocked currencies and barter deals.

War Clouds Gather

If we keep this economic paralysis in mind, we shall understand better one reason why Hitler was not more effectively opposed. The United States had not been blooded in World War I like the British or the French, but now it was deep in a widespread misery from which hardly any American was exempt. America was, moreover, ill-equipped to provide adequate power backing for more active policies even if it had wanted to. Cordell Hull, in a speech on February 16, 1935, captured American sentiment nicely when he said: "Seen from the distance of this hemisphere, the manifold boundary lines . . . of Europe become merged and Europe emerges as an entity. We have no direct concern with the political and economic controversies of the European states. We have time and again expressly disassociated ourselves from these disputes."[40]

This sentiment lay behind the series of neutrality acts enacted into law from 1935 to 1939. Congress took the lead here, providing for an arms embargo to be extended to any and all belligerents, indiscriminately. Well-armed Italy did well out of this when it attacked poorly equipped Ethiopia in 1935. Indeed, since general trade was not prohibited, U.S. exports of oil, steel, and scrap iron to Italy actually increased by 200 to 300 percent in the last months of 1935. Similarly, in 1936, when the Spanish Civil War broke out, Franco's forces had no problem since they received supplies from the Italians and Germans, but the Loyalist government was weakened.

Congress decided to amend things in 1937, giving the president discretion to decide whether "a state of war" or "civil strife" existed. When a full-scale but undeclared war broke out between China and Japan in 1937, Roosevelt used that fiction to continue aid to China.

As things went from bad to worse in Europe, the United States was debating the Ludlow amendment to the Constitution. This would have required a nationwide vote before America could go to war, excepting only for an actual invasion. In January 1938 the House shelved the amendment by the extremely close vote of 209 to 188—again an indication of divided American sentiment. Two months later, in March 1938, Hitler took Austria and in September of the same year came the dismemberment of Czechoslovakia's defenses by means of the Munich Agreement. This event, described by British Prime Minister Neville Chamberlain, as assuring "peace in our time," gave Hitler a new opportunity to repeat his usual assurance that what he had just taken was "the last territorial claim which I have to make in Europe." In the following March, Hitler then took the rest of Czechoslovakia. Congress decided once more to revise the neutrality acts and was still debating in August 1939, when the Soviets concluded a nonaggression pact with Hitler. World War II began on September 1, 1939, with the United States at least as unprepared, militarily, emotionally, or in any other way, as it had been in 1914. Unwelcome world events were continuing to be hard to accept.

A cash-and-carry provision of the third neutrality act had expired as of May 1939, and Congress, in the fourth such act, made it unlawful for any American vessel to carry "any passengers or any articles or materials to any state" named by the president as being in "a state of war." No American citizen without special permission could travel into any "combat area" proclaimed by the president. After such a proclamation, no "American vessel, engaged in commerce with any foreign state" was "to be armed, except with small arms. . . ." Bonds of belligerents could not be sold, or credit extended to them. Arms dealers would be licensed, and arms could be shipped to belligerents only with such licenses. But now at least arms could be sold, though on a "cash-and-carry" basis. This provision avoided the situation brought about under the third neutrality act, when, on September 5, 1939, President Roosevelt, bound by the law, had to embargo all arms shipments, cutting off Britain and France from some $80,000,000 worth of arms already ordered. President Roosevelt had said of that third act that its continued existence was "most vitally dangerous to American neutrality, American security, and American peace," adding: "I regret that the Congress passed that act. I regret equally that I signed that act." The new act, while still very restrictive, at least allowed America to quit aiding a Hitler victory.

The events just described, and the debate in Congress over the fourth neutrality act, show the extent of American confusion in the late 1930s. As we saw in Chapter 2, the disagreements involved the question of when and where to draw the line, but they went deeper than that. They also involved difficulties in agreeing on what the problem was, defining the real issues, and formulating policy alternatives. What obviously was missing was a conceptual consensus about what America faced as the most serious threat to its security, what America wanted the trend of events to be, who America's friends were, which nations were a menace to American security (and in what order of priority), and what the best course of action was to achieve U.S. goals—whatever those were.

One is struck by the *abstract* nature of this debate, particularly its lack of concrete analysis concerning friends and enemies. Even when President Roosevelt provided much needed aid to "our" side by making the Destroyers-Bases Agreement with the British on September 3, 1940, after France had fallen and only the British stood between the United States and Nazi Germany, he gave the usual assurances that these actions were "not inconsistent in any sense with our status of peace. Still less is it a threat against any nation. It is an . . . act of preparation for continental defense in the face of grave danger."[41] How giving destroyers to the British to use against the Germans fit any of these statements would take a metaphysician to figure out.

Eventually, though, the continuing impact of events brought a greater sense of realism. When Roosevelt, on January 6, 1941, called America to become the "arsenal of democracy," a coherent concept was beginning to emerge. The tone was different from earlier messages. He said "that principles of morality and considerations for our own security will never permit us to acquiesce in a peace dictated by aggressors. . . . We know that enduring peace cannot be bought at the cost of other people's freedom." Roosevelt went on to say "we will not be intimidated by the threats of dictators that they will regard as a breach of international law," or act of war, American "aid to the democracies." He then added a very realistic proposition: "When the dictators are ready to make war on us, they will not wait for an act of war on our part."[42] On March 11, 1941, Congress passed the "Lend-Lease" Act, legislation that was designed to aid a Britain that soon would be unable to finance its purchases. It authorized the president to "sell . . . exchange, lease, lend . . . any defense article [to] any country whose defense the President deems vital," and permitted him to determine what, if anything, was required in exchange. Isolationist Senator Wheeler promptly proclaimed this Act a bill to "plow under every fourth American boy," but it passed 60–31 in the Senate and 317–17 in the House.

As 1941 continued, concerns became increasingly immediate and concrete. After Japan took control of Indo-China, on July 25, 1941, FDR, who had already cut off war supplies to Japan, froze all Japanese assets in the United States. As Japanese oil supplies fell, the die was cast, because Japan would either have to give in or attack. So little did congressional or public opinion have a real appreciation of these strategic issues, however, that in August (although the Senate margin was larger), the House agreed to extend Selective Service by only a 203 to 202 vote. But, on December 7, 1941, the Japanese attacked Pearl Harbor. On December 8, the Congress acknowledged that the United States was at war with Japan.

It is difficult even today to say with confidence what would have happened if the Japanese had not attacked, since antiwar sentiment was still very powerful. But, as Roosevelt told Congress on December 8, "There is no blinking at the fact that our people, our territory, and our interests are in grave danger."

Who could any longer deny it, with the smoke from sunken ships at Pearl Harbor still billowing up and the dead not yet even counted?

Summing Up

As we have seen, from 1789 to 1941 the United States moved from a position of minor importance on the world scene to being a major actor. Yet much of the time its role changed more as an almost accidental by-product of America's phenomenal growth and enhanced power than as a consequence of any deliberate policy choices. In the late nineteenth and early twentieth centuries, elements of empire were gained with little real planning. These brought America into close contact with an expanding Japan, with serious later results.

Shortly after World War I, a severe reaction set in to America's first venture in the high-stakes game of European power politics. U.S. intervention was now widely considered to have been a mistake, and the idea of cooperation with other powers, either inside the League of Nations or outside it, was rigorously rejected. For most of the inter-war period, the American people then supported a policy of going it alone, of unilateralism. Only as the prospects for world peace steadily dimmed did it appear more and more likely that a major and sustained internationalist role in cooperation with the other democracies might be required. How grudging and gradual was that realization was graphically shown by the head-in-the-sand neutrality acts and the refusal to take adequate steps in Asia to protect what America continued to proclaim as serious national interests of the United States.

In 1939 the United States was a very long way from the notion so familiar to America since 1945, that America would have to play an involved and responsible role in world affairs. And without Japan's "help" at Pearl Harbor, it is not evident what America's "decisions" would have been about World War II involvement, either.

Notes

1. One scholar calls the Louisiana Purchase Jefferson's "greatest triumph." Walter LeFeber, *The American Age: United States Foreign Policy at Home and Abroad Since 1750* (New York: W. W. Norton, 1989), p. 52. LeFeber goes on to talk of a "brilliant

series of policies that finally forced Napoleon to sell. . . ." (p. 53).

2. James E. Dougherty and Robert L. Pfaltzgraff, Jr., write "European Kings found it an arrogant affront to the Old World for an upstart republic to redefine unilaterally the international law of colonization, especially when that republic lacked the power to enforce its proclamation. But the Americans knew . . . they could count on the support of Britain and its navy." James E. Dougherty and Robert L. Pfaltzgraff, Jr., *American Foreign Policy: FDR to Reagan* (New York: Harper & Row, 1986), p. 5.

3. The Oregon Territory lay between the 42nd parallel, which was the northern boundary of California, and parallel 54 degrees, 40 minutes, the latitude of the southern tip of Russian-controlled Alaska. It had been governed more or less as a U.S.-British condominium since 1818.

4. Not all British commentators have been entirely pleased with the result. Lord William Strang, *Britain in World Affairs: The Fluctuation in Power and Influence from Henry VIII to Elizabeth II* (New York: Frederick A. Praeger, 1961), p. 123, comments: "[T]he Americans succeeded better than their claim warranted."

5. Richard B. Morris and Graham W. Irwin, eds., *Harper Encyclopaedia of the Modern World* (New York: Harper & Row, 1973), pp. 686–89.

6. Thomas G. Paterson, J. Garry Clifford, and Kenneth J. Hagan, *American Foreign Policy: A History* (Lexington, MA: D.C. Heath, 1977), p. 178.

7. Russell F. Weigley, *The American Way of War* (New York: Macmillan, 1973), p. 169.

8. Robert Schulzinger went so far as to say: "Modern American diplomacy dates from the war with Spain in 1898." Robert D. Schulzinger, *American Diplomacy in the Twentieth Century* (New York: Oxford University Press, 1984), p. 16.

9. Jules Davids' succinct discussion is helpful. Jules Davids, *America and the World of Our Time: United States Diplomacy in the Twentieth Century,* 3rd ed. (New York: Random House, 1970), ch. 1.

10. New York *Christian Advocate,* January 22, 1903. According to LeFeber, "It is a dramatic story, but few historians believe it." See LeFeber, *The American Age,* pp. 200 ff. Whether the portrayal is entirely accurate or not, there is no doubt, as Robert Ferrell states, that "A religious factor . . . exerted a considerable influence in the American decision to take the Philippines." Robert H. Ferrell, *American Diplomacy: A History,* 3rd ed. (New York: W. W. Norton & Company, 1975), p. 365. There is also no doubt that the logic of the situation is correctly represented by the quotation.

11. According to H. H. Kohlstaat, McKinley later said: "If old Dewey had just sailed away when he smashed that Spanish fleet, what a lot of trouble he would have saved us." H.H. Kohlstaat, *From McKinley to Harding* (New York: Scribners, 1923), p. 68.

12. *Papers Relating to the Foreign Relations of the United States, 1901, Appendix,* p. 12.

13. U.S., *Congressional Record,* 58th Congress, 3rd Session, p. 19. For an insightful if provocative analysis of this period, see Richard H. Collin, *Theodore Roosevelt's Caribbean: The Panama Canal, the Monroe Doctrine, and the Latin American Context* (Baton Rouge, LA: Louisiana State University Press, 1990).

14. For an excellent and succinct discussion of the background and "Canal Diplomacy" (and intrigue), see Michael L. Conniff, *Panama and the United States: The Forced Alliance* (Athens, GA: University of Georgia Press, 1992), especially Chs. 3–4.

15. President Wilson proclaimed a military occupation.

16. Although the labels "liberal" and "idealistic" are attached to his name, Wilson showed the limits of his tolerance when he said: "I am going to teach the Southern American republics to elect good men." Ray Stannard Baker, *Woodrow Wilson: Life and Letters* (Garden City, NY: Doubleday, Page, 1931), vol. 4, p. 289.

17. The *Lusitania* carried substantial contraband in its storage areas.

18. William Jennings Bryan, Secretary of State in 1915 until he resigned, said in his memoirs that "the administration was lacking in neutrality—not in commission, but in omission. . . ." Quoted in Thomas A. Bailey, *A Diplomatic History of the American People*, 4th ed. (New York: Appleton-Century-Crofts, 1950), p. 577.

19. Richard W. Leopold, *The Growth of American Foreign Policy* (New York: Knopf, 1962), pp. 328–29.

20. Some European leaders, examining comparative losses (Germany 1.8 million, Russia 1.7 million, Britain 1 million, one of every two Frenchmen between twenty and thirty-two in 1914, etc.) said that Wilson had bought his seat at a discount.

21. For the whole address of President Wilson to the Senate, January 22, 1917, see *Papers Relating to the Foreign Relations of the United States, 1917, Supplement,* vol. I, pp. 24–29. For further discussion, see Frederick H. Hartmann, *The Relations of Nations,* 6th ed. (New York: Macmillan, 1983), p. 193–95.

22. Wilson's Fourteen Points are in U.S., *Congressional Record,* 65th Congress, 2nd Session, pp. 680–81.

23. Northedge and Grieve title the 1919–39 period, "The Twenty-Year Armistice." F.S. Northedge and M.J. Grieve, *A Hundred Years of International Relations* (New York: Praeger, 1971), ch. 10.

24. The Lodge Reservations are in the *Congressional Record,* Vol. 58, 66th Congress, 1st Session, pp. 8777 ff. They also consist of 14 articles. The second of the 14 articles laid it down that "The United States assumes no obligation to preserve the territorial integrity or political independence of any other country . . . or to employ the military or naval forces of the United States . . . unless in any particular case the Congress . . . shall by joint resolution so provide."

25. LeFeber's discussion is valuable. LeFeber, *The American Age,* pp. 301–12.

26. See Frederick H. Hartmann, "Away with Unilateralism!" *The Antioch Review,* 11 (Spring 1951), pp. 3–9, which introduces the term.

27. Thomas A. Bailey, *A Diplomatic History of the American People,* 4th ed. (New York: Appleton-Century-Crofts, 1950), p. 628.

28. It could not ensure the United States Navy against Sunday morning lassitude at Pearl Harbor. But, theoretically, the odds were so great against Japan as to give Japan no incentive for such a high-risk venture.

29. U.S., *Senate Document No. 55,* 72nd Congress, 1st Session, pp. 53–54.

30. U.S., Department of State, *Peace and War: United States Foreign Policy, 1931–1941,* Department of State Publication No. 1853 (Washington, DC, 1943), pp. 183–86.

31. For a less sanguine assessment, see Thomas G. Patterson, J. Garry Clifford, and Kenneth J. Hagan, *American Foreign Policy: A History Since 1900,* 2nd ed. (Lexington, MA: D.C. Heath, 1983), Ch. 10.

32. U.S., *Congressional Record,* 70th Congress, 2nd Session, p. 1066 (January 3, 1929).

33. Ibid., pp. 1186–89 (January 5, 1929).

34. For example, the British national debt at the beginning of World War I was 678 million pounds; by the end of March 1920, it was 7,859 million pounds. Witt Bowden, Michael Karpovich, and Abbott Payson Usher, *An Economic History of Europe Since 1750* (New York: American Book Company, 1937), p. 679.

35. *An Economic History of Europe Since 1750,* p. 679.

36. That the reparations burden was "impossible" might seem overstated. Consider this. The final figure was 132 billion gold marks ($33 billion in the dollars of that time). But total world trade in 1913 was only $40.4 billion and Germany's share in 1913 was about $5.3. With very high tariffs now in effect, how could Germany pay? (As long ago as the sixteenth century, Axel Oxenstiern wrote: "Behold, my son, with how little wisdom the world is governed.")

37. U.S. loans to the Allies in cash (pre-Armistice) amounted to over $7 billion. With cash and supplies, and adding post-Armistice, it amounted to over $10 billion.

   Between 1924 and 1931, U.S. private investors loaned about $2.250 billion to Germany. In those same years, the U.S. government received some $2 billion payment on the Allied war debts.

38. The Dow-Jones Industrial Average at its low point in the 1920s was 63.90 (1921). In 1929 it reached 381.17, to plunge to 41.22 in 1932. (It rose again to 194.40 in 1937, only to sink to 92.92 in 1942.) Samuel Eliot Morison, *The Oxford History of the American People* (New York: Oxford University Press, 1965), pp. 942–43.

39. The U.S. tariff rate in 1890, the highest to date, was at 49 percent. In 1913 the level was reduced to 27 percent. The 1922 act again raised rates but gave the president flexibility to make changes. The 1930 Hawley-Smoot Act had complex provisions but its general effect was plain—it was intended to raise rates to record highs. Over 1,000 American economists protested—to no avail.

40. See his speech in U.S., Department of State, *Peace and War: United States Foreign Policy, 1931–1941,* pp. 248–55.

   In early 1939 the Scottish author, Robert Bruce Lockhart, believed the average American's attitude toward Britain's problem was still as follows: "We Americans went into the last war to save democracy. We pulled you out of a hole. . . . At Versailles and after . . . you trampled on democratic ideals. Now, largely through your own fault, you are in trouble again and you want our help. Well, we've learnt our lesson." Quoted in Robert E. Sherwood, *Roosevelt and Hopkins,* rev. ed. (New York: Grosset & Dunlap, 1950), p. 131.

41. Message to Congress, September 3, 1940. *Peace and War,* pp. 564–65. The agreement provided for the transfer of 50 "overage" destroyers to the British in exchange for base rights in British Caribbean territories and Newfoundland.

42. Message to Congress, *Peace and War,* pp. 608–11.

Part II

*Formulating Foreign Policy:
Perceptions and Organization*

The Intellectual Element of Foreign Policy

Perspectives

As we begin Part Two it is time to reflect on what is needed to create and conduct an effective foreign policy.

The first element is certainly intellectual preparation, a true *perspective* or outlook on the problems faced. A people and their officials need to understand the world around them and what it implies. In every nation, past-future linkages always give perspective for decision making, but that perspective may be true or distorted, beneficial or harmful. We have seen that the American people have not always thought in terms such as the four cardinal principles; they have not always appreciated what is meant by the balance of power. They have often approached foreign policy with a strong desire to reduce it to some overriding and abstract formula or guideline. And when the United States broadened its role in the world to great power and then superpower dimensions, because it encountered problems that were remote from everyday knowledge, it tended to use these abstract guidelines whether they fit the situation or not. Given that fact, in this chapter we shall have much to say about perspective.

The second element is an efficient governmental apparatus. This element actually translates into three related needs. First, the White House needs to retain control over major policy decisions while farming out to the executive departments and agencies both the staffing and detail needed to make those decisions. The White House also needs to monitor implementation of such decisions. Second, for any decisions that could potentially result in the use of force, there must be coordination between the State Department, the Pentagon, and the White House for day-to-day planning. Third, the Congress and the executive branch must be effectively linked.

In Chapter 5 we shall begin our consideration of this second element, showing how the experiences of World War II produced very distinct changes in 1947 and thereafter. Part Three will then go on to discuss in detail how day-to-day foreign policy decisions are made.

There is an important reason why Chapter 4 comes before Chapter 5. We will not understand the ways that American governmental and political institutions deal with foreign policy, or anything else, unless we first pause to ask with what special attitudes and expectations Americans approach problems. What do Americans want in this area and with what sense of priorities?

We must resist from the outset a stark "we and they" approach, thinking of American government as quite separate and apart from the American public. That charge reads well in election campaigns but it distorts the reality. People's attitudes do not evaporate or drastically change when they go to work for the government. Common sense reminds us that those in government, like those outside it, share a common American heritage. It is true that holding office makes a person legally and morally "responsible" for what is done or not done. But the leaders of the American government can never for long be far beyond their followers, given the political system that has been developed. The president does not require a translator to talk to the American people or footnote explanations to understand their feelings and attitudes. He, like the heads of his departments, is one himself.

Early Presidents Were Strategically Sensitive

Most of America's early presidents were strategically sensitive, recognizing the dangerous power problem the nation confronted and understanding how various policy alternatives would affect its vital interests. When George Washington was inaugurated at New York City on April 30, 1789, America was technically in alliance with France. The French had forged that alliance with America out of antagonism to Britain. French Foreign Minister Vergennes made that perfectly plain in his advice to his king on how to react to the colonial revolt: "England is the natural enemy of France—she is a rapacious, unjust and faithless enemy.

The invariable object of her policy is the destruction of France, or at least her abasement, humiliation and ruin." Consequently, France should "seize every possible opportunity to enfeeble the might and power of England. . . ."[1] Although Washington did not have access to the French archives, he knew very well how foolish it would be to rely on French support for merely American interests.

All of this was happening in a time of great international turmoil. The outbreak of the French Revolution, which happened the same year Washington took office, was also the beginning of over a quarter century of almost continuous great power war. With France and Britain arrayed against one another, both soon competed in attempting to cut off American trade with the other, seizing ships and, in the British case, impressing American seamen. As we saw earlier, the United States eventually responded by war with England in 1812.

Despite the fact that Thomas Jefferson, third president of the United States, was personally pro-French, he soon found himself having to take hardheaded, security-based decisions in quite the opposite direction from where his sentiments would otherwise have led him. He had hardly taken office when the situation became acute. Napoleon, encouraged by a short peace in Europe, made plans for a new French empire in the New World, centered on the Louisiana territory. Where Spain (which previously controlled the area) had not imposed any real restraints on American river traffic to New Orleans, France was a sufficient threat to cause the Francophile Jefferson to make this warning in 1802:

> There is on the globe one single spot, the possessor of which is our natural and habitual enemy. It is New Orleans. . . . The day that France takes possession of New Orleans, fixes the sentence which is to restrain [the United States] forever within her low-water mark. . . . From that moment, we must marry ourselves to the British fleet and nation.[2]

James Monroe, America's fifth president, also was sensitive to the strategic implications of different choices. He proclaimed the Monroe Doctrine after the Spanish colonies in Latin America threw off Spain's control.[3] In bold words in 1823 he asserted that "the American continents . . . are henceforth not to be considered as subjects for future colonization by any European powers" and that any European intervention in the affairs of the Western Hemisphere would not be viewed "in any other light than as the manifestation of an unfriendly disposition toward the United States." But Monroe acted only after very clear British encouragement[4] and was in no way inhibited by the fact that only a very few years had passed since the British had actually burned the White House.

Lincoln, although he left most diplomatic dispatches to his secretary of state, carefully edited the critical note to London on British recognition of the belligerency of the Confederate States.[5] Plagued by military defeats, Lincoln temporized while awaiting an improvement of the Union's military fortunes.

Every one of these presidents (as well as most of the other early presidents not specifically named) had a hardheaded and realistic appreciation of strategic relationships. They had an understanding of the power and interests of both the United States and the great powers, and knew sovereign states act first and foremost in their *own* interest. To put it another way, they understood "the rules of the game."

A Lessened Strategic Concern

Earlier we made the point that the transformation of America's security status by the end of the Civil War was paralleled by a growing official and public insensitivity to strategic issues. Nowhere is the reason for this more clearly explained than in the 1884 report to Congress of the head of the army, General Sheridan. In it he made this comment:

> Excepting for our ocean commerce and our seaboard cities, I do not think we should be much alarmed about the probability of wars with foreign powers, since it would require more than a million and a half men to make a campaign upon land against us. To transport from beyond the ocean that number of soldiers, with all their munitions of war, their cavalry, artillery, and infantry, even if not molested by us in transit, would demand a large part of the shipping of all Europe.[6]

The awareness of America's increased security was reflected in many ways. As Spain sold Florida to the United States, as America defeated Mexico and gained control of the whole of the continent to the Pacific, as Canada passed out of direct British control to become a dominion in 1867, any immediate threat on America's own frontiers receded, so there was less and less reason to turn attention outward.

By mid-nineteenth century, the approach had almost become to stay out of foreign wars altogether. The Civil War, like the Spanish-American War, revived American awareness of foreign dangers and therefore saw renewed diplomatic activity. But, otherwise, from the end of the Mexican War until the outbreak of World War I, with few exceptions, the United States paid very little attention to the world outside its doors. There was no need to. There was no threat. Who could hurt the United States? America had arrived at a "first plateau" on its path to great power status.

If we were to list all of the important U.S. involvements for virtually the last two-thirds of the nineteenth century, it would fit easily within a single page. Most of these involved disputes near home or what (unrecognized then) were the first moves in the second stage of growing power: the acquisition of coaling stations and other island possessions in the Pacific.

William H. Seward, who handled the diplomatic perils of the Civil War as our twenty-fourth secretary of state, no doubt had his tongue in cheek when he replied to a question on how American diplomats were chosen. "Sir," he said, "some persons are sent abroad because they are needed abroad, and some are sent because they are not wanted at home." But it was certainly already true by Seward's day that America's "best and brightest" did not always end up as representatives of the United States abroad—a tendency that increased in the

| Box 4.1 | Early Presidents Had Foreign Policy Experience | | |

As Secretary of State	Years	Under President	Became President
Thomas Jefferson	1790–93	Washington	1801–09
James Madison	1801–09	Jefferson	1809–17
James Monroe	1811–14	Madison	1817–25
John Q. Adams	1817–25	Monroe	1825–29
Martin Van Buren	1829–31	A. Jackson	1837–41
James Buchanan	1845–49	Polk	1857–61

following decades as political appointees were chosen for their campaign contributions. Certainly, it was increasingly rare for a Benjamin Franklin or a John Jay to be a minister (or, later, ambassador) abroad.

The contrast with colonial times could hardly be more dramatic. Then, it was usual for the president himself to have served a term as secretary of state, and before that he frequently himself had a tour as what we would today call our ambassador. Among our first presidents, Washington was the exception. John Adams served in France, the Netherlands, and Great Britain. Thomas Jefferson served in France. James Madison, although he held no diplomatic post, like Jefferson, served as secretary of state. James Monroe was stationed in France, Great Britain, and Spain before becoming secretary. John Quincy Adams was sent to the Netherlands, Prussia, and Russia before serving on the peace commission with Britain and then becoming secretary.

After J. Q. Adams, Andrew Jackson, like Washington, became president on military rather than diplomatic experience. Martin Van Buren, president from 1837 to 1841, had been secretary of state. After his time, no American president until George Bush, with the sole exception of James Buchanan, had ever held a regular diplomatic post.

It is difficult not to conclude that foreign affairs experience was no longer highly valued once America became more secure, and in the later period, after World War II, when it again entered world affairs in a big way, foreign affairs knowledge was expected of its presidents, but not foreign affairs experience. (The country paid dearly for this with Lyndon Johnson.)

Another way of understanding the lack of concern for American security is to examine the figures for the U.S. armed forces. Before the Civil War the strength of the regular army never exceeded what we today would call divisional size. In 1868, still reflecting the war, it stood at 50,916 but it soon drifted down into the 26,000–28,000 range maintained from 1871 until the Spanish-American War. Reflecting that war, in 1898, it rose to almost 48,000 and reflecting the Philippine insurrection, it was at 81,586 in 1901. In 1914, when European standing armies were on the order of 600,000, the U.S. Army was still below 100,000 men.

All of these developments illustrate the same theme: as America moved from danger to security, from foreign policy as a front-burner issue to foreign policy as an activity remote from the daily lives of the people, the United States became less sensitive to strategic issues and less realistic when confronting them. Even the language of American diplomacy became (as with Secretary Olney's outburst quoted in Chapter 3) more sweeping, more grandiose, and more idealistic.

The Strategic Unusualness of the American Experience

Like a man enjoying good health, America did not reflect much on why it was not sick. The increased security of the United States during the nineteenth century was in part the earned reward of prudent and realistic policy choices. The additional (although unappreciated) factor in this happy development was the strategic unusualness of so much of the international relations of that nineteenth century, a factor which diverted European attention largely away from the United States. For the first three decades or so after the Napoleonic Wars ended, the European powers were primarily concerned with their domestic affairs. They wanted no foreign adventures. They all agreed that any more French-style revolutions must be put down. That solidarity lasted until 1848 and the final overthrow of the Bourbon kings from the French throne. As we saw in Chapter 3, after that, although great power relations resumed traditional (i.e., wary, watchful, rival) patterns in the normal way of the balance of power, Europe's powers remained preoccupied with European affairs. German and Italian unification focused most great power attention far from the Americas in the 1850s and 1860s. And after the Franco-Prussian War, from the 1870s through the end of the nineteenth century, the great powers were absorbed in gaining colonies in Africa and Asia. Colonial imperialism, although not welcomed by the native peoples of those areas, was good for the United States.

The main result of the strategic unusualness of the nineteenth century on American attitudes was in making Americans *insensitive to the role of the balance of power* in their security. Far from Jefferson's attitude about an alliance, even with Britain if necessary, Americans did not think much about alliances or coalitions or think about the balance of power in any form at all.

Nothing shows more clearly the drift away from the realism so typical of the Founding Fathers than the tendency throughout the nineteenth century to consider the British as America's primary potential threat. There was justification for that suspicious attitude through the War of 1812 and again in the period of our Civil War. But precisely because the British thought in terms of the balance of power and were determined to prevent other European nations from encroaching on the Western Hemisphere, the predominant British attitude was one of support for American interests there. In reality, Britain had become more or less a de facto American ally. We are reminded of the Pentagon's definition of threat: capability and intention. The British had the capability, but by and large not the intention. Their position was not due to noble idealism on their part; they had other fish to fry.

The unusualness of the period also effectively shielded America from European interference when America expanded virtually unhindered to continental dimensions. Usually, when any power attempts to expand its national territory as America did in the nineteenth century, that power meets anything but indifference or permissiveness. At the least, it is usually confronted with demands for compensation. A fundamental tenet of the balance of power concept to which all the powers traditionally subscribed was that a gain by one was followed by something for the rest.[7] A classic illustration in the late 1700s was the division of Poland among its three neighbors (Austria, Prussia, and Russia), so as to preserve an equilibrium among them.

President James K. Polk, in his message to Congress of December 2, 1845, remarked that "our rising greatness as a nation" had caused talk in Europe of the need for a " 'balance of power' on this continent to check our advancement."[8] But it remained only talk for the reasons we have listed.

Unfortunately, the term "balance of power," which early American leaders had at least understood, by the mid-nineteenth century had come to mean simply interference from abroad. By the 1870s, any appreciation had dimmed in the United States for the idea that a world of sovereign states, such as we described in Chapter 2, is also a world in which balance of power behavior will reassert itself. When President McKinley sought to make a policy on the future of the Philippines in the Spanish-American War, as we saw earlier, he did not express himself in balance of power terms. Yet, since all nations that are sovereign are able to decide to resort to force to gain their objectives, it is completely unrealistic to assume that no state will ever do so. What logic tells us, history confirms.

With violence always possible, states frequently have formed alliances to augment their power. Indeed, *alliance formation* is perhaps the most common kind of balance of power behavior, the most fundamental symbol of the balance, even more than compensations. Yet, when America confronted World War I and finally in 1917 joined in it, it fought a war "to make the world safe for democracy" and ended its participation by announcing the *end* had come for the balance of power and the alliances ("entangling alliances," Wilson called them) that were the main feature of the balance of power. It would now yield to the League's approach of collective security.

In these crucial decisions Americans were very far indeed from policy conceived in traditional strategic terms. That it served American interests to take the Philippines could be argued. That it served American interests to enter World War I was clearer. But some disagreed, especially a significant number of Americans in the 1920s who, in hindsight and in view of the failure of the League's performance to match its promise, became convinced that the country had gone to war for other and more sordid reasons. They claimed that America had de-

clared war either because of British propaganda or fears for the value of American war loans to the Allies if they lost. (Some Americans darkly hinted that it
was American munition-makers and Wall Street bankers who had maneuvered
the United States into war in order to maximize their profits. One of the sensa-
tions of the time was financier J. P. Morgan being grilled in Washington by a
Senate committee.)

That Americans would come to believe that money had been the prime
moving force in determining intervention showed in still another way how far
the nation had come from an appreciation of power, security, and national interest. But in this, people were only reflecting the logical outcome of a national
experience very unusual in any strategic sense.

To sum up, after colonial days, the United States virtually bypassed one of
the most fundamental political and strategic experiences of other nations. It was
exempted almost entirely from living with the more traditional effects of the balance of power. This gap in the American experience was to make it quite unprepared, for example, to understand how the Soviet Union would behave once
Germany went down to defeat in 1945. In terms of living with the balance of
power, America was ill prepared for its global role.

The Social Unusualness of the American Experience

In addition to this unusual and fortunate *external* context in which to grow to
maturity as a nation, the United States also developed in a unique manner *internally*. This, too, profoundly shaped perceptions. America's public school history
books do not always explain that the United States, even in the beginning of its
history, was not really simply a transplanted English people. True, we may hear
of New Sweden (Delaware, founded by the Swedish West India Company in
1638). The people who settled it were not only Swedes but also many Finns. We
almost certainly hear of New Amsterdam, which became New York when a
British expedition in 1664 took it over. We realize, when we think of it, that
parts of New France became the Northwest Territories of the United States, and
large parts of Spanish America were incorporated into the United States, beginning with Florida. But we still may not take in the extent to which Americans
were a people of many diverse cultures. Samuel Eliot Morison gives us the figures for the rapid increase in colonial population, which grew "from about
85,000 in 1670, to 360,000 in 1713. By 1754 it had quadrupled again to about
1,500,000." He then adds, significantly: "This increase owed much to heavy mi-
gration of non-English people—Irish and Scots, Germans and French—favored
by a liberal naturalization act of the British Parliament in 1740."[9] These peoples
on the whole had no love for England and no special reason for deferring to London's wishes.

The same story is true after the American Revolution, but even more so.
Morison goes on to tell us that in the 1820s, only 129,000 entered the United

States, but "in the 1830s the number swelled to 540,000, of whom 44 per cent were Irish, 30 per cent German, and 15 per cent English." In the 1840s the influx nearly tripled, and in the 1850s, 2,814,554 came in. "Roughly half of the immigrants from 1840 were Irish, with Germans a close second."[10] This tremendous growth, largely non-English, continued in the next decades.

If the new nation was not really simply a transplanted new England, even in colonial times, in later decades it became far less so. The number and ethnic diversity of the people flocking into the United States in the nineteenth century is remarkable.

Immigration in 1873 was less than half a million but between 1880 and 1885, it rose to almost 800,000 a year. The 1880 census figures for Minnesota show 72 percent foreign born or with at least one foreign-born parent. California's figure was 60 percent. Ten years later the figures for the same states were 74.9 and 54.9 percent, respectively. Between 1905 and 1910 it almost topped 1,300,000 annually. The bulk of this later surge—four-fifths by 1910—were immigrants from Italy, Austria-Hungary, Russia, and Poland. In almost every case, they wanted nothing more to do with the countries whose miseries they had just left behind them.

Given this cultural composition (and even ignoring the special conditions in world affairs which made it possible), it is not surprising that between 1848 and 1898, for a whole half century, the United States avoided foreign war. There was no need to get involved or any wish to. Americans had enough to do as it was—settling the country, assimilating the immigrants, industrializing.

The census of 1910 sheds additional light on why President Wilson in 1914, when war broke out in Europe, asked Americans to be neutral in thought, word, and deed. It showed a total population of 91,972,266. Of that number, counting those born abroad or natives with either one or two foreign-born parents, 8,282,618 were of German origin and 2,701,786 of Austro-Hungarian origin (who might or might not be correctly labeled as sympathetic to the Vienna government). On the other side could be counted 3,231,052 of British origin, 2,752,675 from Russia, and 2,098,360 from Italy, for a total of just under 8 million. Then there were 4,504,360 Irish, predominantly hoping the United Kingdom would be defeated. So, depending on how many Austro-Hungarians wanted an Allied victory and how many Irish wanted the German-led coalition to win, perhaps one out of six in the U.S. population was inclined against the Allied cause because of recent nationalistic and cultural ties. On August 15, 1914, the *Literary Digest,* in those days a powerful and respected publication much like *Time* magazine today, reported the results of a poll of 350–400 American newspaper editors. Asked to report sentiment in their area, the results favored the Allies in 189 cases, the Germans in 38, with 140 neutral or undecided.

Effects

Looking at the domestic or internal picture, the diverse composition of America's population produced two distinct results. The first effect was to reinforce the tendency (produced by the external factors we discussed earlier) for America to stay out of Europe's apparently endless quarrels. As the years went by, Washington's Farewell Address seemed more and more appropriate for the United States. When the nation finally went to war in 1917, it was not considered a free and deliberate choice so much as one forced upon America by a foreign power, a foreign power that would not respect its wish to be left alone in peace.

The second effect resulted from the multi-cultured nature of the population and how those diverse peoples behaved and interacted. A mobile people in a vast continent, Americans were peculiarly open to new ideas and new ways of doing things. There were no overlords in the feudal sense in the United States (except for slave-owners). Peasants from Europe encountered few legal barriers and rapidly entered the lower middle class. There was no single cultural heritage to enforce uniformity based on custom. All traditions, from whatever origin, had a more or less equally valid claim to become the American way. But with conditions outside the settled East Coast in particular needing constant adaptation by the settlers, the rule became that all opinions had to be counted and weighed in the balance of the ballot box. Voting for the Senate, at first the prerogative of the states, eventually became everybody's right. Voting for the House or for the state assemblies, at first restricted by gender, property, and other requirements, was broadened to include virtually all adults.

Thus the second effect, given this action-oriented, determined people meeting unprecedented problems as seemed best to those concerned, was to develop a distinctive ad hoc problem-solving method. This method was characterized by open-mindedness about solutions, and rested on debate, negotiation, and compromise. It centered on finding the key correct principle to apply. We are so used to this American method as a fixed way of handling problems that we do not realize how much it sets the nation apart from states with longer histories, more homogenous populations, and tradition-oriented attitudes on foreign policy. This distinctly American way of reaching decisions and striving for a consensus made Americans much more open to changing their minds (since the weight of tradition did not hinder them). It also encouraged them to seek a governing principle to apply to every problem.

The first effect of the diverse composition of America's population allowed it to change the direction, thrust, and content of policy when policymakers thought it wise. As Roosevelt said in asking for revision of the neutrality acts, he frankly regretted making the mistake of signing the restrictions that he now wanted rescinded. The second effect led Americans to approach foreign policy problems with the assumption that they had a method for solving any difficulty, *once the key to the problem was found.*

Winston Churchill commented on this attitude in his war memoirs, when he looked back on his experience with Americans making decisions. Churchill commented that it was his feeling that those Americans in World War II pressing for an invasion of German-held Europe, without any preliminaries, were underestimating the difficulties. (When in late 1942 Churchill himself had suggested the possibility to his Chiefs of Staff for 1943, they made those difficulties only too clear.) The British preferred to soften up the opposition by first threatening Nazi flanks and making them face in more than one direction simultaneously. Churchill pointed out that the American position was logical and based on clear-cut principles. (After all, the most direct route is a straight line. And soonest begun, soonest ended.) Churchill, half-American himself, and an ardent student of history, no doubt knew all about General Nathan Forrest of U.S. Civil War fame. Forrest, a formidable Confederate general, put his ideas of how to achieve victory in succinct terms: "Get thar firstest with the mostest." "But," said Churchill, "we [British] do not think that logic and clear-cut principles are necessarily the sole keys to what ought to be done in swiftly changing and indefinable situations." The British put more stress on opportunism, "seeking rather to live and conquer in accordance with the unfolding event than to aspire to dominate it often by fundamental decisions." Churchill conceded that both views could be argued, and ended: "The difference is one of emphasis, but it is deep-seated."[11]

Some Unique Experiences

America's national experience with the world *outside* its doors also had its effects. To some degree all nations have different historical experiences that give them their distinctive approach to problems. But the American experience contained some very unusual—even unique—factors, at least so far as great powers are concerned.

No great power ever experienced the degree of geographical isolation America enjoyed, separated as it was by great oceans from the locus of possibly hostile moves. We saw earlier how the colonial powers withdrew as the country expanded so that the United States soon had no strong neighbors immediately or almost adjacent to its frontiers. That meant that nearly all of America's development as a nation took place under drastically different conditions than the usual lot of great powers. It had no need of a large standing army and simply did not have to think always of the reactions of other nations in terms of the threat they could be. This situation lasted a long time, creating ingrained habits of thinking. Before the age of missiles, an assault against American territory could only be launched from a land base near at hand or via the sea. But there was no foreign land base that could serve the purpose for some great power willing to take on the task.

The second unusual if not unique feature of America's experience was its freedom from 1815 to 1914 from any serious threat of being involved in great power wars. The balance of power remained stable, as we saw, during those critical decades when America was growing in power. The attention of the British, who might have harmed the United States, was continually diverted. The absence of general war eliminated the major pressure to drag the country into European power politics.

The net effect was to make the American people slowly forget the sense of danger that had marked the nation's early decades, to slowly forget the relevance of the balance of power to national security. American attitudes were reflected in the fact that although the early presidents usually had a great deal of diplomatic experience, by the 1840s it was rare and thereafter virtually unknown. Americans were also spared the need and expense to maintain large armed forces. The nation could afford to pay little attention to foreign affairs in general while people got on with the real business—business. This unusual history also explains why Americans became less sensitive to strategic issues.

"Realism" and "Idealism" as Guidelines

With very little understanding of even the basic operation of the international system, many Americans in the early twentieth century believed World War I had been caused by "power politics," by alliances, arms races, secret diplomacy, and the like. When World War II came along many observers had a very different view. The primary policy error this time was thought to be a *neglect* for power politics, too much wishful thinking coupled with a naive faith in international law, organization, and ethics. This latter school of thought named itself "realism" and became dominant in America for many years. These self-proclaimed "realists" labeled those who believed strongly in law, organization, and ethics "idealists," and to many idealism became a pejorative label. To the realist, power relationships are the critical factors in international relations, and must be the primary concern of any nation's foreign policy.

The terms *realism* and *idealism* are useful to some extent because they focus attention on certain aspects of foreign policy and act as a kind of shorthand for describing whole sets of beliefs about the nature of international relations and the consequent appropriate guidelines for policy. And whole books have been written in the conviction that the "struggle" between realism and idealism helps to explain the pronounced swings we have already observed in both American opinion and American foreign policy.[12] But while such analyses can yield certain insights of value, they have limitations, especially when carried to extremes. Neither writers about foreign policies nor those who make policy are always clear in distinguishing between *describing what is* and *giving prescriptive advice*. And the truth is that few policymakers are one hundred percent concerned with power alone, with no concern for ethics, or vice-versa. Indeed, as we shall see later, many American policymakers link the two (Glenn Hastedt calls it "moral pragmatism").[13] It would be hard to find examples in American foreign policy where ethical and moral concerns have not influenced America's formulation of long-range goals, acting as a constraint and/or sometimes even providing much of the basis for action[14] (as in the U.N./U.S. Operation Restore Hope in Somalia in 1992–93).

But while both power and ethical concerns influence policy choices and their results, there are, as always, many other factors also. By themselves, realism and idealism as explanations are much too inclusive and simplified to account entirely for foreign policy decisions. Realism and idealism are inadequate especially when they are utilized as explanations regardless of the particular historical, cultural, and geographic context. For example, we showed how America's *circumstances* (i.e., the external environment as well as the nation's strength or weakness) in the last two hundred years have altered drastically. And that made a great difference. America went from little power to enormous power and from great insecurity to an easy and largely unearned security—and then back toward less security in the decades after World War II. Obviously, a weak nation that must live in the shadow of strong and willful neighbors can ill afford to be too "idealistic," to depart far from very practical decisions. Considerable "realism" is, if you will, built-in. The degree of "idealism" or "realism" in one's policy clearly is affected by one's circumstances and will vary with them.

Without entirely rejecting these useful terms, then, it is important to realize that the reactions of the American people to various problems also need to be explained in other ways. One is by contrasting how Americans have dealt with clear and obvious problems, such as Pearl Harbor, compared to problems which were vague or remote or quite unclear. In terms of the latter group, which necessarily became larger in number as America grew in power and took on a world role, policymakers searching for the key to a problem tended to reason with generalized abstractions like containment. Like the domino theory. Or like "the war to end all wars." Such guidelines, unfortunately, offer little real help to safely navigate the minefield of murky problems. In such cases, the American tendency to seek a governing principle, noted by Churchill, can get a nation into trouble.

Compare the time of the War of 1812 with Vietnam. If one thinks in terms of just causes, it is reasonable to say that America in 1812 might have fought either Britain or France. In either case, both the president and the people would have been quite clear about the security implications of that choice. However, consider Lyndon Johnson's foreign policy decision to commit combat troops to Vietnam, rather than continue sending more easily withdrawable "advisers." With Vietnam a half a world away, with very few Americans even knowing where it was, let alone understanding its language, its history, or the strength of the contending factions, foreign policy was dominated by such abstract slogans, and the implications of involvement were far less cut and dried. The country plunged into war in ignorance of the serious problems it would soon face.

When a debate over alternatives matches two counterbalancing interests, one of which has the support of a popularly accepted guideline, that alternative acquires added weight in its favor. Since the guideline expresses "known truth," the most pernicious effect is to hamper any serious discussion of what is wrong with it, let alone show why the other alternative has merit. A guideline is assumed to have so much relevance that it becomes almost unthinkable not to apply it. After all, the presumed consequences of an opposite choice are supposedly horrendous. That removes the analysis from any direct consideration of the actual features of the problem by shoving it into a basket of "similar" problems: e.g., any aggression, unopposed, leads to the fall of dominoes, leads to more unopposed aggression, and so forth.

George Kennan, who first provided the intellectual basis for the U.S. policy of containment and then became convinced that it had become too militarized in its implementation, wrote a justly famous book on American foreign policy. In his memoirs he comments on how he came to his opinions:

> . . . I had been struck by the contrast between the lucid and realistic thinking of early American statesmen of the Federalist period and the cloudy bombast of their successors of later decades.

Kennan became convinced that much of the rationale and rhetoric of 1950s American foreign policy dated back to the period between the Civil War and World War II, and that

> much of this [approach] was utopian in its expectations, legalistic in its concept of methodology, moralistic in the demands it seemed to place on others, and self-righteous in the degree of high-mindedness and rectitude it imputed to ourselves.[15]

As illustration, Kennan cites America's love affair with arbitration treaties (of which it made many), the focus on world disarmament, "the attempt to outlaw war by the simple verbiage of the Kellogg Pact," and the nation's naive and unrealistic expectations of a League of Nations or United Nations as a cure-all.

This is an apt summary. What everything he mentions has in common with what we have already commented on is that American foreign policy had drifted from gut reality, with roots firmly planted in soil Americans could see, to a kind of never-never land floating beyond the horizon, which the nation addressed in a series of abstractions.

Past-Future Linkages and the American Character

Past-future linkages, as one of the four cardinal principles, says that the past experience of a nation influences how, in the present, the future results of any foreign policy choice between alternatives will be perceived. That is what Kennan is illustrating when he traces American abstractionism back to the secure conditions that existed between 1865 and World War I.

The past-future linkage principle is, of course, a description of what is universally true. And since every nation has its own individual past, any two or more nations approaching any problem will perceive it differently in some degree. In that sense, there is no such thing as a "common problem." We need to be aware of how these differences set America apart as a nation from other nations. It will sharpen our appreciation of why *they* act as they do, as well as why *we* act as we do. It will make us more aware of how one nation can misread the policies, intent, and determination of another. Winston Churchill once said that the outbreak of any war showed at least one thing clearly: the two antagonists did not read each other's minds correctly. These differences have often been noted by perceptive observers who, in describing the attitudes, traits, and behaviors that set various peoples apart, talk of different *national characters*.

No one who has traveled abroad can come home to America believing that all people everywhere are "just the same." They may be very alike in many things, but they are sure to differ, nation by nation, in many others. Even the two greatest English-speaking nations, America and Britain, use the same words to say sometimes exactly opposite things: the parliamentary phrase, "to lay a paper on the table" is a useful example. For the British it means to quit considering it, while for Americans it means to take it up.

Salvador de Madariaga, a prominent Spanish diplomat in League of Nations days, had many chances to observe his fellow diplomats. In a perceptive book published in 1928, he described his assessment of the national character of his own people and of two others. *Englishmen, Frenchmen, Spaniards* argued that each culture had "a distinctive attitude which determines their natural and spontaneous reactions towards life." As a key to these reactions, he uses three words, each really (as he says) untranslatable. "In the Englishman: fair play. In the Frenchman: *le droit*. In the Spaniard: *el honor*." He describes their respective psychological center of gravity as "body-will" for the English, intellect for the French, and soul for the Spaniard. He adds that "the natural reaction of the three is *action* for the English, *thought* for the French, and *passion* (emotion) for the Spanish.[16]

Whether Madariaga is correct people can judge for themselves. That there *are* differences, though, is beyond dispute. In the same way, although there is plenty of room for argument about the particulars of the American national character and American attitudes, there can be no argument about whether they exist.[17] Although Americans individually differ, as a people they have certain tendencies. We have already shown many examples of American-particular approaches to problems and their solutions, including foreign policy.[18] Trying to be entirely specific about such things as a national character defeats the purpose because there are obviously so many individual exceptions to any generalization. But with that caveat, if there are such generalizations solidly based on the evidence, they are important. Taken together, they provide the basic construct within which a people perceives and attempts to solve problems. To dismiss generalizations is to take the wrong exit from the problem, because there *are* differences. Instead, care is recommended.

If we accept the concept of a distinctly American character, we must accept that the Germans, the Italians, the Indians, the Japanese, the Egyptians, and all the rest have their own peculiarities, too—things that make them different from Americans. Of course, such differences in cultures and attitudes would be merely academic if it were not for the fact that they affect how people see world problems and react to them, each nation through its own cultural lenses.

The American Character

What, then, are the most important features of the American character? We have already mentioned at least one: the determination to face problems head-on. What are the other features? What kind of people are Americans, anyway?

Americans are, above all else, a practical people. If it works, do it. If it ain't broke, don't fix it. Keep it simple, stupid. This practical sense helps to hold America's idealism down closer to the ground—at least where practical experience can be linked to a problem.

Jules Verne, in one of his lesser known works, *From the Earth to the Moon*, sets his scene in Baltimore. He writes in 1865 and his plot turns around shooting a shell transporting a man to the moon. Here is how he describes Americans: "The Yankees, the greatest mechanics in the world, are engineers—just as the Italians are musicians and the Germans metaphysicians—by birth. Nothing is more natural, therefore, than to perceive them applying their audacious ingenuity to the science of gunnery." And, a little later, "Now, when an American has an idea, he looks for another who shares it. If there are three of them, they elect a president and two secretaries. Given four, they name a keeper of records, and the office is ready for work; five, they convene a general meeting. . . ."[19]

Verne is obviously reflecting a generally-held foreigner's view of Americans. He quite correctly identifies two pronounced American traits: a mechanical (or technological) prowess and a strong tendency to improvise organizations to deal with problems, issues, or causes.

In 1902 Theodore Roosevelt said that "From the very beginning our people have markedly combined practical capacity for affairs with power of devotion to an ideal. The lack of either quality would have rendered the possession of the other of small value."[20] Agreeing with Verne on the practical and innovative qualities, Teddy Roosevelt adds idealism.

There is no question but that idealism was alive and prominent in America's *internal* affairs "from the beginning," as the sonorous phrases of the Declaration of Independence and the Constitution amply demonstrate. But its advent in foreign policy, as we have noted and as Kennan has said, is a more recent addition. No Founding Father, however tempted toward eloquence, would have uttered the famous words of John Kennedy's inaugural speech.

> Let every nation know, whether it wishes us well or ill, that we shall pay any price, bear any burden, meet any hardship, support any friend, oppose any foe to assure the survival and the success of liberty.
> This much we pledge—and more.[21]

Words like this warm every American's heart.[22] But to whom is the pledge made? To an abstraction. And after Kennedy pledges all of this he adds: "and more." What more could there be?

Americans also are a proud people, and American pride and American idealism are hard to separate. Herman Melville, in his autobiographical novel, *White-Jacket*, published in 1850, combined praises to American idealism with rather unbridled boasting:

> At a period when other nations have but lisped, our deep voice is heard afar. Long enough have we been skeptics with regard to ourselves, and doubted whether, indeed, the political Messiah had come. But he has come in *us*, if we would but give utterance to his promptings. And let us always remember that with ourselves, almost for the first time in the history of the earth, national

selfishness is unbounded philanthropy; for we cannot do a good to America but we give alms to the world.[23]

To those who might think that Melville is atypical, consider (as we pointed out earlier) what was engraved on the back of America's World War I victory medal: THE GREAT WAR FOR CIVILIZATION. Americans tend to think big, abstractly, and optimistically, both about their motives in taking action and in the assumption that good will surely follow. Churchill once commented on this instinctive American feeling that one should lay out the goals and think big. In his autobiographical overview of World War I, he writes:

> In the military as in the commercial or production spheres the American mind runs naturally to broad, sweeping, logical conclusions on the largest scale. It is on these that they build their practical thought and action. They feel that once the foundation has been planned on true and comprehensive lines all other stages will follow naturally and almost inevitably. The British mind does not work quite in this way.[24]

Idealism, buttressed by technological ability, great resources, and a belief that all problems are soluble, plus a pronounced ability to improvise organizationally, think big, and proceed logically to some goal, adds up to a formidable effect. And, obviously, the more the momentum of policy, the further one can go either in the right or the wrong direction.

There is another important consequence of these beliefs and tendencies: partly because America has been able, with its technology, to significantly reduce or alter some of the effects of geography on policy choice, and partly because of its geographical isolation from threat, Americans also are far less aware of geography, as compared with most peoples in the world.[25] Americans try to overcome geography, whereas other peoples have to adjust to it. Nor do Americans think much about its political implications, since for them there are not many (at least not negative ones). As noted earlier, the United States has no major powers as neighbors, or large armies poised on its frontiers, ready to invade when opportunity presents.

You can see the results of the lack of concern with geography at American universities, where such courses as exist are few and far between and where the academic departments which offer them are small and trying simply to survive. Compare that with, say, Europe. The Geography Institute at Bonn is a very important part of the university, and its evening lecture series always well attended. Compare a standard German road atlas like *Der grosse Continental Atlas* or any Hallwag Euro Map with those put out by the U.S. gasoline companies or the AAA. The great difference is in the geographical detail. An American map features roads and distances and downplays the terrain, the rivers, and the elevations. This reflects a national mindset that hinders an appreciation of how many foreigners react in many situations.

All of these traits are combined in the American character in a unique way. It is highly important to keep that in mind. This is not to say that no other nation can be idealistic or think big or improvise or display technological prowess or be as casual about geography. But it is America's fate, for better or for worse, to have these traits in abundance and in combination. Nowhere else is this true.

Lessons of Experience and Their Effects

America's attitudes and traits, we have said, come from America's experience as a nation. We have already said much about that experience in terms of the external environment. Until now we have only mentioned the domestic context, but it is time now to amplify our discussion, for that, of course, was equally or even more influential.

A first lesson, repeated over and over again as the pioneers moved west, was to be self-reliant. In a country being carved out of the wilderness, rank and class, at first important, soon faded into minor positions. The English gentlemen who came along with the rest to found Jamestown in Virginia and who expected the same deference they received in Britain soon found themselves facing the stark reality of Captain John Smith's dictum: "If they will not work, neither shall they eat." It is probably this experience of having to pitch in that produced both a pronounced American skill at improvised organization and undergirded the ideal of equality in American social institutions. If all were to survive, all were to be equal in that all must produce and work and help.

The very scale of American achievements, too, inevitably produced a kind of boastful pride. Europeans, crossing the American plains by train, day after day, could hardly believe the immensity of the American territory. In this large area, farms were created and mines dug and churches and schools, as well as saloons, built. Areas with extremely crude cultural amenities became sponsors of symphony orchestras and ballet troupes. But, even more important from a power point of view, Americans tapped the enormous riches that nature had provided and created a very high standard of living. Generation after generation of immigrants, pouring into this rich land, took up a toehold on the foot of the economic ladder and then, if they had the ability and they were willing to work, progressed up that ladder. In Europe or Asia, where son followed father in a traditional family occupation, this sort of upward mobility was practically nonexistent. In America, too, of course, there were exceptions, especially among blacks and native Americans. But for most people the generalization was accurate, and the sense of reaching toward the skies cultivated an enormous optimism. That optimism is one root of American idealism. If so much is possible, why not aim high? As Henry Kaiser said as he turned to producing ships in World War II, "The difficult we do immediately; the impossible takes a little longer."

We see here one reason why communism never took a great hold in America. The Communist ideology, of course, as formulated by Karl Marx, was based on a very narrow sample. Marx really generalized from what was happening to England in its worst phase of industrialization. The enclosure movement had forced people off the common lands, they had moved to work in factories, and there were not yet adequate laws to protect them in this new and harsh environment. (Even factory machinery had no guards around instruments which could sever a hand in a flash.) Marx's England is Charles Dickens' England, the England of Oliver Twist. In America something like that phase occurred, too. But any ugly set of working conditions was simultaneously being undermined by the opportunity to simply pull up stakes and move out to take over free land in the West. And the laws came, too, to America.

Another characteristic American attitude, right from the beginning, was suspicion of government. We saw this when we quoted James Madison's Number 51 of *The Federalist Papers,* where he explains why he thinks the American government must be one of checks and balances. It is not surprising Americans would feel this way. They had experienced "taxation without representation" in the British Parliament, as high-handed British governments had sought to impose their will on the colonies. The motto of the Founding Fathers was really "that government is best which rules least." But since government could not be dispensed with altogether, it was vital to keep it under control. That feeling was also shared by the thirteen states who eyed the new Federal power with misgivings and insisted on adding the first ten amendments to the Constitution—the Bill of Rights. These limits on governmental power also played a part in stimulating great economic growth. (Think what it would have been like if Washington for decades had been doing central economic planning and price-setting like the former Soviet Union endured!)

As the suffrage was progressively extended to all or virtually all adults in America, the collective opinion of Americans came to play a great part in politics, both in domestic policy and foreign policy. This is an area where the American character had *substantial* effects on policy. American policy limits in modern times have been much more captive to public reaction than has been the case for other great powers, with the possible exception of Britain.

Recall that we earlier made the point that Americans did not feel bound as a people by a single traditional answer to problems. That meant Americans were flexible in their responses, depending on whether the case seemed proved or not. That meant also that there could be drastic policy shifts, if that really reflected the public consensus. We saw how difficult it was in the 1930s for President Roosevelt to convince the American people that the nation must accept some responsibility for what was happening in the international environment, and how slow Americans were to agree. As late as February 1939, some 48 percent of the people believed that America's entry into World War I was a mistake.

Some 69 percent, however, were willing to aid Britain and France in their new trouble, provided that help stopped short of war. Even in October 1939, after the war had begun in Europe, 59 percent of Americans thought that the U.S. entry into World War I was a mistake. But 21 percent favored American intervention *now,* and 46 percent were willing to go to war if that proved the only way to prevent a German victory. By January 1941, only 40 percent of Americans thought it had been wrong to enter World War I, and by December 1941, that percentage had fallen to 21. Obviously, Americans were now beginning to think of the two wars as a series, the implication being that the United States had failed to finish the job the first time. America adopted its first peacetime conscription act in 1940 by a vote in the Senate of 47 to 25 and in the House by 232 to 124. When the vote came on its extension, August 18, 1941, it was approved in the House by a one-vote margin! Still, as Hitler, aided by Mussolini, had begun to crush neighbors and France had surrendered in mid-1940, the American people were slowly but surely being shaken from their lethargy. Once aroused, they became formidable in their determination to put an end to Hitler, to invade Europe at the first opportunity, and to insist on an unconditional surrender. George Kennan, in his study of American foreign policy, once characterized such extreme pendulum shifts, which can occur in America only because of what we have already said, in these words:

> But I sometimes wonder whether . . . a democracy is not uncomfortably similar to one of those prehistoric monsters with a body as long as this room and a brain the size of a pin: he lies there in his comfortable primeval mud and pays little attention to his environment; he is slow to wrath—in fact you practically have to whack his tail off to make him aware that his interests are being disturbed; but, once he grasps this, he lays about him with such blind determination that he not only destroys his adversary but largely wrecks his native habitat.[26]

A somewhat more tolerant way of characterizing the same pendulum swing would be to say that in a nation where public opinion is very important, swings in sentiment on major issues sometimes take a long time (at least in the absence of a sudden crisis). Although views on specific problems may fluctuate rapidly, in areas involving fundamental change, the public needs time for the meaning of events to sink in.

And swings in public support or opposition to proposed policies have no set timetable of response. Even President Roosevelt, who took the lead in the direction of intervention to aid the Allies, showed ambivalence and confusion. When he asked for the repeal of the neutrality legislation that was obviously giving Hitler an advantage by denying the Allies arms, he said: "I regret that the Congress passed that act. I regret equally that I signed that act." And he described the act as "most vitally dangerous to American neutrality, American security, and American peace." These three—neutrality, security, and peace—were all goals supported by the majority of Americans at the time, but Hitler's actions were in fact forcing Americans to see that they led in incompatible directions; that Americans had to decide which of the three had priority.[27] Changing the law was obviously a departure from strict neutrality, although it increased U.S. security by helping America's friends to survive. It also brought America a step closer toward war and away from peace. What was accomplished by the policy change was definitely in America's interest; but the change was not easy to verbalize in any logical way, given the whole of the American "wish-list" at the time. The second part of Kennan's characterization needs little qualification. Americans are a very "gung-ho" people. Whatever they do, they do as hard, fast, and as far as possible.

American attitudes and goals could and did conflict, but in time the majority of Americans came to a joint conclusion that they would be insecure if they did not risk peace by ditching their neutrality.

Summing Up

Political scientists have often observed that experiences give rise to beliefs, beliefs to attitudes, attitudes to perceptions, and perceptions to decisions. Among the most consistent attitudes of Americans has been a conviction that the American commonwealth stood for principle and represented a new and improved version of government on this earth. Coupled with a vigorous and large population in a vast land enormously rich in resources, Americans have also believed that the limits on what can be accomplished are much smaller than many outside the United States would assume. And the experience of Americans in many ways within the boundaries of the American commonwealth has confirmed this general belief. Americans have moved, perhaps not the mountains, but certainly the hills. They have accomplished many things that to most of the peoples of the earth, who live in poverty, want, and disease, seem impossible dreams. Reality has vindicated much of that idealism first sketched out in the American dream. Of course, it is not Utopia; on every hand, serious problems—some very deep and abiding—await proper remedies. A self-critical people (because they believe so much is possible), Americans often focus on what is wrong, not what is right. But the faith has remained strong for two centuries that they eventually will solve their problems.

America's experience with foreign affairs has been more various. Given the very obvious weakness and insecurity during and after the War of Independence, Americans could not afford to ignore the realities of the world power system, whether they approved of other nations' motivations and actions or not. Regardless of feelings and preferences, and though it took some time, Americans generally realized that England and France and the rest were motivated by selfish interests. If they helped, it was not for reasons of altruism. What people saw, too, of the operations of the balance of power left them dismayed if not disgusted.

George Washington's famous advice, that once America grew sufficiently in power it would be able to chart its own course in the world and stay out of Europe's persistent clashes, struck a sympathetic chord that rang for generations.

As we saw, the lack of a general war for almost a hundred years, and America's geographical distance from meaningful threats, permitted this policy. Not until World War I, when the status quo collapsed, did America have to reconsider. And when it did, it moved to support the Allies against the Germans, citing freedom of the seas as the main reason. What that meant was that Americans had become sufficiently insensitive to strategic concerns and had strayed so far from the language of the balance of power and *Realpolitik* that they had to grope for an explanation of why their vital national interests were in jeopardy. Then, in an attempt to foreclose a repetition of World War I, America's idealistic bent led it to propose the League of Nations while its realistic bent led it, on reflection, to reject it. Between the wars America struggled anew to reconcile these two tendencies, as Hitler's menaces increased. Those who favored neutrality portrayed the coming war as an effort by other nations to serve their own interests at the expense of America's. But gradually the American people came to the realistic acceptance that they inevitably were involved, and after World War II they stayed involved. Most of the time, they stayed wisely involved, but there were some exceptions, as we shall see in Part Four.

Notes

1. Quoted in Samuel B. Griffith II, *In Defense of the Public Liberty* (Garden City, NY: Doubleday, 1976), pp. 255–56.

2. A. A. Lipscomb, ed., *Writings of Thomas Jefferson* (Monticello ed., Washington, 1904), vol. X, pp. 312–15. (Jefferson to Livingston, April 18, 1802.)

3. Ruhl J. Bartlett, ed., *The Record of American Diplomacy* (New York: Knopf, 1948), pp. 168–87, contains all the major documents relating to the Monroe Doctrine.

4. British Foreign Minister George Canning was very frank about the British interests involved. See Canning's speech in December 1826 to Parliament, for example, in Robert Walsh, ed., *Select Speeches of the Right Honorable George Canning* (Philadelphia: Key and Biddle, 1835), pp. 466–67.

5. See the text and reproduction of the U.S. note to Great Britain of May 1861, with Lincoln's handwritten changes, in Carl Sandburg, *Abraham Lincoln: The War Years* (New York: Harcourt, Brace, 1939), vol. 1, pp. 281–82.

6. *Report of the Secretary of War, 1884,* p. 49. Quoted in John Bigelow, *The Principles of Strategy Illustrated Mainly from American Campaigns* (New York: Greenwood Press, 1968; reprint of 2nd ed. of 1894), p. 55. Also quoted in Russell F. Weigley's excellent study, *The American Way of War* (New York: Macmillan, 1973), p. 168.

7. Prince Talleyrand, who served under both the Bourbon kings and Napoleon, is the author of a much quoted definition of the balance of power, which he calls a "combination of the rights, interests, and the relations of the Powers . . . which seeks to obtain . . . that one or several other Powers shall never attain to domination over Europe" and that this "combination shall render a rupture . . . of the tranquility of Europe difficult or impossible." See G. Pallain, ed., *The Correspondence of Prince Talleyrand and King Louis XVIII During the Congress of Vienna* (New York: Plenum, 1881), pp. xv–xvi.

8. Message of President James K. Polk to Congress, December 2, 1845, reprinted in Ruhl J. Bartlett, ed., *The Record of American Diplomacy* (New York: Knopf, 1948), pp. 201–03.

9. Samuel Eliot Morison, *The Oxford History of the American People* (New York: Oxford University Press, 1965), p. 140.

10. Ibid. These figures take on even greater meaning when they are compared against total U.S. population. In 1820 it was 9.6 million, growing to 12.9 in 1830, 17 in 1840, 23.2 in 1850, and 31.5 in 1860. Only in 1921, with the passage of the Johnson Act, was immigration restricted. That act set up quotas based on "national origins."

11. Winston S. Churchill, vol. 3 of *The Second World War.* See *The Grand Alliance* (Norwalk, CT: The Easton Press, 1989), p. 673. This edition is identical with the version published in 1948–53 by Houghton, Mifflin.

12. The purported incompatibility between idealism and realism has led to much scholarly debate. See in particular Hans J. Morgenthau, *Politics Among Nations,* 5th ed. (New York: Knopf, 1973); Hans J. Morgenthau, *In Defense of the National Interest* (New York: Knopf, 1951); Thomas I. Cook and Malcolm Moos, *Power Through Purpose* (Baltimore: Johns Hopkins Press, 1954); and Robert Osgood, *Ideals and Self-Interest in America's Foreign Relations* (Chicago: University of Chicago Press, 1953). For a succinct summary, see Charles W. Kegley, Jr., and Eugene R. Wittkopf, *World Politics: Trend and Transformation,* 3rd ed. (New York: St. Martin's Press, 1989), pp. 12–18.

13. Glenn P. Hastedt, *American Foreign Policy: Past, Present, Future* (Englewood Cliffs, NJ: Prentice-Hall, 1988), pp. 29–31.

14. For a penetrating analysis of the whole issue, see Stanley Hoffman, *Duties Beyond Borders: On the Limits and Possibilities of Ethical International Politics* (Syracuse, NY: Syracuse University Press, 1981).

15. George F. Kennan, *Memoirs: 1950–1963,* vol. II (Boston: Little, Brown, 1972), p. 71. Thomas Paterson, in his discussion of American ideology, writes, ". . . embedded in the American ideology was the belief that the United States was blessed with superior principles and institutions which others should adopt." Later he writes, Americans "saw themselves as benefactors, celebrants of the American success story, spreading their economic and political riches to the less fortunate. . . ." Thomas G. Paterson, *On Every Front: The Making and Unmaking of the Cold War,* rev. ed. (New York: W.W. Norton & Company, 1992), pp. 100, 101.

16. Salvador de Madariaga, *Englishmen, Frenchmen, Spaniards* (London: Oxford University Press, 1928), p. 3.

17. Some analysts prefer the concept of "political culture" to "national character." See Charles W. Kegley, Jr., and Eugene R. Wittkopf, *American Foreign Policy: Pattern and Process,* 4th ed. (New York: St. Martin's Press, 1991), pp. 248–55. Tying the concept of culture to several of our earlier points Arthur M. Schlesinger, Jr., writes: "The United States had a brilliant solution for the inherent fragility of a multiethnic society: the creation of a brand-new national identity. . . . The point of America was not to preserve old cultures, but to forge a new *American* culture." Arthur M. Schlesinger, Jr., *The Disuniting of America* (New York: Norton, 1992), p. 12.

18. This is different, of course, from saying there are typical American policy views about America's role in the world. Although controversial, some research has indicated that since the Cold War consensus was shattered, instead of consensus three basic sets of beliefs have developed among American leaders. See Ole R. Holsti and James N. Rosenau, "A Leadership Divided: The Foreign Policy Beliefs of American Leaders, 1976–1984," in Charles W. Kegley, Jr., and Eugene R. Wittkopf, eds., *The Domestic Sources of Foreign Policy: Insights and Evidence* (New York: St. Martin's Press, 1988), pp. 30–44.

19. Jules Verne, *From the Earth to the Moon* (Norwalk, CT: Heritage Press, 1970), p. 2. As an interesting point of information, Verne had his shell fired from Stone Hill, Florida, only a few miles away from where the Kennedy Space Center was set up a century later. The Verne capsule was to take 97 hours, 13 minutes, 20 seconds to reach the moon; *Apollo* in fact took 103 hours, 30 minutes. In both cases the capsules splashed down in the Pacific and were picked up by American warships. The distance between the two splashdowns was just under two and a half miles!

20. In a speech in Philadelphia, November 22, 1902.

21. Kennedy's whole speech (plus illustrations of the various drafts it went through) can be found in Theodore C. Sorensen, *Kennedy* (New York: Harper and Row, 1965). The full text is at pp. 245–48.

22. Americans often identify their ideals and aspirations with those of all mankind. According to James Nathan and James Oliver, this is what President Wilson did just before World War I. James A. Nathan and James Oliver, *United States Foreign Policy and World Order,* 4th ed. (Glenview, IL: Scott, Foresman, 1989), p. 10.

23. Quoted from the Library of America edition, *Redburn, White-Jacket, Moby-Dick* (New York: Literary Classics of the United States, 1983), p. 506. Also see Daniel S. Papp, *Contemporary International Relations: Frameworks for Understanding,* 2nd ed. (New York: Macmillan, 1988), pp. 169–70.

24. See above, footnote 11. Fiction writers have recorded the same thought. For example, Frederick Forsyth, in *The Deceiver* (New York: Bantam, 1991), p. 261, says: "The search for the single, wonderful solution is a particularly American trait."

25. Having many potentially unfriendly neighbors Russia, having major powers on the flanks (Germany, for so long), extended frontiers and little depth (Israel, pre-1967), unfavorable topography on borders (Goland Heights), or controlling or being able to threaten key assets or choke points (Strait of Hormuz) are all critical geographical factors some nations need to consider—but not the United States.

26. George F. Kennan, *American Diplomacy, 1900–1950* (Chicago: University of Chicago Press, 1951), pp. 45–47.

27. Dougherty and Pfaltzgraff correctly point out that Americans have never been morally indifferent to what was going on. They just had "hoped desperately that President Roosevelt could chart a wise course, preserve freedom of choice, steer clear of war, and somehow make everything turn out right in the end." Dougherty and Pfaltzgraff, *American Foreign Policy,* p. 25.

The Organizational Element

Achieving Coordination

A people who prefer to go it alone and "stay out of Europe's quarrels" are not likely to develop an extensive set of bureaucratic arrangements for conducting foreign policy. And they certainly will see no need for an efficient apparatus to coordinate foreign policy with military needs. So it was that until its experience in World War II the United States had only a very rudimentary policymaking apparatus, and there was little coordination between the State Department and other government agencies. What happened in World War II was to change all of that.

The Background

Today everything about the American government is so large that it is easy to forget how it once was so small. In 1789, the Department of State had exactly six employees. The army and navy were also small, but not, as we saw earlier, because America had no power problem. The reason was there was little money available, except for dire need. Ships were enormously expensive and, since a militia could be raised on short notice, a very small standing army would do: 5,949 in 1823, a little over 8,000 in 1838. It took Barbary pirate interference with American shipping (until then protected by the British navy) to cause the commissioning of four substantial frigates in 1794.[1] With a small-sized government, little money to spend, few diplomatic crises, and very small armed services, coordination was not a serious problem. Formal procedures were not really needed when those who ran American affairs on the whole personally knew one another. Besides, although American diplomacy was very active in the early years, and although America fought a second war with Britain in 1812, thereafter, with the exception of the Mexican war, no foreign war was fought until 1898. And since it is in connection with war that foreign policy decisions are at their most critical, which in turn shows the need for policy coordination, nothing much happened.

Even as late as the Civil War, the president of the United States personally made all or most of the important decisions, even personally rewriting important notes to foreign nations.[2] Abraham Lincoln personally selected officers to be commissioned, and not only those of general rank. But he was also the first president to find himself at a serious disadvantage because there were no institutional arrangements to coordinate diplomacy and the armed services, or even to control and administer armed services of the size then being raised.

Within the government bureaucracy and the armed services, career arrangements were totally inadequate to develop and maintain officials capable of dealing with the kind of problems routinely handled today. Until the Pendleton Act of 1883, the U.S. civil service was crassly oriented toward political appointments. Merit appointments and promotions were almost unknown. In the military, as late as the 1880s, promotion in the navy went directly with length of service. If you lived long enough, you might make admiral or general before compulsory retirement at age 62. In any case the small size of the military offered little promotion opportunity. Professional, mid-career training did not exist, either.

It is not surprising, though, that these rather primitive conditions persisted so long. As we saw, America was a nation fairly immune from attack, with no serious, active threat to cope with across its land frontiers. It was in this frame of mind that the country went to war with Spain, soon finding itself using short-range battleships designed for coastal defense in the far waters of the Pacific. That these ships, re-coaled as they transited, were in position for the battle of Manila Bay was due to the foresight of Assistant Secretary of the Navy Teddy Roosevelt. But the State Department had no idea of what Roosevelt had done and had played no role in the decision.

Ernest May comments on the condition of State Department coordination with the armed forces:

In the archives of the McKinley, Roosevelt, and Taft administrations, I have yet to find a letter from a Secretary of State, asking for a military cost accounting before some diplomatic stroke. Although Taft's Secretary of State did occasionally ask the fleet to back up his diplomacy, he never inquired ahead of time about the fleet's location and makeup.[3]

Nor did the army speak to the navy, or the navy to the army, about their plans or deployments. The years of these three administrations stretched from 1900 to 1913, to the very brink of World War I. Only as that war approached were voices heard within the American government calling for an end to this rather nonchalant approach.

Toward a Rudimentary Organization

The lack of policy coordination in the Spanish-American War showed conclusively the dangers of letting things drift. On the military side, reforms were soon forthcoming. In 1900 Secretary of War Elihu Root was able to force through a reorganization of the U.S. Army. Congress agreed to establish both an army general staff and a chief of staff. In March 1915 a bill provided for a Chief of Naval Operations "who shall, under the direction of the Secretary of the Navy, be charged with the operations of the fleet, and with the preparation and readiness of plans for its use in war." However, since the navy bureaus still went their own way and the CNO had little power, the navy had more the appearance than the reality of an improvement.

These changes also did nothing to coordinate the military departments or keep them in direct touch with the State Department. The State Department itself conducted its business with a nonchalance (or naiveté) that is well illustrated by quoting from Ambassador Robert Murphy's memoirs. Murphy was posted to Switzerland during World War I. He remarks that the legation at Bern was "run, almost literally, by a man and a boy" until the war broke out. In a chapter aptly titled, "Innocents in Wartime Switzerland," he says:

> ... it was child's play for the German Black Chamber [cryptography unit] to break our simple book codes of that period. Moreover, most Americans had never even heard of security, and the Bern legation certainly did not practice it. Foreign employees had the run of the legation, and it would have been comparatively easy for some of them to get hold of our code books.[4]

Several years *after* the war, Secretary of State Stimson, finding that the United States had a code-breaking unit in his department, ordered it totally disbanded. His remark: "Gentlemen do not read each other's mail." That is truly a remark from another, very distant time!

In 1916, spurred on by the actual existence of a war and an increasing likelihood that the United States would take part, the Congress created a Council of National Defense. Admiral Alfred Thayer Mahan, at the time the best known American military leader, testified before the House Naval Affairs Committee, asserting: "It seems to me that there is very little appreciation in this country of the relation between diplomacy and the Army and the Navy." As though to support Mahan's assertion, the secretary of war supported the bill, but he saw no reason why the Council should include the secretary of state!

The Council of National Defense did provide for limited high level civil-military collaboration. But although it continued to exist into the 1930s, it was far from effective. Its first formal working successor, the Standing Liaison Committee, was only slightly better. It consisted only of second-rank officials, rather than cabinet members. General Marshall, army chief of staff, Admiral Stark, chief of naval operations, and Sumner Welles, under secretary of state, served on it. Its great weakness was that each of these officials reported to a different superior officer (i.e., the secretaries of war, navy, and state), and these superior officers did not meet except as part of the whole Cabinet. And Cabinet meetings under President Franklin D. Roosevelt, as under most presidents, were little more than sounding boards for presidential ideas. Moreover, as Washington like a magnet always draws to it people of ambition, there were serious personality clashes in the Roosevelt administration. The friction in the State Department between Welles as number two and Hull as number one kept their contact to rather formal levels. Making everything worse was the fact that Roosevelt himself had his troubles with Hull and had much more confidence in Welles. He retained Hull primarily for domestic political reasons.

Dean Acheson, who became an assistant secretary of state when Hull was secretary and Roosevelt was president, had a ringside seat while all of this was going on. He comments in his usual pithy style:

> Cordell Hull was a handsome man. . . . Suspicious by nature, he brooded over what he thought were slights and grievances, which more forthright handling might have set straight. His brooding led, in accordance with Tennessee mountain tradition, to feuds. His hatreds were implacable—not hot hatreds, but long, cold ones.[5]

Then Acheson adds: "Mr. Hull's feuds grew out of his relations with President Franklin Roosevelt." That antagonism was destined to undercut important American interests, as we shall see.

So, as far as coordination, or its lack, was concerned, this was the situation when World War II broke out, and Roosevelt had to conduct a complex foreign policy plus control the waging of a war involving far-flung military deployments.

Five examples of what happened to America between 1941 and 1945, to which we shall turn shortly, will go far to explain why in 1947 major changes were made in the American government for thinking through the strategic implications of foreign policy and military decisions, advising the president, and coordinating such decisions, government-wide. Before we turn to these examples, however, because the events leading to World War II and the war itself are now a half century behind us and its events are not fresh in everyone's memory, we need a succinct account of these major political-military events. Otherwise, the development of the Cold War, which we analyze in Part Four, would be hard to understand.

World War II

When Adolf Hitler came to power in Germany, he skillfully capitalized on the bitterness with which the German people regarded the Versailles *Diktat* after World War I and the resentment they felt because of the inflation and unemployment they had endured since then. Hitler had ready to hand a geopolitical situation that might have been custom designed for his use. In the east, Russia had been stripped of major territories all along its western frontier. In the middle-south, Austria-Hungary had been dismantled into four weak states. A new Poland had been created in the middle-north. That meant that a corridor of weak states lay between a Soviet Union and a Germany that had been treated harshly in the settlements that ended World War I. The set of weak states between them and a shared sense of grievance were to prove enough for Hitler and Stalin, despite their ideological differences, to agree to divide the set as prizes. That event, the infamous Nazi-Soviet Pact of August 1939, set the stage for World War II.

Hitler had gotten away with his program up to that point for several reasons. Britain and France, so severely bled in 1914–18, wanted no new war. They also found it difficult to agree on tactics against Hitler: Britain concluded a naval treaty with Germany in 1935 that allowed Germany to set aside some of the disarmament provisions in the Versailles Treaty, while France instead entered into a new alliance with the Soviets. Either tactic could conceivably have worked, but going separate routes merely encouraged Hitler. And when Hitler openly challenged Versailles on March 16, 1935, by denouncing its restrictions on armaments, and again on March 7, 1936, by remilitarizing the Rhineland, England and France found it difficult to see in either event a sufficient cause for a bloody war. (After all, the other powers had not fulfilled the Versailles pledge to disarm, and the Rhineland *was* German territory, even if German troops had been excluded from it.) And when Germany began annexing German-inhabited territories such as Austria and demanded the Sudeten area, which formed the western frontier of Czechoslovakia, was Hitler not simply completing the work of German unification?

Italy played a crucial role, too—first as a "good guy," later as spoiler. When Hitler made his first attempt on Austria, in the form of an attempted coup by Austrian Nazis in Vienna in July 1934, Benito Mussolini sent his crack Alpine troops to the Brenner Pass frontier. Hitler, still too weak to fight, backed down. But in 1935 Mussolini began his attack on Ethiopia, which resulted in the League of Nations, openly defied, instituting sanctions against Italy. (England and France, jointly confronting serious counterbalancing interests, still wanted Italy on their side against Germany. Accordingly, they agreed to water down these sanctions by excluding oil from the provisions and leaving the Suez Canal open.) Hitler's move to rearm and to enter the Rhineland took place against this backdrop.

These divisions and ambivalences on the part of the British and French help to explain why, when a crisis over Hitler's demands on the Sudetenland was at its height in 1938, the Munich Conference was held. That conference in September 1938 gave Hitler everything he wanted. British Prime Minister Chamberlain even asked Hitler for a joint declaration that the two nations had no other intentions than to settle all problems peacefully.

Returning from Munich, the French premier thought he would be booed, but his people accepted what was done. Neville Chamberlain, encouraged by the meeting, waved his umbrella as he descended the ramp of his plane, saying "I have brought you peace in our time!" He meant that Hitler had given one of his ritual promises that "this is the last territorial demand I have in Europe." (Hitler even guaranteed at Munich that the rest of Czechoslovakia, now demoralized and deprived of its frontier fortifications, would remain free.)

The chief German interpreter, Dr. Paul Schmidt, the only reputable eyewitness whose memoirs we have, tells us what happened on the German side after Hitler's first elation over the success of his plans at Munich. Hardly two weeks later, at Saarbrucken, Hitler, disappointed over the obvious joy of his own people that war had been avoided, told them bluntly that "the [German] people of 1938 are not the people of 1918." He warned them that it would only take a tougher man than Chamberlain to come to power in England—for instance, Churchill—and his "first aim . . . would be to start a new war." Schmidt adds:

> Hitler was astonished and indignant that the two great countries [England and France], after their transitory relief at the maintenance of peace, were not exactly congratulating themselves on the price they had to pay for it, and that they were naturally determined to do everything possible to see that they were never again in such a helpless position.
>
> It once again became startlingly clear to me during those days how little Hitler understood the mentality of Western Europe.[6]

It only took Hitler until March of 1939 to march into the rest of Czechoslovakia. The British and French again failed to take action. The Soviet Union, which had not been invited to the Munich Conference even though it, like France, had an alliance with Czechoslovakia, became even more convinced that Hitler was turning his war machine in the Soviets' direction, with tacit Western approval.

And it only took Hitler until a year after Munich to show that he would not stop unless he *was* stopped. Putting pressure on Poland, he also in August 1939 entered into secret negotiations with the Soviet Union to ensure that it would not oppose his conquest. The Soviets, wary of the West and willing to buy time in this fashion, agreed. In a secret protocol, Germany and Russia divided the Polish state. To Hitler's great surprise, Britain and France, who had offered a new guarantee to Poland, honored their pledge to that country when he nonetheless invaded it on September 1, 1939.

Hitler's blitzkrieg finished off Poland quickly, while on the western front England and France waited for the attack on them. But in April 1940 Hitler first moved into Scandinavia. This preempted an Anglo-French plan to move into that same area to assist the Finns, who were at war with the Soviets and doing very well against them. Because of the pact between Stalin and Hitler, the Allies considered them both as enemies. Nonetheless, it would have been folly for the

English and French (and the reverse of the conservation of enemies) to take on the Soviets as well as the Germans. Hitler, having heard rumors of the Anglo-French plan, acted first and eliminated the possibility of London and Paris fighting two major powers simultaneously. This was his first great "contribution" to Allied victory (his second was his unilateral decision to declare war on the United States after Pearl Harbor).

Continuing his momentum, on May 10 Hitler invaded the Netherlands, Belgium, and Luxembourg. That same day Winston Churchill became Britain's prime minister. French and British forces advanced into Belgium, but in less than a month's time they were forced back in defeat. By heroic efforts, 215,000 British and 120,000 French troops were evacuated from Dunkirk, abandoning almost all of their equipment. With the Allies reeling from this blow, on June 10 Mussolini declared war and attacked the French from the south.[7] Hitler's panzers now swept in a wide arc behind the French Maginot Line, capturing Verdun on June 15. Meanwhile, Soviet forces moved into Estonia, Latvia, and Lithuania. On June 22, at Compiegne, a German-French armistice was signed in the same railroad car to which the Germans had come at the end of World War I to sign that armistice. France was out of the war, with three-fifths of the country under German occupation.

In the United States, meanwhile, Congress passed a National Defense Tax Bill to raise the enormous sum (for those days) of just under a billion dollars. On September 3, President Roosevelt by an executive order moved to turn over fifty U.S. destroyers to the hard-pressed British in return for British Caribbean bases. The Gallup Poll showed 62 percent of Americans in favor, with 38 percent opposed. The New York *Daily News* said that the United States "has one foot in the war and the other on a banana peel."[8] Nevertheless, on September 16 the Congress passed the Selective Service Act. In March 1941 the Lend-Lease Act was passed, and events moved ever more quickly. In April, America acquired bases in Greenland from the Danish government in exile, and in July United States forces moved into Iceland, replacing British units.

Roosevelt's message to Congress on July 7, 1941, said bluntly: "The United States cannot permit the occupation by Germany of strategic outposts in the Atlantic to be used as air or naval bases for eventual attack against the Western Hemisphere."[9] He also announced that U.S. forces had moved into bases (acquired from the British) in Trinidad and British Guiana to safeguard the Caribbean approaches. In August, after meeting with Churchill at sea off Nova Scotia, the two leaders announced jointly an "Atlantic Charter," setting forth principles for a new postwar order. Then in September, with U.S. naval vessels now routinely escorting merchantmen from American and Canadian ports to Iceland where the British navy took over escort, the U.S.S. *Greer* was "deliberately" attacked "in full daylight" while "flying an American flag." (The words are Roosevelt's.) Americans were indignant at this affront to the flag.

In November, the major restrictions still remaining from the neutrality act of 1939 were removed by Congress in response to Roosevelt's statement that "as we approach full production requiring the use of more ships now being built it will be increasingly necessary to deliver American goods under the American flag. . . ."[10]

American relations with Japan were steadily deteriorating, too. Taking advantage of French weakness after the armistice, Japan took over French Indo-China. In consequence, after diplomacy became deadlocked, on July 25, 1941, the United States moved to freeze Japanese funds and suspend shipments of oil and scrap metal. Since these supplies were fundamental for Japan's war machine, Tokyo's counterbalancing interests were clear: give in or fight. (The strategic opportunity to strike, as we saw earlier, had come with Germany's assault on the Soviets.)

Japan had no hope, or even any plan, of bringing the war home to the American continent. Like it action in going to war against Russia in 1904, Japans hoped to win a local area victory significant enough so that the larger power, in this case the United States, would agree to some peace settlement. The Japanese Navy Chief of Staff on September 6, 1941, made this clear at a high-level staff conference: "Even if our Empire should win a decisive naval victory, we will not thereby be able to bring the war to a conclusion. . . . Our empire does not have the means to take the offensive, overcome the enemy, and make them give up their will to fight." So "what happens thereafter will depend to a great extent on overall national power . . . and on developments in the world situation."[11]

Like the Nazis, filled with Hitler's bombast of inevitable victory, the Japanese set themselves for a war with the United States that they did not know how they could actually win. This was more than *hubris;* it was a misunderstanding of the American national character that is truly incredible.

Confronted with a two-front war, despite the anger against Japan and the anguish over the inability to succor the American troops still fighting in the Philippines, the United States gave first priority to the more dangerous enemy, Germany. The first move was an operation in French North Africa (Operation Torch). This held a promise of defeating the Germans at the periphery of their power and bringing French territory once again actively into the war. Torch was launched in November 1942 as British and American units landed in Algeria (French North Africa). Hitler, defying the principle of the conservation of enemies, had invaded the Soviet Union in mid-1941 (his third great mistake). Confronted in North Africa with the need to either reinforce or withdraw, he decided characteristically to gamble for even higher stakes. He reinforced—his fourth mistake, and a decision that was to cost him the loss of the first large German army to surrender in World War II.[12] By May 1943, the allies had captured 250,000 Axis troops, half of them German, trapped in Tunisia.

With North Africa secured, the Anglo-American discussion turned to "what next?" Since the forces were still not sufficient for a frontal attack from England to France, the logic of their position focused their attention on Sicily. From there it would be possible easily to move over to Italy. That would raise the real possibility of knocking one of the Axis powers out of the war.

In January 1943, Roosevelt and Churchill, in a meeting at Casablanca in Morocco, announced that they were aiming at the "unconditional surrender" of the Axis powers. Even so, after Mussolini resigned once the Allies took Sicily, they negotiated peace on July 25, 1943, with the new Italian government under Marshal Badoglio. Hitler, refusing to accept Italy's surrender, sent reinforcements into Italy to contest the Allied advance up the mainland. On September 15, German troops rescued Mussolini, and a new Fascist government was created in the north of Italy. On October 1, U.S. troops entered Naples.

Meanwhile, in Asia the U.S. Marines landed on Guadalcanal, and in November 1942 the U.S. Navy defeated a Japanese force in a three-day battle of the Solomon Islands. Allied troops landed on Bougainville on October 31 as the Japanese were now pushed back from their furthest advance.

On the Russian front, by January 1943, Germany was encountering a series of defeats as the Soviets counterattacked. On February 2, twenty-two encircled German divisions, ordered by Hitler to fight or die at Stalingrad, surrendered. More than 90,000 Germans were captured, only 5,000 of whom ever saw "the Fatherland" again. The losses of the Germans and their allies in three months of Russian winter fighting exceeded 500,000.

In retrospect we can see that militarily the turning point in World War II came in 1943, even though the fighting continued until 1945.

On June 6, 1944, the Allies invaded Normandy, and on August 15 they landed also on the French Mediterranean coast between Marseille and Nice. From then on it was just a matter of time, as the Allied armies closed in on Germany from every direction. The Western allies crossed the German frontier in September, and by the following January the Soviets were into Germany on the eastern frontier.

In December 1944, Hitler made his last serious mistake of the war. By ordering a strong counteroffensive against the Western armies—the Battle of the Bulge—Hitler necessarily thinned out his forces in the east, which allowed the Soviets an easier advance into Germany. Hitler subsequently made desperate efforts to slow the Soviets down, removing troops from the western front so that now the Allies surged ahead.

Unfortunately, it was just at the time of the Battle of the Bulge, when the Allies were almost up to the German frontier, that the lines of division for the postwar occupation of Germany were being drawn. Given where the armies were, it seemed reasonable to divide Germany at what later became the Iron Curtain line. However, American and British forces actually held territory more than one hundred miles further east in Germany when fighting ceased—all of which they evacuated, allowing many Germans and much of Germany to pass into Soviet control.

In 1943, with the military tide turning, the Big Three conferences (Roosevelt, Stalin, and Churchill) to arrange the outcome began. Though there were many areas of controversy, the most important issue geostrategically was what to do about Germany. At Teheran in November- December, the Allied approach was to dismember Germany, but by the Yalta Conference of February 4–12, 1945, the emphasis was shifting to dividing Germany into "temporary" occupation zones until the Allies agreed on conditions for an eventually restored German state. That approach was continued at the last of the wartime Big Three conferences at Potsdam, from July 17 to August 2, 1945 (we will discuss this event later).

Victory in Europe—V-E Day—came on May 8, 1945, with Germany in ruins and Hitler a suicide in his bunker in Berlin. In Asia, the surrender was not quite so unconditional. When the Japanese, even after the dropping of atomic bombs on Hiroshima and Nagasaki in early August, balked at not retaining the emperor, the Allies agreed that he could keep his throne. On September 2, 1945, formal terms of surrender were signed in Tokyo Bay on the U.S.S. *Missouri*.

With this history firmly in mind, we shall now go back and look at five historical examples in which the inadequacies of America's intellectual preparedness and policy coordination processes hindered making effective policy choices.

Inadequacies Carry a Price Tag: Five Examples

The first example is *Pearl Harbor* itself. The fact that the Pearl Harbor attack came as such a shock demonstrated both intellectual and organizational problems. Intellectually, such surprise was the product of the strategic insensitivity we stressed earlier. After all, the attack came in December 1941, almost exactly six months after Germany had attacked the Soviet Union. That German attack significantly altered the strategic circumstances of Japan—and, therefore, of the United States, which had already emerged in Japanese minds as the greatest threat to their plans to dominate what they called an "East Asia Co-Prosperity Sphere." The Japanese were freed from any concern that they would be attacked from their own rear once they made a frontal attack on America. Since the Japanese had already occupied China, the Soviets were the last threat in their own area. All of that escaped American notice. Washington realized in a general way that tensions were rising. It even, through its code-breaking, knew that the Japanese were preparing for war. But, since America had gotten out of the habit of thinking in strategic terms and had no unit of government responsible to do so, it did not connect the German move with what the Japanese did six months later. (A people more accustomed to thinking strategically would also have realized that six months was what military planners would require to mount such an operation.)

We must be very clear, here. No matter how important it was to remain alert on a daily basis to the possibility that became actuality when Japan attacked the United States at Pearl Harbor on December 7, 1941, we are not talking of such situational unawareness. Nor are we talking of the bureaucratic inefficiencies that developed or the issue of knowing that the attack, if it came, would be at Pearl Harbor. All of these are important matters, but they are subsets of a larger strategic point: knowing that to achieve its objectives Japan had to attack and remove the primary obstacle in its path, the United States, and knowing that once the Soviet threat could be discounted by the Japanese, an attack was almost inevitable.

Although this particular failure (with its various subsets) was not the sole cause of the creation of the Central Intelligence Agency and the National Security Council after the war, it played a primary role.

The second example of inadequacy and what it can lead to was the planning for the *postwar occupation of Germany*.[13] Roosevelt, as indicated above, did not have easy relations with Secretary of State Hull. He also had little faith in the State Department as an institution. As the war continued, he got caught up more and more in his military role as commander-in-chief. As a consequence, State Department planning was conducted with little presidential guidance, and the president's major decisions usually were taken after consultation only with his military advisers (who had no desire to be hobbled by political considerations). Roosevelt's own actions made civil-military coordination difficult. The list of staff that he took to the various Big Three conferences, for example, shows a very top-heavy military group and little else. Look at the Teheran Conference. He did not even invite his secretary of state to come along! Then, on board ship, Roosevelt sat down with his Joint Chiefs of Staff (without any State Department representative at the meeting) to discuss the future zonal frontiers in Germany— a prime political topic. Using a National Geographic map, he sketched out a plan showing the three zones converging on Berlin. That map, unknown to the State Department, was put into an army safe in the Pentagon after the Teheran Conference.[14]

A relatively low-level State Department-War Department coordinating group was established in Washington to staff this question and to make a recommendation as to the future zones of occupation. But the group was not made aware of Roosevelt's map, and it soon deadlocked besides. No higher authority did anything effective about it. Meanwhile, in London, the European Advisory Commission established by the Big Three to settle this issue had a British draft as early as January 1944, which the Soviets accepted on February 18, 1944. The U.S. representative, Ambassador Winant, given no instructions for a month, then was told by the Washington coordinating group to press for three zones (American, British, Soviet) radiating out from Berlin (i.e., essentially Roosevelt's map concept). With two of the three powers already committed to an alternate plan, the American proposal had little chance, even if backed by substantial arguments. But the State Department, still knowing nothing of the idea's origin, only sent it along because the military were now pressing strongly for it. They gave no supporting arguments to Winant.

Winant, justifiably balking at trying to carry the plan without supporting arguments, sent George Kennan back to Washington. When Kennan was allowed to see Roosevelt and told him about the problem, Roosevelt on April 3, 1944, agreed to accept the British-Soviet draft. On April 28, the Joint Chiefs concurred. This is the origin of what became West Germany and East Germany.

Winant, still worried, came himself to Washington in May and raised the question of Berlin access. He found the War Department apparently wanting to leave the issue open so that American forces could, they thought, then use any routes they wished. On June 1, 1944, Winant announced American acceptance of the plan—with no Berlin access. The degree of separation of the military and political aspects of policy and the lack of a coordinated approach to national security matters are truly astounding.

Where Roosevelt did take effective action was to improve the administration of national security affairs on the military level. The Joint Chiefs of Staff came into existence by presidential authority, not confirmed in law until after the war. And there is no question but that he consulted with them and that he, as commander-in-chief, made the overall decisions. But, without a serious and continuous political policy input from the State Department, these decisions were taken almost exclusively on military grounds.

The third example is the "war aim" slogan, announced at the Casablanca Conference, of *"unconditional surrender"* by the enemy powers, Italy, Germany, and Japan. Roosevelt apparently tossed this off with little staffing by anyone. The president told Harry Hopkins that when the press conference was held at which he (Roosevelt) used this phrase, "the thought popped into my mind that they had called Grant 'Old Unconditional Surrender,' and the next thing I knew I had said it."[15] Churchill, in his memoirs, does not contradict this account; he was apparently more concerned to omit Italy from this approach, sensing that a surrender could be negotiated. Elliott Roosevelt, the president's son, says that Churchill at a dinner heard the phrase from Roosevelt and said, "Perfect."[16] Whatever the facts, the formula was applied to Germany but that did not happen with Japan. There, as with Italy, the surrender was negotiated. Critics of the unconditional surrender formula allege that this unwillingness to talk terms discouraged Hitler's enemies within Germany and gave the fanatic Nazis no hope of escaping their fate once they were defeated, thus prolonging the war. That charge is probably correct. In any event, there was no well-staffed analysis of the advantages and disadvantages such a statement or policy might produce. The State Department certainly must have been surprised!

The fourth example is the way in which the *division of Germany into two states,* one allied with the West and one under the Soviets, emerged. The specific problems were several, including lack of a sound geostrategic concept to guide policy, poor policy coordination, unwarranted assumptions of Soviet postwar good will, and decisions based on abstractions instead of clear and concrete ideas about the final outcome.

As the war wound down, the Soviet Union, having suffered enormous casualties (more than *20 million dead*) and widespread destruction during Germany's invasion, was in no mood to coddle its former opponent. Simply dividing Germany was not Stalin's goal. He would have preferred eliminating Germany altogether, as clearly shown at the Teheran Conference, by his toast to the execution of some fifty thousand German officers at the end of the war. Roosevelt attempted to treat the toast as a joke; Churchill knew very well it was not. Germany, Stalin said, should be "broken up so that she could not reunite." Because the Germans fight "like wild beasts," it would be best to "break up and scatter the German tribes."[17]

Churchill and Roosevelt intended that Germany should be de-Nazified, and at Teheran they both talked in terms of dismembering Germany. But as they later contemplated the appalling disarray that would be produced in Central

Europe by a program of truly dismembering Germany, they shrank back. At the Yalta Conference (February 4–12, 1945), Stalin tabled a proposal to divide Germany into three states,[18] but by now Roosevelt and Churchill were having second thoughts. Although the Yalta communiqué still used the word "dismemberment," the whole question was referred to a commission for further study.

When the discussion turned to Germany's future frontiers, Stalin proposed the Oder-*Western* Neisse River as Poland's western border. This would place German Silesia in Poland (which Stalin already planned to dominate with a Communist regime). Churchill, while willing to see Poland's area somewhat enlarged on the west, cautioned against stuffing "the Polish goose so full of German food that it got indigestion." Roosevelt agreed, saying that "there would appear to be little justification for extending [Poland] to the Western Neisse." Confronted with an impasse, the issue was postponed until a new Polish government took power following what were to be free elections.

The other major question concerning Germany at Yalta concerned reparations. The Soviets claimed $128 billion in direct losses. As a famous American politician once said about billions, "pretty soon you're talking real money." Billions in 1945 was indeed real money. Stalin wanted to milk Germany of all movable assets as compensation. Britain and America, facing the problem of feeding a deindustrialized and destitute population in their zones of occupation, insisted on a more moderate agreement. Reparations were to take three forms: "removals" of German "assets . . . within two years" after Germany's surrender, "chiefly for the purpose of destroying the war potential of Germany"; "annual deliveries of goods from current production for a period to be fixed"; and the "use of German labor." As for the total amount of these reparations, it was agreed that the Reparations Commission would use the figure of $20 billion as a basis of discussion, with half of it to go to the Soviet Union. But who would determine the value of any item, especially if "used"? (The Soviets stripped Germany of almost anything movable, claiming it all was worth very little.) This argument was not really resolved and was to cause much more trouble.

The last Big Three conference came at Potsdam (July 17–August 2, 1945). Roosevelt had died and been replaced by Truman. And, in the middle of the conference, Churchill was replaced by Laborite Clement Atlee as the result of the British election. That left Stalin as the only veteran of all the meetings, with the other two severely handicapped by lack of background.

It was apparent by Potsdam that dismemberment had been shelved, although achieving "the complete disarmament and demilitarization of Germany and the elimination or control of all German industry that could be used for military production" was reaffirmed in the agreement made there.[19] But the United States was even more cautious than it had been earlier, on reparations. The protocol at the end of the conference specified that payment of reparations was to "leave enough resources to enable the German people to subsist without external assistance." Each occupying nation was to take reparations from its own zone. In addition, the Soviet Union would get "15 percent of such usable and complete industrial capital equipment" from the Western zones as was "unnecessary for the German peace economy . . . in exchange for an equivalent value of food, coal, potash, zinc, timber, clay products, petroleum products, and such other commodities as may be agreed upon." The Soviets would also get 10 percent of any "unnecessary" industrial capital equipment in the Western zones without any payment or exchange. What was "unnecessary" and what was an "equivalent value" was, of course, in the eye of the beholder. Arguments over the meaning of these words in concrete cases blossomed as soon as the powers tried to implement them.

On frontiers, the Soviets proposed, "pending . . . the peace settlement," that their western frontier should move westward into part of former Poland. This was "agreed in principle." But how much former German territory would go as compensation to Poland remained controversial. Stalin, on the eve of the conference, unilaterally transferred that part of the Soviet zone east of the Oder-Western Neisse to Polish administration—one that was already under Communist control, despite earlier promises of democratic elections.

The American view that the boundary should be the Oder-*Eastern* Neisse had not changed, but at the conference Truman finally agreed to accept the Western Neisse temporarily in return for Soviet agreement on a "package" that included admission of Italy and the East European states to the U.N., and essentially the Western approach to reparations. Stalin agreed. Accordingly, in the protocol, the Big Three reaffirmed their view that "the final delimitation of the western frontier of Poland should await the peace settlement."[20]

We call the protocols issued at the end of such conferences, "agreements." In this instance a more accurate term would be "disagreements." Or agreements with at least serious mental reservations. Or even "agreement for now, but the problem is not really solved."

There is no doubt that the Soviets were in desperate condition. At Yalta, Stalin claimed that 1,710 Soviet towns were completely destroyed, as well as 31,500 factories and 40,000 miles of railroad right-of-way. Moreover, the situation in Poland and in the Soviet zone of Germany was equally bad. It is not surprising that the Soviets would contest every point in interpreting the protocols to their advantage. They needed and wanted everything.

Yet the Western position was equally understandable. They were not prepared to ship food and machinery east in endless supplies while they (especially the United States) had to provide food to keep the German people from starving. The whole approach to Germany was one that could hardly be maintained very long. And it was not maintained very long. Soon restrictions were eased in the zones. But the bad feeling and resulting tension between East and West grew.

Throughout these conferences it was evident that intellectually the United States was simply not prepared to deal with a Soviet Union aggressively looking out for its own particular interests first. Washington did not subscribe to the type of logic associated with the concept of counterbalancing interests so central to an effective policy, nor to the idea that Moscow was a temporary, not permanent, ally. Indeed, for most of the war America looked forward to increased or at least continued postwar cooperation for mutual ends with the Soviets (although Truman was somewhat less sanguine than FDR). Roosevelt never flagged in his efforts to convince Stalin of America's good faith, believing that if

Stalin were so convinced the cooperation could continue. (On many occasions Roosevelt bent over backwards to show Stalin that he did not necessarily agree with Churchill.) Regrettably the most serious concessions *were not even seen as serious concessions.*

The fifth example of intellectual and coordination problems is the way the question of *access to jointly-occupied Berlin* was handled, along with the related question of the withdrawal of American forces from what was to be the Soviet zone of occupation.

These questions arose with Germany's surrender, at a time when the first serious frictions between the United States and the Soviet Union (which were to lead to the Cold War) had already appeared. The focus of these frictions was over German reparations and, more importantly, over the fact that the Soviets were obviously turning Poland and the other Soviet-occupied East European states into satellite states controlled from Moscow. As we shall see in later chapters, the Cold War was to last for decades.

At the end of the war in Europe, Truman, assuming that the arrangements for the occupation of Germany were purely temporary, ordered U.S. troops to withdraw from their advanced positions, to retire back to the agreed Western zone. By doing so, Truman threw away his trump card to offset Stalin's physical occupation of Poland.

With Western forces at the end of the war as much as 150 miles into the proposed Soviet zone, Churchill on May 4, 1945, had urged Truman to delay withdrawal:

> The Polish problem may be easier to settle when set in relation to the now numerous outstanding questions of the utmost gravity which require settlement with the Russians. I fear terrible things have happened. . . . The proposed withdrawal . . . would mean the tide of Russian domination sweeping forward 120 miles on a front of 300 or 400 miles. This would be an event which would be one of the most melancholy in history. . . . [21]

Churchill wanted first to be "satisfied about Poland, and also about the temporary character of the Russian occupation of Germany."

Such balance-of-power thinking was not congenial to Washington. Truman replied to Churchill that the allies were clearly committed on specific zones and that he could not agree to going back on our commitments. Two other things influenced his view: that the United States wanted the Soviets to honor their Yalta pledge to come into the war against Japan, and that (according to the Soviets) the Allied Control Council to administer occupied Germany could not be allowed to function until the American withdrawal was completed.

Now began the second act, as the Allied Control Council did begin to function in Berlin.

As the war had approached its end, the government in Washington left to its military commanders any arrangements for access to Berlin. Accordingly, General Eisenhower sent General Clay to arrange the details. Clay, in his memoirs, recounts his conference with Marshal Zhukov, in which Zhukov took a highly restrictive approach. Clay says:

> We both knew there was no [existing written] provision covering access to Berlin. . . . We did not wish to accept specific routes which might be interpreted as a denial of our right of access over all routes."

So Clay accepted "as a temporary arrangement the allocation of a main highway and rail line and two air corridors, reserving the right to reopen the question in the Allied Control Council." He adds: "I must admit that we did not then fully realize that the requirement of unanimous consent would enable a Soviet veto in the Allied Control Council to block all of our future efforts."[22]

As we shall see later, these arrangements put the United States at the mercy of the Soviets' continued willingness to grant access to Berlin. Before much time had passed, the Soviets were to institute a blockade, which America countered with an airlift. The whole episode, in which the State Department views were not really considered, shows the inadequacy both of the intellectual understanding of what was at issue and of the governmental arrangements for foreign policy decision-making.

The State Department

We have seen that effective coordination demands good and continuous communications *between* the different departments of government. But it also assumes that the departments *themselves* are efficiently organized. We showed earlier that this assumption was not always warranted for the armed services before World War II. The same was true of the State Department as it grew in numbers from the 1930s onwards, trying to cope with the increasing complexity of U.S. foreign relations.

The small size of the U.S. government before World War II really is difficult to comprehend today. Consider that the old granite building just to the side of the White House, known today as the Executive Office Building, was once called the State-War-Navy Building. It was called that because it actually housed all three departments, *plus* the Bureau of the Budget. (And even being in a single building, they did not necessarily keep each other informed!)

U. Alexis Johnson, who rose to become under secretary for political affairs and retired after a distinguished Foreign Service career in 1977, entered the Foreign Service in 1935. He actually took the entrance examinations in 1932, as one of 7,000 applicants hoping for one of fifteen appointments, once vacancies developed—which took three years in his case.[23] Luckily for him, the Foreign Service was now on a professional footing, since legislation in 1924 converted it from "old-boy-network" appointments to a real career service. The 1924 Rogers Act for the first time amalgamated separate consular and diplomatic services into a single service, with definite rules for appointment and promotion. But three years after Johnson was sworn in and sent to his first post in Tokyo, the total number of Foreign Service Officers stood at only 766. Even in 1948, the figure was only 1,360. These FSOs represented the core of the Department, serving primarily abroad as the nation's diplomatic eyes and ears. By 1968, when America was fully engaged in world affairs, the FSO total had reached 3,379—almost a fivefold increase over 1938. This rapid rate of expansion also created a certain administrative turmoil, just because of the growth.

Embassies abroad were not just staffed with FSOs, though, and the total employed by State was much larger. The total included other groups, such as Foreign Service reserve officers and Foreign Service staff officers, as well as representatives from Civil Service and foreign nationals employed abroad. If we count up personnel from these major separate groups working for the State Department itself, and add them to the FSO totals given above, the totals jump to 5,692 for 1938, 20,327 by 1948, and 25,495 for 1968—again, approximately a fivefold increase.[24]

The fact that the FSOs were under one set of laws and the Civil Service under another, created problems. FSOs, for example, had to be promoted up or were out of the service, while the Civil Service worked on the principle that after a probationary period the occupant of the position acquired tenure. This problem was eventually minimized by bringing many of the Civil Service officials into the Foreign Service.

This "Wristonization" procedure, so named after its author, wiped out much of the previous distinction between FSOs serving almost exclusively abroad during their careers, and "home office" personnel (usually titled, Foreign *Affairs* Officers) with little or no foreign experience—a division of responsibility and function largely accounting in the latter case for the high civil service numbers. It was decided, correctly, that such a division produced problems in both groups—for the one, being out of touch with Washington; for the other, being out of touch with conditions abroad.

Another problem, by no means ever completely solved, was how to handle the fact that other government departments, not primarily engaged in foreign affairs, needed to have special representatives stationed abroad in the embassies. Between 1927 and 1935 the United States in effect had four or more foreign services operating abroad. In 1927, the Department of Commerce formed a separate foreign commerce service. In 1930, the Department of Agriculture established a smaller foreign agricultural service. In 1935, the Department of the Interior (Bureau of Mines) set up a similar but still smaller service involving mineral specialists. These services all had congressional authorization. Add to this representatives of the Treasury Department.

Because of the confusion stemming from so many units abroad, all reporting to different seniors in Washington, President Roosevelt in 1939 sponsored a reorganization act that merged the Commerce and Agriculture officers abroad into the Foreign Service. In 1943, the Bureau of Mines representatives were also included. But Treasury kept its own identity, and in 1954, the Agriculture Department created its own Foreign Agricultural Service. When the Central Intelligence Agency was created, it had to have positions abroad, too—along with representatives from Justice, Interior, Defense, the Atomic Energy Commission, the Federal Aviation Agency, and Health, Education, and Welfare. One result of this was that as of June 30, 1964, only 7,200 out of 30,000 federal civilian employees in U.S. embassies abroad actually worked for the State Department.[25]

Again, Dean Acheson's remarks are pertinent: "The prewar State Department was closer to its nineteenth-century predecessors in both what it did and how the work was done than to the department I was later to command. Between the two a great world change and General Marshall had intervened." In the nineteenth century, says Acheson, "what the Supreme Court has called 'the vast external realm'" impinged upon American interests only rarely, "usually only when wars between foreign nations interfered with our commerce or when foreign nations intervened in our hemisphere. . . ." Acheson points as illustration to "the utter triviality of the correspondence between President Harrison and Secretary of State James G. Blaine, from 1889 to 1892," all of it in longhand, in notes written almost every day.

Consequently, most matters concerning the State Department "arose from specific incidents or problems and then evolved into policies, rather than beginning as matters of broad decision and ending in specific action." That gave bureaucratic power to the division chiefs, who were "like barons in a feudal system. . . ." When Acheson came aboard, "the greater part of a day in Old State was devoted to meetings. Where the boundaries of jurisdiction were fuzzy or overlapping, meetings became inevitable." But most questions involved a number of divisions, both functional and geographical. If the meetings went anywhere, it would be in the direction of trying to find a compromise.[26]

Some of this, as Acheson suggests, changed once U.S. foreign policy took off in high gear to deal with the problems of the Cold War. In other respects, though, as we shall see in later chapters, the meetings merely became more interdepartmental, and the problem of reconciling different approaches remained. Much of the problem is built into the way government operates.[27]

Although undoubtedly necessary, such a development toward extra–State Department staffing also caused problems. We shall see that, as more departments had some say in foreign policy and as the foreign policy itself became more active, it created a new kind of strain on the occupant of the chair of secretary of state. It often made a secretary defensive of his sphere of activity, as when Al Haig claimed under Reagan to be the "vicar" of foreign policy—meaning, Haig wanted his cabinet associates and the White House staff to play only a minor role. Haig resented all those others (including the White House staff) who kept "horning in" on what Haig considered his "turf."

When George Marshall was secretary, he, like Dean Acheson, fell at the other end of the spectrum. Both men never forgot they were not themselves the chief executive. George Schultz, too, was very careful about this, as was James Baker. Acheson once stated the relationship this way, apparently describing Marshall's view, who

> saw his own role as chief of staff to the president in foreign affairs, directing and controlling the Department, keeping the president abreast of incipient situations

that might call for decisions or action, acting as a principal assistant in making the decisions and assuring action upon them.[28]

Besides having his ego under control, the secretary of state will not succeed unless he has a well developed concept of government staff work. George Marshall had that to an advanced degree. He usually went home each day at 4:30 or 5:00 P.M. because he devoted his own time only to such things as only he could handle, delegating the rest. He insisted on having a recommendation on a single sheet of paper (to force the staffer to think the issue through). Likewise, he insisted that any question put to him by a staffer had to have a recommended answer along with it—for the same reason. Nor would Marshall listen to only one side of an issue if his staff had divided opinions. Both sides would be heard at the same session. When he was in Paris at a conference with the allies, he once told Rusk (then an assistant secretary) to query the department for instructions on an issue. Rusk was surprised; after all, Marshall was the secretary. But Marshall told him that, in the field as he then was, he could not know all that Washington knew that would affect the decision. Most of these staffing procedures Marshall learned in the army, but they apply anywhere in the government where efficiency is sought.[29]

Acheson was an excellent secretary, but he also wrote that "All presidents I have known have had uneasy doubts about the State Department." These doubts ranged from the president's fear that he was losing control of his own foreign policy to an ambitious secretary, to a fear that the department was so hidebound that it could never get anywhere with any complicated problem. There is much in the record to validate the second concern. Truman actually had the very embarrassing experience when he decided to recognize Israel as a new state, only to find the State Department the next day canvassing for votes at the U.N. to give the area trusteeship status![30] That the charges presidents have levied against State have some basis in fact cannot be denied. At the same time, when we consider that the Department of State is operating with embassies and consulates scattered around the world and representing the varied interests of so many of the major departments in Washington itself, it can hardly be expected to move very quickly on most problems, nor can it be made fully efficient.

Toward an Effective Coordination: The National Security Act of 1947

When the United States emerged from World War II as the leader of the "Free World," the problems of coordination between separate departments of government, so obvious to all, could no longer be safely ignored. As a result, in 1947 Congress passed the landmark National Security Act. Before we consider its specific provisions, it will be useful to reflect on how we, if we had had that task, would have approached the problem. What are the essentials that are needed?

First, of course, the units to be coordinated must themselves have a reasonable degree of efficiency. We have seen that there was some progress in this respect, both in the military departments and in the State Department.

Second, some solution must be found to provide proper advice to the president, on the one hand, and a smooth and efficient implementation of policy decisions on the other. Remove the apparatus for doing this too far from the departments by centering it in the White House, and the decision may never get implemented out in the bureaucracy. But keeping the White House role to a minimum and depending upon the cabinet officials and line departments, particularly State and Defense, puts too much on the shoulders of busy officials working in separate buildings. And how are State and Defense to remain in touch? And at what level or levels? The logic here later led, as we shall see in Chapter 7, to the creation of a National Security Council staff and the interagency committee structure.

Third, to establish an efficient system of coordination on the military side, the services have to speak effectively to one another. Roosevelt's innovation of the Joint Chiefs pointed the way to a solution for this problem, with Admiral Leahy of Roosevelt's staff acting as what we would today call the Chairman of the Joint Chiefs.

The final need is for good intelligence. (And the reverse: a system to ensure that the United States is not too easy a target for foreign espionage.)

All of these needs were in the minds of President Truman and the Congress when they developed the National Security Act.[31] That act created what was at first called the National Military Establishment, headed by a Secretary of Defense with very limited powers.[32] The army and the navy, along with an air force created from the army, remained as separate services, each with its own civilian and military chiefs. The act also created a Central Intelligence Agency, designed to provide appropriate information to the central decision makers. It established a National Security Council specifically charged to "assess and appraise objectives, commitments and risks" involved in alternative policy options, blending military and political considerations in the process. This NSC was to "advise the President with respect to the integration of domestic, foreign, and military policies relating to the national security," with the goal of enabling all pertinent parts of the government "to cooperate more effectively. . . ." The NSC membership consisted (in this first version) of the president, the vice president, the secretary of state, the secretary of defense, the director of mutual security (who then dealt with allied arms supplies), the chairman of the National Security Resources Board, and others whom the president might add.

A final element in the National Security Act was the establishment of the Central Intelligence Agency (CIA), subordinate to the NSC. It was to coordinate the intelligence activities of the several government departments and military intelligence units. In theory, the CIA was to have a predominate role in intelligence collection and dissemination, but it soon ran into resistance from the service agencies in military areas. In 1961 the Defense Intelligence Agency was established to help coordinate on the military side. There was also the technical side of intelligence-gathering, performed by the super-secret National Security Agency. It specialized in the devices needed for codes and ciphers, their safeguarding and their breaking, and in ensuring communication security. To attempt to control all of these intelligence activities, the director of the CIA was also given a second "hat" as the Director of Central Intelligence (DCI), the coordinator of the whole effort. In 1949, after the first revision of the National Security Act and the establishment of a statutory Chairman of the Joint Chiefs (CJCS), the DCI and the CJCS were named as statutory advisers to the NSC.

With these arrangements, the United States hoped to avoid repeating past mistakes. How well they worked out in practice we shall see later.

Summing Up

The record shows that the United States government was ill-prepared for the policy complications of World War II, both in an intellectual sense and in an organizational sense. The five examples given above showed that clearly. These problems in World War II led directly to the National Security Act of 1947.

Notes

1. Edward L. Beach, *The United States Navy: 200 Years* (New York: Holt, 1986), pp. 29–34, gives more detail.

2. See Carl Sandburg's monumental four volume, *Abraham Lincoln: The War Years* (New York: Harcourt Brace, 1939). See especially Vol. I, p. 282.

3. Ernest R. May, "The Development of Political-Military Consultation in the United States," *Political Science Quarterly,* 70 (June 1955), p. 164.

4. Robert Murphy, *Diplomat Among Warriors* (Garden City, NY: Doubleday, 1964), p. 6.

5. Dean Acheson, *Present at the Creation: My Years in the State Department* (New York: Norton, 1969), p. 9.

6. Dr. Paul Schmidt, *Hitler's Interpreter,* ed. R.H.C. Steed (New York: Macmillan, 1951), p. 115. This book is a translation of the second half of Schmidt's *Statist auf diplomatischer Bühne, 1923–45.* The first half is an eyewitness account—the only one—of the important negotiations during the "era of Locarno" in the 1920s, when it seemed possible that France and Germany could be reconciled. Schmidt's German title means *Ventriloquist's Dummy on the Diplomatic Stage.*

7. President Franklin Roosevelt said: "the hand that held the dagger has plunged it into the back of its neighbor." Quoted in Robert E. Sherwood, *Roosevelt and Hopkins,* p. 143.

8. Quoted from Thomas A. Bailey, *A Diplomatic History of the American People,* 6th ed. (New York: Appleton-Century-Crofts, 1958), p. 719.

9. *Peace and War: United States Foreign Policy, 1931–1941* (Washington: 1943),

pp. 686–87. Reprinted in Ruhl J. Bartlett, ed., *The Record of American Diplomacy* (New York: Knopf, 1948), p. 621.

10. Message to Congress, October 9, 1941. *Peace and War*, pp. 761–65. Bartlett, *The Record of American Democracy*, pp. 628–30.

11. Quoted in Fred Charles Ikl, *Every War Must End* (New York: Columbia University Press, 1971), p. 44.

12. His reinforcement was too little to turn the tide in Africa, while concurrently harming his effort in Russia.

13. Frederick H. Hartmann, *Germany Between East and West: The Reunification Problem* (Englewood Cliffs, NJ: Prentice-Hall, 1965), pp. 37–38, contains a detailed discussion of the evolution of the occupation zones and the problems connected with them.

14. John J. McCloy, assistant secretary of war under Stimson, tells us that the same disconnect between the military and political aspects of decisions continued into the first months of Truman's administration. In an appendix to James Reston, *Deadline* (New York: Random House, 1991), p. 502, McCloy tells of the White House decision meeting on how to use the A bomb—as a demonstration, or on a Japanese target. "In connection with the Japanese surrender [terms] . . . it should not have been left up to the assistant secretary of war to bring up the possibility of political settlement [rather than just dropping the bomb]. *The secretary of state should have been present* and proposing such solutions. But during the war, with the military at the center of all attention, political thinking became less keen in the State Department, and the White House came to rely perhaps too heavily on its soldiers for all advice."

15. Robert E. Sherwood, *Roosevelt and Hopkins* (New York: Harper, 1948), p. 696.

16. In his memoirs, (*The Second World War*, Vol. 4, *The Hinge of Fate* [Boston: Houghton Mifflin, 1950], p. 685), Winston Churchill cites Elliott Roosevelt's account. He then adds: "I have no recollection of these private and informal exchanges where conversation was free and unguarded." (In other words, off the record.) He says the unconditional surrender formula was approved by the British Cabinet with the proviso that Italy should not be included. The official communique for the conference did not contain the formula; it was announced at a press conference by Roosevelt, to Churchill's surprise. In any event, Churchill (p. 687) felt he must then concur.

17. Hartmann, *Germany Between East and West*, p. 16. See also vol. 5 of Churchill's memoirs, *Closing the Ring* (1951), pp. 373–74.

18. For the complete text of the Yalta agreement, see Department of State Press Release No. 239, March 24, 1947. Reprinted in Frederick H. Hartmann, ed., *Basic Documents of International Relations* (New York: McGraw Hill, 1951), pp. 169–78. The controversial secret agreement on the Far East, which restored the Soviet Union's position to essentially the 1904 status, is on pp. 177–78. The fact that the Yalta Agreement was made public in *five* installments (February 11, 1945; March 5, 1945; February 11, 1946; March 19, 1947; and March 24, 1947) helps explain the great furor that arose about it. Were there more secrets yet to come? More concessions to the Soviets?

19. For the text of the Potsdam agreement, see Department of State *Bulletin*, Vol. XIII, pp. 153ff. Also reprinted in Hartmann, *Basic Documents*, pp. 242–51. Here, too, although the main text was released at the end of the conference, a section on the Black Sea Straits was not released until March 24, 1947. The full Potsdam documents, released years later, appeared as Department of State Publication 5399, *Foreign Ministers Meeting, Berlin Discussions, January 25–February 18, 1945.*

20. When Secretary of State James Byrnes, after the Soviets accepted this package deal, said at the next meeting of the heads of government that "they all understood that the cession of territory was left to the peace conference," Stalin blandly ignored the qualification. Well he might; he held the land. See Department of State Publication 5399, *Berlin Discussions.*

21. Hartmann, *Germany Between East and West,* pp. 35–36. Churchill discusses the problem in *The Second World War,* vol. 6, *Triumph and Tragedy* (Boston: Houghton, Mifflin, 1953), Ch. 17, beginning at p. 599. Truman's reactions are given by him in Harry S. Truman, *Memoirs,* vol. 1, *Year of Decisions* (Garden City, NY: Doubleday, 1955), pp. 211–15. On May 6 Churchill telegraphed Truman, "We should hold firmly to the existing position obtained or being obtained by our armies in Yugoslavia, in Austria, in Czechoslovakia, on the main central United States front, and on the British front reaching up to Lubeck. . . ." Quoted by Churchill's official biographer Martin Gilbert, in *Churchill: A Life* (New York: Henry Holt, 1991), p. 839.

22. Hartmann, *Germany Between East and West,* pp. 37–38. For further detail, see Lucius D. Clay, *Decision in Germany* (Garden City, NY: Doubleday, 1950).

23. U. Alexis Johnson, *The Right Hand of Power* (Englewood Cliffs, N.J.: Prentice-Hall, 1984), pp. 18–21.

24. Dean Acheson says that in February 1941, counting both home and abroad numbers, there were 1,200 officers and 2,900 other American employees in the State Department. *Present At the Creation,* p. 9.

25. Burton M. Sapin, *The Making of United States Foreign Policy* (Washington, DC: The Brookings Institution, 1966), p. 252. We discuss this issue and the "country team" concept in Chapter 7.

26. Acheson, *Present at the Creation,* p. 15.

27. The generic title given to this and the kinds of questions which follow is *bureaucratic politics.* We also discuss this further in Chapter 7.

28. Acheson, *Present at the Creation,* pp. 734–35.

29. Dean Rusk has many comments on Marshall in his memoirs. See Dean Rusk, *As I Saw It,* as told to Richard Papp and edited by Daniel S. Papp (New York: Norton, 1990).

30. Truman's experience may be the ultimate in a disconnect. While reporters at the White House were told that the United States had just recognized Israel, at the U.N. the United States delegation continued rounding up votes to support partition. How this happened is explained by Clark Clifford, *Counsel to the President* (New York: Random House, 1991), pp. 22.

31. For a succinct and useful discussion of this process see Mark M. Lowenthal, "The National Security Council: Organizational History," Congressional Research Service, June 27, 1978, pp. 9–12.

32. Kinnard calls it "a weekly federated National Military Establishment . . . in charge of three military services who considered themselves autonomous and who had their own individual views. . . ." Douglas Kinnard, *The Secretary of Defense* (Lexington, KY: University Press of Kentucky, 1980), p. 40.

Part III

*How Washington Decides
Foreign Policy Issues*

6

The President and Congress

In Parts One and Two of this book we analyzed the formative experiences that shaped America's outlook before it took on its post–World War II global role. We also briefly examined portions of the American foreign policy machinery before the war and how some key decisions were made during that conflict. We paid particular attention to the problem of policy coordination. Now in Part Three we examine more fully the question of how Washington makes foreign policy. Our emphasis here is primarily structure and process, leaving discussions of policy until Parts Four and Five (although, obviously, we are concerned about how structure and process influence the kind and quality of the policy adopted).

Before we begin to discuss specifics, we need to emphasize a point that, hopefully, will become obvious: how complicated it all is. American foreign policy is formulated and implemented via policymaking machinery and through processes that are perhaps the most fragmented and complex of any modern nation. Nonetheless, one conclusion will stand out. When all is said and done, the president always is central. To use Roger Hilsman's terminology, the president is and must be the "ultimate decider," "ultimate coordinator," and "ultimate persuader."[1]

We shall also see, though, that there are other important actors, their roles and influence depending on the circumstances, on personalities, the issues, their official position, and so on. Especially important are the assistant for national security affairs, the National Security Council, the secretary of state, the secretary of defense, the director of Central Intelligence (DCI), and the chairman of the Joint Chiefs of Staff. Even this list, because it is focused solely on the upper levels in the executive branch, understates the complexity. The bureaucracy is important (and pervasive) in the routine conduct of foreign affairs. The public provides the context for decision, with public opinion, the media, and interest groups playing various roles in varying situations. And, obviously, the Congress exerts significant influence, especially in reacting to or interacting with presidential initiatives or imposing limits on the president's freedom of action.

In Chapter 7 we assess the activities of the bureaucracy and the role of key presidential advisers in the decision process, and in Chapter 8 we examine the public context. But we begin Part Three by analyzing the most central and crucial actors, the president and Congress.

We divide our analysis into three parts:

1. the "powers" of the president and Congress, formal and informal,
2. why, beginning in the late 1960s, Congress became more assertive, and
3. presidential-congressional relations in four key issue areas: international agreements, the use of military force, covert operations, and aid and trade.

Presidential Powers: Formal

The president's central position in foreign policy stems in part from five formal powers.[2] These are his role as commander in chief of the military; his power to make treaties and to make executive agreements with foreign countries; his power to appoint the highest diplomatic, military, and intelligence officials; and those powers that are inherent to his office. The complexities and subtleties of these powers require close examination.

First, the president is *commander in chief.* Article II, Section 2 of the Constitution provides that the president "shall be Commander in Chief of the Army and Navy of the United States" (today this also includes the Air Force). As we mentioned in connection with the Gulf War, authorities have disagreed vigorously about what exactly the framers meant by this language, but most presidents (especially since Lincoln) have interpreted this provision broadly and dynamically.

Although only Congress can "declare war," and although only five "wars" have been declared (the War of 1812, the Mexican War, the Spanish-American War, World War I, and World War II), the United States has been involved in some form of hostilities more than 130 times and nearly so in a myriad of others. Jefferson employed the navy in the Mediterranean to protect American trade against the Barbary pirates. In 1846 Polk ordered troops to occupy disputed territory along the Rio Grande River, an operation that (quite intentionally) led to the Mexican War. McKinley sent troops to China as part of an international effort to crush the Boxer Rebellion. Wilson ordered the marines into a number of Caribbean countries. Even before the United States was in World War II, Franklin Roosevelt ordered the navy to shoot on sight within a defined geographical area. Truman ordered armed resistance in the Korean War, Eisenhower landed U.S. marines in Lebanon in 1958, in 1965 Johnson ordered the marines into the Dominican Republic, in 1975 Ford employed force in the *Mayaguez* affair, in 1980 Carter tried to rescue American hostages in Iran, in 1983 Reagan sent forces to Grenada and 1986 he ordered the bombing of Libya, and in 1989 Bush sent troops into Panama, as well as to Saudi Arabia in 1990, ultimately to fight against Iraq in 1991. And successive presidents from Eisenhower to Nixon increased involvement in Vietnam in the 1950s and 1960s.

In addition to ordering the use of force in undeclared war situations, presidents also have utilized the commander-in-chief power in three other ways. First, they have made decisions that could produce situations in which hostilities might erupt. Kennedy's ordering of a blockade to halt Soviet shipments of additional offensive missiles into Cuba in the 1962 missile crisis is a good example. Second, once America has been engaged in hostilities the president has been the chief strategist. In World War II it was Franklin Roosevelt who decided that the Allies should open a second front by landing in France, rejecting Churchill's plea for an assault against Europe's "soft underbelly" in the Balkans. President Johnson controlled the major outlines of strategy from 1964 to 1968 in the Vietnam conflict.[3] Third, it has been the president's decision when and whether to terminate hostilities, and he has been the one to decide when and if negotiations for peace should ensue. President Bush's decision to terminate hostilities against Iraq in March 1991 is a case in point. Whether his decision was wise was debated; his authority to make that decision was not.

Clearly, on the basis of his authority as commander in chief the president often has exercised great power. Only rarely—until the Vietnam War—was this authority seriously questioned.

Second, the Constitution provides that the president has the power "by and with the Advice and Consent of the Senate *to make treaties,* provided two thirds of the Senators present concur" [emphasis added]. It is not evident whether the founding fathers thought such treaty making should occur sequentially, the president negotiating agreement and the Senate providing "advice" only afterward in connection with debate over concurrence, or if it was expected that senators also would play some role in negotiations.[4] Regardless, except for brief experimentation in the Republic's early years, presidents have believed that negotiations are the prerogative of the president alone, and the Senate should give advice and consent only at the concurrence/disapproval stage.

Although most presidents have viewed the division of *authority* in this manner, because of the needs for senatorial concurrence and domestic support, they often have invited advice earlier. Recent presidents well recall Wilson's failure to include any senators in the delegation to the World War I Peace Conference and the Senate's subsequent rejection of the Versailles Treaty. Indeed, frequently presidents now engage in extensive consultation with the Senate prior to the signature of a treaty, in effect "negotiating" with the Senate at the same time that they are negotiating with a foreign government. In the final stages of the negotiations of the Panama Canal Treaties, President Carter's co-negotiators "consulted with at least 70 Senators."[5]

There often is confusion about the stages in the treaty-making process, so perhaps we should explain before going on. Stage one is the negotiating process and the signature by authorized representatives of the parties. Once the agreement is signed, it is submitted to the Senate for its advice and consent. The Senate can approve the treaty as it stands by the required two-thirds majority, approve but attach reservations and understandings specifying the U.S. interpretation of various provisions, approve but attach amendments that require the treaty's renegotiation, or reject by failing to give the requisite vote. It also may concur with stipulations that are binding on the president though not on the other parties, as it did when it approved the Conventional Forces in Europe treaty in December 1991.[6] Although people often speak of Senate "ratification" of treaties, that is technically incorrect; the Senate concurs or rejects. If it concurs, another step is required for ratification. The treaty then must be signed and proclaimed by the president.

The president retains the initiative throughout the process. He can withdraw the treaty from consideration at any point prior to his signature, as Grover Cleveland did in 1884 with a treaty with Nicaragua for a canal linking the Pacific Ocean to the Gulf of Mexico. He can refuse to sign a treaty the Senate has approved. Or, as Wilson did with the Versailles Treaty, he may make it clear he will not sign a treaty that is amended in a certain manner, forcing a showdown on the agreement as it stands. Once a treaty is in effect, the president has the power (so far as U.S. participation is concerned) to terminate it.[7]

Third, the president may negotiate *executive agreements* with foreign nations. Executive agreements are binding agreements between heads of state that, unless they are made pursuant to statutes or treaties so stipulating, do not require Senate approval.[8] Even when approval is required, it is not two-thirds but only a simple majority. Sometimes such agreements are informal, and occasionally they even are oral, but in most instances they are so similar to a treaty in form that no difference is evident.

The boundary between treaties and executive agreements is not precise.[9] Logically, one might think it would be possible to distinguish on the basis of relative importance, treaties being used for matters of fundamental significance, executive agreements for lesser matters. But it is not so simple. Executive agreements sometimes are as significant as treaties. Witness the momentous Yalta and Potsdam agreements that provided the foundation for post–World War II developments in both Europe and Asia, and the 1978 Camp David Middle East Peace Accords. Crabb and Holt point out that Bush and Soviet President Mikhail Gorbachev had agreements or understandings on such diverse and important subjects as "the future of Communist governments in Eastern Europe, the reunification of Germany, disarmament . . . , and Moscow's role in American-led efforts to respond to Iraqi expansionism. . . ."[10]

The major difference between treaties and executive agreements thus is not the level of importance. In terms of presidential-congressional relations, the major difference is the degree of presidential control: The president has much more flexibility in, and control of, policy in an executive agreement than he does in a treaty. The extensive use of such agreements after World War II produced a congressional backlash in the Vietnam War era, however, and as we shall see later, Congress has become more assertive in this sphere.

Fourth, the president has the *power to appoint,* with the advice and consent of the Senate, the nation's highest ranking diplomatic, military, and intelligence officials. Although senatorial concurrence is required, most of the time it is quickly forthcoming. The general belief is that the president is entitled to choose his team. Even where a large number of senators oppose a particular nominee, usually he or she will not be rejected, although the Senate may give the individual a rough time in the confirmation hearings and use the occasion to advocate its own views. Yet sometimes nominees are rejected, as was the case in 1983 with President Reagan's nomination of Kenneth Adelman to head the Arms Control and Disarmament Agency and President Bush's 1989 nomination of John Tower to be secretary of defense. The power to select who will fill key policymaking positions surely is a matter of great import. It is only necessary to think of Henry Kissinger, John Foster Dulles, and Dean Acheson and to realize how different things might have been if different individuals had held certain positions at certain times.

We also should point out that the president can make a number of appointments that do not require senatorial approval. Key members of the White House staff, for example, are appointed (and removed) as the president desires. Since the mid-1960s the president's (special) assistant for national security affairs has been extremely influential, at times being more influential than the Senate-approved cabinet officers holding the State or Defense portfolios. Since at least President Kennedy's time, the holder of this position has usually been effectively in charge of the work of the National Security Council. It was the assistant for national security affairs (often called the national security adviser)—Henry Kissinger is the best known in the list—who usually coordinated the flow of decision papers from the major departments, through the council apparatus, into the Oval Office, and out again for the implementation in the departments. Yet this powerful individual is not even named as such in the legislation setting up the National Security Council. As we pointed out earlier, you have to know where an individual is placed in the foreign policy process to really assess that person's importance. Organization charts may or may not give the clue. The president can appoint other special assistants (or envoys) too, as President Reagan did with Phillip Habib in an effort to bring peace to Lebanon in the early 1980s.

Fifth, because of his position, the president has certain *inherent powers.* Because he is head of state, he is the individual with whom foreign governments have official contact. Legally, the president is the only official voice of the United States in foreign policy (although in practice, much of his authority is delegated to subordinates). In the landmark *Curtiss-Wright* case, the Supreme Court stated that in external relations the president "alone has the power to speak or listen as a representative of the nation." Indeed, the president is the "sole organ of the federal government in the field of international relations" and can operate with "a degree of discretion and freedom from statutory restriction which would not be admissible" in domestic affairs. There is a "marked difference between foreign and domestic affairs in this respect."[11]

Presidential Powers: Informal

In addition to his formal powers, the president has five important powers of a more informal nature.[12] The first is the ability to *initiate foreign policy.* The president can commit the nation to a policy or course of action largely on his own hook, just because of who he is. Unilaterally, President Nixon can undertake secret negotiations in 1969 with China for a normalization of relations, President Kennedy institute a blockade of Cuba in 1962 in the missile crisis, or President Carter decide that the United States will boycott the 1980 Olympic Games in Moscow. Often by taking action the president leaves Congress with little choice but to support him or run the risk of undermining the nation's position in international affairs. For much of American history the view held by Theodore Roosevelt in 1907 has been dominant. When he sent the Great White Fleet around the world, Congress threatened to cut off funds. Roosevelt informed Congress the fleet could stay abroad if the money did not arrive to bring it back. As Robert Schulzinger put it "of course Congress relented, and the Great White Fleet sailed home triumphantly."[13] As we shall see later, though, since the Vietnam War Congress has been a good deal more willing than previously to confront the president and not worry about undercutting his prestige abroad.

A second less formal presidential power also involves his *ability to initiate,* this time *in the legislative arena.* Although the Congress enacts the laws, it is the president to whom the people (and the Congress) look for the nation's legislative program. He is the "chief legislator," if you will. The Constitution requires the president to provide the Congress with "information on the State of the Union," but that speech is but one of literally hundreds of messages and proposals from the president to Capitol Hill. The old saw that "the President proposes, the Congress disposes," still largely applies. With only rare exceptions, the legislative framework for foreign policy (as for other programs) begins in the White House, not on Capitol Hill.

There is still a third variation on the *ability to initiate* theme: *the budget.* While much is made of the fact that Congress has the "power of the purse" (discussed below), and rightfully so, what rarely receives adequate comment is the fact that Congress is reacting to a presidential proposal. The president's Budget Message is a mammoth document (hundred of pages long) that contains specific and detailed recommendations, requests and (usually optimistic) forecasts. It is built in the executive branch through a long and laborious process that brings together the requirements and hopes of a whole myriad of claimants, a process that in some senses is never ending. Only Congress can authorize expenditures and appropriate funds, and it scrutinizes the president's budget in minute detail, but the point is that *it is the president's budget that it scrutinizes.* The president has the initiative.

The fourth reason "why the president has possessed an advantage over Congress in foreign policy is the vast amounts of *information* he has at his fingertips." [emphasis added][14] The Departments of State and Defense, Commerce and Treasury, the intelligence community, the National Security Council, the White House staff, the Council of Economic Advisers, and so on, all support and work for the president. Although since the late 1960s Congress has enhanced its information gathering and assessing capabilities, it still must rely heavily on the president both for the "facts" and for fundamental interpretations (let alone the nuances and shadings). Although Congress has various means by which it seeks to overcome the president's information advantage, it almost always is in an inferior position. We shall have more to say on this later.

Finally, the president has great advantages in the area of *influencing public opinion.* As a matter of routine, even his smallest activities and comments receive national media coverage. Franklin Roosevelt's "fireside chats" helped his great popularity and brought pressure on Congress in turn. President Reagan was known as the "Great Communicator." If President Bush wants the airwaves to announce military operations against Iraq he can have them, and all major electronic and print media outlets will give him top billing. As we said earlier, the public tends to rally behind the president when he takes strong action. Because usually only he can take that action, here, too he has an advantage. Historically, presidents often have been the most admired people in the country, (while Congress has rarely been held in similar esteem). Asked to choose, the public tends to follow his lead more than that of Capitol Hill where, in the nature of things, many voices will be heard, not all of them by any means in agreement.

Congressional Powers

While the exact intentions of the founding fathers cannot be precisely determined, it is evident that they expected Congress to play an important role in foreign policy. Though its powers do not match those of the president, they nonetheless are substantial.

First and foremost, of course, Congress, the legislative branch, has the *power to legislate.* Sometimes it may seek to the lay the organizational framework for subsequent policymaking, as it did with the National Security Act of 1947 and the Goldwater-Nichols Defense Reorganization Act of 1986. Sometimes it seeks to lay out a policy framework itself, as it tried to do with the Omnibus Trade and Competitiveness Act of 1988. It may get very specific, as in the Nuclear Non-Proliferation Act of 1978, which imposed strict guidelines for the president in negotiating new agreements on nuclear cooperation.

As a general rule, until the Vietnam War Congress usually exercised its legislative function rather broadly, seeking to set outer limits, establish general guidelines, and help provide the overall policy thrust. Given the necessity for executive discretion and flexibility, it was believed unproductive to legislate precise detail. There were occasional exceptions to these rules, of course, as we saw earlier with the neutrality acts of the 1930s, which prohibited arms shipments to all belligerents. The result in that case was to eliminate or curtail effective aid to states with whom America had common interests, Britain and France. Congress's efforts had unwisely limited presidential discretion. But such actions *were* the exception.

The second power is the *power of the purse.* American foreign policy requires the expenditure of great sums of money, and no monies can be spent unless authorized and appropriated by Congress. Congress may decide to provide the funds necessary for existing or planned programs, provide less than requested, or appropriate more than was sought. In March 1992, President Bush could talk about providing aid to Boris Yeltsin's struggling Russian economy, but without congressional action nothing would happen.

Despite its potential utility, for most of American history Congress did not seek to influence significantly the general course of foreign policy through its power of the purse. Partly this inaction was due to the fact that it lacked the staff and expertise to adequately evaluate administration requests, and it was encumbered by an internal structure that treated budgetary matters in an episodic and fragmented fashion. Also, for more than two decades after World War II, Congress generally shared various administrations' strategic conceptions and tended to support the overall policy thrust.

This is not to say Congress's role was unimportant or that it never used its budgetary powers. But it acted sporadically and usually on narrowly defined subjects. Occasionally it tried to set some limits on foreign policy by saying "no" to particular weapons systems, for example, or by providing a foreign aid appropriation smaller than requested. But even these actions were the exception, not the rule, and when they were taken, it was because of concern over some narrowly defined policy issue, not basic differences over long-term policy and strategy. In those areas Congress and the president usually agreed. As we discuss below, things certainly have changed.

The third power relates to military forces, and has two components: *declaring war and maintaining forces.* The Constitution provides that Congress has the power "to declare war," to "raise and support Armies," and to "provide and maintain a Navy."[16] The authority and responsibility to maintain forces involves Congress in the defense budget-making process and allows Congress to directly influence weapons acquisition and allocate funds among the services as it sees fit. Less controversial than the war power, this authority is an extremely important function of Congress, one which will grow in importance in the post–Cold War era.

Congress has exercised the power to declare war on only five occasions. In all the other instances when America has been in hostilities, no declaration of war has been made (nor was it requested). With occasional exceptions, generally until the Vietnam War there was little *constitutional* controversy over decisions concerning the use of American forces in combat, quasi-combat, and near-combat situations. The president, people believed, had the authority to act unilaterally in defense of the national interest.

One reason for the previous lack of controversy was that often the constitutional language was irrelevant to the specifics of the situation. The Constitution refers only to a declaration of "war." It does not deal with the myriad potential conflict situations that develop, nor does it relate readily to the variety of uses of the military in situations short of "war." Although there sometimes were objections on policy grounds, most congressmen (and most observers) long had felt that the president had the power to act in such contingencies in whatever ways he deemed essential. Also relevant here is the fact that in modern times nations seldom issue formal declarations of war. Hostilities are initiated first, and only then, if at all, is there a formal declaration. Once America is attacked a declaration of war would acknowledge a state of belligerency, but an attack would hardly set off some abstract Congressional debate about whether we ought to fight.

Until the Vietnam War, even when the constitutional language was or might have been pertinent, there seldom was much dispute. If the president had asked for a declaration of war, Congress provided it; if he did not ask for it, war was not declared. Usually when he ordered the deployment and employment of the armed forces, Congress agreed with his actions and gave him support. Even when it disagreed, it usually adopted the position that the president had the authority to act as he did. While the policy might be debated, *Congress would still go along,* because to not do so would weaken the president and thus be harmful to the nation. The Vietnam War changed Congress's attitudes enormously, and in 1973 led to the passage of the War Powers Resolution.

The fourth power is *to advise and consent on treaties.* The overwhelming majority of treaties considered by the Senate have been approved. According to one study, out of some 1400 submitted between 1789 and 1982, only nineteen were disapproved.[17] Most of the time, even when senators opposed a treaty, they hesitated to refuse consent because if consent were refused, the effect on relations with the other signatories inevitably would be adverse. After a treaty has been negotiated and signed, the parties assume that at least a basic understanding has been achieved and some quasi-commitments made. Also, to refuse consent at this juncture would weaken the president's future ability to deal effectively with foreign leaders. Since the late 1960s such thinking has carried less weight than it used to, however, and Congress has become more assertive in exercising its prerogatives.

The fifth power is *oversight*. Oversight refers to the reviewing and monitoring of the executive branch's conduct of foreign policy. Although the Constitution does not provide for it in so many words, without question oversight has become one of Congress's most influential functions. In appropriations bills, for example, there are detailed provisions instructing the administration on how to spend certain funds. Then, regular reports must be made on compliance. As James M. McCormick correctly points out,

> In general, oversight has expanded because Congress now has placed more and more reporting requirements on the executive branch, and congressional committees have increased their review activities as well.[18]

The law, as written in 1989, required the president to send to Congress 288 periodic reports on foreign aid alone.[19]

Investigation is a major oversight tool. While in a legal sense Congress's right of inquiry is limited to subjects on which it can validly legislate, this limitation presents no obstacle to a desire to proceed; if Congress wants to investigate, a justification can be found (or created). Through its investigations Congress can bring maximum publicity to bear on various issues and individuals and can examine the historical record in depth and detail. And often these investigations have considerable policy impact. In 1973 and 1974, House and Senate subcommittees investigated the role of CIA operations in Chile, and these investigations resulted in the passage of the Hughes-Ryan Amendment tightening control over covert action (see below). Additional investigations then surfaced further revelations, and these led to the establishment of permanent intelligence oversight committees.

Congress's Growing Role

The events of World War II, the following Cold War, and America's superpower status led the United States to a greatly expanded role in world affairs. Almost always the president was the key decisionmaker as the American role grew, Congress playing a very secondary part. Few people thought this odd. Most Americans believed the president had the authority to do what was necessary to protect the national interest, and because of his sources of information he usually was in the best position to ascertain what that interest was. Moreover, because of the nature of international politics and the fundamental differences between the presidency and Congress, only the president could act with the required speed and decisiveness. Also, and very importantly, for the first two decades of the Cold War there was a widespread consensus on the basic nature of the problems confronting the United States and the role it had to play. In light of these problems, it was essential to give the president full and firm support.

By the late 1960s, however, vast numbers of Americans were questioning presidential preeminence in foreign policymaking, and soon Congress was significantly expanding its role. The Vietnam War, of course, was the factor most responsible. This conflict shattered the underlying consensus. Few took it on faith that it made sense to leave most major policy initiatives to the president. Congress had to take more responsibility.

Although Vietnam was the most critical factor in changing the situation, several other developments in the late 1960s and 1970s were important also. It was becoming increasingly obvious that the Soviet Union was engaged in a massive military buildup and was very active in the Third World, "violating" what many congressmen felt were the requirements of "real" detente (and detente was a *presidential* policy). A number of improprieties and deceptions were revealed about the conduct of American covert intelligence operations, further diminishing trust in the presidency. And, of course, there were the Watergate scandals.[20]

In addition to these developments, there was a second reason for the growing role of Congress: better independent analytical capability. The Congressional Research Service (formerly the Legislative Reference Service) was created in 1970, and it became a useful tool for policy research. The General Accounting Office enabled Congress to have increasingly detailed oversight. The Congressional Budget Office, established in 1974, was a major step forward, providing Congress some real professional capability for analyzing and assessing the president's budget requests. The Office of Technology Assessment was established in 1972 to help Congress wrestle with increasingly complicated technical issues. Moreover, congressional (committee and personal) staffs increased by leaps and bounds. "By 1987, the two houses of Congress had more than eighteen thousand staff members."[21]

The effect of the growth in support agencies and staff assistance is clear. Today Congress has independent sources of expertise and information that have diminished significantly its dependence on the executive for useful information.

The third major cause of Congress's expanding role has been changes in the Congress itself. First, naturally, over time the membership changed. Largely gone is the post–World War II generation that shared the policy consensus with presidents from Truman on and tended to wait for or even seek presidential leadership. Few of the new generation are willing to "serve a proper apprenticeship." Second, congressional operations have become more democratized, and the influence of seniority has declined. This, in combination with the changing of the guard already mentioned, has produced even greater diffusion of power than that which previously existed. The individual legislator today has more impact than at any time within memory. When the president deals with Congress, in some senses it is like dealing with 535 separate secretaries of state.

For all these reasons, Congress's role in the foreign policy process today is quite different from what it was in the first two decades or so of the Cold War. This change has produced significant tensions in presidential-congressional relations in four major issue areas, which we shall now examine.

Issue 1: International Agreements

The first area of increased presidential-congressional tension is in the making of international agreements. Take treaties. As we saw, although the Senate never believed consent to a signed treaty was obligatory, usually such consent was soon forthcoming. And while Congress was never favorably disposed toward different presidents' considerable use of executive agreements, it seldom raised much fuss. And, while at least some congressmen would have liked to have played some part during the negotiation stage, most never really expected to. To some extent all these things have changed. Because the Senate will not automatically defer to presidential wishes, the president now must carry on two sets of negotiations: one with foreign nations and one with the Senate. In the midst of the legislative struggle over the Panama Canal Treaties, President Carter's diary reveals these comments:

> It's hard to concentrate on anything except Panama . . . I asked Cy [Vance] to go and spend full time on the Hill, and also to ask Henry Kissinger to do the same thing. I then asked Harold Brown and the Joint Chiefs to join them there, and Fritz [Mondale] will be spending full time—all working personally with members of the Senate . . . I had lunch with Senator Stennis to try to get his vote on the treaties, but failed . . . President Ford promised to use his influence with Heinz, Bellmon, and Schweiker . . . [22]

It is not only at the approval/rejection stage that the Senate has become more assertive. It is not unusual for senators to become involved during the negotiations phase. Often congressmen are appointed by the president to be official or unofficial members of the negotiating team. On a few occasions, individual senators have even taken it upon themselves to enter into unauthorized direct negotiations with foreign officials.

Interestingly, the House also has become assertive in this area. While it cannot participate directly in the advice and consent process, the House still has tried to influence the outcome through its debates and hearings. Committees opposed to the Panama Canal Treaty were holding public hearings well before the negotiations were completed. And, most treaties require considerable implementing legislation. Here, too, the House may be influential.

While Congress's enhanced role frequently has increased presidential-congressional tension, that has not always been the case. Indeed, if the White House and Capitol Hill are largely in agreement, a high degree of cooperation may result, with Congress simply making sure it shares the limelight with the president. They may even work together on the preliminaries. The Strategic Arms Reduction Treaty was signed by the United States and the Soviet Union on July 31, 1991, and sent to the Senate in November. A host of hearings dealing with aspects of the treaty's subject matter actually had been held since April, and Senate leaders were anxious to move things along quickly. But because of the failed Soviet coup in August, the establishment of the Commonwealth of

Independent States (CIS), subsequent negotiations of the United States and the CIS, and so forth, the Senate Foreign Relations Committee cooperated with the Administration and repeatedly postponed the opening of official hearings.

A connected area of change involved Congress's increasing unwillingness to acquiesce in the use of executive agreements instead of treaties. For years this was not a big issue. Although executive agreements have outnumbered treaties by perhaps as much as ten to one, such a quantitative comparison can be misleading because many of these agreements were made pursuant to congressional legislation or treaty provisions. Also, although it is clear that in the early Cold War years presidents frequently bypassed the Senate through such arrangements, Congress usually would have concurred if it had been consulted, because of the underlying consensus that existed. In fact, in the pre-Vietnam era, only once did Congress raise major objections. In 1954, the Bricker Amendment, which stipulated that Congress would have the power to regulate all executive agreements and that all treaties and executive agreements could become effective domestically only by congressional legislation, failed Senate approval by only one vote.

But, in the Vietnam years, things began to change. In June 1969, the Senate passed a sense-of-the-Senate National Commitments Resolution, which provided that no future foreign commitments could be made without congressional approval. Although nonbinding, it signaled clearly that the Senate would not acquiesce passively to commitments unilaterally made by the president. Shortly thereafter, a Senate Foreign Relations subcommittee discovered that a number of secret executive agreements existed, some with security commitments. The real issue, here, was commitment-making, the degree to which the president could commit the nation, in law, without cooperating with or even informing the Congress.

The result was that in 1972 Congress passed what is popularly known as the Case Act. The Case Act requires that all international agreements other than treaties be submitted to Congress within sixty days of entering into force. However, such agreements may be provided under an injunction of secrecy to the Senate Foreign Relations and House Foreign Affairs Committees, if the president decides that public disclosure would be harmful to national security.[23]

Although the Case Act demonstrates Congress's determination not to acquiesce passively to presidential initiative, it does not really alter the executive-legislative balance. While Congress must be informed, it still has no role in the making of such agreements, nor any approval/disapproval function. And, apparently, most members of Congress do not want any. All efforts in recent years to legislate a larger role in such matters have been defeated. Congress recognizes that sometimes speed and flexibility in presidential initiatives are useful, and congressional debate is not always in the national interest. But Congress does want to be informed, and there is no doubt that treaties still are preferred over executive agreements. This is not just parochialism. In addition to the desire to participate in the decision process, when an agreement entails issues of major import, the treaty route has an important advantage: Because the Senate *has* been involved, the media and public opinion alerted, and so on, a treaty signifies a broader consensus, a degree of national commitment that may not be there with an executive agreement.

Issue 2: Military Force

A second issue area that has caused increased tension involves decisions to use military force. Here, too, the primary catalyst for change was disenchantment over the Vietnam War and retrospective disillusionment with the policy making that resulted in the American commitment, then escalation, there. As a result of that disenchantment and disillusionment and of an American–South Vietnamese military incursion into Cambodia in 1970,[24] legislators introduced a number of bills to restrict the president's role and enhance their own. The result in 1973 was the passage, over President Nixon's veto, of the War Powers Resolution.[25]

The War Powers Resolution was designed to ensure that the "collective judgment" of Congress and the president would apply to decisions concerning the introduction of American forces into hostilities or into situations in which hostilities appeared imminent and concerning the continued use of military forces in such contingencies as well. It stated that the president could employ American forces only pursuant to "(1) a declaration of war, (2) specific statutory authorization, or (3) a national emergency created by attack upon the United States, its territories or possessions, or its armed forces." Except in the case of a declaration of war, once the president had acted, he was to report fully to Congress within 48 hours. If Congress disapproved, it could order the forces withdrawn by concurrent resolution (a majority vote in each house, not subject to presidential veto). Even if it did not so act, troops had to be withdrawn within 60 days—90 days if "unavoidable military necessity" so required—unless Congress declared war, extended the 60-day period, or was unable to meet. Both prior to the introduction of forces and after, the president was to consult with Congress "in every possible instance."

Because of the War Powers Resolution, the president presumably was less free than previously to unilaterally order American forces into combat or near-combat situations. Presumably also, Congress would be consulted more frequently than before, prior to military actions, and would be informed once they were undertaken. If it disapproved, it could terminate American involvement by various methods. But suppose Congress ordered termination and the president refused to comply. What then? The consultation requirement posed another uncertainty. With whom should the president consult? The party leadership? Foreign Relations and Affairs Committees in each house? All of Congress? The more people involved, the more time would be taken, the more the likelihood of leaks, and the less likely that a consensus would be established. But if only a few members were consulted, Congress's views as a whole would not be accurately ascertained or represented. And when should consultation occur? And what happens then? None of this was clear.

The historical record since the resolution's passage has done little to clarify.[26] There have been some cases, such as the transfer of refugees from DaNang, Vietnam, in 1975 and participation in the multinational force in Beirut in 1982, when Presidents Ford and Reagan both adhered fairly closely to the provisions of the resolution. But these were incidents when such presidential action was convenient. In other cases, when presidents would have found consulting to be a problem and the resolution's provisions too restrictive, presidents have found ways to act anyway. In 1975, when President Ford decided to undertake military operations in response to Cambodia's seizure of the freighter *Mayaguez,* he just went ahead. Only a small number of congressmen were informed, and then only after orders to begin operations had been issued. In April 1980, as President Carter and his aides were planning a mission to rescue American hostages held in Iran, he had to decide how to handle Congress.

> On April 18, I had quite a discussion with my closest advisers about how to deal with the congressional leadership on the Iran decisions. . . . One or two key members of Congress might be consulted when our final plans were under way, but I would notify a larger group of the leadership . . . only after the rescue operation had reached the point of no return. . . . It was absolutely imperative that there be no leaks.[27]

Congress was similarly informed by President Reagan in 1983 in the Grenada operation.[28] So much for "consultation."

The record of presidential "compliance" with reporting requirements also has been "mixed," to say the least. It is important to remember in this regard that no president has considered himself bound by the law. Without exception, they have believed it to be an unconstitutional infringement of the commander-in-chief power. Still, as we mentioned earlier, in several cases presidents have submitted reports in accordance with their interpretation of its provisions, anyway. But we stress "in accordance with their interpretation," because in no case has any president said he is acting "under" the law. The reports are always phrased very carefully to make this point and to avoid setting the 60-day clock in motion. Indeed, the relevant provision, 4(a)(1), has only been mentioned once. And while Congress in the 1983 Lebanon crisis passed legislation declaring the WPR was operative, when President Reagan signed that legislation, he stated he was *not* ceding any of his power as commander in chief.

The most egregious provision of the law (Congress's right to order troops out by a concurrent resolution) is probably a dead letter, because of a 1983 Supreme Court decision ruling one-house legislative vetoes unconstitutional.[29] But what conclusions can we draw about the remainder? While presidents now are required to perform more procedures than before the WPR's passage, they have really not had their freedom to act diminished very much. President Bush did report to Congress after having American air forces assist Philippine president Corazon Aquino stay in power in 1989, after invading Panama, and after ordering troops to Saudi Arabia in 1990. But in all of those cases he felt he had the authority to do whatever was necessary, and he was in no way hindered in doing it. Even many congressmen are uneasy with the WPR. In the 1987 Kuwaiti-tanker episode (discussed in Chapter 17), as Barry Blechman points out, the "majority of the Senate employed an extraordinary series of . . . maneuvers to avoid invoking the 'war powers' it had been granted . . . only fourteen years before.[30]

Congress realizes that the WPR has not fulfilled it promise, and a host of recommendations for reform have been made. But none have been successful. Of course, when the president and Congress are largely in agreement on policy, the point is essentially moot. And, Congress rarely protests much when the operations are quick strikes that involve little possibility of long-term involvement. But when operations are likely to be more extended, Congress wants to play an active role in the decision process. If it cannot do so through the WPR, it may use other means, as it did in the Gulf War.[31]

Issue 3: Covert Operations

A third area of increasing presidential-congressional tension is covert operations. From the time of the creation of the Central Intelligence Agency in 1947 until well into the Vietnam War, covert operations only rarely were an issue. Most Americans, including most congressmen, believed that the Cold War required an effective intelligence apparatus and that covert operations sometimes were necessary. About the only time much interest was shown was when some policy debacle caught the public's eye, such as the abortive Bay of Pigs invasion in 1961.[32]

The general disenchantment in the late 1960s provided a favorable context for a greater congressional role in intelligence matters, however, and a number of developments in the early and mid-1970s brought this about. Investigations revealed that the CIA had covertly sought to prevent the election of the Marxist, Salvador Allende, in Chile. Evidence of other covert activities was disclosed also, surfacing developments that surprised many legislators (and their constituents). It also became evident that the president's command and control arrangements for covert actions were vague and imprecise, and that sometimes the president himself was not fully aware of what was happening.

In consequence, in 1974, Congress passed the Hughes-Ryan Amendment. Under Hughes-Ryan, before a covert operation could be launched, the president had to determine specifically that it was important to national security and issue a "finding" to that effect. Hughes-Ryan also required that all covert actions be reported by the president to the appropriate committees of Congress in a "timely" manner.[33] Soon after, Congress went beyond just requiring that it be informed. The CIA had been providing aid to the FNLA/UNITA coalition in its war against the Soviet-backed MPLA in Angola. Unhappy with this, Congress cut off the agency's funding. It followed by establishing permanent select committees on intelligence in both the House and the Senate, committees given broad oversight mandates and financial power. All authorizations for funding of intelligence activities now were to be made by these committees instead of the respective armed services committees, which had tended to be favorably disposed toward CIA operations.

It soon became evident that Hughes-Ryan had several flaws, and in 1980 Congress passed what is popularly known as the Intelligence Oversight Act (IOA). IOA reduced the number of committees to be informed from eight to two, and changed the reporting to Congress requirement from in a "timely fashion" to keeping Congress "fully and currently informed." Significantly, IOA required the president also to inform Congress of "significant anticipated activity" (although notification could be limited to the committee and chamber leadership in extraordinary circumstances or to protect sources and methods).

While the IOA did not give Congress authority to approve or reject covert operations, there was a widespread belief that because of the informing and reporting requirements, presidents would be extremely reluctant to order operations without congressional support.[34] But many congressmen believed that is exactly what Reagan did in 1984 in ordering the mining of Nicaraguan harbors. Legislators said they had not been "fully" and "currently" informed; the administration said they had. To preclude future problems of this sort, DCI Casey and the Senate Intelligence Committee agreed on new informational procedures, and everything appeared settled. Then in 1986 it was revealed that in 1985, without informing Congress, President Reagan had authorized the secret sale of weapons to Iran. As Barry Blechman writes:

> The Congress had been kept completely in the dark about the secret sale of arms to Iran. Notification was withheld . . . for at least ten months . . . it [the "finding"] was revealed only after a Lebanese newspaper broke the story. President Reagan had specified in the "finding" that the Congress was not to be informed until he had determined otherwise.[35]

Since that time, Congress has regularly considered the notification issue, and on some occasions legislation requiring notification of *any* covert operation has passed one house. Although at this writing there has been no change in the law, it is apparent that the issue is far from dead. Congress reluctantly understands the president's need for control, speed, and flexibility in decisions on covert operations, but the Congress wants to be informed, both before and after covert operations are undertaken. Presidential-congressional tension over such matters will be with us for sometime to come.

Issue 4: Aid and Trade

A fourth area of increased presidential-congressional tension is aid and trade. Both aid and trade involve a mixture of foreign policy and domestic considerations, and they also involve both economic and political concerns. When

Congress and the president deal with so-called "security assistance" and with arms transfers, military factors must be assessed as well.

Let us look first at foreign aid. As we shall see in more detail in Chapter 9, after World War II foreign aid became a major foreign policy instrument of the United States, the Marshall Plan being the most famous example. Such aid proposals and programs usually are drawn up in the executive branch, often after considerable consultation and negotiation with potential recipients. But because Congress must authorize and appropriate all foreign aid monies, it inevitably is an important player in such matters. And it has been, throughout the postwar period.

Since the mid-1960s, however, there has been a significant difference in the role of Congress, because it has moved beyond simply reacting to presidential initiatives and occasionally questioning total funding amounts or specific items. Since the mid-1960s Congress has made major efforts to influence the substance of the policy of both the United States and of potential recipients. In some cases it has flatly prohibited aid to certain nations (Cuba, Angola) or to nations engaging in certain practices or behaviors such as violations of human rights (in 1976, Congress prohibited security assistance to Chile on those grounds). In some areas aid has been prohibited unless the president declares that the aid is essential to national security. One example is aid to states with nuclear reprocessing or enrichment facilities that are not under multilateral safeguards. In an effort to bring about policy change Congress has occasionally terminated existing programs, as it did with aid to Turkey after that nation invaded Cyprus in 1974. In the spring of 1975 it refused President Ford's plea for supplemental aid to Cambodia and Vietnam, effectively ending U.S. involvement in that war.[36]

But it is not just in the providing or not providing of aid that Congress is important. Today when Congress provides aid, it usually does so with detailed instructions on its use and with stringent reporting requirements.[37] This results in what its critics call "micro-management." During the 1980s the Reagan administration sought to aid the opposition rebels in Nicaragua, the "Contras," as they were called. This policy (and how it was carried out) was a subject of much dispute and rancor.[38] But for our purposes the point is that when aid was provided, Congress was deeply involved in the nuts-and-bolts of the operation, "writing lengthy documents that outlined policy, defined what was military and nonmilitary aid and gave detailed prescriptions for what items could and could not be delivered."[39]

In arms transfer policy, too, Congress began to be a major actor. In the Arms Control Export Act, as amended, Congress required the president to report to Congress offers (above a certain value) for the sale of weapons and defense articles and services. Congress then had 30 days in which to consider the proposed sale, during which time it could veto the sale by a concurrent resolution. Though no major sale was ever so vetoed, frequently presidents had to alter their policy as a result of congressional opposition. In 1978, for example, President Carter wanted to sell F-15 fighter aircraft to Saudi Arabia, but before Congress would go along he had to assure it that those aircraft would not be based at Tabuk (the Saudi base nearest Israel) and would not be configured for major bombing raids.

As we saw in our discussion of the War Powers Resolution, in 1983 the Supreme Court declared that one-house legislative vetoes were unconstitutional. Recognizing this decision might have invalidated the concurrent resolution procedure, in 1985 Congress amended the Arms Control Export Act to require only a joint resolution to prevent a weapons sale.

Since joint resolutions are subject to a presidential veto, one might have thought Congress now would become less influential. But that really has not been the case. In 1985 the Reagan administration tried to sell previously denied weapons to Jordan. Despite a personal visit by King Hussein to convince Congress the weapons would not be used against Israel, a joint resolution opposing the sale was passed and signed by the president.[40] On some occasions a president, seeing great opposition, will just pull in his horns. But, sometimes he will fight. In May 1986, Congress voted to bar the sale of certain missiles to Saudi Arabia. But Reagan used his veto. Eventually that veto was upheld by one vote, but to be successful the president had to delete $89 million worth of Stinger antiaircraft missiles from the package.

Congress also has grown more assertive in matters of foreign trade. But in this area our conclusions are more qualified, because Congress has long played a significant role in trade policy, especially in regard to setting tariffs. And that impact has been significant.

Tariff policy has been the subject of popular passions—and thus pressures on Congress—since the earliest days. Agricultural interests (who wanted tariffs low) have battled manufacturing interests (who wanted tariffs high). Foreign interests have sometimes suffered severely in the result. That happened, for example, when a business panic in 1893 led to a tariff act in 1894 that almost ruined the Cuban economy.[41] In Chapter 3 we briefly discussed the worldwide depression of the 1930s. Nation after nation attempted to export while restricting imports. The Smoot-Hawley Act of 1930, which nearly doubled tariffs and provoked retaliation by other nations against American goods, was an important contributor to the paralysis that followed.

The modern history of trade legislation really begins with the 1934 Trade Agreements Act. Through this legislation Congress authorized the president to negotiate reciprocal tariff reductions with other nations of up to 50 percent. Under what was called the "most-favored-nation" principle, concessions granted to one nation would be automatically extended to all. The delegation of such authority "represented a considerable shift of power from the legislative to the executive branch. . . ."[42]

Since 1934, the Trade Agreements Act has been the cornerstone of American trade policy, and since that time Congress has continued it through a number of extensions.[43] Two major policy premises generally underlay these extensions. First, there was the concept of continual, if limited, tariff reductions. The second was a "no injury" philosophy—safeguarding domestic industry and workers.[44] Obviously, these premises could easily become incompatible (and they often did).

As we discuss later, after World War II the United States and twenty-three other nations established the General Agreement on Tariffs and Trade, the purpose, among other things, to provide a multilateral framework for the liberalization of trade.[45] Within this framework important tariff reductions were negotiated, the president receiving the requisite negotiating authority via extensions of the Trade Agreements Act. The 1962 Trade Expansion Act was particularly important. Under its terms the president was permitted to cut duties by up to 50 percent of their July 1962 level, and negotiations could be conducted on broad categories rather than on a product-by-product basis. It was on the basis of this legislation that America later participated in the multi-year "Kennedy Round" of GATT negotiations, which ultimately resulted in an average reduction of 35 percent in industrial tariff rates. This legislation also created the position of the special representative for trade negotiations, removing that function from the Department of State.

The increased congressional assertiveness of the early 1970s soon found its way into trade policy also, with the Trade Reform Act of 1974. Although known primarily for its linkage (through the Jackson-Vanik Amendment) of Jewish emigration from the Soviet Union to the granting of most-favored nation rights to Moscow (discussed later), the 1974 act was important for several other reasons. First, and rather traditionally, it gave the administration new tariff-reducing authority (and thereby paved the way of the Tokyo round of GATT talks). But second, it placed much greater emphasis on nontariff barriers, recognizing the changing nature of the trade problem America was facing. Those would become increasingly important, as we shall see later. Third, "fast- track" rules were provided, so Congress could consider certain trade matters far more expeditiously than usual. Finally, the 1974 act offered a Generalized System of Preferences for developing countries, where they would get preferential treatment without having to reciprocate.[46]

With Congress's evident effort to grasp the policy initiative, the 1974 Trade Reform Act was a clear reversal of Congress's 40-year record of largely just reacting to presidential initiative in trade matters. With the worm now turned, in the Trade Agreements Act of 1979, the 1984 Trade and Tariff Act, and especially the Omnibus Trade and Competitiveness Act of 1988, this increasingly proactive stance continued. Indeed, in the 1988 legislation, as in the 1974 and 1979 acts, Congress went well beyond trade matters and ventured into overall economic and foreign policy. Congress also has acted more indirectly, amending administrative procedures and pressuring administrators to make subtle but significant changes that impact particular market segments. As Pietro Nivola comments, by such methods ". . . members of Congress can control the flow of dispensations without being branded protectionists. Congress can have it both ways, retaining opportunities for constituent service without being directly answerable for flawed or controversial policies."[47]

We shall analyze these important trade-related economic and political issues (and related economic/political issues, such as the trade deficit, the budget deficit, relations with trading blocs, and free trade agreements) in Parts Four and Five. Here the point is simply this: With respect to these matters, as in so many others now, Congress intends to play a major role in establishing the direction and thrust (and frequently the details) of policy.

Summing Up

With all the changes since the late 1960s, it is easy to lose perspective. Although Congress has enhanced its role in many areas, the president remains the central figure in policymaking. It was the president or his representatives who negotiated SALT I and the INF, START, and CFE treaties; normalized relations with the People's Republic of China; mediated the Camp David Accords and the Egyptian-Israeli Peace Treaty; ordered U.S. forces into action in Grenada, Panama, and the Persian Gulf; began the SDI program; persuaded Israel not to join in the 1991 Gulf War; and so on. Still, things are different. Because of Congress's assertiveness, even when the president grasps the initiative, he cannot do so without one eye on Capitol Hill.

But though Congress today is often very assertive, its inherent weaknesses remain. Congress's analytical and information-processing staff and support capabilities, while much improved, pale beside the president's; it is more decentralized than ever, it is necessarily slow moving, and it is equipped not so much to initiate and direct as to react and limit. The president, as before, must play the dominant role.

What Congress can and should do is effectively debate the major policy alternatives at those turns in the road when major choices face the United States. Through such debate Congress can help assess the anticipated costs and benefits of key counterbalancing interests, as well as participate in the formulation of broad policy guidelines.

Congress in modern times has not always done this essential job. To illustrate: Congress did not adequately assess the implications of either the Truman Doctrine or the Gulf of Tonkin Resolution, two of the most far-reaching policy developments of the postwar era. In the first case, in March 1947 President Truman, perceiving a communist threat to Greece and Turkey, went far beyond the particular case to state that it should be American policy "to support free peoples who are resisting attempted subjugation by armed minorities or by outside pressures." A more open-ended mandate for global involvement can hardly be imagined. But while Congress debated the Greek-Turkish Aid Act for several weeks, the long-term implications of the Truman Doctrine's concepts and language were barely touched. The act passed the House, 287–107, and the Senate, 67–23.

In the case of the Gulf of Tonkin Resolution, in August 1964, after apparent attacks by North Vietnamese torpedo boats on American destroyers, Congress authorized the president to take whatever measures were necessary to protect American forces in Vietnam. The resolution was adopted unanimously by the House and by an 88–2 vote in the Senate. Altogether, the total estimated committee and Senate floor consideration was 8 hours and 22 minutes! As we see in Chapter 11, the Gulf of Tonkin Resolution later was used by President Johnson as what amounted to a functional equivalent of a declaration of war. Unfortunately, at the time of passage the debate was superficial and the implications of the decision being made were left obscure. While Congress's actions in 1991 and 1992 after the collapse of the Soviet empire showed little coherence, the fact that it was *considering* the future course of American post–Cold War policy was a definite plus.

Congress also plays an important role in giving attention to selected specific issues. Here, too, it may pose alternatives for presidential consideration. It also can help keep the executive accountable through the exercise of effective oversight. Performance can be monitored and assessed through careful scrutiny of the record. Whether commitments were or were not made, policy was or was not appropriate, new policies, legislation, or guidelines are needed, etc.— insights into all this and more can result from careful assessment. The danger here really is that Congress will do *too* much, micro-managing to such an extent that national policy is hamstrung.

If Congress effectively exercises its functions of debate and oversight, there will be other benefits. Because Congress in many ways is a microcosm of informed public opinion, it can act as a vital link between the people and their government. As it represents America's diverse peoples, it gives policies a stamp of legitimacy, a crucial matter in a democratic system. If Congress participates effectively, it ensures at least a modicum of domestic support for whatever the policy adopted; without this, at some point, the policy will fail. And ultimately, effective debate will have a positive effect on national morale. Without it, in circumstances such as Vietnam, in which public opinion is severely fragmented, national morale will be seriously affected.

With the pre-Vietnam policy consensus a fading memory, the United States is groping for a new conception of its role in foreign affairs. Unless there is an underlying consensus over that role, the level of tension and struggle between Congress and the president will be enormous. The effort must be made, despite the fact that establishing a new consensus will not be easy, because of the importance of the task. Surely Congress should participate strongly in that effort.

But for progress to be made, effective leadership will be necessary on both sides. Regardless of the particular organizational systems and processes employed, it still is people who make decisions. When the Senate in 1948 supported President Truman's determination to establish a new alliance to help stabilize Europe and provide deterrence against a threat from the Soviet Union, the Senate did so largely because of the leadership of Republican Senator Arthur Vandenberg, a former isolationist. Although his position as chairman of the House Armed Services Committee was important, it was also the *competence* of congressman Les Aspin that gave him such clout in 1992.

For the United States to deal effectively with the changing world of the post–Cold War era, the president and Congress need to spend less time in conflict and more in cooperation. While effective coordination *within* the executive branch is certainly important (a subject we deal with in several places in this book), *some coordination between branches* is also essential. That comes down to people and their ideas. Neither end of Pennsylvania Avenue has a monopoly on wisdom. Given human nature and the structure of our checks and balances system, some degree of presidential-congressional tension is inevitable. But there also is room for meaningful cooperation and a reasonable degree of coordination between the branches. Utopia is not possible, but progress is.

Notes

1. Roger Hilsman, *The Politics of Policy Making in Defense and Foreign Affairs* (New York: Harper & Row, 1971), pp. 18–22.

2. There is a sixth formal power, the power to recognize foreign governments. While recognition *policy* has sometimes been controversial, no one questions the president's authority in such matters, so discussion is not necessary.

3. He also got involved in tactical detail, picking bombing targets from the White House.

4. For a useful discussion, see Norman A. Graebner, "Negotiating International Agreements," in George C. Edwards III and Wallace Earl Walker, eds., *National Security and the U.S. Constitution: The Impact of the Political System* (Baltimore: Johns Hopkins University Press, 1988), pp. 204–209.

5. I. M. Destler, "Treaty Troubles: Versailles in Reverse," *Foreign Policy* (Winter 1978–79), p. 50.

6. *Arms Control Today,* December 1991, p. 23.

7. With the establishment of diplomatic relations with China, Carter notified Taiwan that their mutual security agreement would be allowed to lapse. Several members of Congress challenged this action in court, arguing that termination required approval by two-thirds of the Senate. The Supreme Court in *Goldwater et al v Carter,* although divided in its reasoning, upheld the president's action.

8. In the post–World War II period, executive agreements have far outnumbered treaties. See Loch Johnson and James M. McCormick, "Foreign Policy by Executive Fiat," *Foreign Policy* (Fall, 1977), pp. 117–38.

9. Arthur M. Schlesinger, Jr., calls them one of the "mysteries of the constitutional order." See his comments in Arthur M. Schlesinger, Jr., *The Imperial President* (Boston: Houghton Mifflin, 1973), pp. 85–86.

10. Cecil V. Crabb, Jr., and Pat M. Holt, *Invitation to Struggle: Congress, the President, and Foreign Policy,* 4th ed. (Washington, DC: CQ Press, 1992), p. 15.

11. *United States v. Curtiss-Wright,* 299 U.S. 304 (1936).

12. Although conceptualized in a somewhat different manner, the analysis by Crabb and Holt is similar in thrust.

13. Schulzinger, *American Diplomacy in the Twentieth Century,* p. 37.

14. John Spanier and Eric M. Uslaner, *American Foreign Policy Making and the Democratic Dilemmas,* 4th ed. (New York: Holt, Rinehart and Winston, 1985), p. 54.

15. See John E. Mueller, *War, Presidents and Public Opinion* (New York: John Wiley & Sons, 1973), ch. 8.

16. See Hobart B. Pillsbury, Jr., "Raising the Armed Forces," Daniel J. Kaufman, "Organizing the Armed Forces," and Harvel M. Sapolsky, "Equipping the Armed Forces," in Edwards and Walker, *National Security and the U.S. Constitution,* pp. 73–135.

17. *Congressional Quarterly's Guide to Congress,* 3d ed. (Washington, DC: CQ Press, 1982), pp. 291–92. Cited in Crabb and Holt, *Invitation to Struggle,* p. 43.

18. James M. McCormick, *American Foreign Policy and Process,* 2nd ed. (Itasca, IL: F.E. Peacock, 1992), p. 331. McCormick's discussion of the expansion of reporting requirements, pp. 331–33, is worth reading.

19. *CQ Weekly Report* (February 18, 1989), pp. 333–34.

20. Richard Melanson wrote: "The scandal gradually destroyed Nixon's ability to govern as it effectively replaced Vietnam as a national obsession." Richard A. Melanson, *Reconstructing Consensus: American Foreign Policy Since the Vietnam War* (New York: St. Martin's Press, 1991), p. 69.

21. Crabb and Holt, *Invitation to Struggle,* p. 272.

22. Jimmy Carter, *Keeping Faith: Memoirs of a President* (New York: Bantam Books, 1982), p. 171. One of the better analyses of the process is William L. Furlong and Margaret E. Scranton, *The Dynamics of Foreign Policymaking: The President, the Congress, and the Panama Canal Treaties* (Boulder, CO: Westview Press, 1984).

23. In 1977 the act was amended to require that all agreements made by agencies of the executive branch be reported to the State Department within 20 days, for ultimate transmittal to Congress. McCormick's discussion in *American Foreign Policy and Process,* pp. 308–13, is worthwhile.

24. See Chapter 12 for further discussion.

25. It took more than three years to get the WPR passed. As thus would be expected, the product was very complicated and in many instances unclear in effect. For a provocative but well-founded analysis, see Robert F. Turner, *Repealing the War Powers Resolution: Restoring the Rule of Law in U.S. Foreign Policy* (Washington, DC: Brassey's, 1991).

26. According to Barry Blechman, prior to the 1991 war with Iraq there were fifteen incidents in which the resolution was cited, and six more to which it was relevant. Barry M. Blechman, *The Politics of National Security: Congress and U.S. Defense Policy* (New York: Oxford University Press, 1990), p. 172.

27. Carter, *Keeping Faith,* p. 511.

28. See Michael Rubner, "President Reagan, the War Powers Resolution, and Grenada," *Political Science Quarterly* (Winter 1985–86, pp. 627–47.

29. In *Immigration and Naturalization Service v. Chadha,* one-house legislative vetoes were ruled unconstitutional. The full implications for the concurrent resolution provision are not clear, but most observers believe it has been nullified.

30. Blechman, *The Politics of National Security,* p. 3.

31. Discussed in Chapter 1. There are some who believe *both* the president and Congress acted irresponsibly in that conflict. See Michael J. Glennon, "The Gulf War and the Constitution," *Foreign Affairs* (Spring 1991), pp. 84–101. He writes that this episode "represented a textbook example of how an audacious executive, acquiescent legislature, and deferential judiciary have pushed the Constitution's system of separation of powers steadily backwards toward the monopolistic system of King George III."

32. See Chapter 10.

33. The "appropriate committees" were those on foreign relations or affairs, armed services, appropriations, and intelligence, in each house.

34. Former DCI Stansfield Turner was reported to have stated that under congressional pressure, "three times Reagan signed, then cancelled, covert action operations." Loch K. Johnson, "Covert Action and Accountability: Decision-Making for America's Secret Foreign Policy," *International Studies Quarterly* (March 1989), p. 100.

35. Blechman, *The Politics of National Security*, p. 159.

36. For a useful discussion see P. Edward Haley, *Congress and the Fall of South Vietnam and Cambodia* (Rutherford, NJ: Fairleigh Dickinson University Press, 1982).

37. See the discussion in Gerald Felix Warburg, *Conflict and Consensus: The Struggle Between Congress and the President Over Foreign Policy Making* (New York: Harper & Row, 1989).

38. For a neat little analysis, see Charles W. Kegley, Jr., and Eugene R. Wittkopf, *American Foreign Policy: Pattern and Progress*, 4th ed. (New York: St. Martin's Press, 1991), pp. 417–20.

39. *CQ Weekly Report* (January 12, 1989), p. 12.

40. This example is based on Blechman, *The Politics of National Security*, p. 126.

41. Ferrell, *American Diplomacy*, p. 349.

42. Crabb and Holt, *Invitation to Struggle*, p. 199. For a discussion of the context and philosophy of Roosevelt's policy, see Ferrell, *American Diplomacy*, pp. 540–44.

43. Our discussion of the subsequent extensions is largely based on Mordechai E. Kreinin, *International Economics: A Policy Approach*, 5th ed. (San Diego: Harcourt Brace Jovanovich, 1987), Ch. 15.

44. The "no injury" philosophy emphasizes protecting industries and workers from the competition of imports. Often there are countervailing pressures on congressmen, because other groups want to be able to buy the imported product at lower prices (or because they think it is better), and some groups want freer trade so they can sell more goods overseas.

45. See Chapters 16 and 19.

46. As the American deficit grew with the four dragons (Hong Kong, Taiwan, Singapore, and South Korea) in the late 1980s, President Reagan withdrew the GSPs for them.

47. Pietro Nivola, "Trade Policy: Refereeing the Playing Field," in Thomas E. Mann, ed., *A Question of Balance: The President, the Congress, and Foreign Policy* (Washington, DC: The Brookings Institution, 1990), p. 246.

7

Policymaking
and the Bureaucracy

In Chapter 6 we described the major powers of the president in conducting foreign policy, as these derive from the Constitution and from custom. We also noted how the Constitution defines the congressional role, and how that role has grown in recent times. Part of the reason for the wide grant of authority given the president is that in one person he combines two offices normally separated in the larger and more powerful nations: head of state and head of government. That doubling-up alone means that he has much to do. On a single day he may in one role or the other have to host a state dinner for the Chancellor of Germany, give policy guidance on the Israeli-West Bank issue, consider alternatives for handling the civil war in Yugoslavia, meet with the Group of 7 to discuss international debt relief measures for Russia, prepare for a state visit to Japan (where he will also discuss trade problems), accept or alter a draft of a proposed free-trade agreement with Mexico, confer with his re-election campaign team, meet with the congressional leadership on tax legislation, and read and digest many of the documents that go with all of this. And, if there is a sudden crisis, that has to be shoe-horned into his day as well. How does he manage to cope?

With that kind of heavy load, anyone who has never read the Constitution of the United States will probably expect that the powers and duties of the president will be the first thing in it, taking up a good share of the document. They would be wrong. It is only after a lengthy discussion of the Congress and the powers denied to the federal government and other powers denied to the states, that the Constitution turns in Article II to the "Executive Department." That article says that "the executive power shall be vested" in the president (whence the label, "Chief Executive"), tells how he is elected, and then in one long sentence names him commander in chief, says "he may require the opinion, in writing, of the principal officer in each of the executive departments" on subjects relating to their duties, and gives him the treaty-making authority discussed earlier, plus the power to appoint officials. In a third section it says "he shall take care that the laws be faithfully executed, and shall commission all the officers of the United States."

And there you have the main points. From these brief sentences springs the whole panoply of power we today associate with the president and the Executive Branch. Like the institution of the Cabinet (which came about from the simple fact that President Washington liked to meet his chief officers in a body), much of what we see today is an elaboration from this simple constitutional basis.

The Constitution is perfectly clear on the essentials: (1) the president runs the bureaucracy to execute the laws and (2) the heads of the bureaucracy will advise him of his policy alternatives. Although the president cannot conceivably know all that is done in his name, he is *responsible*. It is why Harry Truman was fond of saying "The buck stops here." And since the president's authority is wider in dealing with foreign affairs than with anything else, it is highly important how he organizes his administration to funnel advice to him and to assist him in carrying out the laws.

For obvious reasons, the most important of the president's advisers are usually also cabinet members. Always prime among these today are the secretary of state and the secretary of defense. Other heads of major departments, like the secretary of the treasury, may rank with this group. Then there are appointed officials, like the assistant for national security affairs, who may under certain circumstances become more influential advisers than even the primary cabinet officers.

The government departments, like State in "Foggy Bottom," and Defense in the Pentagon, along with a number of agencies, employ the vast majority of the bureaucracy. But since World War II there has grown up a large bureaucracy attached directly to the president and near to him physically—the White House staff. This staff is of two kinds: one group, like the Secret Service agents, serves the president as such; the other group, like the National Security Council Staff mentioned in Chapter 5, is there to assist the president by funneling the views of the bureaucracy to him and, in turn, instructing the bureaucracy in what the president has decided. Being in the White House, however, it is very easy for members of this staff to exercise a power not originally intended when the post was created. As we go on, we shall see how this in fact happened with the position of assistant for national security affairs. This also explains in part how a relatively low-ranking official, a lieutenant colonel of marines, Oliver North, was able to direct the Iran-Contra operation.

The creation of this second group of White House staff, especially as it grew in size, posed an important organizational problem for the president. In Chapter 5 we explained why the NSC was created. That was not the only possible solution to the planning and coordination problem; instead, members of the executive might have tried to make the cabinet system function more effectively. However, once the NSC was created, suppose it took on more than a mere paper-shuffling role (as happened in the Iran-Contra case). Then it would be doing the job of the line departments when it should only be staffing, not carrying out the policy. Or is it impossible in practice to maintain that division of responsibility? (We shall be examining this issue, so fundamental to the policy process, as we go on.) But even if this problem of a staff group taking on line responsibilities is solved, *how* should the White House role be coordinated with the line departments? That is not altogether easy to decide. In principle, the White House staff process merely instructs who is to do what and when, then sees that that in fact happens. But that principle still does not say exactly what process will be followed. Should all communications be made through the cabinet officer who will then push the problem down through the organization (and transmit progress reports through the same channel in reverse)? That is wasteful, and the realization that it would not work well is probably one significant reason why the NSC was invented in the first place. The NSC—as distinguished from its *staff*—is really the partial cabinet approach under another name.

For this reason, all the presidents since Truman have tried variants of a single organizational scheme to link the White House and the line departments. They have sought to organize a "principals group" as the top level (sometimes separate from the NSC itself, sometimes not), supplemented with what might be called a "senior working-level" group (at the deputy secretary or under secretary level), and sometimes with a third level of the assistant secretaries, who are the principal actual action officers in the departments. This structure can promote a process that works well, especially since no level is bypassed. We shall see this two-level or three-level system in use, with variations in the titles assigned each group. As we shall also see, in a crisis situation most presidents frequently relied on a more informal small group.

In the sections that follow, we shall first examine how the senior advisers and the bureaucracy affect the making of foreign policy as they interact with the president. At the same time, we shall continue to emphasize important features of "bureaucratic politics," meaning how the very organization and processes of the bureaucracy and its incumbents affect the decision process and how the nature of the process affects the *kinds* of policies produced. Finally, we shall assess two more intangible but critical influences on policy: the human factor and the factor of timing.

The State and Defense Departments

In principle, as stated above, the whole executive branch exists for the sole purpose of assisting the president. In practice, as we shall see, that does not always quite happen.

Of all the departments and agencies of government, the Department of State is senior. Founded in 1789, and specifically charged with the foreign policy function, by law State has the primary responsibility for advising the president for both formulating and implementing foreign policy.

The home office of the Department of State is organized in a classical bureaucratic pyramid (see Diagram 7.1), with the secretary of state at the top. Beneath, in descending order of importance, are a number of subordinate officers and units. Recognizing that both area and subject matter expertise are required for effective policymaking, State has major bureaus for both geographic and functional areas. Authority and responsibility tend to correspond closely to the hierarchical structure displayed on the organization chart. Very structured superior-subordinate relations exist, so that decision making also tends to be hierarchical in nature. Standard operating procedures (SOPs) guide most daily activities, and they emphasize the need for elaborate coordination. To illustrate, for the secretary in the early 1990s to respond effectively to the European Community's proposed establishment of a single European currency, inputs are needed from the Bureau of Economic and Business Affairs, the legal adviser, the Bureau of European and Canadian Affairs, and many others (and usually interaction with other departments such as Treasury). Consequently, the process almost always makes decision making very time consuming in State, while innovation is rare.

The State Department has the responsibility of representing the United States abroad. It maintains more than 200 embassies and other diplomatic posts throughout the world. Such diplomatic "missions," as they are called, provide the official communication links between the United States and the foreign nations in which they are located. American diplomats stationed there function technically as the personal representatives of the president, the American head of state. As such, they represent the United States at various ceremonial functions. More critical is the "eyes and ears" function—keeping the home office fully and accurately informed about developments and conditions in the host country and the policies and views of its leaders. U.S. diplomats also have an implementation function. They are expected to do as they have been instructed, even to implement policies they feel are unwise.

America's diplomatic missions are not organized identically and vary greatly in size. But they all carry out certain common functions: political affairs, economic/commercial affairs, consular matters, and administration, and have at

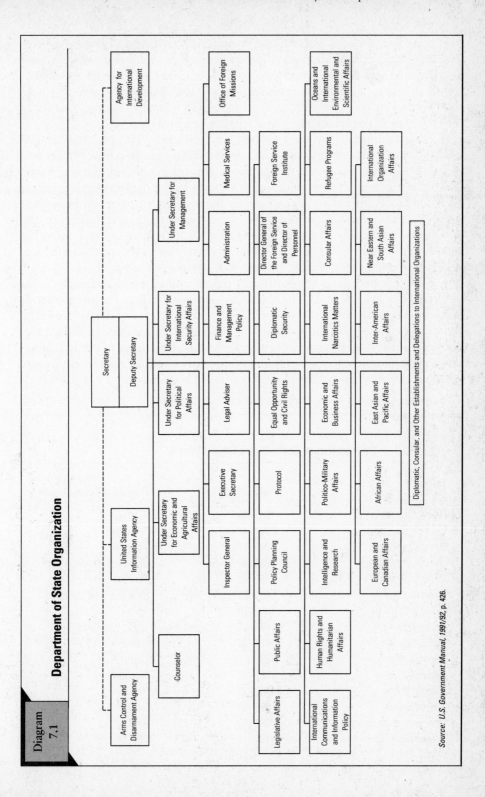

Diagram 7.1

Department of State Organization

Source: U.S. Government Manual, 1991/92, p. 426.

least these four sections. For obvious reasons, the political and economic/commercial affairs sections are especially important. U.S. diplomatic missions have another and difficult major function: to *coordinate* the activities of representatives from many Washington agencies who are attached to the embassy. Under the "country team" concept, ambassadors have formal in-country authority over all mission personnel, no matter what their home agency.[1]

State's influence with the president (and, therefore, with the other departments) depends to a great extent on the personality and competence of the secretary. Because he heads a powerful hierarchical organization, the secretary's leadership and management abilities are important. But the secretary's power is based on much more than how efficiently the department operates. Because of his formal position as the president's principal official foreign policy advisor, the secretary can normally count on access to the Oval Office. But, once there, the secretary must gain and retain the president's trust and confidence. And the secretary must never forget that he or she *works for the president.*

Different presidents want different things, and different secretaries bring different backgrounds and role expectations to the job. (Box 7.1 lists the secretaries of state since 1945.) In Chapter 5 we told how General Alexander Haig, Reagan's first secretary, did not last long. On the other hand, Nixon's first secretary, William Rogers, brought neither diplomatic experience nor a determination to be preeminent to the position. Because Nixon did not really want Rogers to influence policy much, that worked out well. Those secretaries who have been

Box 7.1	**Secretaries of State Since World War II**	
Name	Held Office In	President Served Under
James Byrnes	1945–47	Truman
George Marshall	1947–49	Truman
Dean Acheson	1949–52	Truman
John Foster Dulles	1953–59	Eisenhower
Christian Herter	1959–60	Eisenhower
Dean Rusk	1961–68	Kennedy and Johnson
William Rogers	1969–73	Nixon
Henry Kissinger	1973–76	Nixon and Ford
Cyrus Vance	1977–80	Carter
Edmund Muskie	1980	Carter
Alexander Haig	1981–82	Reagan
George Shultz	1982–88	Reagan
James Baker	1989–92	Bush
Lawrence Eagleburger	1992–93	Bush
Warren Christopher	1993–	Clinton

most successful, such as John Foster Dulles and Henry Kissinger, were individuals in whom "the Man" had great faith. Of a secretary's many roles (administrator, policy spokesman, adviser, policy implementor)[2] *his or her most important job is to do well whatever the president wants him or her to, whether it be little or much.*

The second department with a major input to foreign policy is the Department of Defense (DOD).[3] Until 1947, the United States had two departments for military affairs: the Departments of War and Navy. In Chapter 5 we examined some of the major problems of military and political-military coordination that arose during World War II, problems that played an important role in bringing about the National Security Act. This act created a National Military Establishment with a secretary of defense at the top, presiding over three separate military departments (army, navy, and air force). The same act gave the Joint Chiefs of Staff a statutory base, and created a small Joint Staff to coordinate interservice activities. In 1949, this National Military Establishment became the Department of Defense (DOD).

Even though DOD is often called "the Pentagon" it is far from a homogenous mass of faceless ciphers, all speaking from the same script. As Diagram 7.2 indicates, there are four primary elements:[4]

1. the Secretary of Defense (SecDef), supported by the largely civilian Office of the Secretary of Defense (OSD);
2. the military departments and services (army, navy, and air force);
3. the Chairman of the Joint Chiefs of Staff (CJCS), and the Joint Chiefs of Staff (JCS), as a body;
4. unified and specified (military) commands—forces in the field.

The first element in DOD is the secretary of defense and supporting staff. As initially established in the National Security Act of 1947, the position of secretary of defense was weak, its powers strictly limited so as not to be more than a minimal constraint on the autonomy of the individual military services. However, over time, especially because of the particular influence of Robert McNamara during his tenure as secretary in the Kennedy-Johnson years, the secretary's power expanded enormously. Today, the SecDef has complete authority, direction, and control over the entire department, including the key officials heading the other elements we discuss below. The SecDef is not only the principal assistant to the president in all military matters, he and the president are known as the National Command Authorities. The operational chain of command for military operations runs directly from the president to the secretary and from the secretary to the Commanders-in-Chief (CINCs) of the forces in the field. The SecDef is supported by the Office of the Secretary of Defense. It is a large, mostly civilian staff element, and it is responsible for executing all of DOD's functions.

The second element in DOD consists of the military departments—the departments of the Army, Navy, and Air Force. These military departments are headed by civilian secretaries who report to the SecDef, with the four-star generals and admirals who head their services (the chiefs) being the administrative No. 2s. In the Navy's case, since the Navy Department contains both the Navy

Diagram 7.2

Department of Defense Organization

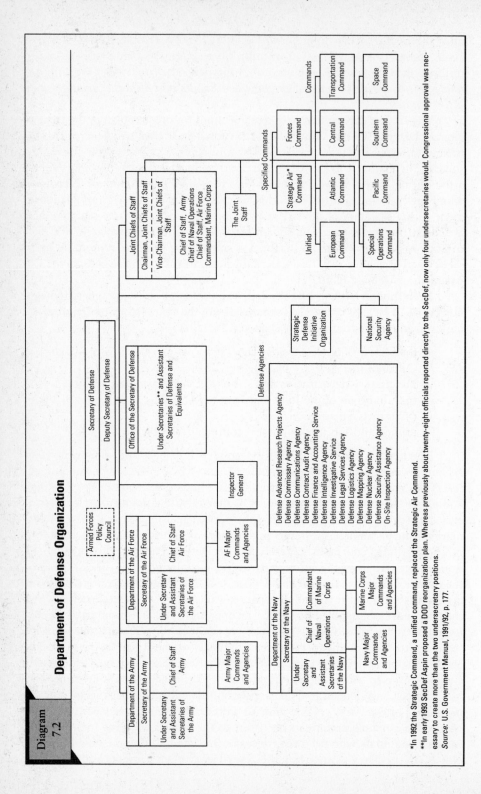

*In 1992 the Strategic Command, a unified command, replaced the Strategic Air Command.

**In early 1993 SecDef Aspin proposed a DOD reorganization plan. Whereas previously about twenty-eight officials reported directly to the SecDef, now only four undersecretaries would. Congressional approval was necessary to create more than the two undersecretary positions.

Source: U.S. Government Manual, 1991/92, p. 177.

and the Marines, there are two four-star officers. These secretaries and chiefs do not command forces in military operations, but they are responsible for *administrative* functions such as recruiting, organizing, training, and equipping the forces that ultimately will do the fighting. Thus, contrary to public perceptions, neither the civilian department heads nor the senior military men are in the chain of command as such, and cannot order forces into action. But their recruiting, organizing, training, and equipping responsibilities make them major players in the preparations for military activities and in the budget and resource allocation processes.

The third element in DOD is the Joint Chiefs of Staff (JCS). It is composed of a separately appointed chairman (CJCS), a vice-chairman (as of 1986), the chiefs of staff of the Army and Air Force, the chief of naval operations, and the commandant of the Marine Corps (the last four of whom were mentioned above as the administrative No. 2s). The reporting chain of the chiefs of service in the JCS is via the CJCS to the secretary of defense—which means that on those matters their civilian secretary need not be specifically informed (although he generally is). The JCS, even though not *in* the chain of command, normally staff the secretary's orders, ensuring coordinated field activity. (And the CJCS *is* in the *communications* chain of command.)

We saw that the JCS was founded on an ad hoc basis by President Roosevelt in World War II and established by law in the 1947 National Security Act. From 1947 until 1986, the JCS, corporately, fulfilled the critical role of principal military adviser(s) to the president, the National Security Council (NSC), and SecDef. Most of that time the JCS also acted as a participant without formal authority in the operational chain of command. Supported by a Joint Staff composed of officers from the four services, it also played an important role in strategic planning.

In the 1986 Goldwater-Nichols Defense Reorganization Act, Congress mandated several changes. It created the position of vice chairman, with four-star rank. Since 1986 that office has become very important, especially in the interagency arena and the resource allocation and weapons acquisition areas. The 1986 law made a second (and enormous) change by designating the chairman *alone* as the principal military adviser to the president, NSC, and SecDef, instead of the JCS as a body. A third change for the first time gave the CJCS full control over the Joint Staff. Along with that, responsibility for a host of duties previously performed by the corporate JCS was also transferred to the chairman. In addition, he received the new task of preparing fiscally constrained strategic plans. It is clear why today the CJCS is by far the most influential military man in the government—by 1993 some complained that the CJCS was *too* powerful.

The fourth element in DOD consists of the unified and specified commands. It is to these commands that the military departments and services provide the forces they have organized, equipped, and trained. These "combatant commands," under the direction of the national command authorities, have operational control over the actual deployment and employment of U.S. military forces.

Unified commands are composed of significant forces from more than one service. In 1992, there were nine unified commands, five of which had geographical responsibilities: Atlantic Command, European Command, Southern Command, Central Command, and Pacific Command. The other unified commands were the Space Command, the Transportation Command, the Strategic Command, and the Special Operations Command. Specified commands have functional missions and are composed of forces from only one service. The only specified command in 1992 was the Forces Command.

Treasury, the USTR, and Commerce

Because political and military affairs have long been recognized as key elements of American foreign policy, discussions of the State and Defense Departments are traditional in texts on the subject. But it is evident that for the United States today, economic affairs also are of great importance. (In both Parts Four and Five below, we pay considerable attention to economic problems.) The key executive branch departments and agencies in foreign economic relations are the Treasury Department, the Office of the U.S. Trade Representative, and the Department of Commerce.[5]

The Department of the Treasury is the preeminent agency dealing with foreign economic relations. Its responsibilities include balance of payments and trade, tariffs and exchange rates, as well as domestic issues. The secretary of the treasury is not only the chief financial adviser to the president, but the treasury's role is critical in the development of international monetary and fiscal policy. Given the importance of economic questions in both foreign and domestic matters, the secretary is usually in the inner circle of presidential advisers. In the department itself, the key day-to-day unit (in foreign policy) usually is the Office of the Assistant Secretary of International Affairs. It "assists the Secretary, Deputy Secretary, and Under Secretary for International Affairs in the formulation and execution of policies dealing with international monetary, financial, commercial, energy, and trade policies and programs."[6]

The 1980s not only confirmed the secretary's important modern day role as a key presidential adviser; those years also saw two other (interrelated) developments of note. First, in mid-decade with a strong personality at the helm who enjoyed the president's confidence—James Baker—the treasury chief on occasion played an important foreign policy role of his own. For example, the 1985 growth-oriented Baker Plan represented a marked departure from previous policy. It also "demonstrated . . . that the Treasury Department was taking the lead on foreign economic policy."[7] Second, Treasury became dominant in the interdepartmental arena. Stephen Cohen saw this development as due in particular to the relative global decline in American economic strength and the growing recognition that international economic factors were increasingly affecting the

American people in a very direct sense. These factors naturally increased interest by policymakers in economic issues.[8]

The Office of the U.S. Trade Representative (USTR) is the second important economic agency. Established in 1963 by President Kennedy as part of the Executive Office, over time the USTR has had its powers and responsibilities expanded, eventually being charged "with responsibility for setting and administering overall trade policy."[9] With Clinton's establishment of a National Economic Council in 1993, it was not immediately clear how things would sort out, but no one doubted the USTR would remain a major player. The USTR also serves as the chief U.S. representative in all major international trade negotiations. Such activities cover a broad range, including the GATT, negotiations in the United Nations Conference on Trade and Development, and, when the talks deal primarily with commodity and trade issues, negotiations in other multilateral institutions. With the passage of the Omnibus Trade and Competitiveness Act of 1988, the USTR also became the lead actor in judging the desirability of retaliating for unfair trading practices. Because the USTR is a presidential appointee with cabinet rank as an ambassador and answers directly to the president, to the extent he wishes, the president can keep trade policy tightly in his own hands, balancing relationships among the USTR and NEC as he sees fit.

The Department of Commerce is the third agency playing a particularly important role in trade matters. It is Commerce, rather than the State Department, that is responsible for U.S. commercial representation overseas (even though its personnel are attached to the embassy). It has primary responsibility for managing import-export programs, where its International Trade Administration plays the lead role. It handles the enforcement of antidumping and countervailing duties statutes.[10] Despite these extensive duties, the Commerce Department generally plays a secondary role in the area of trade policy *formulation*. With so much of trade policy formulated through the interaction of the president and the USTR (and now the NEC?), Commerce's role usually is primarily that of implementer.[11]

Policymaking and the NSC, 1947–76

These executive branch departments and agencies play important roles in the policymaking process. But the kinds of fundamental decisions we discussed in Chapter 2 are made at higher levels, by the president and his senior advisers, in part because individual departments and agencies, operating largely in their own assigned spheres, see only part of any problem. Then also, as we detail below, presidents frequently prefer to operate in small groups of their own choosing, outside normal bureaucratic confines. Such groups, small and hand-picked, have relatively few viewpoints to reconcile or procedural barriers to overcome. Since their members are typically close to the president and understand his thinking and desires, they require less direction from the president. He can count on the small group to act quickly and to keep his confidence. (Anyone who fails to abide by the rules is quickly out.) A third reason is that from the president's perspective the coordinating machinery set up after World War II, especially the NSC, sometimes leaves something to be desired.

It follows from this that the NSC's impact on decision making has varied considerably according to presidential preferences and style. Since it was created in 1947 the NSC has often been a participant in the policy making process, both in planning and coordination. But, especially in its first three decades, the NSC fell short of its founders' expectations. With every president deciding how he wants his decision process structured, this variation of both method of procedure and impact on policy is built-in.

The Truman Years

President Truman, the first president to work with the new machinery, approached the NSC with considerable skepticism. He wanted to be quite sure that it did not begin to erode the president's authority to make decisions. From its initial meeting in September 1947 until the Korean War began, Truman attended less than one-fourth of its meetings. When he did attend he seldom participated "in order to emphasize that . . . he was not bound by its advice."[12] Although the Korean War brought greater attendance and a presidential directive that all major policy recommendations should be coordinated by the NSC and its staff, Truman's most important decisions were made outside the NSC framework. He relied primarily on his secretaries of state (George Marshall, Dean Acheson), and selected key individuals as the case warranted. In crises, he usually convened small ad hoc groups external to the NSC structure.

The Eisenhower Years

Eisenhower, with his military background, initially planned for the NSC to have a more important role. Though he did not expect it to be a formal planning body, he did want the NSC to integrate the policy recommendations from the departments and from his senior advisers to produce a set of general policies to provide overall policy guidance. To help achieve this objective, a formal NSC committee system was established. The NSC staff, naturally, increased in importance in this period.

During Eisenhower's tenure the NSC met frequently. Policy papers, already having been properly staffed and coordinated, were discussed vigorously.[13] The president participated actively in these discussions, keeping his subordinates attuned to the directions he wanted policy to take. But the overall study and recommendation process was highly formal and structured (its critics said "cumbersome") and was really suited only to long-range planning or program decisions. Informal "special NSC meetings" were held to deal with current problems. During crises, decisions usually were made by the president outside the NSC, in consultation with Secretary of State Dulles, Secretary of Treasury

Humphrey, or others such as the Chairman of the JCS (CJCS) or Director of Central Intelligence (DCI).[14]

The Kennedy Years

Kennedy, with a personality and background very different from Eisenhower's,[15] felt that the Eisenhower system produced neither useful advice nor sound decisions. Where Ike favored a chairman-of-the-board approach, in which he dealt with only the major issues, the action-oriented Kennedy wanted to be in the middle of things. Eisenhower's NSC subunits (the Planning Board and the Operations Coordinating Board) were dismantled. Though formal NSC meetings were held, they rarely were occasions where serious advice was heard or major decisions made. With the NSC staff under National Security Adviser McGeorge Bundy playing a major supporting role, Kennedy himself made as many decisions as possible, making "policy" as he went. Crisis management was handled through ad hoc groups such as the "ExComm" of Cuban missile crisis fame, the participants selected more for their individual abilities and loyalty to the president than their organizational position or responsibilities. While the Kennedy "system" (or lack of it) had the advantages of speed, decisiveness, and keeping control in the president's hands, it had the drawback of bypassing the in-house expertise of the bureaucracy.[16] Too often issues were not fully debated, and frequently coordination and staffing were inadequate (as the Bay of Pigs showed.)

The Johnson Years

Lyndon Johnson's view was similar to Kennedy's in some ways. He, too, believed more in personal relationships than organization charts. Still, he believed some organization was necessary and revamped the NSC machinery, creating a two-tier interagency committee structure to help in coordination. Unfortunately, the system never functioned effectively.[17] Indeed, under LBJ formal meetings generally received short shrift. Johnson made his most important decisions and received his most influential advice *outside* the NSC, using the "Tuesday Lunch" as his key decision forum. Besides the president, regular attendees included Secretary of State Rusk, Secretary of Defense McNamara, and usually the DCI, the CJCS, and the national security adviser, plus the president's press secretary. Others with particular expertise might be invited if the president desired. This group was the president's creature, providing the president advice from people whose views he wanted.[18] The old saw, "where you stand depends on where you sit," rarely applied. But the closed and select nature of the group produced a major disadvantage: counterbalancing interests were seldom considered.[19] The debate took place within a commonly accepted set of policy assumptions like containment and the domino theory. Once Johnson and his advisers become preoccupied with Vietnam, a siege mentality set in, and the advisory channels constricted even further. This was very different from Kennedy's freewheeling search for analyses of the options.[20]

The Nixon Years

Nixon came to office determined to revive the NSC. His experience as Eisenhower's vice president had a major effect on his approach. Like Ike, Nixon believed in clear lines of authority and responsibility, but he wanted a process that presented a menu of options for consideration, not a consensus. Moreover, in part because he thought the CIA incompetent and the State Department untrustworthy,[21] Nixon wanted a tightly centralized system to ensure White House control. An elaborate system of NSC interagency committees and subcommittees was established to help achieve these objectives. And, for most of 1969 and 1970 the system functioned more or less as envisioned, although in order to emphasize that the NSC was an advisory and not a decision making body, Nixon usually waited until after meetings were over to announce his decisions.[22] However, with the press of events (discussed in Chapter 12), by the early 1970s the NSC had largely fallen into disuse as a major decision forum. Now key decisions were made privately by Nixon and Kissinger. Advice was formulated and conveyed primarily by and through Kissinger and the NSC staff. Although Ford later opened up the decision process, convening the NSC fairly frequently, Kissinger maintained his preeminence as policy adviser. The NSC remained on the periphery.[23]

The end of the Ford administration marked the completion of approximately three decades of experience with the NSC. Various presidents had used or circumvented the machinery in different ways, each with its own advantages and disadvantages. The general conclusion was that, quite in contrast to its founders' hope, the NSC seldom had been the central forum for decisions on crucial issues or the primary source of advice.

Policymaking and the NSC, 1977–

The Carter Years

When President Carter took office he was determined to set the nation on a new course, both in how it did business as well as in the direction it would take. No more would there be an extreme centralization of power or dominance by one or two individuals; collegiality would be the hallmark of his administration. Consistent with this philosophy, the NSC would be "the principal forum for international security issues requiring presidential consideration."[24] The NSC would bring things together and "integrate and facilitate" decisions.[25]

But the reality was that under Carter, like most of his predecessors, the NSC rarely was the most important decision forum. Nor was it a major decision facilitator or integrator. Instead, the president, who by temperament liked to be deeply involved in the details of daily activities, operated very informally. Generally he bypassed the NSC. Frequently he operated in catch-as-catch-can sessions, or in ad hoc small groups. As with Johnson, regular working lunches became customary, with Secretary of State Vance, national security adviser

Brzezinski, and SecDef Brown attending. (These three also lunched on Thursday without the boss.) Regular Friday morning breakfasts with the same group (with others being invited if the issue required) were soon instituted. Much was decided in these sessions. Even crises usually were handled on an informal personal basis, outside the NSC. Certain members of the White House Staff, such as Press Secretary Jody Powell and Presidential Assistant Hamilton Jordan, often had influence far out of proportion to their official positions.

During much of Carter's term there was significant tension between Vance and Brzezinski over the roles and influence of the national security adviser and the secretary of state, with each competing for the president's ear. Because Carter did not exercise effective leadership, many times a discordant cacophony of views was heard; coordination was either minimal or nonexistent. During much of the Iran hostage crisis, for example, the president went one way, Vance a second, and Brzezinski a third. Although there were meetings of the NSC Special Coordination Committee (which was supposed to handle crisis coordination), the president neither took an active role nor provided clear guidance, so the committee floundered. Carter's initial plan to have Brzezinski act primarily as a facilitator and coordinator went by the boards. With Brzezinski playing a policy-determining role second only to the president, the secretary of state was pushed into the background. Carter's rather naive hope that he could rely primarily on collegiality to achieve the necessary coordination did not work; as Alexander George pointed out, more than cordiality is needed for effective policymaking.[26]

The Reagan Years

Ronald Reagan came to the presidency convinced that Carter's policies had been weak and ineffective and that his decision processes had been equally inept. Reagan planned a very different operation. The secretary of state would be the principal foreign policy adviser, with the national security adviser and the NSC staff functioning as coordinators and facilitators. Because he believed enhancing the nation's military capability was a top priority, the SecDef and JCS would play more prominent roles in decision making than under Carter. The NSC would use revised versions of the two-tier structure of interagency committees and subcommittees that had existed since the Johnson years, but use them more effectively. Their functions would be to advise on policy objectives, develop options, make recommendations in their respective areas, and help oversee implementation.[27] Reagan planned to attend NSC meetings personally and participate regularly, although he would not involve himself much in the details. As president, like Eisenhower, Reagan would focus on the essential questions for decision. Details of Reagan's organization are set out in Diagram 7.3.

A few parts of the system worked out more or less as planned. When NSC meetings were held, the president usually was in the chair, participating actively. The views of the military did carry more weight, and Reagan generally did focus on fundamental issues, leaving the details to subordinates. But many things worked out quite differently than he had hoped. The NSC, as such, was not used

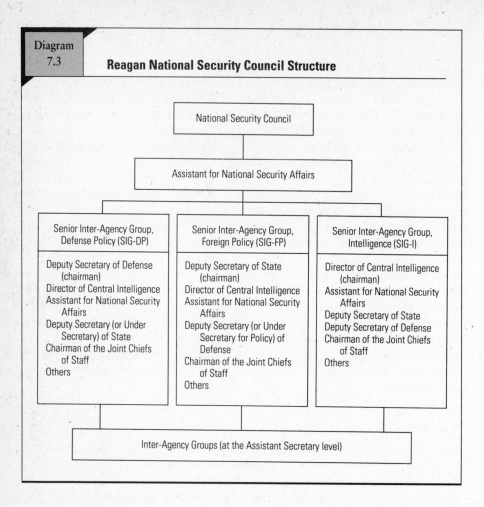

Diagram 7.3

Reagan National Security Council Structure

National Security Council

Assistant for National Security Affairs

Senior Inter-Agency Group, Defense Policy (SIG-DP)	Senior Inter-Agency Group, Foreign Policy (SIG-FP)	Senior Inter-Agency Group, Intelligence (SIG-I)
Deputy Secretary of Defense (chairman) Director of Central Intelligence Assistant for National Security Affairs Deputy Secretary (or Under Secretary) of State Chairman of the Joint Chiefs of Staff Others	Deputy Secretary of State (chairman) Director of Central Intelligence Assistant for National Security Affairs Deputy Secretary (or Under Secretary for Policy) of Defense Chairman of the Joint Chiefs of Staff Others	Director of Central Intelligence (chairman) Assistant for National Security Affairs Deputy Secretary of State Deputy Secretary of Defense Chairman of the Joint Chiefs of Staff Others

Inter-Agency Groups (at the Assistant Secretary level)

much. Like his predecessors, over time Reagan turned increasingly to a smaller and less formal body, the National Security Planning Group (NSPG). NSPG meetings were structured to maximize the exchange of ideas and positions prior to presidential decision, and often they were quite effective. But if that development was a plus, there were also a number of negatives. Because Reagan much of the time was so uninvolved in the details,[28] the policy machine sometimes lacked a clear sense of direction. As Secretary of State Haig later wrote:

> But to me, the White House was as mysterious as a ghost ship; you heard the creak of the rigging and the groan of the timbers and sometimes even glimpsed the crew, on deck. But which of the crew had the helm?[29]

Sometimes it was worse. The Iran-Contra affair (discussed in Chapter 13), indeed showed a policymaking machine out of control. As the Tower Commission so kindly put it, "[R]eviews of the initiative by all the NSC principals were too infrequent."[30]

Several other difficulties developed, too. Hardly ever did the small informal decision groups that the president created keep adequate records or follow normal government staffing procedures for coordination and the dissemination of decisions reached. Indeed, it was not infrequent that the principals went away from such meetings with divergent ideas of what *had* been decided, or who was to do what. This result was not unique to the Reagan administration, of course. It tended to be true of all small groups.

Another problem was that the three initial and major NSC Senior Inter-Agency Groups (i.e., the level just below principals) were not used effectively.[31] That probably was connected to the major bureaucratic and personal tensions, which characterized the opening phase of the Reagan years.[32] Secretary Haig immediately came into conflict with the White House "troika" (Counsel to the President Edwin Meese, Chief of Staff James A. Baker, and Deputy Chief Michael Deever). Haig also found himself in conflict with Secretary of Defense Caspar Weinberger. Later, after Haig was gone, tensions recurred between the new secretary of state, George Schultz, and Weinberger. And so on. Finally, in the Reagan years, the in-fighting was partly responsible for an unusual turnover in the office of national security adviser. Moreover, with the changes in personnel in that office came changes in the adviser's functions. As incumbents came and went, their roles ranged from background coordinator (Richard Allen) to management specialist (Colin Powell). Admiral Poindexter's role in the Iran-Contra affair would not have been as likely to happen under a president less inclined to delegate authority without at the same time checking to be sure that the delegation was warranted. Besides, Reagan was the opposite of Carter: strong on choice on major policy direction, weak on detailed implementation.

Three quotes from George Schultz's account of his years as secretary of state are illuminating. The first one goes to the point that the president's "decision" counts only to the extent that he tracks what the bureaucracy does with it. Schultz laments:

> The President agreed [but] I encountered yet another series of big interagency meetings . . . on the same old fundamental question [to which the] NSC staff answer was, as ever, a resounding no.
>
> I was beginning to realize that nothing I could do or say, and nothing the president would decide, would ever change their minds. The task before me was to make them irrelevant. . . . [33]

Schultz meant that his strategy would have to be to attain direct access to the president. Yet that would not solve everything because he needed "a working relationship with the NSC adviser, too."

And *that* was not easy, either. With Judge Clark, the problem was Clark's relative ignorance about national security affairs. With McFarlane, who followed Clark, the problem was different.

> Bud [McFarlane] seemed to want the NSC staff to run foreign policy, with the secretaries of state, defense, and treasury—and the director of central intelligence —as bit players.[34]

But Schultz, unlike Haig, retained his chief's confidence. And Schultz, unlike Haig, stuck it out.

The Bush Years

When President Bush took office, although his policy intent was essentially to continue the format of the Reagan administration, he intended to play a more active and direct role in the decision process. Like Kennedy and Nixon, Bush wanted the White House in control. His initial key appointments were all pragmatists who understood "how Washington works" and knew the value of loyalty to the boss. James A. Baker, former secretary of treasury, White House chief of staff, and presidential campaign manager, became secretary of state. Lieutenant General (ret.) Brent Scowcroft, whose military background and previous experience as President Ford's national security adviser provided an understanding of staff and interagency processes, again became the national security adviser. When Senator Tower's appointment as SecDef was rejected by the Senate, Bush picked Dick Cheney, a five-term member of the House and former chief of staff to President Ford (when Bush was DCI and U.S. representative to China). The appointment of Robert Gates, deputy director of the CIA and a former NSC staffer, to be Scowcroft's deputy, was further evidence of Bush's desire to have a strong interagency process. A three-tier NSC committee system was established to this end, the Principals Committee at the top, the Deputies Committee (made up of No. 2s) next, and a third tier of functional and regional Policy Coordinating Committees at the assistant secretary level. (Diagram 7.4 sets out the Bush NSC structure.)

We are still too close to the Bush administration to view it with much perspective, but some tentative conclusions are possible. First, the president's determination to use the interagency process more effectively than his predecessor was reasonably successful. In the Persian Gulf War, for example, the NSC Deputies Committee met quite frequently (usually via teleconference) and was a major plus in the coordination process. While there were several exceptions, a number of the assistant secretary level Policy Coordinating Committees performed well also. Second, Bush was quite successful in keeping the control of policy in his hands, to a great extent remaining the "ultimate decider." In part at least, this desire explained the president's near obsession with secrecy. However, the insistence on secrecy had its downsides, as when decisions were made without key aides being informed. Reportedly, when Bush sent Scowcroft on a secret mission to China in July 1989, he did not even inform chief of staff John Sununu. Another characteristic of Bush's style was its very personal nature. In Chapter 1 we discussed his "reach out and touch someone" use of the telephone to communicate with foreign leaders. In a manner reminiscent of Franklin Roosevelt, Bush strongly believed in the importance of personal contact, and in his ability to influence others as well.

Finally, Bush, like most of his predecessors, made most of his critical time-urgent decisions in an informal manner outside the NSC framework. Small ad hoc groups were established as needed, with only a small circle of advisers par-

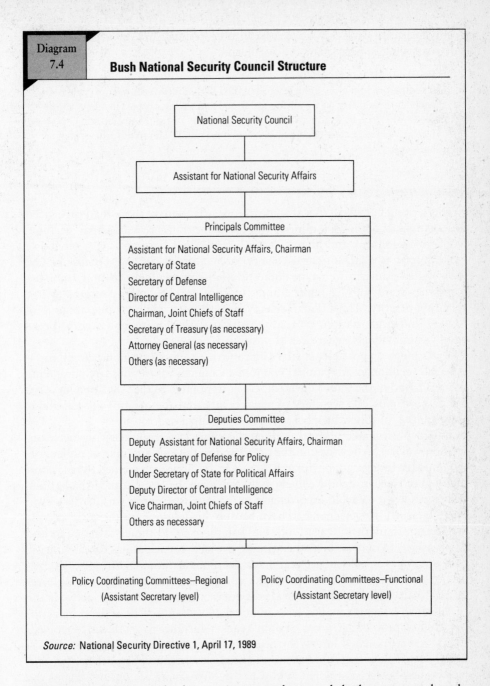

Diagram 7.4

Bush National Security Council Structure

National Security Council

Assistant for National Security Affairs

Principals Committee

Assistant for National Security Affairs, Chairman
Secretary of State
Secretary of Defense
Director of Central Intelligence
Chairman, Joint Chiefs of Staff
Secretary of Treasury (as necessary)
Attorney General (as necessary)
Others (as necessary)

Deputies Committee

Deputy Assistant for National Security Affairs, Chairman
Under Secretary of Defense for Policy
Under Secretary of State for Political Affairs
Deputy Director of Central Intelligence
Vice Chairman, Joint Chiefs of Staff
Others as necessary

Policy Coordinating Committees–Regional
(Assistant Secretary level)

Policy Coordinating Committees–Functional
(Assistant Secretary level)

Source: National Security Directive 1, April 17, 1989

ticipating and with standard operating procedures and the bureaucracy largely ignored. Decision making in the failed 1989 coup against Panama's Manuel Noriega was a case in point—no NSC meetings occurred. In the Persian Gulf War, the "Big Eight" (or "Gang of Eight") were the key players (Bush, Baker, Cheney, Scowcroft, Gates, Sununu, Powell, and Vice President Quayle). In routine matters, too, Bush worked hard to keep things under his personal control. According to Kellerman and Barilleaux:

> Bush uses his staff to explore problems and identify options, which are then debated before him at Cabinet sessions called "scheduled train wrecks." He participates in these meetings by asking questions and taking notes. Then he retires to the Oval Office to "shop around" for further advice from associates in Congress, foreign leaders, and friends whose counsel he values. Ultimately, the president decides. . . .[35]

The Clinton Years

At this writing in mid-1993 it was much too early to make more than superficial observations about the Clinton system, but some things seemed apparent. First, like Lyndon Johnson and Jimmy Carter before him, Clinton was very obviously handicapped by a lack of knowledge of foreign affairs. Second, because he had been elected primarily to handle domestic issues, especially the economy, and because they were both his interest and expertise, foreign policy concerns were a very low priority. Third, like Kennedy, Clinton was almost contemptuous of routine and organization, preferring informal decision practices with inputs from key individuals, regardless of position.

As much as possible, at first Clinton tried to focus on domestic affairs—especially economic. A National Economic Council was established, paralleling the NSC. And of the three new members he appointed to the NSC, two had economic portfolios, the secretary of the treasury and the head of the Economic Council (the third new member was the U.N. ambassador).

When economic and other domestic subjects were under consideration, Clinton was deeply involved in the detail and in the give and take of policy formulation. In foreign policy matters, however, his approach seemed to be a combination of Reagan's and Kennedy's. Like Reagan, he laid out the broad guidelines but sought to avoid involvement in the details. Clinton was perhaps even more detached than Reagan had been because he did not have the same *interest* in foreign affairs that Reagan did. He was there to do things as required and when asked, of course, but otherwise he avoided participating. Like Kennedy, Clinton often solicited advice and made decisions without regard for organization or position. Clusters of friends and advisers were relied on for counsel, frequently including individuals outside the government who had been active in the presidential campaign and/or were political consultants. Within the official apparatus it appeared that, given Clinton's early reluctance to get directly involved, policy was formulated largely by Secretary of State Warren Christopher, National Security Adviser W. Anthony Lake, Lake's deputy, Samuel Berger, and (sometimes) SecDef Les Aspin, with Clinton only saying yes or no. Perhaps the most telling indicator of his lack of interest in organization and process was that it was weeks before an NSC meeting was held.

But while a president may desire to concentrate on economic and other domestic issues and put foreign policy on the back burner, as Woodrow Wilson,

LBJ, and others discovered, the world does not always cooperate. And, when fundamental decisions are required, only the president can direct policy effectively. Unfortunately, when a context such as we have just described is combined with a native ebullience and action-oriented temperament, the odds on a decision making process that produces effective policy are not good. The administration's early 1993 decision making concerning the Bosnian crisis, discussed in Chapter 13, provided a useful illustration.

Bureaucratic Politics

Although the president and his senior advisers decide the critical issues, providing the fundamental policy thrust and direction, most routine daily activities are handled by the foreign relations bureaucracy, outside the White House. It is here that "bureaucratic politics," a term we used earlier, has its most important meaning. But how, specifically, does bureaucratic politics affect the process of making foreign policy?

In any large bureaucracy, standard operating procedures (SOPs) play an enormously important role. Large and complex organizations such as State, DOD, or Treasury would be lost without SOPs, because any large organization needs standardized policies and procedural rules. Such rules, regulations, and guidelines govern the handling of everything done. Without SOPs, chaos would soon result. However, with SOPs, a certain stagnation effect is inevitable. Once any policy is established, flexibility tends to evaporate; policy becomes difficult to alter; it tends to be reinforced. Leslie Gelb correctly described this effect when he commented on what happened after President Johnson decided to escalate the war in Vietnam: "The bureaucracy became like a cement block in the trunk of a car—it added tremendous momentum."[36]

The second consequence of SOPs is that the vast majority of lower level decisions will be made without the president's specific knowledge. He simply cannot know what everyone is doing in his name. Nor is it either possible or desirable for him to try to find out; the important decisions would soon go unmade.

SOPs have a third effect. They are, naturally enough, status-quo oriented. With SOPs established on the basis of past procedures, employees generally conform to those procedures rather than rocking the boat. That pattern feeds at each level a strong tendency to weed out more extreme ideas and to develop a consensus. Finally, when SOPs guide policymaking, so many bases must be touched, so many agencies and individuals consulted, and there is so much to do, that it takes "forever and a day" for anything to happen. A major difficulty with SOPs, to put it mildly, is that they are terribly time-consuming.

But SOPs are not the only major characteristic of bureaucratic policymaking. There is also what can be called "bureaucratic competition." For easily understandable reasons, instead of working together across agency and departmental lines, individuals and units sometimes compete with one another, or even try to shut others out.

There is no doubt that such bureaucratic competition sometimes takes place, but it is very important to address this subject in a balanced manner. Two factors lie behind this competition. First, organizations have interests of their own. Quite naturally, although it is not their primary function, leaders and members will seek to develop such capabilities and advance such policies as will achieve and protect those interests. The result of the interaction of these policies can be a process of competitive bargaining, with each unit seeking to maximize its position and influence. At the same time, one must not automatically assume an avowedly selfish or unpatriotic motivation behind this bargaining (although that *is* often what critics assume). Indeed, usually the analysis or position advocated is thought to be in the broader national interest. An illustration may clarify the point. Suppose the Arms Control and Disarmament Agency (ACDA) advocates a larger role for ACDA in the decision process and greater emphasis on arms control. Fueling that wish is the belief that the change will make arms control a higher priority in the nation's foreign policy. Are not arms control agreements "obviously" in the national interest?

The second factor is what we might call the results of partial perspective. Different organizations deal with different aspects of problems, have different responsibilities, and operate from different perspectives. As a result, in a sense the various groups do not even see the same "reality." It would only be natural in such circumstances for different units to develop and advocate different policy recommendations. And they frequently do. The oft-repeated phrase "where you stand depends on where you sit" thus can reflect something quite different from the personal ambition that people often associate with departmental jockeying for power (although sometimes it reflects that, too). People argue from what they know and from what they are required to do; not surprisingly, they attach less importance to needs and tasks outside their range.

Throughout this book we have stressed how policy coordination or its lack affects the results of policy. Operating via SOPs and bureaucratic competition can affect both coordination and policy content. The extreme fragmentation of America's policymaking machinery, with so many units and individuals involved in the process, also has an effect. The right hand may not know what the left hand is doing. Overlapping jurisdictions may occur, engendering duplication, waste, and unnecessary interagency friction. Or the reverse can happen. Each unit may assume a task is someone else's responsibility, so it "falls in the cracks." As we saw in Chapter 5, it is not unknown for different units to go their own way with no coordination at all. In April 1967 during the Vietnam War, with a diplomatic initiative underway and restraint seemingly in order, a bombing raid was scheduled against power plants in Hanoi. "There was just no interest or effort expended in orchestrating military and diplomatic moves; everyone was doing his own thing."[37] Secretary of State George Schultz, in discussing the aftermath of the Israeli occupation of Beirut in 1982, describes in detail similar disconnects within both the U.S. and Israeli bureaucracies.[38]

Besides the impacts of SOPs, bureaucratic competition, and fragmentation, three other characteristics of the bureaucratic policymaking process influence results. First, in the bureaucracy most "decisions" are the product of interacting inputs from a host of sources over some period of time, rather than clear-cut discrete choices by a single person. Policy evolves continuously, as a sort of decisional flow.[39] We saw in Chapter 2 how change tends to be incremental. The second characteristic is that the participants in the process frequently have too much to do and too little time to do it. The consequence is that the real nature of the problem may not at first be recognized,[40] let alone dealt with effectively. Third, since bureaucracies' desire to fashion a consensus is normally very powerful, any accommodation or compromise achieved may be at the lowest common denominator. This bureaucratic tendency is called "minimalizing;" its result is deciding as little as possible.

It should be evident now why "bureaucratic politics" have important results. But it is essential to keep this all in perspective. In quantitative and cumulative terms, the bureaucracy and "bureaucratic politics" dominate the policymaking process. But it would be inaccurate to describe them as preeminent in the most fundamental decisions affecting America's vital interests. As we said initially, it is the president and his key senior advisers who usually make those decisions, within the various intellectual and organizational constraints we have already discussed and the public context we shall discuss in Chapter 8.

It would certainly be very wrong to believe that the president is hardly more important than anyone else in policymaking, just another, if more senior, cog in the bureaucratic machine. As we saw in Chapter 6, the president is ultimately responsible, he is the one to whom critical information is funneled, he is the one to whom the experts report. Not only does the president have a wide range of powers that enable him to take action, initiate, and sustain policy; but no bureaucrat can legally or practically perform those functions (unless the president is asleep at the switch). By determining the overall thrust for the bureaucracies to follow in the first place, the president and his senior advisers are also the source of the procedural and substantive guidance within which those lower level daily decisions are supposed to be made.

To complete our analysis we now need to switch gears. In discussing bureaucracies and policymaking to this point, we have focused on organization, structure, and process. This for good reason—those things are important. But as our discussion in earlier chapters showed, there is more to it. The intellectual element of foreign policy is critical, and sometimes the rush of external factors intrudes to hinder even the most logical of decision-making methods. We turn next to a discussion of the human factor, and then to the problem of timing.

The Human Factor

Governmental machinery has to be run by people, and people are not always logical, reasonable, or unbiased. Nor do they all react the same. Even if a position and its authority and usages are well defined, as with the presidency itself or with the office of secretary of state, the person who holds that position makes a great deal of difference. So do the conditions under which the office is held.

An in-depth look at developments in the Truman administration will help make the point. In 1945–48, Harry Truman was president, put into that office by the death of President Roosevelt in April 1945. Truman was an unelected president following a president with great prestige who had been elected to an unprecedented four consecutive terms. In many ways, Truman was initially an unknown quantity to the American people (and to foreign leaders as well).

Truman soon proved he had a very positive attribute: he knew quality, and he attracted talented people to his administration. One was General George Marshall, the army chief of staff during World War II. Truman first sent Marshall to China after Japan's defeat, to attempt a negotiated settlement between the Chinese Communists and the Chinese Nationalists, who were embroiled in what would turn out to be the last act of the long-continued civil war. Marshall failed in that task—success would have been astounding—and returned to claim his well deserved retirement. But Truman then asked him to become secretary of state, and Marshall, with a great reverence for the presidency, felt that the request could not be refused. And this collaboration turned out well, as Truman sought to find a new policy to deal with the Soviet threat after World War II. Marshall, ably assisted by his undersecretary, Dean Acheson, led the way to the North Atlantic Pact and gave his name to the imaginative U.S. economic collaboration with Europe that restored that continent's economic life. Only on one important issue did Marshall hold views directly and even vehemently opposed to those of President Truman: recognizing the new state of Israel.

Clark Clifford, perennial counselor to presidents, tells in his memoirs of the serious clash that occurred.[41] It was May 12, 1948. At midnight, May 14— at 6:00 P.M. Washington time—the British would relinquish Palestine, a League of Nations mandate in their charge since the end of World War I. One minute later, David Ben-Gurion would proclaim a Jewish state. What would the United States do? That was the subject on May 12, as President Truman sat at his desk in the Oval office in the White House. Gathered together were Marshall, his deputy, Robert Lovett, Clifford, and several others. To the State Department (and most of the senior advisers in the U.S. government), it seemed fairly clear-cut. There were many times more Arabs than Jews, and the Arabs also controlled most of the territory and a great deal of the world's oil. Recognition should be withheld. In addition to Marshall, sharing this position were Lovett and Acheson, the chief of the Policy Planning Staff in the State Department, Charles Bohlen, George Kennan, Secretary of Defense James V. Forrestal, and Dean Rusk (who would become secretary of state under Kennedy and Johnson).

Truman had asked Clifford to present the case *for* immediate recognition of the about-to-be-born Israel, a position the president himself endorsed. The meeting soon became heated. Marshall, usually well in control of himself, was furious to think that Truman was prepared to disregard the collective wisdom arrayed against the proposal. With the room stunned into silence, Marshall said: "If you follow Clifford's advice and if I were to vote in the election, I would vote against you." Clifford, with good reason, calls this the "most remarkable threat I ever heard anyone make directly to a President."[42]

Truman put an end to the meeting. Seeing how agitated Marshall was, Truman said "I understand your position, General, and I'm inclined to side with you in this matter." With his weak political base, Truman did not feel he could risk an open confrontation with the war hero, Marshall. But in his heart he believed he ought to recognize Israel, so he set Clifford to work in the next days to break the deadlock, working via Lovett. Finally, almost at the last hour, Marshall agreed to a formula whereby he would not endorse the move but neither would he publicly oppose it.

The critical point for us is not the outcome of these "discussions," of course. It is that decisions are made by particular human beings with their own unique personalities, attributes, and policy views. The effective president must take advantage of his advisers' strengths and expertise and ensure a reasonable degree of policy coordination, while being sure to remain the ultimate decider. Surrounding oneself with talented and energetic people and devising a policy-making system that shows respect for their informed opinions is important, of course, but it does not necessarily produce harmony, especially when key advisers' views are rejected.[43] In such situations, in the interest of having an effective decision-making apparatus for the long haul, the president sometimes finds it productive to operate indirectly and obliquely.

Timing: Everything Has to Be Done at Once

Another "wild card" in decisions is the conundrum represented by timing. When we think of a rational decision process, we visualize a picture of logical, progressive steps in the treatment of problems. We visualize the lower level moving the decision higher for guidance or decision, or the higher one moving it lower for staffing. This is how all departments and agencies are presumed to function. But there always is a complicating factor. Even assuming that a problem will in fact be routed in this way and that officials will use the machinery put into place for that purpose (which does not always happen), how are the various steps to be related to actors and events outside the control of the United States? We made the point earlier that the world is decentralized politically. There is no master playwright, directing all the actors. Every state, instead, follows its own inclinations, in terms of its own view of its national interests. So how will the decisions and policies of foreign leaders be factored into the American decision process?

In the Persian Gulf War case, President Bush, of course, had to keep one eye on domestic public opinion. He knew what he wanted to do, and what Americans generally wanted to do, but he could hardly send a large number of troops to a foreign country regardless of international reaction.[44] He certainly could not do so without scrupulous regard for the wishes of the state that

America would presumably be defending: Saudi Arabia. So, almost simultaneously, the public presentation of the case had to be managed from the White House in conjunction with pressing the issue at the United Nations. Both had to be coordinated with the evolving opinion of King Fahd of Saudi Arabia about whether he wanted American troops to be sent. How far to commit the United States depended on King Fahd's willingness to commit his nation as a base from which American forces could operate. Logically, again, one can say that Fahd "had to" recognize the threat and invite U.S. forces in. But Saudi Arabia had a whole history of keeping America "over the horizon." Would that position be reversed this time? And, should Bush wait for Fahd to make up his mind before he made up his own mind? Should Bush wait to make up his mind until the U.N. took action? Or until the Congress took a position? But what would the Congress do unless Bush took the lead in the first place, asking its support for some particular action? (And, given the time it takes to build up the forces for operations, if Bush waited too long he would preclude certain options.)

The days when President Johnson could go to the Congress and ask for a blank check because North Vietnamese torpedo boats (allegedly) attacked a U.S. destroyer (see Chapter 11) are over. Everyone knows that the open-ended Gulf of Tonkin resolution, which Congress passed in response to Johnson's request, played an important role in allowing over a half million U.S. troops to fight a confusing war in an obscure corner of Southeast Asia, in Vietnam. So Bush had to be more exact in his request. But what should it be? When should it be presented? What should come first?

Of course, the president can at any point tell the armed forces to prepare a plan for an offensive option against Saddam Hussein, to be used if Saddam refuses to pull out of Kuwait. But if the president gives these orders, it will probably leak out to the media, sooner or later. Worse than that in its complications, a plan is only a plan. Until an "execute order" goes out, nothing will happen to put it into effect. But if America deploys, say, another quarter of a million troops into Saudi Arabia in order to prepare for an offensive if the president so directs, the very movement of all of those troops implies some follow-through if Saddam still refuses to leave Kuwait. In a cumulative sense, each step, psychologically and politically, implies more than the step per se indicates. Logically there may be no reason why a plan, once prepared, should raise the prospect of it being implemented. But in the real world, it does. So what steps should be taken in what order?

Bob Woodward, in his book *The Commanders,* although he does not raise this question in this way, provides us a chronology of important decisions, illustrating how these problems present themselves in real life.[45] One of the first issues was how to convince the Saudis that the threat facing them was active and real. With its satellite capability, the United States could "see" the Iraqi armored divisions swinging around to approach the Saudi border after overrunning Kuwait. SecDef Cheney was authorized to show Prince Bandar, the Saudi ambassador, these photos. Bandar then went off to Saudi Arabia to tell King Fahd, but Fahd wanted to see the evidence with his own eyes. How ironical that the Saudis knew so little about what was happening just across their frontier, while the Americans knew it all in detail! Meanwhile, the White House decided that the best way to accelerate a Saudi decision was to send a high-level American emissary.[46] (The higher the level, the harder for the Saudis to temporize or refuse to request troops.) So on Sunday, the third day after Iraq's invasion of Kuwait, the Saudis did receive Cheney. General Powell, the chairman of the Joint Chiefs, watching CNN that day, was surprised to hear President Bush go beyond his previous private guidance to his staff. Now Bush said that Saddam would be forced to leave Kuwait, whereas the previous decision centered on defending Saudi Arabia. That same day, with King Fahd agreeing to an American deployment, General Schwarzkopf, contacting his Saudi counterpart, found him uninformed about Fahd's decision, and they had to get that straightened out, too.

Or take the problem as it was shaping up in November, as the U.N. Security Council moved toward an authorization to use force to expel Iraq from Kuwait unless Saddam withdrew by January 15. The Soviet foreign secretary, Eduard Shevardnadze, although in principle on the same wave length as the United States, told Secretary of State Baker that the Soviet Union could not endorse a resolution specifically authorizing the use of force because Russian public opinion, still reacting to the unfortunate experience with the Afghan war, would object. So a formula had to be found. The words were of more consequence, at least at the moment, than the action.

Or take the problems in December. The United States forces deployed to the Middle East had initially been sent to deter Iraqi attack. If the U.S. intent was to go over to the offensive, to attack in order to free Kuwait, new plans had to be made final, especially choosing a D-day and H-hour (the day and hour for launching the operation). On December 29, General Powell was authorized to send out the preliminary, or "warning" order. It named a mid-January date that General Schwarzkopf had indicated would be acceptable for his forces. But Congress had not yet taken any action. On Thursday, *January 3,* President Bush met with the leaders of Congress. On *January 9,* Secretary Baker met Iraqi Foreign Secretary Aziz in Geneva (for six hours of useless discussion). Only after that did Congress begin a debate. It lasted three days and ended only on Saturday, *January 12,* with the Senate vote of 52–47 and House vote of 250–183, authorizing Bush to use force if Saddam did not withdraw. Four days later, at the time set in the warning order, the fighting began.

In such situations the enormous time pressure, with so much happening at once, makes decision making even more difficult. But senior policymakers have no choice; they *have to* make a decision. Monday morning quarterbacking is left to others.

Summing Up

In Chapters 6 and 7 we have discussed the major governmental actors in the formulation and implementation of foreign policy. We have seen that while the president is the most crucial player, the NSC, Congress, and the bureaucracy also play important roles. One thing must always be remembered, though. In the American system, the public provides the context within which governmental actors operate. We turn in Chapter 8 to a discussion of that public context.

Notes

1. Indeed, the rationale for the country team concept is to enable the ambassador to coordinate all elements of the mission effectively. See John H. Esterline and Robert B. Black, *Inside Foreign Policy* (Palo Alto, CA: Mayfield Publishing, 1975), pp. 79–81, for an effective, succinct discussion.

2. Because of his many roles, all "sorts of demands impinge on the life of the secretary of state and restrict his ability to set his own agenda: the events overseas . . . time spent with the president and the Congress; weeks of foreign travel; and meetings with the press." Cyrus Vance, *Hard Choices: Critical Years in America's Foreign Policy,* (New York: Simon & Schuster, 1983), p. 14. Competing demands exist even during crises. As George Schultz writes "[n]o crisis can ever get undivided attention." George P. Schultz, *Turmoil and Triumph: My Years as Secretary of State* (New York: Scribner's, 1993), p. 741.

3. For a more detailed discussion see Frederick H. Hartmann and Robert L. Wendzel, *Defending America's Security,* 2nd ed., rev. (Washington, DC: Brassey's, 1990), Chapters 8 and 10.

4. There also are defense agencies and DOD field activities within DOD.

5. While the Treasury and Commerce Departments have important "foreign responsibilities," in each case their primary focus is domestic. This emphasizes once again the interrelated nature of foreign and domestic policies. The Agriculture and Labor Departments also have very specifically focused international economic responsibilities.

6. *U.S. Government Manual 1991/92,* p. 487.

7. McCormick, *American Foreign Policy and Process,* p. 384. McCormick also cites the 1985 Plaza Accord and the 1989 Brady Plan.

8. Stephen Cohen, *The Making of United States International Economic Policy,* 3rd ed. (New York: Praeger, 1988), especially pp. 60–64.

9. *U.S. Government Manual 1991/92,* p. 97. The following description of duties is from the same source, pp. 97–98.

10. "Dumping" refers to selling exports at prices lower than those in one's own market. "Countervailing duties" are import taxes designed to offset the advantages a product may have because of subsidies by the exporter.

11. Of course, Congress plays a role, too, as we discussed in Chapter 6.

12. Lincoln P. Bloomfield, *The Foreign Policy Process: A Modern Primer* (Englewood Cliffs, NJ: Prentice-Hall, 1982), p. 46. For an excellent discussion of how various presidents used the NSC, see John Prados, *Keepers of the Keys: A History of the National Security Council from Truman to Bush* (New York: Morrow, 1991).

13. All major papers were accompanied by a CIA estimate bringing together intelligence from State, DOD, and the CIA. Robert R. Bowie, "The President and the Execu-

tive Branch," in Joseph S. Nye, Jr., ed., *The Making of America's Soviet Policy* (New Haven, CT: Yale University Press, 1984), p. 75.

14. Eisenhower established the later-to-be famous position of (special) assistant for national security affairs (ANSA), but in the Eisenhower system the ANSA was more manager than policymaker.

15. In his classic study of presidential character, James David Barber classifies Kennedy as an "active-positive commitment" and Eisenhower as a "passive-negative." See James David Barber, *The Presidential Character: Predicting Performance in the White House,* 2nd ed. (Englewood Cliffs, NJ: Prentice-Hall, 1977).

16. Initially, Kennedy had planned to give the State Department more responsibility, but he became frustrated with its unresponsiveness and lack of innovation. Kennedy would say that giving State an instruction "is like dropping it in the deadletter box." Arthur M. Schlesinger, Jr., *A Thousand Days: John F. Kennedy in the White House* (New York: Fawcett ed., 1967), p. 377.

17. The two-tier structure of LBJ, though, provided the pattern for the NSC interagency system until Bush.

18. As Barbara Kellerman and Ryan J. Barilleaux write, "because attendance . . . was by presidential invitation only, Johnson used the occasions to exclude those officials whose advice he simply did not want to hear." Barbara Kellerman and Ryan J. Barilleaux, *The President as World Leader* (New York: St. Martin's Press, 1991), p. 123.

19. In 1964 Johnson asked the CIA if the remainder of Southeast Asia would likely fall if Laos and South Vietnam were lost. The answer, in essence, was "no." The CIA's view was not asked again. Leslie H. Gelb, with Richard K. Betts, *The Irony of Vietnam: The System Worked* (Washington, DC: The Brookings Institution, 1979), p. 230.

20. LBJ was similar to Kennedy, though, in his increasing use of the national security adviser as a policy adviser and member of the team. When Walt Rostow replaced Bundy, he became one of the leading public spokesmen for the administration's Vietnam policy.

21. See Henry Kissinger, *White House Years* (Boston: Little, Brown, 1979), pp. 14–15.

22. This was done also, in part at least, so Nixon could avoid anyone challenging his orders. Kissinger, p. 491. Also see Prados, *Keepers of the Keys,* p. 266.

23. In 1975, Kissinger, who had been both ANSA and secretary of state since 1973, was replaced as national security adviser by General Brent Scowcroft. Scowcroft was primarily a facilitator and coordinator, with little policy influence.

24. U.S. Congress, Senate, Committee on Foreign Relations, *Hearings on the National Security Adviser: Role and Accountability,* 96th Cong., 2nd sess., 1980, p. 30.

25. Presidential Directive/NSC-2, quoted in ibid., p. 81.

26. See the discussion of Carter's system in Alexander L. George, *Presidential Decision Making in Foreign Policy: The Effective Use of Information and Advice* (Boulder, CO: Westview Press, 1980), pp. 159–62.

27. Under Reagan, the three principal committees were the Senior Interagency Group—Foreign Policy (SIG-FP); the Senior Interagency Group—Defense Policy (SIG-DP); and the Senior Interagency Group—Intelligence (SIG-I).

28. Richard Neustadt wrote "But as Carter's alleged need to master every subject once gave detail a bad name, Reagan . . . has perhaps restored its reputation." Richard E.

Neustadt, *Presidential Power and Modern Presidents: The Politics of Leadership from Roosevelt to Reagan* (New York: The Free Press, 1990), pp. 290–91.

29. Alexander M. Haig, Jr., *Caveat: Realism, Reagan, and Foreign Policy* (New York: Macmillan, 1984), p. 85.

30. *Report of the President's Special Review Board* (Washington, DC: USGPO, February 26, 1987), p. IV-1.

31. After he became ANSA in 1987, Frank Carlucci acted to supersede the largely nonfunctioning interagency system. He created the Policy Review Group, chaired by his deputy, to act as the final review body for studies and issues moving up the chain. It was quite effective.

32. In a well-founded analysis, one author called this tension "perhaps the most characteristic and enduring problem in the management of national security affairs under the Reagan administration." (Carnes Load, *The Presidency and the Management of National Security* [New York: Free Press, 1988], p. 80.) Prados is very critical. He writes "Reagan allowed his administration to become paralyzed by the policies and egos of NSC principals. . . . The key became being the last to see him." Prados, *Keepers of the Keys,* p. 481.

33. Schultz, p. 274. The next quote is on p. 269.

34. Schultz, p. 524.

35. Keller and Barilleaux, *The President as World Leader,* p. 214.

36. Gelb, with Betts, *The Irony of Vietnam,* p. 239.

37. Chester L. Cooper, *The Lost Crusade: America in Vietnam* (New York: Dodd, Mead, 1970), pp. 373–74.

38. George P. Schultz, *Turmoil and Triumph: My Years as Secretary of State* (New York: Scribner's, 1993). See pp. 43–114.

39. See the discussion of developments leading to a December 1979 "dual track" decision in the Carter administration in Robert E. Hunter, *Presidential Control of Foreign Policy: Management or Mishap?* (Washington, DC: Praeger, with CSIS, 1982), pp. 47–48.

40. See Charles F. Hermann, "New Foreign Policy Problems and Old Bureaucratic Organizations," in Charles W. Kegley, Jr., and Eugene R. Wittkopf, eds., *The Domestic Sources of American Foreign Policy: Insights and Evidence* (New York: St. Martin's Press, 1988), p. 257.

41. Clifford, *Counsel to the President,* pp. 3–25.

42. Clifford, p. 13. This is corroborated in David McCulloch, *Truman* (New York: Simon & Schuster, 1992), p. 616.

43. A wise president with talented and experienced advisors will encourage them not to confine their advice to their areas of specialization. Otherwise he may too narrowly restrict the range of useful opinion. We will see this later in our discussion of the Vietnam War. Truman may have been guilty of this in Korea. See George, *Presidential Decision Making in Foreign Policy,* p. 123.

44. Clearly the cardinal principle of third-party influences is very important here.

45. Woodward, *The Commanders.* See especially pp. 225, 238, 249, 251–52, 259–60,

275, 285, 298–99, 319–20, 333–34, 353–54, 361. Also, while one may question the accuracy of some of the details in his account, clearly he has captured the thrust.

46. The interagency advisory and coordination process was very active in this period. The NSC Deputies Committee, for example, met regularly and in some periods almost continuously.

8

The Public Context

American foreign policy to a considerable extent is formulated in a public context. As with any democratic government, in principle the United States government exists to serve the people. Therefore, presumably at least, the views of those people will have some influence on the choices made by policymakers. The mass media will affect public views in a variety of ways, and perhaps policymaker perceptions as well. And in the American system, large and small "interest" groups, too, will seek to influence decisions and policies on specific issues.

In assessing the nature of the public context and its role and impact, we proceed as follows. First, we examine public opinion's major characteristics, looking especially at how those characteristics affect the impact of opinion. Second, we examine the mass media and how they affect public opinion. Third, since the media are so often critical of policy, we examine the question of policymaker-media tension. Fourth, we bring our conclusions to bear on the relationship between public opinion and the policymaker, both in the Executive Branch and in the Congress. Fifth, we turn to an assessment of the role of interest groups. Finally, we analyze special cases in which the influence of interest groups is often said to be an exception to the usual rule.

Characteristics of Public Opinion

What are the major characteristics of public opinion in the area of foreign policy? The first and most obvious characteristic is that most of the public has very little knowledge about most foreign policy matters. Although Loch Johnson's comment that "the American people remain in a state of blissful ignorance about most aspects of foreign affairs"[1] may be a bit too strong, the lack of understanding of even the most basic facts at times is rather astounding. A 1964 Gallup poll showed that less than 60 percent of the population knew that the United States was a member of NATO. Only 38 percent knew the Soviet Union was not a member, and 28 percent had never even heard of the organization.[2] In 1978, with attention presumably focused on the oil situation because of events in Iran, only 60 percent of the American people thought the United States really had to import oil, at a time when almost half the nation's oil needs had to be met by imports.[3] Even these figures exaggerate the degree of knowledge. Of the 60 percent who knew that some oil had to be imported, only about one third had even the roughest approximation of the percentage of consumption being met by imports.[4] In 1979 only 23 percent of the public knew which countries were involved in the SALT talks.[5] In 1983, 45 percent thought the United States was supporting the Sandinistas in Nicaragua, not the Contras.[6] And so on.

The second characteristic is that the public's interest in foreign policy varies enormously. Much of the time it really does not care very much. After leaving office Dean Acheson wrote:

> In the State Department we used to discuss how much time that mythical "average American citizen" put in each day listening, reading, and arguing about the world outside his own country. Assuming . . . a fair education, a family, and a job in or out of the house, it seemed to us that ten minutes a day would be a high average.[7]

The fact that people often are not very concerned with foreign policy is understandable. They are, after all, involved with the practical concerns of everyday living. Whether Johnny makes the basketball team or the plumber came to fix the sink are their immediate concerns. Indeed, if people are interested in any kind of public affairs matter, their concern usually is with issues that have a direct impact upon them, such as drugs, unemployment, crime, and so on. Yet, this having been said, two caveats are in order. First, although often people are relatively uninterested in foreign affairs, there *are* times when foreign policy

Box 8.1	**Getting Involved in El Salvador?**	
America should stay out		29%
America should assist the government		27%
No opinion		6%
Uninformed		38%

Source: George H. Gallup, *The Gallup Poll: Public Opinion 1981* (Wilmington, Delaware: Scholarly Resources, 1982), p. 69.

concerns take first place, the Vietnam and Persian Gulf wars being cases in point. Too, when affected directly, such as by having a child in military service or standing in gas lines created by an Arab oil boycott, citizen interest perks up. Second—and somewhat paradoxically—even when their interest in particular situations or problems is low, people still may believe that international issues are very important. Despite much comment and conventional wisdom to the contrary, people do not always believe domestic issues are more important than foreign policy matters.[8]

A third characteristic is that, in terms of what the government actually should do, much of the time the public does not hold a single, coherent view. No clear signal can be transmitted from the public to policymakers because there is no consistent and clear signal to transmit. By 1967 and early 1968 the majority of the American people saw the initial decision to enter the Vietnam War as an error, but opinion was strongly divided on what to do next. A significant minority wanted a total withdrawal, but a majority wanted to end the war by escalating, if necessary even by invading North Vietnam.[9] In 1981 public views on what to do in El Salvador were similarly fragmented (see Box 8.1 for a sample of public opinion on this topic). What was "the public will"?

A fourth characteristic is that on many issues the public tends to be relatively acquiescent and at least mildly supportive of the president. Rather than importantly influencing presidential policy decisions, in most situations the public looks to the president for guidance and (usually) supports the actions he undertakes.[10] With only rare exceptions, the public is more a follower than a leader. On several occasions the public even has done a complete reversal, approving policies undertaken that, before their initiation, it had opposed. In 1968 only 40 percent favored reducing the bombing of North Vietnam, but when that reduction occurred, 64 percent were in favor.[11] Before the Bush administration's 1989 invasion of Panama only 32 percent favored using force, but after the invasion occurred 82.5 percent gave it their approval.[12]

The fact that public opinion tends to be supportive of the government is of great importance in crises, and often at such times that support is pronounced. In what is sometimes called the "rally-round-the-flag" effect, if the public perceives an important threat to the United States, the public generally will close ranks behind the president. But this response is not universally true. If a crisis is long lasting, and if the objective is perceived to be out of proportion to the time, resources, and effort required, support may decrease. Indeed, over time public support may disappear altogether and even turn into opposition. In the early phases of both the Korean and Vietnam wars the president received strong support, but as it became clear that the wars were not being "won," the mood changed drastically. This pattern means that in the short run presidents normally have considerable flexibility and can assume that public support usually will be forthcoming. But if a crisis is not resolved quickly, or if the public cannot be convinced that at the least considerable progress is being made, there may be a withdrawal of support and growing antagonism. This puts great pressure on the president to act quickly, to try to resolve issues decisively, and to give an appearance of success. World War II was an exception to this rule, in that support was maintained over a long period of time, but there it was entirely apparent that national survival was at stake. If the threat is not so clear and present, the public's patience wears thin.

One interesting aspect of all this is that usually when the president takes strong action, he tends to be supported almost without regard to circumstances; it is taking action that matters. It is obvious why President Kennedy's actions were strongly supported in the Cuban missile crisis and President Bush's after the deployment of troops to Saudi Arabia. What is less evident, though, is why President Kennedy's popularity rose enormously after the Bay of Pigs debacle or Carter's after the failed hostage rescue effort in 1980. Or why, with dissent being so strong and the troop withdrawal well underway, nearly 60 percent of those polled supported Nixon's 1972 mining of Haiphong Harbor. The answer seems to be that strong actions are almost automatically supported. Apparently there is some truth to the saying that Americans believe one should "do something, even if it is wrong." This reaction explains why, despite considerable skepticism over the nature of the objectives and whether the action was really necessary, the public still strongly supported President Reagan's October, 1983, decision to invade Grenada.

Though the foregoing is generally true, two qualifications must be kept in mind. The first, mentioned earlier, is that even when strong action is taken, over extended periods of time public support may decline unless certain conditions are met. Second, as Bruce Jentleson argues quite persuasively, since the decline of the Cold War consensus and the diminution of the anti-military Vietnam syndrome, public support varies more directly according to the perception of the policy objective being sought. The "American public is much more likely to support the use of force for the restraint rather than the remaking of other governments."[13]

The fifth characteristic of public opinion is that opinions about particular issues and policy choices occasionally can be quite volatile. In 1976, still reeling from the Watergate scandals and the war in Vietnam, the public was anxious for detente. It was unhappy about the level of defense spending, and determined to avoid "more Vietnams." By the end of 1980, though, an enormous turnabout had occurred. Its pride wounded as American strength and honor were apparently challenged by the Soviet invasion of Afghanistan, the Iranian seizure of U.S. hostages, and the Soviet military buildup, the public shifted to an aggressive mood. Now it supported both a major *increase* in defense spending and a "tougher" stance in dealing with the Russians. It also showed much more willingness to use military force as well as to have the CIA engage in covert operations. This shift, in only four years.

It is important not to jump to the conclusion that this volatility is intrinsically either negative or unwarranted. Given the changing global environment and the ineffectiveness of so many of Carter's policies (see Chapter 12), there were good reasons for public views to change. Indeed, perhaps what the rapid shift demonstrates best is that the American people learn quickly, adjusting their views according to changed circumstances. Moreover, as we shall see, this volatility is the exception, not the rule. Public opinion about foreign policy more generally is rather stable, unless something disturbs it.

The Mass Media

The mass media are so prominent today that one almost automatically assumes they affect the public's attitudes and beliefs very significantly. Since the press and national television networks are the major vehicles for transmitting current information to the public, it seems almost axiomatic that they will have a powerful influence on public opinion, shaping American ideas of the nature of the problems faced in fundamental ways. But do they? The answer depends in part on whether we are talking about the kind of very fundamental attitudes, beliefs, and perceptions we examined in Chapter 3, or the public's views of a particular immediate issue such as the 1968 Tet offensive in the Vietnam war.

Despite some misconceptions to the contrary, the media have not much altered the kinds of fundamental attitudes and beliefs Americans have derived from their unique national experience. Deeply ingrained attitudes and images produced by fundamental historical and societal factors are very resistant to change. Information tends to be selectively interpreted, incorporated, or rejected in a manner consistent with one's preconceptions; existing attitudes tend to be reinforced, whether they be negative or positive, and it takes more than media activities to change them. Indeed, a prime characteristic of American public opinion in addition to those already mentioned is that fundamental American beliefs, although sometimes volatile on specific issues, over time are remarkably stable. Not that all Americans agree with each other, of course,[14] but the fundamental beliefs of individuals change little. Too, once they have made up their minds, the American people are stubbornly resistant to pressures to change.[15]

But while the media do not *directly* determine *fundamental* images, attitudes, and beliefs, they unquestionably can be important in influencing opinion on particular issues (especially network television.)[16] They also are important in determining what the public will think about, in setting the agenda for public consideration. Not that the media can make something an issue if the people have no (even latent) interest, but they can certainly stimulate and intensify public interest if some degree of concern already exists. Clearly, by focusing the public's attention and raising its level of interest, the media intensified public disenchantment with American policy in Vietnam. The "nuclear freeze" issue of the early 1980s became a major issue in large part *because* of media attention.

Perhaps equally significant is the fact that if issues are not presented, the public may not appreciate their importance (or even know of their existence). In March 1977, President Carter held a news conference at which he proposed a withdrawal of American forces from South Korea, a compromise on the Arab-Israeli dispute, and some compromises on arms control. The media were preoccupied with the seizure of three buildings and holding of 134 hostages in Washington, D.C., by the Black Muslims, however, and gave the President's important statements little coverage.[17]

Policymaker-Media Tensions

Senior policymakers almost inevitably complain, sooner or later, that the media treat them unfairly. So we must ask: to what extent do print and electronic journalism present coherent, accurate, and impartial accounts? To what degree do they inform the public in a fashion that permits the formation of rational, evidence-supported opinions? And what is the media's role vis-à-vis the President and other senior policymakers?

There is no doubt that senior officials pay a great deal of attention to the media and consider them one of the fastest sources of information on many important events around the world. Watching CNN today is almost SOP. In *The Commanders* Bob Woodward portrays a 1988 conversation that took place between General Colin Powell and Alexander "Sasha" Bessmertnykh, immediately after Powell received his fourth star, in this way:

> "Sasha, that's very kind of you, I'm surprised you learned of it so quickly. Yuri . . . must be reporting more quickly than he usually does, or maybe you're using the new fax machine you guys put in."
>
> "No," Bessmertnykh said, laughing. "I saw it on CNN." "Come on," Powell replied, "you only had CNN during the [Moscow] summit in May. . . . You had it in all hotels."
>
> "No we have it there permanently. I have it in my office and I watch it all day long."
>
> Powell said he did too, joking that the two countries could save a lot on communications just by relying on CNN.[18]

Senior policymakers may watch CNN, but that does not mean they like what they see there or on the other channels. Nor do they always approve of how various stories are presented by the press. The truth is that most presidents at one point or another have had tense, if not adversarial, relations with the media. President Carter was "disgusted" by the "negative" treatment his efforts to bring about the Egyptian-Israeli Peace Treaty received.[19] President Truman once wrote a reporter, "I wish you'd do a little soul searching and see if at *great* intervals, the President may be right."[20] President Kennedy was so angry over his treatment by the *New York Herald Tribune* that he ordered the White House subscription canceled, and during the Vietnam War President Johnson tried (unsuccessfully) to persuade the *New York Times* to transfer David Halberstam to another assignment. Further examples are legion.

To some extent, tension between the president and the media is inherent in the nature of things. The media, in addition to reporting what the government is doing, act as a watchdog and check up on those in power. Investigative reporting leads to questions, which often result in criticisms. Those on the receiving end, though, may feel that *all* the media does is criticize.

There is another side to this story. A considerable amount of tension between the media and the government is balanced by a good deal of cooperation. During wartime the press has usually tried to accommodate government requests that it refrain from releasing sensitive information and that it not write certain stories deemed potentially harmful to national security. This is, naturally, a very controversial area. First Amendment freedoms of speech and press are enormously important and yet, in some situations, policy needs to be formulated and implemented in secret. Balancing these factors is difficult anytime, especially so in war. In the Vietnam War, ground rules for reporters were established by the military, but as press criticism mounted the military became more and more angry. The military's decision in the Grenada operation not to permit a media presence for the first two days aroused much controversy. In the aftermath a national media pool was agreed to, and in modified form that approach was used in the Persian Gulf War. But there, too, the media felt unreasonably restrained. So this issue is far from permanently decided.[21]

Two other factors exacerbate the inherent policymaker-media tension. One is governmental efforts to "manage" the news. The president and his senior advisers, wanting to project the most favorable image they can, use a whole host of techniques. These include the careful timing of information releases, selective access to inside news for cooperative reporters, and the deliberate leak of favorable information. Often the flow of detrimental data is restricted. In the Cuban missile crisis, Kennedy instituted a "systematic control over the flow of information . . . until the crisis was over. Control, in blunt terms, meant lying. . . ."[22]

The other factor has been the development of adversarial or, as some call it, the "new" journalism.[23] Although many journalists still subscribe to the traditional concept of impartial factual reporting with personal opinion restricted to the editorial portions of the medium, the "new" journalists seek to discover "truth," not just "facts." That sometimes means that the personal views of journalists control both the content and thrust of their work. Some seem convinced that the media are the social unit best equipped to give the nation direction. In that situation, no administration, regardless of what it does, will be deemed satisfactory.

Regardless of the policymaker-media relationship, do the media provide the public with enough high-quality information to satisfy those who want a solid basis for an informed opinion?

Consider first the inherent limitations of the mass media. They are severely hindered in any effort to inform the public adequately because of quantity, access, space, and time constraints. Far too much is happening in the world for more than a small fraction to be reported, so judgments have to be made about what to include and exclude. Besides material excluded for quantity reasons, in some situations the media have no access. With few American journalists in Kampuchea (Cambodia) to report on the holocaust perpetrated by the Pol Pot regime in the mid-1970s, for a long time most Americans were simply unaware of it. Closed societies, such as China, consider nearly all information about public affairs a state secret. In such cases, when the media cannot obtain adequate access, many of the most significant developments will go unreported.

Newspapers have space limitations. Moreover, they must make a profit to survive. Decisions concerning how much and what to print must be based, in part, on the expected effect on profits. The newspaper managing editor must decide how much space to allocate to new vis-à-vis sports, the society page, amusements, and so on. Within the news category, further allocations must be made between local, state, national, and international features. Even "prestige" newspapers such as the *Washington Post* seldom give as much as 25 percent of their news coverage to international stories; most papers give much less. Foreign policy news often is but a small part of a small part.

The national and cable television networks, which are the primary sources of international information for the public, suffer from severe (although self-imposed) time constraints. Regardless of what happens on a given day, if a broadcast is only a half-hour long, it has to be compressed into twenty-two minutes or so of airtime. Because time is lost introducing and terminating stories, and the majority of hard news time is usually devoted to domestic issues, how much can be left? Perhaps half a dozen or so thirty-second to two-minute segments will focus on different international events at various points in the program, and usually that will be it. Obviously, only a tiny fraction of what has happened on a given day can be covered, and that which is can be covered only superficially.

The result is that the media provide only a partial and superficial picture, a picture that highlights stories that are exciting and dramatic. But it is more than a matter of coverage. There also are serious problems of quality. With occasional exceptions, issues seldom are presented in context or in an analytical/historical perspective. The average citizen learns next to nothing about the basic causes of events or the underlying factors at work. Television's world especially is simple and personalized; intellectual depth is almost nonexistent.

What about bias? We saw that many presidents have felt that the media treated them in a biased manner, but to some extent this perception is inevitable. Whether the evidence indicates any systematic distortion by the media, either generally or in particular cases, is not easy to answer. Although many of the leading journalists describe themselves as liberals,[24] the elite newspapers such as the

New York Times and the Washington Post generally provide reasonably accurate and balanced factual reports (although they hold differing editorial views). Local newspapers, however, are far less even in their coverage and often are far from neutral or balanced.

Studies of the electronic media have not been as extensive as for the print media. What work has been done does not demonstrate any clearly observable general bias here, either. The conclusion one must draw is that on the national level there is no demonstrated general and systematic media bias, although on the local level occasionally there may be.

Conclusions that there is a lack of a general national media bias hold up fairly well with respect to the handling of particular cases, too. There have been some significant exceptions, cases in which journalists have sought sources supporting one position while downplaying the alternatives or interpreting events according to their own views.[25] But the number of such instances that can be substantiated is small.

A more common problem is a presentation that is *unintentionally* distorted. That treatment stems either from a lack of adequate perspective on the reporter's part or from premature judgments that filter out competing views. The Tet offensive of January–March, 1968, proved to be a turning point for America's Vietnam War policy, for the psychological and symbolic effects of the North Vietnamese–Viet Cong attacks were enormous. These battles increased war-weariness among the American people and accelerated the beginning of the peace talks. The media accurately portrayed these facts. What it did *not* do, however, was give the same coverage and emphasis to the fact that, after some early military successes, the North Vietnamese–Viet Cong forces suffered substantial losses, failing to hold any of their major objectives.[26] Although the United States and South Vietnamese scored a considerable *military* victory, this received less "play" than the psychological and symbolic effects of Tet. Ultimately the psychological impact of Tet did far outweigh the military impact. In light of public opinion at the time, that may have been inevitable. But, what would the impact have been in the absence of the powerful but incomplete image conveyed by the media?

How do these comments add up? Our earlier conclusion (that most of the time, for most people, the media are not determinative of fundamental views) stands; but, as we have seen, that statement is not the whole story. The media, as the source of most current information for most Americans, to some extent have an agenda-setting function. They often also have an intensity-altering impact. Because of their nature and function, it is almost inevitable that they are perceived by presidents to be somewhat hostile unless the agenda and priorities of the president and media happen to coincide—something relatively rare. With respect to those views of the public the media do influence, because of quantity, access, time, and space constraints the media can provide only a partial and superficial picture. Reality inevitably is filtered through a somewhat distorted lens that is lacking in perspective. Deliberate and systematic bias on the national level does not exist, although in particular cases a distorted image may be presented.

Public Opinion and Policymaking

We have explored the linkages between public opinion, the mass media, and the policymaker with a specific question in mind. We want to know to what extent, and in what ways, public opinion influences the president and other senior policymakers.

The very characteristics of public opinion discussed earlier—lack of knowledge, more a follower than a leader, frequent lack of any coherent view, a tendency toward acquiescence and support—ensure that senior policymakers usually get little clear and specific guidance from the public. This is especially true of guidance for particular situations. In this sense, there is little direct linkage between public opinion and policy decisions.

It follows that most of the time policymakers have great latitude. Indeed, the room for maneuver may be so wide that decisions can run counter to the public's views. For example, although the majority of adult Americans opposed the Panama Canal Treaties, the agreements were negotiated, approved, and ratified. On the other hand, one must not carry this concept too far—Jimmy Carter was not reelected and some of Reagan's support in that election was due to voter displeasure over those treaties. As we pointed out earlier, the American public's willingness to be supportive does not extend to passivity in any and all circumstances.

And even if the public usually has little direct impact on specific policy decisions, that does not mean the policymaker can disregard public opinion. If the public is often vague about details, sometimes is uninterested, or has widely varying opinions on given issues, *it does* have general views and fundamental beliefs that policymakers will disregard at their peril. Even when knowledge and interest are low, ordinary citizens can have reasonably coherent attitudes.[27] In some situations the public's general attitudes and fundamental beliefs become very significant *by providing the boundaries for permissible action*. Behind the casual facade, the public will have notions (sometimes latent) about what policies, methods, and objectives it will tolerate or accept. These are transgressed only at considerable risk. For example, the American people in the early years after the Holocaust simply would not have permitted the American government to follow a course of (in)action that would have allowed Israel's destruction. Again, once the withdrawal from Vietnam began, a massive escalation would not have been tolerated. Similarly, during the Reagan years, the public's consistently low level of support for aid to the Contras made it clear that a massive American involvement just was not in the cards. In each of these cases, public opinion set some limits, precluded certain options, and narrowed the range of policy choice.

Sometimes policymakers are influenced by what they *anticipate* the public's reaction would be. During the 1945 Yalta Conference, President Roosevelt, Winston Churchill, and Joseph Stalin were discussing plans for the postwar occupation of Germany. Roosevelt's belief that the American public would not permit American forces to remain for more than two years after the end of hostilities seriously influenced some of his decisions.

The boundaries set by the public are not immutable, of course. Even deeply ingrained images and attitudes can be altered over time, in turn changing the policy limits. We saw earlier how the United States was doing everything it could in the mid-1930s to avoid becoming involved in Europe's conflicts. But as war clouds gathered, more and more people began to doubt the wisdom of existing policies. Gradually, as the evidence supporting the need for a policy shift accumulated, the policy limits began to change. Incrementally, in tandem, as the limits altered so did the policy, the administration at each step asking for as much as it felt possible. What eventually became a complete change in policy reflected a parallel complete change in public opinion.

Sometimes the public plays another very important role: *marking out the general direction policy should take.* This influence is the exception, of course, for all the reasons discussed earlier, but when it happens it is very important. For example, once opinion had reached a firm and vigorously displayed consensus on the necessity of withdrawing from Vietnam, the ultimate direction of American policy was fixed. Room existed for tactical variations, but the strategic course was set. We shall see in detail in Chapters 12 and 13 how the American public, angered and frustrated by events in Iran and Afghanistan in the late 1970s and early 1980s and convinced the United States was becoming "weaker" than the Soviet Union, strongly supported a "tougher" stance in dealing with the Soviets. Ronald Reagan was elected with a mandate to restore American "honor," rebuild its military, and undertake initiatives that would reverse America's "decline." As in the Vietnam example, there was considerable latitude in terms of specifics, but the general thrust was clear. In both cases the pressures the public applied were sufficiently clear to mark out a general direction. When such a movement in public concern happens, it is a very bold president who does not see his options as limited. Ultimately, in the United States, policy cannot succeed without public acceptance.

Interest Groups

Interest groups in the United States exist literally in the thousands, all sharing the goal of influencing government. There are economic groups, ethnic groups, single issue groups, religious groups, and so on, as well as major coalitions. Given the number of groups and the volume of activity, it would be easy to conclude that policy is largely a product of interest group interaction and bargaining. Individuals of a cynical mind, especially, find it easy to attribute policy in general and in particular cases to the conspiracies or machinations of "special interests." But although interest groups can play a role in the policymaking process, that role generally is far smaller than the suspicious would believe. In fact, when it comes to foreign policy decisions, interest groups are almost uniformly insignificant. A key reason is that on most issues only a few groups really care, so the vast majority simply make no effort to influence policy. For example, although business groups are concerned with foreign trade matters, human rights issues are of little concern (unless they affect economic relationships); the National Council of Churches is concerned with the plight of refugees but is not directly interested in whether tariffs should be increased on imports of footwear from Korea.

Even in the many cases in which interest groups do make a strenuous effort to exercise influence, they usually are not very successful. This is true even of groups that are popularly believed to have an enormous and nearly continuous impact. One study of United States policy in the 1967 Middle East war concluded: "Noteworthy by their unimportance during the crisis were the allegedly powerful pro-Israeli interest groups and the oil lobby."[28] (We shall return to this subject later.)

One reason many interest groups have less influence than their membership numbers imply is plain to those who think about it. Most groups, especially large groups such as the AFL-CIO or Chamber of Commerce, have members who also belong to several other groups. Overlapping memberships demonstrate that people have multiple interests and competing loyalties. As a result, their allegiance to any one group normally is qualified by their other interests. In fact, quite frequently by virtue of multiple affiliations and interests an individual "belongs on both sides" of a question. That factor can severely limit the ability of the leaders of an interest group to have its members act as a cohesive body in any direction. As a consequence, on many issues there can be no effective group position. Or, if there is one, it is so vague and unenthusiastically advocated that its practical impact is nil.

There is a second reason for the general lack of impact of interest groups. On most important issues a great many groups will be involved, advocating a number of divergent positions. Take a trade bill. Some will demand generally higher tariffs, while others will want only selective increases. A third set will advocate fewer restraints, hoping for a reciprocal diminution of restraints by other countries. A proposal in the 1973 Trade Reform Bill to reduce tariffs was supported by such varied groups as the U.S. Council of the International Chamber of Commerce, the League of Women Voters, the National Feed and Grain Association, and the Aerospace Industries Association of North America. Groups that wanted to maintain the existing structure or increase duties were equally diverse. They included the American Iron and Steel Institute; the United Rubber, Cork, Linoleum and Plastic Workers of America; the Liberty Lobby; the Nationwide Committee on Import-Export Policy; and the AFL-CIO.[29] In the 1980s when the Reagan administration's program of aid for the Contras was so controversial, the same phenomenon occurred. Groups such as Citizens for Reagan, the American Defense Lobby, the Conservative Caucus, the Eagle Forum, and the U.S. Defense Committee were in favor. But many religious groups, the

ACLU, SANE, Common Cause, and OXFAM America were against.[30] In the Contra case, as in most cases, the composition of the coalitions was also somewhat fluid; different groups altered their participation over time.[31]

These situations are typical. Counterbalancing coalitions form on almost all issues that concern interest groups. Many times, the result is that the coalitions largely balance or neutralize each other, leaving policymakers great latitude to reach their own decisions.

There is a third reason that limits the ability of interest groups to affect foreign policy. On domestic issues, interest groups frequently are in a position to provide specialized expertise and information, which is one of the main reasons they can be influential. But with foreign policy, the situation usually is quite different. The government's foreign policy apparatus generates detailed information, employing large numbers of highly trained specialists to interpret the meaning of events and assess their significance. By contrast, with some exceptions, interest groups normally are markedly inferior in such matters. They have neither the specific policy-relevant information nor the specialists to assess its meaning. Even when they do, they usually are dealing with people already overwhelmed by "expert advice," with no need or wish for more.

A fourth limitation on the power of interest groups to influence decisions on foreign policy is crucial. Where vital interests are at stake, interest groups almost never have access to senior policymakers. Occasionally this is simply a matter of time constraints. When the United States finds itself in a crisis such as at the beginning of the Korean War, decisions must be made very quickly; there is no time for groups to obtain access or to form a coherent view in a rapidly changing situation. Sometimes the lack of access is due to the need for secrecy. In the early stages of the Cuban missile crisis as in the negotiations preceding President Nixon's trip to China, interest groups were not aware of what was happening. For good and obvious reasons, President Bush did not involve interest groups when he was planning his responses to the 1990 Iraqi attack on Kuwait. The more the urgency of the crisis, the less it lends itself to giving many voices a hearing. Just as we pointed out in Chapter 7 that bureaucratic politics are largely irrelevant to most key decisions on vital security issues, interest groups, too, usually play no role.

Interest Groups: Exceptions to the Rule?

There are occasional exceptions to the rule that interest groups have much less influence on foreign policy than popularly is supposed. One "occasional exception" is when the focus is on foreign political-economic issues with a major domestic impact. Energy policy is a good example. Although policy decisions in such an area are not *controlled* by interest groups, both Congress and the President can be caught in a maelstrom of conflicting internal and external pressures that forces them to *pay attention* to interest group arguments. A second exception can occur when Congress is deeply involved and a well-organized interest group not only has an axe to grind but is determined to have an impact. If only a few members of Congress can be swayed, it may be enough. Following the Turkish invasion of Cyprus in 1974, a well-organized lobby led by the American Hellenic Institute Public Affairs Committee was crucial in convincing Congress to suspend military aid to Turkey.

Some few groups have had more influence than our overall analysis would indicate. Two of the more famous have been the Committee of One Million (the China lobby) and the Jewish lobby. The Committee of One Million, for two decades after 1949, fought vehemently against the extension of diplomatic recognition to the People's Republic of China and against its admission to the United Nations. The Committee's cause gained impetus when the strong American anti-communist consensus interlocked with a generally favorable and somewhat romanticized view of China and Chiang Kai-shek and was reinforced by popular anger because American missionaries had been expelled from China. All this more than sufficed to gain the China lobby a sympathetic hearing. In the second case, before 1948 the Jewish organizations mounted a well-organized campaign to convince American policymakers to support the creation of a Jewish state in Palestine. Later, they actively sought to maximize pro-Israeli sentiments and policies. In both situations, Jewish groups could count on initial American sympathy for the underdog. Clearly, both the Jewish lobby and the Committee of One Million drew much of their strength from a special set of circumstances.

Nonetheless, while American policy, especially following the introduction of Communist Chinese "volunteers" in the Korean War in 1950, was strongly anti-Beijing for nearly two decades, it would be hazardous to attribute this position solely to the China lobby. And while the United States supported the creation of Israel and had largely cooperative relations with that country for much of its existence, such support was not a direct result of the Jewish lobby's pressures, either. The fact that a policy was adopted which interest groups in both cases could endorse *proved nothing other than that the pressure groups found the policy congenial.* No cause-and-effect relationship is demonstrated by this simple correlation. Much more important in shaping the policy was the fact that the President, many other senior policymakers, and most of Congress, along with much of the general public, *shared* these particular policy views. The views of these interest groups fitted into the mainstream of the views held by nearly all Americans.

This final point cannot be overemphasized. When, after a number of years, policymakers began to reassess both their China and Middle East policies and undertook policy alterations for strategic reasons, their views paralleled similar changes in attitude by large segments of the public. When that happened, these same interest groups discovered they had little policy-influencing impact. The China lobby, objecting to Nixon's move toward normalization of relations with Beijing, could do nothing much about it. Similarly, during and after the 1973 Middle East war, when the United States adopted a more evenhanded stance in the Arab-Israeli dispute, the Jewish lobby proved unable to stop it. That is why

Mitchell Bard remarks: "The truth, however, is that the Israeli lobby is unable to affect major foreign policy decisions and is actually capable of influencing only a narrow range of policies that benefit Israel."[32]

Another group sometimes alleged to have influence far in excess of the norm is the "military-industrial complex" (MIC). In his farewell address of January 17, 1961, President Eisenhower warned of the acquisition of unwarranted influence by a military-industrial complex. The potential for the "disastrous use of misplaced power by this complex," he said, "exists and will persist."

With the annual defense budget in the United States exceeding $280 billion as the 1990s began, it is evident why the conglomeration of industries, bureaucratic agencies, labor unions, legislators, states, cities, and military personnel composing the military-industrial "complex" tried to influence matters in ways beneficial to their interests. Policymakers expect to be the targets of influence efforts by such groups, and frequently they are. Occasionally the pressures are considerable, and once in a while a decision is crucially altered. But this is very much the exception, despite some misconceptions to the contrary. Although the level of activity is great, usually the impact is minimal.

The primary reason for this is that the military-industrial "complex" *is not a "complex" at all; most of the time it is rent with strife and competition.* On many issues the various interest groups, corporations, and community leaders align themselves with whichever military service they believe will be most useful to them. But the services often are in competition with one another, and the addition of these factional pressures intensifies any natural interservice rivalries that already exist. As a result, with pressures offsetting pressures, senior policymakers can pick and choose. This effect is even more pronounced in other cases where fragile, fluid, issue-based coalitions struggle for advantage within and across industry, service, and politico-community lines. What actually forms is an unstable subsystem of conflicting and self-neutralizing "minicomplexes." Anyone who has witnessed the intense competition between group coalitions for a government contract to produce a new fighter airplane has quickly seen how wide of the mark the notion of *a* complex can be.

Even where substantial consensus reigns, the "complex" often loses. In the late 1970s much of the military, especially the Air Force, plus a number of industrial and politico-community groups, wanted production and deployment of the B-1 bomber. President Carter labeled the B-1 lobby "one of the most formidable ever evolved in the military-industrial community."[33] But, with the president opposing production, the B-1 was not produced. Add that a strong countercoalition of three dozen groups as diverse as the Federation of American Scientists, Clergy and Laity Concerned, and the National Taxpayers Union similarly opposed production, and you have another reason why the MIC frequently is unsuccessful. There are counterbalancing coalitions.

Although the MIC is neither universally nor automatically dominant, it *sometimes* plays an important role, especially in weapons development and procurement. The role is complicated and difficult to describe. Perhaps the best way to put it is that, instead of the MIC *influencing* policymakers, what happens is a very complex maze of interactions. Various elements of the MIC work and bargain with each other and with parts of the government from the beginning of the research process all the way through weapons production and deployment. (And even here the MIC is subject to most of the constraints discussed earlier.)

Although parts of the MIC may affect choices at various points in the process, the fundamental decisions about military strategy, force planning, procurement, and deployment are still made by the president and his senior advisers in a much broader national security context, and in these the MIC seldom plays *any* role. The MIC, although it differs somewhat in size and wealth from other groups, is not really a special case in terms of its influence on major policy issues.[34]

Interest Groups and Congress

There is one point that deserves further elaboration: the influence of interest groups on Congress. We saw in Chapter 6 that Congress is extremely fragmented. Because of this, many observers believe Congress is very susceptible to interest group pressures. Members of the House are thought to be especially vulnerable because of the nature of single-member districts and the fact that representatives have only two-year terms. Yet earlier in this chapter we said that although a few members sometimes can be swayed, most cannot, most of the time. How can we explain this? It is true that House members frequently vote as their more politically active constituents wish. But that does *not* mean they have been *influenced*. Indeed, much of the time the reason is that they *share the same attitudes and preferences of those constituents*. They are, in other words, representative. When a legislator holds the same view as the Jewish lobby and votes as it desires, it may very well be because he or she believes in the Israeli position or already has sympathy for the Israelis. Or, it may be that he or she is reflecting and representing the constituents' will.

What is the significance of Congress being so fragmented, in terms of the policy effects of interest group pressures? Take any issue working its way through the Congress, such as foreign aid for Russia. It must pass the scrutiny of several committees, ultimately for both authorization and appropriations, each of which has subcommittees that have examined specific items even before the parent committees meet. It must also fit the confines of any budget agreements that are in effect. Because of the complexity of the legislative process, it is rare for any single member of the Congress to have a great deal of influence on the outcome (even though, obviously, some legislators are more important than others). To a considerable extent, any one member has only a limited and passing voice in what is being done.

The point of this is that in order for interest groups to really be influential—since the individual legislator is such a small part of the process—a large number of legislators would have to be influenced. But as we noted earlier, normally only a few members are influenced, at most. Moreover, any success an interest group has in influencing Senator "Jones" may be offset by the views of

Senator "Smith." And success in influencing members in one house may be off-set by actions in the *other* house. Finally, of course, if it is a matter of new legislation, the conference committee must meet to reconcile the divergent bills passed by each house, removing things even further from the hurly-burly of group politics. The conference committee may even jettison an item that has survived all of the previous hurdles. Legislative action on American foreign policy issues is a very uncertain process, a process that is extremely difficult for interest groups to influence more than marginally, except in *very* exceptional cases.

Summing Up

How shall we sum up? Looking first at the main characteristics of public opinion, it is clear that most of the time the public is not very knowledgeable about foreign policy matters, and the level of interest varies enormously from case to case. Moreover, the "public will" often is filled with contradictions and tends to be inconsistent and fragmented on specific issues. As a result, most of the time public opinion cannot provide policymakers with clear and precise guidance in advance. Once in a while, though, public opinion will set boundaries for policy or mark the general direction policy should take.

Policymakers have discovered that public opinion on specific issues can be highly volatile, sometimes fluctuating greatly in a very short period of time. Usually the public supports major policy initiatives, especially in their early stages. But if positive results are not forthcoming as quickly as the public would like, that support may erode drastically. This puts pressure on policymakers to take strong action and to seek quick, clear-cut solutions.

What influence do the mass media have? Though they provide much of the public's current information, the media usually do not decisively affect the public's most fundamental views. But they still are important because they set much of the agenda that the public considers, and they may affect the intensity with which views are held. Because of inherent limitations, the mass media generally can present only a partial and rather superficial picture. They do not really inform the public sufficiently to allow people to make solidly based judgments. Still, the media can convey a general sense of things and some basic data.

Overall, it does not appear that there have been many deliberate attempts by the media to present information in a biased manner, although most presidents, sooner or later, have believed that the media were treating them unfairly. Because the media seek to act as a watchdog and check on government, and because presidents want to project the most favorable image possible, there is an inherent tension in their relationship. In recent years tensions with the media have been exacerbated even further by the development of adversarial (or the "new") journalism, in which the journalists' personal views often strongly influence both the scope and the content of their work.

Turning to interest groups, it is evident that "special interests" occasionally have an important influence on policymakers, but this occurs much less often in foreign policy than is sometimes assumed. The general rule is that interest groups do *not* significantly influence foreign policy choices, at least on the most important questions (especially during crises). Not that they are completely irrelevant. On certain political-economic issues with a major domestic impact such as trade legislation, interest groups may be quite important, and in rare cases they may even play a major role. And even when they do not importantly influence policy choice, they can raise the salience of certain problems, compel policymakers to pay attention to certain aspects of issues, provide information to the public and raise its interest level, and on occasion increase the domestic political stakes in policy choices. But the general rule still holds: On matters of fundamental importance, interest groups rarely have much influence. On these kinds of issues one is hard put to find examples of groups influencing senior policymakers to the extent that they adopted a policy they would not have adopted for other reasons, anyway. This is true even of "special interests" like the military-industrial complex and the Jewish lobby, which so often are alleged to be exceptions to the rule.

Notes

1. Loch K. Johnson, *America as a World Power: Foreign Policy in a Constitutional Framework* (New York: McGraw-Hill, 1991), p. 161. David Gergen writes that the American people "have an abysmal understanding of the world," and show "little appetite for increasing their understanding." David R. Gergen, "Diplomacy in a Television Age," in Simon Serfaty, ed., *The Media and Foreign Policy* (New York: St. Martin's Press, 1990), p. 52.

2. Lloyd Free and Hadley Cantril, *The Political Beliefs of Americans* (New York: Simon & Schuster, 1968), p. 60.

3. George H. Gallup, *The Gallup Poll: Public Opinion 1978* (Wilmington, DE: Scholarly Resources, 1979), p. 138.

4. Gallup, p. 129.

5. Robert Erikson, Norman Luttbeg, and Kent L. Tedin, *American Public Opinion,* 2d ed. (New York: John Wiley, 1980), p. 19.

6. Richard Sobel, "The Polls—A Report: Public Opinion about United States Intervention in El Salvador and Nicaragua," *Public Opinion Quarterly* (Spring 1989), p. 120.

7. Acheson, *Present at the Creation*, p. 489.

8. For the relative importance of foreign and domestic issues in 1982, 1986, and 1990, see John E. Rielly, ed., *American Public Opinion and U.S. Foreign Policy 1991* (Chicago, IL: The Chicago Council on Foreign Relations, 1991), p. 10.

9. Gelb, with Betts, *The Irony of Vietnam*, p. 172.

10. See the useful discussion in John Spanier and Erik M. Uslaner, *American Foreign*

Policy Making and the Democratic Dilemmas, 4th ed. (New York: Holt, Rinehart, and Winston, 1985), pp. 156–62.

11. Thomas L. Brewer, *American Foreign Policy* (Englewood Cliffs, NJ: Prentice-Hall, 1980), p. 80.

12. Bruce W. Jentleson, "The Pretty Prudent Public: Post-Vietnam American Opinion on the Use of Military Force," *International Studies Quarterly* (March, 1992), p. 55. Bruce Russett provides a discussion of the public's frequent willingness to accept *any* of several alternative policies and its willingness to change views if the president changes course, in "Doves, Hawks, and U.S. Public Opinion," *Political Science Quarterly,* pp. 515–38.

13. Jentleson, p. 50.

14. Eugene Wittkopf divides the public into four basic segments: internationalists, isolationists, accommodationists, and hard-liners. The percentage of the population in each has remained quite stable in recent years. See Eugene R. Wittkopf, *Faces of Internationalism: Public Opinion and American Foreign Policy* (Durham, NC: Duke University Press, 1990). Also see the discussion in Donald L. Jordan and Benjamin I. Page, "Shaping Foreign Policy Opinions: The Role of TV News," *Journal of Conflict Resolution* (June, 1992), pp. 227–41.

15. Even from the president. Despite Reagan's enormous efforts to persuade people to support aid to the Contras, the percentage who supported his position in 1988 was about the same as that which did in 1984.

16. See Jordan and Page, especially p. 237.

17. See James Reston, *New York Times* (March 11, 1977), p. A27.

18. Woodward, *The Commanders,* p. 53. For a discussion of the enormous global reach of the U.S. media and its impact, see Patrick O'Heffernan, *Mass Media and American Foreign Policy: Insider Perspectives on Global Journalism and the Foreign Policy Process* (Norwood, NJ: Ablex Publishing Corporation, 1991), ch. 1.

19. Carter, *Keeping Faith,* p. 426.

20. Quoted in Roger Hilsman, *To Govern America* (New York: Harper & Row, 1979), p. 307. Some argue that because of journalists' natural desire to have the United States succeed, when policy appears to be failing, critical analysis is both understandable and desirable. Indeed, "Flagging ineffective or costly foreign policy is patriotic." See Nicholas O. Berry, *Foreign Policy and the Press: An Analysis of The New York Times Coverage of U.S. Foreign Policy* (Westport, CT: Greenwood Press, 1990), pp. 141–42.

21. After six months of talks, the media and the military agreed on nine principles for proposed coverage of battlefield operations, although they continued to disagree on the issue of prior review. See Debra Gersh, "War Coverage Guidelines," *Editor and Publisher* (March 21, 1992), pp. 18, 24.

22. John Tebbel and Sarah Miles Watts, *The Press and the Presidency: From George Washington to Ronald Reagan* (New York: Oxford University Press, 1985), p. 481.

23. William Dorman pooh-poohs this idea, arguing that what developed in the post–World War II period was a "journalism of deference to the national-security state." See William A. Dorman, "Playing the Government's Game: The Mass Media and American Foreign Policy," in Kegley and Wittkopf, eds., *Domestic Sources of American Foreign Policy,* pp. 79–86. For the view that adversarial or "attack" journalism is very signifi-

cant, see Larry J. Sabato, *Feeding Frenzy: How Attack Journalism Has Transformed American Politics* (New York: The Free Press, 1991). Jim Lederman points out that the "relationship between media and politics is a dynamic one." In its coverage of the Palestinian *intifada*, the press not only covered news but created news. Still, Lederman believes, the press will have to have strategies of its own "if it is not to be carried along by a rush of events, many of which will be staged or contrived, each time a new crisis breaks." Jim Lederman, *Battle Lines: The American Media and the Intifada* (New York: Henry Holt, 1992), pp. 311, 312.

24. See Sabato, Chapter 3.

25. This appears to have been the case in the Vietnam War, with respect to the 1972 Christmas bombing of Hanoi. See Martin F. Herz, with Leslie Rider, *The Prestige Press and the Christmas Bombing, 1972* (Washington, DC: Ethics and Public Policy Center, 1980). There is no question that media people meet and discuss what issues they think are worth investigating. One of the authors sat at lunch at a table of well-known editors, who discussed the coming media probe of the U.S. intelligence agencies—which broke into print six months later. On another occasion the military editor of one of the big weekly magazines told how, at their weekly lunch, they discussed how they felt about public personalities. At the beginning of the Reagan administration, they said they printed without comment what Haig said (even if it raised problems with what he had previously said), but they always reminded Weinberger if he contradicted himself. *Haig they disliked.* For the view that the media are very biased, see Martin A. Lee and Norman Solomon, *Unreliable Sources: A Guide to Detecting Bias in News Media* (New York: Carol Publishing, 1990).

26. See the massive, well-documented work by Peter Braestrup, *Big Story: How the American Press and Television Reported and Interpreted the Crisis of Tet—1968 in Vietnam and Washington* (Boulder, CO: Westview Press, 1977). Berry holds quite a different view, arguing that Braestrup "misses the overall policy implications of Tet," p. 145. It is conceivable that the communists were not especially interested in holding their "gains," content instead with the propaganda impact.

27. See McCormick, *American Foreign Policy and Process,* pp. 495–98.

28. William B. Quandt, *Decade of Decisions: American Policy Toward the Arab-Israeli Conflict, 1967–1976* (Berkeley, CA: University of California Press, 1977), p. 70.

29. David H. Blake and Robert S. Walters, *The Politics of Global Economic Relations,* 3rd ed. (Englewood Cliffs, NJ: Prentice-Hall, 1987), p. 219.

30. McCormick, *American Foreign Policy and Process,* p. 459.

31. For a provocative analysis of this phenomenon in the rise of the nuclear weapons peace movement, see Daniel Wirls, *Buildup: The Politics of Defense in the Reagan Era* (Ithaca, NY: Cornell University Press, 1992), Ch. 3.

32. Mitchell Bard, "The Influence of Ethnic Interest Groups on American Middle East Policy," in Kegley and Wittkopf, eds., *Domestic Sources of American Foreign Policy,* p. 58.

33. Carter, *Keeping Faith,* p. 81.

34. This is our judgment of course. It is not universally shared. For a provocative explanation of a major cause of the great defense expenditures in the Reagan years, see Gordon Adams, "The Iron Triangle: Inside the Defense Policy Process," in Kegley and Wittkopf, eds. *Domestic Sources of American Foreign Policy,* pp. 70–78.

Part IV

Cold War Problems

Part Four focuses on the "Cold War" period in American foreign policy, which began shortly after World War II and lasted through the 1980s, approximately, 1945–90. During that almost half century the *primary* focus of American policy was on the Soviet Union and the Communist bloc.

In this period (as the subheads in the following chapters will show) U.S. policy addressed *four major problems:*

Problem I: Provide worldwide deterrence against Soviet pressures or threats, with special emphasis on Europe;

Problem II: Ensure a minimum stability in areas of great strategic and/or economic interest, especially the Middle East;

Problem III: Coordinate defense needs with foreign policy and cap a spiralling arms race through arms control;

Problem IV: Encourage stability in the international economic system and promote world trade.

More minor concerns also existed, although generally overshadowed by the Cold War issues: strengthening the United Nations, improving the world environment ecologically, advancing respect for the rule of law, and exploring space.

Every American president from Truman through Bush addressed these four problems, although unequally from one administration to another. A dramatist would see these forty-five years as a play with three acts. In Act I, Americans reluctantly but then vigorously take on the role of deterring what is seen as Moscow-led Communist bloc subversion and aggression. Act I ends in the despair of a failing Vietnam venture. Act II opens with efforts to disengage from Vietnam but soon passes to an emphasis on detaching China—a highly significant change because it abandons the idea that the Communists are a monolithic bloc. Act III sees the United States raising the stakes to match the Soviets in a dangerous game of armament escalation, followed by the Soviets deciding that the game is not worth the price.

9

The Cold War
and the Korean War

For almost a half century, from shortly after World War II to the administration of President Bush, one problem preoccupied U.S. foreign policy-makers above all others: the Soviet Union and the military and security threat it appeared to represent to American and allied interests. In a complex world, this concern was naturally not the only focus of U.S. policy, but many of the other problems and issues seemed or were closely tied to the Soviet one. Moreover, policy alternatives on almost *any* problem were weighed in the light of possible Soviet actions. In any other bilateral policy action of the United States, the Soviet Union's shadow hovered over it as a perennial third-party influence. Thus the Middle East was not seen as a problem simply centering on Arab-Israeli relations or on the region's importance as a major source of needed oil. Everything that happened there also had overtones for U.S.-Soviet relations. Another problem which consumed much U.S. attention throughout these years, arms control, was even more directly tied to those relations. Even such issues as foreign aid and the U.S. approach to the United Nations or international law or ecological and space and environmental questions were not free of Cold War concerns. From this perspective, the ending of the Cold War with the breakup of the old Soviet Union, while it did not (and should not) eliminate military and security concerns from U.S. policy, did allow a significant change in the thrust of much of the previous policy, as we shall see in Part Five, when the contemporary scene is examined.

How and Why the Cold War Began

Historians in particular and scholars in general still argue over exactly how the Cold War began. For present purposes it is enough to note two important reasons. First is that, in a system dominated by power units called nation-states, with each necessarily being wary of the possible threat from others, balance of power effects are always present. The defeat of Hitler's Germany "automatically" enhanced the power of the Soviet Union, especially since China was in disarray and the Japanese had also been disarmed. Even apart from ideology, friction between two states significantly powerful enough militarily to be commonly called "superpowers," was to be anticipated. What, however, multiplied the effect of that friction significantly was the heavily ideological orientation of both of these superpowers. That was the second reason why the Cold War became so intense and lasted so long.

Earlier we explained the historical and sociological reasons why, in the United States, ideology is woven into the very fabric of American attitudes. Although Woodrow Wilson ultimately failed in his efforts to reform the international system, and whether his solution to international problems was realistic or not, he expressed very well an American approach to such problems, an approach squarely based on abstract principle. It was therefore natural that Americans would tend to take Soviet communism at worst-case face value.

That Americans soon came to see the Soviets as a threat to their security, a condition that endured for decades, is a fact. But the reverse was also true. Communism came to power in the Soviet Union through bloodshed, through a revolution finally spawned by a devastating and lost World War I. It endured through a prolonged civil war and Western hostility. No nation lost more territory at the end of World War I than the Soviet Union. If Soviet behavior before World War II had shown a clearly hostile face toward capitalist society, it was a stance that was fully reciprocated. But Lenin, the first ruler of the new Soviet state, had made it abundantly clear that Communists were in a "state of partial war" with every capitalist nation, that Communists intended to exploit divisions in capitalist societies through propaganda and subversion.[1]

Russia's Communist ideology reinforced xenophobic tendencies cultivated by Russia's historical experience as a nation. As the cardinal principle of past-figure linkages tells us, events do not simply "occur" and vanish like the sands of the desert swept by a wind. Their legacy is to produce attitudes that are then applied to the future. To the Russian people, their recurrent and prolonged suffering and the long series of invasions and wars they encountered justified an intense suspicion of the outside world. Even Russia's expansion to continental dimensions from the sixteenth century onward came primarily as a response to exterior threats. Russia traces its very roots to the incursions of the Vikings. When the Mongols came, they swept over much of Russia, almost subjugating it. Both in 1382 and 1571, the Tartars sacked and burned Moscow. In the early 1700s, Charles XII of Sweden mounted a serious and prolonged invasion. The French came under Napoleon, the Germans in World War I, the Poles right after that, and again the Germans in World War II. This was a much fought-over country, with few natural barriers to discourage invasion and with a perhaps justifiable inclination to distrust foreigners. Communism took up where national experience had left off.

Under Stalin, Lenin's successor in 1924, relations with the capitalist West for years were no better, although the rise of Hitler and the obvious threat of Germany to the Soviets finally induced the Soviets to examine the possibility of closer (although temporary) relations with the capitalists. That new line of policy resulted in the establishment of diplomatic relations with the United States under Franklin Roosevelt, followed by the Soviet Union's admission to the League of Nations on September 18, 1934. But the Soviet Union was also the first nation to be actually expelled from the League—for invading Finland. And when the Soviets decided that the failure of the British and French to defend Czechoslovakia in 1938 meant that the Western nations were hoping to embroil Germany and the Soviets in a war that would bleed them both to weakness, the Soviets turned around in 1939 and agreed to the infamous Nazi-Soviet Pact. War then became a matter of days.

Despite these past events, the legacy of U.S.-Soviet wartime cooperation against Hitler initially produced an American postwar attitude of goodwill toward the Soviet Union. Roosevelt in particular had cherished a role in the new world order for the Soviets as one of the "Four Policemen," who would guarantee peace (along with the United States, Britain, and China). But even before the war had ended, signs of increasing discord appeared. The Soviets resented the abrupt termination of Lend-Lease under President Truman. But the main focus of an emerging quarrel was Germany.

With the Soviets no longer fearing their defeated German and Japanese neighbors, and their conviction on ideological grounds that more than temporary cooperation with capitalists was impossible, Stalin began to act in what to an increasing number of Americans seemed a very highhanded fashion. What especially had a negative effect on American attitudes was the discovery that Soviet agreements to foster "democracy" in Poland and the Balkans meant to the Soviets installing puppet Communist regimes. That, in American eyes, was a cynical and deliberate perversion.

Thus the stage was set for serious disagreements, waiting only for the fuse to be lit. What set it off initially was the threatened loss of Greece and Turkey to

Communist pressures. And once begun, the Cold War accelerated drastically in an all-out contest for influence in Germany.

Containment Supplies a Concept for a Cold War

The change in the American public's view of the Soviet Union from a wartime ally of the United States against Hitler, to a threat, did not come overnight or without debate. It was to form the principal issue in the election of 1948, during a time when the Soviet challenge to force the United States out of Berlin was in full swing. But even during World War II, American military leaders and diplomats had found the Soviet attitude puzzling. It did not seem to square with Roosevelt's easy optimism. By 1947, America's leadership saw evidence accumulating that instead of cordial cooperation the Soviets intended a hostile competition. As the Soviet intention to dominate as much as possible of Europe became ever more obvious, their attitude had two major effects. One was to cause Washington to search for a governing principle or guideline formula that would make sense of what they were experiencing. The other major effect was to spark a new great debate in the United States over whose fault it was that relations were deteriorating.

A governing principle or guideline was soon to be furnished. George F. Kennan, a philosophically-inclined senior foreign service officer in Moscow, sent a detailed analysis of the Soviets to Washington in 1946.[2] This "long telegram" both "explained" Soviet behavior and recommended a specific response. Kennan advocated a policy of patience and firmness to *contain* the Soviets. Secretary of Defense James Forrestal, seizing upon Kennan's argument, gave it wide circulation in senior governmental circles. Most reacted that Kennan had put his finger on it. Kennan was soon brought back to the State Department's policy councils. Then, in July 1947, through an article in *Foreign Affairs* (under the pseudonym, "X"), Kennan went public, arguing that "the main element of any United States policy toward the Soviet Union must be that of a long-term, patient but firm and vigilant containment of Russian expansive tendencies."[3] America needed to respond to Soviet pressures "by the adroit and vigilant application of counter-force at a series of constantly shifting geographical and political points, corresponding to the shifts and maneuvers of Soviet policy. . . ."[4] That policy "would promote tendencies which must eventually find their outlet in either the break-up or the gradual mellowing of Soviet power. For no mystical, messianic movement . . . can face frustration indefinitely. . . ."

Kennan's containment argument was to be central to the new policy that President Truman would announce in 1947, the Truman Doctrine. And that doctrine, and its implications, would be the central point of the debate which would accompany the election of 1948.

American Opinion Hardens

Harry Truman had become president in 1945 simply because he was vice president when Roosevelt died. At the time, the "haberdasher from Missouri," as the press often unflatteringly called him, had no established reputation with the American people. (Compared to FDR's public opinion approval rating of 66 percent when he died, Truman in office averaged 41 percent approval and ended with only 31 percent.)

An ardent reader of history, Truman had no personal experience with foreign affairs when he went to the Potsdam Conference and met Stalin. Kept out of highly secret, compartmentalized developments like the "Manhattan Project," which produced the atomic bomb, an unprepared Truman was suddenly faced with momentous decisions like whether to use it or not, and if so, how—as a demonstration or on a target.[5]

In particular, Truman had no set views about the Soviets when he took over the Oval Office. He had sat on the platform when visiting dignitary Winston Churchill gave his hard-line speech in 1946 at Fulton, Missouri, the speech in which Churchill characterized the Soviet arbitrary actions in Eastern Europe as bringing down an "Iron Curtain." But Truman himself, as Clark Clifford, his right hand counselor in these years, tells us, "was not ready to proclaim the end of the era of wartime collaboration with the Soviets. He knew the American public was not ready to hear its President deliver the same bleak message that Churchill had made at Fulton," that a prolonged struggle was now inevitable. At a staff meeting on July 12, 1946, though, Clifford records an increasingly frustrated Truman remarking that "The Russians are trying to chisel away a little here, a little there."[6]

But other prominent Americans thought that the source of the multiplying frictions lay in American inflexibility in responding to the needs and interests of the Soviet Union. Chief among these was a cabinet holdover from Roosevelt's time, a man then of influence, Henry Wallace. In a letter to Truman on July 23, 1946, he asked: "How would it look to us if Russia had the atomic bomb and we did not, if Russia had 10,000-mile bombers and air bases within a thousand miles of our coast lines and we did not?"[7] Wallace was arguing that the Soviets were merely reacting to provocations. But to Wallace's left-wing views, the right-wing replied by quoting long-dead Lenin that "the existence of the Soviet Republic side by side with imperialistic States for a long time is unthinkable. One or the other must triumph in the end." And that would come in "a series of frightful collisions. . . ." That, the right-wing said, was ample proof that the Soviets were incurably aggressive.

When Truman refused to agree with his views, Wallace took the issue to the American public in the election of 1948, heading an independent ticket of Progressives. After Truman won that election in the face of predictions of a Republican (Dewey) triumph, American opinion hardened, swinging toward the right.

With a policy course determined and a useful descriptive formula found in the containment concept, a quite new policy toward the Soviet Union began to be put into effect.

Problem I: Formulating the Truman Doctrine

The immediate cause for Truman making the March 12, 1947 speech, which became known as the Truman Doctrine, was the need to decide how the United States would respond to the British request that America take over the security backing of the Greeks, then fighting a civil war against the Communists. What made this decision momentous was the fact that it would involve the United States in an area, the Eastern Mediterranean, where previously it had had no real commitments.

Truman saw the insurgency in Greece as one more example of the heavy hand of the Soviets in the Balkans.[8] The Soviets had already put great pressure on Iran, failing to withdraw from the northern area according to their World War II agreements, assisting efforts to create a breakaway state near the Soviet frontier, and demanding oil concessions from Teheran. Only a strong American response had made them back down. And now, certainly, they were pressing the Turks hard for a concession on passage through the Dardanelles. Truman argued that "totalitarian regimes imposed on free peoples, by direct or indirect aggression, undermine the foundations of international peace and hence the security of the United States." He then pointed to how, "in violation of the Yalta Agreement," that progression had already occurred in Poland, Romania, and Bulgaria, with similar developments elsewhere. Truman saw "the present moment in world history" as one when "nearly every nation must choose between alternative ways of life," democratic or totalitarian. He then laid down a potentially very far-reaching principle:

> I believe that it must be the policy of the United States to support free peoples
> who are resisting attempted subjugation by armed minorities or by outside
> pressures.

Truman went on to say that it was "necessary only to glance at a map to realize that the survival and integrity of the Greek nation" were of "grave importance in a much wider situation." For, "If Greece should fall under the control of an armed minority, the effect upon its neighbor, Turkey, would be immediate and serious. Confusion and disorder might well spread throughout the entire Middle East."[9]

Notice that Truman weighs two alternatives and visualizes opposite outcomes. From these projections, he makes his choice of two counterbalancing interests and decides that the United States should and must be involved.

In the discussions of the time, the issue of whether or not to aid Greece and Turkey was not really controversial. But the open-ended nature of Truman's principle did provoke questions. Truman's own secretary of state, Dean Acheson, clearly did not think the United States was binding itself to aid *any* country *anywhere* that was under siege from an armed minority. In the hearings which followed the speech, Acheson was questioned specifically on this point.

> Senator Connally: This is not a pattern out of a tailor's shop to fit everybody in the world and every nation in the world, because the conditions in no two nations are identical. Is that not true?
>
> Mr. Acheson: Yes sir; that is true, and whether there are requests, of course, will be left to the future [and will] have to be judged, as you say, according to the circumstances of each specific case.[10]

There is no question that Acheson was sincere. Nor is there any evidence that Harry Truman wanted to apply his principle everywhere, regardless of circumstances. But events were now moving things in a different direction than Truman or Acheson envisioned first with the Berlin blockade, which heightened the tension level in the world, and then with events in Asia.

The Fast Pace of Events

Dean Acheson's title for his memoirs, *Present at the Creation,* catches very well the feeling in these years in Washington that momentous decisions were being taken to create a new world order.[11] It is difficult to grasp the fast pace of events, even with a chronology. Without it, things become quite blurred.

Consider 1947. A serious argument with the Soviets over their delayed refusal to withdraw from northern Iran had ended the year before with the Soviets moving out. Then in March 1947 came the problem of Greece and Turkey, which led to the Truman Doctrine.[12] On May 8, 1947, Undersecretary of State Dean Acheson made a speech outlining a possible U.S. response to Western Europe's extreme economic dislocation. Secretary Marshall followed up with a speech at Harvard on June 5, making it explicit. By July 12 a conference was beginning in Paris to decide on Europe's reaction, a conference that went on until September 22. About that same time, the United States concluded the Rio Pact on collective security in the Americas (September 2). Late in 1947, a meeting of the Foreign Ministers Conference (which included the Western allies and the Soviets) met in London to discuss the German problem. It ended in deadlock.

The next year, 1948, was even more dramatic. It began with the Communists toppling the democratic government of Czechoslovakia in an internal coup in February. It continued in June with the Soviet blockade of Berlin and the Berlin airlift response.[13]

The year 1949 was an especially active year. The blockade ended in a Soviet defeat on May 12. Only about a month earlier, on April 4, the North Atlantic Pact was signed, coming into effect on August 24. And less than a year after that the Korean War began.

Box 9.1	**Major Foreign Policy Events After World War II**	

Years	President	Events
1945–52	Truman	Truman Doctrine, Marshall Plan, GATT, Berlin Blockade, NATO formed, "loss" of China, Korean War begins
1953–60	Eisenhower	End of Korean War, Indochina War "ends," Quemoy-Matsu crises, Suez War, Hungarian uprising, Lebanon intervention, second Berlin crisis, advisers to Vietnam
1961–63	Kennedy	Bay of Pigs fiasco, new Berlin crisis, more advisers to Vietnam, Cuban missile crisis, Sino-Soviet split, Hot Line Agreement
1963–68	Johnson	Vietnam involvement escalates into overt combat, Middle East War, NonProliferation Treaty
1969–74	Nixon	Fosters detente, plays "China card," SALT agreements, ends Vietnam War, Watergate, Middle East War and Disengagement Agreements
1974–76	Ford	Helsinki Agreements (CSCE)
1977–80	Carter	Attempts human rights program, defense deemphasized, Camp David accords on Middle East, Panama Canal treaties, Soviets invade Afghanistan, SALT II signed and withdrawn, Iranian hostage crisis
1981–88	Reagan	Military buildup, intervenes in Grenada, begins SDI program, Lebanon disaster, supports Contras against Sandinistas, Libyan raid, Iran-Contra affair, negotiates INF treaty
1989–92	Bush	Intervenes in Panama, enters Persian Gulf War, CFE Treaty, Berlin Wall falls, Soviet Union disintegrates, START signed, Cold War ends, Germany reunified

Count it up: multiple crises with the Soviets, including one in Germany, where both the United States and the Soviets had substantial troops; a commitment in southeastern Europe; two ground-breaking pacts for collective security; and the ambitious Marshall Plan, followed by a major war in Asia—all in three years time. Such a series of events would, over time, take the Truman Doctrine (and Kennan's containment concept) much further than was originally foreseen.

The Truman Doctrine Applied: Greece and Turkey

The language actually used by Truman was to prove prophetic (a struggle between "two ways of life"). But its expression of determination to support democracy focused on Greece and Turkey. Greece was being threatened first from within by an indigenous Communist movement. But the Greek communists were aided from abroad. Turkey was being pressured by the Soviets to revise the convention governing the Dardanelles Straits, to allow Soviet warships easier access to and from the Black Sea and Mediterranean. What Turkey needed, in addition to money for arms, was a clear sign of support. It got just that when the United States, returning the body of the Turkish ambassador, chose to do so using the U.S.S. *Missouri,* the most powerful battleship in the world. To drive home the point, the *Missouri* was accompanied by a task force which stayed in the Sea of Marmara for some time.[14] The Greek problem took longer but was handled equally successfully. A combination of economic aid and military advice stabilized the situation.

The total appropriation Truman requested for this first implementation of the Doctrine does not sound impressive in today's terms: $250 million for Greece, $150 million for Turkey. But in 1947, when America's total national budget was only $41 billion, that represented a staggering 1 percent.[15] That the American people had become convinced that efforts of this magnitude were necessary was shown by the vote in Congress: 67 to 23 in the Senate, 287 to 107 in the House. Equally a testimony to the changed views was the rapidity of the action. Truman's request came on March 12, 1947, and Congressional approval in a little over two months. The president signed the act on May 22.

Problem IV: The Marshall Plan

The next development was the Marshall Plan. With the European economy steadily deteriorating,[16] French grain acreage had fallen to a quarter of prewar totals. Until the European economy could be rebuilt, Europe's needs amounted to two and a half billion dollars *annually* of coal, bread grains, and shipping services. Moreover, with currencies deteriorating, their real values in terms of one another was a question mark. In a memorandum written within the State Department by Will Clayton, which impressed both Acheson and Marshall enough to spur them to action, Clayton proposed the enormous sum of 6 or 7 billion dollars for three years.[17] He proposed that Europe should jointly come up with a plan acceptable to the United States and that the United States should run it.

Secretary of State George Marshall's speech on June 5, 1947, incorporated these ideas. He said that "before the United States Government can proceed much further in its efforts to alleviate the situation . . . there must be some agreement among the countries of Europe as to the requirements of the situation and the part these countries themselves will take. . . ." He added that it would be "neither fitting nor efficacious for this Government to undertake to draw up unilaterally" such a program. That was the business of the Europeans. The initiative, therefore, "must come from Europe" and the program should be "a joint one, agreed to by a number of, if not all, European nations." America's role would "consist of friendly aid in the drafting of a European program and of later support" so far as it could.[18]

The program that began with these words was impressive in many of its features. The most impressive of all, though, was the fact that the Soviet Union and its satellites were not excluded. Whether, in the end, Congress would have agreed to pour American dollars into Soviet coffers is a good question. The Soviets did attend the conference the Europeans hastily assembled, sending Foreign Minister Molotov as their representative. The Czechs and the Poles showed great interest in the proposals. But after several days of discussion, Molotov walked out, saying that it was all a plan to keep everyone under American tutelage and control. Shortly after this the Foreign Ministers Conference over Germany deadlocked, and a half year or so later the full blockade of Berlin was in effect. In retrospect, it is apparent that the Soviets wavered and then decided on a hard line. Whether any cooperation with the West, even if Congress was willing, would have endured and triumphed over Western-Soviet arguments in the next years is what President Roosevelt loved to call "an iffy question."

Sixteen European states (all of noncommunist Europe except Spain, but including Iceland and Turkey) did prepare a plan, and Congress approved U.S. participation in the Economic Cooperation Act of April 3, 1948. Even decades later, the memory of this action was still very fresh in the minds of Europeans (and many people in the nations that had not even participated). When, in 1991, Secretary of State James Baker came to Albania, which was at last throwing off the shackles of rigid communism, a crowd of 300,000 turned out spontaneously to greet him in the public square. (The German foreign minister's visit, at about the same time, went unremarked by the public.) This was a tribute to the enormous good will generated by the Marshall Plan abroad. Clark Clifford says of this effort that "the scope of it defies modern budgets; it cost nearly $10 billion in 1948–49 dollars, the equivalent of more than $50 billion today. It was 16 percent of the federal budget."[19]

Europe Rebuilds

Nothing the United States might propose would have been of much use if the European powers had approached their economic problems after World War II as they did after World War I. The vindictive spirit with which Germany was loaded with an impossible reparations burden was mentioned earlier. The great change in 1945 and the half decade that followed was the general realization that this kind of approach would again doom them all.

The most statesmanlike element in the Marshall Plan approach was the U.S. decision not to run it all, but to ask Europe to work out a collective approach detailing what was needed to prime Europe's pumps. Even with this approach and substantial U.S. aid, great problems had to be overcome.

For example, to restore a vigorous international trade, currencies would have to be made convertible, exchangeable on a more or less stable basis. But in the aftermath of World War II, the relative worth of currencies was difficult to reestablish. Nor was it feasible to simply establish a direct link to a gold exchange basis and remove controls. That would mean exposing national economies to market forces that could sweep all reserves away in weeks or days—just like the problem Russia was struggling with in the early 1990s. In fact, that just about happened to England in July 1947, when it decided prematurely to free the pound.

Because America's role was so important and the dollar was rapidly becoming the main international currency (taking the prewar place of the British pound), the availability of dollars was a vital key to convertibility. By the end of 1958 the "dollar shortage" had been overcome, especially because of U.S. Marshall Plan aid and of the ability of Europe's industry to produce goods again for export that would earn dollars. After 1958, Western European currencies could be freely converted into dollars (and dollars had a fixed relationship to gold). That system worked well for a number of years.

Problem I: Serious Trouble Begins Over Germany

The Truman Doctrine (March 1947) and the Marshall Plan (proposed in June 1947, with a European conference on it from July to September 1947) were hardly over when serious trouble began over Germany.

As early as September 1946, Secretary of State James Byrnes, speaking in Stuttgart, had complained bluntly that the Soviets were failing to administer Germany as a single economic unit. Yet the whole agreement on Germany turned on that assumption, for the Soviets were being given reparations out of German current production, in return for which they were to supply food. But by 1947 Secretary of State George Marshall, Byrnes' successor, was complaining that the United States and United Kingdom were paying "some [$]700 millions a year to provide the food . . . to prevent starvation and rather complete disintegration" in Germany. "We put in and the Russians take out." With the Soviets not yielding an inch, the Western occupying powers met in London on March 6, 1948, and announced that they had agreed on "a federal form of government" in their Western zones.

In dramatic response, on March 20, Soviet Marshal Sokolovsky, after delivering a tirade, walked out of the Allied Control Council in Berlin. Then, on March 31, 1948, the Soviet Military Administration declared that military passenger trains would not be allowed across the border en route to Berlin (110 miles inside the Soviet zone) unless baggage and passengers were inspected by Soviet personnel. That clearly contravened Marshall Zhukov's earlier oral agreement with General Clay. The next day the Soviets ordered that no rail freight could leave Berlin without approval. When the United States tested Soviet resolve with a train with a few armed guards on board, it was shunted to a siding until, a few days later, it was withdrawn.

Nevertheless, the West completed its plan for a West German government on June 1, 1948. Fifteen days later the Soviets walked out of the Kommandatura, the Four-Power organ governing the city of Berlin. On June 18 the Soviets tightened rail restrictions with the bald excuse that facilities were in "bad order."

June 18 was also the day that the new Deutsche Mark currency law was promulgated, to become effective on June 20. On June 18, too, the Soviets were informed that the new Western mark would *not* be used in Berlin. At a meeting of experts on June 22, the Soviets announced a new currency of their own, which would be used in *all* of Berlin. With no agreement possible, the Eastern mark went into use in the Soviet areas on June 23, and in response on June 24, the Western mark was introduced into West Berlin. That day, *all* Western rail traffic with Berlin was suspended by the Soviets.

With Berlin holding food stocks for only 36 days and coal stocks only for 45, the Soviets were confident the West would either have to give in or see some 2.5 million people in the Western areas of Berlin starve. The blockade was a stark reality.

The Allied response was a tremendous airlift. In 1948, an average daily lift of 4,500 tons was needed. By December, even with the winter weather, the daily average delivery had exceeded the 4,500 tons, and by February it had reached 5,500. By Spring 1949, it was 8,000 tons—equivalent to what had entered Berlin by rail and water before the blockage. On the record day, some 13,000 tons were flown into the three airports (Tempelhof, Gatow, and a new one at Tegel, built during the airlift). By the time the blockade was lifted on May 11–12, 1949, after eleven months, some 1,402,644 metric tons of food, coal, and other supplies had been flown into Berlin in 277,728 flights. At the height of the airlift, planes were coming in or leaving every thirty seconds!

The ending of the blockade was an admission of Soviet defeat, underlined even further by the fact that the East German offer of ration cards to West Berliners was accepted initially by only 21,000 people—a figure which never rose above 70,000. It was during this period that the saying arose: "In Berlin there are no Germans and Americans; there are only Berliners." It is certain that the cooperation of Germany and the United States in a common cause eradicated much of the wartime hostility and forged a new bond between the two peoples. Whatever chance the Soviets ever had to win over West Germany had evaporated.

Problem II: And Who "Lost" China?

America's attention, focused on Europe in the first postwar years, was soon to be switched abruptly to Asia.

During World War II, the United States had given what aid it could to the Chinese Nationalist government of Chiang K'ai-shek. Chiang, as a Christian and noncommunist, was popular in the United States, and his wife was a charming woman with a flair for favorable publicity. All during the 1930s he had fought an up and down civil war with the Communists. While Chiang emerged as the recognized leader of China at the end of World War II, he quite rapidly began to lose control of China. This was partly due to the Soviets, who turned over captured Japanese war equipment in Manchuria to their friends, the Communist Chinese. But Stalin had indicated a definite willingness to work with the Nationalists, and it is unlikely that he was trying very hard to overthrow Chiang. Chiang had gone in for very large armed forces at the expense of a smaller, more useful, and better disciplined army. Conditions in the countryside soon disintegrated, with many elements of Chiang's army deserting and even taking sides thereafter with the Communists in the fighting in 1947 and 1948. At the end of 1949, Chiang, with the remnants of his forces, fled to the island of Taiwan (Formosa).

This set of exterior events was to interact with developments within the United States to have a profound effect on how the United States reacted to the Korean War, which broke out only seven months after—as the American extreme right wing was to put it—*"we* [i.e., America] lost China."

Right after World War II the United States was caught up in serious labor unrest and a four-way political party split in the election of 1948. Besides the question of how to handle the Soviet Union, a question that had produced the Henry Wallace movement, there were many other issues, such as the race issue. Furthermore, the growing conviction that Americans were not going to be able to simply relax into their prewar posture, fanned fears of subversion by domestic Communists. This issue was pushed very heavily by the head of the FBI, J. Edgar Hoover. Hoover was making no secret of his belief that America needed a permanent investigatory tool to root out Communists who might have infiltrated into positions of authority in the U.S. government. Ably seconded by many conservative politicians, they clamored for action by President Truman.[20]

The House had already established an Un-American Activities Committee, whose hearings received copious media publicity. The pressure resulted in the issuance of Executive Order 9835 on March 21, 1947, only nine days after the Truman Doctrine speech.[21] The order established a Loyalty Program, with the

Civil Service Commission authorized to look into the loyalty of any new federal employee. The Commission was to set up loyalty boards in every department and agency. These were to recommend the removal of any employees whose loyalty was in any way questionable. But who was to define loyalty? Of what did it consist? If a federal employee in the State Department, say a foreign service officer serving in China, wrote a memorandum saying that Chiang's government was corrupt and that the Communists were gaining, was that to be considered disloyal? Unfortunately, as it turned out, the answer was a resounding yes! Every one of America's Chinese experts had eventually to walk the plank into career oblivion, as this program went on.

Assisting this whole movement to the right with its increasing hysteria was McCarthyism. Senator Joseph McCarthy literally terrorized the U.S. government in the late 1940s and early 1950s. It is extremely difficult for anyone reaching maturity in the 1990s to understand the tensions of these times and the dimensions those tensions finally reached. Very large numbers of Americans, convinced that the Soviets were bent on trouble and knowing that the Soviets could call on Communist movements everywhere, supported the call to nab the subversives before they could stab America in the back.

McCarthy's initial charges were made in a speech in Wheeling, West Virginia, in that brief period of time between when Chiang lost the mainland in 1949 and when the Korean War began in June 1950. Thereafter, McCarthy, holding up a piece of paper, would again and again proclaim: "I have here a list of xxxxx Communists in the State Department"—or anywhere else. The number would vary, but the theme did not. And everyone scurried for cover.[22] Even President Eisenhower, who succeeded Truman in 1953, would not defend his old chief and friend, General George Marshall, when McCarthy impugned Marshall's patriotism!

By the time of McCarthy's West Virginia speech, very few Americans still felt that America needed to be more accommodating to the Soviets. The Soviet attempt to wrest West Berlin away had only ended on May 12, 1949. Most everyone now agreed that the Soviets were embarked on a serious confrontation with America, and, as often in the past, once a former view was discarded, opinion shifted very far indeed. It shifted further than the author of the containment formula, George Kennan, himself was prepared to support. In his memoirs published in 1967, he describes how "the movement of the pendulum of official thinking from left to right" brought it close to Kennan's own views in 1946–48, only to continue on into an "oversimplified and highly militarized view of the Russian problem . . . after 1949."[23]

So two things were going on in parallel. In foreign affairs, Americans began to think more and more that they were in a contest with the Soviet Union that would be waged with all weapons, and anywhere that opportunity beckoned.[24] Cumulatively, the crises in Greece, Turkey, and Iran, the consolidation of Soviet control in Eastern Europe, the Czech coup, the Berlin blockade, and the "fall of China" had convinced U.S. policymakers of an inherently aggressive Communist bloc controlled and directed by the Kremlin.[25] The detonation of an atomic bomb by the Soviets only added to the growing anxiety. Meanwhile, in domestic affairs, Americans feared that subversive elements had crept into positions where they could do harm. This Communist scare fed on occasional bits of harder evidence of subversion or, at least, disloyalty, of which the Alger Hiss case was the most prominent. Hiss had officiated as secretary-general at the San Francisco conference creating the U.N. In 1948, Elizabeth Bentley and Whittaker Chambers, both self-confessed former Communists, testified before the Congressional committees about Communist penetration of the government, and in August, Chambers accused Hiss of being a Soviet spy. Hiss protested his innocence but ultimately was found by a court to have perjured himself.

McCarthyism and McCarthy himself were primarily a product of the Korean War years, but while his influence lasted, he created enormous harm. In the spring of 1954, for rather trivial reasons, he made his great mistake. He decided to take on the U.S. Army. It was one of the first national events to be carried on television live. When he began, public opinion polls showed he had 50 percent of the people approving what he was doing, with 29 percent opposed and 21 percent with no opinion. By hearing's end, he had destroyed himself as a political force in America. On December 2, 1954, the U.S. Senate finally took courage and condemned McCarthy's behavior as "contrary to senatorial ethics," and as having obstructed the constitutional processes of the Senate and impaired its dignity. Before three years had passed, Joe McCarthy literally drank himself to death.

So, when the Korean War broke out, and during the entire time it was fought, the circumstances in the United States were, to say the least, unusual.

Acheson Makes a Speech

Dean Acheson made a speech to the Press Club in Washington on January 12, 1950. As its title shows, it was designed to explain why the U.S. side in the Chinese civil war had lost. It was called "Crisis in China—An Examination of United States Policy."[26] Acheson argued that what had happened was "that the almost inexhaustible patience of the Chinese people in their misery ended. They did not bother to overthrow this government [of the Nationalists]. . . . They simply ignored it throughout the country." Besides, the Nationalist military command had been grossly incompetent. "The Communists did not create this condition. . . . But they were shrewd and cunning to mount it, to ride this thing into victory and into power."

All of this was anathema to the American right wing—especially to a well-organized group, called "the China lobby." Spearheaded in the Senate by Senator William Knowland of California and in the House by Representative Walter Judd (a former missionary in China), it was a potent lobby. As with McCarthyism, it is difficult today to understand the political power of the China lobby, but it was very great—especially with McCarthyism interacting with it. The main difference between the two was that the China lobby was pressuring for U.S. support for Chiang's utopian idea, that he would regroup and return to the Chinese mainland to "liberate" it.

This much of Acheson's speech, while anathema to the China lobby, might not have aroused them to the full-scale attack they mounted on him. But Acheson went on. Addressing the perennial question of where to draw the line to protect American interests in the area, he said America's "defensive perimeter runs along the Aleutians to Japan and then goes to the Ryukyus" and then "from the Ryukyus to the Philippine Islands."[27]

As Acheson correctly argues in his memoirs, General MacArthur had said much the same thing on March 1, 1949, in an interview in Tokyo.[28] Where once the United States based its defensive positions on the West Coast, said MacArthur, "Now the Pacific has become an Anglo-Saxon lake and our line of defense runs through the chain of islands fringing the coast of Asia. It starts from the Philippines and continues through the Ryukyu Archipelago, which includes its main bastion, Okinawa. Then it bends back through Japan and the Aleutian Island chain to Alaska." Neither description mentioned Korea.

That was not accidental. In the judgment of the Joint Chiefs, it would have been very difficult to fight a war on the Asian mainland, and they did not advise that America do so. MacArthur's "line" and Acheson's "line" were consistent with the JCS judgment. Because leaving out something might be construed as a lack of interest, however, Acheson went on in his speech to say: "So far as the military security of other areas in the Pacific is concerned, it must be clear that no person can guarantee these areas against military attack." If that happened, the "initial reliance" would be on the people attacked and then upon U.N. reaction.

But when North Korea attacked South Korea in June of that same year, Acheson's critics charged that his January speech had "given the green light" to that attack.

This was the last straw for the right wing. Not only was Acheson explaining that it was Chiang's own weaknesses that had brought about his mainland collapse. Now Acheson was actually encouraging the Communists to attack Korea! McCarthy began to refer to Dean Acheson regularly as "the Red Dean."

Behind such views, of course, was a premise: that it was in the power of the United States to control China's destiny, to make the decades-long Chinese civil war turn out in America's favor.

Dennis Brogan, an acute British observer of the American scene, wrote in *Harper's*, just before the 1952 election, that this attitude, which he called the American "illusion of omnipotence," was "best illustrated by a very common American attitude toward the Chinese Revolution. In this attitude—apparently the dominant one at the moment—there is a curious absence of historical awe and historical curiosity. The Chinese Revolution, an event of immense importance, is often discussed as if it were simply . . . the result of American action or inaction. . . ."[29]

Acheson's critics imply, in suggesting that North Korea attacked South Korea because of what was or was not in Acheson's speech, that nations go to war because of the oral statements of intention on the part of other nations, rather than for compelling reasons of their own. Acheson, not without reason, describes these reactions to U.S. policy and to his speech in a chapter entitled "The Attack of the Primitives Begins."

Problems I and II: The Korean War Begins

When the news of the North Korean assault reached Washington at 9:26 P.M., EST, on Saturday night, June 24, President Truman had no trouble making up his mind how to respond. The action he took was through the United Nations, which he supposed—correctly—would support the United States. But the official American view was that the Soviet Union was undoubtedly behind the attack, choosing an area of unquestioned strategic value for its assault, with the deliberate aim of shifting the balance of power in Asia.

That Korea was strategic no one could argue. It lay at the junction of three powers: China, Japan, and the Soviet Union. The U.S. government, advised of the assault, went into high gear, centered at first on rounding up U.N. delegates who had scattered for the weekend. A first meeting of the U.N. Security Council was held at 2 P.M. Sunday.[30] Earlier, the Soviet Union had decided to boycott all Security Council meetings to protest the fact that China's seat was still occupied by the Nationalist Chinese; therefore, the Soviets could interpose no veto. By a 9–0 vote the Council adopted a U.S.-sponsored resolution calling for an end to the "breach of the peace" in Korea and calling on "all members to render every assistance to the United Nations in the execution of this resolution and to refrain from giving assistance to the North Korean authorities."

Quoted earlier was President Truman's reaction to the news of the attack. Setting aside JCS plans, he ordered U.S. forces based in Japan to prepare to deploy to Korea to defend it.

This was not the first time American troops had been in Korea. After World War II the United States had accepted the surrender of Japanese forces in South Korea (while the Soviets did the same for North Korea). These surrender arrangements, assumed to be purely temporary, like so many things about the wartime arrangements, did not work out that way. Later, in the hope that the U.N. could find a basis for a peaceful unification of the two parts, American troops had evacuated Korea, as the Soviets also did. But the antagonism between the new governments in the north and south steadily deepened and tension along the 38th Parallel "border" increased.[31] Now it had come to open war.

With the U.N. committed, President Truman announced on June 26 that he had ordered General MacArthur, the United States commander in the Far East, to furnish military supplies to South Korea. Then on June 27, at noon, he announced that he was sending air and sea forces "to give the Korean Government troops cover and support." With further reports now available at the U.N., the Security Council on June 27 recommended that "the Members of the United Nations furnish such assistance to the Republic of Korea as may be necessary to repel the armed attack and to restore international peace and security in the area." Again, the Soviets were not there to veto. When they finally returned to the Council on August 1, 1950, everything essential by way of U.N. action was already accomplished. In the months that followed, about two thirds of the sixty U.N. members responded with help of one sort or another, including supplies and medical units or actual forces. Some fourteen quickly sent armed forces, with two more doing so later. These sixteen were almost all allies of the United States, either already or soon to be. In addition to the allies, South Africa and Ethiopia also sent troops. By early 1951 these U.N. forces totaled 250,000 from the United States, 26,000 from the other thirteen states, plus the South Korean army. Policy was coordinated among this group by twice-weekly meetings in Washington.

Turning back to the initial reaction, when North Korea's attack began, those U.S. troops in Japan that were sent to Korea were not combat ready. But they were the only ones in position to act soon enough. Now they were thrust into the fighting. With the North Koreans enjoying the initiative, the South Korean and American forces were pushed back steadily until they held only the very southern port of Pusan. But reinforcements arrived and dug in to form the famous "Pusan perimeter." The attack was stopped.

The next move was highly dramatic. On September 15, 1950, General MacArthur mounted a daring amphibious assault on Korea's west coast, at Inchon, near South Korea's capital of Seoul. It was daring because the tides there must be caught just right.[32] And it was fully successful. Outflanked, the North Koreans retreated helter-skelter northwards, hoping to gain sanctuary before they were encircled. This sudden reversal of military fortunes outstripped the U.N.'s ability to agree on exactly what should happen next. The Chinese reaction would be important if the U.N. troops crossed the inner Korean border, but the Chinese Communists were not members of the U.N. In this situation, and with the Security Council again subject to a Soviet veto, action shifted to the veto-less General Assembly. A resolution was passed, 47 to 5, with 7 abstentions, approving "hot pursuit" by implication. It promised that "United Nations forces should not remain in any part of Korea otherwise than so far as necessary for achieving the objectives specified"—that is, a united and independent Korea. The Indians warned that China might intervene but the warning was not taken seriously.[33]

As the U.N. forces advanced rapidly into North Korea, the disorganized North Korean forces were not able to mount much serious resistance. By early November the North Korean armies were dispersed and fleeing, and U.N. forces had penetrated far into North Korea. At one point they reached the Yalu River (the frontier with Manchuria). Then, on November 5, the Unified Command reported "a new foe" in the form of "Chinese Communist military units." It was unclear how many units or what their orders actually were. Were they about to launch an offensive, or were they there to prevent further U.N. advances?

With the Chinese Communists charging repeated violations of their air space over Manchuria, China demanded a hearing at the U.N., to which the Security Council reluctantly agreed. The situation was now extremely delicate.

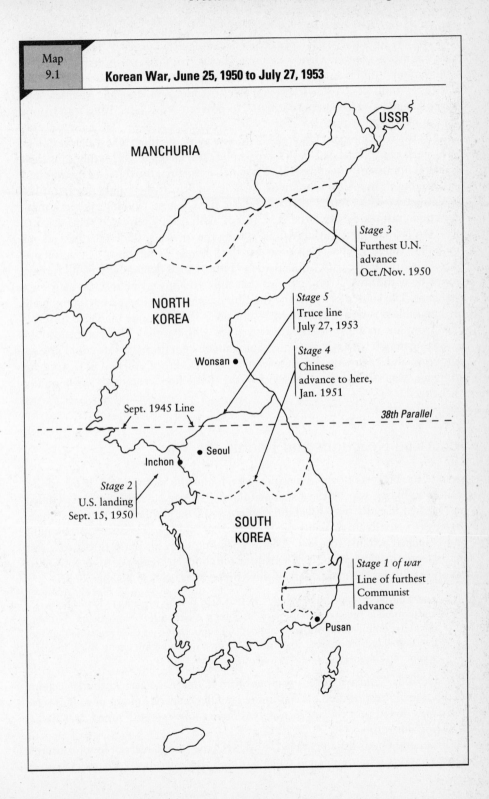

Map 9.1

Korean War, June 25, 1950 to July 27, 1953

USSR

MANCHURIA

Stage 3
Furthest U.N.
advance
Oct./Nov. 1950

NORTH
KOREA

Stage 5
Truce line
July 27, 1953

Wonsan •

Stage 4
Chinese
advance to here,
Jan. 1951

Sept. 1945 Line

38th Parallel

• Seoul

Inchon •

Stage 2
U.S. landing
Sept. 15, 1950

SOUTH
KOREA

Stage 1 of war
Line of furthest
Communist
advance

Pusan

MacArthur's military position was risky because he had divided the troops in the advance into two forces, whose command was from Tokyo. Actually, the JCS had cautioned him not to use American troops to reach the frontier, knowing that that would be extremely provocative to China.[34] (After all, America supported Chiang and his supposed return to power.) Now some American troops were in fact at the Yalu.

At the very moment when the U.N. was awaiting the Chinese delegation in New York and a clarification of China's position, General MacArthur launched a general offensive (November 24). He called it the final blow to end the war and get "the boys" home for Christmas. Striking swiftly at the vulnerable point between the two U.N. forces in North Korea, the Chinese "volunteers" in a massive counterattack defeated the U.N. forces, who hastily retreated southward.

On November 28, MacArthur, stating the obvious, said: "We face an entirely new war." That was also the day the Chinese Communist delegation appeared before the Security Council and in bitter words demanded that all foreign troops be withdrawn from Korea so that the two Koreas could settle their own problems. The United Nations and the Chinese were now locked into completely incompatible positions, and the war went on as the U.N. side managed to stabilize a front line in the approximate area of the 38th Parallel. The war settled into a slugging match with neither side reaping much benefit. Each side could always reinforce, and each side did. It was a stalemate. From April, 1951, until an armistice was signed in July, 1953, the battleline remained substantially unchanged.

American Reactions and Ending the War

Despite the bickering over Acheson's speech and the fact that the JCS had not wanted to fight a war on the Asian mainland, Truman's decision was welcomed and backed initially by a substantial majority of the public. In the government there was virtually no dissent from the view that Stalin with malice aforethought had launched a flank attack in Asia after failing with his main thrust to wrest Berlin from the U.S. grasp. U. Alexis Johnson, undersecretary of state for political affairs during the major part of the Korean War, says in his memoirs:

> There has been some talk recently . . . that Kim Il-sung [the North Korea leader] masterminded the invasion more or less on his own, with the knowledge, but not the active connivance, of the Kremlin. . . . I suppose it is at least arguable that the invasion was a bit of local adventurism by an overexuberant client. But I do not accept this theory.[35]

He adds: "But whatever prompted Kim to order the attack, this is certain: At the time no responsible official in the United States or among our allies seriously questioned that the aggression was Soviet-inspired and aimed principally at testing our resolve."[36]

General Omar Bradley, then chairman of the Joint Chiefs of Staff, recounts in his memoirs what happened when Truman convened his chief policymakers to advise on how to react to the invasion. Bradley says that he said at the meeting: "We must draw the line somewhere" and Korea "offered as good an occasion for action in drawing the line as anywhere else."

Bradley went on:

> In those days we held the rather simplistic view that *all* communist moves worldwide were dictated from Moscow by Stalin personally. The guessing that night was that Stalin had temporarily set aside his designs on Europe and the Middle East for an all-out push in the Far East conducted by his satellites. Korea might only be one phase of this push.

Taiwan might be next, or Indochina or the Philippines. Bradley concludes by saying: "But we did not believe Stalin wanted all-out global war."[37]

The domino thinking here is very clear, as is the view that the Cold War moves of the whole Communist camp were orchestrated in Moscow. (These ideas prevailed for many years and played an important role in prompting U.S. intervention in Vietnam).

The first response to China's entrance into the struggle was that it confirmed the notion that there was a unified Communist bloc. Logically, then, if China had intervened in that role, the war should now be extended to China. So, General MacArthur now argued, in an effort to convince the American people, the United States had no alternative but to end the stalemate by attacking the "privileged sanctuary" of the Chinese in Manchuria.

Logic might lead one way, but prudence led another. Strategically, MacArthur's recipe offered only a larger war instead of a stalemated war, and since he proposed the United States should become fully engaged with the Chinese while leaving the Soviet Union fully free to make trouble anywhere else, his arguments fell on deaf ears in the White House and Joint Chiefs. Where it did have an appeal among those able to influence government thinking was in the China lobby and in the Republican extreme right wing. MacArthur, encouraged by the fact that an increasingly restive American public was looking for some solution to end an endless war, made a conspicuous visit to Taiwan to consult with Chiang. His last act of defiance was to write to the Republican minority leader Congressman Joseph Martin, replying to Martin's request for MacArthur's opinion on using Nationalist Chinese troops in Korea—a course of action Truman had ruled out because it would dramatically increase Chinese Communist anger. MacArthur wrote back that Martin's view of using those troops neither conflicted with "logic" nor with the American tradition "of meeting force with maximum counterforce as we have never failed to do in the past." He added "that here in Asia is where the Communist conspirators have elected to make their play for global conquest. . . . As you point out, we must win. There is no substitute for victory." In his memoirs MacArthur says that Congressman Martin, "without consulting me, released my letter."[38] The confrontation between Truman's policy and MacArthur's preferences was now public knowledge. It caused a media sensation. Six days later, Truman relieved MacArthur of his commands.

The second result was public disenchantment with the United Nations.

What was happening in the Korean War did not conform to expectations about collective security. That idea held that an aggression against one would be treated as an aggression against all, that the collective military power of the world would smash the aggression in quick order with overwhelming strength. But in this actual case, only two thirds or less of the U.N. membership at the time did even as much as send soap. And one major power, a nonmember (Communist China), was contributing military support to the aggressor, while the Soviet Union, a superpower, was supplying military equipment to the aggressor side and trying to stymie U.N. action. The disillusionment that came with the stalemate only half a decade after the U.N. began its existence was to continue for many years. Real reliance for security, the American people concluded, came from alliances, not from the U.N.

Once both sides recognized that the war was stalemated, the stage was set for a negotiated peace. Here again public expectations took a jolt. How could America justify negotiating with the aggressor? Collective security thinking held that the aggressor was to be abjectly defeated; it did not call for discussions to see how he felt about it and what he was willing to agree upon in order to end the hostilities. Worse, once the negotiations began, they were protracted. As one month passed into another, each of them accompanied by casualties, American public opinion about the war turned ever more negative.

The public initiative for ending the war came from the Soviets in the form of a speech over U.S. radio by the Soviet representative at the U.N., Jacob Malik. He suggested a cease-fire and an armistice allowing mutual withdrawal of forces from the 38th Parallel. In other words, restore the pre-hostilities border. The new U.N. commander, General Ridgeway, suggested meeting aboard a Danish hospital ship. Beijing radio agreed to a meeting, but at Kaesong—one of the few towns in Communist hands below the 38th Parallel. On July 10, 1951, the U.N. agreeing to Kaesong, negotiations began. Disputes about the neutral zone in which the parties were meeting led soon to a two-month delay. Resumed at Panmunjom, the negotiations then went on intermittently for most of two more years until an armistice was signed. It is possible that they would have gone on even longer had not Dwight D. Eisenhower become president with a promise to end the war in Korea. That he meant it was obvious. There was even talk that atomic weapons might have to be used. The final agreement, which followed the battlelines, left somewhat more territory in the hands of South Korea than before the war.

Problem I: The North Atlantic Pact Becomes NATO

The third result of the Korean War was to transform the North Atlantic Pact into NATO, changing it from a promising paper alliance to an organization in place in Europe for defense.

To say that the North Atlantic Treaty was a paper promise does not mean it was ineffective as a deterrent. After all, the United States at the time was still way ahead of the Soviet Union in the nuclear weapons field. There was no doubt that the promise in Article 5 was seriously intended. It provided that "an armed attack against one or more . . . shall be considered an attack against them all. . . ." The parties pledged "separately and jointly, by means of continuous and effective self-help and mutual aid" to "maintain and develop their individual and collective capacity to resist" any attack. They provided for consultation "whenever, in the opinion of any of them, the territorial integrity, political independence or security of any of the Parties" was threatened. A council, on which each member would be represented, would set up subsidiary bodies as needed. Any party to the treaty, after twenty years, could give one year's notice of withdrawal. Thus the treaty term was, in effect, indefinite.

But it cannot be doubted that an organization in place is militarily more competent to deter than a simple promise. Once the decision was made in December 1950, to establish SHAPE (Supreme Headquarters, Allied Powers Europe), with General Dwight Eisenhower as its head, the organization grew rapidly, both in members and in strength. The first amendment to the treaty came on October 22, 1951. By the London Protocol of that date, the original parties agreed to invite Greece and Turkey to join, thus also enlarging the area covered by the treaty. Greece and Turkey came in on February 18, 1952, adding a Greek army of 165,000 and a Turkish army of 400,000. West Germany joined in 1955. When Spain joined in 1982, total NATO membership grew to sixteen.

Summing Up

There is much more that could be discussed. For example, the whole story of the prolonged argument in the Korean War peace talks over whether prisoners of war have to return to their homeland—a serious issue because most of the Chinese prisoners did not want to go back to China.[39] That issue was "solved" when Syngman Rhee, the leader of South Korea, told his guards to open the gates of the POW compounds. The Chinese, who had lost much "face" by the fact that their soldiers did not want to go back let this one pass without prolonged protest.

And there is academic debate in the scholarly community over how to describe this "limited" war. The war had indeed been limited in important ways: by the fact, first of all, that neither China nor the United States participated in it under national flags. Americans came as soldiers of the U.N.; Chinese came as "volunteers." That made it much easier to disengage. Anyone who thinks this is a frivolous distinction can learn much from the negotiations over Vietnam, where the United States *was* fighting under its own flag.

More could also be said about collective security theory and whether and how much it worked in this case. The bottom line on this war was that North

Korea (or, if you prefer, the Communist camp) did not profit from its aggression. Whether it should have been "fined," say 10 percent or 20 percent of its territory for having attempted the conquest is debatable. It comes down to whether one thinks that frustrating an aggression is itself sufficient punishment.

What the Korean War did do in American foreign policy was to strengthen the belief with which Americans started the war, that the United States had been engaged in frustrating a Moscow-orchestrated attack on its Asian flank. It also deepened differences with the Chinese Communists, thereby delaying for years establishment of normal diplomatic relations with them. Eisenhower, for example, was to remain bitterly opposed to the Chinese Communist regime. When the transition took place at the end of his eight years in office and Kennedy took over, he told Kennedy bluntly that if Kennedy proposed to recognize China, he, Eisenhower, would come out publicly against it.[40]

In retrospect, though, the most important result of the Korean War for American foreign policy was that it did not clarify the issues that the domino theory so blithely covers over by claiming that one aggression, unopposed, leads to more. Because Korea unquestionably was an important strategic area, because South Korea's conquest would certainly have altered the whole strategic balance of power in Asia, those who understood that fact were happy enough to accept the American action there, whatever the grounds of justification. But those who saw its justification as arising from its frustration of Communist plans for worldwide aggression were equally content to accept the action on that ground. By failing to separate the two justifications, the resulting ambiguity was to come back to haunt the United States the next time, over Vietnam.

Notes

1. Lenin's comments, of course, were made in a time of great capitalist hostility.

2. Useful is John L. Gaddis, *Strategies of Containment: A Critical Appraisal of Postwar American National Security Policy* (New York: Oxford University Press, 1982), pp. 19ff. For an effective but succinct analysis see Walter Isaacson and Evan Thomas, *The Wise Men: Six Friends and the World They Made: Acheson, Bohlen, Harriman, Kennan, Lovett, McCloy* (New York: Simon and Schuster, 1986), pp. 352–56.

3. "X," "The Sources of Soviet Conduct," *Foreign Affairs,* Vol. 25 (July 1947), pp. 566–82. The quote is from p. 575.

4. Kennan later expressed regret for a poor choice of words in referring to "counterforce," arguing that his meaning was far from the military-confrontation context in which it was implemented. This is a matter of some dispute because, in the Long Telegram, military strategy was the first strategy discussed. Soviet power, Kennan wrote, was "impervious to the logic of reason" but "highly sensitive to the logic of force." Moscow was likely to back down "when strong resistance was encountered an any point." An opponent of the Soviets would "rarely" have to use force if he "makes clear his readiness" to use it. See Walter Isaacson and Evan Thomas, *Six Wise Men,* Ch. 12.

Kennan's two analyses were similar but neither identical nor entirely consistent, thus muddying the waters. See the excellent analysis in John Lewis Gaddis, *Strategies of Containment,* Chs. 1 and 2.

5. Truman biographer David McCullough says that when Roosevelt went to the Yalta Conference, Truman was told that he could contact Roosevelt through the White House, but only if it was "absolutely urgent." He adds that "Since taking office, Truman had seen nothing of Roosevelt [by then] nor had he been told anything at all about the conference." In the eighty-two days Truman was vice president he met with Roosevelt twice (except for cabinet meetings): March 8 and March 19. In both meetings nothing of consequence was discussed. David McCullough, *Truman* (New York: Simon & Schuster, 1992), pp. 333, 339.

6. Clark Clifford, *Counsel to the President* (New York: Random House, 1991), pp. 109–10. Clifford was a close adviser to President Truman.

7. Clifford, p. 131.

8. Lefeber's interpretation is quite different: that Stalin had earlier adopted a hands-off policy toward Greece, and Truman, with Acheson, saw this as a "historic opportunity to launch an offensive against the Soviet Union." Lefeber, *The American Age,* p. 453.

9. *Congressional Record,* Volume 93, 80th Congress, 1st Session, pp. 1980ff. Reprinted in Hartman, *Basic Documents,* pp. 275–82.

10. Dean Acheson, *Present At the Creation,* p. 225. Acheson says (p. 219) that he told the congressional leaders gathered at the White House that "Like apples in a barrel, infected by one rotten one, the corruption of Greece would affect Iran and all to the east. It would also carry infection to Africa through Asia Minor and Egypt, and to Europe through Italy and France. . . ." Acheson's figure of speech anticipates Eisenhower's "domino" metaphor.

11. Acheson's title, *Present at the Creation,* comes from King Alphonso X of Spain's quip: "Had I been present at the creation I would have given some useful hints for the better ordering of the Universe." Acheson was a very interesting person to talk to. His style, though, infuriated Senators of the homespun variety. Not surprisingly, his memoirs, after Acknowledgments, has a page entitled *Apologia Pro Libro Hoc.* He does not offer a translation.

12. Many American policymakers already had come to believe that the United States and the Soviet Union were locked in a bipolar struggle for survival, with the Greek and Turkish problems only part of that larger picture. See the discussion in Joseph M. Jones, *The Fifteen Weeks* (New York: Viking, 1955), pp. 138–41.

13. Frederick H. Hartmann, *Germany Between East and West: The Reunification Problem* (Englewood Cliffs, NJ: Prentice-Hall, 1965), pp. 24–25, examines this crisis in detail.

14. Clifford, *Counsel,* p. 101.

15. Clifford, p. 131.

16. The U.S. intelligence community considered this the most dangerous threat to American security at the time. A then-secret CIA report of September 26, 1947, titled "Review of the World Situation as it Relates to the Security of the United States," stated on p. 1: "The greatest danger . . . is the possibility of economic collapse in Western Europe and the consequent accession to power of Communist elements." (The report was declassified on November 18, 1977.)

17. Acheson, *Present At the Creation,* pp. 231–32.

18. Acheson, pp. 232–35. See also Frederick H. Hartmann, ed., *Basic Documents of International Relations* (New York: McGraw-Hill, 1951), pp. 284–86 for excerpts from both Acheson's speech and Marshall's.

19. Clifford, *Counsel,* p. 145.

20. Clifford, pp. 176, 177.

21. Clifford, p. 178. Clifford gives the preamble text of the executive order on p. 179.

22. McCarthy failed to prove that even one person on his so-called "list" was a Communist. For a succinct discussion, see Davids, *America and the World of Our Time,* 4th ed., pp. 437–39.

23. George F. Kennan, *Memoirs, 1925–1950* (Boston: Little, Brown, 1967), p. 134.

24. One might have thought that defense spending would have increased sharply. Such was not the case until the Korean War began.

25. This view, also widely held in Europe, led to the signature of the North Atlantic Pact in June 1949. It also led President Truman to authorize a comprehensive study of America's national security situation. That study eventually produced the much-noted NSC-68, which, after the outbreak of the Korean War, provided the conceptual framework for the massive American military buildup. Declassified in February 1973, the text may be found in the *Naval War College Review* (May–June 1975), pp. 51–108.

26. Acheson himself gives substantial quotes from the speech in *Present At the Creation,* pp. 355–57. The whole speech is in *Department of State Bulletin,* vol. xxii (1950), pp. 112–15.

27. Acheson, *Present at the Creation,* p. 357.

28. Acheson, p. 357.

29. This article by Dennis W. Brogan, "The Illusion of American Omnipotence," *Harper's* (December 1952), pp. 21–28, was widely reprinted in the 1950s, summing up so well as it did the feelings of those Americans outraged by the whole extreme right-wing movement.

30. Acheson's memoirs is among the many shedding light on U.S. reactions. Truman's memoirs were mentioned earlier. The most detailed inside account by a participant is U. Alexis Johnson, *The Right Hand of Power* (Englewood Cliffs, NJ: Prentice-Hall, 1984). It is excellent on the subsequent developments; see pp. 99–170. Johnson, incidentally, got along well with John Foster Dulles and never ran athwart the loyalty-security problem that ensnared so many of his contemporaries in the State Department. A very valuable scholarly account of the first week's decision making is Glenn D. Paige, *The Korean Decision: June 24–30, 1950* (New York: The Free Press, 1968).

31. Useful on the historical background is Carl Berger, *The Korea Knot: A Military-Political History,* rev. ed. (Philadelphia: University of Pennsylvania Press, 1964), Chs. 1–7.

32. Because of the tide problem and other military reasons—the precarious military situation in the south, ease of enemy movement to the battlefield, difficulties of reinforcement—not everyone in Washington supported MacArthur's concept. For an excellent discussion of combat operations in Korea, see Clay Blair, *The Forgotten War: America in Korea, 1950–1953* (New York: Times Books, 1987).

33. For an insightful assessment of "why," see John G. Stoessinger, *Nations in Darkness: China, Russia, and America,* 4th ed. (New York: Random House, 1986), Ch. 4.

34. The issue of MacArthur's entire strategy was controversial, and remains so. Despite their concerns, however, the president's advisors apparently hesitated to cross the general. Isaacson and Thomas wrote: "Between November 10 and December 4, the Secretaries of Defense and State and the Joint Chiefs of Staff met three times . . . the two Secretaries met five times with the President, and Acheson himself talked five more times with the President. The minutes . . . repeatedly reflect concern with MacArthur's moves, yet there is about them a sense of drift, almost helplessness." Isaacson and Thomas, *The Wise Men,* p. 537. On pp. 537ff, one sees an advisory system that served the president very poorly.

35. Johnson, *The Right Hand of Power,* p. 98. Johnson correctly describes Washington's reaction. The reason he had come across other views is that Nikita Khrushchev's memoirs, published in 1970 and 1974, give an insider's account of what happened at the Moscow end in 1949. Khrushchev says:

> . . . at the end of 1949, Kim Il-sung arrived with his delegation to hold consultations with Stalin. The North Koreans wanted to prod South Korea with the point of a bayonet. Kim Il-sung said that the first poke would touch off an internal explosion in South Korea and that the power of the people would prevail. . . . Naturally, Stalin couldn't oppose this idea. It appealed to his convictions as a Communist all the more because the struggle would be an internal matter which the Koreans would be settling for themselves.

Khrushchev adds: "I must stress that the war wasn't Stalin's idea." See Nikita Khrushchev, *Khrushchev Remembers,* trans. and edited by Strobe Talbott (Boston: Little, Brown, 1970), pp. 367–70. In his massive and very well-documented analysis, Bruce Cumings concurs. See Bruce Cumings, *The Origins of the Korean War, Volume II: The Roaring of the Cataract, 1947–1950* (Princeton, NJ: Princeton University Press, 1990), Ch. 19. Cumings stresses the essentially civil character of the war.

36. Johnson, *The Right Hand of Power,* p. 99.

37. Omar Bradley and Clay Blair, *A General's Life: An Autobiography* (New York: Simon & Schuster, 1983), p. 535. (This is actually Bradley's *second* autobiography. His first one, written soon after World War II, was far less informative and, of course did not cover so many years.) See Seyom Brown, *The Faces of Power: Constancy and Change in United States Foreign Policy from Truman to Reagan* (New York: Columbia University Press, 1983), p. 55.

38. General of the Army Douglas MacArthur, *Reminiscences* (New York: McGraw-Hill, 1964), pp. 385–89.

39. Johnson, *Right Hand of Power,* gives the statistics on p. 170. The U.N. held a total of 171,000 prisoners, including Korean civilians impressed into the Communist armies. Of these, 87,000 refused repatriation. Approximately *three out of four* Chinese prisoners were in this group.

40. Clifford, *Counsel to the President,* p. 345.

Escalating Tensions

*Eisenhower, Kennedy, and the
Cuban Missile Crisis*

For most of the Eisenhower and Kennedy administrations, the global tension level was high. Both presidents believed that the "Free World" was locked in a long term struggle with Moscow-directed International Communism just as Truman had, although they used somewhat different approaches in dealing with the problems they confronted.

Problem I: Germany Again

With the Korean War settled, attention now shifted back to Europe, especially Germany. Eisenhower took office knowing that the breaking of the Berlin blockade, while successful in and of itself, had done nothing to resolve the basic problem. Indeed, the strategy had deepened the differences between the West and the Soviets. After the June 1949 meeting of the five-power Council of Foreign Ministers, no new meeting was held until January 1954. This was almost a year after Stalin had died and had been succeeded by a group leadership, including Molotov but nominally led by Georgi Malenkov.

Much had happened to Germany in the meantime, including in June 1953, an uprising in East Berlin and East Germany against the Communists. Young boys came out in the streets to hurl Molotov cocktails (bottles filled with gasoline and having a cloth wick) at Soviet tanks. In the first confusion the jails were raided by the rebels and many political prisoners released, who promptly fled to the West. But the revolt was soon suppressed.[1]

Meanwhile, German rearmament began. In the East, as early as 1948, the Soviets had 50,000 Germans under arms, complete with artillery and tanks. The West countered with a French plan for German rearmament within the framework of a European Defense Community (EDC). West German rearmament would occur only with definite controls (a point the French understandably insisted on, given the history of France-Germany relations since 1871). Bonn would not have any separate, full-scale divisions; rather, German battalions would be integrated into multinational divisions run by a European command. In return, West Germany was to become sovereign. These provisions became part of the Bonn and Paris Conventions in May 1952. But even limited German rearmament was a stumbling block for Paris, and in the end the French themselves did not ratify the very EDC they had proposed. However, as part of NATO's forward defense concept, German rearmament was considered essential by the West. New arrangements were made to allow German forces under NATO control. Then Germany then was admitted to NATO, in May 1955.[2]

At the same time, with the Soviets in transition from Stalin's dictatorship to something less arbitrary, the West was anxious to explore whether the division of Germany could be healed. But when the Berlin Conference of Foreign Ministers met from January 25 to February 18, 1954, no common ground was found.[3] Molotov laid various proposals on the table. Their common theme was that the two existing German governments should consult on a treaty to establish an all-German government. (In other words, no arrangements would be made that were not acceptable to the Soviet Union's German satellite.) Whenever Molotov mentioned elections he would stipulate that it would be necessary to take measures to prevent "the rebirth of activity on the part of Fascist and militaristic organizations" as well as "by large monopolies." In other words, the elections would be Soviet-style. Molotov also proposed that the all-German state thus created would be neutral.

The main response of the West was the Eden Plan. It was a straightforward proposal for free elections in the Western sense, following which the united Germany would decide with whom it would align. (No one on either side doubted that the answer would be to join NATO.)

Molotov made a new offer on February 10th. Foreign troops should be evacuated from both Germanies. Germany would remain divided, with both parties neutralized. Given the West's determination to maintain a forward defense at the Iron Curtain line, this was summarily rejected. Deadlocked, the conference ended.

Problem II: Indochina

Following on the heels of this meeting was another Foreign Ministers Conference, this one concerning the Far East. It was called to settle the thorny issues resulting from the collapse of French power in Indochina. The conference commenced in Geneva on April 26, 1954. Although it met in an atmosphere of considerable international tension and developed the so-called Geneva Accords (discussed later), it is remembered today as much for the fact that John Foster Dulles snubbed Zhou Enlai, the Chinese Communist foreign minister, as for any concrete agreements of lasting effect.

The French had taken Indochina in the heyday of European imperialism in the nineteenth century. Defeated by the Germans in World War II, the French could do nothing to prevent the Japanese occupying the area.[4] After the war, the French tried to reassert their colonial rule, against stiff indigenous resistance led by the Viet Minh.[5] The resulting war posed a dilemma in counterbalancing national interests for the United States. It could not support colonialism, but it wanted the French to accept German rearmament and a firm policy against the Soviets. If America gave France aid, though, it could not prevent the French from using it to fight in Indochina. Unfortunately, with successive French governments weak and divided, the French could not muster the political courage or strength to make any serious decisions in any direction. With neither a majority to pull out of Indochina nor a majority to stay in and try to win, French counterbalancing interests deadlocked. The halfhearted policy actually pursued, like most such, did not work.

With French politics stalemating real decision, the French military determined to bring matters to a head with the "Navarre Plan." By occupying the fortress of Dienbienphu and challenging the Communist forces to a fixed battle, the French generals were sure they could win.[6] Previously the French had had to fight against guerrilla assaults, hit and run. A fixed battle, it was thought, would allow France to use its assets and destroy the opposition. But what actually was happening at Dienbienphu, where the rebels obligingly showed up to fight just as the French had hoped, was that the French were losing. A frantic French government urgently requested American help. On April 3, 1954, while Eisenhower at Camp David worked on a speech to quiet domestic fears about Communists and a possible economic depression, Secretary of State Dulles convened a meeting of congressional leaders to consider possible responses. At the time, the U.S. carriers *Boxer* and *Essex,* with two hundred planes, were in the South China Sea. Eisenhower queried Churchill on British participation, sending Dulles to London to make the case, but there was no interest. And there was little support in Congress for intervention. Eisenhower, who had made intervention dependent on both congressional and allied (especially British) support, thus decided to stay out.

Three weeks later, with the battle over Dienbienphu still going on, the Geneva Conference convened. When Dienbienphu finally fell on May 7, the French government soon collapsed. On June 19, 1954, Pierre Mendes-France, one of the most remarkable French leaders after World War II, took power, pledged to what seemed to be a utopian promise to achieve peace in Indochina in thirty days or resign. Astonishingly, he succeeded. The conference agreed to "temporarily" divide Vietnam at the 17th Parallel.

This result is less astonishing if we remember that Dulles on March 29 had said the United States would not "passively" accept the "loss" of Indochina. That Eisenhower had ruled out an air strike earlier did not guarantee American inaction if the Communists pressed too hard. Indeed, even the use of nuclear weapons was not entirely impossible. Besides, the various Communist participants felt they had done enough. Communist China already had been severely drained by its effort in the Korean War and was, therefore, reluctant to throw down the gauntlet. The Viet Minh, having gained so much and been promised elections (which they were sure they would win), were willing to accept less than they might have won by arms. And the Soviets, still coping with the aftermath of Stalin's death, needed peace, too. So the arrangement was made—to come apart later, as we shall see.

Problem III: Defense and Arms Control

Simultaneously with handling the German question, Indochina, and other area problems, the administration was deeply concerned about the growing costs of national security.

When Eisenhower took office in 1953, America was in the midst of a military buildup begun during the Korean War. The creation of NATO had also resulted in a substantial deployment of American troops in Europe. In the strategic area, a large nuclear stockpile and forward-based bombers ensured America's superiority. As a result, in FY 1953, U.S. national security spending was more than $50 billion (more than 13 percent of GNP).

Eisenhower believed that such a level of effort and expenditure could not be sustained indefinitely. Seeing the Soviet threat as much economic as military, and believing that America's economic health required a balanced budget, he advocated what was quickly labeled "the great equation"—a balanced economic-military emphasis maintainable over the long haul. His "New Look" approach coupled a continued emphasis on strategic superiority with major conventional force reductions (especially in the army).

Eisenhower's view was that America should never again fight a protracted war like Korea. Instead, it would retaliate quickly and effectively against the real culprit, who stood behind the nominal aggressor. Accordingly, the president largely abandoned previous distinctions between nuclear and conventional conflict. He authorized the military to plan to employ nuclear weapons as the situation required. America's strategic superiority and technological edge would permit more capability at less cost, more "bang for the buck."

This emphasis on nuclear weapons and a professed willingness to use them came to be known as "massive retaliation," a phrase that John Foster Dulles added to the American vocabulary. The Communists would be deterred by America's capability to retaliate instantly and massively, at times and places that the United States chose. By the same token, this policy would also provide "extended deterrence" for U.S. allies.

With nuclear forces as the ultimate backup, Eisenhower also sought further bilateral alliances that could furnish local frontline forces to take any first blow. Treaties were signed with South Korea and Nationalist China. In addition, a Southeast Asia Treaty Organization (SEATO) was set up, aid agreements were signed with several Middle East states, and the Baghdad Pact, later renamed CENTO, was formed.

Eisenhower also renewed U.S. efforts to reduce international danger and lower the world tension level through nuclear arms control. The earliest plans, under Truman, had envisaged an international authority (under the U.N. Security Council) controlling all phases of atomic energy production and use. Allowed unhampered inspection throughout the territories of all U.N. members, the U.N. inspectors would ensure that no clandestine activities were taking place. Once this inspection and control were fully effective, all atomic weapons anywhere would be destroyed. But the Soviets refused this plan. Wary of any plans for inspection, they advocated instead summarily outlawing the production of nuclear weapons, followed quickly by their destruction.

The U.S. plan would have allowed inspections on Soviet soil *before* U.S. weapons (the only ones in existence) were destroyed; the Soviet plan had weapons being destroyed before anyone could be sure cheating was not taking place. Not surprisingly, each side's proposals were unacceptable to the other.

Over the next several years, arms control and disarmament proposals were (or seemed) formulated more for their political impact than for any real steps toward agreements. Still, both Washington and Moscow recognized the dangers of a growing nuclear arms race. Eisenhower, hoping for a breakthrough at the Geneva summit meeting in 1955, unveiled an "open skies" proposal. It would have permitted U.S. planes to overfly the Soviet Union and Soviet planes to overfly the United States, thus reassuring each in the days before space satellites that neither was secretly mobilizing. The Soviets showed little interest in Ike's proposal (or any other proposal that meant foreign intrusion into their land, sea, or air spaces). Eisenhower's presidency ended without any comprehensive arms control agreements.

Problem II: Middle East Crises

In May 1955, the superpowers were able to agree to an Austrian State Treaty. With it, the Allied occupation ended. Austria would henceforth be neutral. And with the wars in Korea and Indochina "finished" and the Berlin situation quiet, tensions relaxed further. It was in a hopeful vein that the great powers agreed to their summit meeting at Geneva in July 1955.

By this time Malenkov had been forced out of power in the Soviet Union (February 8, 1955). With Nicolai Bulganin as titular chief of the Soviet delegation, it soon became apparent that the real boss was Nikita Khrushchev, First Secretary of the Soviet Communist Party. At Geneva, both sides renounced initiating a nuclear war as a policy option. Although little of substance was agreed, tensions relaxed further.

But it was all too good to be true, and 1956 turned out to be a very traumatic year. Crises developed that not only strained superpower relations but that disrupted the unity of the West at a critical time.

The problem began in Egypt. There, as elsewhere in the Arab world, Israel's victory in the 1948–49 Palestine War was considered unacceptable. In 1952 a military junta overthrew Egyptian King Farouk. By 1954 Gamal Abdel Nasser was firmly in charge. He was interested in the Cold War from only one angle: It provided maneuvering room to play off one side against the other.[7]

Nasser's initial goal was to get the British out of Egypt. Ultimately, he wanted much more: to drive out the Israelis entirely and to control the Middle East. In his book, *The Philosophy of the Revolution,* Nasser described the role he wished to play: "The vicissitudes of history are full of heroes who create for themselves roles of great glory and heroism, playing them at decisive moments on the stage of history. . . . For some reason, it always strikes me that in this area in which we live is a role running around aimlessly looking for a hero to give it being." Nasser listed the elements of Arab strength, particularly oil and a strategic position, plus "the hundreds of millions [of Muslims] united by a single creed" who, working together, could "wield a power without limit."[8]

Nasser saw the Baghdad Pact, which linked Turkey and Iraq, and later Britain, Pakistan, and Iran, as a thinly veiled pretext for continued foreign influence. Angered by the pact's formation and unable to get arms on his terms from the West, Nasser in September 1955 signed an agreement with Moscow to receive Czech-made arms.

Nasser's second step evolved from his desire to build a High Dam on the Nile at Aswan. Foreign aid would be needed, and both East and West showed interest. In December, the United States and Britain gave Nasser clear assurances of support.[9] But Nasser continued with his tactics of playing one side against the other, and in May 1956 he compounded American irritation by recognizing Communist China. In July an irritated Dulles suddenly announced the withdrawal of the American offer, Britain and the World Bank hastily following suit. Explaining himself later, Dulles argued that Egypt's recognition of China "posed an issue to which . . . there was only one proper response: That issue was, do nations which play both sides get better treatment than nations which are stalwart and work with us?"[10]

Nasser, of course, saw things differently. Five days after this rebuff, in an angry answer, he rejected "the domination of force and the dollar." He told Washington "Drop dead of your fury for you will never be able to dictate to Egypt."[11] Then, catching the world by surprise, he nationalized the Suez Canal Company, putting its operations under Egyptian national control. Egypt would build the High Dam itself, financing construction from the proceeds from operating the canal. Thus Egypt would build a "dam of dignity, freedom and grandeur" and eliminate "humiliation and servility."[12]

The resulting situation was far from simple. Nasser undoubtedly had a right to nationalize the canal company if he compensated the stockholders. (The British were the largest stockholder. The French, who had built the canal, also had heavy holdings.) Thornier was the issue of freedom of navigation. The Constantinople Convention of 1888 guaranteed unimpeded navigation of the canal, both in war and peace. Although Nasser said he would honor the treaty, Britain and France were highly skeptical. Egypt had already barred Israeli shipping since 1950, despite U.N. resolutions. Anthony Eden, the British prime minister, saw Nasser's action as parallel to Hitler's. Such a man must not again be allowed "to have his thumb at our windpipe."[13] Since in 1955, over 107 million tons of cargo (three-fifths of it oil destined for Western ports) went through the Suez Canal, what Nasser did with his thumb was quite important.

Looming over these issues was Nasser's role and power in the Middle East. America, from a Cold War perspective, worried whether Nasser's neutrality would enhance Soviet influence. Britain, long the area's leading foreign power, with strong ties to Jordan, Iraq, and the smaller nations along the Persian Gulf, saw it this way, too, but even more as an imperial challenge of the first magnitude.

The national interests of Israel, France, and Britain now converged. The Israelis, who at the birth of their nation had defeated much of the forces of the Arab world,[14] knew Nasser's ultimate goal was to destroy them. Why wait when such a threat demanded action? France, having endured the trauma of Indochina (and a revolt in Algeria, where Nasser had provided significant aid to the rebels), was in no mood to tolerate any further blow to French pride. The day after the nationalization, Prime Minister Eden of Britain cabled Eisenhower that the West "must be ready, in the last resort, to use force."[15]

The reaction of the United States was ambiguous. In terms of past-future linkages, America was against colonialism and for the "rule of law." Eden's statement seemed flavored by old-fashioned imperialism. Then again, the canal traffic was far less important to Washington than to Europe. On the other hand, Dulles was still angry at Nasser's playing off of the superpowers and said he was determined that Nasser must "disgorge" the canal. And it would not be easy to oppose America's most important allies. Between August and October, the United States took the lead in efforts at a diplomatic solution that would avoid the need to choose between two American counterbalancing interests. But to no avail. Nasser, for whom compromise would have required surrendering what he had just gained, frustrated every proposal. In September, in a statement that encouraged Nasser's unwillingness to make concessions, Dulles said the United States did not intend "to try to shoot its way through the Canal."[16] Meanwhile, in late 1956, British, French, and Israeli determination grew.

On October 29, Israel launched a preemptive strike against Egypt.[17] London and Paris demanded both belligerents withdraw their troops ten miles from the Canal (which, of course, flowed *through* Egypt, the Sinai Peninsula on one side, the rest of Egypt on the other). They also asked Egypt's "permission" to occupy the area "temporarily" to protect canal transit. When Egypt quite under-

---

Box
10.1
Illustrating Counterbalancing Interests

In 1956, with Nasser nationalizing the Suez Canal Company, Israel, Britain, and France attacked Egypt, while President Eisenhower opposed their use of force.

British Prime Minister Eden's two alternatives:

Not Oppose Nasser	Oppose Nasser
Advantage: avert involvement with unforseeable consequences	Advantage: prevent worse trouble later
Disadvantage: Nasser encouraged to conduct more "aggression" and Suez trade jeopardized	Disadvantage: costs blood and money now

President Eisenhower's two alternatives:

Oppose U.S. Allies	Not Oppose U.S. Allies
Advantage: demonstrate U.S. faith in "rule of law" and impartiality toward Arabs in Middle East	Advantage: will not disrupt important coalition
Disadvantage: undermines prestige of allies; probably projects U.S. more into Middle East responsibilities	Disadvantage: U.S. superpower image tarnished by lack of action

---

standably rejected the proposal, England and France began on October 31 to bomb Cairo, which was followed rather tardily by an actual landing of troops.

Complicating matters further, on October 21, following months of unrest, an uprising against Soviet control began in Hungary. Revolt was ready to explode in Poland, too. The Soviets initially responded with concessions on Poland and a withdrawal of Red Army units from Hungary. But with the West now embroiled in its own crisis, plus the new Hungarian government's astonishing idea of actually joining NATO, the Soviets soon went over to a massive counterstrike and ruthlessly ended the rebellion against Soviet overlordship. The United States could do little more than condemn the Soviet actions.[18]

The U.N. now became the focal point for the Middle East debate. Demonstrating American idealism, Eisenhower on October 31 declared there would "be no law if we work to invoke one code of international conduct for those we oppose and another for our friends."[19] America now decided between the two alternatives of supporting its allies or supporting the rule of law. Taking the lead in the U.N., the United States put pressure on the British, French, and Israelis.

On November 5 the General Assembly voted to create a multinational Emergency Force "to secure and supervise the cessation of hostilities," giving the humiliated French and British a tiny fig leaf to hide behind. The Soviets, meanwhile, were issuing threats of military intervention (and even rocket warfare) if the allies did not retire. The allies, isolated diplomatically, agreed to withdraw.

American policy decisions in the crisis relied heavily on the abstract principle of respect for law. Unfortunately, as with any shorthand formula response, the other values tended to be ignored. Looked at in terms of counterbalancing interests, the disadvantage of being the prime mover against one's own allies might well have loomed larger. Although the United States might not be expected to condone the invasion, it was not under any obligation to respond by undermining the regional balance of power—which is what happened.

The consequences of Suez were enormous. In a regional context, Eisenhower's policy may have temporarily gained some Arab favor. But from a Cold War perspective, the results were distressing. Relations with Britain and France were badly strained. In addition, whatever opportunity had existed to discourage Red Army reentry into Hungary was lost because the West was in total disarray. That lack of American action made hash out of Dulles' repeated calls for liberation from the Soviet yoke. Of course, relations with Israel were not helped. And Suez increased Nasser's prestige in the Arab world, where "face" is at least as important as it is in the Orient. After all, Nasser had successfully defied the Israelis and two great foreign powers, all at once! Suez also weakened British influence in the region, and thus those regimes in Iraq and Jordan tied so closely to them. And, of course, Nasser was still working with Moscow.

In the aftermath of Suez, with British and French influence so damaged, Washington saw it had helped create a power vacuum into which Moscow could easily step. Eisenhower, seeking a remedy, in January 1957 proposed what became known as the Eisenhower Doctrine. He asked Congress for advance authority to halt Communist aggression in the Middle East.[20] After two months of debate, Congress gave Eisenhower most of what he wanted, authorizing $200 million in mutual security funds. The doctrine asserted that "the United States regards as vital to the national interest and world peace the preservation of the independence and integrity of the nations of the Middle East." If necessary, the United States would use armed force to assist any such nation or group of nations requesting assistance "against overt armed aggression from any nation controlled by International Communism."[21] [Note the capitalization.]

Like the Truman Doctrine, the Eisenhower Doctrine implied potentially extensive commitments. It did not identify which countries were controlled by international communism. Nor did it try to rank the nations of the area in order of importance to the United States. Instead of establishing priorities, it provided a general principle, a new shorthand formula for deciding policy. If anyone asked, the United States was to respond.

The Arab reaction, not surprisingly, was generally negative.[22] True, there had just been an overt armed attack against an Arab nation—but by whom? Certainly not a nation controlled by international communism. It was the Soviet

Union who had been one of the strongest political defenders of Egypt when the attack had been mounted by Israel, France, and Britain. Along with the United States, the Soviets had helped lead the United Nations effort to condemn the aggressors. But nothing was more remote from actual Arab experience (either in the Suez crisis or in their history) than overt armed attack by a nation controlled by international communism. Even the very phrasing of the doctrine showed a lack of empathy for the way Arabs viewed events, for Arab past-future linkages. Not surprisingly, only one Arab nation, Lebanon, officially endorsed the doctrine, and only in Lebanon was it actually implemented.

The Lebanon case is instructive. In the 1950s, Lebanon was often called the Switzerland of the Middle East. Well situated as a funnel for regional trade, its banking institutions also served regional financial needs. Its growing wealth, though, was predicated on the stability of a very precarious political arrangement that shared power between the Muslim and Christian populations. When a revolt began in May 1958, Lebanon claimed that Egypt and Syria were trying to undermine Lebanese independence. Washington readily accepted this notion, ignoring evidence to the contrary. By now Washington was sure that Nasserist and/or Communist machinations were behind any Middle East unrest. Soon actual fighting began in Lebanon. Then, in July, a brutal coup occurred in neighboring Iraq. Brigadier General Abdel Kassim took power, removing Iraq from the Baghdad Pact and raising the sudden specter of a new ally to reinforce Nasser's ambitions (and add to Soviet influence). Pro-Western Jordan now appeared in serious jeopardy; perhaps also Saudi Arabia. Washington, seriously concerned about regional stability, decided on armed intervention in Lebanon.[23] The British decided to act simultaneously, airlifting troops to Jordan to prevent a possible Nasserist coup.

Sixth Fleet marines began landing on July 15. British paratroopers landed in Jordan on July 17, their numbers rising to 3,000 in short order.[24]

Even today, whether these deployments were required or wise remains controversial. While Washington believed it enhanced stability by preventing Nasserist takeovers, its actions both gave the illusion of validity to earlier charges that the crisis was just a pretext for Western intervention and raised suspicions about the West's ultimate intentions. In the aftermath, Iraq moved into the Soviet orbit and (temporarily) drew closer to Nasser. Lebanon was stabilized for a time, but its day of reckoning was only postponed. The mutual Anglo-American resentments from Suez were in some degree mitigated by the parallel actions they took. Driven by the Cold War, the United States, for better or worse, had become a prime actor in the Middle East.

Problems I and II: Crises in the Far East and Europe

The year 1958 brought the Eisenhower administration two more almost simultaneous crises, one in the Far East and the other in Europe.

The Far Eastern crisis began first. When in 1949 Chiang Kai-shek lost China and retreated to Formosa (Taiwan), he kept control of two small islands just off the Chinese mainland, Quemoy and Matsu. These islands were of no real strategic significance, but any change in control over them could undermine a precarious status quo. In 1954 and 1955 the Communist Chinese bombarded those offshore islands. Washington, already committed to the defense of Formosa and the nearby Pescadores, wondered if this was the prelude to further action. The crisis subsided in April, but the problem remained unresolved.

In August 1958, violence erupted again, when the Chinese Communists unleashed an artillery barrage, killing 200. As the confrontation escalated, Chiang asked for help. Eisenhower, feeling that Chiang had too many troops in these islands for defensive purposes, was not prepared to offer categorical support of all actions Chiang might undertake. With the resupply problem worsening, Dulles flew to Newport, Rhode Island, where the president had gone to play golf. Dulles presented a memorandum to Eisenhower that heavily stressed the domino theory: If Quemoy went, then Taiwan, and then more would follow. "The consequences in the Far East would be even more far-reaching and catastrophic than those which followed *when the United States allowed the Chinese mainland to be taken over* by the Chinese Communists." (Italics added.) Eisenhower abandoned his usual caution and approved the memorandum as policy, with minor changes. At a press conference that followed, Dulles made it clear that the United States would not allow Quemoy and Matsu to pass into Chinese Communist hands by force.[25]

As the crisis deepened, the British probed as to how far the United States was prepared to go. (They considered that Beijing had a valid claim to all Chinese territories, including the islands.) Dulles said that if the Communists were to attack Quemoy from the air, America would retaliate against mainland airfields. He raised the threat of the use of tactical nuclear weapons. "I hope," said Dulles, "no more than small air bursts without fallout."[26]

Beijing now understood the seriousness of the American position. With the Seventh Fleet escorting Nationalist supply ships to the three-mile limit off the islands, the defense situation was strengthened even though bombardment by Communist artillery continued. Khrushchev weighed in with a warning against a nuclear attack on China, pointing out that "the other side too has atomic and hydrogen weapons. . . ."

But with public opinion now turning against the announced policy in the United States, Eisenhower began backing away from the talk of tactical nuclear weapons.[27] Dulles on September 30 told a press conference that the United States had no legal commitment to defend the islands and "no commitment of any kind" to help Chiang return to the mainland. The Chinese responded with a cease-fire and gradually the crisis faded away.[28] Whether American policy in this instance served American national interests depends in part on whether one considers the whole policy of antagonism and confrontation with Communist China made sense. But the Cold War paradigm, the legacy of the Korean War and the popularity of the domino theory, combined with the pro-Nationalist pressures of the China Lobby, made consideration of the counterbalancing interest alternative infeasible.

Problem I: Ultimatum on Germany

Now attention shifted to Germany. Little had changed since 1949. The 1954 Berlin Conference had merely registered superpower disagreements, in no way easing the tensions. The Soviet Union, worried over the unrest in East Germany, Poland, and Hungary, confronted a classic set of alternatives: make concessions (or perhaps even withdraw) or get tougher. Molotov had set a tough tone at the last conference: There were now two Germanies, he said. That was a fact of life. Don't expect us to cooperate in giving up what we have. The Soviet position was that Berlin, the question of elections, and all others concerning unification, should be left up to the "two" German states. The only matter for the Four Powers to consider was a peace treaty with the "two states."

There had been one moment, in February 1955, when the course of history might have been changed, if the West had been willing to settle for a unified but neutral Germany. At a Warsaw interparliamentary conference on the German question, 150 delegates (including Soviet representatives) voted unanimously to offer negotiations "on free, controlled elections in Germany, such as were proposed by Sir Anthony Eden. . . . The resolution also suggested that the territorial integrity of a neutralized Germany should be guaranteed by the European states and the United States." The newspaper account closed by saying: "The Warsaw resolution . . . went far beyond any offer made publicly by Vyacheslav M. Molotov on the reunification of Germany."

This account appeared in the *New York Times* on February 11th, five days after the conference ended on February 6th. Obviously, since the Soviet delegates would not have gone against governmental policy, some high Soviet official was behind the offer. But Malenkov was suddenly forced out on February 8, 1955, two days after the conference. Unfortunately, the U.S. ambassador to the Soviet Union, Charles Bohlen, was at that time on vacation in France.[29] If there was an opportunity, it was gone almost as soon as it appeared.

In any case, with Khrushchev in control, a hard line Soviet policy was asserted. On November 10, 1958, he began the most dangerous crisis of the Eisenhower years. In a speech he charged the West with having violated all of the "basic provisions of the Potsdam Agreement" but one: The "so-called Four-Power status of Berlin, that is, a position in which the three Western powers . . . have the possibility of lording it in Western Berlin, turning that part of the city, which is the capital of the German Democratic Republic, into some kind of state within a state and, profiting by this, conducting subversive activities from Western Berlin. . . ." It was time to end this and "create a normal situation."

In a note to the West on November 27, Khrushchev spelled out the details of what "normal" meant. *West* Berlin would become a "free city" with no armed forces permitted there. To avoid "haste and unnecessary friction" and to assure "maximum possible consideration for the interests of the parties concerned," the Soviets would "make no changes in the present procedure for [Western] military traffic [to and from Berlin] for half a year." If the West did not utilize this time to accept, the Soviets would carry out the "planned measures through an agreement with the German Democratic Republic [which], like any other independent state, must fully deal with questions concerning its . . . sovereignty on land, on water, and in the air." The Soviet Union would no longer discuss Berlin questions with officials of the West. Once Western rights of access terminated, any Western violation of the new situation would "immediately cause appropriate retaliation."[30]

Precipitating this new confrontation was a difficulty neither the Soviets nor the East Germans had been able to solve. Not only was West Berlin a "bone in the throat"; the population of their puppet state was also slowly but surely eroding. East Germans were "voting with their feet," going to the West in droves. Although from the beginning of the Cold War the main roads across the Iron Curtain in the middle of Germany were stringently controlled, anyone could still easily cross over via hundreds of secondary roads. But these were closed by the Soviets the day after the EDC Treaty was signed at Paris on May 26, 1952. Even so, in the ten years from 1949 to 1959, some 2,188,425 East Germans escaped and registered with the West German authorities for resettlement assistance. From 1949 to early 1961, the refugee flow averaged annually 230,000. Fifty percent of these were under the age of 25, and 74 percent were under 45! East Germany, with a population of something more than 16 million near the end of this period, could not afford the loss of the most vigorous segment of the population. But this was exactly the group least willing to sit and be stifled in the Communist world, especially since there was an attractive alternative. After the secondary roads were cut, most of these refugees left by simply coming to East Berlin and taking the rapid transit train into West Berlin. The diminishing of East German population is the essential clue to understanding why the Soviets were so anxious in this period to close off Berlin.

In mid-December the West responded that it would not yield to threats. On December 31 a U.S. note spelled out that America would "not accept a unilateral repudiation on the part of the Soviet Government of its obligations in respect of . . . freedom of access. Nor will it accept the substitution of the regime which the Soviet Government refers to as the German Democratic Republic"— a state and a status that the West did not recognize.[31] The note went on to say that the United States could not negotiate under duress but assumed that the Soviets had not really intended that. If that were so, the United States was prepared to meet.

The Soviet response on January 10, 1959, was considerably milder than the previous note. More notes were exchanged, more speeches made. On March 16, on television, Eisenhower ended by saying: "We will not retreat an inch from our duty. We shall continue to exercise our right of peaceful passage to and from West Berlin." More notes were exchanged, and finally a May conference in Geneva was agreed.

The Geneva Foreign Ministers Conference was devoted exclusively to the

German question. It was the longest such conference ever held, lasting from May to August. The most dramatic feature of the conference, apart from the deadlock which terminated its first phase, was the fact that the six-months "ultimatum" quietly expired during the discussions without ending them.

When the final work session met on August 5, other proposals had been exchanged, but the deadlock remained. Khrushchev at the beginning of the affair had obviously thought the West, in disarray after the dual crises of 1956 and visibly shocked by the successful launching of *sputnik* (Soviet space vehicle) in 1957, would be unable to hold together. Disillusioned, he came to the United States at the end of September 1959 to discuss the situation at Camp David with Eisenhower. In a news conference on September 28, Eisenhower said they had both agreed "that these negotiations should not be prolonged indefinitely but there could be no fixed limit on them." Khrushchev, next day in Moscow, concurred: "We agreed indeed that talks on the Berlin question should be resumed, that no time limit whatsoever is to be established for them, but that they also should not be dragged out for an indefinite time." And that ended that temporarily.

The United States now agreed to hold a summit meeting in Paris in May 1960. Only days before it was to begin, Khrushchev in a speech at Baku again went over to a hard line. If the Soviets were forced to sign a separate peace (with East Germany) and the West refused, "they will not retain the rights. . . . They naturally will forfeit the right of access to West Berlin. . . ." All that was lacking now was a date for it to again be an ultimatum.

Suddenly there was an unanticipated complication. Until satellites were perfected, the United States used U-2 airplanes to photograph the Soviet Union from high altitudes. Reportedly the U-2 could fly up to 4,000 miles at altitudes of more than 14 miles, using less than 1,000 gallons of fuel. Its cameras could photograph the terrain below for 3,000 miles with a width of 125 miles. The photos were sufficiently detailed so that, with enlargement, one could read a newspaper headline from eight to ten miles in space.[32] U-2s were not normally flown before important conferences; there was always some risk. But it was presumed that the Soviets could not reach the plane's altitude with any rocket fire. In any event, one was launched over the Soviet Union on May Day. Flying at high altitude over the Soviet Union, that U-2 was not only shot down by Soviet rockets but the pilot was captured—a fact that Khrushchev cunningly concealed. Then shortly after the American cover story was released, it was also "shot down" when the Soviets revealed that they had captured the pilot alive. An embarrassed Eisenhower accepted responsibility and Khrushchev, now at the Paris summit, demanded that the "guilty" be punished and an apology made. That statement ended the meeting before it really began—which may well have been Khrushchev's intention because he really had no hope of accomplishing anything useful at the summit. He had painted himself into a corner.[33]

At the end of Eisenhower's second term, few Americans seriously questioned the fundamental imperative of containment. Although there might be (and were) differences over how policy should be implemented and what tactics should be employed, "everyone knew" the "Free World" was confronted by an inherently aggressive Communist bloc controlled and directed by Moscow. The "lessons of Munich" had made forward deployment, global involvement, and quick action essential.

Problem I: Kennedy—Hard Beginnings and a Missile Crisis

When Kennedy became president in 1961, the Cold War was at its height. In those days the threat of a nuclear war seemed very real—correctly so, for Khrushchev was by no means through stirring the pot over Berlin. He knew he had a formidable opponent in Eisenhower, who had, incidentally, been strongly supported by de Gaulle when the pressure was most acute.

General Vernon A. Walters reports a conversation between Eisenhower and de Gaulle on the evening of September 3, 1959. The two heads of state were relaxing in their bathrobes before the fireplace in Rambouillet Castle, some 35 miles from Paris. Walters says the conversation "drifted to the efforts France was making in the nuclear field. . . . General de Gaulle said he was determined to go through with the effort to develop a nuclear capability for France as he felt it was essential to the defense of her interests and to her survival." He specifically mentioned the Suez debacle of 1956. Then de Gaulle added:

> You, Eisenhower, would go to nuclear war for Europe because you know what is involved and what is at stake. But as the Soviet Union develops the capability to strike the cities of North America, one of your successors will be unwilling to go to nuclear war for anything short of a nuclear strike against North America. When that comes, I or my successor must have in hand the nuclear means to turn what the Soviets may want to be a conventional war into a nuclear war.[34]

De Gaulle always assumed that the Soviets would not be deterred from a conventional war but would shrink from a nuclear one. His comment shows clearly that even one of the closest allies of the United States had clear doubts that America would stand up to a nuclear threat if Khrushchev forced the issue. De Gaulle, in this case, was wrong. But it is easy to see why Khrushchev thought that Jack Kennedy, the new and young president of the United States, would be a pushover, for Kennedy began by mishandling things very badly indeed.

Kennedy hardly had time to catch his breath after the election and get settled into the White House, before he had to make a critical decision about Cuba. Relying heavily on the advice of senior officials, he gave the green light to the Bay of Pigs invasion of Cuba by Cuban exiles opposed to Castro and trained by the CIA. The operation ended in complete disaster.[35] When the invasion was going badly and the basic assumption that the Cuban people would greet the landing as a liberation and rise up against Castro proved false, the only further option was the direct use of U.S. military force (especially air cover). At the last minute Kennedy drew the line and refused. Furious that he had not probed very deeply into the details (which had all been arranged under Eisenhower), Kennedy vowed never to take staff reports at face value again.[36]

Khrushchev now pressed Kennedy for an early meeting, and one was arranged for Vienna in early June 1961. At Vienna, Khrushchev again pushed for a German peace treaty and for making West Berlin a free city. After the treaty was signed, Khrushchev said, the West would have to take up access questions with the GDR. Kennedy on television called the meeting "a very somber two days" although not marked by any loss of tempers.[37] Khrushchev, nine days later on *his* television, ended with a new threat: "We ask everyone to understand us correctly: the conclusion of a peace treaty with Germany cannot be postponed any longer. A peaceful settlement in Europe must be attained this year." On June 21, in a new speech, he added: "At the end of this year, we . . . will sign a peace treaty" with the GDR.

As the new crisis accelerated, Kennedy reiterated the U.S. refusal to allow the Soviets to change American rights in Berlin. On July 25 he stated calmly: "We do not want to fight, but we have fought before. And others in earlier times have made the same dangerous mistake of assuming that the West was too selfish and too soft and too divided to resist invasions of freedom in other lands." Kennedy made it clear that the freedom of West Berlin was a vital interest of the United States. The United States was there not on anyone's sufferance but due to its victory in World War II. Abandoning West Berlin would mean abandoning Europe, which America had deemed so essential to its security that it fought two world wars. It would not accept an ultimatum. To be ready for any contingency Kennedy said he would seek an additional $3.25 billion for the defense budget and call up certain National Guard and reserve units. In response Khrushchev, becoming even more bellicose, said the United States had declared preliminary war on the Soviet Union. If war occurred, Kennedy would be the last American president.[38] On August 11, Khrushchev said: "We shall not be the first to press the buttons at our rocket installations, we shall not start a war; but if the imperialists force a war upon us we shall meet it bravely and deal a devastating blow to the aggressor." If America wanted war, that is how it would be.

In July the flow of refugees from East Germany ran at about twice the usual monthly average. In August it set new records. Khrushchev was right that the Soviets could not just keep waiting. So, on August 13, 1961, having failed in all other ways to stop the flow, he closed off East Berlin and began building the Berlin Wall. The days that followed were tense, as both American and Soviet tanks faced off at the Wall. Allied military patrols, though, were not shut out of East Berlin (nor were the Soviet military excluded from West Berlin). Although the crisis marked the commencement of many years of tragedy for East Germans who attempted to scale the Wall and were shot down, the situation was kept within bounds.

It was soon clear, though, that Khrushchev was not content just to stop the refugee flow, critical as that was. As Craig and George put it "Instead of making a dead set at Berlin, he [Khrushchev] chose the indirect approach. He decided to try something in Cuba, hoping apparently to win Berlin as a by-product of an American humiliation in the Caribbean."[39]

In the summer of 1962 U.S. intelligence became aware of greatly increased Soviet shipping to Cuba. That it was military in nature was clear; whether it was defensive surface-to-air missiles (SAMs), or something else, was not clear. On September 11, responding to U.S. concerns, the Kremlin said: "There is no need for the Soviet Union to shift its weapons for the repulsion of aggression, for a retaliatory blow, to any other country, for instance Cuba." But TASS, the Soviet news agency, did admit that "defensive" arms were being sent. In fact, 42 medium and intermediate-range ballistic missiles were actually en route to Cuba.

Why Khrushchev decided to do this and thought he could succeed is still in dispute.[40] Maybe it had to do with altering the nuclear balance. The Soviet position in *intercontinental* missiles was decidedly inferior to the United States. Perhaps Khrushchev hoped to make up the deficit by placing medium and intermediate-range missiles 100 miles from the American coast. If he had succeeded secretly, as a suddenly revealed surprise one day in conjunction with a new attempt to force the allies to recognize East Germany, the strategy would have definite psychological possibilities. Americans might feel outflanked, caught in a potential cross fire. Having missiles in Cuba also might influence Latin American nations. Khrushchev had shown himself throughout his tenure as bold and willing to take risks. Here he did it again and brought the world very near to a nuclear war.[41]

There had been rumors, press reports, and unconfirmed human intelligence indicating that something unusual was happening in Cuba, but not until October 14 was there definitive evidence. A U-2 flight over western Cuba showed that a medium-range missile base was under construction in the San Cristobal area. Increased U-2 coverage of Cuba soon verified the existence of five other MRBM (1,100 mile) and three IRBM (2,200 mile) sites. As Graham Allison was to write some years later, Soviet missile base construction followed a very definite pattern, making it possible if one found the initial steps to predict what would follow in due course.[42]

Kennedy had a previously scheduled meeting arranged with Andrei Gromyko, the Soviet foreign minister, for October 18. He decided to hold the meeting as scheduled and not let Gromyko know that he knew what was happening. Gromyko reiterated a Khrushchev promise that the German question would not be reactivated until after the American November 6 elections. Twice he said that after that, if no agreement could be reached, the Soviets would be "compelled" to sign a separate peace treaty with East Germany that would end Western rights in Berlin. On Cuba, Gromyko stressed that Soviet missiles *in Cuban hands* were purely defensive.

Closeting with his close advisers (soon to be called "the ExComm" of the NSC, although some of its members like Dean Acheson held no government position), Kennedy listened to the debate over his alternatives.[43] Early-on opinion swung toward a "surgical" air strike. But that would kill Soviets at the sites and make it harder for the Soviet Union to retreat.[44] An amphibious assault had the same drawback, would be even more bloody, and would involve American casualties. Yet, if it came to force, each would be needed. As the group pondered, they concluded that it would help to separate the problem into two phases. First, stop the Soviet ships still en route. Second, persuade the Soviets to dismantle and remove the missiles already being emplaced. The plan would involve delicate timing: suppose the Soviets stopped their ships en route but still pressed ahead to complete and activate the sites in Cuba? Still, the phased approach had the merit of avoiding immediate casualties and giving the Soviets some warning and some hours to think through their reaction. It would also avoid provoking Khrushchev into a "spasm" reaction.

Accordingly, Kennedy on October 22, in a television speech, grasped the initiative.[45] His speech was calm, firm, and to the point.

> Good evening, my fellow citizens. This Government, as promised, has maintained the closest surveillance of the Soviet military build-up on the island of Cuba. Within the past week unmistakable evidence has established the fact that a series of offensive missile sites is now in preparation. . . . The purpose of these bases can be none other than to provide a nuclear strike capacity against the Western Hemisphere. [This] . . . sudden, clandestine decision to station strategic weapons for the first time outside of Soviet soil, is a deliberately provocative and unjustified change in the status quo which cannot be accepted by this country, if our courage and our commitments are ever to be trusted again by either friend or foe.

Kennedy continued. A selective naval "quarantine" (blockade) would be imposed to prevent further shipment of "offensive weapons."[46] This nation would "regard any nuclear missile launched from Cuba against any nation in the Western Hemisphere as an attack by the Soviet Union on the United States, requiring a full retaliatory response upon the Soviet Union." This was strong stuff. The superpowers were now eyeball to eyeball.

The next days were hectic. The Organization of American States (OAS) met and cast a unanimous twenty votes to support the quarantine. Wednesday, October 24, when the blockade went into effect, was a highly dramatic day. All the world waited to see what would happen as the Soviet ships got nearer the interception line. In the Pentagon, too, tempers were frayed. Secretary of Defense McNamara and the Chief of Naval Operations had a falling out over McNamara's unwillingness to give the orders and leave the tactical decisions to the navy. The actual line of deployment for the quarantine was a little different from what the president intended. But, regardless of such details, the plan was working. There were some tense moments, particularly when Soviet submarines were spotted. On Thursday a Soviet tanker was hailed and allowed to proceed. On Friday a Lebanese-registered freighter under Soviet charter was boarded, inspected, and allowed to pass. By that day sixteen of the eighteen Soviet cargo ships, including all five with large hatches, had turned around.

Although phase 1 was working, work on the Soviet missile sites already in Cuba continued. If anything, it was being pushed. Then a U.S. U-2 was shot down by a SAM, adding further tension.

In those days communications were a problem. The relaying of the Soviet and American notes was agonizingly slow. A critical point came with the delivery of two Khrushchev letters, one on Friday at 9:00 P.M., October 26, and a second the next day. The Friday letter seemed to be saying that, since the missiles had been put into Cuba to defend against an American attack, they could be withdrawn if the United States promised no invasion. The Saturday letter, though, seemed to take a harder line, demanding that the United States withdraw its Jupiter missiles from Turkey in exchange. On Saturday Kennedy, ignoring the Saturday letter and putting his own interpretation on the Friday letter, answered that "the key elements of your [Friday] proposals . . . seem generally acceptable as I understand them." In a letter to Khrushchev, Kennedy spelled it out:

1. You would agree to remove these weapons systems from Cuba under appropriate United Nations observation and supervision; and undertake, with suitable safeguards, to halt the further introduction of such weapons systems into Cuba.
2. We, on our part, would agree . . . (a) to remove promptly the quarantine measures now in effect, and (b) to give assurances against an invasion of Cuba.[47]

In the evening of October 27 Robert Kennedy met with the Soviet Ambassador to Washington, Anatoly Dobrynin. Kennedy said the United States did not want war and had done everything it could to avoid it. But there were limits. The Soviets had constantly deceived America. The Soviets should understand that "if they did not remove those bases, we would remove them. . . . Perhaps his country might feel it necessary to take retaliatory action; but before that was over, there would be not only dead Americans but dead Russians as well." Kennedy went on to say that time "was running out. We had only a few more hours—we needed an answer immediately from the Soviet Union. I said we must have it the next day."[48] At the same time he added a "sweetener," telling Dobrynin that the president had long been thinking of phasing U.S. missiles out of Turkey (and Italy).[49]

On Sunday morning, October 28, the Soviet answer came, announced first over Moscow radio. The Soviets had accepted and had "given a new order to dismantle the arms which you describe as offensive and to crate them and return them to the Soviet Union." The Soviets agreed to the verification procedures, but *both* superpowers in the sequel were frustrated when Castro vetoed the plan. Nonetheless, the Soviets did as promised, and the United States was satisfied.

Problem III: Changing National Security Policy

From well before he became president, Kennedy was convinced the Soviets constituted a fundamental military threat to the West. The Berlin and Cuban missile crises only strengthened this view. Kennedy believed Eisenhower's defense policy had been seriously flawed. Massive retaliation simply was not credible as a deterrent because of its all-or-nothing characteristics. Unfortunately, the reduction of America's conventional war capabilities had left the nation with the terrible dilemma of either being ineffective in the face of attack or having to escalate quickly to nuclear war. Instead of this Hobson's choice, what America needed was a broad range of capabilities that would enable it to deter or fight across the entire spectrum of conflict. A wide range of weapons, conventional and nuclear, should be available so the president could choose the level and nature of response appropriate to the particular contingency. Borrowing a title coined earlier by General Maxwell Taylor, Kennedy called his policy "flexible response."[50]

Kennedy, like Truman's earlier implementation of NSC-68 in 1950, immediately initiated a massive across-the-board buildup. For conventional war, planning was now based on a "2 1/2 war" concept. The United States needed the capability to fight major wars with the Soviets in Europe and the Chinese in Asia and handle a "1/2 war" elsewhere, *simultaneously*. With this capability, nuclear weapons, rather than being used like "any other munition," would be employed only as a last resort. Limited war and counterinsurgency capabilities also had to be increased. In 1961 Khrushchev had advocated "wars of national liberation," and America had to be able to counter Communist and Communist-proxy guerillas whenever and wherever necessary. Various "special forces" were soon developed for this purpose, the Green Berets being only the most well known example.

Kennedy also ordered a major buildup in strategic nuclear strength. During the presidential campaign he had charged that there was a "missile gap," but after taking office he learned that was not the case. Indeed, the United States was "ahead." But even with that being true, he was still concerned. There was the possibility that the Soviets might move to a sudden and major increase in missile production. Strategic superiority was essential, so Kennedy greatly accelerated the submarine-launched ballistic missile program and slightly increased procurement of land-based missiles. Strategic Air Command ground alert and short-notice airborne capabilities were enhanced also. In order to have effective deterrence, it was necessary to have sufficient "assured destruction capability" that could survive and be able to retaliate after a Soviet attack. To assure this survivability, the United States diversified its forces into what was called a strategic "Triad" of bombers, land-based ballistic missiles, and sea-based (submarine) ballistic missiles.

Greatly concerned as he was with building military strength, Kennedy also pushed for certain kinds of narrowly focused arms control measures, in areas such as crisis communications. As noted earlier, during the Cuban missile crisis American and Soviet leaders could not communicate rapidly and accurately.[51] In the aftermath of the missile crisis, American policy makers proposed establishing direct communication links between Washington and Moscow. The Soviets saw the merits of this proposal, so negotiations quickly commenced, resulting on June 20, 1963, in the so-called "Hot Line" agreement. Telegraph-teleprinter equipment subsequently established at terminals in the two capitals provided facilities for the direct transmission of encoded printed messages, thus minimizing the chances for accidental escalation.

The crisis had a second, positive effect. In 1963, the United States, Britain, and the Soviet Union began serious negotiations for a ban on nuclear testing. Such a ban could reduce environmental damage and radioactive fallout while also helping to lower superpower tensions. The attempt at a solution was not new; the many roadblocks had included verification issues, the military need for continued testing, and the problem of cheating, to name just a few. Even now, in the aftermath of a first class crisis, efforts to achieve a *comprehensive* test ban proved futile, but a partial ban was agreed upon. The agreement banned tests in the atmosphere, in outer space, and underwater. Tests underground, within limits that did not contaminate the atmosphere, were still permitted. Washington saw the new treaty (correctly) as an opportunity to limit proliferation (since it is difficult to *develop* reliable nuclear weapons without above-ground testing).

Summing Up

Now that the Cold War is over and some missiles are actually being destroyed, it is hard to appreciate fully the sense of antagonism and tension that permeated superpower relations in these years. They were very hard times indeed. John Foster Dulles, with his lurid vocabulary, threatening "massive retaliation" if the Soviets orchestrated an aggression by proxy (i.e., the way the United States saw the Korean War), caught the spirit of the times. Dulles, encouraging unrest in the Soviet bloc, castigated the Democrats for being willing only to *contain* the Soviets. He proposed captive peoples should be liberated, that the Communists should be rolled back from the areas they had enslaved. That talk ended abruptly when America stood by, inactive, as the Hungarian freedom fighters were suppressed. Not that the United States could be blamed. What could it have reasonably done about it, short of all out war?

As Dulles was winding down his years on the world stage in the late 1950s, Nikita Khrushchev's role was increasing. An earthy peasant who had risen from the ranks, he was to shock the U.N. by going there in person and banging his shoes on the table for attention. That was typical of the man and his approach to problems. Khrushchev tried very hard to bulldoze his way into a settlement of the German problem on his own terms. He took great risks, but in the end he made few gains.

On the American side Eisenhower and Kennedy were contrasts in many ways. But cautious Eisenhower told Kennedy at their transition meeting that the situation in Laos was very dangerous and might necessitate U.S. intervention. And Eisenhower began the use of advisers to South Vietnam and refused to push the South Vietnamese to hold the promised elections. Kennedy was a distinctly American blend of pragmatism and idealism. His inaugural speech, in which he said America would aid any friend and oppose any foe to protect freedom, was as open-ended as any of Dulles' promises or threats. But, when it came down to the wire, he was, like Eisenhower, very careful with his commitments.

In the end, both administrations remind one of Churchill's comment, quoted earlier, about the difference between Americans and Britons. Americans seek the governing principle; the British are more inclined to see each situation in its unique features. Propositions like containment or liberation or the domino theory all have in common that they are governing principles; so is the idea that America will defend any friend or oppose any foe in the cause of freedom. Ideas like that take the place of looking directly at a given threat in a given situation in a given locality at a given time and assessing its specific features. At least, such ideas would if not tempered by that peculiarly American counterbalancing tendency toward pragmatism. But because of Ameican pragmatism neither Eisenhower nor Kennedy, at least during the times when, as president, they held the responsibility, was prepared to implement these abstract propositions wholeheartedly, regardless of when or who or where.[52] That was because each had some experience with the international scene and each had a certain sophistication in dealing with foreign affairs. After Kennedy was assassinated, however, a very adept politician who happened to be vice president and who knew domestic affairs like the palm of his hand, had to make serious decisions about foreign affairs like Vietnam: Lyndon Johnson. Woodrow Wilson, an expert in domestic affairs like Lyndon Johnson, said when he was elected, how ironic it would be if, in his administration, foreign affairs dominated. Even more so, and with unhappier consequences, with LBJ.

Notes

1. By the Soviets; the East German troops would not fire on their own people.

2. First Germany had to join the Western European Union, which limited the size of the German army and would enforce Germany's pledge not to produce ABC weapons. As part of the arrangement, Britain pledged to keep troops on the continent, and so on.

3. For detail on the Berlin Conference see Frederick H. Hartmann, *Germany Between East and West,* pp. 52–66.

4. Much of the actual domestic government was administered by Vichy, however.

5. During World War II the Vietnamese Independence League, or the Viet Minh as it was generally called, led the resistance against the Japanese (and their Vichy collaborators). The Viet Minh was, in effect, a national front organization dominated by the Indochinese Communist Party under the guidance of Nguyen Ai Quoc (Ho Chi Minh). At the Potsdam Conference it had been stipulated that after the war ended, British troops would occupy Vietnam up to the 16th Parallel and the Chinese nationalists in the north, to round up and disarm the Japanese. The British and Chinese were there along with the French, the Viet Minh, and several other Vietnamese units. The confusion was enormous.

6. The U.S. JCS were skeptical, but by now Washington felt compelled to go along. See George C. Herring, *America's Longest War: The United States and Vietnam, 1950–1975,* 2nd ed. (New York: Alfred A. Knopf, 1986), p. 27.

7. His approach became known as positive neutralism. He sought a policy free "from all alien determinants" and would not be aligned with, or committed to, anyone (in the Cold War). See Fayez A. Sayegh, "Anatomy of Neutralism—A Typological Analysis," in Fayez A. Sayegh, ed., *The Dynamics of Neutralism in the Arab World: A Symposium* (San Francisco: Chandler, 1964), p. 39.

8. Gamal Abdel Nasser, *The Philosophy of the Revolution* (Cairo: Dar Al-Maaref, n.d.). Pages 59–77 give a representative sample of both style and content. Nasser visualized Egypt as acting in three circles—Arab, African, and Islamic.

9. For the text of the announcement see Department of State, *American Foreign Policy, 1950–1955: Basic Documents,* Vol. II, p. 2230.

10. *New York Times,* April 3, 1957. Also quoted in Townsend Hoopes, *The Devil and John Foster Dulles: The Diplomacy of the Eisenhower Era* (Boston: Little, Brown, 1973), p. 337.

11. Hoopes, p. 345. Hoopes is quoting Kenneth Love, *Suez,* p. 338.

12. For the text of his speech, see Royal Institute of International Affairs, *Documents on International Affairs, 1956* (London: 1958), pp. 77–113.

13. Richard W. Leopold, *The Growth of American Foreign Policy: A History* (New York: Knopf, 1962), p 787.

14. Israel saw that war as an attempt to strangle the new baby in its crib. Most Arab nations, however, sent only portions of their armed forces into the fray, needing to keep units at home because of other domestic and international concerns.

15. For complete text see Anthony Eden, *Memoirs: Full Circle* (Boston: Houghton-Mifflin, 1960), pp. 476–77.

16. For text of the Dulles speech see Department of State, *The Suez Canal Problem, July 26–September 22, 1956, Documents,* pp. 339–41.

17. Dulles, who still had been hoping against hope that war could be avoided, reportedly was furious. See Herman Finer, *Dulles Over Suez: The Theory and Practice of His Diplomacy* (Chicago: Quadrangle Books, 1964), p. 354.

18. Washington had developed covert action strategies and assets to support Eastern European rebellions against Soviet control, but chose not to employ them.

19. The circumstances in which the speech was prepared are described in Hoopes, *The Devil and John Foster Dulles,* pp. 377–78.

20. Whether the president "needed" this congressional authorization, although discussed, was not a major issue. Later, with Vietnam, this subject became highly controversial, of course. See our discussion in Chapter 6.

21. Department of State, *United States Policy in the Middle East, September 1956 June 1957: Documents,* p. 20. Dulles had told Congress that unless the president's proposal passed immediately, the chances of war would be greater than they were at the time of the Berlin airlift. Any major delay by Congress would mean that the area would "be in a short time dominated by International Communism." Quoted in U.S. House of Representatives, Committee on Foreign Affairs, *Hearings on H.J. Res. 117, A Joint Resolution to Authorize the President to Undertake Economic and Military Cooperation with Nations in the General Area of the Middle East in Order to Assist the Strengthening and Defense of Their Independence,* 85th Cong., 1st Sess., 1957, p. 34.

22. Although Jordan was brought under its protective umbrella, it never officially accepted it.

23. Note that the trigger for American action was not a major change in Lebanon, but events in Iraq and Washington's projection of what the consequences might be. In other words, third party influences.

24. Hoopes, *The Devil and John Foster Dulles,* p. 436.

25. See Hoopes, pp. 444–49.

26. Hoopes, p. 450.

27. It is clear that Eisenhower was determined to control the situation without employing force, if at all possible. See his comments in Dwight D. Eisenhower, *Waging Peace, 1956–1961* (New York: Doubleday, 1965), p. 295. At the same time, "domino theory thinking" still compelled a firm position. See the "Memorandum on the Formosa Straits Situation" in Appendix O, pp. 691–92.

28. There have been a number of useful scholarly analyses of the "bargaining process" in this crisis. Carsten Holbraad says it was an example of "graduated reciprocation in tension-reduction" in action. Carsten Holbraad, *Superpowers and International Conflict* (New York: St. Martin's, 1979), p. 46. The discussion in Stanley E. Spangler, *Force and Accommodation in World Politics* (Maxwell AFB, AL: Air University Press, 1991), Ch. 6, is valuable.

29. Ambassador Bohlen, asked at a lunch at Newport, R.I., by one of the authors (Hartmann) why there was no real U.S. reaction to this interesting development, explained that he was on vacation. Events certainly must have moved rapidly in Moscow. Ambassador Nathaniel Davis, now teaching at Claremont, went over the Russian-language periodicals for that time period, but there was no follow-up in them on the Warsaw Conference by the Soviets, either.

30. For more extensive quotation of Khrushchev's speech, see Hartmann, *Germany Between East and West*, pp. 92–94.

31. This and the next documents are from Hartmann.

32. Elie Abel, *The Missile Crisis* (Philadelphia: Lippincott, 1966), p. 21.

33. Eisenhower reportedly said later that the U-2 affair had been a "stupid . . . mess" that had ruined his efforts to end the Cold War. Gaddis, *Strategies of Containment*, p. 197.

34. Vernon A. Walters, *Silent Missions* (Garden City, NY: Doubleday, 1978), p. 491.

35. On the Bay of Pigs episode, see Peter Wyden, *The Bay of Pigs: The Untold Story* (New York: Simon & Schuster, 1979).

36. Lower level analysts had been excluded from the advisory process. See Wyden. The discussion by Irving Janis in footnotes 1–4 to Ch. 2 of his *Groupthink* is really worth examination. It discusses both his views and those of other analysts of the Bay of Pigs decision process. Irving L. Janis, *Groupthink: Psychological Studies of Policy Decisions and Fiascoes*, 2nd ed. (Boston: Houghton Mifflin, 1982), pp. 277–84.

37. Arthur M. Schlesinger, Jr., *A Thousand Days: John F. Kennedy in the White House* (New York: Fawcett, 1967), p. 348, reported in the 1960s how tense that meeting had been. Secretary of State Dean Rusk in 1990 published a fuller and more definitive account. He tells how Khrushchev told Kennedy he would turn over control of the access routes to Berlin to the East Germans and if the West interfered, "there will be war." Rusk says that Kennedy "looked him in the eye, and said: 'Then there will be war, Mr. Chairman. It's going to be a very cold winter.'" Dean Rusk, *As I Saw It* (New York: Norton, 1990), p. 221.

38. Schlesinger, *A Thousand Days*, p. 365.

39. Gordon A. Craig and Alexander George, *Force and Statecraft: Diplomatic Problems of Our Time*, 2nd ed. (New York: Oxford University Press, 1990), p. 127.

40. See the classic analysis of alternative explanations in Graham T. Allison, *Essence of Decision: Explaining the Cuban Missile Crisis* (Boston: Little, Brown, 1971), especially pp. 40–56 and 230–44. Khrushchev's own version became available in 1970, with the publication of Strobe Talbott, ed., *Khrushchev Remembers* (Boston: Little, Brown, 1970). See especially pp. 492–505. Khrushchev does not link Cuba, the missiles, and Germany. He essentially argues that after the Bay of Pigs it was obvious that the United States would never rest until it had overthrown Castro with military force, and that such an event would set back the cause of socialism in the whole of the Western Hemisphere. He speaks of the Soviet cargo ships as transiting right through the American navy (presumably, though, before the blockade). He puts a great deal of stress on the communications between Robert Kennedy, speaking for his brother, and the Soviet ambassador to the United States. In Khrushchev's version, Kennedy is almost in tears as he tells the ambassador that President Kennedy is having great difficulty resisting the calls of his generals to use force. Khrushchev's actual words, attributed to Ambassador Dobrynin, were that Kennedy said "The President is in a grave situation and he does not know how to get out of it. . . . President Kennedy implores Chairman Khrushchev to accept his offer and take into consideration the peculiarities of the American system. . . . The American army [otherwise] could get out of control." Khrushchev goes on to say: "We could see that we had to reorient our position swiftly. 'Comrades,' I said, 'we have to look for a dignified way out of this conflict. At the same time, of course, we must make sure that we do not compromise Cuba.'" (p. 497–98)

41. Adam Ulam wrote "On the Soviet side, the gamble was stupendous." Adam B. Ulam, *The Rivals: America and Russia Since World War II* (New York: Viking Press, 1971), p. 331. The CIA's opinion on October 20, 1962, was that the Soviets intended to "demonstrate that the world balance . . . has shifted so far . . . that the U.S. can no longer prevent the advance of Soviet offensive power even into its own hemisphere." See U.S., Central Intelligence Agency, *CIA Documents on the Cuban Missile Crisis, 1962*, Mary McAulife, ed. (Washington, DC: October 1992), p. 214.

42. Allison, *Essence of Decision*, pp. 102–17.

43. Abel, *The Missile Crisis*, was written from Robert Kennedy's notes taken during the crisis.

44. According to (Attorney General) Robert Kennedy, this option was opposed by the president and the attorney general on ethical grounds also. It reminded them of an American-perpetrated Pearl Harbor. Robert F. Kennedy, *Thirteen Days: A Memoir of the Cuban Missile Crisis* (New York: Norton, 1971), p. 15. John Stoessinger believes this was an important factor. See John Stoessinger, *Nations in Darkness: China, Russia, and America*, 4th ed. (New York: Random House, 1986), p. 196.

45. Roger Hilsman's analysis of the events of October 22–28 remains one of the best. Roger Hilsman, *To Move A Nation: The Politics of Foreign Policy in the Administration of John F. Kennedy* (New York: Delta, 1967), Ch. 16.

46. According to Brugioni, the JCS "were unanimous during the crisis in calling for immediate military action. . . . [t]he strike plan they advocated was a massive attack on all missile sites, all air fields, and all military camps, and invading the island. With the specter of Soviet nuclear weapons in Cuba a probability, prudence called for strikes to eliminate all sources of retaliation." Dino A. Brugioni, *Eyeball to Eyeball: The Inside Story of the Cuban Missile Crisis*, ed. by Robert F. McCort (New York: Random House, 1990), p. 263. A U.S. invasion fleet was steaming near Cuba in the final hours of the crisis.

47. For the full text see Robert F. Kennedy, *Thirteen Days,* pp. 80–82.

48. Kennedy, pp. 86–87.

49. Raymond L. Garthoff, *Reflections on the Cuban Missile Crisis,* rev. ed. (Washington, DC: The Brookings Institution, 1989), p. 86. On page 88, Garthoff states that the decision to add the "sweetener" was made in a small group of ExComm members after the ExComm meeting of the 27th.

50. See Maxwell D. Taylor, *The Uncertain Trumpet* (New York: Harper, 1959).

51. In 1961 during the second Berlin crisis, communications "were so primitive that the State Department's new Operations Center heard almost nothing about the events in Berlin until about midnight Washington time—six hours after the border sealing began." Michael R. Beschloss, *The Crisis Years: Kennedy and Khrushchev, 1960–1963* (New York: HarperCollins, 1991), p. 272.

52. It was in the middle of the Dienbienphu crisis that Eisenhower made his famous falling dominoes speech, yet he chose not to intervene. Clearly, if he had followed his own guidance totally, intervention would have occurred.

11

Into and Out of Vietnam

When John F. Kennedy was assassinated at Dallas on November 22, 1963, the United States was heavily (but not irretrievably) involved in Vietnam. It is important to understand how that happened, what caused the United States to involve itself even more deeply, the problems that it in turn created (both at home and at the "front"), and its long-range effect on U.S. foreign policy.

How it happened is comparatively clear. *If* Americans in general and an administration in particular addressed problems in foreign policy under the assumption that the United States faced a unified Communist bloc, directed from Moscow, which tirelessly searched for opportunities to challenge the "Free World" in inconvenient places, then the insurgency in Vietnam could, without too much trouble, be considered exactly that. *If* the administration also believed in the domino theory, it would not pause in its reaction simply because the place of the challenge was strategically unimportant; the place would not count very much since a row of dominoes could begin to fall anywhere and spread everywhere. Shorthand formulas such as the belief in an aggressive, orchestrated Communist bloc and the belief in a domino effect were sufficient grounds for concluding that the United States must act militarily.

Dean Acheson had said, when asked about the far-reaching propositions that studded the Truman Doctrine, that every case would be examined on its merits. But the merits of any case would not appear very significant if one fully believed in these shorthand formulas. This is even more likely if the president knows relatively little about foreign or military affairs, which was the case with Lyndon B. Johnson.

In the American system of government, no vice president is ever fully ready to take over the reins if tragedy strikes. Until President Carter gave Walter Mondale an office in the White House, vice presidents did not even have their own space there.[1] Johnson, not popular with Kennedy's "ivy league" inner circle, had not always been included in their councils and did not know all the details or origins of many of the policies he now had to implement or change.[2]

Yet, in other ways, Lyndon Johnson has to rank as one of our best prepared vice presidents. A former Senate majority leader after serving in the House, he knew American politics better than almost anyone else. He knew how to get Congress to carry out his program (something most presidents have a lot of trouble with). What he did not know much about was foreign policy and national security.[3] As fate would have it, he was to make *the* critical decision about Vietnam.

A Deepening Commitment

Not that Johnson began America's commitment there, of course. When the United States began to slide down the slippery slope into what later was aptly called "the Vietnam quagmire," Eisenhower was in office and the United States was still fighting the Korean War. Eisenhower began what was called a "limited-risk gamble" of aiding the French in Indochina but he stopped short of overt armed intervention. The Geneva Accords, which "ended" the war, "temporarily" divided Vietnam into northern and southern zones (thus "North" Vietnam and "South" Vietnam), provided for force withdrawals and prisoner exchanges, and made provision for free elections (which, in theory, would unify the country). But the United States refused to be a party to these agreements, believing they "legitimized" a Communist territorial base.[4] After the Geneva Accords the president sought to prevent any further "losses" and sent advisers to the South Vietnamese. These advisers, 685 when Kennedy came into office, rose to 22,000 in Kennedy's 34 months in office.[5] In Kennedy's time, too, clandestine operations began against North Vietnam and the United States became involved in the overthrow of South Vietnam's first leader, Ngo Dinh Diem.[6] That was

November 1963, on the eve of Kennedy's assassination. Thus the United States had a substantial involvement by the time Johnson was sworn in.

But it is not numbers alone that count in involvements. Even more it is *form*, or mode. Those who doubt this should remember the Korean War. It took years to arrive at an armistice there, when neither the United States nor China were belligerents, as such, but only part of a U.N. force on the one hand, and "volunteers" on the other. It is easy to imagine how the difficulties would have multiplied if they had been in a formal state of war with each other but neither had won an outright military victory.

When the form of U.S. involvement was in an advisory role, the United States needed no one's permission to withdraw if it changed its mind. It was up to America, unilaterally. But once the form was changed to an overt combat role, as Johnson changed it in 1965, the enemy had to be "consulted" if America wanted it to end. (The United States had to consult, if only to get its mounting number of prisoners back.) That change of form, plus the fact that many Americans were now being killed in combat and dollars were being spent in huge amounts, made Vietnam quite a different situation in the Johnson years, when over two and a half million Americans went to Southeast Asia.

Because the involvement came only incrementally, Congress never did declare war, but that does not mean that it would have refused to do so. When it passed the Gulf of Tonkin Resolution in 1964, it certainly did not have in mind conflict in the dimensions reached the very next year, but that, too, does not mean that any majority was present in Congress that was ready to quit, cold-turkey. The Congress only came to confront the question of the merits of fighting a real war in Vietnam *after* the fighting had become both extensive and bloody, with the nation already very restive. Where such a war as this has no clear and obvious purpose (as this one, shorthand formulas aside, did not), and if that war is also greatly prolonged (as this one was), there will surely be trouble.

So it is hardly surprising that the Vietnam War was beyond any question America's most controversial foreign policy commitment. It caused a split in the American public that took years to heal; it began the situation (now seemingly "permanent") in which people came to distrust what their own government told them was the truth. And it spent more than 55,000 American lives and over 150 billion American dollars for no obvious positive return.

Judging What Makes a War Worth Fighting

There are many retired three- and four-star U.S. military officers today who firmly believe that the war was being won in Vietnam when the home front faltered and cut off their support.

Propositions like that remain almost impossible to assess well unless some distinctions are made at the outset. It might be true that the war was fought in highly efficient fashion, given the political constraints under which the military labored, and that if the war had been continued, it would have produced a military victory. But, even if that were so, it is only a secondary level question. Much more important is that no amount of brilliance on the battlefield could have offset the negative effects if the war itself was ill-chosen and not in the interests of the United States. The overriding consideration on which the war has to be judged is the strategic issue: whether the war *should have been fought at all.*

How that question is answered is critical. No president ever faces a more serious question than whether, with or without a declaration of war, to commit Americans to combat. He has to have a very convincing reason before he can decide that it is worth American blood and American dollars.

It is of no use for him to decide he will commit up to a certain level. Because it is by no means foreseeable whether once that level is achieved one can quit, can disengage. Estimates of "what it will take" to win (or even, not lose) have a way of escalating. What happens in wars, declared or undeclared, has the inconvenience of depending only partially on the will of a single party. The opponent, too, has a vote. He can raise the ante or refuse to "behave logically." Wars have both unpredictable consequences and unpredictable lengths. So the decision to participate or not is as critical as one can get.

To make a war with its attendant killing and destruction worthwhile, one ought to have a very clear and convincing reason for participating in it. Earlier, it was pointed out that any decision by any government is made on the basis of *projections* about what will happen if something is done or not done. In the Vietnam case, no one could have argued persuasively at any point in that war that the enemy fought there could do the United States the slightest harm if America simply did not land troops on his shores for him to shoot at. It was not an issue of self-defense in the sense of, say, Pearl Harbor, where U.S. troops and ships were under physical attack. Nor was the area of obvious importance. George Kennan, on February 10, 1966, near the beginning of the U.S. involvement, said that "if we were not already involved . . . in Vietnam, I would know of no reason why we should. . . . It is difficult to believe that any decisive developments . . . would be determined in normal circumstances by what happens on that territory."[7]

So the concept of being threatened necessarily had to rest on more abstract grounds and some kind of chain reasoning. We have already showed how American leader after American leader said that they believed in containment and the domino theory: the proposition that aggressive world communism, run from a malevolent Moscow, was the enemy, and immediate frontline involvement by the United States was required to halt the aggression and prevent the dominoes from falling. This belief also shows up clearly in the position papers of the National Security Council as early as February 1950, and in the Eisenhower administration, when it was decided to extend military aid to the French in Indochina.[8] A typical statement in early 1952, highly classified at the time, said in part:

> 2. Communist domination, by whatever means, of Southeast Asia would seriously endanger in the short term, and critically endanger in the longer term, United States security interests.

> a. The loss of any of the countries of Southeast Asia to communist aggression would have critical psychological, political and economic consequences. In the absence of effective and timely counteraction, the loss of any single country would probably lead to relatively swift submission to or an alignment with communism by the remaining countries of this group. . . . [9]

The analysis went on to add India and the Middle East to what "would in all probability progressively follow," thus also endangering "the stability and security of Europe." That is what would happen if a single country was lost!

If the argument was correct, any war against Communist aggression was certainly justified. That senior policymakers in Eisenhower's time and Kennedy's and Johnson's believed these statements to be true underscores the stress in this book on *how* policy decisions are made through visualizing alternative futures. Believing in what might be probable, the policymakers in this case *acted on these projections as though they were incontestably true.*

This NSC paper was written in 1952, when Eisenhower was president and John Foster Dulles was secretary of state. Dulles had developed the concept of "massive retaliation" to deal with Communist aggression, but once the Soviets had amassed a sufficient nuclear arsenal to make any war with nuclear weapons prohibitively damaging to all involved, using such weapons in anything short of an extreme case became a formula for mutual suicide. The logic of this changed strategic ratio led President Kennedy to build up U.S. conventional forces beyond the Eisenhower budget limits. It led military analysts to conclude that, if big wars are suicidal, then little wars would be fought instead, and they would have to be kept limited by deliberate steps up a "ladder of escalation." That would constitute "graduated deterrence." No longer would the United States use all the force available, but just enough. (That would have the added advantage of keeping the fighting from escalating automatically to the point where a neighboring power, like China in the Vietnam case, might feel it necessary to intervene—with or without the "volunteer" fiction.)

Not all of these ideas about limited war were held by all of the analysts. The center of gravity of their critiques, though, was the danger of not having sufficient conventional forces to fit the needs that might arise. The leading critique of the ideas of massive retaliation, written by retired General Maxwell Taylor, pointed out the folly of relying on nuclear weapons for all contingencies.[10] Taylor, recalled to active duty, would later become Kennedy's chairman of the JCS, as Kennedy sought to broaden his military options.[11]

With this background, the next events become clearer. Not long after the Geneva Accords divided Vietnam at the 17th parallel[12] and the first advisers were sent by President Eisenhower to assist the South Vietnamese, the corruption and ineptness in South Vietnam was becoming obvious. When Kennedy in November 1961 sent General Maxwell Taylor, then still his personal military adviser, to Vietnam, Taylor returned to argue in a secret report that Kennedy should send American ground troops whose "initial size should not exceed about 8,000, of which a preponderant number would be logistical-type units."[13] The Joint Chiefs correctly commented that "If we act in this way, the ultimate possible extent of our military commitment must be faced." They estimated that might require, worst case, six divisions or 205,000 American soldiers. They thought that even if Hanoi and Peiping directly intervened and the war broadened, the logistical difficulties the Communists would face would still make that size U.S. force sufficient.[14] Secretary of State Dean Rusk and Secretary of Defense Robert McNamara sent a joint memo to Kennedy on November 11, 1961, stating that "The United States should commit itself to the clear objective of preventing the fall of South Vietnam" to the Communists by assisting the government of South Vietnam "to win its own war against the Guerrillas."[15] They, too, urged sending combat troops. It is interesting, in the face of this combined pressure, that Kennedy said no. But this did not mean any lack of serious concern, only a difference about means.[16] It is also interesting that, without any real Chinese involvement (other than furnishing arms), later the 205,000 "maximum" was almost trebled before the United States decided that enough was enough and began to withdraw.

Johnson kept Kennedy's major officials in office, so that both Rusk and McNamara, as well as Walt Rostow, continued to offer policy advice.[17] All three were what would later be called "hawks." Naturally, as the situation in Vietnam worsened after the coup, they advised stronger measures by the United States to compensate.

The situation in Vietnam in 1964 continued downhill. By March, Secretary McNamara, convinced that the new government of General Nguyen Khanh in South Vietnam was faltering, urged "new and significant pressures" on North Vietnam.[18] Bombing of the North was now being seriously studied.[19] Then, at sea, in the first days of August, the destroyer *Maddox* was attacked by two North Vietnamese PT boats responding to a South Vietnamese raid. There was an apparent second attack on August 4 on *Maddox* and the *C. Turner Joy,* although there is still controversy about that. Less than 12 hours later, U.S. bombers were on their way from U.S. carriers to bomb North Vietnam. The Tonkin Gulf Resolution, requested by President Johnson, was introduced into Congress and passed both houses on August 7, by a vote of 88–2 in the Senate and 416–0 in the House.[20]

The very rapidity with which the resolution passed shows that many in Congress thought of it as a gesture of support to the president, rather than as a decisive step toward war. Senator Fulbright, who sponsored the resolution in the Senate, was later to complain vehemently that it had been misrepresented to him. Yet the language of the resolution is not all that vague. The important sections read as follows:

> Resolved . . . that the Congress approve and support the determination of the President, as Commander in Chief, to take all necessary measures to repel any armed attack against the forces of the United States and to prevent further aggression.
>
> Sec. 2. The United States regards as vital to its national interest and to world peace the maintenance of international peace and security in Southeast Asia. Consonant with the Constitution of the United States and the Charter of the United Nations and in accordance with its obligations under the Southeast Asia Collective Defense Treaty, the United States is, therefore, prepared, *as the President*

determines, to take all necessary steps, *including the use of armed force,* to assist any member or protocol state [of SEATO] requesting assistance in defense of its freedom. [Italics added.][21]

In what might be called the "functional equivalent" of a declaration of war, the president was clearly given authority to use force at his own discretion. The most interesting other point (besides the totally inadequate Congressional discussion before voting), is that the SEATO treaty provided for consultation among the signatories in the event of an aggression, but it did not require any of them to do more than that. Moreover, neither South Vietnam nor any of the other states in former French Indochina were members of SEATO. That is why the curious added phrase, "or protocol state," is inserted. The actual members of SEATO were Australia, France, New Zealand, Pakistan, the Philippines, Thailand, the United Kingdom, and the United States. They had agreed, after the 1954 Geneva "settlement" by protocol to extend military protection to the Indochinese states. But the United States was not a party to the Geneva agreements, refusing to sign (and thus presumably endorse) the division of Indochina agreed there.

To sum up: The United States' *obligation* to defend South Vietnam did not exist. That did not preclude the United States from doing so; it just did not have to if it did not want to. Congress's action left it up to President Johnson to decide.[22]

One Thing Leads to Another

President Johnson's decision is well known: It was to not allow a Communist victory. After the Viet Cong attacked the American military barracks at Pleikku on February 7, 1965, American bombers attacked North Vietnam.[23] Two more retaliatory raids were launched in the next week. In early March sustained raids began.[24] On March 8, 1965, 3500 marines landed at Danang to protect the airfield there. On March 29, Viet Cong guerrillas blew up the American Embassy in Saigon. The president, responding to the media inquiries about dramatic new U.S. commitments, on March 31 said that he knew of "no far-reaching strategy that is being suggested or promulgated." Johnson was, of course, being less than candid, and at a White House strategy conference on April 1 and 2 he changed the mission of the marine battalions at Danang from *defense to offense.* He also decided to send in two more marine battalions and to increase support forces by 18,000 to 20,000 men. North Vietnam, meanwhile, announced its terms for a settlement. America had to withdraw, dismantle its bases, cancel its alliance with Saigon, and end its policy of aggression. Pending reunification, neither "zone" (North and South Vietnam) could enter an alliance. The South's internal affairs had to be settled according to the program of the National Liberation Front. Finally, peaceful reunification of Vietnam would be settled by the Vietnamese people, without foreign interference.[25] At the very time America's commitment was deepening, Hanoi was throwing down the gauntlet.

And the commitment *was* deepening. Advisers could defend themselves and still remain advisers, but an offensive role was a combat commitment. One idea at the time was that the offensive use of the troops would be modest. A "coastal enclave" strategy would give the United States bases that the troops would defend, being prepared to go to the rescue of South Vietnam forces as far as 50 miles outside the enclave. But there were crosscurrents here: General Westmoreland had already asked for a reinforcement of two divisions, and the JCS had discussed sending three. With forces on this scale, "offensive" would mean much more than is implied by an enclave strategy. By April 20, a Honolulu conference meeting without the president began to discuss "an expanded enclave strategy." In a message from Saigon, Taylor, now the U.S. ambassador to Saigon, expressed surprise that the new marine battalions had come ashore with tanks, self-propelled artillery, and various other equipment "not appropriate for counterinsurgency operations." Westmoreland and the JCS were moving toward "territorial clear and hold" operations, while Taylor now was trying to hold the line. At the time of the Honolulu conference 33,500 American troops were actually in Vietnam and 40,200 had been authorized. The conference recommended going to 82,000 and on April 30 the JCS formally recommended 48,000.

In May the Viet Cong launched an assault that made mincemeat of the South Vietnamese forces that opposed them. By June, General Westmoreland was asking for a total force of forty-four battalions. On June 9, the White House issued a statement claiming that there had been "no change in the mission of United States ground combat units in Vietnam in recent days or weeks. . . . The primary mission of these troops is to secure and safeguard important military installations like the air base at Danang. They have the associated mission of . . . patrolling and securing actions in and near the areas thus safeguarded." The statement added that Westmoreland had authority to use these troops to aid South Vietnamese forces "faced with aggressive attack."[26]

The *Pentagon Papers* documentation makes clear that, since the meaning of "offensive action" had not been carefully defined, different officials were placing different interpretations on it. Westmoreland, for his part, had requested the 173rd *Airborne* Brigade. (You do not need an airborne brigade unless you are planning deep operations.) Having gotten it, he used it from June 27 to June 30 in what could only be described as a search and destroy operation into Viet Cong base areas.

With the argument over strategy and troop levels now escalating, on July 28 Johnson held a news conference at which he said: "I have asked . . . General Westmoreland what more he needs. . . . He has told me. We will meet his needs." The president went on: "I have today ordered to Vietnam the Airmobile Division and certain other forces which will raise our fighting strength from 75,000 to 125,000 men almost immediately. Additional forces will be needed later, and they will be sent as requested."

U.S. strength in Vietnam in 1964 was 23,300. In 1965, the year of the decision to go over to overt combat status, the number jumped to 180,000. In 1966 America had 389,000 troops there, and in 1967, 475,000. The peak strength, reached in 1969, was 543,000, according to General Westmoreland, who

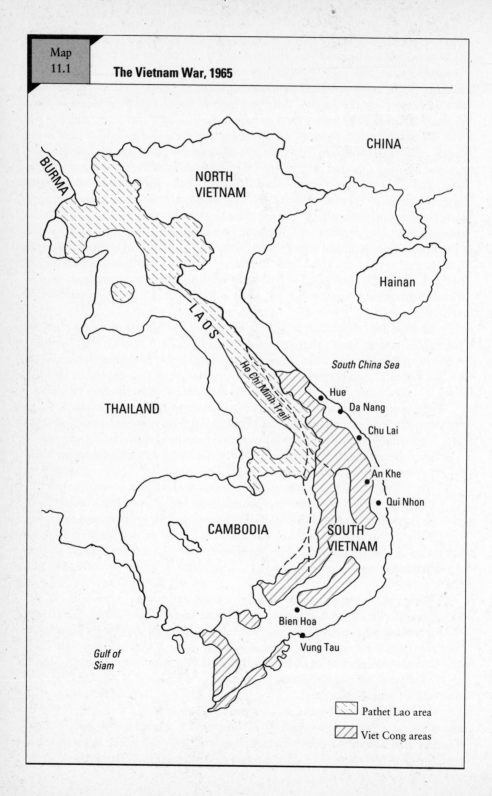

Map
11.1

The Vietnam War, 1965

BURMA

CHINA

NORTH
VIETNAM

Hainan

LAOS

THAILAND

South China Sea

Ho Chi Minh Trail

Hue

Da Nang

Chu Lai

An Khe

Qui Nhon

CAMBODIA

SOUTH
VIETNAM

Bien Hoa

*Gulf of
Siam*

Vung Tau

Pathet Lao area

Viet Cong areas

commanded them. It was only when General Earle G. Wheeler, Chairman of the Joint Chiefs, returning in 1968 from an inspection in Vietnam, recommended a new reinforcement of 205,179 troops that a halt was called in the buildup.[27] Wheeler's *reinforcement* figure, almost a half a decade into the war, was ironically almost precisely the JCS estimate, given above, for the *maximum* total needed to win the war.

Since General Wheeler's reinforcement figure meant, as President Johnson well realized, that the reserves would have to be mobilized, Johnson turned to a trusted adviser for a new look at the problem. That adviser was Clark Clifford, who became secretary of defense after McNamara "resigned." Clifford carefully asked everyone whether the reinforcements would, if fact, *end* the war. Hearing no assurances, he decided that enough was enough.

Clifford argues at various places in his memoirs that the military failed to brief the president properly on where the first steps could eventually lead. That argument is not convincing in light of the documents. It is true that Johnson's own military experience was limited to navy service in World War II and that he did not always fully appreciate the implications of each step. But Johnson was a very strong-minded president who was quite in charge any time he wanted to be. The truth seems to be, not that he in particular was misled, but that almost all who took part in the policy deliberations, civilian and military alike, shared the same optimism that anything America set its mind and hands to would succeed.[28] The documents certainly show this cultural bias growing out of a successful past experience (past-future linkages). It is equally certain that the Joint Chiefs would repeatedly come back from an inspection in Vietnam, proclaiming: "We have had our problems out there, but I can tell you that we know now what to do about them. There is light at the end of the tunnel." The words might vary; the theme did not.[29] No member of the JCS could or did believe that America would not achieve its goal, provided that it poured in its resources and kept working at it.

On the other hand, in one sense it might be argued that the initial proposals to go beyond the adviser role were misleading to anyone without a real military background. Once it was decided to bomb North Vietnam, it made military sense to employ both carrier-based and land-based air. Once America had established land bases in South Vietnam, it made military sense to provide forces to defend them. And to defend them, in the American military tradition, implied forward deployments to search for and destroy enemy forces. And so, logically, one thing led to another.

In this one sense, Johnson may have been misled. But he was already misled by his belief in the domino theory.

Did the Commitment Make Sense?

Whether all this effort was worthwhile depended on what came of it, or what it prevented from happening. That the reasoning of the domino theory was far off the truth is clear today from the present situation in Southeast Asia. With America totally out of the picture, the whole area has not fallen—as predicted—to communism, even if the United States did not "win." America did not in the end prevent South Vietnam from falling into the hands of the Communists and, when it did, it made very little difference to America or the rest of the world.

One of the most serious problems with the policy was its negative goal. It is hardly necessary to add that, if the goal was worthwhile at all, it certainly was not worth what it cost. The loss of the Vietnam War by the United States came about because in the end America cut its losses, rather than because it ran out of additional resources it could have committed.

The main argument given for defending South Vietnam was, as noted, strategic: the whole balance of power in the world would be undermined if America did not intervene. Yet, in the deliberations of the Washington policy makers in these years, hardly a voice was raised to look at the implications of Vietnam for the *other* key actors in that balance, i.e., third-party influences. The question was not seriously asked: What would be the effect on China and the Soviet Union?

The policymakers *knew* that the Communist countries were a bloc; they *knew* that they were collectively engaged in aggression at suitable times and places; and they *knew* that the whole effort was orchestrated from Moscow. Knowing all this, the policymakers did not seriously question *any* of these premises. They went instead to "the bottom line" of what the United States should do about it and how best to do it. When they said they were only going to back up the South Vietnamese, or when they said later that they would have to give them a lot of help, or when they said still later that Saigon would have to make out without America but the United States would still provide the weapons, they were merely shifting from one mode of commitment to another. But suppose America had stayed out of the whole mess? Suppose America had let matters take their course?

Well before the United States chose to shift to a combat role in 1965, the Chinese were openly quarreling with the Soviets. The foundations for dispute had existed for years in the vast territorial claims Beijing had against Moscow from Tsarist times, disputes over trade and aid, and the Soviets' refusal to help China develop its own nuclear capability. Other factors involved the only lukewarm Soviet support in the 1955 and 1958 crises over the offshore islands of Quemoy and Matsu (see Chapter 10), and its support for India *instead of China* in the 1962 Sino-Indian War. But the straws that broke the camel's back, so to speak, were the Soviet "appeasement" of the West in the Cuban missile crisis and the signature the following year of the Limited Nuclear Test Ban Treaty.

The Moscow conference that led to the Nuclear Test Ban Treaty began on July 15, 1963. Even before the conference started, relations between the two Communist giants had disintegrated enough so that on June 14, attempting to get around the controlled Soviet press, the Chinese took the extraordinary step of scattering leaflets from the Trans-Siberian express as it crossed Russia! The Test Ban Treaty itself was initialed on July 25, and signed on August 5. The Chinese had not completed their nuclear testing by that time and were outraged that the Soviets had looked after their own narrow interests at the expense of China's. Before the end of September, the treaty had been ratified by the U.S. Senate and signed by ninety-nine states. The Chinese, who had sent a delegation to Moscow to observe and confer on July 5, recalled them on July 20.

On July 14, the Soviets published various Chinese charges and their defense.[30] Some of the argument was about trade relations and Soviet assistance to China. The Soviets argued that Sino-Soviet trade and deliveries of promised industrial plant to China had "dropped forty times." But it was "on the initiative of the Chinese leaders." The Soviets dismissed the Chinese charges that the Soviets had made an " 'adventurist' mistake by supplying rockets to Cuba and then allegedly 'capitulated' to American imperialism." Actually, Moscow said, the Soviets by their action had "made it possible to frustrate the plans of the extreme adventurist circles of American imperialism that were ready to go the whole hog" and invade Cuba. Now, instead, the Americans were publicly pledged not to invade.

A critical and sometimes underemphasized part of the dispute, however, was over ideology—especially the doctrine of the inevitability of war. Up to the time of Khrushchev, the orthodox Communist belief, reaffirmed by Stalin on the eve of his death, was that there could be no lasting peace with capitalists. Whatever temporary accommodations that might be made, the capitalists, for structural class reasons, would always in the end make war on the socialists (i.e., Communists). Khrushchev, in February 1956 at the Twentieth Congress of the Soviet Communist Party, retired this theory to the dustbin of wornout Communist dogmas. He declared at that time that there was "no fatal inevitability of war [because] the Socialist camp is invincible." The West would not attack the Soviet Union because the Soviets were too well armed for an attack to succeed.

There are many implications to this revision of Communist dogma; here we are concerned with its impact on Soviet relations with China. The Soviet public letter to the Chinese on July 14 explained why war was no longer inevitable: "This conclusion is not the fruit of good intentions but the result of a realistic, strictly scientific analysis of the balance of class forces in the world arena; it is based on the gigantic might of world socialism." The Chinese argument was that "an end cannot be put to wars as long as imperialism exists; peaceful coexistence is an illusion. . . ." Also, "the Chinese comrades obviously underestimate all of the danger of a thermonuclear war. "The atomic bomb is a paper tiger, 'it's not terrible at all,' they contend." The Chinese were ignoring the human costs but we "would like to ask the Chinese comrades, who offer to build a wonderful future on the ruins of the old world destroyed by a thermonuclear war, if they have consulted the working class of the countries where imperialism dominated on this matter?"

Behind this argument over ideology was a profound difference in attitude and circumstances, which is exactly what irritated the Chinese to the point where they said they did not fear a nuclear war. After the Cuban missile crisis, the Chinese felt that the Soviets had brought themselves and everyone else to the brink; they feared that the Soviets were making common cause with the capitalists on the spurious proposition that the Soviets could no longer be successfully attacked. That would leave the Chinese, who still had not re-covered Taiwan, in the lurch. "I've got mine, Jack" was, in the Chinese mind, the message.

There were many more exchanges of serious charges between the two Communist giants. For example, the official Chinese *People's Daily* in January 1966 said: "The Soviet Union is preparing the ground to strike a new deal with U.S. imperialism just as the Lyndon Johnson administration is quickening its pace toward a wider war of aggression against Vietnam." In May 1970 *Pravda* said: "But we cannot turn a blind eye on the fact that a militaristic psychosis is being stubbornly fanned in Peking and demands are made of the people 'to pre-pare for hunger, to prepare for war.'"[31] Meaning here: war between China and the Soviet Union.

So, at the very time when tensions were building up between the two Com-munist powers, the United States deflected Chinese attention by building up a force of over a half million men on their southern flank. Recall, too, that Amer-ica still maintained diplomatic relations with Taiwan as the *de jure* government of China. Under the influence of the domino theory, the buildup also completely ignored the age-old tensions between China and Vietnam, which later brought them into serious border clashes—just as later, too, after it became clear the United States was going to de-escalate, the Soviets and Chinese had border clashes.

Since the landing of combat forces in Vietnam and the changeover to an overt combat role was in 1965, and since the Sino-Soviet dispute, with its ex-change of acrimonious letters was public in 1963, it cannot be argued that Amer-ica took its action in ignorance. The best excuse that can be offered is that the policymakers believed the dispute was superficial, or no more than transitory. But the real truth, unfortunately, is probably nearer what Churchill said about the American tendency to find a governing principle (like the domino theory) and go full speed ahead. The saddest yet perhaps best conclusion one can come to is that America would have been better off not having been involved at all.

The Military Strategy

Whether the war was fought correctly remains today in dispute.[32] We have seen already the argument between maintaining enclaves and sending units on search and destroy missions. There was also the approach of "strategic hamlets," towns and villages organized with U.S. help for effective self-defense. Both the enclave approach and the hamlet approach ultimately went by the boards; the hamlets being progressively overrun by the Viet Cong and North Vietnamese and the en-clave approach permitting the enemy to take the initiative. We need to add that the idea of standing still on the defensive also runs contrary to the American way of war. After all, as Americans say, "the best defense is a good offense." Perhaps the most serious defect of the enclave idea, though, was that it was designed to outwait the enemy, letting them come to the conclusion that they could not win. And the enemy had far more patience than the American people.

Undoubtedly, then, the American military favored going in there and taking the war aggressively to the enemy.[33] The problem here was that the enemy was only partially to be confronted in organized, sizable units. One man in black pajamas was a Viet Cong, and another man in black pajamas was not. Which was which? In the end, with so much of the war a conflict between guerrilla forces and organized American units, the United States began to fire its artillery and drop its bombs without confining what was done only to known enemy targets.[34] This was not done deliberately or because Americans were unfeeling; it came as the natural consequence of the kind of war the Vietnam War was. But the more indiscriminate bombing there was, the less chance there also was to "win the hearts and minds of the people."

Another military problem was that the U.S. Army, to give its officer corps chances at active combat commands, rotated its commanders, often at six month intervals. That was hardly long enough for them to learn the problems the military faced, and it was short enough to expose them to the temptation to make their reputation quickly. Enlisted men grew progressively more wary of having new platoon commanders. Fragging—deliberate grenade throwing at officers who wanted more aggressive tactics—was not unknown, especially in the later years as disillusionment grew both in the enlisted ranks and at home in the general public from which these draftees came. In actuality, it is an impressive testimonial to the American character that much worse things did not happen.

The American military, like the French before them, hoped for pitched battles. The basic approach was to inflict casualties on the enemy at a rate he could not sustain. By the middle of the war, McNamara, with his preference for "hard" data, had the military doing body counts. But whether these figures were reliable is another question. For example, in March 1968, a special panel of advisers (the so-called Wise Men) was meeting in the State Department. General William E. DePuy, who had commanded troops in Vietnam and was the special assistant to the JCS for counterinsurgency, briefed them on the recent Tet Offensive. He said the Communists had lost 80,000 men killed in action. Arthur Goldberg, one of the Wise Men, asked what was the normal ratio of wounded to killed? Conservatively, three to one, answered DuPuy. Goldberg asked then how many regular soldiers the Vietcong probably had left. DuPuy said 230,000 to 240,000. Goldberg then took the 80,000 killed figure, multiplied it by three, and arrived at the figure of 320,000 enemy killed or wounded. His question then was: "Who the hell is there left for us to be fighting?"[35]

The Tet Offensive of January–February 1968 was extraordinary by any standards.[36] Intelligence reports had predicted that the Communists would use the customary relaxation of vigilance by the South Vietnamese during the lunar new year to launch a broad-ranging assault. The American military, who had established a strong marine-held position at Khe Sanh, were waiting in hopes that this would be the climax of the war, as Viet Cong and regular North Vietnamese units (mostly at Khe Sanh and Hue) attacked. But enemy forces also launched attacks on the cities and provincial capitals. It cost the enemy dearly, but they attacked 5 out of 6 of the major cities, 36 out of 44 of the provincial capitals, and 66 of the 242 district towns.

The American military, comparing estimated enemy losses of 58,000 to U.S. losses (3,895 killed in eight weeks), called the battle a victory. And militarily it was. But politically and psychologically it was a disaster. What the American public concluded was that, after years of war, the enemy could still go anywhere he chose and attack anywhere he wanted, and in that case America was just as far from winning the war as ever.[37]

The American military in Vietnam fought the kind of war they were trained to fight and fought it in the traditional American way. They were not, however, prepared to fight a guerrilla war, and they operated under severe political constraints. Moreover, from the beginning, the percent of South Vietnamese who were really willing to fight the Communists was substantially overrated.[38] Where the military can be faulted in the war years is their persistent optimism that increasing the commitment would ultimately achieve U.S. goals.[39] Without the kind of expansion or escalation that probably would have provided a much wider war, no numbers of troops could have turned this situation around.

The Beginning of the End

By the fall of 1967, McNamara himself was losing faith that the policy could yield success. Diplomatic efforts had gotten nowhere, and the war was not being "won." Johnson, displeased by McNamara's "desertion," named him to the World Bank and nominated Clark Clifford to succeed him.

Clifford, a perennial adviser to presidents (at least Democratic ones), had been a "hawk," sharing the view that the war was necessary. But when he took office in January 1968, he became responsible as secretary of defense for recommending to the president either more troop increases or for finding some alternative.

As an adviser, Clifford had sat in on the previous policy decisions. In June 1965, at the time America was sending combat units to Vietnam, Clifford asked General Wheeler, CJCS, what if it works, what then? Halberstam says Wheeler looked puzzled. "I don't understand the question." Clifford repeated: If we won what do we do? Were we still involved? Did we have to stay there? Wheeler answered, yes, a major force would have to stay, perhaps for twenty or thirty years.[40]

Clifford's own account of the meeting on July 21 begins by pointing out that Westmoreland was requesting thirty-two additional combat battalions (100,000 men) by the end of that year, and more in 1966, plus intensified bombing of the North and a partial mobilization of guard and reserve units.

Near the end of the meeting . . . I asked General Wheeler a simple question: "If the military plan that you propose is carried out, what is its ultimate result if it is 'successful?' Wheeler answered that, in all likelihood, we would be able to withdraw most of forces, but there was a chance that we would have to stay for a long time with a smaller number of troops to help secure a stable government.[41]

That would be the prize for winning.

When Clifford took over at Defense, we saw earlier that his first important decision was what to do with General Westmoreland's new request for another massive infusion of troops. General Wheeler, returning from Vietnam, told the president that General Westmoreland required over 200,000 more men. When Johnson asked Clifford to do a complete review of U.S. policy in Vietnam, Clifford could find no one able to say that sending the new reinforcements would change the course of the war. He reported that to the president. Meanwhile, the request for the additional forces leaked, and the *New York Times* published it on March 10, to the fury of President Johnson, who by now felt trapped no matter what he did. With a presidential speech on Vietnam scheduled for March 31, an intense in-house staff battle continued over its content. The meeting of the Wise Men culminated with debriefing the president. One after another, they expressed their misgivings about a war they once had supported. The president was deeply shaken. After much heart-searching, what he said on March 31 was this:

> Tonight I have ordered our aircraft and our naval vessels to make no attacks on North Vietnam, except . . . north of the demilitarized zone where the continuing enemy buildup directly threatens allied forward positions. . . . [42]

That was an area covering almost 90 percent of North Vietnam's population and most of its territory. It was a bid for Hanoi to open negotiations for an end to the war, an admission that America could not or would not try to win. Johnson ended his speech: "I shall not seek, and I will not accept, the nomination of my party" for reelection.

On April 3, Johnson announced that North Vietnam had expressed willingness to confer. This was the beginning of the end of the most traumatic episode in American foreign policy since the beginning of the nation. After several preliminaries, American and DRV representatives began substantive negotiations. Many procedural obstacles still had to be overcome before full-fledged peace talks among all the parties could begin, but eventually they were. On January 25, 1969, the first substantive sessions of Paris Peace Talks began.

What Went Wrong?

The analysis in this chapter has emphasized that U.S. policy in deciding to play a combat role in Vietnam was decisively influenced by two shorthand formulas used as guiding principles: Communist bloc containment and the domino theory.

Consequently, U.S. policy was clearly based on a dual assumption. First, that the Vietnam situation was ultimately one more move in the Soviet Communist chess game to win control of the world. Second, that this, therefore, made the area of great strategic interest for the United States and its allies. Yet both assumptions were questioned by many scholars, both at the time and later.

It is fairly obvious that the Vietnam commitment, if analyzed through the lens of the *four cardinal principles* instead of through that of these *shorthand formulas,* would have yielded quite a different bottom line. The cardinal principles assert that any important foreign policy decision, especially one involving vital interests (i.e., whether to go to war or not), can best be understood as a choice between two fundamentally divergent alternatives. Counterbalancing interests, as one of those four cardinal principles, in particular points out that such a choice, if done carefully, must involve examining *four* separate values. Each alternative has its own plus and minus; in modern jargon, its up side and its down side.

In Vietnam, as so often with such significant choices, the choice came down to get involved or stay out. But the choice to go in was really made because of the negative value of only one of these alternatives—the foreseen and dreaded cost of not taking up the challenge in Vietnam. At best, the plus side of that alternative was preserving South Vietnam as an independent state. But what of the other two values? What would have happened if the United States had pulled its advisers out and let events take their course?

If this analysis had been carried out, the important data added would have focused on third-party influences (another of the cardinal principles). It would have focused on the *real* relationship between Communist China and the Soviet Union, and between China and Vietnam. After all, deterring the Communist bloc was the whole purpose of the involvement. The fighting may have been in Vietnam, but the message being sent was for Moscow and Beijing. The question that was ignored, then, by not doing the total analysis was whether there was a cheaper and more cost-effective way of deterring.

If the real relationship between China and the Soviet Union was based on suppressing a growing mutual antagonism in the face of the common threat of an America bent on deploying forces around China's periphery, then deploying those forces retarded a Sino-Soviet split. Yet the evidence that there was such a split in the making was available and beyond dispute. Moreover, such a Sino-Soviet split was clearly in America's interest. It not only would mean the breakup of the major alliance link in the Communist bloc; it would also cause both the Soviets and the Chinese to shift a wary attention to their mutual frontier, thereby limiting the ability of the Soviets to pursue their interests elsewhere.

In the Korean War, for better or worse, U.S. forces had moved up to the Yalu, to China's frontier with Korea. Now, in Vietnam, there was the threat of U.S. forces on China's southern periphery. By such deployments the United States inevitably complicated any Chinese split with the Soviets, causing China to act more prudently. At the same time, the American action increased the number of U.S. enemies instead of keeping them as low as possible (conservation of enemies).

Summing Up

It is important to remember that foreign policy assumptions are in a fundamental sense culturally determined (past-future linkages). It is not surprising, therefore, if American leaders share certain American biases. From this point of view, President Johnson was eminently American. The assumptions he made about an inevitable American victory, however faulty, were initially shared by 90 percent of his fellow citizens. James Reston, one of the most respected reporters during this period, says of Johnson:

> First, he knew little or nothing of the enemy or the guerrilla war he was fighting. Second, he had supreme confidence that the United States could do anything it set its mind to, and thought money and machines were the answer to any test of power, and third—a touch of racism here—that America was superior and that "these little brown men," as he called the Vietnamese, would run into the rice paddies at the sight of American troops and modern weapons.[43]

The Vietnamese, for their part, also made their culture-bound assumptions, but they saw Americans more clearly than Americans saw them. For cultural reasons, they were willing to trade any number of lives to win their point, and they had the patience to do so. Seeing America through the eyes of an underdog who has to use every possibility to make up for superior American power, the Vietnamese drew the conclusion that the vulnerable point in American armor was American unwillingness to sacrifice a substantial number of lives and continue a struggle indefinitely.

Such national differences have to go into any foreign policy analysis. It is not correct or prudent to assume that other peoples think like Americans.

There is something about a phrase like the one used in the Gulf of Tonkin Resolution—using "all necessary means"—that is quintessentially American. It implies that you can determine exactly what is "necessary" to solve the problem. Then, you just use what is required. And, if you need more, just ask for it. The phrase reflects a conviction that Americans need not pay much attention to a means-results ratio. McNamara in the Pentagon installed "systems analysis," whose function was to decide through quantification and statistics which weapons systems to buy and when enough was enough. His objective was not primarily to find out whether America could afford it, but rather to see that America did not spend redundantly. "Obviously," the nation could afford whatever it determined was "necessary" in Vietnam. But it did not turn out that way, there, or necessarily anywhere else.

Notes

1. Clifford, *Counsel to the President,* p. 54.

2. David Halberstam, *The Best and the Brightest* (New York: Random House, 1969), p. 305 says: "McGeorge Bundy [Kennedy's NSA], sensing grave doubts about Johnson

in his White House shop . . . lectured some of them, telling them not to be such Eastern snobs about Johnson, to cast that arrogance aside. Perhaps he did not have the elegance of his predecessor, but he got things done, and perhaps, being somewhat weak in foreign affairs, he would need them more. . . ." Halberstam's book, one of the earlier serious studies on our Vietnam involvement, holds up quite well, still. Johnson's experience as vice president was reminiscent of Harry Truman's under FDR, when the vice president was not even aware of the Manhattan (A-bomb) project.

3. Johnson addressed domestic issues with confidence. On foreign policy and national security, the record shows clearly that he tended to go with the most well argued, majority advice. That made Secretary of Defense Robert McNamara the second most important man in Washington in these years. Clifford, *Counsel to the President,* has ample illustrations. The documentary record shows the same thing. See especially Neil Sheehan, et al., *The Pentagon Papers* (New York: Quadrangle Books, presumably 1975; a Bantam Books edition came out in 1971). These papers were highly classified documents leaked from the Pentagon files to the *New York Times* which, after a famous court battle, won its case under the freedom of press provisions of the U.S Constitution. The papers include presidential memos and NSC papers but are more inclusive on JCS and military command memos. For the White House side, Clifford's account is much more complete.

Townsend Hoopes, who held a senior position in the administration, wrote of Johnson: "In matters of war and peace he seemed too much the sentimental patriot, lacking Truman's practical horse sense, Eisenhower's experienced caution, Kennedy's cool grasp of reality." (Hoopes, *The Limits of Intervention,* rev. ed. (New York: David McKay, 1973), p.8.

4. The United States was not a party to the Final Declaration, and Eisenhower explicitly stated it was not "bound by the decisions taken by the Conference." See U.S., Congress, Senate, Committee on Foreign Relations, *Background Information Relating to Southeast Asia and Vietnam,* 6th rev. ed., (Washington, DC: GPO, June 1970), p. 172. Hereinafter cited as U.S. Senate, *Background Information.* It was partly because of the "losses" at Geneva that the SEATO treaty was signed in September 1954.

5. Almost all Vietnam figures disagree sooner or later. Here we have almost always used *The Pentagon Papers* statistics, which are taken from the official documents. For a quick overview of the growth of U.S. forces in Vietnam, see the front and rear inside covers of the *New York Times* edition.

6. Even after all these years the exact nature of the American involvement remains controversial. The most generally accepted interpretation is that at first Washington sought to encourage the coup without overt involvement. Aware of the various intrigues that had been occurring, Washington took indirect actions that decreased Diem's support and made it clear it would not intervene to prevent his overthrow. Later its role became more direct. See the helpful discussion in Stanley Karnow, *Vietnam: A History, The First Complete Account of Vietnam at War* (New York: The Viking Press, 1983), Ch. 8. Also recommended is Chester L. Cooper, *The Lost Crusade: America in Vietnam,* revised and updated (Greenwich, CT: Fawcett, 1972), Ch. 9, and William J. Rust, *Kennedy in Vietnam* (New York: Charles Scribner's Sons, 1985), Chs. 9–10.

7. U.S. Congress, Senate, Committee on Foreign Relations, *Hearings on Supplemental Foreign Assistance, Fiscal Year 1966—Vietnam,* 89th Congress, 2nd Session, 1966, p. 331.

8. *Pentagon Papers,* p. 7.

9. *Pentagon Papers,* pp. 28, 29.

10. See Maxwell Taylor, *The Uncertain Trumpet.*

11. The new policy was called "flexible response." For a valuable discussion of the impact of limited war theory on the conduct of the war, see George C. Herring, " 'Cold Blood': LBJ's Conduct of Limited War in Vietnam," *The Harmon Memorial Lectures in Military History,* No. 33, 1990, pp. 1–34, U.S. Air Force Academy, 1990.

12. This was to be temporary, until free elections occurred within two years. They never took place, of course.

13. The quotation is from Taylor's cablegram from the Philippines, to President Kennedy, November 1, 1961. The secret report then gave amplifying details. For text, see *Pentagon Papers,* pp. 146–48. Taylor was accompanied by White House adviser Walt W. Rostow. Their instructions were to find out what was needed to strengthen South Vietnam. Maintaining the status quo or de-escalating were not options.

14. Memorandum from Secretary McNamara to the president, November 8, 1961, including the JCS views. *Pentagon Papers,* pp. 153–55.

15. Memorandum from Secretaries Rusk and McNamara to the president, November 11, 1961. *Pentagon Papers,* pp. 155–58. The issue of who was in operational control of the enemy forces, which would bedevil America for years to come, was already evident. While Rusk and McNamara spoke of "Guerrillas," Kennedy, in a letter to Diem dated December 14, said the campaign was "directed by the authorities at Hanoi." See U.S. Senate, *Background Information,* p. 189.

16. Neil Sheehan's belief, in fact, is that to Kennedy, "Vietnam in 1962 was a test of whether the 'Free World' or the 'Communist World' would prevail." Neil Sheehan, *A Bright Shining Lie: John Paul Vann and America in Vietnam* (New York: Random House, 1988), p. 59.

17. There was much optimism in Washington. As McNamara said on his first visit to Vietnam (1962), "Every quantitative measurement we have shows we're winning this war."

18. Beginning with a Buddhist uprising against "Catholic dominance and Diemist oppression" in May 1963, for nearly two years there was great turmoil and conflict between various *South* Vietnamese factions. This only added to the general confusion. General Khanh had overthrown General Minh (Diem's successor) in January 1964. Not until the spring of 1965 was the South Vietnamese government stabilized (Khanh held no position in that government).

19. This became very controversial. In the midst of a presidential campaign Johnson was projecting the image of a man who would not rashly escalate the war, and was characterizing his opponent, Senator Barry Goldwater, as a man who would. The general judgment is that LBJ had not yet *decided* to expand the war but knew it might become necessary. For a more critical view, see Nathan and Oliver, pp. 269–70.

20. *Pentagon Papers,* p. 275. For an excellent yet succinct discussion of the Gulf of Tonkin crisis, see Guenter Lewy, *America in Vietnam* (New York: Oxford University Press, 1978), pp. 32–36.

21. *Pentagon Papers,* pp. 272, 273.

22. Congress came to regret its careless choice of words in the Tonkin Gulf Resolution, which allowed Johnson full discretion. But there is no doubt it gave him that power.

23. As John Schlight put it so carefully, "The Pleiku raid brought a change of heart to

most members of the National Security Council. . . . Those who had formerly insisted that political reform must precede attacks on the north now agreed to immediate reprisal." John Schlight, *The United States Air Force in Southeast Asia, The War in South Vietnam: The Years of the Offensive, 1965–1968* (Washington, DC: Office of Air Force History, 1988), p. 17.

24. For a useful analysis of the background and early stages of the bombing campaign (known as "Rolling Thunder"), see Mark Clodfelter, *The Limits of Air Power: The American Bombing of North Vietnam* (New York: The Free Press, 1989), Ch. 2.

25. For the text see George McTurnin Kahin and John W. Lewis, *The United States in Vietnam: An Analysis in Depth of the History of America's Involvement in Vietnam* (New York: Dell Publishing Company, 1967), pp. 432–33.

26. *Pentagon Papers*, p. 421.

27. This is the figure Clark Clifford uses. See *Counsel to the President*, pp. 482, 483. General Wheeler's memorandum uses the figure of 206,756, for a new ceiling of 731,756. *Pentagon Papers*, p. 633.

28. Because Johnson believed in the domino effect, he was convinced that from it he understood the Vietnam situation. He reportedly said: "Yet everything I knew about history told me that if I got out of Vietnam and let Ho Chi Minh run through the streets of Saigon, then I'd be doing what Chamberlain did in World War II." Quoted in Doris Kearns, *Lyndon Johnson and the American Dream* (New York: Harper & Row, 1976), pp. 252–53. Most key foreign policy decisions in Johnson's time were made unilaterally or in the "Tuesday Lunch Bunch." This small group was essentially permanent and closed. Because of this, information from "unfriendly sources" was precluded. Fundamentally different views were rarely considered. Even so, Leslie H. Gelb and Richard K. Betts, in their book, *The Irony of Vietnam: The System Worked* (Washington, DC: Brookings, 1979), argue that the "bureaucratic system did what it was supposed to: select and implement means to a given end" (p. 354). The authors argue earlier that the end—consistently followed for 25 years—was preventing a Communist victory in Vietnam. They are correct; yet that merely shows that the policymakers, thinking within containment parameters, did not really consider the "opportunity costs." They should have, and the system would have "worked" to better purposes if they had. The authors also argue that the policymakers were consistently pessimistic about *winning*. That is harder to accept. Walt Rostow, for example, was hardly ever pessimistic. Neither were our generals, provided the president kept sending more troops. (The generals certainly *would* have been pessimistic if President Johnson had given them a firm, final quota for troop strength of, say, 150,000.)

29. One of the authors had what we think was a unique experience. As a permanent member of a war college faculty all through the Vietnam War years, he had the opportunity to hear the JCS members in then-classified briefings. This is an accurate summary of their individual and collective views.

30. The Chinese charges and the Soviet defense of July 14 can be found in David Floyd, *Mao Against Khrushchev* (New York: Praeger, 1964), pp. 406–20. See also *Two Major Soviet Statements on China* (New York: Crosscurrents Press, 1963), and *Statement of the Soviet Government, September 21, 1963, Reply to a Statement of a Chinese Government* (New York: Crosscurrents Press, September 1963), pp. 3–40.

31. *New York Times*, May 19, 1970.

32. Sheehan's *A Bright Shining Lie* is very penetrating in this regard. Of the myriad of

books focusing on strategy directly, one of the more provocative is Harry G. Summers, Jr., *On Strategy: The Vietnam War in Context* (Carlisle Barracks, PA: 1981).

33. This was one of the reasons the air force so disliked the way Rolling Thunder actually was implemented. Initially conceived by the military as a bombing campaign to achieve clear military objectives, it became a White House-controlled and manipulated off-and-on operation designed to achieve the political objective of bringing Hanoi to the bargaining table on Washington's terms. With air targets picked by Johnson, the controlled escalation at some point was supposed to inflict the correct amount of pain to achieve the desired result. It did not. See Bruce Palmer, Jr., *The 25-Year War* (Lexington, KY: University Press of Kentucky, 1984), p. 37 on the targeting issue.

34. See Robert Galucci, *Neither Peace Nor Honor: The Politics of American Military Policy in Viet-Nam* (Baltimore: Johns Hopkins Press, 1975), p. 118.

35. Recounted in Clifford, *Counsel to the President,* p. 513.

36. See Don Oberdorfer, *Tet!* (Garden City, N.Y.: Doubleday, 1971).

37. The accuracy, fairness, and influence of media coverage of Tet was and remains an issue. Useful is Peter Braestrup, *Big Story: How the American Press and Television Reported and Interpreted the Crisis of Tet–1968 in Vietnam and Washington,* 2 vols. (Boulder, CO: Westview Press, 1977).

38. On p. 549 of the second edition of Hartmann's *The Relations of Nations,* published in 1962, there is a three-panel map of Vietnam, showing Communist-held territory in 1949, 1950, and 1954. In 1954, at the time of the Geneva Accords, the Viet Cong [Minh] is shown as holding a third of South Vietnam. This estimate, widely at variance with the common assumption at that time, proved to be correct. The map was based on open-source Swiss military intelligence data, which, during this whole period, was much more accurate than anyone else's. Again, Sheehan's *A Bright Shining Lie* is valuable.

39. Of course, civilians too were overly optimistic. See George C. Herring, *America's Longest War: The United States and Vietnam, 1950–1975,* second edition (New York: Alfred A. Knopf, 1986), Ch.5. Reporter James Reston, in the field with the troops at the time that General Paul Harkins was U.S. top commander, found junior officers singing a ditty to the tune of "Twinkle, Twinkle, Little Star," which is really a tribute to their spirit in the face of adversity, with no real end in sight.

> We are winning, this we know,
> General Harkins tells us so.
> In the Delta, things are rough,
> In the mountains mighty tough.
> But we're winning, this we know.
> General Harkins tells us so.

James Reston, *Deadline* (New York: Random House, 1991), p. 318.

40. Halberstam, *Best and Brightest,* p. 596.

41. Clifford's somewhat less dramatic version—still substantially the same as Halberstam's—is in *Counsel to the President,* p. 414.

42. Clifford had the most influence on this speech, which originally started out like the rest to emphasize that "we would stay the course" and send more men. Karnow's discussion of the period from Tet through Johnson's speech is particularly insightful. See Karnow, *Vietnam,* Ch.14. Johnson never forgave Clifford.

43. Reston also says that President Johnson inherited the interventionist policy from Kennedy, that he was influenced by the anti-communist atmosphere of the country, that he believed in the domino theory notion "that defeat in Vietnam would be followed by the collapse of American authority in the Pacific," and that Johnson acted therefore "from a combination of ignorance, vanity, and booze. . . . The drink didn't improve his judgment." James Reston, *Deadline,* pp. 310–11.

12

A New Approach to Cold War Problems

The prolonged national trauma over Vietnam made a policy reassessment absolutely necessary. The most pointed question of all was whether America had to continue to oppose by force *every* Communist aggression, no matter where or by whom. In a nutshell, the shorthand formulas came under review.

Richard Nixon and his national security advisor, Henry Kissinger, have both written extensive memoirs. They show, despite the men's personality differences, that they had one trait much in common: pragmatism. Although each was strongly on record, Nixon as a politician, Kissinger as an academic, as convinced opponents of communism, the question they now addressed in their White House offices was not one lost in clouds of rhetoric but very much down to earth. How was the United States, through its foreign policy, to avoid bleeding to death or bankrupting itself? For what Eisenhower had warned against—

an excessive dependence on military forces as a weapon of foreign policy—had proved sadly true. It *was* possible for even a rich nation like the United States to overextend itself in commitments.

Labels Are Often Misleading

Academics have long used the terms "realism" and "idealism" to show polar tendencies in American foreign policy. Earlier discussion in this book showed both realism and idealism *as attitudes* with deep roots in the American experience. These traits are, of course, not mutually exclusive. Any given policy, conducted in the name of realism or in the name of idealism, is very likely to contain elements of both, just as, for instance, the Truman Doctrine did. Or the Marshall Plan. Each combined help to others with results that directly benefited the United States. So, although idealism is usually equated with moral and ethical considerations, while realism at its worst is considered a synonym for power politics, and at best as meaning pragmatism and practicality, actual policy almost always has to combine both. That is true in the nature of policy decision; it reflects the way the world operates, and it is in the last analysis congenial to the American temperament and outlook. The American people are not in the habit of endorsing foreign policy goals that they explicitly recognize as strictly self-centered and self-serving. But in any event, the analysis in Chapter 11 does not show the United States formulating and implementing policy either in the name of idealism or realism, but under the influence of abstract and shorthand formulas used as guiding principles. Of course, either idealism or realism can be expressed as an abstract formula, also. After all, "power politics" is just as abstract a concept as anything that can be put forward under the label of idealism. Abstract formulas, based on *either* supposed realism or supposed idealism, can just as readily lead to foreign policy disasters. It is the results that count, not the supposed motivation, goals sought, or labels used.

That is the point where Nixon and Kissinger sought to turn around the thrust of American foreign policy.

Extrication from Vietnam

It was obvious that no new departures in foreign policy could be made without also solving the Vietnam problem.

The American public reaction against Vietnam came about slowly, but by 1967 and early 1968 the majority of Americans considered the initial decision to enter the war as an error. But opinion remained severely divided on what to do next, the "doves" and the "hawks" offering highly opposite "solutions." By the time Nixon became president in 1969, these differences had by no means been resolved, but more and more people wanted withdrawal. By midyear of 1969, once public opinion had coalesced around that idea, the administration's general policy direction was fairly well determined. "Vietnamization" would permit withdrawal "with honor," assuming the enemy cooperated.

In seeking "peace with honor," Nixon believed he could count on the support of what he called the "silent majority." Ever thin-skinned when it came to criticism, he reacted with a curious compound of arrogance and defensiveness. He was sure

> his own intentions were noble, and that his New Class opponents—intellectuals, the national media, bureaucrats, ultraliberal Hollywood celebrities, nonbusiness professionals—wished to destroy him and the values of his heartland supporters.[1]

But throughout Nixon's first term there was much public unrest, especially in the aftermath of American/South Vietnamese military actions against North Vietnamese sanctuaries in Cambodia in 1970. That really divided the public (although 50 percent approved). The panic shooting by the Ohio National Guard of four students at Kent State University that same year fanned these winds of discontent into a blaze of public outrage. Yet Nixon himself remained quite popular; in 1972 he was reelected in a landslide.

There is no question but that a divided public made the job of withdrawal more difficult. But there it was. The North Vietnamese, observing all of this, held out for maximum concessions, beginning with the proposition of even negotiating in earnest. They had already made one bad bargain in agreeing to the "temporary" division of Vietnam at the 17th Parallel after they had decisively defeated the French in 1954. Then, the lure was the elections, which they were sure they would win. But, especially because of American policy, those elections were never held. This time the Hanoi government was determined that they would not only gain their goal but would humiliate the United States along the way. That was one of the goals of their costly but politically effective Tet offensive of 1968.

The proposals and counterproposals that were surfaced through all kinds of mediators finally resulted in the Paris Peace Talks. These talks did not reach a serious stage until mid-1972. Kissinger, who was chief American negotiator, dates the "breakthrough" as October 8, 1972, when Le Duc Tho, the chief North Vietnamese negotiator, suggested that the two nations sign an agreement that settled the military questions (withdrawal, prisoners, cease-fire) while treating the political questions (especially the survival of the South Vietnamese government after a cease-fire) in terms only of "main principles."[2] In his memoirs Kissinger comments that "After four years of implacable insistence that we dismantle the political structure of our ally and replace it with a coalition government, Hanoi had now essentially given up its political demands."[3] But, Kissinger adds, Hanoi had said "nothing about withdrawing its troops," not even admitting they were there.[4]

Despite Kissinger's implication that Hanoi had made a significant concession, it is plain to see that if Hanoi got Washington to ignore the question of North Vietnamese troops in South Vietnam, the eventual result would be Saigon's collapse. Which is what happened.

The terms of peace that were agreed to in Paris on January 23, 1973, were very far from earlier American proposals. On May 14, 1969, Nixon had proposed on national television withdrawal of "the major portions" of U.S. forces within one year of an agreement, with simultaneous withdrawals by both sides from South Vietnamese soil.[5] But by May 1972, three years later, all American forces would leave in four months, while the North's troops could stay. Ultimately, the withdrawal period was 60 days. This was not a very glorious ending to the war, from an American standpoint. But it got U.S. prisoners of war back.

In the sequel, even though American forces began to withdraw and the POWs to return, the war did not really stop. In the spring of 1975 there was an all-out North Vietnamese offensive. On April 30, with the American evacuation complete, the Saigon government surrendered. "Reunification" was proclaimed little more than a year later. In Cambodia and Laos, too, Communist forces triumphed. All Washington's efforts to bring a "peace with honor" had failed. Thus the Nixon-Kissinger (and Ford) Vietnam policy accomplished little except to extricate the United States from an unpopular and unsuccessful war. Even so, until the Vietnam involvement was liquidated, nothing much else was possible, for it was all-absorbing. And the end of the war did not bring about the extremely negative and scary predictions put forward by the advocates of the domino theory. Not only did the Southeast Asia area fail to exhibit a continuing "fall of dominoes," but as time passed it became ever more obvious that what happened in former French Indo-China would ultimately have very little effect on the rest of the world.

Problem I: A More Subtle Approach

By the time the Vietnam peace terms were announced, a more subtle approach to the American power problem was well underway. Neither Nixon nor Kissinger in their memoirs used the term "conservation of enemies." But it was this cardinal principle that they in fact implemented. Nixon's was the first American administration to seriously consider whether it made sense for the United States to continue to automatically consider China as a potential enemy simply because China was firmly Communist. The new approach marked a distinct turn away from the military emphasis that the containment approach had taken in both Korea and Vietnam. It sought rather to "contain" the Soviet Union more deliberately by exploiting the "natural" features of any system of sovereign nation-states.[6] This reversion to classical balance of power thinking was not designed to isolate the Soviet Union but to constrain it. Accordingly, the Soviets would be presented with more need to be prudent while being encouraged to cooperate with the United States in ensuring a more stable equilibrium.

This complex objective turned upon reaching an arrangement with Communist China. Hitherto in the postwar period, China had been ostracized, with American influence directed to its isolation. But President Nixon, less than two weeks after his January 20, 1969, inauguration, instructed Kissinger to begin privately exploring the possibility of a rapprochement with China.[7] Not until the middle of 1971 did this approach pay off. Then, on July 15, 1971, Nixon was able to announce what he correctly called "one of the greatest diplomatic surprises of the century." Revealing that Kissinger and Premier Zhou Enlai of China had held talks in Beijing from July 9 to 11, Nixon added that he himself would soon visit China to "seek the normalization of relations. . . ." With that visit, which took place in February 1972, came the beginning of significant changes, not only in U.S.-Chinese relations, but also in Sino-Soviet and Soviet-American relations. In history, these events are called "the China card." It was all the more remarkable when we remember that Nixon's visit occurred months before the breakthrough in the Vietnam talks and at a time when China was still sending arms to America's opponent.

The China card was a great surprise, as Nixon said. But it was implicit in the state system at the time, as all such surprises must be. For Communist China, although technically allied to the Soviet Union since 1950, was very uneasy about the relationship, particularly after the Cuban missile crisis, as we saw earlier. The Chinese were becoming convinced that the Soviets were their primary threat. Confronted with U.S. military forces in Korea and Vietnam, the Chinese naturally also felt uncomfortable about that. But if the United States was intent on withdrawing from Vietnam and was willing to make some accommodation with China, China could "conserve enemies" and gain much. Instead of uneasy relations with both superpowers, a rapprochement with the United States would put pressure on the Soviet Union, at the very least, to treat China with more respect. Both the United States and China, by making this move, were smoothing relations with a possible secondary enemy in order to concentrate on the primary threat.

The normalization of U.S. relations with China ended a Sino-America hostility that had little solid basis. It also came at a time when the Sino-Soviet dispute was both open and bitter and when armed clashes had occurred on their disputed frontier. By now freeing the Chinese to act adversely against the Soviet Union if they so decided, the change drastically curtailed Soviet strategic freedom. After the fighting in August 1969, Moscow even asked the United States what it would do if the Soviets were to launch a military strike against China's growing nuclear facilities.

There was no good way the Soviets could derail the improving Sino-American relations. Although the move now made toward warmer relations with India was an obvious effort to counterbalance the China card, Moscow had no real place it could turn to produce an equivalent strategic ploy.

The Soviet response had both a "soft" component and a "hard" component. This duality was natural enough. Softening the tone of diplomacy may lower the tension level, but it does not increase national security. To make the nation more secure, only two possibilities exist. One is "to play a card" to "conserve" enemies. But the Soviets had nothing equivalent to America's card to play. The other possible response is to increase the size and combat readiness of the armed forces—which is what the Soviets did. For what the diplomats fail to deliver to keep a nation secure is customarily demanded of the generals (if not demanded *by* the generals).

The pace of the increased Soviet defense effort, rather complacently disregarded by the American government at the time, was rapid. United States defense outlays, which in 1960 were comfortably ahead of Soviet spending, decreased (in constant dollars) after 1968—a trend that continued every year thereafter until 1977. But Soviet spending, which overtook America's in 1968, thereafter shot ahead. By 1981, Soviet spending (almost $260 billion) exceeded U.S. spending ($170 billion) by a whopping $90 billion a year. The United States, smugly comfortable with its card and its obvious effects on Moscow, was ultimately to find itself dangerously behind in the armaments race.

Problem III: Overhauling Defense Policy and New Arms Control Efforts

The Vietnam War had not only been costly in American lives and in shattering the popular consensus on foreign policy. It had also been enormously costly in

Diagram 12.1

U.S. Defense Spending as a Percent of GNP (1950–1997)

······· *1993–1997 Projected*

Source: Office of Management and Budget

dollars, well beyond the ability of even a rich nation like the United States to continue indefinitely. Although not explicitly renouncing domino theory thinking, President Nixon quickly turned away from its implication that the United States would deploy military forces in virtually automatic strategic commitments. In what came to be called the "Nixon Doctrine," he said:

> The United States will keep all its treaty commitments. We shall provide a shield if a nuclear power threatens the freedom of a nation allied with us, or of a nation whose survival we consider vital to our security and the security of the region as a whole.
>
> In most cases involving other types of aggression we shall furnish military and economic assistance when requested and as appropriate. But we shall look to the nation directly threatened to assume the primary responsibility of providing the manpower for its defense.[8]

With the primary threat decreased through the China card, a significant shift in conventional forces defense policy seemed feasible. The 2 1/2 war concept of the Kennedy and Johnson years had been based on the assumption of a war against the Soviet Union in Europe, China in Asia, and a "1/2 war" somewhere else—simultaneously. (If this seems hard to believe in today's perspective, it nonetheless was the fact.) Because it now seemed reasonable to assume that the Soviets and Chinese would not field forces as allies against the United States, a new planning formula was adopted: a 1 1/2 war strategy. Not yet aware of the way Moscow was reacting in terms of its own armed forces, the United States now made very deep cuts in its conventional forces.

Problem III: Strategic Arms Control, SALT I

In his memoirs Nixon wrote: "The Soviet Union will always act in its own self-interest; and so will the United States." That did not mean, however, that no common interests existed or that no usefully beneficial agreements could be made. This approach, *detente* as it was soon christened, was not a pipe-dream about achieving permanent cooperation and eliminating all conflict. Rather it was designed to minimize confrontation in as many areas as possible.

Two areas were high on this policy agenda. One was arms control. Up to this time, for many reasons, no international agreements limiting central strategic weapon systems had proved possible. Nations who arm for security are not easily persuaded to disarm. Other kinds of agreements had been made: "Hot line," Antarctic Treaty, Outer Space Treaty, even a Limited Test Ban Treaty. (A Nuclear Non-Proliferation Treaty had also been signed, although not yet ratified.) But nothing on central strategic systems.

Nixon (and Kissinger) believed that establishing a balance in nuclear arsenals would not only be valuable in its own right. It could also encourage a larger pattern of cooperation under detente. Domestic pressures on defense spending (another legacy of Vietnam) and the administration's belief that "sufficiency" would have to replace strategic superiority, added additional reasons for trying for an agreement. Washington continued to cling to the idea of "essential equivalence" in strategic weapons, enough to make a retaliatory strike credible —what was called "mutual assured destruction," usually abbreviated to MAD. But as long as these objectives were achieved, the administration was less concerned with specific numbers than with achieving some balanced agreement.

With Strategic Arms Limitation Talks (SALT) beginning in 1969, by May 1972, two agreements had been signed. The first, the Interim Agreement on Certain Measures with Respect to the Limitation of Strategic Offensive Arms, focused on controlling the *number* of fixed ICBM and SLBM *launchers,* although it did not provide for *equal* limits. For five years the number of launchers would be capped at the level of those operational or under construction on July 1, 1972. For the United States, this was 1,054 ICBMs and 656 SLBMs. For the Soviets it was 1,618 ICBMs and 740 SLBMs.[9]

The Interim Agreement was enthusiastically hailed, worldwide. Although it was limited in scope, even excluding entire systems (such as bombers), and left uncontrolled a number of other variables that impact strategic capability, the agreement was a big first step. To have tried for more at the time, like dealing with multiple warheads on one missile, or throw-weight comparisons, or accuracy, would have introduced far too many variables. Most commentators approved what had been done, with criticism coming only later.

The second agreement, which would become very controversial later, was an Anti-Ballistic Missile (ABM) Treaty. This ABM Treaty allowed each side two antiballistic missile sites, with no more than 100 ABMs at each site.[10] This, of course, severely limited what could be done in a defensive mode against incoming missiles.

To many observers, arms control was both the centerpiece and litmus test for U.S.-Soviet relations. To Nixon, it was a key tool in Washington's effort to give the Soviets a stake in stability.

Problem IV: Grain Exports

A second tool was trade. But here the results were to be far less impressive.

The Soviets obviously desired and needed American trade, technology, and credits. Their rapid economic growth rate of the 1950s and 1960s had declined drastically, with their Achilles' heel their seldom adequate grain harvests. Western capital and technology could help develop Siberia's vast resources. Trade by itself could be mutually beneficial, but it would also add one more reason for the Soviets to act with restraint. In July 1972, an agreement was reached permitting the Soviets to buy $750 million of American grain. Later announcements raised that total to more than $1 billion. In October a comprehensive trade agreement granted the Soviets most-favored-nation status.

But problems soon arose. The relatively sudden and very large Soviet grain purchases drove American food prices dramatically higher. The media called it the "great Russian grain robbery." And a painstakingly negotiated trade agreement, which required legislation for implementation, was sidetracked by the U.S. Congress. Senator Henry Jackson, believing detente was becoming a one-way street in favor of the Soviets and unhappy about Soviet restrictions on Jewish emigration, tried to extract a *quid pro quo.* He introduced an amendment (as did Representative Charles Vanik in the House) requiring the lifting of restrictions on Jewish emigration to Israel as a precondition for easier trade conditions. The Jackson-Vanik Amendment, attached to the Trade Act of 1974, was approved by large majorities in both houses. The Soviets responded by rejecting the entire package on the grounds of interference in their internal affairs.

Problem II: Linkage and Regional Developments

Both President Nixon and President Ford (as well as Henry Kissinger, who bridged both presidential terms as secretary of state) said they believed in linkage. In an era of detente they hoped that leverage in one area could be linked to advantages in another. And from this point of view, the "China card" certainly paid off. But Washington had already found that the idea that Moscow would really assist the United States to disengage from the Vietnam War had been taking the point much too far. After all, as any hardheaded observer could see, it had been very much in Moscow's interests to keep the United States bogged down in Southeast Asia.

In other areas where the Soviets and Americans had obvious divergent interests, no great change was observable, either. Although Nixon and Kissinger claimed credit in the Jordan crisis of 1970, when Syrian-trained Palestine Liberation Army tanks failed to halt the Jordanian pursuit of Palestinian *fedayeen,* what probably turned the tide was an Israeli threat to intervene and a decisive Jordanian air strike against the tanks (which had no air cover).

In a second Mideast crisis in 1973, precipitated by an Egyptian-Syrian attack on Israeli forces, Moscow clearly knew the attack was coming but chose not to warn Washington. When the Israelis counterattacked and surrounded a whole Egyptian army, superpower tension was extreme.

In a third incident, a confrontation over Cuba in 1970, the Soviets had started constructing a submarine base there. The U.S. Joint Chiefs objected strongly, and Kissinger took up the cudgels. He characterized "the Soviet move as going beyond its military implications; it was part of a process of testing underway in different parts of the world."[11] Kissinger informed the Soviet ambassador that the United States would not tolerate such a base in Cuba, and the Soviets decided it was not worth contesting the issue.

A fourth development was in Angola, where the Soviets had supported the anti-Portuguese Popular Movement for the Liberation of Angola (MPLA). After Portugal's withdrawal, Soviet aid increased; so did American assistance to a counter-coalition. When South African forces intervened against the MPLA, the Soviets introduced more than 10,000 Cuban combatants. Since the U.S.

Congress refused to appropriate funds to support the rival coalition, the MPLA/Cuban coalition gained the upper hand. It was hard to see detente producing much regional cooperation in any of these cases.

A fifth development was the India-Pakistan War of 1971. The Bengalis in East Pakistan, separated from West Pakistan by more than 1,000 miles across India, rebelled and proclaimed an independent state, Bangladesh. In a brutal civil war, the Pakistani army sought to crush the rebellion. But India, which in August had signed a friendship pact with the Soviets, aided the rebels, in November launching an all-out offensive. The United States, believing the Soviets were encouraging India "to exploit Pakistan's travail in part to deliver a blow to our system of alliances [and] in even greater measure to demonstrate Chinese impotence,"[12] decided to "tilt" toward Pakistan. A U.S. carrier task force entered the Bay of Bengal to signal opposition to any Indian efforts to dismember *West* Pakistan and Washington took action to persuade Moscow to put significant pressure on India to stop. On December 16, India agreed. Whether India did so because of Soviet pressure or simply because it had limited objectives remains controversial. But it did stop.

In all five cases it is hard to find any real "linkage" between detente's goal of enhancing stability and equilibrium and the actual results in the various regional crises.[13] Whatever American success was achieved was accomplished largely outside the detente framework. In none of these cases did linkage work, any more than it had in the efforts of the United States to get the Soviets to help end the Vietnam War. Moreover, the very fact that such crises continued to occur encouraged the American right wing to deride the very idea of detente.

A Changing Political Scene: The Congress and Foreign Policy

Part Three showed how the Vietnam War significantly changed the American domestic political landscape. Its net effect was to set narrower boundaries to presidential power, in some respects with lasting effect.

Congress, mirroring popular feelings to which an outspoken and critical media added its voice, became increasingly assertive of its prerogatives, belatedly regretting its open-ended grant of authority to President Johnson in the Tonkin Gulf Resolution.[14] Chapter 6 gave four illustrations of this new assertiveness of Congress: in the use of military force,[15] the making of international agreements, tighter controls over covert operations, and policy on aid and trade.[16] Mentioned just above was how Congress attached the Jackson-Vanik amendment to the Trade Reform Act.

In the changed atmosphere, any major foreign policy agreement submitted to Congress was potentially controversial. Congress agreed to the SALT I offensive arms agreement only after another Jackson amendment, this one urging that future agreements not limit the United States to intercontinental strategic force levels inferior to Soviet levels.[17] To ensure that foreign policy commitments made by the president would be made known to Congress (in contrast to what had happened with the notorious Yalta agreement), in 1972 Congress passed the Case Act. All international agreements other than treaties had to be submitted to Congress within sixty days of coming into force.

Any one of these changes by itself was of consequence. Collectively, they constituted a drastic change in the attitude of Congress toward the presidency and in the ability of the president to shape foreign policy. Coupled with the Watergate scandal and Nixon's resignation under fire, the new relationship between Congress and the president led his successor, Gerald Ford (who had himself been appointed to the vice-presidency after his predecessor had resigned under pressure) to say that the imperial presidency (alluding to what critics said of Nixon) had been replaced with an imperiled presidency.

As president, Ford had no popular mandate at all. Although he retained Kissinger and leaned on him heavily, with Congress in its assertive mood as a major and continuous player in policy formulation, it was clear that foreign policy would no longer be left largely to the president in the immediate years to come.

Ford's decision to remove the stigma of possible trial still hanging over Nixon's head by granting him a presidential pardon, although undoubtedly taken on principle, also probably doomed any chance he had for election in his own right.

So it was that the national election of 1976 was filled with cries for reform. As always in the United States, one extreme tends to encourage the other—at least in political campaigning, where issues in any event are frequently oversimplified. Many people threw into one pot both discontent over Vietnam (that America had quit, that it had not won, that it had gone there to begin with, that it fought the wrong way, that it spent too much, that it did it essentially alone) and disgust over the lack of dignity in the White House. They looked for a newer and cleaner image. They had had enough of "power politics" and "realism." When, in the wake of the lies and deceit that accompanied the final stages of the Watergate scandal, Jimmy Carter promised that he "would not lie or deceive," he hit a responsive chord with the American people.

Carter: Idealism, Again

Jimmy Carter—he insisted on the "Jimmy"—was an "unorthodox" Democrat who made it to the White House with no real assistance from the Democratic Party national apparatus. He owed no obligations to vested interests and his announced program focused on decency, fair dealing, and no deceits. A former nuclear submarine officer and an agricultural businessman in Georgia, he had served as governor of his state. Although possessed of a quick mind, he had no actual experience with foreign affairs. Where Nixon, Kissinger, and Ford had sought to achieve a stable equilibrium via a "realistic" mix of pressures and rewards, Carter vowed to pursue a fair and humane policy that, like Wilson's, would be based squarely on ideals.

In a key speech at the University of Notre Dame in May 1977, Carter sounded that theme: "I believe that we can have a foreign policy that is democratic, based upon fundamental values, and that uses power and influence . . . for humane purposes. We can also have a foreign policy that the American people both support and, for a change, know about and understand."[18] America would become "free from that inordinate fear of communism which once led us to embrace any dictator who joined us in that fear." The idea of containment had been overemphasized, and policy in consequence partly misdirected. Since the Soviets, he said, were essentially a "status quo" power now, defense issues had become secondary.

Carter considered the world far more interdependent than most of his predecessors. To him, economic forces were increasingly more important than military, and "North-South" relations were as important as "East-West" concerns, meaning there had to be greater emphasis on the needs and interests of the Third World.[19] Achieving meaningful arms control agreements would be his primary national security goal. Regional issues would be handled within a framework of justice and self-respect largely outside the outworn Cold War framework. Central to all of this, Carter would *promote human rights, worldwide.* As he wrote in his memoirs:

> As President, I hoped and believed that the expansion of human rights might be the wave of the future throughout the world, and wanted the United States to be on the crest of this movement.[20]

These were certainly desirable *goals.* But as his administration progressed, it became apparent that Carter lacked any carefully worked out program for achieving them. One of Carter's speechmakers reportedly said: "Carter has not given us an *idea* to follow. The central idea of the Carter Administration is Jimmy Carter himself . . . since the only thing that gives coherence to the items of his creed is that he happens to believe them all."[21] Whether that was correct or not, Carter's administration was to be remembered for one solid achievement (on the Middle East), one prolonged mess (Iran), and one action (on Panama) that has remained controversial in part ever since.

Problem IV: Foreign Aid and Human Rights

Carter's idealism was shown immediately. Acting to promote human rights, he gave little regard to the objections of foreign nations that he was interfering in their "internal affairs." He pressured them to change their policies or suffer the consequences. A tacit but persuasive assumption was that if America remained thus faithful to "humanity's goals" (as unilaterally interpreted by the United States), it *must* ultimately win a net friendship.

The prime thrust of his human rights approach fell on foreign aid, particularly with Latin American nations. Aid to Argentina and Uruguay was cut off because of alleged human rights violations. Guatemala and El Salvador, realizing they were scheduled for similar treatment, beat Washington to the punch and rejected aid first. Brazil, the most powerful nation in Latin America, soon did likewise. Only in the Dominican Republic did the human rights emphasis improve the American position. Hardly a net gain in friendship.

The human rights emphasis provoked adverse responses from many other nations. It also had a spillover effect, for Carter soon found his strategic arms control efforts with the Soviets stymied. In early 1977, when Soviet dissidents protested against human rights abuses by the Kremlin, Carter, seemingly oblivious to Moscow's sensitivity on this issue, openly and vigorously condemned Soviet policies. He went so far as to bypass Soviet officials, *directly* assuring leading dissident Andrei Sakharov that the United States would continue its "firm support to promote respect for human rights not only in our own country but also abroad."[22] Carter even invited ex-dissident Vladimir Bukovski to the White House. The Soviets, outraged, responded that Washington's "pretensions" to "teach others how to live were unacceptable to any sovereign state."[23] Such attempts at "interference in our internal affairs," they said, were categorically "rejected."

Carter's human rights initiatives in Latin America also continued to have counterproductive effects. In Central America his policy toward Nicaragua helped bring about dictator Somoza's downfall but failed to convert the Sandinistas, who took power then, to a favorable view of the United States. This development laid the basis for a problem, one of whose ultimate consequences was the Iran-Contra controversy. In El Salvador, following a 1979 coup, Washington worked to moderate the almost pathological violence that followed.

Carter's "idealistic" approach to African and Latin American problems vastly underrated the complexity of the conflicts he was to encounter. Although he placed a high priority on improving economic relationships, the results (except for enhanced ties to Nigeria and Mexico—because of their oil) were very disappointing. On racial-colonial issues in Africa the administration's hard line got it nowhere. It was unsuccessful in persuading South Africa to modify apartheid. It did not move Namibia or Rhodesia toward independence (although British action later helped transform Rhodesia into Zimbabwe). Suspending aid to Ethiopia for alleged human rights violations, Washington saw the Soviets take its place and help defend Ethiopia's territorial integrity against a Somalian invasion. As in Angola, Cuban soldiers were employed, along with Soviet military technicians and several Soviet generals on the ground.

Problem III: Arms Control, SALT II

Against this background, the United States now encountered more undesirable "linkage" from the Soviets. Secretary of State Cyrus Vance, jouneying to Moscow for arms control talks, found Washington's proposals summarily dismissed. The Soviets made it perfectly clear that if the United States wanted progress on arms limitations, it would have to cease its "violation" of the Soviet "right" to treat its own people as it would.

With arms control so important to Carter, though, the administration changed tactics, becoming less directly and openly critical. It also refashioned its proposals.

Previous negotiations had been conducted within the guidelines of a 1974 Vladivoskok agreement in principle. These guidelines had set overall limit goals for strategic nuclear delivery vehicles and MIRVs. The assumption then was that SALT II would be concluded soon. When that did not happen, the creation or proliferation of so-called peripheral systems (cruise missiles, the Soviet Backfire bomber) had complicated negotiations further. Now Washington proposed a three-tier formula in an eight-year treaty, plus a three-year protocol for the new systems, and a statement of principles looking forward to further agreements.

The Soviets accepted this formula, and after further negotiations the SALT II Treaty was signed in June 1979. It provided overall limits on strategic nuclear delivery vehicles, with various subceilings on MIRVed missiles, and provisions on how many ICBMs could be MIRVed. Construction of additional fixed ICBMs was prohibited, the maximum number of warheads on various missiles was fixed, and limitations were set on throw-weight. The three-year protocol banned the deployment of mobile ICBMs or flight-testing from such launchers. Finally, the range of all ground- and sea-launched cruise missiles would be limited.

A whole host of arguments now began in Washington over the merits of the treaty. But the treaty's content did not determine the treaty's fate. Instead, SALT II was doomed by growing public and congressional disillusionment with the Soviets. Moscow's continuing military buildup was now not only obvious but frightening. Even less consistent with Carter's view that the Soviet Union was a status quo power were its policies in Africa. So, too, in Latin America, where Cuba, allied to and heavily dependent on the Soviets for support, was a major player in supporting leftist revolutions. The Soviet invasion of Afghanistan in December 1979 was the last straw. It took place during America's continuing humiliation over the Iranian hostage affair (discussed below). These events eliminated all prospect of Senate ratification. In early 1980 Carter withdrew SALT II from the Senate.

Now the inadequacy of Carter's defense program became glaringly obvious. A vigorous critic of the American military effort in Vietnam, Carter had canceled the B-1 bomber program (with air-launched cruise missiles scheduled to be deployed on B-52s by the early 1980s). In conventional forces he had allowed readiness and sustainability to deteriorate to the point that the United States had what critics called a "hollow force." Vetoing appropriations for a super-carrier, he justified the limited number of carriers by embracing a "swing strategy" for the navy. In the event of a war with the Soviets, U.S. Pacific forces would move to support NATO reinforcement runs—but leaving Japan and Korea at risk. Only in the strategic nuclear area did Carter continue what critics accepted as an adequate program. Research and development work continued on the 10-MIRV MX ICBM, a Trident missile came on line, and work continued on the new Trident submarine.

The cumulative effect of the Soviet buildup, plus the Iranian crises and the Soviet invasion of Afghanistan (not yet discussed), finally led Carter to a major turnabout in his defense budgets.

Where (as a percentage of GNP) these budgets had declined from 9.3 percent in FY 1968 to 5.0 ten years later, Carter's last budget asked for 5.3 percent *real* growth in obligational authority. Postponing troop withdrawals from South Korea, he signed new base agreements with both Turkey and the Philippines. To compensate in part for the fall of the Shah of Iran, with its corresponding destabilization in the Middle East, he established a new contingency planning force focused on the area. Initially called the Rapid Deployment Joint Task Force and later the U.S. Central Command, it eventually would play an important role in the Persian Gulf War.

Announcing the "Carter Doctrine," he made a new, explicit American commitment in the Middle East. Any outside power attempting to control the Gulf would henceforth be viewed as acting with hostile intent to undermine America's vital interests. It would be repelled by any means necessary. These were significant changes back toward a more militarily-oriented policy.

Problem II: Two Regional Initiatives, Panama and Israel

The Carter administration also took two important regional initiatives. Both sought to settle existing tensions through encouraging compromise.

The first initiative—and high on Carter's list of priorities—was the negotiation of Panama Canal treaties. Since 1903 the United States had operated the Panama Canal and controlled the ten-mile wide Panama Canal Zone as "if it were the sovereign of the territory." (The wording is in the 1903 treaty.) This grant of authority was in perpetuity, but over the years anti-American feeling in Panama, sparked by this situation, had grown. Bloody riots broke out in 1964. Negotiations for a new treaty had followed intermittently. Carter, "convinced that we needed to correct an injustice," thought time was running out. "Our failure to take action . . . had created something of a diplomatic cancer. . . ."[24] What America did about Panama, Carter thought, would be a "litmus test" of how the United States intended henceforth to treat small and relatively defenseless nations.

Spurred by presidential interest, negotiations now went forward more rapidly, even in the face of strong domestic opposition.[25] Two treaties were signed, and both of them were eventually ratified. The first was mostly economic in thrust, providing that Panama would assume control over the Canal Zone once the treaty became effective. The United States would operate and control the Canal itself until the year 2000, but with a progressively greater Panamanian participation. By the end of 1999, the Panamanians would take over entirely. It was also stipulated that until that time the United States would retain primary responsibility for the defense of the Canal.

The second treaty was primarily security-oriented in thrust. It provided that the Canal would be permanently neutral. Each party was given the right to defend that neutrality, and American warships were provided a right of "expeditious passage."[26] Unfortunately, both treaties were purely bilateral, thus losing the opportunity to multilateralize responsibility for the strategic aspects of the canal on a hemispheric basis. The dangers in these security arrangements showed up a decade or so later. By that time, control of Panama (and therefore, prospectively, of the canal) was in the hands of Manuel Noriega, a military dictator and drug dealer. Although the United States eventually (under President Bush) took military action to remove Noriega and install a new democratic government in Panama, the control of the canal remained non-hemispheric.

The other regional initiative was highly successful. It brought Egypt and Israel to the peace table. After the 1973 war, although Kissinger's shuttle diplomacy had led to partial disengagements between the Israelis and Egypt and Syria, most of the territorial issues resulting from Israel's victory in 1967 remained unresolved. With the Arab states and Israel holding widely divergent interpretations of Security Council resolutions 242 and 338 (which would govern any further negotiations), the Palestinian issue remained a pile of tinder, waiting for a match to set it aflame.

Believing initially that Soviet cooperation would be vital to any progress in this area, Carter sought to bring them in instead of shutting them out of the negotiations, a la Kissinger. Seeking a comprehensive settlement, he wanted to reconvene the Geneva Conference (which, meeting shortly after the 1973 war, had then collapsed), including some way for Palestinians to participate. On October 1, 1977, Washington and Moscow were able to announce principles for settlement acceptable to the superpowers, but the announcement went over poorly in the region where parties not only did not agree with each other but dislike the "meddling" of "outsiders."

It was this deadlock that Egypt's Anwar Sadat broke. Egypt disliked Israel; Egypt also needed peace. Weighing these counterbalancing interests, Sadat astounded observers by proclaiming his willingness to go "to the end of the world," even "to the Israeli parliament itself," for peace. The stunned Israelis, weighing *their* counterbalancing interests, invited him to come. On November 20, 1977, the Egyptian leader, speaking to the Israeli Knesset, said, "we accept living with you in permanent peace." Syria, the PLO, Iraq, Algeria, South Yemen, Libya (and the Soviets) were all highly critical.

Egyptian-Israeli negotiations followed immediately, but serious problems developed. Here, Carter, at his best and seizing a historical opportunity, offered to mediate. After exhaustive bargaining, on September 17, 1978, this initiative ended with two Camp David Accords signed. One accord dealt with the West Bank and Gaza, providing procedures for developing some degree of Palestinian autonomy and the termination of Israeli administration, along with relocations and withdrawals of forces. This clearly was to be only a stepping stone, avoiding as it did critical issues such as sovereignty, territorial boundaries, and the status of Jerusalem. The second agreement laid the groundwork for an Egyptian-Israeli peace treaty, the exchanging of Israeli-held land for peace.

Arab reaction generally was adverse to both agreements. However, Sadat had too much invested to turn back now. The Israelis, though sacrificing territory, also were very anxious. How better to implement the conservation of enemies principle than to remove their most capable enemy from the opposition coalition? If Egypt was isolated diplomatically in the Arab world as a result, that was not Israel's problem. On March 26, 1979, the Egyptian-Israeli peace treaty was signed. The Israelis would withdraw completely, Egypt resume sovereignty, and there would be buffer zones to keep strictly limited area forces apart.

Without Carter's efforts (and America's influence), this progress would not have been possible. Although Washington had to make a commitment to Israel to serve as a last resort source of petroleum for a 15-year period, and had to promise considerable financial aid to both countries (on top of existing programs), the administration believed, correctly, that it was worth it. With less chance of a major Arab-Israeli war, the risk of a Middle East confrontation with the Soviets had also shrunk. On the negative side, little progress had been made in resolving the Palestinian issue, the Israelis went on building more settlements in the West Bank, and Sadat was now under increasing pressure at home and abroad. Furthermore, as Nathan and Oliver observe, the Camp David negotiations had ended up excluding "the Russians . . . yet again," thus pinning "the most radical Middle Eastern groups and states closer than ever to the Soviets."[27] Still, on balance, the peace treaty was an important step forward.

In the Far East the administration showed itself sensitive to strategic requirements. It reversed its initial plan to reduce the force level in South Korea, moving instead to strengthening defense ties in South and Southeast Asia. After difficult negotiations, full diplomatic relations were resumed between the United States and China on January 1, 1979, with Washington now maintaining only unofficial ties with Taiwan. Limited progress was made with Japan on Washington's aim of persuading Tokyo to increase slightly its defense efforts.[28] But the U.S.-Japanese trade balance tilted further against the United States, the deficit increasing from just over $5 billion in 1976 to more than $10 billion by 1980—with no sign of stopping there.

Problem II: The Hostage Crisis

If progress in the Middle East was Carter's most obvious success, by the irony of fate it was also the scene of his greatest failure.

Since the early 1970s, American policy toward the Persian Gulf had rested on the so-called "twin pillars" of Iran and Saudi Arabia. With the direct commitment of American power thought to be improbable for domestic reasons, Teheran and Riyadh were seen as surrogate keys to maintaining Gulf stability.

Throughout 1977 and 1978 there were many indications of popular discontent in Iran, but Washington generally was not alarmed.[29] Nonetheless, as it became clear things were deteriorating, Carter told the Shah that Washington would "back him" all the way. What this would mean *in practice* was not clear, however. As the situation deteriorated further, it became obvious that real revolution was possible; it became equally obvious that Washington had no clear policy. The Shah by now was receiving contradictory signals; UN Ambassador Andrew Young was even calling the Iranian opposition leader, the Ayatollah Khomeini, a "saint." With conflict between the NSC and State increasingly heated, the American ambassador sat in Teheran without instructions. In late December the aircraft carrier *Constellation* was dispatched, but a few days later it turned around. On January 16, 1979, the Shah fled. Khomeini returned to Iran to set up an Islamic Republic, determined to eliminate all American influence.

The ineffectual leadership and poor decision making in Washington lowered American prestige abroad. The Saudis had nervous second thoughts about their American "ally." Worried about Khomeini and what his Shiite Islam fervor might do to Gulf stability, they saw a distinct threat to their own regime. Adding to their disenchantment was the conclusion of the bilateral Egyptian-Israeli Peace Treaty in March. Because that treaty affected Saudi interests negatively (as an inevitable third-party influence) by decreasing the threat to Israel, the Saudis now became a strong political opponent of the Egyptians. The Saudis also reduced efforts to keep OPEC oil prices stable. From 1974 to 1978, the price of crude had risen only slightly: from $10–11 per barrel, to $12–13. Now prices jumped to the $30–35 range.

The situation in the Middle East now went from bad to worse. After Carter agreed to let the Shah come to America for medical treatment, Iranian "students" seized the American Embassy in Teheran, taking its incumbents hostage. Hardly had Washington caught its breath when the Soviets invaded Afghanistan (December 1979). The timing and bold nature of the Soviet attack, plus the fact that it was the first use of regular Soviet military forces outside the Soviet bloc since World War II, thoroughly shocked the president and his advisers.

Political and economic pressures applied to both the Soviets and Iranians produced no results. On April 24, 1980, the United States finally attempted a hostage rescue mission, only to have to abort it after three of the eight helicopters had troubles. They had not even reached Teheran. To America's growing frustration was now added humiliation. This was the bitter fruit of allowing the U.S. armed forces to deteriorate.

Near the end of the year, with Iran now fully engaged in a bitter war with Iraq, Teheran became more willing to end the hostage affair. With enormous help from Algeria, an agreement was reached and the remaining 52 hostages released. Whether as a deliberate gesture of contempt for the Carter administration or not, the hostage return date was January 20, 1981, just after Ronald Reagan was sworn in. (In 1991 a dispute was to erupt as to whether Reagan's staff had intervened to deliberately postpone the release until then!)

Carter's average public opinion approval rating of 47 percent had fallen by this time to 34 percent—three points above Truman's at term's end and a stalemated Korean War, and only ten points above Nixon's when he resigned his office in disgrace.

Summing Up

Chapter 12 has discussed two rather different new approaches to Cold War problems.

In the first approach, under Nixon, the old Cold War shorthand formulas as guidelines to U.S. policy were jettisoned in favor of a hardheaded look at American interests. Clearly, the Vietnam War needed to be phased out and, if possible, the world balance of power changed. The early years of the Nixon administration were highly successful in changing the strategic position of the United States from its dismal condition during the Vietnam War, when the United States had its hands full in a very questionable and expensive war while, as a byproduct, the Soviets enjoyed great freedom to pursue their goals.

Nixon's disengagement of U.S. forces from Vietnam came at a price to U.S. prestige and was accompanied by deceit (for example, over the bombing of Cambodia, which was denied and shrouded in military secrecy). There was parallel deceit in handling the Watergate scandal. Combined, these deceits undermined popular confidence in the integrity of the American government—a distinct disservice to the country.

Henry Kissinger proved an adroit diplomat, but his contribution (apart from the "China card") did not do much in healing or resolving problems on any permanent basis. As watchwords of the day, "linkage" and "detente" eventually fell into disrepute.

Nixon and Kissinger were "realists," and their successes came from that way of looking at problems. But it was by no means inevitable that in the end the political benefits of a realist approach would be swallowed up in deceits. The problem here was not the realism; the problem was a lack of closely balancing principle.

Following Ford's caretaker government, Jimmy Carter was elected on a wave of revulsion against the "realist" and "power politics" approach, determined to reestablish American policy squarely based on wholesome American values. He proposed to deal in a new and positive way with what he saw as a changed international system. But with the exception of the Camp David Accords and the Egyptian-Israeli peace treaty (and mixed results in the Far East and with the Panama Canal treaties), most of his results were highly disappointing, to say the least. Ironically, as his failures mounted, Carter was forced back to certain fundamentals, such as a recognition that the weakness of U.S. armed forces was, intended or not, apparently seen by the Soviets as an encouragement to armed adventures. By the end of his term, Carter sounded very much like any Cold War president of the 1950s. Was it Carter's idealism which was at fault? Not really; it was his pursuit of particular principles apart from whether they could produce the desired results in a particular context. Idealism of *this sort* does not work. Nor is it really in the American tradition, which has more usually combined principles and national interests without too much strain on either.

Notes

1. Richard A. Melanson, *Reconstructing Consensus: American Foreign Policy Since the Vietnam War* (New York: St. Martin's Press, 1991), p. 41.

2. Henry Kissinger, *White House Years* (Boston: Little, Brown, 1979), p. 1343.

3. Kissinger, p. 1344.

4. Kissinger, p. 1344.

5. Kissinger, p. 270.

6. See also the useful discussion in John Lewis Gaddis, *Strategies of Containment: A Critical Apprisal of Postwar American National Security Policy* (New York: Oxford University Press, 1982), Chs. 9, 10.

7. Richard M. Nixon, *RN: The Memoirs of Richard Nixon,* vol. 2 (New York: Warner Books, 1978), p. 8.

8. Richard Nixon, *U.S. Foreign Policy for the 1970s: A New Strategy for Peace, February 25, 1971* (Washington, DC: GPO, 1971), pp. 12–14. Useful is Jeffrey Record, *Revising U.S. Military Strategy: Tailoring Means to Ends* (Washington, DC: Pergamon-Brassey's 1984), Chap. 3.

9. Each party could expand the number of SLBMs, the Soviets to 950 and the United States to 710, if it dismantled an equal number of older ICBMs or launchers of SLBMs on older submarines.

10. In July 1974, the parties signed a protocol reducing the number of sites to one for each party. Moscow used its site for a defensive ring around Moscow, while the United States, after deploying a system in North Dakota, eventually retired it.

11. Kissinger, *White House Years,* p. 641.

12. Kissinger, p. 886.

13. John G. Stoessinger, *Henry Kissinger: The Anguish of Power* (New York: W.W. Norton, 1976), assesses the same five occasions (plus Vietnam) but frequently reaches conclusions quite different from ours.

14. Another reason for Congress' increased role was its enhanced analytical capability. The Congressional Research Service replaced the Legislative Reference Service, the General Accounting Office provided more effective supervision, and in 1974 the Congressional Budget Office was created. Moreover, congressional staffs increased by leaps and bounds.

15. The War Powers Resolution was key in this effort. Having taken over three years to pass, the resolution was very complicated in its provisions and unclear in its effects. For an excellent analysis, see Robert F. Turner, *Repealing the War Powers Resolution: Restoring the Rule of Law in U.S. Foreign Policy* (Washington, DC: Brassey's, 1991).

16. Useful on this topic, especially in relation to Middle East issues, is Cecil V. Crabb, Jr., and Pat M. Holt, *Invitation to Struggle: Congress, the President, and Foreign Policy,* 3rd ed. (Washington, DC: CQ Press, 1989), Ch. 4.

17. The SALT I offensive arms agreement technically was an executive agreement, which normally would not have required any congressional action. However, when Congress established the Arms Control and Disarmament Agency in 1961, Congress also legislated that the United States could not agree to disarm or limit its armed forces

or armaments except pursuant to the treaty-making power of the president or unless authorized by congressional legislation.

18. See *Weekly Compilation of Presidential Documents,* May 30, 1977.

19. See Cyrus Vance, *Hard Choices: Critical Years in America's Foreign Policy* (New York: Simon & Schuster, 1983), p. 256.

20. Jimmy Carter, *Keeping Faith: Memoirs of a President* (New York: Bantam, 1982), p. 144.

21. Quoted in Seyom Brown, *The Faces of Power: Constancy and Change in United States Foreign Policy from Truman to Reagan* (New York: Columbia University Press, 1983), p. 460. For the view that Carter and his advisers *did* initially possess a grand design which, unfortunately, was "poorly articulated," see Melanson, *Reconstructing Consensus,* pp. 91ff.

22. The president's letter to Sakharov is quoted in U.S., Department of State, *Special Report: Second Semiannual Report to the Commission on Security and Cooperation in Europe, December 1, 1976–June 1, 1977,* June 1977, p. 6.

23. See the statement by Leonid Brezhnev in Novosti Press Agency Publishing House, *L. I. Brezhnev: Speech at the 16th Congress of the Trade Unions of the USSR. March 21, 1977,* Moscow, 1977, pp. 27–28, 30–31.

24. Carter, *Keeping Faith,* p. 155.

25. Carter, pp. 162–78, provides a fascinating discussion of Carter's *domestic* negotiations. Useful is William L. Furlong and Margaret E. Scranton, *The Dynamics of Foreign Policymaking: The President, the Congress, and the Panama Canal Treaties* (Boulder, CO: Westview Press, 1984).

26. Conservative critics, saying Carter gave away "our" Canal, charged the strategic costs outweighed the political gains. How an America at war would defend the *neutrality* of the Canal was also not clear.

27. James A. Nathan and James K. Oliver, *United States Foreign Policy and World Order,* 4th ed. (Glenview, IL: Scott Foresman, 1989), p. 366.

28. The increase in Soviet nuclear capabilities in the Far East, the enhanced power of its Pacific Fleet, and its systematic buildup in the "northern territories" were major contributing factors.

29. Ambassador William Sullivan, Israeli intelligence, and Anwar Sadat all indicated there was real trouble. For an insider's account of the developing crisis and the fall of the Shah, see Gary Sick, *All Fall Down* (New York: Random House, 1986).

13

The Last Decade
of the Cold War

When Ronald Reagan became president in 1981, the Cold War was well into its fourth decade. Few would have guessed that the Cold War was also beginning its last decade. Reagan had been elected on a program of reversing America's weakness, and his views of the Soviets were reminiscent of those held by Americans in the 1950s, with rhetoric to match. There would be no more "naive" talk of North-South relations replacing East-West, or economic factors being more important than military, or of Soviet-American cooperation. The Soviets were, in his view, the "focus of evil" in the modern world. They were, as always, inexorably expansionist, driven by unrestrained ambition. He saw the "Vietnam syndrome" and misguided American policies under Carter as weakening America just when the Kremlin's relentless military buildup and regional forays had actually increased the threat.

Given this situation, revitalizing containment was Reagan's first order of business. Now, more than ever, especially because of the military threat, the United States had to play the lead role. Hopefully the day would come when the Soviet Union's great internal economic and social problems would induce the Soviets to reconsider what they were doing. Perhaps then they would look again at the "shelved," or counterbalancing, alternative of cooperation with the West.

Reagan believed part of the challenge was psychological. The United States had to restore its own pride and reassert its own willpower. His extremely effective communication skills soon produced significant results. In particular, his portrayal of America defending democracy against the "evil empire" controlled by the Soviets struck a responsive chord in much of the American populace. Against the evil empire, in Reagan's vision, would be arrayed a newly aroused America, like a "shining city on a hill."

Reagan simplistically, but effectively, portrayed the contest as a drama more or less reduced to black and white terms—a drama in which the hero's role and the villain's roles were laid out for none to miss. As Melanson writes: "According to Reagan, American foreign policy reflected the selflessness, goodness, peacefulness, and generosity of the American people."[1] Not just America's ideals would see it through, though. As Secretary of State Haig later wrote, Soviet diplomacy was "based on tests of will. Since Vietnam, the United States had largely failed these tests."[2] It no longer would do so.

Problem III: Defense Buildup

But psychological rejuvenation unsupported by a rebuilt military capability would have little value. The Reagan administration believed it was necessary to begin at the beginning with a realistic assessment of the threat, rather than what they labeled as the wishful thinking of the Carter years.

With the Soviet threat worldwide and Soviet forces sufficient, they could launch simultaneous attacks in Europe, the Pacific, or Southwest Asia. To meet this threat, America needed a true multifront capability. But in Reagan's first year in office, it had nothing of the kind. Shortages of spare parts was one crippling element, for stocks used up in Vietnam had not been replaced in the lean budget years that followed. Besides a U.S. capability to respond effectively to any Soviet attack anywhere, it also needed to be able to launch counteroffensives in other areas where it could maximize American strengths against Soviet weaknesses. That meant, among other things, turning away from the risky "swing strategy" developed under Carter, which provided that once the "main event" occurred (i.e., a Soviet attack across the Iron Curtain or into the oilfields of the Middle East), America would swing its forces from the Pacific, where they supposedly would not be needed, to the active theaters. On the face of it, of course, the swing strategy was a rationalization of a dilemma caused by inadequate funding.

A true global strategy, on the other hand, would require not only building up the individual service forces in terms of readiness and sustainability. It also meant supporting those expanded and reinvigorated forces with sufficient strategic mobility, especially airlift and sealift.

The navy's newly developed "maritime strategy" fitted right into this view. Rejecting the notion popular in the Carter administration that the navy's major function was to escort NATO reinforcements across the Atlantic, fighting off Soviet subs on the way, the navy boldly proposed carrying the fight to the enemy. The Soviet blue-water navy was to be defeated quickly and decisively by aggressive forward deployments to gain control of the seas. For this purpose the administration proposed a 600-ship navy that would include 15 carrier battle groups and 100 nuclear attack submarines. Similarly, the air force was to activate additional tactical fighter wings so as to be able to press a forward-area battle with sufficient strength. The army goal of 16 active-duty divisions included also five division-equivalents to be deployed in Europe plus five more slated for rapid deployment as reinforcements. They would "marry up" with prepositioned equipment.

To support this "flexible response, forward defense" strategy, the air force and army had together created an offense-oriented Air Land Battle concept. NATO, in like spirit, paralleled these changes in doctrine with a Follow-on Forces Attack concept known as FOFA. FOFA emphasized initiative, maneuver, and deep strikes to disrupt enemy forces.

Although these ambitious administration force goals always fell well short of the maximum security ("minimum risk") proposals of the Joint Chiefs of Staff, the goals still required expenditures of awesome magnitude.[3] During Reagan's first term, Congress supported most of his proposals in the conventional forces area. (We shall have more to say about the role of Congress later.)

Reagan also was worried about the strategic forces, where the Soviets by now had a big lead in many categories. Determined to "modernize" all three legs of the so-called Triad (ICBMs under ground, SLBMs at sea, and bombers), Reagan announced his program in October 1981. He envisioned deploying 100 MX ICBMs (rather than Carter's proposed 200), but with the first 40–50 in hardened Minuteman III silos.[4] He also proposed constructing more Trident submarines while accelerating research on the new, highly accurate D-5 SLBM; procuring 100 B-1B bombers; continuing research on the Stealth Bomber (B-2); and continuing equipping modernized B-52s with cruise missiles.

Congress was generally supportive of the president's strategic initiatives, too. It strongly endorsed his efforts to enhance the sea-based leg, and while there was some controversy about the B-1B, Congress eventually fell into line. But the MX and how it would be based was another story. Critics argued that the MX deployed in silos would be vulnerable. Its multiple warheads, since it was MIRVed, made it an excellent target for a single enemy warhead. That also made MX "destabilizing," in the jargon of arms control analysts. They meant that the enemy would be tempted to fire first, using his own multiple warheads, independently targeted to hit a half dozen or more American targets. Thus MX would be counterproductive to arms control efforts.

After a good deal of debate, Congress "accepted" the recommendations of the president's Commission on Strategic Forces (the Scowcroft Commission). Their recommendation was to put 100 MXs in superhardened silos while also pushing ahead to develop a new small and single-warhead mobile ICBM. This new missile, the Midgetman, would be deployed beginning in 1992. Accepting, at least for the moment, these recommendations allowed the Congress to turn to other business. But everyone knew that the issue was not really resolved.

By 1985 most aspects of the defense buildup were well along toward completion. The only really major disagreements involved the ICBM and basing mode issues. But by 1985, another program had arisen that provoked enormous controversy: the Strategic Defense Initiative (SDI).

The Strategic Defense Initiative

For most of the post–World War II period in the strategic arena, Americans and Soviets alike had been preoccupied with offensive nuclear capability. Defensive measures had been considered generally infeasible and unwise, except in the very limited amounts permitted in the ABM Treaty. An enormous and continuing offensive arms race had occurred, neither side willing to be second best. Since the late 1960s, Washington had believed that peace unfortunately rested on the capability for "mutual assured destruction," or MAD. Assuming an ability on each side to survive a first-strike, each would then be able to retaliate and destroy an unacceptably large amount of the other side's valuable targets. *If* each side believed the other had that ability, each would presumably be deterred and that would ensure peace. That *if*, though, was a very large condition indeed.

When he was governor of California, Ronald Reagan had learned that the United States had no real defense against a missile attack, other than to retaliate, and he had been very uncomfortable with the MAD doctrine from that time on. The issue of MX basing, which he inherited from the previous administration, made the issue of current importance. As the Soviets pushed ahead with their multi-warheaded nuclear missiles, which were equipped with much more powerful warheads than the American arsenal, all of the land-based American ICBM weapons were in increasing jeopardy. The MX would not change that, and there was incontrovertible evidence that Soviet capabilities, far from slacking off, were increasing at a rapid rate. If the Soviets believed in MAD, they certainly were exceeding any reasonable measure of deterrence. There also was the problem that the proliferation of systems like mobile missiles and easily hidden cruise missiles undermined confidence in traditional "bean counting" approaches to arms control. Accidental launching might also occur, despite safeguards. And there was the uncomfortable knowledge that Soviet nuclear doctrine emphasized considering all the options, including what had to be done to "win." Under these conditions MAD sounded more like a promise of mutual slaughter than an effective means of deterrence.

At the same time that these factors were throwing doubt on existing policies, continued research into defensive possibilities (by both the United States and Soviet Union) revitalized the possibility that some defense might really be possible. As the Joint Chiefs considered the problem of the ongoing strategic weapons race in 1982 and early 1983, they could draw no comfort from the thought of merely more of the same. In their view, the Soviets could much more easily build large ICBMs. They had less political pressures to consider, less money restrictions on building, less arguments over where to site the new ICBMs, and they were very good at producing very large numbers of such weapons. By following their lead America would not be utilizing the great strength that it had and the Soviets did not—technical innovation.

Mulling the problem over, after 43 meetings of the JCS sufficiently serious as to be principals-only (no staff), on February 11, 1983, they advised the president that it was time also to explore defensive options. Such a defensive development by the United States had the potential of undermining Soviet confidence in the effectiveness of any first strike they might be tempted to launch. It would also degrade and offset the Soviet advantage in heavy missiles.[5]

President Reagan immediately embraced the concept. He was so eager to explore this option out of a dead-end offensive arms race that shortly thereafter (in what was christened his "Star Wars" speech), the president went public saying: "I am directing a comprehensive and intensive effort to define a long-term research and development program to begin to achieve our ultimate goal of eliminating the threat posed by strategic nuclear missiles." SDI was born.[6]

Proposing a revolutionary concept that would break the mental shackles of four decades of strategic thinking would have created controversy even if the concept had been clearly defined. Unfortunately (and even inevitably with something this bold), the president's initial formulation was unclear. Was he proposing to defend all Americans or just American missile bases? In Congress and the media, a plethora of arguments soon raged. In Europe, pundits claimed that the United States was proposing to create a security umbrella over American territory, while a nuclear war was fought over in Europe. Proponents pointed out that if the Soviets could not be confident about the fairly complete success of an initial attack, they would not likely take the enormous risk of beginning a conflict. But opponents questioned whether a defensive system could really be technically feasible. Arms control gurus speculated on whether it would increase or decrease "stability." The general public asked whether it would escalate or slow down the arms race. And would it help or hinder arms control? Almost everyone asked whether it would not be prohibitively expensive.

To most of these questions there were no easy or convincing answers. How could there be, at the start of such a program? Yet, if SDI worked as a deterrent, the payoff in American security would be enormous. Looking for the moment ahead, the Soviets strenuously attempted to get the United States to abort the SDI program. It is virtually certain that the American refusal also finally helped to convince Gorbachev that the Soviets must give up the arms race.

Reagan's actions in regard to SDI illustrated well his whole approach to the presidency. He knew what he wanted when he heard it, even if he was no master of the details.

Problem I: New Toughness, Poland

To Reagan, rebuilding America's military strength was essential not only for military reasons. It was needed also to convince the Soviets that they could not act as they had in the 1970s in Angola and Ethiopia, Afghanistan and Nicaragua, with no concern for how America might respond. But actions to reverse America's decline could not wait until the defense buildup was completed. The Soviets had to be shown right away that a new era had dawned. Events in Poland provided the first opportunity.[7]

Domestic changes were sweeping Poland, threatening the Communist party's monopoly on power. Lech Walesa's *Solidarity* trade union, once legalized, began pushing hard for further reforms. Seeing Solidarity beginning to support workers in other East European countries, the Kremlin worried over the danger of the "contagion" spreading. The threat of a Soviet military intervention in Poland now became very real. Extensive Warsaw Pact military maneuvers brought back painful memories of suppression actions in Hungary in 1956 and Czechoslovakia in 1968. Washington responded by sending the Kremlin some very strong signals indicating that intervention would be considered a very unfriendly action. When the actual crackdown came in 1981, it was instituted by Poland's own President (General) Jaruzelski, using the Polish army. (In 1992 it became known from Soviet sources that he acted just in the nick of time to prevent a Soviet move.) Whether the American strong stand had any effect is not known; what is known is that it was a faithful indicator of how the administration intended to proceed.

Problem II: Lebanon

It was largely in the Third World that the new policy of seizing the global offensive was demonstrated. In the Middle East, America moved to fashion a "strategic consensus" to oppose Soviet inroads. It sought to persuade the regional powers that there was a significant Soviet threat and that additional capabilities and coordinating mechanisms were needed. Unfortunately for the Reagan approach, most regional powers did not agree. In their view, the Soviets were not the primary cause of most of the region's difficulties; indeed, usually they were not even a major player. Because of these differences in perspective, in early 1982 (although the threat was still considered real and planning for the Rapid Deployment Force continued), the administration adopted the alternative tactic of a low profile approach. It now emphasized quiet informal cooperation and developing stronger links to the Israelis. The policy focus shifted to ensuring the completion of the Israeli withdrawal from the Sinai, as per the 1979 peace treaty.

Then, on June 6, 1982, Israel invaded Lebanon.[8] Initially this operation may have been designed only to secure the 25 mile zone in southern Lebanon from which Palestinian guerrillas in the past had raided Israeli settlements. In any event, Israeli forces now smashed their way to the outskirts of Beirut. Whatever the initial objective, the goal became the elimination of the PLO.

But the United States stepped in to prevent further bloodshed, mediating a cease-fire. Defeated PLO leaders and combatants were allowed to depart Beirut, while American forces were dispatched as part of a multinational force to ensure safe withdrawal and to protect the Palestinians left behind. President Reagan, believing the moment was propitious, chose this time to launch a new Arab-Israeli peace initiative.

Suddenly everything went wrong. After the PLO withdrawal and the withdrawal of the multinational force, Lebanon's new president, Bashir Gemayel, was assassinated.[9] Then the Israelis stood by and permitted Lebanese Christian forces to massacre hundreds of Palestinians (including women and children) in refugee camps at Sabra and Shatila. The Israelis also summarily rejected the Reagan peace initiative. The Arabs hinted at some flexibility, but they, too, gave little reason for optimism.

In response to the chaos, a new multinational force, again including U.S. Marines, was stationed in Lebanon. The American commitment, initially quite limited, now began to deepen. Washington sought the withdrawal of all foreign forces from Lebanon, the restoration of Lebanese sovereignty over the entire country, and security for Israel's northern border. The administration launched a new mediation effort, and a Lebanese-Israeli accord was achieved in May 1983. But Israel said the accord's implementation depended on withdrawal by Syria and the PLO. Since they clearly were not leaving, it became a dead letter. Then in October a serious tragedy occurred when terrorists bombed U.S. Marine headquarters in Beirut, causing 241 deaths. Still, President Reagan said that keeping the marines in Lebanon was "central to our credibility on a global scale." Naval bombardments and air strikes against suspected terrorist positions soon followed. Initially noncombatants, American forces were now taking sides in Lebanon's civil war. In language reminiscent of the domino theory, Reagan said:

> If others feel they can intimidate us . . . in Lebanon they will become more bold elsewhere. If Lebanon ends up under . . . forces hostile to the West, not only will our strategic position in the eastern Mediterranean be threatened, but also the stability of the entire Middle East including the vast resources of the Arabian Peninsula.[10]

The situation on the ground continued to deteriorate, however. In early 1984, after talks with the Syrians, the Lebanese government cancelled the 1983 accord with Israel. Lebanon was now *de facto* partitioned, and it was evident that neither Syria nor Israel planned to pull out soon. Faced with a seemingly hopeless situation, the American marines were withdrawn. Clearly, Reagan's Middle East policy had been unsuccessful.

Given all the complications in the Middle East, though, the American failure was not surprising. Furthermore, the Lebanese case had lacked any unwavering and concrete objective. Certainly it is not feasible to insert peacekeeping forces into any situation where all the belligerents are not willing to accept them. Once such a force is itself involved as a participant, it loses credibility in its peacekeeping role. That happened in Lebanon.

Problem II: A Caribbean Communist Triangle?

Now came an issue both more obviously important to the United States and more subject to its control.

In 1983 the Reagan administration was convinced that the Soviet Union was involved in a new attempt to put United States defenses in jeopardy from the Caribbean flank, a replay of the Cuban missile venture with a different scenario. The U.S. Joint Chiefs, observing the construction of a 10,000 foot runway on Grenada being rushed to completion by Cuban army engineers, saw it as one link in a developing triangle. The other two parts rested on Cuba itself and on Nicaragua, where the Sandinista government was being heavily supplied with armaments by the Soviets. The Pentagon was concerned primarily because of the strategic importance of the American Gulf of Mexico ports: In the event of war in Europe, forty percent of U.S. NATO reinforcements would depart from those ports, then transit the Caribbean as they moved east to the Atlantic. If the Soviets based bombers in the Communist-dominated areas, U.S. transports would be exposed to attack. That prospect gave the Pentagon nightmares, for there would not be any easy solution except probably a head-on invasion of at least Cuba, to remove the menace.

But since the Grenada runway was still incomplete, there was time to act. President Reagan did so only a week after the legitimate government of Grenada was overthrown in a coup by the New Jewel leftist movement. Nominally, the action was taken at the request of several other small Caribbean states.

Two days after the Beirut marine bombing, operation "Urgent Fury" forces hit Grenada on October 25, rushing also to protect some 1100 Americans caught up in the crisis. The Cubans resisted and some 600 Cuban troops were captured. The operation was quickly successful and, although not without controversy,[11] was well supported both by Congress and the public.[12]

In the Grenada case, as well as later in Libya, the administration always had two additional and broader goals that reached beyond the specific objectives in each. The first was to demonstrate that in carefully chosen situations military force remained an effective and necessary policy tool—one which the United States could and would use as required. Second, the United States had to show the Soviets, Cubans, and other "outlaws" that the "Vietnam syndrome" no longer would prevent America from countering their machinations.

Problems II and IV: Libya, Terrorists, and Freedom of the Seas

Libyan behavior was a specific case in point. Not only was Colonel Qaddafi in back of much of the terrorism that was claiming innocent victims in many areas, he had also laid claim to a huge piece of the open seas in the Mediterranean, the Gulf of Sidra. Drawing a line across the gulf from headland to headland he claimed some 85 to 90 miles of international waters. Such claims, uncontested, could quickly shrink the open oceans of the world to a point where maritime nations like the United States would be confronting serious problems. The first incident had occurred in August 1981, when Libyan planes challenged U.S. F-14s from the Sixth Fleet. Two more incidents took place in 1986. What triggered them was the bloody bombings, instigated by Libya, at the Rome and Vienna airports in December 1985. In March 1986 the Libyans fired a surface-to-air missile at U.S. planes many miles outside Libyan territorial waters. The planes evaded the missile and destroyed the radar at the launch site. In April, a much larger operation took place, with U.S. planes converging from the Sixth Fleet and from U.S. Air Force bases in England for a coordinated strike against Libyan targets, including Qaddafi's headquarters and one of his homes. The precision of the operation was in marked contrast to the fumbling that had flawed the rescue operation of the Iranian hostages. It showed that the money spent on defense had produced an enormous change in efficiency. Qaddafi obviously got the message and quickly adopted a much lower profile.[13]

Problem IV: The Law of the Seas and the Deep Seabed

The strong response of the United States to Qaddafi was triggered emotionally by the terrorist issue, but it also reflected the strategic judgment that Qaddafi's infringement on the open seas had to be decisively rejected.

Ever since World War II, the law of the sea had been changing as states tended to extend their claims on the open seas. The traditional 3-mile limit for territorial waters was one of the first casualties, as nation after nation began claiming 9 miles or 12 miles. Where there were offshore islands, that could mean, if they were no more than 9 or 12 miles off the coast, extending the territorial waters eighteen or twenty miles to sea. These efforts particularly caused troubles for the United States when island nations embracing traditional international straits were tempted to proclaim exclusive jurisdiction. This is exactly what Indonesia and Malaysia did in March 1972, each reiterating its claim to the very important and well used Strait of Malacca as national property. The United States itself formally abandoned advocacy of the 3-mile limit in August 1971, suggesting agreement be made on a new, uniform, 12-mile limit. As a consequence the United States proposal specifically exempted the character of any international strait from being altered, a policy the Reagan administration reiterated.

Even without such claims to exclusive jurisdiction, states were also beginning to claim extensive areas seaward, where they would exercise some sort of less-than-exclusive jurisdiction—perhaps fishery zones, or petroleum extraction areas, and the like. The traditional (more conservative) approach to the mouth of bays or gulfs also began to be questioned by many of the newer nations, who saw opportunities for extending their control.

All of these moves, without exception, were in the direction of shrinking the "common property of mankind," as the phrase had it for the now-shrinking open oceans.

The incentives for a country to extend its national jurisdiction were obvious: to protect fishing areas against voracious modern factory ships, to expand the national territory, to lay claims to minerals and other riches of the seas. As early as 1958, the multilateral Geneva Convention had produced a definition useful for one troublesome area, the continental shelf. That definition stated that the shelf started at low tide and extended to where the ocean bottom sloped abruptly downward. Within such limits, the shelf varied from zero to 938 miles in width, with an average width of 48 miles. At the outer edge, the depth varied from 65 to 1800 feet, with an average of 436 feet. Although the extent of continental shelves varied greatly among those nations favored with any at all, this agreement was acceptable. The United States, with one of the greatest shelf areas, was particularly well off.

Given this agreed definition, that left the deep seabed outside the continental shelf for countries to fight over. This is where the most dramatic controversy occurred. By 1975, with the end of the Third United Nations Conference on the Law of the Sea, the parties had evolved what was called an "informal single negotiating text." It reflected a deadlock on the question of ocean-floor mining in the deep seabed. The developing nations wanted it managed by an international organ that they could control. The industrial nations, fearing that they would have to put up a great deal of the money and expertise, but have no control over how that money was used, balked. There was also a split over the proposed 200-mile exclusive economic offshore zones proposal, with the landlocked and "geographically disadvantaged" states generally opposing. Since more than seventy nations were already claiming exclusive economic zones, the United States, pending some agreement, began to supervise a commercial-fisheries zone that extended 200 miles out to sea in 1977.

In 1981, the Reagan administration withheld its consent to the draft treaty, making proposals for revision at the resumed U.N. sessions in March 1982. These proposals rejected especially the draft provisions on seabed mining. The

United States insisted on voting provisions that would prevent any project from escaping the control of the industrial nations.

When the final vote was taken in April 1982, the developing nations, believing that the United States would have to accept the final verdict, pushed ahead with their own plan. The vote was 130 in favor, 17 abstaining (including the Soviet Union, Britain, and Italy—all of whom really opposed), and only four nations against. Those four were the United States, Turkey, Israel, and Venezuela. But of the key industrial nations, only France, Canada, and Japan actually voted with the majority.

The net result from the point of view of exploitation of the seabed was nil. Mining would not happen in fact with the industrialized nations against it. From the point of view of American foreign policy, the event again showed Reagan's determination to insist on American views where he thought them soundly based. But dozens of the smaller nations used to deciding U.N. issues were offended. For better or worse, the United States had shown it would not shrink from being in an obvious minority if it felt strongly about an issue.

Problem II: Central American Policies Become Controversial

Part of the incentive for the Grenada operation was the Reagan administration's conviction that Communist subversion was gaining ground on America's own doorstep. Reagan always viewed regional conflicts in the larger U.S.-Soviet framework. Convinced that the Soviets were overextended, he believed also that the Kremlin would not risk a confrontation in what to them was a peripheral area; he felt that Washington could act without much risk. Underlying everything was Reagan's idea that cumulative pressures by America, given Moscow's inability to match the West economically and its own internal needs, would eventually outclass Moscow's ability to compete. It was through this lens that the continuing civil war in El Salvador was viewed.

Events in El Salvador were seen as important in their own right, as a struggle against communism. But it was also considered an important test of U.S. ability and resolve. Acting on that belief, Washington increased both economic and military aid significantly, also pushing for democratic reforms at the same time. Joint U.S.-Honduran military exercises were conducted and U.S. "training facilities" were established in Honduras.

What was done in Honduras was done in some degree or other everywhere else that the administration saw the hand of communism behind insurgencies. In what became known as the "Reagan Doctrine," covert as well as overt aid was given to the mujahadeen, the anti-Soviet rebels in Afghanistan. In Angola, Jonas Savimbi was similarly supported. In both cases, the results were mixed, but the administration remained convinced that its policy was correct. As it saw it, aiding insurgents could accomplish the twin objectives of preventing their defeat and making it more costly for the Soviets to underwrite the continuing struggle. And the strategy did that.

In the case of El Salvador, success in preventing insurgent gains was closely connected to stemming the flow of arms to the guerrillas from Cuba via Nicaragua. Washington had solid evidence of the Sandinista connection with Cuba and other Communist states. It believed the Soviet-Cuban-Nicaraguan troika was intent on and capable of creating further instability, throughout Latin America, unless it was stopped. That brought Washington's focus of concern squarely back to Nicaragua, the transit point. There the existence of an insurgency group opposed to the Communist-oriented regime offered a lever to disrupt Sandinista plans for El Salvador. This opposition group, soon to become well known across America, was called "the Contras" ("those who were against"). The decision to support these Contras soon also brought the Reagan policy toward insurgency in general and toward Nicaragua in particular into controversy.

A majority in Congress was by no means persuaded that a hard-line approach would solve the problems in an area where the gulf between rich and poor was so tremendous and where the insurgency certainly had major aspects of a desperate attempt at minimal living conditions. Many in Congress were willing to grant that the Communist hand behind the insurgency in El Salvador was hardly concealed. But communism, even with its subversive techniques and its open-handed distribution of weapons, could hardly cause the collapse of established governments if they paid at least minimal attention to the needs of their own people. Was that not true, too?

Because of this belief in Congress, which as always reflected a wider public skepticism, the funds provided were always given half-heartedly and on a meager basis. And in Nicaragua, Congress actually prohibited military aid to the Contras altogether in 1984. But after the last funds were spent by May 1984, Congress relented enough to provide minimal funding again in October 1986.

Within the administration, influential figures such as the national security adviser and the director of central intelligence began to explore alternative ways to continue adequate funding for the Contras that held some prospect of escaping congressional controls, such as foreign funding. This effort was to lead shortly to the biggest domestic scandal in American politics since Watergate.

The Iran-Contra Episode

Congress had, as Part Three showed, made serious attempts to curb covert actions that were presidentially-authorized (or presidentially-concealed). When President Reagan authorized the mining of Nicaraguan harbors in 1984, Congress charged that it had not been "fully" and "currently" informed, as the law required. To prevent future disagreements, DCI William Casey signed an agreement with the Senate Intelligence Committee detailing information procedures more closely. Everything seemed settled. Then rumors became more insistent that somehow funding to the Contras was continuing. Administration members queried by the intelligence committees of Congress provided "categorical—but false—assurances" that the law was being observed.[14]

Then, suddenly, over a period of several months, one revelation after another shocked the American people. They were astounded to hear the following:

1. As appropriated Contra funds ran out, the administration had obtained money from private donors and foreign governments, including the Saudi royal family and Taiwan.

2. During the arms embargo against Iran (because of its support for terrorism) the administration, in cooperation with Israel, secretly sold arms to Teheran, anyway. When this violation of its own policy was discovered, the administration first said the purpose was to establish contacts with "moderates" in the Khomeini government. It soon became clear that the real motive was sentimental-humanitarian: the hope of bringing about the release of some American hostages.

3. The president gave Congress "timely" notice of the sales only after they were revealed in a Lebanese newspaper, more than 10 months after the decision was made. The administration deliberately withheld information from Congress and told it outright lies.

4. The plan went ahead despite the strong opposition of both the secretary of defense and the secretary of state.

5. Some of the funds from the arms sales were diverted to the Contras through secret Swiss bank accounts at a time when Congress had forbidden all military aid.

6. The activities of Iran-Contra were conducted largely by the NSC staff, especially national security adviser, Admiral John Poindexter, and Marine Lt. Col. Oliver L. North (called by one critic the only "five-star" lieutenant colonel in the military). Elements of the NSC became a "shadow government" that ran a secret "private" war. When the Poindexter-North activities were discovered, a cover-up to minimize or disguise the degree to which the president was informed was attempted. Throughout, information was withheld from Congress or Congress was actually misled.

As the various events surfaced, a number of congressional investigations were instituted, and the president appointed a Special Review Board (the Tower Commission) to look into the mess. An independent counsel was appointed to see if crimes had been committed. But President Reagan's reputation remained essentially unscarred. The "teflon president," some called him. (Eisenhower enjoyed the same sort of tolerance.)

What finally emerged was, in the words of one congressional committee, a picture of "pervasive dishonesty and extraordinary secrecy."[15] There had been conscious and deliberate decisions to violate the laws banning sales to states supporting terrorism. The president had ignored the requirement to notify Congress of covert operations. Information had been withheld from Congress, and it was deliberately deceived. In fact, Poindexter and North made it quite clear that they believed Congress had been a hindrance to effective policy, and the nation would be far better off if Congress would give the president a free hand. Throughout, it was shockingly apparent that the executive branch policymaking process had been thoroughly distorted, with lower level officials going in divergent directions with little guidance from the top. As the Tower Commission said, "(R)eviews of the initiative by all the NSC principals were too infrequent."[16] It was never entirely clear how much Reagan knew about some of the facets of the operation, but he was the president. If he did not know, he should have. He was responsible.

Whether Reagan really had no idea (as he repeatedly claimed) that funds were being diverted remains controversial. Much in the routine conduct of foreign affairs does occur, especially at the lower levels, without any specific knowledge or concurrence of the president. But Iran-Contra was run by people in the NSC, key members of the presidential advisory system. Outsiders without government experience thus might logically ask how then the president could not know?

But it really is possible, for two reasons. First, because of Reagan's decision style. His preference to lay down general principles, letting his staff work the details, is well known. Many executives in other lines of work do the same. So Oliver North, with the concurrence of Poindexter, and knowing the president *had* approved the initial arms sales to Iran and wanted the Contras sustained, might rather easily have done what he did from the desk he occupied. After all, when an NSC staffer tasks some other office in the government, the normal assumption is that the president authorized it. The second reason is that the operation was covert, therefore heavily compartmentalized. "Need to know" rules apply. In such circumstances, most of those involved will know only a piece of what is going on. Naturally, such a system is open to abuse.

Finally, besides the ethical and legal questions raised and the operation's political absurdity, Iran-Contra violated a fundamental bureaucratic principle. It utilized *staff* to mount an *operation*. An NSC staff is there to provide alternatives to a president; it is the line departments and agencies such as the CIA and State and Defense that should implement the alternative the president chooses. It was this very departure from good bureaucratic practice that helped allow such an unorthodox operation to proceed. The uproar that followed is why the existing restrictions on the NSC staff handling operations were subsequently made even more restrictive.

Problem I: The Soviet Threat Lightens

Throughout Reagan's presidency the one foreign policy constant was the focus on the Soviets. But change was now at hand.[17]

Any existing situation, particularly if it has lasted for a while, encourages the assumption that it will continue. Inertia's effect discounts alternatives. Yet the counterbalancing interest principle reminds us there is always an alternative to every policy, whether it is ignored or not. Like the United States, the Soviets could always alter policies in Europe and the Third World, at some sacrifices to be sure, but also with certain gains. There has to be a real incentive to overcome the inertia, but it can happen.

It did happen with the Soviets, beginning in early 1984. When Mikhail Gorbachev became General Secretary of the CPSU, he came in with a strong agenda for changes. Writing later about Central Committee discussions in April 1985, he said that their analysis led them "to the only logical conclusion, that the country was verging on crisis."[18] Drastic change was needed "if the country was not to sink further into the morass of stagnation" that past domestic policies had produced.[19] *Perestroika* (restructuring) was required, which depended upon *glasnost* (openness) in discussing reforms. Gorbachev did not spell it out, but in foreign policy, where the Soviets had overstretched themselves most obviously in global aid to non-Communist regimes, serious cutbacks would soon be required. He did spell out that reducing tension with the United States would not only allow a breathing space so that the Soviets could move in on their domestic reforms; it would also permit meaningful arms control agreements that would in turn conserve scarce resources.

Problem III: INF and START

As Gorbachev sought to streamline his economy in 1985 and 1986, he had to deal with a bureaucracy and a military reluctant to support his overall aims. At this juncture, Reagan was struggling through the Iran-Contra affair and its aftermath. Each leader now saw an advantage in pursuing arms control talks, both to take important steps to reduce tension and to deflect attention from their domestic problems. With each providing strong leadership from the top, considerable progress was made, confounding the myriad naysayers who considered arms control a lost cause. After strenuous efforts, in December 1987, an Intermediate Nuclear Forces (INF) Treaty was signed. INF provided for the elimination of all intermediate range missiles in Europe (500 to 5,500 kilometer range) and the elimination or conversion of INF missile-related facilities within three years. INF was precedent setting in three ways. First, it eliminated a whole class of weapons. Second, it was asymmetrical in America's favor, requiring much greater reductions on the Soviet side. Third, echoing the president's oft-used phrase "trust but verify," it provided for an unprecedented exchange of data and a comprehensive and intrusive verification program.

In the START talks, too, serious progress occurred. The Soviets had discontinued negotiations in late 1983, when American INF deployments in Europe had begun (as they had stopped participating in the INF talks). But because of Gorbachev's agenda, the evident American determination to proceed with SDI research and development regardless of Soviet behavior, and the continued INF deployments, the Kremlin reentered negotiations. By September 1986 substantial progress had been made, and at the Reykjavik summit in November Gorbachev and Reagan discussed reducing strategic weapons by 50 percent in five years. Delivery vehicles would be capped at 1,600 and warheads at 6,000. But important differences remained over verification, the treatment of mobile missiles, and warhead sublimits. The critical difference between the superpowers, though, was Gorbachev's attempt to link his concessions to U.S. abandonment of SDI—something Reagan adamantly rejected. Even so, the logjam was beginning to break on disarmament.

Problem II: Disengagement in Afghanistan and Angola

Progress in arms control was an important indicator of better Soviet-American relations. As these relations warmed, of course, the bilateral tension level declined. Those factors, along with growing evidence of the depth of Gorbachev's domestic problems, helped create a more favorable climate for settling regional disputes. And Gorbachev, overextended and having higher priorities at home, believed retrenchment was necessary. In 1988, Moscow decided it was necessary to withdraw from Afghanistan. The last detachment pulled out in February 1989. The Kremlin also put pressure on Cuba to end its African adventures. This pressure, along with continued "constructive engagement" by Washington, eventually produced an agreement for the withdrawal of Cuban and South African forces from Angola and the implementation of Namibian independence. Also on the plus side, there was overwhelming evidence that the nations of the Third World finally had realized that the Soviet model of development was hardly worth emulation. If they were to receive substantial economic help, it would have to come from the industrialized democracies, not the stumbling Soviet economy.

As Reagan left office, the Contra war in Nicaragua had collapsed (even though the incompetent Sandinista regime was in perilous condition). In El Salvador, violence had increased. In the Middle East, Arafat had publicly accepted Resolutions 242 and 338. And the Iran-Iraq war finally ended in a state of exhaustion. The most important point, however, was that U.S.-Soviet relations were much improved. Moscow still possessed enormous military power, but the increasing evidence that Soviet problems were both broad and deep encouraged a swing of the pendulum of American attitudes toward considering aid to encourage democratic development in Russia.

Changes of this magnitude take time to absorb. When George Bush took office in January 1989 it was still too early to say that the Cold War was "really" over. Washington views still differed widely as to the degree to which irreversible changes had occurred in the USSR and Eastern Europe. Some questioned Gorbachev's sincerity, others his staying power. Having seen hopes for better Soviet-American relations dashed so many times in the Cold War, American officials were cautious. It was not only that events were moving rapidly and unpredictably. Many events also were largely outside America's ability to control. Perhaps the only certainty was that the Soviet position was a declining one. Meaning, unless President Bush was incredibly foolish, he had a wonderful opportunity to advance America's interests.

Problems I and II: The Transformation of Europe

Europe had been the prime stake throughout the Cold War, with control of Germany the key lever. The basic reason the tension level had remained so high for so long was because Soviet forces were deployed far beyond Soviet borders, deep into the heart of Europe, and NATO's necessary counterdeployments made Europe an armed camp. These deployments, in turn, had existed only because of Europe's arbitrary division. The Soviets had never been willing to withdraw from East Germany while Western troops remained in West Germany, nor had they been prepared to see a free and united Germany allied with the West. The United States had never been in a position to *compel* a settlement of the German problem. An alternative to the status quo did exist, though, as it always does. Recognizing that under certain conditions an overextended USSR might have an interest in Soviet withdrawal, the alternative was to work to help produce conditions that would bring about a change in the status quo *with Soviet consent*.

In 1989 the appropriate conditions were suddenly to develop, though not as a direct result of an American policy designed to produce them.[20] Instead, internally generated nationalism and anti-Communist desires for independence swept over Eastern Europe at a dizzying pace. In September the Polish Parliament approved a Solidarity-led government, the first non-Communist government in Eastern Europe since 1948. In Hungary the Communist Party was renamed the Democratic Socialist Party and soon advocated Western-style democracy. Czechoslovakia scheduled elections. The contagion soon swept through Bulgaria, producing the resignation of hard-line Communist leader, Todor Zhikov. Before the year was out, Romania's dictator Nicolae Ceausecsu was overthrown and executed.

The most critical events, though, occurred in East Germany. When the Honecker regime stubbornly refused to follow the liberalizing tendencies in Poland and Hungary, thousands of East Germans fled the country. As the pressures increased, Honecker resigned. But it was too late. When the new regime lifted restrictions on travel and emigration, hundreds of thousands of East Germans went across to discover or rediscover the West so long known to them only on television. Then, on November 9, 1989, a truly historic event occurred: The Berlin Wall was opened. It would soon come down altogether.

That security relationships had been changed significantly and the Warsaw Pact was dying was apparent. The increasing Soviet willingness to permit the dismantling of its East European empire was a clear signal of determination to forge a new relationship with the United States. But what would the Soviets do about the central issue: the future of Germany? With the Wall breached, East and West Germans alike demanded (re)unification. But think how powerful a reunified Germany would be. Such a Germany would dominate Europe. Moreover, both Germans and Americans insisted that the new Germany had to be free to join NATO—a major sticking point for four decades. The Soviets, who already were promising that they would withdraw their forces from their Eastern European "allies" territory in the near future, at first said no. Absolutely out of the question. But Gorbachev held a weak hand, and what was the point of stopping halfway? Better to cut any losses and move on to deal with the most pressing issues. In July 1990, Gorbachev agreed. All that the Soviets had once held on to so tenaciously in Europe would now soon be freed from their physical control. But with these "losses," as with any shift of counterbalancing interests, would come certain gains: for one thing, a drastically reduced tension level, which would allow the Soviets to slash spending on armaments; for another, Western aid in converting the Soviet economy. That all assumed, of course, that all of Gorbachev's promises would actually be carried out.

Problem III: Reduction of Conventional Forces

To the Bush administration, achieving the transformation of the European balance of power, with Soviet consent, was a critical facet of ending the Cold War. A second was the negotiation of constructive arms control agreements, agreements that should become feasible in tandem with the decline in tension.

Although to the Congress and the general public "arms control" mostly meant limiting strategic systems or maybe SDI, to many defense experts negotiations on conventional forces in Europe were equally or more important. Mutual and Balanced Force Reduction Talks on reducing conventional arms in four Western nations (West Germany and the Benelux), along with three Warsaw Pact countries (East Germany, Poland, and Czechoslovakia) had begun in 1973, with little progress made. In 1986, to break this stalemate, both NATO and the Warsaw Pact agreed to a new forum. New momentum also came from an agreement at the Stockholm Conference on Confidence and Security Building Measures and Disarmament in Europe.

Although it took two more years before talks in the new forum (Conventional Armed Forces in Europe, or CFE) began, it soon became clear that the technical details would no longer be decisive. Both Bush and Gorbachev were determined to reach agreement. Following intense and exhaustive bargaining, on November 19, 1990, the CFE Treaty was signed.[21] Twenty-two countries became signatories: the sixteen NATO states and the six nations of the Warsaw Pact.

NATO's primary objective had been to achieve an agreement that would reduce the threat it faced by reducing Pact capabilities for surprise attack and quick victory. CFE set equal limits in five armament categories crucial to such operations: battle tanks, armored combat vehicles, artillery, combat aircraft, and attack helicopters. To reach these equal limits, the Pact would have to make larger and grossly asymmetrical cuts. CFE set lower limits on the number of weapons any *one* nation in the alliance could possess. This, in effect, placed special limits on the Soviets, because they were the only nation with forces large enough to be affected. Because the treaty encompassed the area from the Atlantic to the Urals, its provision also would limit Soviet forces *in the western third of the USSR.* The Soviets could not simply move their weapons out of Europe onto Soviet territory.

Even though it was crowded off the front pages by the Persian Gulf Crisis and developments in Eastern Europe and the Soviet Union, CFE was important and was a major step in ending the Cold War. But with the demise of the Pact and the subsequent collapse of the Soviet Union and its East European empire, the treaty (which was signed in 1990) was more or less in limbo for a while. This worried American officials. In light of the instability in the region, if CFE was not approved, with the reductions actually carried out by the newly independent states of the former USSR and former Pact nations, there was the potential for real trouble. Fortunately policymakers recognized this danger, and in June 1992, the signatories, plus several of the former Soviet republics, pledged to carry out the accord.

A START Treaty Agreed

Bush was successful in the START talks, too. Much progress had already been made under Reagan so that Bush began his term with a well-defined Joint Draft Treaty. Building on that, negotiations were resumed in June 1989. The most critical unresolved issues were how to control mobile ICBMs, whether to include sea-launched cruise missiles, some counting rules, sublimits on ICBMs, some ALCM issues, and verification.[22] What would or would not constitute a "new" missile also became a bone of contention.

Negotiations continued in 1990, with considerable progress being made. At the U.S.-Soviet summit in Washington from May 31 to June 3, Bush and Gorbachev agreed to the general START framework. Although all the major substantive issues were resolved, many technical details still had to be worked out. The more than 400 pages of draft treaty text guaranteed that process would be no small feat. It in fact took a whole year.

The START treaty, signed by Bush and Gorbachev on July 31, 1991, was precedent shattering. It was the first treaty ever to require actual *reductions,* not just ceilings, on strategic nuclear weapons. And the cuts were significant. It required the reduction of Soviet warheads by approximately 50 percent, American warheads by about 35 percent. Each side also had to eliminate hundreds of missiles. Additionally, there were limitations on throw-weight, sublimits on ballis-

Box 13.1	**Reducing Nuclear Warheads**					
	Pre-START		START I		START II	
	U.S.	USSR	U.S.	RUSSIA	U.S.	RUSSIA
Warheads on MIRVed ICBMs	2,000	5,958	1,100	2,460	0	0
Total Warheads on ICBMs	2,450	6,612	1,400	3,153	500	504
Total Warheads	12,646	11,012	8,556	6,163	3,500	3,000

Source: CQ Weekly Report (January 2, 1993), p. 34

tic missile warheads, sublimits on warheads, on mobile ICBMs, and (in a separate declaration) limits on SLCMs. Moreover, the United States made no SDI concessions.

As we noted in Chapter 6, because of the turmoil in the former Soviet Union and Eastern Europe, the U.S. Senate hesitated in giving its approval, but few doubted it would. In October 1992, the treaty passed easily, 93–6. In mid-June 1992, even before the Senate had acted, President Bush and Russian President Boris Yeltsin announced a new agreement. Whereas under the START I treaty the two nations together would come down to about 15,000 warheads (from about 23,600), under the new accord, they would be reducing to 3,000–3,500 each. Additionally, Bush and Yeltsin pledged to eliminate all land-based MIRVed ICBMs, the heart of the old USSR's nuclear arsenal.

Shortly before President Bush left office, this START II agreement was officially signed. Substantively, it adhered closely to the broad outlines announced at the June summit. But there remained a fly in the ointment. START I had not even entered into force yet, and that had to precede effectuating START II. Initially, of course, START I was a bilateral treaty between the United States and the Soviet Union. But with the collapse of the USSR, it was decided to make it a five-party treaty involving not only Russia and America, but also the three USSR-successor republics on whose territory nuclear weapons were still located: Ukraine, Kazakhstan, and Belarus. In May 1992, those states signed a protocol agreeing to ratify START I, to remove all nuclear weapons within seven years, and to accede to the Nuclear NonProliferation Treaty (NPT) as nonnuclear weapon states. By early summer 1993, however, Ukraine still had not ratified START I, nor had it acceded to the NPT. Ukraine, with its 176 strategic missiles, was a key actor here and obviously was considering strongly the alternative of keeping its nuclear weapons. Meanwhile, Russia, although it had ratified

START I, said it would not exchange the instruments of ratification (the final step necessary to bring the pact into force) until all the necessary precedent actions with these other republics had taken place. In September 1993, President Yeltsin and Ukranian President Leonid Kravchuk discussed a deal granting Ukraine debt relief if Ukraine would ship the 176 missiles to Russia for dismantling. But because parliamentary consent is required, neither START I nor START II were "done deals."

Problem III: Reorienting NATO and U.S. Defense Policy

The *NATO Review* for December 1991, has the content title listed on the cover as: "The Rome Summit, NATO Transformed."[23] That says a good deal. And NATO headquarters had taken on a new look, too, as representatives (both political and military) from the former Soviet bloc made visits. Both East and West were searching for new forms of association, recognizing also that the well established NATO organization could provide a key element in a new approach. It would be dangerous to leave the East dangling in a security vacuum. The exact nature of these new links remained to be discovered. At NATO's Rome summit itself, on November 7–8, 1991, delegate speeches stressed that if NATO was needed less for short-term protection, it was needed more for long-term stability. Recognizing the uncertainties ahead as Europe was transformed, no one wanted to see a severing of the links between Europe and the United States and Canada.

At the same time that these issues were being examined, the instability in Eastern Europe also was causing NATO concern. Especially troublesome was the breakup of Yugoslavia in 1991 and the ensuing civil war (discussed further in Chapter 15). But all the members were aware of the problems that can arise with intervention in a civil conflict and were hesitant to become seriously involved. Some of the ships in NATO's Standing Naval Forces for the Mediterranean and Atlantic were helping implement U.N. sanctions and the trade embargo, and some aircraft were monitoring a "no-fly" zone over Bosnia. Individual members also contributed to the U.N. "peacekeeping" operation. But the alliance wanted to find a meaningful role short of serious intervention.

Meanwhile, in the United States the implications of the collapse of the Soviet empire and breakup of the USSR continued to be studied. The 1992 *National Military Strategy*, prepared by the Chairman, JCS, acknowledged the strategic changes that had occurred.[24] Listing the national interests and objectives of the United States in the 1990s, in addition to dealing with the threat of terrorism and improving stability through arms control, it added such items as fostering restraint in global military spending, preventing the transfer of critical military technologies, and reducing the flow of illegal drugs into the United States. Critics dismissed the list as an attempt to justify a level of military power no longer needed, since the Soviet Union was no longer a threat. In a sense, the

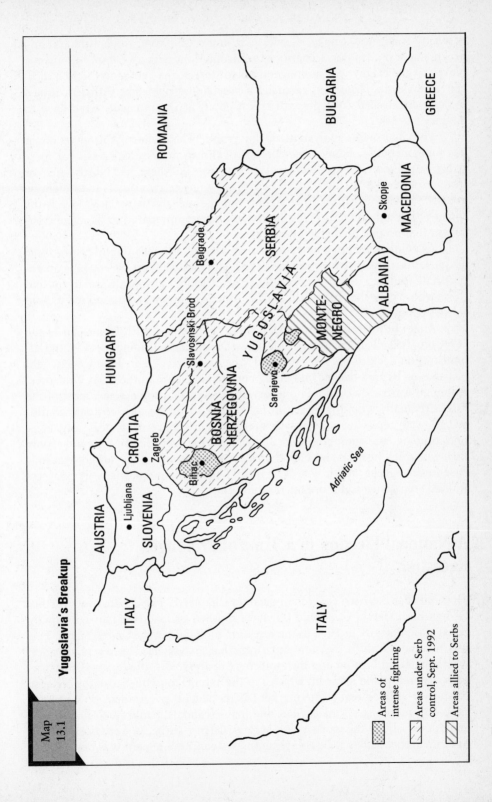

Map 13.1

Yugoslavia's Breakup

Legend:
- Areas of intense fighting
- Areas under Serb control, Sept. 1992
- Areas allied to Serbs

Pentagon was the victim of its own past practices: basing force estimates and procurement needs upon scenarios of confrontations with a very specific enemy. Now that the enemy was no longer a potent threat, the Pentagon found it difficult to make the argument (actually a very sound one) that sufficient armed forces were needed to cope with threats that, at the moment, were hard to define.

The Chairman's analysis made that point. "The decline of the Soviet threat has fundamentally changed the concept of threat analysis as a basis for force structure planning." There were still a few threats out there, like North Korea or Iraq, or perhaps a hostile Iran. "There may be one or two others that might be added . . . without straining credulity. But the real threat we now face is the threat of the unknown, [of] instability and being unprepared to handle a crisis or war that no one predicted or expected."

As pointed out elsewhere, it is difficult to create a meaningful armed force as quickly as threats may appear. As president, George Bush was seeking an appropriate middle ground between those who wanted abrupt disarmament and those who argued that the world outside America's doors had not ceased to hold serious dangers.

After considerable internal discussion and debate, with Chairman of the JCS Colin Powell and Secretary of Defense Dick Cheney leading the way, the administration decided on what it called "the base force." This base force would be achieved by mid-decade and be 25 percent smaller than the Cold War force. Although America would retain a forward presence in some areas, most of the force eventually would be based in the United States. Because regional contingencies were replacing general war as the primary concern, strategy, organization, training, and equipping were all being altered accordingly. Of course, only time would tell how close the final product would come to the administration's base force concept, and it was clear from the beginning that many in Congress wanted even faster and more far-reaching cuts.

A National Election in a Time of Prolonged Recession

The Gulf War has been covered in detail in Chapter 1. The debate over whether George Bush should or should not have finished off Saddam Hussein rapidly faded in significance in 1991 as the recession took hold in the United States. This was not the "usual" recession Americans had experienced in recent decades, where things hit bottom and then improved sharply. One drag on recovery was the severe retraction in credit, which was the natural consequence of the collapse of an over-inflated real estate market. As the federal government poured huge sums into mopping up the savings and loans scandals, bankruptcies increased. Simultaneously, at the worst possible time, defense cutbacks were beginning to have their effects. Bases closed, weapons system procurement was curtailed or cancelled, and defense firms trimmed thousands of jobs. Japanese investment in the United States, which had helped to fuel the heady expansion of the 1980s, was drastically cut back as the Japanese economy encountered its own problems. Germany, busy trying to digest a ramshackle East German economy, was being strained financially, especially because Germany had promised to aid the former Soviet Union in return for the withdrawal of Soviet troops from German soil. Countries like Canada and the United Kingdom were encountering fairly high inflation rates, and their unemployment rates were higher than that of the United States. In short, as 1992 began, the whole world economy was in a condition that hampered the American effort to come out of recession.

Making it all worse was President Bush's ill-conceived trip to Japan, bringing the presidents of the Big Three U.S. automakers in his entourage. Whatever Bush's intent, the trip was a public relations disaster. The Japanese interpreted it as a request from the United States for a handout of some sort. They responded with vague promises of importing a few more American cars and, as soon as the American delegation had gone home, began a series of public statements guaranteed to irritate the American public. America's troubles, the Japanese said, were due to lazy American workers, overpaid (and presumably inefficient) American corporate heads, and a tendency to spend too much and save too little. Whether there was any truth to this did not matter at all. Meanwhile, Japan-bashing continued in the United States, in some cases meaning a literal bashing of Japanese cars, in other cases meaning a campaign to "Buy American." The relations between the two most powerful economic nations in the world fell to a low ebb.

It was in this context that President Bush fought and lost to Bill Clinton in an election campaign focused on his most vulnerable area—the domestic front. When Bill Clinton took office in 1993, he promised even further "down-sizing." As a result, Secretary of Defense Aspin on September 1, 1993, announced further defense cuts. These reductions fell harder on the army than on the other forces but emphasized retaining a capability to fight and win two major regional conflicts nearly simultaneously.[25]

Clinton's First Crisis

Although he took office intending to focus on domestic affairs, President Clinton had not long to wait until his first foreign policy crisis caught up with him. When it did, during his first hundred days, it was a difficult one to deal with. It focused on Bosnia (a subset of the larger problem brought about by the breakup of Yugoslavia discussed in Chapter 15) and the determination of the Serbs to succeed in their long-frustrated ambitions to create a Greater Serbia. (The Serbs had actually achieved much of that ambition in the Balkan Wars, just before World War I, only to be frustrated at that time by the intervention of the great powers.)

The Bosnian crisis was almost a case study in demonstrating both American idealism and American realism, for it launched a debate in the United States along classic counterbalancing interest lines. It was a debate between those who considered any U.S. intervention to be the path to a "new Vietnam," and those who cried out that America could not possibly stand by while "ethnic cleansing" produced a "new Holocaust." The debate was a classic one because it focused on getting involved or staying out, because it sought to set a direction for policy, and because it involved unforeseeable consequences.

Although the end of the Cold War had at least removed the usual insertion in U.S. debates of a "domino theory" argument, what was quite apparent was the continued American predilection for summarizing points of view in guideline slogans or formulas. As we have pointed out repeatedly, this is a dangerous, even if ingrained, American habit. It was dangerous in this case in particular because no one of the slogans really spoke efficiently to either the American national interest or to the realities of civil wars. The implied assumption in the argument that the United States had to intervene was that somehow it was the world's moral policeman. The implication, further, was that America had some direct responsibility for the Holocaust, or at least for preventing any repetition. Would that argument hold, regardless of the cost in American blood? How many American lives were worth losing in return for saving how many lives in Yugoslavia? Or was the assumption being made that "ethnic cleansing" could be terminated without much cost in American blood at all?

Labels or formulas like "ethnic cleansing" or "Holocaust" lead attention *toward* a foreign situation that Americans find offensive and *away* from considerations about whether it makes good sense for the United States to intervene, and at what costs in blood. To argue that America must intervene because America has the military force to do so effectively may or may not be factually correct; but, in any case, such arguments bypass the questions of *why,* and *at what acceptable cost.*

The repetition of these slogans by the media also obscured the fact that most Americans were apathetic about intervening, especially given the continuing recession.

Again, these slogans effectively disguised the problem by renaming it. Instead of calling it what it was—a civil war—it became something immoral, particularly because one side in the civil war was winning, while the losing side was suffering greatly.

It is instructive, however, to look at civil wars and the reality of what happens when they occur. The first thing about such wars is that they are fought inside a country, usually by two opposing groups, but sometimes (as in this case) by three. It does not help to add a new foreign combat force, firing in every direction needed. In short, the only possible use of foreign intervention is either (1) to separate belligerents with their consent and cooperation—*all* the belligerents—or, (2) to pick a side and go in with massive force to aid that side against the other. The first use of intervention follows the U.N. peacekeeping model, which is really designed to enforce an agreed and stable truce. That much the United States could do, if it seemed desirable. The second use of intervention is, clearly enough, a nonstarter in terms of even the most loose interpretation of American national interests.

The early attempt of the president to seize the initiative and lead the way to international intervention failed. That Clinton was following an old American attitude, in trying to take the lead, did not make any difference in the outcome, which was a serious setback to his own prestige. The European nations, obviously, since they are there, had the greatest responsibility for action. Even if the Bosnian situation was not so dangerous, it was hardly required for the United States to play more than a supporting role. The very fact that the European nations did not leap into the fray illustrates very well that they knew how much of a bloody sinkhole intervention in anyone's civil war can be.

Summing Up

There were few overt signs when Ronald Reagan became president that the Soviets were overextended in their commitments, although the strains on the civilian economy were quite obvious. Yet these strains had existed for some time as the Soviets poured a very disproportionate percentage of their resources into weapons and foreign involvement. The huge U.S. rearmament effort, especially the SDI concept, proved to be the handwriting on the wall, for the Soviets knew that while they could outbuild the United States in missiles (for political and other reasons, such as basing complications), they could not really compete in the field of technological innovation, where the United States could hold the lead. The recognition of their own problems and the realization that a continuing arms competition would do no good brought about successful efforts on the part of a new Soviet leadership to begin to reform the system and enter into meaningful arms control agreements.

Thus it was that Reagan, followed by Bush, was given a great opportunity to move away from the wasteful arms race, an opportunity they both effectively embraced. As with any seminal event or watershed in the life of a nation, this change called for new analyses and new policies as the Clinton administration assessed the needs of an altered international environment. Part Five addresses U.S. policy in this post–Cold War world.

Notes

1. Melanson, *Reconstructing Consensus,* p. 134.

2. Alexander M. Haig, Jr., *Caveat: Realism, Reagan, and Foreign Policy* (New York: Macmillan, 1984), p. 95.

3. For further discussion of the defense planning and resource allocation processes, see Frederick H. Hartmann and Robert L. Wendzel, *Defending America's Security,* 2nd ed., rev. (Washington, DC: Brassey's, 1990), Chs. 8–9.

4. The basing-mode issue was an unresolved legacy from Carter. He had proposed 200

missiles in a "racetrack" system of 4,600 multiple protective shelters, a proposal that was stopped by both technical and political criticism.

5. For a more detailed discussion of how the JCS saw the problem, see Frederick H. Hartmann, *Naval Renaissance: The U.S. Navy in the 1980s* (Annapolis, MD: The Naval Institute Press, 1990), Ch. 14. Reagan's own account of this meeting, given in his memoirs, *An American Life* (New York: Simon & Schuster, 1990), pp. 547–48, does not square altogether with the recollections of the other participants whose interviews are recorded in *Naval Renaissance*. The major difference is that Reagan's account describes him as taking the initiative, rather than vice-versa. But it is true that Reagan had already commissioned an NSC study group to examine the issue. Reagan says:

> Early in my first term, I called a meeting of the Joint Chiefs of Staff—our military leaders—and said to them: Every offensive weapon ever invented by man has resulted in the creation of a defense against it; isn't it possible in this age of technology that we could invent a defensive weapon that could intercept nuclear weapons and destroy them as they emerged from their silos?
>
> They looked at each other, then asked if they could huddle for a few moments. Very shortly, they came out of their huddle and said, "Yes, it's an idea worth exploring." My answer was, "Let's do it."
>
> So the SDI was born, and very shortly some in Congress and the press named it "Star Wars."

6. "Peace and National Security: A New Defense," *Vital Speeches,* (April 15, 1983), p. 390.

7. Useful for understanding the administration's perspective is Caspar Weinberger, *Fighting for Peace: Seven Critical Years in the Pentagon* (New York: Warner Books, 1990), Ch. 1.

8. The extent of American foreknowledge is controversial, especially whether or not Secretary of State Haig gave the Israeli Defense Minister a "green light," explicitly or implicitly.

9. According to Bob Woodward, Gemayel had received covert aid from the CIA for several years. Bob Woodward, *Veil: The Secret Wars of the CIA 1981–1987* (New York: Simon and Schuster, 1987), Ch. 10.

10. *New York Times* (October 24, 1983), p. A10.

11. As an example, it is interesting to compare two quite different analyses of the Grenada operation in two of the leading textbooks. Compare Spanier, *American Foreign Policy Since World War II,* 12th ed., pp. 306–07, and Nathan and Oliver, *United States Foreign Policy and World Order,* 4th ed., pp. 423–24.

12. The international reaction was something else, again. And in the Grenada operation, except for the tiny eastern Caribbean nations who assisted, there was little Latin American support.

13. See Hartmann, *Naval Renaissance,* pp. 244–46, for further discussion of the operational details.

14. Cecil V. Crabb, Jr., and Pat M. Holt, *Invitation to Struggle: Congress, the President, and Foreign Policy,* 3rd ed. (Washington, DC: CQ Press, 1989), p. 185.

15. U.S. House Select Committee to Investigate Covert Arms Transactions with Iran and Senate Select Committee on Secret Military Assistance to Iran and the Nicaraguan Opposition, *Iran-Contra Affair,* House Report 100–433, Senate Report 100–216, 100th Congress, 1st Session, p. 13. See also Edwin Meese, *With Reagan: The Inside*

Story (Washington, DC: Regnery Gateway, 1992), Chs. 18–20. Meese, Reagan's attorney general, although an interested party and suspect in liberal circles, does an excellent job of setting forth the convoluted legal issues involved.

16. *Report of the President's Special Review Board* (Washington, DC: GPO, February 26, 1987), p. IV–1.

17. See Terry L. Deibel, "Reagan's Mixed Legacy," *Foreign Policy* (Summer, 1989), pp. 34–55, for a first-rate discussion.

18. Mikhail Gorbachev, *Perestroika: New Thinking for Our Country and the World* (New York: Harper & Row, 1987), p. 24.

19. *Strategic Survey, 1986–1987* (London: International Institute for Strategic Studies, 1987), p. 10.

20. Very interesting is John Lewis Gaddis, *How Relevant Was U.S. Strategy in Winning the Cold War?* (Carlisle, PA: U.S. Army War College, 1992).

21. For a perceptive and succinct assessment, see Lee Feinstein, "The Case for CFE," *Arms Control Today*, (January/February 1991), CFE Supplement, pp. 2–4.

22. Some of these issues had split supporters *within* the U.S. government. For example, the military favored mobile ICBMs (and the administration's modernization program included two), but the arms control position was to ban them. That debate explains why the JCS had urged Reagan to go slowly in the strategic talks.

23. *NATO Review,* "The Rome Summit, NATO Transformed," (December, 1991). Distributed in the United States by the Department of State.

24. Chairman, Joint Chiefs of Staff, *The National Military Strategy, 1992,* pp. 4–5.

25. The Aspin plan would reduce the total U.S. forces from 1.4 million in 1993 to 1.2 million by 1999. Army divisions would reduce from 14 to 10; aircraft carriers would drop by 1, to 12; air force tactical fighter wings would decline to 20 (from 28); while marine troop strength would drop only 6,000, to 174,000.

Summing Up
the Book So Far

Before going on to contemporary American foreign policy problems, it will be useful to look now, in connected fashion, at the analytical tools this book has used, and which will be applied again in Part Five. Linking these tools here in an organized fashion will serve as a useful review as well as a preparation for what comes next. For if anything should be clear from the last thirteen chapters, it is that foreign policy, examined simply as the history of events or incidents or anecdotes, yields no useful fruit. As Salvador de Madariaga once said about the cliche that travel broadens: "Nothing travels as much as a suitcase, but learns as little."

Four kinds of observations have been emphasized in the previous pages:

first, how Americans see problems, and how they came to look at them that way;

second, how decisions are made and the nature of choices in foreign policy;

third, how the world functions, and what makes that exterior environment, to which policy is addressed, what it is;

fourth, how these first three observations bear on the efficient and effective conduct of American foreign policy.

On the first point, recall that Dennis Brogan spoke of America's "illusion of omnipotence." That, however, was before Vietnam knocked some cockiness out of American attitudes. Add Winston Churchill's assessment, contrasting the American habit of trying to find a fundamental guiding principle to apply to problems, with the British habit of "muddling through." Churchill said that Americans thought that once they had defined some guiding shorthand formula, they would then plunge ahead. Certainly, the Communist bloc containment idea or the domino theory falls under this head.

The history of American foreign policy contains many such formulas, highly abstract propositions like "unconditional surrender." Because such formulas reflect culture-biased assumptions about cause and effect, they automatically provide the answer to any policy question. The formulas describe where alternatives will lead, shortcutting, if not eliminating, the analytical process. Since "everybody knows" these truisms, they are rarely questioned effectively until it is quite obvious that they are not working out well. The consensus that springs from "everybody knowing" is good for getting on with a policy. But, if the policy rests on false assumptions, it merely accelerates going in the wrong direction. Such false assumptions, incorporated in such truisms, are difficult to detect outside of a context, especially because normally they are themselves abstractions.

American abstractionism probably finds its source in the very way of life in the United States. Abstract concepts permeate the American political culture in particular, and have done so since colonial days. Primarily because Americans had multi-cultural national origins, it was impractical to decide controversial questions by recourse to custom and precedent, as is the case in much older nations. Moreover, the conditions in America were themselves without precedent. In a new land with almost limitless horizons, people could do much more what they pleased. With many points of view being advanced, and with some really new kinds of issues to settle, there was no other way than to follow the will of the majority. That meant Americans would live by "the rule of law." That meant that the law could and would change as the majority view of proper solutions altered. "Separate but equal" could change in the course of time to "equal rights" legislation. "Socialized medicine," condemned by almost all conservatives in the 1950s, would yield to Medicaid and Medicare by the 1980s. The rule of law was an idealistic way to go; but for a country like America it was the only realistic way to go. Americans grew used to assuming the two extremes could be melded together, much as they accepted the idea of contributions to charity being tax-deductible. They grew used to the idea of an abstract approach to problems.

An abstract approach has one frequently overlooked but serious disadvantage: it encourages looking at problems on their supposed merit rather than in a cost-effective context. The emphasis then easily shifts to whether something deserves to be done rather than what it will take to accomplish it. These habits of mind also make Americans prone to try to find once-and-for-all solutions to problems. It is important to remain sensitive to such biases.

In this background lies the source of the recurrent American vacillation between "realism" and "idealism," and of the persistent later attempts to follow policies that reconcile both. In earlier times, before Americans took on an active role in world affairs in the twentieth century, they tended to reconcile these traits by a division of function: foreign policy for the most part remained practical and realistic; popular opinion expressed through the media stressed the idealistic. That satisfied a largely immigrant population, which wanted no involvement in the affairs of the old world but was still close enough to it emotionally to have strong feelings about events there. The policy was sensible enough, and it did not occur to Americans to take moral judgments of European behavior and connect them to actual commitments. Since these judgments were ethical in nature, they could be as idealistic (and impractical) as anyone cared to take them.

After World War II, on the other hand, with America pursuing a global policy and being altogether the strongest power on earth, it was an easy step to bring ethical judgments and practical considerations together into actual commitments. If this is a correct view, the habit is relatively recent. It was all the more easy to fall into this habit because the American role *was* global. All other things being equal, the further from U.S. shores a problem is, the less Americans will know from immediate experience what the problem really consists of and how it is likely to develop. And the less the immediate and agreed data, the more abstractionism also tends to predominate.

Every nation has such cultural biases, stemming from its own historical experiences, ethnic makeup, and geographical location. Quite involuntarily, American perceptions of the cultural biases of other nations will be filtered through American culture-shaped notions.[1] (The exchange of insulting comments between prominent Americans and Japanese in early 1992 was a case in point.)

This book has repeatedly stressed the importance of such filtering devices, such *past-future linkages*. They determine not only what people see now but what people imagine their choice of alternatives will make true of the future. Because of these filtering devices, nations can and do attach very diverse interpretations to events abroad. Policies made without reference to this basic fact of international life court trouble, even disaster.

No problem's parameters are therefore defined merely by the facts of the situation, even if the facts themselves are not in dispute. And cultural filters have a strongly directive effect. They shape the critical assumptions by which nations define problems and assign values to handling them one way or another. Prime Minister Anthony Eden, for example, saw Nasser's nationalization of the Suez Canal Company in 1956 as another Hitler starting on a new series of aggressions. Eden resolved to use force to stop that supposed aggression. But President Eisenhower saw Britain's use of force as an outmoded response of a colonialist power to a provocation. There was no dispute about the actual facts; cultural filters made the difference.

The assumptions made because of these filters play a role in people's perceptions much like the air in car tires. They inflate the facts to usable dimensions. But like the tires, part rubber and part air, only the facts are solid. Albert Einstein once said the same thing about the physical world, arguing that people come to every set of phenomena with assumptions about its structure and nature because they cannot understand anything without giving it some preliminary structure through their imaginations.

The second set of observations centers on the nature of decision making. Two kinds of errors are often made in describing the nature of choice. The first oversimplifies, reducing decisions to a mere yes-or-no. But every serious decision necessarily involves at minimum evaluating the advantages and disadvantages of both the "yes" and the "no." The mistake made here is to assume that the disadvantage on the "yes" side is the same as the advantage on the "no" side, and vice versa. But a little thought will show that that cannot be true. Perhaps a homely illustration will illustrate this fact. Suppose a person is about to buy an automobile. Auto X has very quick pickup, low maintenance, and great design lines. It is also very, very expensive. Auto Y, on the other hand, has moderate appeal in terms of everything, including price. Its disadvantage is that it does not make the prospective owner's blood surge with delight; it is basic transportation.

Now think of this distinction in foreign policy terms. When the United States decided not to become a member of the League of Nations after World War I, the chief advantage of the decision was believed to be that the United States would be able to remain essentially uninvolved in the affairs of the great powers (which, of course, comes down to saying that a nation can effectively exclude itself from world affairs by its own say-so). The chief disadvantage was believed to be very slight: America would not be consulted, despite America's status as a great power. But if the United States had chosen membership instead, the chief advantage was that the League would be strengthened and would be more resistant to challenges by law-breakers. The chief disadvantage, however, was that the United States might be called upon to participate in League sanctions decided upon only in part by Washington. These are really four separate values. Or, take another more recent illustration: President Bush's decision to resist the Iraqi invasion of Kuwait by force, without waiting to see if sanctions would suffice. The chief advantage of acting quickly was that it had the best chance of keeping the allied coalition intact. The chief disadvantage was that armed action is always risky. But if Bush had waited, the chief advantage would be that American lives would have been spared, and the chief disadvantage would have been that Hussein might have used the interlude to launch an invasion of Saudi Arabia, on whose border his troops were already poised. Again, there are four values.

The other mistake made about choices is to assume that decisions involve many alternatives. In one sense this is an acceptable notion: a person trying to decide whether to jump into the water can compromise by putting his or her toe in first. Or he or she can ease into the water, a step at a time, over five or ten minutes. All these are gradations, though, along a spectrum labeled "getting wet." The important part of the decision is the initial phase: whether or not to get wet at all. Alternatives usually, if not always, really reduce to two. They involve a choice between doing it or not, being committed or not. Such alternatives could be called *directionally-oriented in terms of involvement,* meaning that you cannot go in both directions at once, or be involved and not involved simultaneously. Either you send arms to the allies, or you do not. Either you agree to let the Chinese Communist regime be seated in the U.N., or you do not. Either you aid Yeltsin's Russia, or you do not. There are still four separate values here, but the alternatives they weight are only two on any such important issue. And because such choices lead in opposed directions, the name used for them in this book is the same given to one of the four cardinal principles, counterbalancing national interests. It should now be entirely clear why.

One reason all of this needs emphasis is that otherwise one cannot adequately understand the nature of a breakdown in a popular consensus on foreign policy. If important choices could really be made so gradually that no one really noticed, there would be no need for debates. It is true, again, that changes can be made in a series of gradations, such as the gradual amendment of America's neutrality acts before World War II or the gradual disengagement from the Vietnam venture. But each such gradual change ultimately comes to the point where the fundamental choice must be made. Indeed, when gradational change is proceeding, that is the very mark of a breakdown in a popular consensus; it shows that the public is beginning to change its mind.

The other reason why it is necessary to understand these fundamentals about the making of choices is that otherwise one cannot understand the way in which significant shifts in international affairs come about, like the playing of the China card or the Soviet decision to allow Eastern Europe the freedom to choose its own path. It is here that we come to the third group of observations.

The third set of observations has been intended to explain the nature of the international environment to which foreign policy is addressed and in which it must function. In that system, the most basic source of tension stems from the fact that each sovereign nation-state, large or small, has the ability to decide to attack another. That creates a power problem for each state—in a philosophical sense, the power problem is a permanent condition so long as the multistate system endures, but is a changing condition insofar as the specific nature of the threat to any particular state. The general level of tension in the system also varies with the appearance or disappearance of a state that is ambitious to alter the environment through threats to others, as with Hitler, or as with the Soviet Union (in American eyes, at least) during the Cold War.

The third set of observations focused on how to conduct an effective foreign policy in this kind of world. The concept of national interests was introduced as a prelude to an explanation of the four cardinal principles.

The concept of national interest (or interests), as well as the cardinal principles themselves, is an abstract proposition. At first glance, therefore, all would seem to share the same kinds of disadvantages as the American habit of using guiding formulas like the domino theory. But there is an important difference. A formula like the domino theory skips over a serious analysis of specific alternatives in a specific problem setting and jumps instead to conclusions about what action to take. It identifies certain kinds of actions automatically as being in the national interest and certain alternatives among counterbalancing interests as preferable to any others. It makes generalized value judgments that are assumed to apply automatically to specific cases falling within the generalities.

As a concept, national interests does not do that. It merely provides a label for *claims* that alternatives will do useful and cost-effective things for a nation, claims that need to be discussed and compared. But the term *national interest* is itself really value-free as an analytical device. Even when one set of alternatives is judged better than the other set and is incorporated into foreign policy, there is no guarantee that the national interest will prosper. The only thing that can be concluded is that the nation has decided that the set chosen offers the best chance.

As with national interest, the four cardinal principles, too, are value-free. They merely tell you what to take into account about world affairs and foreign policy. The principles have the merit of being a checklist against inadvertent strategic insensitivity.

The concept of cultural biases of nations has already been discussed. That is what is meant by the first cardinal principle, *past-future linkages.* From the point of view of strategic sensitivity, it is particularly important to bear in mind the second cardinal principle, *third-party influences.* This is a 360-degree world, and every national decision, every bilateral relation, takes place in the context of reactions by third states. Especially significant to study is what third states at the moment are *not* doing, but which they might instead choose to do.

It was remarked earlier that *counterbalancing national interests,* the third cardinal principle, are sets of alternatives leading in opposite directions so far as commitments are concerned. Since every nation choosing foreign policy alternatives from such counterbalancing interests has necessarily "shelved" another choice, the momentum and the surprises in the state system (like a China card, like a German-Soviet pact in 1939 that allows World War II to begin) are always there for the acute eye to see. But it takes imagination, for one of the traps people most easily fall into is to believe that the future will be much like the present. That the curve will continue, more of the same. (For instance, the belief that the Soviets will *never* give up control of East Germany.) When the balance of the four values in any set of *counterbalancing national interests* changes, so too will the stage be set for a quite different extension of the curve. The change will be initiated by some dramatic international event, as two parties shift their basic orientation to each other. But often that change and that shift will occur because both have reappraised their bilateral relationship in the light of some third party.

And, lastly, *conservation of enemies* as a principle, although it states the obvious, is no less important for that. When America with its domino and containment formulas went to war in Vietnam (and considered itself as facing a hostile, unified Communist world), the United States was multiplying enemies automatically. Any new Communist state joined the list of opponents. Through using such abstract guidelines rather than an analytical device such as the cardinal principles, the United States also lost effective control of its own decisions.

These three sets of observations explain how easy it is to mistake the surface of events for the reality underneath. A change in the general tension level is never permanent. Tensions come and go in the world—and then come again in a different form. It is tempting to look at the present world through rose-colored glasses. After all, communism has collapsed almost everywhere except China. Arms in the hands of the principal powers are being reduced (although not in the "developing" areas). Perhaps a new world is coming into being, where security and defense problems will really and permanently take a back seat to pressing social concerns. After all, where is the enemy? The history of the state system, though, tells us that although the millennium may be reached someday, the reality has been that the decline of one power is always offset by the rise of another, that the end of one threat is always, sooner or later, succeeded by another.

In turning now to problems clearly already on the horizon and with which the Clinton and succeeding administrations must cope, applying these three sets of observations can provide needed orientation to the real nature of the issues by providing a checklist of things to be taken into account in any analysis. The checklist will keep us more aware of American biases and attitudes toward problems, of the American tendency towad quick solutions. Americans may be an impatient people but that does not alter the fact that most of the serious problems will not easily be resolved in any short time frame. Quick and easy solutions sometimes simply create new problems. The Third World, for example, may desperately need an infusion of Western technical advice and funds. But if the nation involved is a dictatorship, much of what is granted will end up in Swiss banks or squandered at home on a luxurious life-style. If that seems doubtful, simply look at America's savings and loan scandals. Not just power corrupts; money does, too, if it is not accountable. As the states of the former Soviet Union transition to a free market economy, they need emergency help. But how long the emergency lasts is significantly dependent upon how long they string out the transition. If they move too slowly or too quickly, no amount of aid will stave off terrible conditions downstream.

The problems to be addressed in Part Five will show clearly that, despite changes for the better in world affairs, it would be highly premature to think that Utopia is dawning. Even so, there are real possibilities for improvement in world affairs through a wise American foreign policy. That policy will probably prosper best if Americans are careful to restrain their bent for abstract formulas and once-and-for-all solutions.

The United States no doubt should take a leading role, but it cannot do everything, and, no matter what an administration's preferences, a good deal of what happens will be thrust upon America (like Somalia), like it or not. Difficult choices are inevitable, given the many problems "out there."

For better or worse, because America is a global superpower, the major problems confronting United States foreign policy today stretch completely around the world. Arms control continues to rank high on the agenda in rela-tions with the Soviet successor states, as does the question of aid and support for the conversion to a free market economy. In Europe, the decision of the nations of the European Community to continue their integration in 1993 and the im-plications for the United States have to rank high on the agenda. In the Middle East, which still contains the seeds for much violence and where arms expendi-tures have been very high, the Israeli-PLO agreement in September 1993 offers real hope for peace. Foreign policy questions in that region will focus on further reducing decades-old tension. Africa, on the other hand, with its great problems of overpopulation and hunger, must have a different focus. In Latin America, the age-old battle between democracy and military rule, and the struggle between the very rich and the very poor, is far from over. In the Far East, Japan suffers already from the first signs of economic indigestion from an overheated econ-omy, while China balances orthodoxy with material progress in a nation of over a billion people.

In making decisions about these complex problems, to which this book now turns, Americans will need all the wisdom the analysis above can provide. The same is true of global issues, such as the international economy, pollution, and the environment to be dealt with in Chapter 19.

Notes

1. On perception, Thomas Kuhn's work is seminal. On p. 111 he says: "Examining the record of past research . . . the historian of science may be tempted to exclaim that when paradigms [substitute, for us, the truths that "everybody knows"] change, the world itself changes with them. Led by a new paradigm, scientists adopt new instru-ments and look in new places. Even more important, during revolutions scientists see new and different things when looking with familiar instruments in places they have looked before." Thomas S. Kuhn, *The Structure of Scientific Revolutions*, 2nd ed., enlarged (Chicago: University of Chicago Press, 1970); 1st ed. was 1962. Kuhn goes on to describe how, between 1690 and 1781, on at least 17 different occasions, as-tronomers had seen a star where Uranus must have been. Some were among Europe's most eminent scientists. Finally, in 1781, Sir William Herschel detected motion that was planetary rather than cometary. Kuhn comments (p. 115): "When that suggestion was accepted, there were several fewer stars and one more planet in the world of the profes-sional astronomer."

See also Robert Jervis, *Perception and Misperception in International Politics* (Princeton, NJ: Princeton University Press, 1976). This very extensive treatment of the whole problem includes much fascinating information and penetrating analysis.

Finally, Bernard W. Anderson, the distinguished biblical analyst, in discussing faith also says something significant about perception. In *Rediscovering the Bible* (New York: Association Press, 1951), p. 206, he says: "When men see meaning in history or discern values in their social experience, they do so from a *standpoint* which is taken by faith." And on p. 210 he adds: "Historical events do not just 'occur'; they occur with a meaning in the experience of individuals or a community."

That certainly applies to foreign policy.

Part V

Contemporary Problems in U.S. Foreign Policy

Eight Major Decision Areas

For almost a half-century American foreign policy was dominated by the Cold War. But, beginning in the late 1980s, breathtaking changes within the Soviet Union were to change all that. Reforms in Moscow intended to improve unworkable internal conditions spread quickly to be manifested as fundamental political changes in both the Soviet Union and its former East European satellites. These changes culminated in the dissolution of the USSR, the withdrawal of the Soviet military from the territory of its former Warsaw Pact allies, and the reunification of Germany. Such drastic changes created both new problems and opportunities for new choices on the part of U.S. foreign policy.

In Western Europe, the decision of the European Community to move forward steadily toward economic and monetary union posed a different set of problems for the United States. There was the future of NATO to consider and the consequences for trade relations with this gigantic new single-tariff, single-market area.

These changes also had spinoff effects elsewhere. In Asia, the dissolution of the Soviet Union made Japan less dependent on the United States. In the Middle East and in much of the developing world, the subsiding of Cold War tensions made it possible for the first time in years for the United States to look at problems around the world without the distortion of Cold War imagery.

With the Cold War "won," America was in the fortunate position of not having a clearly defined major adversary. This "blessing" was, of course, mixed. For the removal of what had for so long been a primary policy focus created a great deal of uncertainty about the shape of the emerging international environment.

Thus, as the 1990s began, *the United States faced eight major decision areas,* which are the focus of Part Five. They are listed, together with their alternatives, essentially in the order in which they are analyzed in the chapters which follow.

1. *Policy toward the USSR's successor states.* The major alternatives turn on how much aid to give and how much to assume that the turn toward democracy will last. Alternatives also turn on how best to assure the destruction of much redundant military material spread across the region.

2. *Policy toward Eastern Europe.* The major alternatives turn on how to assist the change-over to a market economy and democracy with limited resource commitments, and what approach to take toward regional conflicts, especially whether to involve U.S. troops as "peacekeepers."

3. *Policy toward a presumably increasingly politically integrated and independent Western Europe.* The alternatives turn on how much America should remain engaged (and whether it should seek a leadership or a partnership role), particularly on how it should deal with the changed roles of a unified Germany and NATO.

4. *Policy toward trade, especially with Western Europe.* The major alternatives turn on how hard to push for even freer trade and how much to adopt limited protectionist measures.

5. *Policy toward the Middle East.* The major alternatives turn on how to continue 1993's progress on a resolution of the Arab-Israeli conflict without exacerbating inter-Arab and Gulf stability problems or endangering access to Middle East oil.

6. *Policy toward Japan.* The major alternatives turn on how to defuse the friction caused by the trade imbalance while maintaining cooperative security relationships.

7. *Policy toward China.* The major alternatives turn on how to deal with China's growing economic and security importance in Asia while simultaneously encouraging its movement away from totalitarianism.

8. *Policy toward "new" items on the agenda, such as national economy, energy, and quality of environment issues.* The major alternatives turn first on how to maintain a strong national economy to sustain foreign policy requirements in an increasingly interdependent world economy. They also turn on how the United States is to juggle the economic cost of progress in controlling adverse effects to the environment while making that progress, and how to ensure the acquisition of adequate energy resources at tolerable prices.

15

The Soviet Union Dissolved and Eastern Europe Freed

Implications

The changes that have swept over what was once the Soviet Union and all of Europe east of the former Iron Curtain since 1988 are truly breathtaking. Within the Soviet Union communism totally collapsed, the union itself fragmented into separate parts, and the former satellite countries became free. The implications for U.S. foreign policy of these enormous changes *are the focus of the first of the eight major decision areas.*

Major Decision Area 1: Implications of the Second Soviet Revolution

When Mikhail Gorbachev took the helm of the Soviet Communist Party and then in 1985 began to institute fundamental reforms, he did not have in mind what actually followed. Because what followed, besides a coup attempt that failed to stop the momentum of change,[1] was the dissolution of the Communist Party as well as the breakup of the Soviet Union itself and its East European empire.[2]

Although from an American point of view these changes also diminished the Soviet military threat, the successor states of the former Soviet Union still possessed enormous military power, including a nuclear arsenal whose keys were potentially less securely held by central government authorities. Even though the one right-wing coup had collapsed, with changes going on of this magnitude, no one could confidently assert that no danger to the United States could result. What, too, about the possible multiplication of armed forces as the old union came apart, and, again, especially as that multiplication affected nuclear weapons? No matter what the eventual result, the United States would have major power problems to deal with.

As another by-product of this second Soviet revolution, Poland and Eastern Europe were struggling with a free-market economy, while the integration of former East Germany into a single German state was having enormous impact on everything else in Europe, affecting even U.S. interest rates. Whether the fragmentation of the Soviet Union itself was at an end with the establishment of a "Commonwealth of Independent States" (CIS) was another question mark, for the old Soviet Union was not a "natural" single unit in any cultural sense, but was the product of military conquests. Within the new CIS, regional and ethnic antagonisms soon surfaced. In November, 1991, for example, Chechen-Ingush, a rebellious Muslim region of Russia in the Caucasus Mountains, claimed its right to go its own way. Even the new "Russia," the largest single member of the CIS, was a conglomeration of nationalities, although predominantly Russian. There was much uncertainty here for U.S. policymakers.

The answers to such questions and uncertainties were largely tied up with considerations of which way the future would develop. And, as has been pointed out in discussions of the cardinal principle of past-future linkages, the best clues to an unknown future are to be found by examining the past, for despite the many changes that have occurred and the different nationalities and ethnic groups involved, the common historical experience of all, as members of the same nation and participants in its history, will still be very important. Since many Americans have little idea of why, historically, Soviets came to behave the way they did and to look at problems through a quite unfamiliar perspective, it is important to fill in the background before going on to the contemporary problems that the United States faces as it deals with the USSR's successor states.

Backgrounds

Before 1917 the nation we learned to call the Soviet Union was called simply Russia. Historians of Russia have pointed out that the enormous territorial expansion of that country was largely the result of fighting off incursions from abroad. As an organized political entity, Russia traces its roots to the incursions of the Vikings, who used Russia's great cities to extend their control. Their capital was at Novgorod. When the Mongols came, they swept over much of Russia, almost subjugating it.[3] Both in 1382 and 1571, the Tatars sacked and burned Moscow. As late as the seventeenth century, when Charles XII of Sweden invaded Russia, the country was recurrently fighting off enemies.[4] This experience encouraged a military-style government, with unquestioned power in the hands of the Tsar.

Peter the Great (1672–1725) is remembered today as the father of modern Russia. In less romantic terms, he forced Russia to modernize to avoid being conquered by more advanced nations. As Adam Ulam observes, it was during Peter's reign that the "Russian Empire entered the ranks of the Great Powers."[5]

But, great power or not, in the next centuries Russia was to be invaded by Napoleon and by the Germans (twice), as well as having to fight the Japanese in the Far East. Each invasion cost Russia dearly and left its mark, not least in reviving sensitivity about vulnerable frontiers. For even if Russia, once small, became large, it still had no real natural frontiers to inhibit invasion.

Yet history was kind to Russia in one very important sense. In the 1700s, when Russia split Poland with Austria and Prussia, taking the largest share, there was no strong power in Asia.[6] Japan was still in isolation, China in political decay. Of the European great powers, Austria was recurrently locked in struggle with France, and France equally often with England. Spain's attention was on the New World and its colonies there. And Sweden lost its taste for military heroics. What all this meant was that Russia could expand to the east, ultimately across Siberia, and to the south, incorporating vast territories with scores of foreign peoples, without any real foreign opposition. Only in the nineteenth century, as British imperialism converted much of the rimland of Asia into colonies and protectorates, from India and Burma to the spheres of influence on the Chinese mainland, did the Russians find their advance contested. That change became clear in Afghanistan in the 1880s, for instance, when England and Russia narrowly avoided war.

So Russia's past made it an autocratic state covering a vast territory that included many non-Russians. It also made Russians extremely sensitive to the recurrent threat of invasion and inclined, as a consequence, to dominate their possible invasion routes wherever possible.

This was Russia's stance as the twentieth century began. Then came two disastrous wars for Russia, the first with Japan in 1904 and 1905. (It is significant that in Moscow's Museum of the Revolution, during the Cold War era, the displays showed the 1917 Communist revolution starting with the coal strikes of 1905.) Next came World War I. The terrible casualties and destruction of that war,[7] the complete incompetence shown by the government, the corruption in military supplies that put sand instead of gunpowder into cartridges, brought about communism. Finally, the Tsar was not so much overthrown as ignored. He abdicated on March 15, 1917. A provisional government took over, which would carry on the war. Germany, however, allowed Vladimir Lenin and other

Bolshevik leaders to transit from Switzerland to Russia, counting on them taking over the country and making peace. The Russian people found the Communist slogan of "Peace, Bread, and Land" irresistible. Either shooting their officers or merely ignoring them, the Russian armies voted with their feet and abandoned the battlefield to the advancing Germans.

Leon Trotsky, one of Lenin's close associates who organized the Red Army, was chief armistice negotiator with the Germans. However, in effect, Trotsky refused to actually negotiate, so the Germans, for their part, wrote the drastic Treaty of Brest-Litovsk that gave Germany enormous concessions.[8] Russia would lose Finland, the Baltic provinces, Poland, and the Ukraine. It was to demobilize its army. Having no real option, Russia signed the treaty on March 3, 1918. Four days later, to keep Russia in the war and keep Germany facing two fronts, a British force landed at Murmansk to aid the counterrevolutionary White Russians. Landings of British and French forces in the south were soon supplemented by other Allied interventions in the Far East. A large Japanese army moved in, and 10,000 U.S. troops landed at Vladivostok. President Wilson acted reluctantly, not with the thought of dismembering Russia but of keeping Russia in the war, and keeping a wary eye on the Japanese troops (whose ultimate intentions were more suspect).[9] But the net effect of all of this intervention was to convince the already ideologically suspicious Soviet Communists that if the capitalist nations could have stamped out their new regime, they would have.

The intervention prolonged a very bloody civil war, which lasted from 1918 to 1920. In the west, the Ukraine changed hands from White to Red to White and Red again, only to be invaded unsuccessfully by the Poles in May 1920. At one time the Japanese alone had over 72,000 troops on the mainland, and the Japanese did not withdraw until October 1922. They left behind them a devastated land.

No nation lost more territory at the end of World War I than the Soviet Union. Although because Germany was defeated the Brest-Litovsk Treaty never took effect, many of its provisions came to pass anyhow after the Allied victory, except that the Ukraine remained Russian. That Finland, Poland, and the Baltic states became independent seemed reasonable, but other territorial transfers included changes in favor of Rumania, which acquired Bessarabia, and Turkey, which received Kars-Ardahan.

These historical events help a good deal to explain the problems that developed later, especially as the West ineptly tried to come to grips with the menace of Hitler. It is not surprising that the Soviet Union, which had seen France create a "Cordon Sanitaire" of alliances along the Soviet frontiers, should remain suspicious of Western intentions.

After Lenin died on January 21, 1924, Josef Stalin took over. Absolutely ruthless, Stalin forcibly collectivized agriculture, bringing on a famine when farmers resisted. Millions died. In 1933–34 he purged the Communist Party, expelling one million members. Then, in a new drastic move to quell all internal resistance, he instituted summary trials and executions, of both old Party members and the Red Army officer corps. A conservative estimate is that 30 percent of the officer corps were shot. Figures for Party executions became public in February, 1956, when Nikita Khrushchev, in the wake of Stalin's death and the transition to a new leadership, revealed that 70 percent of the 139 members and candidates of the Central Committee (98 persons) were arrested and shot in 1937–38.[10] What happened to the Central Committee happened also to the larger body, the Soviet Congress. "Of 1,966 delegates . . . 1,108 were arrested," said Khrushchev, "on charges of anti-revolutionary crimes. . . ." Most of these, too, probably were shot. (The transcript of this speech at this point records: "Indignation in the hall.")[11]

Only very gradually and reluctantly did Europe's powers extend diplomatic recognition to the Soviet regime. One reason for the slowness was the Soviet refusal to recognize the validity of the old regime's debts. Only under Franklin Roosevelt did the United States agree to resume relations.[12]

The Soviet Union might have remained a pariah if it had not been for the rise of Adolf Hitler. France made a treaty of alliance with the Soviets, and they were admitted to the League of Nations on September 18, 1934, almost a year after Germany had given notice of withdrawal. Now the Soviet Union watched Adolf Hitler grow in power as Britain and France, shrinking from the prospect of a new world war, appeased him. Today, the extent to which Britain and France went is hard to believe. Neville Chamberlain, the British prime minister, was far more concerned with keeping a tight budget than with buying airplanes, and the rank and file refused to believe lone voices, like Winston Churchill, calling out like Cassandra the doom that lay ahead if the response to German actions did not change.[13]

This affected the Soviet Union in the conclusion it reached when it assessed the Munich Agreement and the subsequent dismemberment of Czechoslovakia. The Soviets had not even been invited to the Munich Conference. Half a year later, when Hitler violated his pledge and took over the rest of Czechoslovakia, it brought German troops to within a short distance from the Soviet frontier. At the same time Hitler took over Memel and Danzig, so that he now literally had Poland surrounded. Even if no one in Russia had ever read Hitler's *Mein Kampf*, it would have been obvious what was coming next.

The Soviets believed that the Western agreement in Munich was designed to turn Hitler's aggression eastward, so they determined to buy time by settling with Hitler in the infamous Nazi-Soviet Pact of 1939. That same year, on December 14, after putting pressure on the Baltic states and attacking Finland, the Soviet Union had the distinction of being the first and only nation ever expelled from the League of Nations. When the war began, the Soviets took the half of Poland given to them by the Nazi-Soviet Pact. What they gained from all of this was a bit more than a year and a half of peace. Then began a time of great bloodshed and destruction for the Soviet Union. The course of the war had long-ranging results because the Soviet Union emerged from the war determined to have Eastern Europe under its own control. Thus began the forty-five years of domination that ended in 1990.

Intellectual Clues to Change

The principle of past-future linkages does not refer merely to the events of history. As we have argued consistently, events do not simply "occur." They are seen to "mean something," to have significance. To the Russian people, their recurrent and prolonged sufferings and the recurrent invasion and war to which they were subjected encouraged a deep suspicion of the motives of outside states. This historically-ingrained paranoia was deepened further by the tenets of communism. Fundamental to Communist thinking was the argument that the capitalist world would never leave the socialist world in peace, that war was therefore "inevitable." We mentioned earlier how, in Khrushchev's 1956 "secret speech," he altered that fundamental Communist dogma, arguing that war was no longer inevitable because in power terms the socialist bloc was now "invincible." The Soviet Union was so strong militarily that it could administer (in Soviet jargon) a "massive rebuff" to the imperialists if they dared to attack the Soviet Union. Therefore, no attack would be made.

Khrushchev's 1956 doctrinal revisionism had a limited but immediate purpose. But in any case the older doctrine was outmoded. As Nogee and Donaldson point out, Khrushchev "recognized that nuclear weapons had fundamentally altered the character of international politics."[14] For no matter who began nuclear war, and no matter with what degree of surprise, there would inevitably be a second strike. Even a few warheads getting through would be devastating. And how could anyone really appeal to a Communist audience by telling them that after a devastating war, communism would be victorious? So Khrushchev, saddled with an outdated doctrine that specifically prophesied a coming war, moved to drop that doctrine. What he did not have in mind was changing the Soviet mind-set, either on international problems or toward the United States. But, in the end, exactly that was to happen.

When Khrushchev argued that war was not inevitable because the capitalists, observing the Soviet pile of weapons, would reach the realistic conclusion that war would not pay off, he was necessarily changing the whole way the Soviets thought and approached foreign policy problems.

During the Cold War many Americans were under the impression that Communist ideology, with its forthright declaration of hostility to capitalism, implied or asserted that the Communists were only waiting for their best opportunity to take war to the United States. But that was never part of Communist doctrine. What they believed—and what their historical experience encouraged them to believe—was that *capitalists* would never rest until they had eliminated communism. In other words, the warmonger role was reserved for their opponents, not for them. Indeed, the very reason why they thought communism would triumph in the end was because capitalists were incapable of any other policy. Lenin specifically traced the recurrence of world wars to one group of capitalist nations seeking to take away the markets and colonies of another group.[15] War with the victor capitalists was inevitable because finally the capitalists would take on the Soviet Union.

The reason the word "inevitable" flavored so many pages of Marxist analysis is that it presented capitalists as wooden creatures, two-dimensional creatures, doomed to act out a built-in class role. They were on automatic pilot, so to speak. Individual capitalists might be friendly, but as a class there was nothing to be expected from them by Communists except permanent hostility. Whatever tactical variations might occur, that was the long-term prospect.

This is a curious idea, really, from an American perspective. But Communists believed that the private ownership of the means of production—such as factories and farms—was the essential capitalist, war-mongering clue to behavior as greed spurred them on.

What Khrushchev did in discarding the basic Communist tenet of inevitability was to credit the opponent with *an ability to analyze situations and to choose between policy alternatives* on the basis of what promised better results. But if the capitalist did not have to act out a class role, willy-nilly, then out the window also went the proposition that communism's victory was inevitable. If the capitalist can choose, he can make choices that retard or reverse his "inevitable" demise. No longer could the Soviets believe with the same confidence what Brezhnev nevertheless said as late as 1976, that "the developments of recent years forcefully confirm that capitalism is a society without a future."[16]

Even more, if capitalists were able to make choices based on their analysis, then Communists, too, had to look at the same situations in objective terms if they were to compete. Granting freedom of will to the opponent ultimately then freed the Communists themselves from the shackles of orthodox Communist thought and encouraged analysis that was free altogether from Communist dogma.

Consequently, the *ultimate* effect of Khrushchev's revisionism was intellectual. It laid the foundations of freer thought, without which it is highly unlikely that Mikhail Gorbachev could have pushed a lethargic Soviet Union into new ways of thinking. When Gorbachev introduced his reforms, he buttressed his policies with liberal quotations from Lenin, but when the reforms began to be realized in a society becoming used to freer thinking, events led quickly to a revamping of Soviet society. They led to the astounding situation in 1991, that when the KGB and armed forces leaders, along with most other top Soviet officials, attempted their coup, the people refused to go along.

Counterbalancing National Interests

If one reason for the second Soviet revolution was that the Soviet citizens had learned freer ways of thinking, a second reason was that communism by Gorbachev's time had clearly failed in its most basic boast: sharing the increased wealth that would be communism's payoff.

Khrushchev, who once argued that America's grandchildren would be Communists, did not live long enough to see what really happened. Simone Weil once said of communism that "the great mistake of the Marxists and of the whole of the nineteenth century was to think that by walking straight on one mounted upward into the air." Marxism, developed before the bloody tragedy of World War I, did not die alongside much of the prewar optimism about "onward and upward." By the 1980s, what was begun in the spirit of humanitarianism and in the name of progress for the common man had disintegrated into a police state and shabbiness everywhere at home, and the foreign heel of the oppressor abroad.

Khrushchev, as we just saw in the "secret speech," did attempt to breathe a limited breath of liberalism into this autocratic structure. But he was not prepared to change any of the system's fundamental features or free any of the client states. His successor, Leonid Brezhnev, said that détente did not "in the slightest cancel out, nor can it cancel out or alter, the laws of the class struggle." The purpose of détente, he continued, was "to create more favorable conditions for peaceful socialist and communist construction."[17] Brezhnev also gave his name to a doctrine that said in so many words that no country once brought under communism would be allowed its freedom.

That Brezhnev Doctrine was announced in the wake of the "Prague Spring" of 1968, when Warsaw Pact troops descended on the Czechs to suppress their "new socialism," which included a free press! But Czechoslovakia's bid for freedom was only the latest in a series that began in East Berlin and East Germany in 1953, and continued on in Poland and Hungary in 1956. Yet not a single one of these uprisings was successful, and Moscow's rule seemed firmly entrenched when Gorbachev took power. Then why did it all change, and change so fast?

One prime reason is that the Soviets could not afford what they were doing, and the price tag finally caught up with them.[18] Anyone who did not actually visit the Soviet Union and in the 1970s and 1980s heard it referred to repeatedly as a "superpower," can be pardoned for thinking that it must have resembled the United States and its infrastructure and economic resources in at least major ways. The truth was and is otherwise. Even today, outside Moscow, there are few paved roads. The railroad system is completely inadequate, and so is the highway system. The quality of life and the standard of living, widely known today to be very poor, was much the same before the West heard about it. The only stores that were always well stocked were those that sold for hard currencies only. The only individuals and families who were well off were those with high party rank. The housing was substandard and in short supply. Only in the area of national defense was there abundance. It had a corner on the brains and the funds, while food rotted on its way to market because the transportation system could not move it in time.

The Straw That Broke the Camel's Back

Conditions in the Soviet Union were not very pleasant at any time after the Revolution. But in 1955, the Soviet decision to extend arms to Nasser, a non-Communist, marked a fundamental change in Soviet policy that was ultimately to help bankrupt the Soviet Union. For the idea of extending aid widely to non-aligned nations as well as Communist allies was in time to be the straw that finally broke the camel's back. It put the Soviet Union into a new arena of competition with the United States where the economy played a much more important role. It diverted abroad aid that was much needed at home.

Now the Soviets began to compete worldwide with the United States, in an effort to extend communism into Africa, the Middle East, and Latin America. It was a very costly policy; the subsidy to Castro's Cuba alone was in the billions of dollars. And, as time went on, the Soviets had very little to show for all of this. Eventually, they had nothing to show for it. In the meantime, the high price continued to drag down the already low standard of living at home.

With the Communist policy of equipping non-Communist troublemakers around the globe with free weapons and subsidies proving very costly in itself let alone compared with its results, Gorbachev could and did use the intellectual vehicle Khruschev had unwittingly supplied to express the need for change. For Khrushchev's doctrinal reform made it acceptable and possible to examine counterbalancing national interests in an objective fashion previously completely alien to Soviet thought. Once the pluses and minuses of the alternatives could be compared, the prospects for change in view of communism's poor showing became overwhelming.

Halfway Reforms

To decide to reform a society is easy compared to doing it. Institutional inertia anywhere is difficult to overcome. An American who did not actually visit the Soviet Union in those earlier days cannot easily appreciate what it was like, for the visitor and for the Soviet citizen. *Everything* was regulated. If you arrived in Moscow, equipped with visa and Intourist reservation, you were put into a taxi that went to your hotel without any word between you and your driver. While you were in the Soviet Union, the Intourist guides were highly reluctant to see you venture out on your own. If you wanted to leave Moscow for Leningrad, you needed reservations—*before* you left for the train or plane. When you departed your hotel, you entered a taxi with a special license plate, and the driver already knew where you were going. You could exchange money in certain amounts only, and only at certain times. You could eat only at certain restaurants, with coupons. Any taxi in Moscow available to a tourist was licensed for within-the-circular road area only. Woe to the tourist or visitor who wanted to improvise an agenda. Naturally, there was no news in the Western sense on either radio or television or in the newspapers. All the media, as often as not, were featuring the need to liberate some obscure Communist who was being victimized somewhere. And the money, non-convertible, cost many times more than it was worth, making the whole visit an unwilling subsidy for the Communist system.

But the visitor could leave. The Soviet citizen, crammed into his tiny apartment (if he was lucky enough to have his own rather than live with his in-laws), could only live where his internal passport permitted, and that passport was issued only for where he had a job. He lived in an atmosphere where he automatically got on the end of a line he passed, knowing that it meant that something scarce was for sale. He put his name down for car purchase, knowing it would be several years before he would be offered one, and that he had better take that one because otherwise he went to the foot of the line again. (As Henry Ford once said, "They can have any color they want, so long as it's black.") Only party functionaries lived well, and the higher ones lived exceedingly well, with special stores and many privileges, including official cars with chauffeurs and dachas in the countryside. Anyone who did not like the system had the secret police, the KGB, to contend with.

A system like that, which had endured for seventy years, is hard to change. It should not have surprised anyone that Mikhail Gorbachev seemed to go at it so slowly. All power to approve or disapprove his suggestions was in the hands of those who stood to lose their privileges if he prevailed.

There is a second reason why Gorbachev moved so slowly with his domestic reforms: he did not really want to dismantle the socialist system. What he wanted was to give it a humane face. This is perfectly clear from his book, *Perestroika: New Thinking for Our Country and the World,* which appeared in the United States in 1987.[19] ("Perestroika" means "restructuring.") In the book, Gorbachev names April, 1985, as the time the Central Committee faced the fact that the Soviet Union was "verging on crisis," and made the decision to change course.[20] The need to enlist popular support led to the "all-round democratic changes in public life," in this way aiming to unite socialism with democracy. Gorbachev rejected the argument that perestroika signified "disenchantment with socialism."[21] Rather, it was the realization by the reformers that the "potential of socialism" had been "underutilized."

It was almost too late when Gorbachev, to his dismay and at the risk of his life, learned that socialism with a humane face was, for the Soviet Union at least, virtually a contradiction in terms. In deciding how to proceed, Gorbachev and his colleagues soon found a whole range of not-easily-reconcilable views. As he tried to steer a mid course between the conservative right and the liberal left, he lost support on both sides.

The fact was that halfway measures, especially stretching out over a long period, are inherently unsatisfactory. There was no prospect that they would work. Even if the intent from the beginning had been to make radical reforms very quickly, the problems would have been highly formidable. Stretching them out with partial solutions simply undermined central authority without producing local agencies and arrangements capable of taking their place.

Take the economic system, built around central planning, with military and military-related activities absorbing the lion's share of the product. How could the government convert that? Years ago, back in the 1950s, one defector to the United States explained his abrupt departure by the fact that he was just ahead of the police. He had been the manager of an auto tire factory in the Ukraine, but he had not been given an adequate supply of raw rubber to make his quota of new tires. Afraid of what would follow, he and a companion went out on the city streets at night and stole tires off existing autos, retreading them and passing them off for new! That's the problem with a central planning system: You don't get what you need to produce what you are supposed to send. Also, the system is practically impervious to consumer preferences. The famous illustration is baby buggies. Huge supplies of ugly baby buggies were produced, but few mothers wanted one.

How do you reform a centralized planning system like that? It probably cannot be done; you can only abolish it all once and for all and go through a period of chaos until trading links are reestablished in accordance with supply and demand. But try doing that in a Soviet Union where for decades Moscow has organized everything with the special intention of keeping outlying areas dependent, even if the organization was completely inefficient from an economic point of view. But unless Moscow copes with this problem effectively, how is the United States to do much about it?

In dealing with such problems *glastnost* (openness) made a beginning. It opened peoples' minds to other possibilities in all fields of activity. But recognizing that the very small private plots allowed to farmers on state farms and collectives produce ten times or more per acre than the state-run acres did not automatically also provide the knowledge or the mechanisms for change. To improve agricultural production substantially and immediately, these state-held areas must be sold or leased to the peasants already working them, but such a change cannot happen overnight. And such a reform will not in itself ensure that a good part of what is produced gets to market. The whole transportation and distribution system has to be overhauled. On the bright side, everyone knows that somehow the private produce makes it to market. Given an incentive, problems tend to be overcome.

Gorbachev's Problems Multiply

Despite the fact that Gorbachev was unwilling to push reforms at the needed pace, to his many opponents he seemed to be proceeding at breakneck speed. But Gorbachev faced an entrenched enemy tied to its positions. To accomplish his program he had to take on a bureaucracy well wedded to its prerogatives and powers. He had to cajole an armed force that was being cut back in men and weapons, both through arms control agreements and withdrawals from Eastern Europe. He had to keep in check the separatist tendencies in the multi-cultured, multi-national Soviet Union, knowing full well that most of the non-Russian population of the Soviet Union had been brought into association with the Russians by coercion or force. He had to keep production going while the economic transition took place. This is a list of enormous proportions. It also explains Gorbachev's willingness to make unprecedented concessions to the West in arms control and withdrawals of Soviet troops.

One of the problems which came to occupy a good deal of his time was the devolution of the centrally controlled economic, bureaucratic, and political system. As the republics came to enjoy more freedoms, they pushed for more. Soon they were defying Moscow altogether. It was natural enough that the Baltic republics, incorporated by Stalin quite against their will, would move fastest and furthest. But as fighting broke out between different national groups in the south, and as the Russian Republic under Boris Yeltsin went its own way, difficulties that were not as easily foreseen multiplied.

Various political reforms were instituted, some in rapid succession. All tended to increase presidential powers as conditions deteriorated, especially in terms of the food supply. The most dangerous development of all was in that last point, for economic reform had bogged down in the middle of an argument between one group that wanted quicker reforms and another that wanted to move slowly. Gorbachev agonized between the two and on this critical point appeared to be more indecisive than on anything else.

The Coup Attempt and the Aftermath

The result by early 1991 was that the easy optimism about the "new" Soviet Union had more or less evaporated. Those in the United States who had begun to discount any Soviet threat began to take a new look at the problem. Those in the Soviet Union who felt most threatened by changes also were taking a new look. It was clear to the Communist office-holders that their personal situation would continue to deteriorate. Joining this group were (perhaps) sincere patriots disturbed at the Soviet Union's new vulnerability. To others, the problem was Gorbachev's "traitorous" acts in giving up all the hard-won gains of World War II. As the summer wore on, the possibility of a coup could not be ruled out.

At 4 A.M. Monday, August 19, 1991, Moscow time, Vice President Gennady Yanayev and seven other principals, including Defense Minister Marshal Dmitri T. Yazov, Interior Minister Boris K. Pugo, and Chairman of the KGB Vladimir A. Kryuchkov, made their move.

Gorbachev himself was placed under house arrest at his vacation dacha in the Crimea, along with his wife and other members of his family.[22] In Moscow itself, the first target of the coup was the first freely elected president of the Russian Republic, Boris Yeltsin. As about 100 tanks began to surround his headquarters in the Russian Parliament building, Yeltsin succeeded in communicating with supporters, who flocked to the parliament building to defend it with their bodies and a few guns. Meanwhile, some of the tanks and army units sent to cow Yeltsin or kill him changed sides. Other KGB unit commanders refused orders to storm the building. By Tuesday, August 20, hundreds of thousands of protesters had rallied in cities around the nation, including Moscow, Leningrad, Minsk, and Kishinev. Four people were killed in overnight clashes near Yeltsin's headquarters.

By Wednesday, August 21, the eight major coup plotters realized that they had failed.[23] Tanks and armored carriers began to move away from the Russian

Parliament, and soon a two-and-a-half mile column of tanks and trucks was moving out of Moscow, cheered by the people as they went. By Thursday, August 22, Gorbachev was back in Moscow, and the coup was over. Interior Minister Pugo had committed suicide, and the others were soon under arrest.

Yeltsin was, of course, the hero of the hour. But it should not be forgotten that there would have been no Yeltsin in that position or with that kind of popular support if Gorbachev had not led the nation into reform, however half-hearted or incomplete his efforts. The economy was in chaos, but the attempt to bring the common people to associate themselves with what happened in the Soviet Union was a spectacular success. After more than a thousand years of being told what to do, the Soviet citizen was beginning to think and act for himself or herself.

Gorbachev's prestige was seriously damaged by the coup, particularly since the principal plotters were all men he had personally chosen and put into office. He could not say he had not been warned: the liberals who had left his side when he turned to the very hardliners who were coup leaders had specifically and publicly spoken of the threat of a coup.

Gorbachev at first tried to shield the Communist Party from categorical guilt, but it soon became apparent that the Party had simply stood by or cooperated in the coup. On August 24, Gorbachev resigned as head of the Communist Party, disbanded its leadership, and in effect banned the party from any role in ruling the Soviet Union. Party archives were sealed and placed under police control, while party assets were seized until its future could be decided. All of this was done with Gorbachev and Yeltsin acting together.

In the wake of the coup and its failure, the roll call of republics within the Soviet Union opting for "independence" or "sovereignty" grew longer. Virtually every unit was on the list by the middle of September. These units, of course, took their actions for a variety of reasons and with a range of seriousness about actually departing from the Union. The Baltic republics did definitely want out, and they were given that right in September. The rest agreed on the need for much greater autonomy from central control in Moscow. Given effective freedom over many of their primary concerns, they were almost all actually ready to remain in a revamped Union, where Moscow would retain control over the armed forces and foreign policy, but taxation and economic decisions would be largely in the hands of each constituent republic.

In the first week of September, a completely new central government was put into place on an interim basis. These arrangements were hardly in place before they became obsolete. Convinced that the pace of reform was completely inadequate, Boris Yeltsin met with the leaders of Ukraine and Byelorussia (now Belarus) for two days in early December 1991. What they agreed to do was establish a new Commonwealth of Independent States, open to all the other Soviet republics to join. On Thursday, December 12, Gorbachev threatened to resign if this went through, but the same day the Russian legislature voted 188–6 to ratify the Commonwealth agreement. They also annulled the 1922 treaty establishing the Soviet Union. Gorbachev's protests were brushed away, and by December 21, at a second meeting in Kazakhstan, eleven republics agreed to the new arrangement. The top governmental bodies were to be councils of heads of state and government. They would be assisted by committees of republic ministers in key areas like foreign affairs, defense, and economics. The Baltic states opted to remain out of the new arrangements. So did Georgia. Gorbachev, bowing to the inevitable, resigned so that the new system could come into operation with the advent of 1992.

No one better summed up Gorbachev's contribution than did Yeltsin himself:

> We, like the whole world, respect him for what he did, especially in the first years of perestroika. [But] he thought to unite the impossible: Communism with the market, public property with private property, political pluralism with the Communist Party. These are incompatible couples, but he insisted on them, and therein lay his fundamental strategic mistake.[24]

Major Decision Area 1: The Former Soviet Union

The new arrangements left open more questions than they resolved. For example, although the strategic forces of the Soviet Union, it was agreed, would remain under a central Commonwealth control and other forces could presumably be divided up if the republics so wished, Ukraine almost immediately made a grab for the Black Sea fleet. Yeltsin reacted vigorously, declaring that the navy was a strategic force. Even the control over strategic forces sounded more improvised than permanent. To use them it would take first Yeltsin's agreement, which would be concurred with by the other republic heads. That arrangement was obviously a political formula. It would hardly do in the event of a threat of imminent war. But then, all of the Commonwealth republics, by elevating their wish for independence above their security fears from abroad, were making a clear assumption that they would not be the victim of an attack by the West. (This view contributed to the 1992 pledge of the non-Russian USSR-successor states with nuclear weapons to ratify START I and accede to the NPT, discussed earlier.)

The issue of control of strategic forces was illustrative of the uncertainties that lay ahead. The CIS had no charter, nor did it have any mechanisms to ensure that any agreements reached by its members would actually be observed. Moreover, many of the documents signed in its first year were signed by only some of the members, including a collective security pact. Although some members wanted to develop economic coordinating structures, progress here, too, was slow.

The creation of the Commonwealth of Independent States reflected the pent-up wishes of the Soviet Union's diverse peoples to go their own ways. But going one's own way was easier said than done. Just the redeployment of weapons required by the changes was a formidable problem, especially as some of the republics created "national" armies. Then there was the issue of bringing the Russian forces home. Of the 3,846,000 members of the Soviet armed forces, for example, there were 170,000 in the Baltic states. They had to be repatriated. So, too, a large part of the nearly 1,000,000 stationed in Ukraine-Moldavia. Smaller numbers were elsewhere. And this is on top of what had to be withdrawn from Eastern Europe. (And what would Moscow do with them once they arrived home?)

Another complication was the fact that Russians formed a large minority in many of the republics.[25] Ukraine's population was 22.1 percent Russian. Russians formed about a third of the population of Estonia and Latvia, and 37.8 percent of that of Kazakhstan. Except for Armenia (below 2 percent), the Russian minority elsewhere tended to run 8 or 9 percent. There was the potential for real trouble here.

Also, the economies of many of the new CIS members were heavily intertwined. Most of the new republics had an adverse trade balance with Russia, the major exceptions being Belarus and Ukraine. By way of comparison, where Britain's trade with the rest of the EC was 22 percent of its output, Ukraine's inter-republican trade was 60 percent. Armenia's situation was even worse. These figures just hint at the extent of the problems that had to be ironed out. In 1992 most of the attention of the people was focused elsewhere, though—on the struggle to simply live, to feed themselves and their children.

As is true with most critical policy changes, what was needed was decisive action, not halfway measures. The requirement was a clear decision for, first, a fundamental transition from the old controlled economy to a free market economy tailored specifically to Russia's needs and national character, and, second, movement to a convertible ruble honored on international exchanges. But, unfortunately, the human tendency is to temporize and split the difference, and the problems faced were enormous. Throughout 1992, GDP and living standards declined. As printing presses turned out bales of currency, the ruble sank to a penny apiece. Most prices were freed, and they then shot up much beyond the ability of the average Russian to handle. In mid-July 1992, the Russian Parliament legalized payment of workers in dollars and other hard currencies (within Russia). The Central Bank simultaneously supplemented the 1,000 ruble banknote with a new 5,000 ruble note—which speaks for itself. At a session of the Russian Congress in December, Yeltsin's program was severely criticized (and his executive powers challenged).

The determination of the peoples of the old USSR to go their own way also manifested itself in a number of nationalist/ethnic conflicts. In the midst of this, though, there was one particularly interesting development, with a peacekeeping effort by the CIS. More than a thousand Russian paratroopers were deployed along with Georgia national guard units to try to stop the fighting between Georgian and Ossetian irregular forces. But such operations were hardly the overall answer, and throughout 1992 conflicts abounded. Private armies, which already had helped bring down the government in Azerbaijan, kept Tajikistan in turmoil, and fighting continued in several other areas also. In November Yeltsin declared a state of emergency in two warring regions of the Caucasus. The situation truly was precarious.

U.S. Secretary of State James Baker, in a speech at Princeton on December 12, 1991, summed up the situation eloquently and well:

> If, during the Cold War, we faced each other as two scorpions in a bottle, now the Western nations and the former Soviet republics stand as awkward climbers on a steep mountain, held together by a common rope.
>
> A fall toward fascism or anarchy in the former Soviet Union will pull the West down, too. Yet equally as important, a strong and steady pull by the West can help them to gain their footing. We must strengthen that rope and not sever it.[26]

Baker's figure of speech is interesting, reminding one of FDR's announcement of Lend-Lease, to help America's "neighbors." He posits Washington's perception of the two fundamental alternatives—to make a serious commitment to help, or not—and the consequences that would flow from the choice. Baker advocates help, for (as he says) "as much as we will benefit if this revolution succeeds, we will pay if it fails. . . . We are not the leaders of this revolution, but neither are we mere bystanders." Baker called for, in effect, a new Marshall Plan, jointly supported by the West and Japan.

With economic conditions in Russia and the other former Soviet republics continuing to deteriorate, as early as April 1992 President Bush proposed a major foreign aid package, including a $24 billion multilateral initiative for the G-7 nations (the United States, the United Kingdom, France, Germany, Japan, Canada, and Italy). Shortly thereafter, the IMF and World Bank offered membership to Russia and most of the other republics. But by midyear Congress had not acted, and the IMF was imposing severe conditions on Russia as the price for assistance. In October, though, Congress passed the American portion of the package (but the IMF said more than $100 billion was needed over the next four years). In April 1993, the G-7 nations pledged another $28 billion in aid. But much of this was contingent on more reforms. Also, Russia's armies were shrinking. That was a good news and bad. Most frontline troops were still based in now independent nations like Ukraine. Weapons and ammunition were finding black market outlets on a large scale. With conscription cut back, in August 1993, the chairman of Russia's parliamentary defense committee estimated that by year's end the army would have 630,000 officers but only 544,000 men![27]

There was bound to be stormy weather ahead, regardless of U.S. policy.

Major Decision Area 2: Eastern Europe

The sweeping pace of political change in Eastern Europe was almost unbelievable, even in retrospect. Take the events of the last four months of 1989.

- In September, Romanian President Nicolae Ceausescu was still trying to rally the Warsaw Pact to stop the Solidarity movement from taking power in Poland.

- That same month, however, the Polish Parliament approved a Solidarity-led government. It was the first non-Communist government in Eastern Europe since the 1940s.

- That same month, Hungary, the other non-German satellite state in Stalin's empire that had tried to gain freedom, opened its border with Austria, thus setting in motion a continuing flow of political refugees that destabilized East Germany.

- In October, the Hungarian Socialist Party voted to abandon Communist theories in favor of Western-style democracy. Opposition parties were legalized.

- That same month, the Solidarity-led government of Poland made public plans for a free market economy, Western-style.

- Six days later, on October 18, German Communist Party hard-liner leader Erich Honecker, 77, resigned.

- Five days later, on the anniversary of the suppressed 1956 uprising, Hungary proclaimed a new status for itself as an independent republic, rather than a "socialist people's republic."

- By early November, the leaders of the former ruling (Communist) party in Poland agreed to change the party into a socialist party committed to Western-style parliamentary democracy.

- On November 7, the East German government resigned, followed the next day by the Politburo. On November 9, the Berlin Wall was opened and free travel allowed.

- By November 24, Communist leader Milos Jakes and the rest of the Czech Communist Party leaders were resigning. Alexander Dubcek, leader of the "Prague Spring" of 1968, returned from exile to address 300,000 cheering Czechoslovaks in Wenceslas Square in Prague. Four days later the Czechoslovak Communist Party agreed to give up its 41-year monopoly on political power. The opposition was given the right to publish its own daily newspaper. Three days later, Czechoslovakia announced it would dismantle the fortifications along some sections of its 240-mile border with Austria.

- On the first day of December, East Germany's Parliament abolished the Communist party's monopoly on power.

- Three days later, meeting in Moscow, the Warsaw Pact nations that had intervened militarily in Czechoslovakia in 1968 denounced their own action. The Kremlin, in a separate statement, called the Soviet-led invasion "unfounded" and "erroneous."

By Christmas Day virtually every Communist state in East Europe had announced plans for free elections by the spring of 1990. The Brandenburg Gate, the very symbol of divided Germany, had been opened, and the last visa and currency requirements previously imposed by the East German government had been abolished. In Moscow, the Soviet Congress of Peoples' Deputies stood for a moment of silence in memory of Soviet troops killed in Afghanistan. Then, by a vote of 1,678 to 18, with 19 abstentions, they said that the invasion deserved "moral and political condemnation."

On Christmas Day itself, after a bloody struggle in Romania in which as many as 60,000 may have died, ousted President Nicolae Ceausescu and his wife (who was also his deputy) were executed. He was the last hard-line Communist leader in the Warsaw Pact.

Eastern Europe was now free to rebuild its own institutions in its own way. Freedoms had been gained. What was necessary now was to establish political and economic systems to institutionalize and build on those gains. That was to prove difficult. It is not easy to take centralized institutions, dismantle them, and replace them with free market and democratic institutions. Poland, for example, which had led the way, found itself very divided in the election of late 1991.[28] In the rural areas of Poland, the attitude is very conservative, indeed. Small processing plants for milk, meat, and vegetable oil are much needed, but in one town, Tykocin, where the mayor sold $25 and $50 shares to begin a dairy, in a whole year he sold 17 shares.[29] Traditionally, in prewar Poland, the Jewish merchants did the buying and selling, not the peasants. But today, with the old state-run dairies in collapse, younger villagers, taking their milk directly to the city markets, have begun to find out how profitable it is to cut out the middleman.

All of Eastern Europe now shares similar problems and dilemmas: how fast to go to a full free market, how much to subsidize bread and necessities (and for how long), how much of a social security system to maintain, what to do about the unemployed, what governmental structures and processes to create. On the plus side, they are able to borrow innovative ideas from each other.

Czechoslovakia, for example, in 1991 developed an ingenious idea to assist the economic transformation. Already, in 1990, the government had sold many shops and small enterprises in direct auctions. Now came the larger companies. The plan was to "privatize" 2,285 companies early in 1992, followed by 1,842 companies in a second phase. Although the Czech government intended to encourage Western investment in these assets, it also determined to save at least 20 percent of the shares for the people. In order to give the people a stake in these companies and avoid having them pass into the hands of rich bidders, the government sold "coupon books" for $30. These give the buyer 1,000 points that can later be converted into shares in these companies.

That the general line of economic development through privatization of national assets was something the United States could welcome, goes almost without saying. But that the United States could as a government contribute very much to assist was doubtful. Not only was the United States caught up in economic difficulties of its own; there were also far too many nations simultaneously needing aid.

Major Decision Area 2: Bosnia-Herzegovina and Resurgent Nationalism

The end of the Soviet totalitarian grasp on Eastern Europe has also let loose from Pandora's box repressed nationalism. The contagion has spread widely, not only inside the former USSR but outside. Yugoslavia is the leading case.

Before World War I, Yugoslavia did not exist. "Its" land was divided between the Turkish and Austro-Hungarian empires, roughly on a line running through Belgrade. A host of ethnic groups populated the area, with different cultures and often bitter enmity. Slovenia and Croatia, with relatively little minority population, used the Roman alphabet. Bosnia-Herzegovina, as the frontline province of Turkey until the mid-1400s, acquired a large Muslim group (in 1991, around 40 percent); in the 1990s there were also 32 percent Serbs and 18 percent Croats. Ethnic hatreds still run deep. In World War II, fighting between Serbs and Croats killed more people than the number of occupying Germans. And Bosnia-Herzegovina, unlike its northern sister provinces, uses the Russian alphabet, providing an additional cultural reason why the Serbs have determined to dominate it if they can.

The above description hardly scratches the surface of the complexities involved. But it illustrates the problem. And anyone who has visited Yugoslavia knows that the difference between Dubrovnik on the coast and Skopje in Yugoslav Macedonia (itself 67 percent Macedonian and 20 percent Albanian) is a difference of two cultural worlds not even connected by a decent all-weather road.

Conflict began in the summer of 1991, when the provinces of Croatia and Slovenia elected noncommunist governments and voted for independence. The Serbs, who dominated the Yugoslav government, sought to prevent these secessions by force, and civil war ensued. Following the dispatch of U.N. peacekeepers (and many failures) a precarious cease-fire was arranged, but then Bosnia-Herzegovina (and Macedonia) declared independence. Civil War erupted now in Bosnia-Herzegovina, with the deep hatreds all too evident. Soon Serbian forces were in engaged "ethnic cleansing" operations (i.e., moving large numbers of Muslims, in particular, out of areas of Bosnia controlled by Serbia), and as the mistreatment and killings were reported daily in the American press and television, the always latent pressures in the American public grew for the United States to take some action. As always with a foreign affairs question, the fundamental issue was being obscured by discussion of many secondary issues—like whether ground forces might be used rather than air strikes and a blockade and tightened sanctions.

During the 1992 presidential campaign it was difficult for either President Bush or Governor Bill Clinton to refrain from comment in this situation, although both were well aware of the danger of competing in announcing some bold and inexpensive solution to a morally painful problem. Yet, as one assistant secretary of defense testified to Congress, the fundamental issue was whether the United States and Europe were facing a "Kuwait" (i.e., aggression)

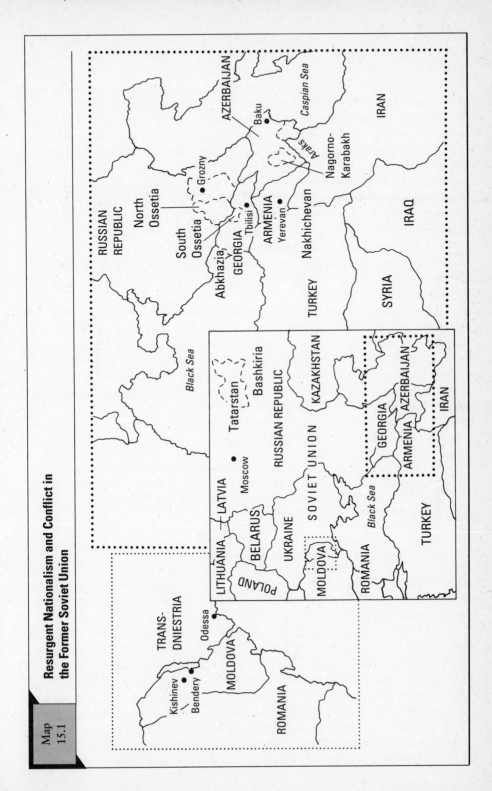

Map 15.1

Resurgent Nationalism and Conflict in the Former Soviet Union

or a "Lebanon" (i.e., fragmentation). Just as some Americans, confronting Kuwait, had thought in terms of Vietnam, now in confronting Bosnia-Herzegovina they thought in terms of Kuwait. The fact was that any serious intervention in a civil war is always very unsatisfactory, let alone one as confusing and uncertain as this. As with the Israeli question, one was also dealing with a problem with very extensive and entangled historical roots. World War I started over the same issue in 1914: Serbia was unwilling to accept a Bosnia-Herzegovina outside of Serbian control. The question for the United States and Europe was not whether people were suffering in the conflict or whether Serbia was at fault, but whether American interests were involved and whether inserting third-party armed forces would in the end make for less or more killing. A less controversial subset of this issue was the possibility of military escort for relief columns (or even humanitarian airdrops of emergency supplies). But that would not end "ethnic cleansing" and would require thousands of troops. For the larger mission of pacifying the area, the Canadian general who had shortly before commanded the U.N. forces already in Bosnia, reckoned that it would take 400,000 ground troops. And then what?

Here, again, we see the limits of military force. It is very dangerous for Americans to think that any military operation that acquires the label "peacekeeping" thereby becomes less bloody or costly *unless* the most basic requirement for successful peacekeeping is assured: the willing consent of belligerents to be separated from each other by a U.N. military presence. For it is not the label that keeps costs down; it is the agreement of those who want to quit fighting but need help in an orderly way to do so.

What this means is well illustrated by Paul Mohn's observation about the 1947–49 war over Israel in the Middle East:

> . . . seven governments had to act simultaneously and orders had to go down through the military hierarchy of as many armies to the front commanders. Some confusion also resulted from the fact that Arabs and Israelis were divided by a difference of time. . . . Further divergencies arose over the proper hours for a cease-fire order. In the Middle East rifle shooting seems to reach its climax at night . . . for that reason the lull of the early morning was held to be the most suitable moment for inaugurating a truce.[29]

These are the problems a U.N. peacekeeping force can settle. But otherwise? The fact that some of a U.N. force are Americans will not change the picture one way or the other.

Three other peoples in Eastern Europe with a proud cultural past have been forced to live divided among several neighboring states: the Macedonians, the Armenians, and the Kurds. But these are just the most obvious. Most people would be astonished to see what a complete map of Europe would look like if all "suppressed" national groups suddenly obtained independence. Beginning in the west, there are the Scottish nationalists, who some years ago carried off the Stone of Scone (on which Scottish kings had been crowned from time immemorial) from Westminster Abbey, under the noses of the police guard. The Normans and Bretons of France and certainly the Basques of Spain have very strong nationalist traditions. Or compare Naples and Sicily to Genoa and Turin and it becomes clear that their differences are enormous in every respect.

But it is along the southern perimeter of the former Soviet Union that conflicts based upon nationality, suppressed when the Red Army was in control and when communism reigned, provide the strongest potential for serious conflict. In the Muslim republics, Islamic forces were urging closer relations with their southern neighbors in Turkey, Iran, Pakistan, and Syria. A former generation spoke about the "Balkanization" of Europe, referring to the successor states that emerged from the old Austro-Hungarian empire. That Balkanization would be nothing compared with what could emerge now. Many even doubted the CIS would last. In such instability, trade and peaceful relations often take a back seat. One could not help but remember the power vacuum in Eastern Europe in the 1920s and 1930s. Could this develop again, tempting a new aggressor, or might events snowball out of control and escalate to terrible violence? No one knew, but none of this kind of instability would be good for the United States. But how much could America do about it?

Summing Up

For years the "Soviet problem" for the United States was defined in terms of the "threat." It was, correctly or incorrectly, assessed in terms of Soviet intentions and capabilities and the external foreign and military policies the Soviets might pursue. As a result of the second Soviet revolution and the collapse of its empire, however, America's focus has shifted almost entirely. While the external policies of the evolving entities in the former USSR and in Eastern Europe cannot be ignored, internal factors and their impacts must now hold center stage.

Two opposite mistakes are possible for the United States as it chooses policy alternatives to cope with these changes—first, to try to do too much; second, to do too little. The transition to market economies in the ex-Soviet Union and Eastern Europe is bound to be rough. It will not help to prolong it with aid given as a Band-Aid. And pouring money in as gifts can only be useful to relieve distress, and then only temporarily. But neither can the people be allowed to starve as they grope with the problem. That implies two kinds of aid are necessary: food and the like for the immediate future, and capital investment and technological aid once the economy is sufficiently privatized so that the money used to achieve change will not simply disappear.

Much more useful in the longer term is to provide expertise, both public and private. America is, after all, the most experienced and successful free market economy in the world. It has a lot to contribute.

Concerning resurgent nationalism and ethnic conflicts, there are no abstract guidelines that are suitable for every situation. In the case of the (former) Soviet Union, it is evident that, whatever the ultimate shape and configuration, there will be a major power in Russia, and other entities will have to be dealt with also. America cannot determine the outcome. But it can provide diplomatic and economic encouragement to help achieve a stable situation involving at least mixed economies and some sort of political system consistent with democratic values and indigenous cultures and desires. The United States' role toward Eastern Europe for the most part must be equally encouraging and equally indirect. Here, however, working primarily through multilateral institutions (perhaps occasionally unilaterally), the United States also may sometimes be able to use its good offices and diplomatic clout to help resolve conflicts. The words "may sometimes" and "help" in the preceding sentence are crucial, however, because there will be many cases when the best choice is to avoid involvement.

With the CIS or its successor, the United States must still maintain a wary eye on developments that might again convert the area to a primary threat to American security. To the extent that America can influence, the alternatives are clear. Either encourage or discourage a continued union of at least most of the ex-Soviet republics. The choice turns on the question of which result will bring more trouble if it occurs. Of these two possibilities, fragmentation would almost certainly be more adverse to U.S. national interests, since it would multiply power problems in the area by vesting sovereign decisions in a greater number of actors. Even if only Russia is left of the old USSR, it will remain a powerful entity. But if the CIS did come apart, leaving only Russia, the likelihood would be constant conflict within the former Union area. That would not be highly desirable from the standpoint of the United States.

Whatever the future, the "dead hand" of the past will play its part. It is utopian to expect that the inbred wariness of foreigners will disappear, given Russia's history. While some foreign assistance is necessary, there will be broad concern that too much foreign influence will lead to foreign domination. The attitude, then, will be strongly ambivalent as the former Soviet entities explore a new relationship with outside nations.

Optimists in the United States, looking at the end of the Cold War, have once again "spent the peace dividend" in anticipation. But we have already warned that the future may not be so untroubled. The history of international relations and the balance of power shows rather vividly that when one nation loses power, others automatically gain. So, if "the Soviets" lose power, others gain. And how those others will choose among *their* policy alternatives is simply not knowable in advance.

Notes

1. See Jerry F. Hough, "Assessing the Coup," *Current History*, October 1991, pp. 305–10.

2. Particularly useful is Martha Brill Olcott, "The Slide into Disunion," *Current History*, October 1991, pp. 338–44.

3. One Russian historian, writing more than a century ago, says that Russia was invaded *forty-eight* times by the Tartars between 1236 and 1462. Cited in Michael T. Florinski, *Russia: A History and an Interpretation* (New York: Macmillan, 1953), vol. 1, p. 61.

4. Charles XII ruled over a Sweden whose military reputation was very high. He was an early practitioner of the conservation of enemies: "I intend to finish first one of my enemies and then will talk with the other." Quoted in Robert K. Massie, *Peter the Great: His Life and World* (New York: Knopf, 1980), p. 319.

5. Adam B. Ulam, *Expansion and Coexistence: The History of Soviet Foreign Policy 1917–67* (New York: Frederick A. Praeger, 1968), p. 4.

6. In a series of three partitions, in 1772, 1793, and 1795, Poland was divided among Prussia, Russia, and Austria (Austria was involved in only the first and third partitions).

7. See Chapter 4, footnote 4. Adelman and Palmieri write that by early 1917 the Russian army "had suffered the staggering sum of over 7 million casualties, including nearly 2 million fatalities. . . ." Jonathan R. Adelman and Deborah Anne Palmieri, *The Dynamics of Soviet Foreign Policy* (New York: Harper & Row, 1989), p. 34.

8. A preliminary armistice was signed in December 1917, but the Bolsheviks then refused to negotiate. Soon what one author called "the first momentous Bolshevik debate on foreign policy" occurred. Eventually Germany, irritated by the Bolsheviks' delaying tactics, launched a general offensive. Shortly thereafter the treaty was signed. The quote is from Alvin Z. Rubinstein, ed., *The Foreign Policy of the South Union,* 3rd ed. (New York: Random House, 1972), p. 41.

9. The best succinct analysis of the entire episode remains George F. Kennan, *Russia and the West Under Lenin and Stalin* (New York: Mentor, 1962), Chs. 5–8. B. M. Unterberger, *America's Siberian Expedition, 1918–1920* (Durham, NC: Duke University Press, 1956) is also a key source.

10. Nikita Khrushchev, First Secretary, Communist Party of the Soviet Union, *Special Report to the 20th Congress of the Communist Party of the Soviet Union,* published by U.S. Department of State, June 4, 1956. Substantial sections of the secret speech are reprinted in Frederick H. Hartmann, ed., *World in Crisis: Readings in International Relations* (New York: Macmillan, 1962), pp. 253–61. The full text is also reprinted in Strobe Talbott, ed., *Khrushchev Remembers* (Boston: Little, Brown, 1970), Appendix 4, pp. 559–618.

11. According to Roy Medvedev, *Let History Judge: The Origins and Consequences of Stalinism,* rev. and expanded ed., ed. and trans. by George Shriver (New York: Columbia University Press, 1989), p. 454, "[B]etween 1936 and 1938 Stalin broke all records for political terror." No one will ever know the exact number of victims but at a minimum it was several million. See the excellent discussion in Walter Laqueur, *Stalin: The Glasnost Revelations* (New York: Charles Scribner's Sons, 1990), pp. 123–27.

12. As one would expect, perception and misperception, on both sides, played a major role in this process. See John G. Stoessinger, *Nations in Darkness: China, Russia, and America,* 4th ed. (New York: Random House, 1986), Ch. 10.

13. William Manchester, in *The Last Lion: Winston Spencer Churchill,* vol. 2, *Alone* (Boston: Little, Brown, 1988), tells a well documented and appalling story of how Prime Minister Chamberlain, by his actions, made the Soviet decision almost inevitable. The British press in those days was also resolutely avoiding the line in the sand that Hitler was repeatedly drawing. On May 28, 1938, Lord Beaverbrook, the publisher of the *Daily Express,* said in a front-page, signed editorial: "Britain will not be involved in war. There will be no major war in Europe this year or next year. The Germans will not seize Czechoslovakia. So go about your business with confidence in the future and fear

not." Then, the day after the Munich agreement, the *Express* headline on the front page was a single word, two inches tall: "PEACE." See James Reston's eyewitness account in his book, *Deadline* (New York: Random House, 1991), p. 62. No wonder the Soviets had doubts about England's real intentions. The discussion of this entire period by Robert Rothschild, a junior Belgian diplomat at the time, is worth reading. Robert Rothschild, *Peace for Our Time,* trans. [from the French] Anthony Rhodes (New York: Brassey's, 1988).

14. Joseph L. Nogee and Robert H. Donaldson, *Soviet Foreign Policy Since World War II,* 2nd ed. (New York: Pergamon Press, 1984), p. 27.

15. Lenin gives this argument in *Imperialism: The Highest Stage of Capitalism* (New York: International Publishers, 1939).

16. Compass Publications, Reprints from the Soviet Press, *L. I. Brezhnev: Report of the CPSU Central Committee and the Party's Immediate Objectives in Defense and Foreign Policy, XXVth Congress of the CPSU, 24 February 1976* (White Plains, NY: 1976), p. 40.

17. See *L. I. Brezhnev,* pp. 45–46.

18. See Gertrude E. Schroeder, "A Critical Time for Perestroika," *Current History,* October 1991, pp. 323–27, and her earlier "The Soviet Economy Under Gorbachev," *Current History,* October 1987, pp. 317–20, 344–46.

19. Mikhail Gorbachev, *Perestroika: New Thinking for Our Country and the World* (New York: Harper & Row, 1987). A fresh approach to problems was also being made in Soviet "think tanks" by the late 1950s, as Georgi Arbatov, the best-known Soviet expert on the United States, relates in his memoirs. See his *The System: An Insider's Life in Soviet Politics* (New York: Random House, 1992), for example, p. 211.

20. *Perestroika,* p. 24.

21. *Perestroika,* p. 10.

22. As Hough points out, since Gorbachev was placed under arrest the evening *before* the coup, one wonders why the radicals were not arrested in the many hours before the coup. See Hough, "Assessing the Coup," p. 305.

23. Among the most critical factors was the division in the military. Hough, 306. See the useful discussion in Seweryn Bialer, "The Death of Soviet Communism," *Foreign Affairs,* Winter 1991/92, pp. 177–78.

24. *The New York Times,* December 22, 1991.

25. *The Economist,* February 1, 1992. A June 14, 1992 article in *The New York Times* estimates that 82 percent of the 150 million people living *inside* Russia are ethnic Russians, meaning that there is a substantial minority problem there, too. It gives the figure of 25 million more Russians as scattered around the former parts of the USSR.

26. *The New York Times,* December 13, 1991.

27. *The Economist,* August 28, 1993.

28. In 1991, the Polish Parliament's lower house, the Sejm, had 460 seats divided among scores of parties on a proportional representation basis. Two of these had just over 12 percent of the vote, another four had just under 9 percent, and all the rest had less.

29. *The Economist,* November 9, 1991.

30. Paul Mohn, "Problems of Truce Supervision," *International Conciliation,* February, 1952.

16

The European Community

For more than four decades after World War II the world lived with an explosive unresolved problem. That problem was the division of Europe between East and West, with its accompanying tensions, including the deployment of large numbers of foreign troops on the soil of a divided Germany. That division was unnatural in the most basic sense of world politics. What was clear, though, was that in any condition, divided or united, from a priority point of view, there was no other region of the world so obviously of critical importance to the United States, especially Western and Central Europe. History confirmed this. The United States had intervened on the continent of Europe in two world wars to restore a threatened balance of power. And, after the postwar recovery period, Western Europe again became rich in those elements that provide the basis of political, economic, and military power. Western Europe became a prize player in the game, as well as a great prize.

Within this framework, until the late 1980s America's primary European concern was East-West relations. Then came the astounding changes detailed in Chapter 15. New priorities are now being established in Europe, and new political, economic, and military configurations and regimes proposed or created. To these the United States must have some policy response.

Major Decision Area 3: The European Community

Western Europe today is simultaneously attempting to move toward a closer union of Europe west of the old Iron Curtain line, while trying to digest both the addition of East Germany (caused by German reunification in 1990) and the pressures from states east of the old Curtain line to establish new relations with that "Western" community or even become part of it. The problem this poses for the United States is complicated. As Europe transforms itself into a single large scale market with no internal barriers, what changes does that imply for America's relations with it?[1] Another problem is, to the extent that there is no threat to the NATO nations, or that Western Europe develops a more common defense outside NATO, what role does that leave for NATO and what role for the United States in NATO? Unified Germany poses another problem. Germany will be a key actor in both the political-military and economic arenas. What will be the new American-German relationship? These and the other European problems America faces will make Washington's life interesting, to say the least.

A Confusing Array of Memberships

How should we think about these matters? It will help if we first pause to identify the players in Western Europe's confusing array of organizations.

Starting with the economic organizations, the first and most prominent is the European Community (EC), sometimes called "the Twelve." The EC has developed in several increments, with several name and structural changes. The first step was the establishment in 1952 of the European Coal and Steel Community. In 1958 came step 2, the establishment of the European Economic Community, or EEC (usually called the Common Market), with a core membership of West Germany, France, Italy, Holland, Belgium, and Luxembourg. The European Atomic Community was also established at this time, with the same core membership. In 1973, Ireland, Denmark, and the United Kingdom joined the Common Market, followed in 1981 by Greece. Then, in 1986, the membership was enlarged once more to include Spain and Portugal.[2]

Second, there is a European Free Trade Association (EFTA). EFTA in 1992 had seven members: Austria, Finland, Iceland, Liechtenstein, Norway, Sweden, and Switzerland. Obviously, these members fall into two main groups: peripheral states and neutral states, some being both. EFTA, as a free trade organization, has no internal tariffs between the members, but each member can set its own individual tariffs with the rest of the world.

On the political-military side, we have NATO. The EC Twelve, except Ireland, belong to NATO, whose membership, besides those eleven, includes Iceland, Norway, Canada, Turkey, and the United States. The EC Twelve, minus Denmark, Greece, and Ireland, are also members of the Western European Union (WEU), which antedates NATO (initially as the Western Union) and was its forerunner. The creation of NATO did not dissolve WEU, and WEU's future is now being discussed in connection with NATO's future.

There also is the Council of Europe, which is focused primarily on topics such as human rights and immigration. In 1991 it included all the West European countries already named, plus Czechoslovakia and Hungary (with other eastern nations prospectively joining). It is based in Strasbourg.

Finally, there is the Conference on Security and Cooperation in Europe (CSCE). Initially only a meeting of 35 nations convened in Helsinki from 1973 to 1975 to discuss various Cold War issues, CSCE did not become an "organization" in the usual sense because no permanent organs were established. A regular series of follow-up meetings occurred, however, and in the early 1990s CSCE began to change and permanent institutions and structures to be established.[3] CSCE is composed of *all* European countries (including the nations of central Europe and the European successor states to the old USSR), plus the United States and Canada. With this broad membership and the integrative and peaceful trends apparent after the Cold War, some saw the CSCE eventually becoming a major player in conflict resolution, perhaps even a sort of European security council or collective security organization.

Before concluding this introduction to European organizations, it is important to point out just a few facts and figures about the most significant economic actor, the EC, to show how important it really is. With 345 million people, the EC has a gross domestic product (GDP) of $6 trillion.[4] It provides 39 percent of world exports. Unlike EFTA, it combines aspects of three international intergovernmental mechanisms, each implying more unity than a free trade area among sovereign nations: a common market, a confederation, and a federation. Where a customs union has a common external tariff but no internal customs, the EC is that but more. It also has a common system of commercial law, adjudicated in a European court. The intent is to permit freedom of movement of goods, services, labor, and capital anywhere within the EC. Yet the Twelve retain most individual governmental functions, especially autonomy in foreign and military affairs (although there is considerable consultation). They are moving toward but have not yet achieved a common currency (discussed later). So they have some features of both the federation and the confederation.[5] Furthermore, they are not all of the same mind as to how fast or far to move toward greater unity, as we shall see.

An Evolving Western Europe: Politico-Military Features

The movement toward Western European integration, so much taken for granted today, has been neither steady nor rapid. Instead, it has been like a slow and turgid stream easily interrupted by rapids, side eddies, even beaver dams. It has flowed on, but very unevenly. Again, past-future linkages will be helpful. We shall first look back in order to see ahead more clearly.

The initial impetus for European integration came as a by-product of a fear that an unprepared Western Europe could once again be engulfed in war. The first step (an entirely European initiative), was the establishment of the Western Union (WU).[6] Signed on March 17, 1948, the WU entered into force on August 25, 1948. It linked Belgium, the Netherlands, Luxembourg, France, and the United Kingdom in an unprecedented 50-year military alliance. WU broke ground in its linking of France and the UK in an outright alliance (rather than a mere "understanding" as before World War I, or the equally vague arrangements before World War II). But even just its extraordinary duration set the WU apart from the usual 20-year alliance typically entered into on the brink of conflict. This agreement was really looking ahead to the long term, indicating that Western Europe was settling down quickly to face up to a potential threat, for Germany would surely grow strong again in time.

Two things changed this perspective. First, the fear-induced expectations that Germany's division would end fairly quickly proved incorrect. Second, the Cold War, especially with the Czech crisis and Berlin blockade in 1948, forced rethinking about who was really the threat. That new thinking led to the signing of the North Atlantic Pact on April 4, 1949 (in effect as of August 24, 1949). Then, as we saw in Chapter 9, came the North Korean assault on South Korea in June 1950. That was seen in the United States in particular as a "left-field play" to hit a Communist home run in the Far East once the "right-field play" over Berlin had failed. Although the initial impetus for defense organization had come from Europe, the United States now took the lead and was determined to convert the North Atlantic Treaty from a simple set of legal obligations into a permanent and broadly functioning organization.

The next logical question, especially in view of the Soviets' creation of an East German army (called by them, "police"), was what to do about some West German contribution. In September 1950, the United States proposed that the West Germans be allowed to rearm up to a ten-division level in an independent German army, while Germany would join NATO.[7] France reacted very negatively to this proposal and proposed the European Defense Community (EDC) treaty we discussed in Chapter 10. Paris saw the EDC as a way to rearm West Germany with minimum risks. As we also saw in Chapter 10, that EDC arrangement, agreed to in treaty form in May 1952, was repudiated by France at the end of August 1954. So, in 1955 West Germany was brought into NATO.

North Atlantic Treaty Organization

Within NATO a very complex command structure soon came into being. To show how this sometimes worked out in practice, in Operation WELDFAST in 1953 (which covered a thousand-mile radius around Athens) some fourteen separate commands were directly involved. These commands, based at Malta, Naples, Izmir, Algiers (then still under the French), Athens, Ankara, and Salonika, reported variously to Paris, Naples, Malta, or Izmir. But the major attention in NATO was focused in Germany, in NATO's Central Command.

The military problem NATO's far-flung membership faced was a difficult one, both on the critical central front in mid-Germany and also on the flanks in Norway and Turkey. The central front area configuration and order of battle gave an attacking force from the east an initial advantage. Although for most of its history NATO armed forces in total numbers exceeded Warsaw Pact numbers—in 1971, for example, for 14 NATO members versus 7 Warsaw Pact members, 5722.9 thousands versus 4788.0 thousands—*all* of the Eastern European and major concentrations of Soviet Warsaw Pact troops were in one area, while a large part of NATO's strength was on the flanks or in the United States, 3,000 miles away from the battlefield. For these reasons, among others, NATO evolved a military doctrine reserving its right to "first-use" of nuclear weapons to offset the conventional forces superiority of the Soviet-led pact.

Although various military strategies were developed, the problem of how to defend NATO's flanks was not adequately dealt with for years. Especially the northern flank. This NATO problem was intimately connected to American military strategy, especially the roles and missions of the navy. President Carter saw the U.S. Navy's Atlantic-area role essentially as one of escorting NATO's reinforcements. But President Reagan made a substantial improvement in what came to be called the "maritime strategy." The heart of that strategy was to deny the Soviets the chance to deploy their large submarine fleet into vast areas of the Atlantic, where they would be difficult to find. Instead, the U.S. Navy would take the war forward at the outset including, therefore, a defense of Norway, which would be critical to fencing the Soviets in.

The military strength of the alliance grew substantially over the years.[8] When General Eisenhower first activated his headquarters on January 7, 1951, he had but twelve divisions in his command, about 400 planes (few of them jets), and about the same number of ships. By 1954 there were significant improvements in army capabilities, most of the planes were now jets, and from virtually no jet-capable airfields, the number had increased by 1954 to 120 and to 160 by 1959. By 1960, as part of the joint infrastructure program, over 4,600 miles of fuel supply pipelines were working, some 26,500 miles of signal network was in place or nearly so, and storage tanks for over a half billion gallons of fuel had been constructed.

And progress continued. Indeed, over the years NATO succeeded in developing some common military doctrine, in creating a formidable, jointly-financed infrastructure, and in welding together units from various countries under a common command. Not that all problems were overcome. There continued to be variations in equipment and different national military doctrines. But there was substantial progress in standardizing weapons systems. And, in comparing NATO to Warsaw, we must also remember the critical fact that people of the Communist bloc nations, such as the Poles and Hungarians, let alone the East Germans, might or might not have fought for the Soviets if war had come.

But while substantial progress was made in the military area, there were a number of political problems. Some had significant military implications. We have mentioned the North Atlantic Council. The highest body in NATO, it makes decisions by unanimous votes. It meets at the ministerial level or at the permanent representative level. Between ministerial gatherings, the permanent representatives, all ranked as ambassadors, meet once or twice a week. Military policy is concerted in the Defense Planning Committee, consisting of the chiefs of staff of each member. *Except France.* The reason France is not in the Military Committee is that in 1966 President de Gaulle, angered at his inability to get NATO to accept his strategic concepts, withdrew France from the integrated defense arrangements. That forced a very expensive relocation of NATO headquarters to Brussels.

The removal of non-French forces from French soil, which was a part of de Gaulle's requirement, also compounded the NATO central front command problem. For it meant that NATO would have very little room for falling back once a massive Soviet attack was made. As a result, in military terms, NATO would have had to resort to nuclear weapons almost immediately. (That is precisely what de Gaulle wanted, for he was convinced that the Soviets would never attack if they were sure of being in a nuclear war almost from the outset.) There was still discreet military cooperation between French forces and NATO units, especially out of sight at sea. But there was no doubt that the military problem had become more difficult for outright political reasons—specifically, French pride.

The "French problem" was far from the only political problem NATO faced. For example, although both Greece and Turkey had joined the alliance, they continued their ancient feuds. (Turkey once held all of Greece, under the Ottoman Empire.) Their feuding became particularly intense over Cyprus, with its part-Greek, part-Turk population. What made the situation worse was the fact that some of the Greek islands are as little as five miles off the Turkish coast. Friction was built in, for both historical and military defense reasons. Both Greece and Turkey feared the Soviet colossus; but in times when the tension level between East and West went down, that between Greece and Turkey always went up. For years, the NATO commander in Naples, CINCSOUTH, spent much of his time on the political aspects of this feuding, rather than getting on with the military job.[10]

A third political problem came in the form of arguments over what to do about so-called "out-of-area" problems. NATO's defense responsibilities were defined in the treaty in geographical terms. The obligation for a common defense did not extend to other areas where one or more of the members might have interests. For example, if the Soviet Union attacked Japan, NATO obligations would not apply. But the United States, a member of NATO, has a treaty guaranteeing Japan's defense. What would NATO do in that case? As we saw, the question arose when Eisenhower was president as to what the European allies would do if America committed forces to aid France in Indochina. In 1990 when Iraq seized Kuwait, the obvious threat to all overcame this caution in that the NATO nations were solidly opposed to Saddam Hussein. But while Germany accepted the removal of U.S. heavy armored units from the NATO defense zone for use in that conflict, Germany was unwilling to become involved militarily itself. So these problems persist, some of them for historical reasons and some of them because the interests of the members of the alliance are often far-flung and of varying importance to those not directly and immediately affected.

Now that the military threat from the former Soviet Union has disappeared, NATO ponders its future role. We shall come back to this question later.

An Evolving Western Europe: Economic and Financial Features

We have mentioned earlier the positive role of the United States after World War II in helping Europe to its feet economically and financially. But Europe, remembering the 1930s, was also determined on its own to do it better this time.

It is useful at this point to elaborate on the development of the EC, mentioned briefly earlier. The European Community came about in several stages, beginning with the creation of the European Coal and Steel Community in 1952.[11] Then on March 25, 1957, the Common Market and Euratom treaties were signed in Rome, the EEC and EAC beginning operations the next year. The principle of a common external tariff on coal and steel, coupled with no tariffs on such products *within* the Community, was now extended to other goods. By the end of 1961, progressive tariff cuts within the Common Market had already reduced tariffs by 40 percent. At the same time, the Market moved toward its goal of a common external tariff. The transition period in the Rome Treaty ended on schedule, on December 31, 1969. Even before that, by July 1, 1968, all customs duties and quantitative restrictions on trade in industrial goods had been abolished within what was now termed the "European Economic Community," or EEC. The common tariff for imports from nonmember nations went into effect as well. By this time the benefits of increased economic integration and rapidly growing productivity were apparent. "In 1966 the Common Market overtook the United States to become the world's largest exporter."[12]

The union of the "inner six" confronted the rest of Western Europe with a problem. Less inclined to the kind of more organic union implied by the EEC arrangement, the "outer seven" (Austria, Denmark, Norway, Portugal, Sweden, Switzerland, and the United Kingdom—with Finland as an "associate") had in 1960 formed the already mentioned European Free Trade Association. EFTA had less ambitious goals than the EEC arrangements. In particular, it lacked the overtones of eventual political unity.

Britain's position remained particularly ambivalent. In mid-1961, the United Kingdom requested discussions looking toward joining the Common Market. President de Gaulle, always suspicious of the British, vetoed the British request on January 14, 1963. The requests of other EFTA members to join were also not acted on. Now EFTA exports stagnated while EC *intra*community trade grew 168 percent between 1958 and 1964.

After de Gaulle retired in April 1969, the issue was reopened and on January 1, 1973, after difficult negotiations, the United Kingdom, Denmark, and Ireland entered the EC, bringing the total then to nine. Austria, Norway, and Finland were given loose links to the EC. As we saw earlier, in 1981, Greece became a full member, and in 1986 Spain and Portugal made it twelve.

The decade since has brought conflicting tendencies and major problems to the Community. One crosscurrent has been created by the incompatibility of simultaneously moving toward a closer economic and political community and admitting most of the nations of Eastern Europe who say they wish to join.[13] With the Community also attempting to reach agreement on a common currency, admission of these nations, most of whose currencies are nonconvertible into hard currency, might wreck such a project.

The second crosscurrent is the very old argument about agricultural policy. A common EC agricultural market was established in 1964, with uniform prices beginning in 1967. Subsidies were widespread. That issue took a new turn when Spain was given membership and Spanish wine began to compete more directly with French wine. With almost two-thirds of the Community budget spent on agriculture, the EC took these issues seriously. But agriculture subsidies, particularly dear to the hearts of German and French farmers, were also a major stumbling block to the "Uruguay Round" of GATT, where the United States had fundamental interests at stake.

Major Decision Area 4: GATT, Trade, Subsidies

Earlier, in mentioning GATT, the General Agreement on Tariffs and Trade, we described its successful beginning. After that first effort in 1947, others followed. Over the years many sets of discussions have taken place and the number of parties involved has grown. These discussions are, reasonably enough, called "rounds." Sometimes such rounds are spread over considerable periods of time—it all depends on when all those necessary to progress have agreed on the next steps. Already, by 1961, there were 37 contracting parties. After the United States in 1962 replaced the old Reciprocal Trade Agreement Act with a new

Trade Expansion Act authorizing a further 50 percent reciprocal reduction in tariffs, GATT went into high gear. The "Kennedy Round," which lasted for three years and ended in May 1967, involved almost half the nations of the world. The EC (then still known as the EEC or European Economic Community) bargained as a bloc. About $40 billion of trade, especially between industrialized countries, was liberalized. Over a four year period beginning in January 1968, tariffs were reduced about a third. In the "Tokyo Round," concluded in 1979, there were 99 parties. By 1979, seven rounds had been conducted.

The long negotiations that began in 1986, the "Uruguay Round" (named after the country in which the negotiations began) has been as difficult as any and in some respects more difficult than any. That is because it has taken place in the shadow of Western Europe's move toward its goal of more complete economic unity, bringing U.S.-EC divergent interests to a focus over the agricultural subsidies question. As analysts have pointed out, as the 1990s began the United States was no longer willing to subordinate its economic objectives to its security concerns.[14] There are three main reasons why: the continuing U.S. trade imbalance, the lessening of security concerns, and the need to reduce the flood of American dollars in foreign hands, which could, under certain conditions, destabilize the U.S. economy and undermine international currency transactions. These considerations, not surprisingly, are all interrelated.

Trade, Money, and Gold

Take the supplies of dollars issue first. The dollar was indisputably the key and indispensable world currency in the 1950s (and for some time thereafter). Gold no longer reigned supreme. As Europe sought to recover from World War II, it had to make large purchases from the United States. The dollar was in great demand, and the shortage of dollars was acute.

Eventually, however, the shortage was replaced by a dollar glut. This came about, mostly for two reasons. First, the United States poured $4–5 billion a year into Europe in the Marshall Plan and to support its forces in Germany. Second, American private investment abroad exceeded foreign capital inflows, adding another $2 billion annually. Then, over time, another factor contributed to the problem: an "adverse" (i.e., more imports than exports) balance of trade added still more dollars abroad.[15] These factors, combined, eventually produced an overall U.S. balance of payments deficit.

The balance of payments deficit, of course, was a phenomenon with ramifications far beyond America's European policy. Indeed, it demonstrated two interrelated and quite fundamental principles (which have become increasingly important with the passage of time): (1) there is a significant interconnection between regional and global economic issues; (2) America's overall international economic position affects its regional policies, and vice-versa.

The European dollar glut threatened to undo the careful work with which the Western world, under U.S. leadership, had prepared to face its economic future after World War II. In July 1944, at Bretton Woods, New Hampshire, two institutions were created by international agreement to deal with money and finance.[16] The first of these, the International Bank for Reconstruction and Development (now called the World Bank), is a publicly owned financial institution that sells bonds on commercial terms and lends the proceeds for investments to countries in need. Its function was to promote development. We shall return to the World Bank in Chapter 19.

The second institution was the International Monetary Fund (IMF).[17] Remembering the financial chaos of the 1920s and 1930s, the Western nations now sought some order and cooperation so they could have a mutually beneficial and smoothly operating trading system. The IMF was created to help bring that about. It was designed to lay down the ground rules for international finance and serve as a instrument of advice and cooperation. It could provide financial assistance to countries in external deficit.

Initially, the IMF charter provided for fixed exchange rates. What actually developed was a system in which currencies were pegged to each other but rates were allowed to adjust by discrete amounts whenever the system moved out of equilibrium. Within this framework, members settled their debts in dollars, which could then be exchanged for gold. Central banks maintained the value of national currencies in terms of the dollar. At bottom, this system was based on the dollar's convertibility to gold. When necessary, the United States stood ready to buy and sell gold (from and to foreign central banks) at a fixed price. The dollar at that time was valued at a fixed $35 dollars an ounce and that fixed conversion rate stayed in effect for years.

This linkage of the dollar to gold was practical, provided no great surplus of dollars developed in world reserves at a time when gold prices were increasing. But even though *individual* trading in gold by U.S. citizens was prohibited and the dollar-to-gold conversion was the privilege of central banks, gold's price in the world's free market could not be controlled. And there gold was steadily increasing in value. The strain of this widely divergent, two-price system would have caused trouble even apart from what soon began to happen to the U.S. trade balance. But as the years went by, foreign nations held increasingly large dollar surpluses and began to convert dollars into gold. The United States, which in 1949 had held two-thirds of the world's monetary gold, by 1967 had only $12.1 billion left, less than one-third.

As the 1960s ended and the 1970s began, therefore, two actions were taken to disconnect the direct link of the dollar to gold. First, the IMF severed the link between the central bank transactions of IMF members and the free market in gold. Although the U.S. dollar link to gold was still in place then, gold could be traded in many markets like any other commodity. Its price fluctuations became highly volatile. For example, early in 1974, it was already $114.75 an ounce. By the end of that same year it was $197.50. In 1980, in a single day's trading in New York on January 17, gold prices fluctuated $105 an ounce! The London market price, $524 on the last day of 1979, was $835 nineteen days later. Where the November 1980 price was $637, it fell to $494 on January 29, 1981, and to $346.50 on March 4, 1982. Although the price was much more stable over the next decade,[18] any crisis at any time could cause its price to soar beyond any *economic* justification.

The outflow of U.S. gold was, as indicated, linked to what was happening to the U.S. balance of trade and payments. Where, between 1950 and 1958, U.S. merchandise exports had increased 64 percent against increased imports of only 44 percent, by 1955 a change was setting in which was to prove persistent. Between 1955 and 1959, exports increased only 14 percent while imports went up 33 percent. In dollar terms, the gap was narrowed from $2.9 to $1.1 billion. (Meanwhile, for comparison, world trade between 1948 and 1969 increased from $121.1 billion to $553.0 billion—certainly a tribute to U.S. efforts.) By mid-1971, as the trend continued, the *United States* trade balance had actually turned adverse.[19] Gold reserves had also sunk to the lowest level since 1938—$10.5 billion. On August 11, 1971, President Nixon, took the second action, suspending dollar convertibility into gold. Then he also devalued the dollar.

The IMF, already seeing the handwriting on the wall, as early as 1967 had introduced a new gold "substitute" in what was called Special Drawing Rights (SDRs). These SDRs were to alleviate some of the strains in the world's banking system by providing an alternate way to amass reserves. SDRs allowed member nations to draw on each other's currencies while being required to repay only 30 percent of a nation's first five-year net use. The idea was that world reserves would expand by the amount not repayable. Between January 1, 1970 and January 2, 1972, a total of $9.5 billion was thus added to world reserves. (This helped finance a world trade that by 1979 had reached $1.6 billion.) These moves, while desirable, did not go to the heart of America's trade imbalance or take away the problem that Nixon confronted by severing the dollar's convertibility to gold.

The establishment of SDRs (and the end of the dollar link to gold) put more emphasis than ever on the problem of currency convertibility. (And convertibility rests, for one of its pillars, on some stabilization of rates of exchange. In turn, rates of exchange fluctuate with domestic economic conditions. And, for most nations, economic conditions are largely the result of domestic political and economic factors.) Given the volatility of gold values alone, it would not be possible to go back to a link based on gold. But free convertibility, resting on free markets in currency, is not a good answer, either. Shifting exchange rates constitute one of the most serious restraints to trade. What free markets in currency do add to the picture, however, is an outside standard that casts skepticism if the official rates of currencies are too obviously high or low.

It has been necessary to examine the Bretton Woods system and follow-on developments in some detail to provide the context for understanding EC concerns. What the EC actually attempted was to create values that have a certain range, within which each major EC currency could fluctuate. That did not do away with fluctuation. For example, in December 1991, the British pound was pushing the lower limit of its set range, while the German mark was at its upper limit. But the system set limits. For a while the European Monetary System (or EMS) worked quite effectively. In October 1992, however, severe problems arose. When the British pound's value declined drastically and the government was unable to keep it at the minimum price, London dropped out of the EMS. Italy soon followed suit. Then in November, Spain and Portugal devalued their currencies. While this helped temporarily, as long as Germany (the key economic power) kept interest rates high, the future of the other EC currencies, and the EMS itself, were in question. As long as *national* priorities took precedence, the system's integrity would be in question.

Fluctuations in currency values against trade show how volatile the changes can be and, therefore, how disruptive. Consider that the ability of the dollar to command goods in international trade rose 67 percent between 1980 and its high point in the first quarter of 1985. Then, by 1987, it had fallen below the level at which it had begun its rise. The fluctuations for some of the principal Latin American currencies and their changes between 1985 and 1991 were enormous. The ups and downs are driven largely by the various divergent domestic policies of these nations and reflect varying degrees of inflation and divergent approaches to national debt servicing.

Political Complications

As the United States dealt with the evolving EC, political factors further complicated the already complex interplay of domestic, regional, and global economic factors. With the United States trade balance already adverse, the fourth round in the Arab-Israeli wars, as we saw earlier, led Middle Eastern Arab states in 1973 to impose an oil embargo on nations considered friendly to Israel. They also restricted supplies by cutting back production. Next, the Organization of Petroleum Exporting Countries (OPEC), which is dominated by Middle Eastern oil, raised prices fourfold in less than one year!

The results were devastating to the world economy. The industrial West, including Japan, had been riding the crest of a substantial boom, bringing with it already some inflationary pressures. Then came the Arab and OPEC actions, throwing the industrial nations into a worldwide recession. Raw material prices in underdeveloped nations crashed. Finished goods prices in developed countries shot up. The poorer nations, already paying $22 billion for oil before these events, and heavily in debt, now faced drastically higher oil prices just as their incomes sank. Inflation in the industrial nations hit hard. Using 1970 prices as 100, by mid-1974 Japan's cost of living figure was 148. The United Kingdom's figure stood at 143. Italy was 138. The United States was 123. But Chile's figure was 3730 and Argentina's was 385.

The United States, which had managed a trade surplus again ($1.4 billion in 1973), found itself with a $3 billion trade deficit in 1974. The cost of its oil imports alone in that same period increased by almost $17 billion.

With the dollar glut persisting and made much worse by these developments, the OPEC nations blindly continued to raise prices (especially to finance the increasing arsenals in the Middle East). That increased the price of a barrel of oil more than 150 percent more in 1979 and 1980. And by 1979, the United

States was importing vastly more oil than it produced. (The subsequent ins and outs of this topic we shall return to in Chapter 19, as we examine the economic effects first of the Iran-Iraq War and then of Iraq's devastation of Kuwait.) These fluctuations were major dislocations to trade and to financial stability, and they show on the one hand the interdependence of nations in today's world economy and, on the other hand, the interlock between politics and economics. That interlock is highly important in what is going on today with the EC as it seeks to achieve a single currency and perhaps even political union; the interlock is also highly important to the connected question of agricultural subsidies, which lies at the heart of the disputes in the Uruguay Round.

Trade and Politics: the United States and the EC

As the EC moves toward closer integration, then, a rather complicated foreign policy problem confronts the United States. It is not a just a question of tariffs, although that remains important. Nor is it just a question of subsidies. It is both larger and smaller. It is larger in the sense of the question of what kind of Europe will the EC be, and what will its relation to America be? Will it be a large inward-looking "fortress" that keeps the United States out as much as possible, essentially a competitor? Or will the EC be more open? The issue is smaller because it also deals with the narrower issues of daily business operations.

As we continue to stress, America cannot deal with EC issues in isolation from the U.S. international economic position in general. There, too, sometimes specific issues seem small, but they really are not. The difficulties that the United States has had in penetrating the Japanese rice market are one illustration among many. That specific problem has particular importance because of the persistent imbalance of trade between the United States and Japan.

Many American businessmen, contemplating doing business abroad, are more concerned with these kinds of problems than with tariff or even currency complications. And the president and Congress must be, and are, sensitive to the concerns of business. What if the EC, as it moves toward standardization in commercial law, sets standards that American business cannot readily meet or does not wish to meet? Suppose, for example, there are compulsory added costs per employee for benefits not customary in the United States. True, the American businessman has the option of not doing business under such circumstances. But that means opting out of a very large market. These questions will need much further study.

Thus, the argument over agricultural subsidies was only one aspect of America's complicated relations with the EC and the world outside U.S. doors. Even here the United States is not alone in its concern. Australia, Argentina, Brazil, and Canada—all of them agricultural exporting countries—also clamor for reforms in subsidies. And the developing nations want subsidy reductions as well. Within the EC itself there is no unanimity. France has the most to lose if the subsidies are reduced, followed by Germany. As negotiations continue, all sides are still struggling to find some compromise formula.

Crosscurrents Within the EC

What makes it even harder for the EC to reach agreement on the agricultural issue is that there are competing crosscurrents. Simultaneously, the EC has been dealing with three separate but interrelated problems: the GATT issue of subsidies, with its internal aspects as with Spain; a proposed treaty for a closer political union; and a proposal for a single currency.

The idea of real political union is very controversial. Britain, to say the least, has been at best lukewarm. It debated for years whether to ask for EC membership and, once it did was admitted, for years thereafter voted consistently against enlarged EC powers. Germany and France have been the primary promoters of closer union, but Germany's unification has revived much of Germany's historical interest, economically and politically, in Eastern Europe. This has not been received with unmitigated joy in the East,[20] however, but the reality is that Eastern Europe has little choice except to seek aid and trade from Germany. Germany's role in the development of central and eastern Europe (and the former states of the Soviet Union) will be enormous.

It is abundantly clear, therefore, that Germany is not interested in tying itself exclusively to Western Europe, although it certainly is loath to revive fears of a new German European dominance—fears fanned into flames as the Soviet Union dissolved and a Commonwealth of Independent States was formed. At the same time, there also is no doubt that making the EC function effectively is a top priority in Berlin. As Robert Livingston correctly writes "As the world's second-largest exporter, Germany has every interest in keeping the EC's trading practices open. . . ."[21] But in the EC, too, the issue of potential German dominance weighs heavily. Regardless of perspective, it is evident that Germany will be one of the two dominant powers in Europe, and perhaps the leader. That prospect makes some of the other EC nations wonder whether it is wise to have the giant new German power inside a political union, where it might "legitimately" dominate their affairs.

Another question yet to be resolved concerning union is how far very different national cultures can really be combined. Even the proposal for a single European currency has implications for a more unified social policy within the various states. Common currency assumes substantially similar standards of living (or at least, no enormous highs and lows from one country to the other). It assumes rates of inflation that are in reasonable harmony with each other. (As 1991 was ending, consumer-price inflation in some of the EC countries was as follows: Belgium, 2.2; France, 2.6; Germany, 3.5; Holland, 4.4; Italy, 6.1; Spain, 5.5; U.K., 4.1.) And it assumes a national willingness to have the national currency replaced by a multinational currency, something many Europeans object to.

Western Europe, with its fairly fixed exchange rates, has had some experience with this problem, as we pointed out earlier. But Poland, Czechoslovakia, and Hungary, admitted as "associate members" to the EC in November 1991, constitute a different case altogether. They wanted full membership before long, but they were nowhere near establishing stable currencies and controlling inflation rates.[22] In fact, the associate members are still in the early stages of going over to a free market economy, so they can only be admitted after quite a long transition period. But not all the EC members look at the problem in the same way. Germany, always also looking eastward, would probably like to move faster than the rest.

The political union and single currency issues came to a head in December 1991, as the Community met at the Dutch town of Maastricht to consider two draft treaties. The first of these was the single currency proposal to create a European Monetary Union, or EMU. The process would occur in stages, moving toward the creation in the third stage of a European Central Bank. That third stage, to come some time after 1997, would be preceded by more flexible arrangements arranged under the European Monetary Institute, or EMI. On December 9 the members agreed that the common currency would be in effect by January 1999, but they included a provision that allowed members to choose not to take part. (The British clearly had reservations; so did the Danes.) The switch to the ECU (European currency unit) would occur as early as 1997, provided that a majority of EC nations voted for it and that at least seven EC nations had inflation rates and budget deficits within defined limits.[23] If that did not happen, those nations that were within the defined limits would automatically make the switch in 1999, without further vote. As few as two nations could form the initial group, with other nations joining as they qualified.

The ECU has been used as a statistical measure since the move to stabilize European currency exchange rates. It has represented a "basket" of these currencies (much like the device used by the World Bank). What will be new is that actual ECU bills and coins will be issued. On one side will be the symbol of EC—twelve gold stars in a circle. On the other side, individual national symbols can be retained. One estimate put the savings that would be achieved in intra-community trade at $18 billion a year, simply from not having to juggle currencies.[24] Another estimate expressed the point this way: If you currently took 1,000 English pounds and went from one country to another through the whole EC, changing the money in and out each time, by the time you got home, assuming you spent nothing in each country, you would still only have 500 pounds. Half the money would have gone simply into transfers! Whether such statistics are accurate or not, there can be no question that the use of the ECU would represent a huge savings.

The second treaty was equally ambitious, providing for a European Political Union that would try to harmonize the foreign policy interests of EC members and give the EC a voice in international affairs by creating common foreign and security policies.

What was particularly controversial about the second treaty was its extensive grant of power to the Community, allowing the Community to do what it likes in its assigned areas of competence, rather than utilizing provisions similar to those in the U.S. Constitution that (can) restrict "federal" power to areas where the federal government must obviously operate (foreign affairs and defense, among others).

What actually will happen and how far this all will go remains uncertain, though. When it comes right down to doing it, to what extent will these nations voluntarily surrender their sovereign power over their countries' internal affairs, foreign policy, matters of national defense, and so on? Will Germans cheerfully give Frenchmen authority for key decisions about Germany's future in these areas? Or, vice versa? Is nationalism *kaput* in Western Europe? (In June, 1992, Danish votes *rejected* the treaty on European union, and shortly thereafter French voters approved by only the slimmest of margins. Although in May 1993, Danish voters reversed course and ratified the treaty, it was a version with many of the commitments removed. Denmark would not have to accept a common defense policy, single currency, or common immigration and justice policies.)[25]

Handling the sovereignty/multilateral economic benefits issue is not nearly as easy as media reports sometimes imply. The British have been especially vocal on the issue, even when the discussion focuses only on economics. *The Economist* of November 2, 1991, said: "It is foolish within the existing Community, let alone in an expanding one, to seek to impose from the centre a uniform system of labour relations, equal opportunities, working hours and minimum wages." At the Maastricht meeting, British Prime Minister John Major made this very point, objecting strongly to plans to create EC-wide norms on social policies such as paid holidays and health benefits.[26] Spain's Prime Minister Felipe Gonzalez indicated that Spain would vote against the second treaty if Spain, Greece, Portugal, and Ireland did not gain assurance from the rest that their share of development funds would be substantially increased above the current annual $15 billion. (This was a problem that would surely recur if and when the EC was further enlarged.)

There is another side to the question of enlarging the Community's powers, for one of the incentives for the EC to move to closer economic unity was, interestingly enough, the feeling that Europe was losing its competitive edge to America and to Japan. American global businesses in particular were establishing branches in various European countries—something European companies were doing only on the most restricted scale.

To prepare the way for establishing branches on some similar scale in Europe by European companies meant abolishing restrictive practices and non-tariff barriers within the Community. Many Americans assume that the EC would have done all of this years ago, but it is not so. In June 1985, the European Commission still listed roughly 280 such measures. In the years that followed, the Council of Ministers and European Parliament approved 198 of 282 proposed single-market directives. But these, to be effective, have to be passed into law by European national parliaments, and not all are responsive or quick to do so. Italy, in particular, lags. By the end of June 1991, only 37 of the 126 proposed laws had been enacted by all 12 EC states.[27]

Even so, great progress was being made. A "Single Administrative Document" was in place by the end of 1991, replacing seventy pieces of paperwork formerly required at customs posts. But these are not the kinds of changes Prime Minister Major was pointing out; everyone knows these changes will simply have to be made if the EC is to get on with its program.

Beyond the issues being handled at the Maastricht meeting, some of the other issues also are causing problems. The EC is split on how far to proceed to create a European army, for example. It also is divided on the question of creating a more unified foreign policy approach to out-of-area crises. The civil war in Yugoslavia in the second half of 1991 was particularly humiliating to the EC. Some who argued for more effective political union (with Germany in the lead) wanted foreign policy issues to be *chosen* by unanimous vote but *handled* for implementation by majority vote in the EC Council of Ministers. Naturally, Britain was the most skeptical of this approach. The EC intervened in the Yugoslav crisis in an effort to bring about a compromise, but it failed. Then, when Croatia and Slovenia seceded, the majority of the EC advised a go-slow approach, avoiding quick diplomatic recognition. Germany, however, took a different tack and quickly granted recognition.[28] Somewhat sheepishly, the rest of the EC followed.

These complicated arguments and problems will take a long time to sort out, but the *direction* in which Western Europe is moving and the nature of the fundamental foreign policy decisions that will, therefore, confront the United States, are becoming clear enough.

Summing Up

The American association with Western Europe since World War II has been a close and continuing one, embracing military, political, and economic interests. Without the Marshall Plan and other constructive policies of the United States designed to prime the pump to restore European production after the war, the history of the last decades would have been vastly different. Khrushchev's crude boast that our grandchildren would be Communists might, after all, have come true. It was the United States that led the way, via the World Bank and IMF, to the stabilization of currencies, so fundamental to a revival of world trade. It was the United States, in its decision to move to lower tariffs as far as possible, that made GATT rounds feasible. It was America's prime role in NATO that allowed Europe to be sufficiently free of threat to make the economic progress we have noted.

But, of course, it was not a unilateral American show. Ultimately the Europeans had to make it work. Remembering the problems caused by the policies of the victors after World War I, the victorious Europeans this time turned away from the idea of reparations "to the last farthing." While America played the prime role in NATO, the alliance was established only after the European nations already had shown their willingness to ally to defend themselves. Behind

NATO's protective shield, the Europeans expended great efforts and made enormous economic progress. It was European ideas promoting European integration that led step by step to the present-day EC. There is enough credit to go round.

We have focused much of our attention in this chapter on economic matters, largely within the framework of multilateral organizations. This is because, as the United States faces the future, that clearly is the direction events are taking. The security-focused bilateral U.S.-Soviet relationship, which for so long had dominated European affairs, has become "old history." Indeed, with the end of the Cold War—the dissolution of the Soviet Union and demise of the Warsaw Pact—the future (and even the existence) of NATO was uncertain. What was the threat? It was certain, though, that a major American force withdrawal was in the offing, although no one knew exactly how far it should or would go.

Thus, as the United States looked ahead in 1993, much was unclear. What *was* clear, though, was that even if geopolitical circumstances had changed significantly, America's interests in maintaining the European balance of power and some degree of regional stability had not. And there still were many problems. Although the Soviet threat as such was gone, very powerful military forces still existed in several of the former Soviet republics. Unified Germany now, inevitably, would play an increasingly powerful role in European affairs. What would that mean for American interests? Would the Eastern European instability we examined in Chapter 15 explode into more violence? Moreover, it was just in the nature of things that there would be unexpected problems. Throughout history, crises and conflicts have occurred that no one could reasonably have anticipated. The "bottom line" was that despite the truly enormous and in many ways positive changes that had occurred, the United States could not blithely assume that peace and harmony would now and forever characterize European relations. Security concerns could not be ignored.

Because of this, both the Bush and Clinton administrations believed America had to remain productively engaged. While some observers believed NATO was becoming largely irrelevant, Washington's assessment was that this judgment was too premature. NATO had a long-standing record of success, and its members recognized its value, even if perhaps its form and function might have to change somewhat. Furthermore, they also realized that maintaining NATO was the only sure way of keeping the Americans in Europe, something they all desired (at least, to some extent). They knew that the EC, though perhaps the organization others would *someday* look to in matters of security as well as the economy, was not able to act in that capacity *now*.

NATO, meanwhile, was adapted quickly to the changing circumstances. It adopted a new military strategy emphasizing mobility. It also established the North Atlantic Cooperation Council (NACC) to expand and facilitate relations with the former Soviet bloc countries. The NACC's membership consisted of the NATO nations, CIS states, the Baltic republics, and several nations in Eastern Europe. Early meetings showed considerable promise.

The central policy issue for the United States in all these various political-military matters was the role America would play in shaping and managing the new security landscape. The primary policy alternatives were, on the one hand, seeking the play the *lead* role as it had done in NATO in the Cold War, as opposed to a policy of *relatively equal partnership* working cooperatively to develop and alter policies and processes.

Although political-military matters certainly could not be ignored, there still was no doubt that (barring entirely unanticipatable events) the primary focus of America's European policy for the next several years would be economic issues, within an interconnected domestic/regional/global framework. In this arena some might have said the United States had a choice between two very divergent alternatives: continue its long-standing advocacy of freer trade, or retreat into a considerably more protectionist stance. But this would have been a poor way to frame the decision, because in today's interdependent world the second option was simply not feasible. With the share of trade in the U.S. economy having risen by two and a half times since 1960 and exports and imports of goods and services amounting to nearly one-quarter of GDP,[29] America simply could not adopt protectionist policies that would severely reduce trade. The *real* alternatives were an advocacy of even freer trade versus *relatively* free trade with selectively imposed restrictions.

Given the economic recession of 1990–93, many voices in the United States were heard advocating increasing trade restraints. That was understandable, but to go too far in that direction would be a mistake. But it would also be a mistake to overlook the fact that the United States it not always competing on a level playing field. We have already stressed the role of agricultural subsidies within the EC. Since the United States for years has been very efficient in agricultural production, providing great surpluses over domestic needs, and since the American trade balance has been adverse, the United States is quite right to push this issue. Free trade has to mean freedom in both directions. To get an idea of the extent of this particular problem, consider that at the end of GATT's "Kennedy Round," the reductions in dutiable agricultural imports were significantly less than those on industrial products. For the EC, for example, reductions in duties on manufactured imports went down by 2.9 percent and reductions on other imports except agricultural went down 3.2 percent. But duties on agricultural imports went down only 2.1 percent. Since the United States equivalent figures were 2.5, 2.1, and 1.5 percent, it is not a case that the EC did nothing and the United States something. It is simply that to get to freer trade, agriculture is an obvious area to work on. (This is even more obvious if we look outside Western Europe at Japan. Their figures were 1.8, 0.1, and 0.5.)

Recognizing this, American and EC negotiators worked the problem hard, and in November 1992, a general agreement (which, they hoped *eventually* would lead to a resolution) was announced. It was said that differences had been resolved on the "main elements" concerning domestic support, export subsidies, and market access. But two things still had to occur: (1) further successful negotiations on the respective country schedules, and (2) eventually, multilateralization and agreement by all the GATT participants.

Free trade is important, but a laissez-faire approach to international economic problems is not a panacea. Nor is it appropriate at all times and in all places. It is a sobering thought that in the 1991 Persian Gulf War, in one particular "American" weapon system, eighty-three microchips were used. Eighty-two of these were of Japanese manufacture.[30] The other one came from a British firm backed by Japanese capital. It is well here to remember the cardinal principle of counterbalancing national interests, especially that there are pluses and minuses for *each* alternative, and that they are not the simple reverse values. The four values are separate and distinct. That means that there is a disadvantage to assuming that, given free trade, everyone everywhere will prosper because the international division of labor will be efficient. A completely free trade view also assumes that it makes no difference who produces what, but from a national perspective it surely does make a difference. Such a view forces one to overlook everything but the question of international economic efficiency, and that is too narrow.

It was a very positive contribution by the United States to supply the dollars for world economic reconstruction after World War II, but those days of dollar shortages are long past. As America goes on importing more than it exports, it inevitably piles up dollars abroad which, when in great surplus as now, form IOUs on the future. Increasing exports (or cutting down imports) cannot easily be done without causing a decline in the American standard of living. Goods made abroad at wages far less than U.S. wages, which then enter freely into the United States, will ultimately either cost American jobs or depress American wages, or both, with many attendant social and psychological effects as well (which is one reason Congress is so involved, as we saw earlier). Some balance is necessary here.

In an overall sense though, in trade and other political-economic matters, there is little reason for the United States to oppose the general direction Europe is presently taking, even if certain specifics require careful attention. In the area of movement toward greater unity, America must always remember that although it can somewhat affect the pace and contours of developments, it cannot unilaterally change the ultimate outcome. The days of America determining Europe's future are gone.

As events unfold, Washington is faced with the problem of maintaining a reasonable degree of influence while not overstepping its bounds. A key issue in this regard will be how to deal not only with the particular nations of Europe, but also how much and how to deal with the EC as an entity. It will be important to avoid the long-ingrained habit of basing policy on some abstract generalization and deducing the specifics from there. Actually, no useful generalization can be developed in this area yet, because the situation is too much in flux. Indeed, the Europeans themselves do not know where and how fast things will go. The answer here is to have a flexible approach that *takes its cue from the Europeans, themselves.* Where *they* act within the framework of the EC as an entity, America must treat it as such. Where they do not, more traditional bilateral and multilateral approaches are recommended.

To return to political-military issues for a minute, America must keep a cautious eye on Europe's occasional desire to revive the idea of a European army to function as an alternative to NATO. Particularly important here will be how to respond to the increasing Franco-German security cooperation. In the late 1980s, a 4,200-man joint Franco-German brigade was established outside NATO, and a Franco-German Defense and Security Council as well. In 1992, France and Germany carried things one step further, announcing plans for a 35,000-man French-German "Eurocorps" by 1995. These developments, along with the changes in NATO to smaller, more mobile, multinational forces, left the European security architecture quite unclear.

Nonetheless, and despite the obvious drive for a greater and more independent European defense capability, America's position was that NATO was still very valuable. Even though in early 1993 President Clinton's new secretary of defense, Les Aspin, ordered DoD to reduce the American troop presence in Europe to 100,000 by 1996, Washington still intended to play a major role in Europe and give NATO strong support. There is, after all, a long track record of cooperation. To begin again from scratch, if that became necessary, would throw away much of the investment so laboriously and expensively made in infrastructure and multinational exercises with U.S. forces.

There is one more issue to be addressed, one we have mentioned several times in passing but that needs further exploration: American policy toward Germany. As we have said repeatedly, in the next few years unified Germany will become the dominant power on the continent (if it is not already). As Germany becomes more independent and assertive, America's role will be somewhat reduced. Accepting this change in roles and power and developing a productive if different relationship will be difficult for the United States.[31] It is not clear yet, of course, exactly what courses German policy will take. In the early aftermath of unification, Germany's foreign policy was essentially regional, focused particularly on the EC and Eastern Europe, and was concerned primarily with economic interests and maintaining stability. That all may continue. It may well be, as Elizabeth Pond has stated, that all German policymakers and major political parties "agree that the German future can be secured within a uniting Europe . . ."[32] and that its reluctance to join the American-led coalition in the Gulf War "will typify its approach outside Europe for the foreseeable future: pay, if it must, but not play."[33] But, maybe not. Maybe once the travails of unification have been overcome, German policy will become more globalist. Or, maybe Germany will try to dominate the EC to advance narrow German interests. Or, something else.

America cannot yet know the direction German policies will take, because the Germans themselves do not yet know. But for America that is not the real issue. The real issue is what approach will be most beneficial in forging a productive new relationship that will maintain a reasonable degree of American influence bilaterally, within a multilateral context that includes the EC and NATO. The primary alternatives are attempting to exert American leadership, or pursuing the counterbalancing interest of a genuine partnership, of seeking to be a "co-leader" in Europe, if you will. Our judgment is that the latter is preferable, although this will be very hard for Americans to accept, psychologically. This is the direction in which the Clinton administration was fitfully moving in 1993, however.

When we assess America's foreign policy choices toward Europe, then, we come out with the conclusion that there is, on balance, far more reason to press on in the directions already taken, than to make drastic alterations. The most important caveat to that judgment is to examine much more carefully the effects of almost wholly free trade on the American domestic economy.

Notes

1. Until the early 1990s this was thought of primarily in terms of the 12-nation European Community's (EC) creation of a single market by the beginning of 1993. In October 1991, however, the EC and the European Free Trade Association agreed to merge and form a new and larger common market, to be known as the European Economic Area, by 1996. This would constitute a market of about 360 million people, which would account for some 45 percent of world trade. As an economic bloc, it also would have great clout internationally.

2. The EC today is a framework organization including all three separate legal entities: EEC, ECSC, and Euratom.

3. A conflict prevention center, as secretariat, and an office of free elections were established, among others. Various means of tying NATO, the EC and CSCE together into a structure of interlocking security institutions were being studied also. For a useful discussion of some of the key issues that would be raised by enhancing the CSCE's role, see Peter Corterier, "Transforming the Atlantic Alliance," *The Washington Quarterly,* Winter 1991, pp. 34–37.

4. In December 1991, the United States officially changed over from GNP to GDP in its statistical data. That brought the United States into line with practice in all the major nations of Europe. The difference between the two measures is that the Gross National Product measures what American firms produce, regardless of where these firms are producing, whereas the Gross Domestic Product, as the name indicates, counts whatever is produced within the United States, regardless of whether it is by American or foreign firms.

5. These statistics above are taken from *The Economist,* vol. 321, no. 7732, November 9, 1991, pp. 59–60 (with one correction: they left out Spain from NATO). This article is an excellent briefing on the EC in particular. Indeed, for up- to-date assessment of the EC outside official channels, it is hard to find any better source.

6. The Western Union is discussed with commendable thoroughness in Lawrence S. Kaplan, *The United States and NATO: The Formative Years* (Lexington, KY: The University Press of Kentucky, 1984). With the formation of NATO, the WU was relatively dormant for several years, but it reemerged in the mid-1950s in its Western European Union incarnation as the vehicle for West Germany's admission to NATO.

7. Secretary of State Dean Acheson's memoirs provide the best single account of all of these events. Dean Acheson, *Present at the Creation* (New York: Norton, 1969).

8. One of the more penetrating discussions of NATO's early years is Andrew J. Goodpaster, "The Foundations of NATO: A Personal Memoir," in James R. Golden, Daniel J. Kaufman, Asa A. Clark, IV, and David H. Petraeus, eds., *NATO at Forty* (Boulder, CO: Westview Press, 1989), pp. 22–35.

9. For example, look at the location of Samos. It is a long way away from what we

think of as Greece and is nestled against the southern shore of Turkey. The problems this island was causing well before the birth of Christ is told in very interesting fashion by the earliest historian of all, Herodtus.

10. This statement is backed by more than one four-star officer who has held the CINCSOUTH command. One of the authors spent two weeks some years ago following CINCSOUTH through his daily routines, and that is exactly what was happening.

11. Initially a French concept proposed by Foreign Minister Robert Schuman, the ECSC was far from an idealistic attempt to lay the foundation for broader European integration. The French believed international arrangements regulating the production and marketing of coal and steel would be an effective check on future German warmaking potential.

12. Thomas M. Magstadt, *Nations and Governments: Comparative Politics in Regional Perspective* (New York: St. Martin's Press, 1991), p. 135. The end of the transition period did not, however, end all restrictions on intra-Community trade. Trucks continued to line up at frontier posts, for example, to be examined for compliance with divergent national regulations. In 1992, efforts were going full-bore to create EC-wide regulations that would make these delays unnecessary.

13. The former East Germany became part of the Community when Germany was reunified.

14. See the excellent article by C. Michael Aho and Bruce Stokes, "The Year the World Economy Turned," *Foreign Affairs, America and the World, 1990–91*, pp. 160–178. Some now subordinate security to economics. See C. Fred Bergsten, "The Primacy of Economics," *Foreign Policy*, Summer 1992, pp. 3–24.

15. The term "adverse" has been used for many years now to delineate a trade balance where more is imported than exported. In a sense, of course, this is not adverse at all, because it brings in more goods than it sends out, leaving more for the party with the "adverse" balance. The early economists known as the mercantile school used to argue that buying more than was shipped out was a serious mistake because the difference had to be paid in precious metal, gold and sliver, needed more importantly to pay the armed forces.

16. For a succinct discussion of the Bretton Woods system and its economic impact, see Mordechai E. Kreinin, *International Economics: A Policy Approach,* 5th ed. (San Diego, CA: Harcourt Brace Jovanovich, 1987), pp. 53–61.

17. The IMF is not a bank. It is essentially a financial club of nations who hold shares. These nations can borrow under certain conditions from the pool of subscriptions, but the main idea behind the IMF was to stabilize the international monetary system.

18. On December 4, 1991, it was $367.40. Not much change.

19. The adverse trends proved to be difficult to reverse or even contain. In 1972 the deficit increased. Then a surplus reappeared in 1973. After that there was a deficit *each* year, actually surpassing the hundred billion dollar mark in 1984. In early 1991, it fell as low as $4 billion a month. In September 1991 it was $6.79 billion.

20. As German entrepreneurs and industrial giants moved into Eastern Europe following the collapse of Soviet control there was an undertone of worry, especially in Czechoslovakia and Poland.

21. Robert Gerald Livingston, "United Germany: Bigger and Better," *Foreign Policy*, Summer 1992, p. 169.

22. For a thoughtful discussion of whether the EC model of integration is appropriate

as the basis for eventually incorporating other European states, see Helen Wallace, "The Europe That Came In from the Cold," *International Affairs,* October, 1991, pp. 647–63. With Czechoslovakia's breakup into two states, the problem increased.

23. The 1990 budget deficits of the EC members, as a percent of GDP, shows a great range. The lowest is Britain (–0.7), followed by France (–1.6) and Germany (–1.9). Several are at 4 or 5 percent. On the high side are Italy with –10.6 percent and Greece with –19.8 percent. See *The Economist,* November 30, 1991, p. 69.

24. Other estimates say $10 billion, rather than 18. Either sum is "real" money.

25. Walter Goldstein argues that it was "inevitable" that the Maastricht Treaty would run into trouble. "The pact was premature in conception to survive intact." But even if the treaty should fail, "the community will remain as a functioning body, and its goal of union will be preserved." Walter Goldstein, "Europe After Maastricht," *Foreign Affairs,* Winter 1992/93, pp. 117, 118.

26. As with any issue of politics, there is a tug here between those who want the EC to do more and those who want it to do less. The Meuse River, which flows through Maastricht, is heavily polluted, primarily becuase of dumpings and runoffs from other countries, upstream. Those who are trying to get action, the environmentalists, find it very hard going because the Community organs have no sufficiently precise criteria. On the other hand, the EC bureaucrats are near agreement (whether one is needed or not) on a uniform size for condoms.

27. *The Economist,* December 7, 1991.

28. The growing German assertiveness (and, when it desired, unilateralism) was plain to all. Elizabeth Pond argues that Germany will now assume some of the burden of leadership in Europe previously shouldered by the United States. Thus, she writes, "Yes, Germany is becoming more assertive in foreign policy. This is all to the good for the United States." Elizabeth Pond, "Germany in the New Europe," *Foreign Affairs,* Spring 1992, p. 114.

29. Bergsten, p. 4.

30. See *The Economist,* November 30, 1991, p. 22. The figures are in a guest article by Shitaro Ishihara, a Liberal Democrat member of the Japanese Diet. Ishihara, a former transport minister, is also coauthor with Akio Morita, chairman of Sony, of a book called *The Japan That Can Say No*—a best-seller in Japan.

31. Catherine McArdle Kelleher wrote, "For the United States, perhaps the hardest adjustment will be to form a new relationship with the Federal Republic of Germany, the key actor in all future European circles." Catherine McArdle Kelleher, "U.S. Foreign Policy and Europe, 1990–2000." *The Brookings Review,* Fall 1990, p. 7. If this was true then, before unification, it must be much more true now.

32. Pond, p. 118.

33. Livingston, p. 173.

17

Ancient Cultures and Enduring Enmities

The Middle East

Throughout recorded history the Middle East has been an area of great significance. It was the cradle and remains the center of three great world religions: Judaism, Christianity, and Islam. Great empires of antiquity originated there (Egyptians, Assyrians, Babylonians, Persians). Geostrategically it is the transportation and communication crossroad to Europe, Asia, and Africa. Great empires, from the Hittites and the Persians, from the Greek and Romans to Napoleon, to the British and later Hitler, have fought to dominate the region. Controlling the strategic approaches to three continents, the Middle East has been a highly desirable prize. Because it has the largest concentration of proven oil reserves in the world and is the leading oil-producing region as well, since World War II its value has been enhanced even further.

American national interests in the Middle East since World War II have remained quite stable. The first and foremost priority has been preventing control of the area by any hostile power. With the development of the Cold War, that usually meant the Soviets. But the interest is the same whether the adversary is the Soviets or not. Other major interests have included ensuring access to the area's oil for the United States and its friends at tolerable prices, minimizing regional instability and the negative consequences it produces, and containing regional disputes in order to prevent an escalation that might bring about a U.S.-Soviet military confrontation. Only the concern about escalating to a confrontation with the Soviets has been changed by the altered circumstances of the 1990s.

Although American interests have been quite clearly delineated and remain fairly stable, achieving or protecting those interests has not always been easy, as we shall see.

Major Decision Area 5: Three Interrelated Problems

In pursuing these national interests, the United States has confronted three fundamental foreign policy problems in the Middle East for almost the entire post–World War II period: the Arab-Israeli dispute, various inter-Arab rivalries, and difficulties caused by the policies of other nonregional nations such as the Soviets or the British. Each of these problems is complex and difficult to deal with by itself. But in many cases the problems are interrelated, exacerbating and complicating matters far beyond what they would be if these interrelationships did not exist. Moreover, since the late 1960s American policy has been complicated even further by (1) the growth in prominence of the Palestinian problem, and (2) the significantly increased importance of the Persian Gulf and Arabian Peninsula as a result of Western (and Japanese) requirements for foreign oil. Clearly, both the Palestinian issue and problems of Gulf stability and oil interconnect to the first three problems.

These several overlapping problems are all important, but it would be a mistake to conclude that they are of equal significance. In many ways the key problem has been and remains the Arab-Israeli conflict. Solving this problem will not guarantee regional peace and stability, but without some solution peace and stability are just not possible. Solving the Arab-Israeli problem would also lessen other tensions, since some of the causes of conflict *among* Arabs stem from their disagreements over how to deal with the Israelis. Persian Gulf stability and oil issues, too, would be affected, for the Saudis want Arab sovereignty over East Jerusalem and some form of Palestinian self-determination. Even if in 1993 Saudi goodwill toward Washington in the aftermath of the Gulf War lingered, over time these other issues were bound to regain their former importance. The extent to which Riyadh would continue to be willing to accommodate an American forward presence and America's oil interests would in part be a function of its view of American policy on the Arab-Israeli dispute.

The prominent role of the Palestinian issue in the Arab-Israeli problem is of comparatively recent origin. The 1948-49 Arab-Israeli War, fought in and around Palestine, created the Palestinian refugee problem as a festering sore. But until the aftermath of the 1967 war, the major actors in the Arab-Israeli conflict were Israel and the surrounding Arab states. The Palestinians, as such, were not major players. Although the Palestine Liberation Organization (PLO) was founded in 1964, until that 1967 war it was essentially a creature of the Arab states. The decisive Arab defeat in 1967, however, convinced many Palestinians that the Arab states would never be able to "liberate" Palestine. Consequently, various Palestinian guerilla units began to act independently, soon undertaking a variety of small-scale military forays or "terrorist" operations. Then, as the Palestinian cause gained strength, many in and outside the Middle East came to believe that the Palestinian issue was the heart of the Arab-Israeli problem. That view found formal expression in 1974 when Arab heads of state recognized the PLO as the "sole legitimate representative" of the Palestinian people. For the last twenty years or so, the Palestinian issue has remained central to the Arab-Israeli dispute.

The second problem facing American foreign policy is inter-Arab rivalries. Although Arabs often have similar policies toward Israel, they frequently disagree on a wide range of other issues. Inter-Arab relationships are very fluid, so uncertainty and the changing of alignments are typical. The on-again, off-again "friendship" of Jordan with the PLO and Syria in the 1980s (discussed later) is a case in point. An analogy to Europe's classical balance of power operations in the eighteenth and nineteenth centuries is not too farfetched.

Non-Arabs can easily underestimate the depth and importance of inter-Arab rivalries. But to many Arab leaders they are equally or more important than the Arab-Israeli conflict. In 1948 inter-Arab enmity prevented effective Arab coordination in the first Palestine war, and inter-Arab concerns were the primary driver in many of Egypt's decisions that led to the second (1956) and third (1967) wars with Israel. Syria's long and bitter rivalry with Iraq is a second illustration. That rivalry had much to do with Assad's willingness to join the anti-Iraq allied coalition in the 1991 Gulf War. Such examples amply demonstrate that inter-Arab rivalries clearly impact and are impacted by the other problems in the region. Third-party influences are crucial here.

The third kind of problem is the impact of the policies of other nonregional powers on America's Middle East interests. An obvious example during the Cold War was the Soviet role. With Moscow the primary global threat to the United States, Americans usually viewed events in the Middle East through the prism of the containment guidelines and the domino theory. America's most fundamental policy objective was preventing Soviet control of the Middle East and its strategic positions and oil resources. But the Soviet Union was not the only external power whose policies the United States had to take into account. Throughout the 1940s and 1950s the British and French played major roles, for example. Since change is the hallmark of the international system, one would expect still others to be important actors in the future. For example, it would not be unreasonable to speculate that with the demise of the Cold War, the decline of Soviet power, and the increasing importance of oil-related economic issues, oil-dependent major powers such as Germany and Japan will play significantly larger roles, at least in Persian Gulf and Arabian Peninsula matters.

What happens with all these problems affects oil supplies and Persian Gulf stability. Where the other problems discussed above have long historical roots, for the United States involvement in the security of oil supplies is a problem of relatively recent origin. Until the late 1960s and early 1970s, the British were the primary nonregional power in the Gulf. Whatever the difficulties that might develop and escalate to involve "Free World" interests, London was assumed to be the lead player for their resolution. Then also, while many of its allies were heavily dependent on foreign oil (much of it from the Gulf), prior to the 1970s the United States was not even a net oil importer. But in the 1970s, as Britain withdrew "East of the Suez" and as the United States became dependent on foreign oil, Gulf stability decreased. The overthrow of the Shah of Iran was followed by the long Iran-Iraq War, and then by Operations Desert Shield and Desert Storm. As America looks ahead, oil requirements and Gulf stability appear to have gained a permanent niche on the policy agenda.

The Creation of Israel

Several times in this book we have made the point that for most of its history before World War II, United States foreign policy had a modest scope. Not surprisingly, until the late 1940s America knew, and cared, very little about the Middle East. It was the developing Cold War and increasing tensions in Palestine that changed this.

The growing American interest began with Arab-Jewish (Zionist) enmity and the war in Palestine. The Jewish story is well known. From the time of their "final" dispersion by the Romans in 135 A.D. until the twentieth century, the Jewish people did not have their own independent state. They never gave up their hope of returning to "the Promised Land" and establishing their own state, though, and in the nineteenth century the Zionist movement began with that as its primary objective.[1] During World War I the British (who were fighting the Central Powers, including Ottoman Turks who had controlled the area) promised their help in establishing a "national home" for the Jewish people in Palestine.[2] The United States, which had been consulted, was pleased.

Unfortunately there was another major claimant for this land, the Arabs, who constituted more than 90 per cent of the population living in the area. They, too, received promises from the British.[3] The Arabs wanted an independent Arab nation, to include Palestine, and believed that was what the British had promised. On this basis they in turn pledged to rebel against the Turks (which they did). Various British-Arab promises were exchanged in a series of letters (the Husein-McMahon letters), and enough ambiguities and inconsistencies existed for historians even today to debate what actually was and was not promised. But that debate really is irrelevant because it is clear that the Arabs *believed* this area was promised to them and that Palestine was included. Obviously, the British promises to the Zionists and the Arabs were incompatible. For good measure, in 1916 in the secret Sykes-Picot agreement, Britain and France agreed to divide most of the region into their own spheres of influence.[4]

When World War I ended, Britain was militarily and politically preeminent in the Middle East. Except for Syria (and "Lebanon"), which was under French control, London directly or indirectly ruled most of the Arab world. Palestine soon became a British Mandate (under the League of Nations), and small scale Jewish immigration began. The Arabs in Palestine got nothing, however. Zionist conflict with the Arabs was immediate, frequent, and bitter. Once the Holocaust began in Europe in the 1930s, Zionist immigration into Palestine increased, and after the war what was once a trickle became a flood.

After World War II the British, despairing of resolving the Palestine problem, turned it over to the still-new United Nations. On altruistic grounds, President Truman and much of the American public supported the idea of an independent Jewish state. A number of prominent American diplomatic and military figures opposed it, however, arguing it would endanger western strategic interests, alienate the (majority) Arabs, jeopardize access to oil, and possibly encourage Russian penetration.[5] In spite of these crosscurrents, on October 11, 1947, U.S. Ambassador Johnson told the U.N. General Assembly that America supported partition into separate Arab and Jewish states. On November 29, the General Assembly, with very strong American support, voted 33-13 to partition, with Jerusalem to be internationalized. All the Arabs were in opposition. The Zionists were ecstatic, although they knew tough times lay ahead.[6]

Limited clashes and small battles occurred immediately, their intensity and scope picking up as the official end of the Mandate in May approached. With proposed partition lines already overtaken by events, the American administration was debating the merits of quick diplomatic recognition of Israel,[7] and once the Mandate ended, America immediately granted recognition. As open war began it was obvious that the Arabs were bitterly divided and little coordination was possible. The Israelis, although fighting against long odds, triumphed decisively. Four separate armistice agreements were signed, the last on July 29, 1949.

The consequences of the war were enormous (see Map 17.1). An independent Israel was established, possessing approximately 77 percent of prewar Palestine—considerably more territory than had been allotted to it under the partition resolution. Jordan (then known as TransJordan) annexed the West Bank, while Egypt governed the Gaza Strip as an administered territory, fueling inter-Arab enmity. Jerusalem was divided (a solution satisfying no one), with Israel ruling the new city and Jordan the old. The Palestinian Arabs, as such, again got nothing. Nearly three-fourths of a million Arabs became refugees. Crowded into camps near Israel's borders, they quickly became a malignant cancer. The Arabs said they had lost round one, but round two would be different.

It was clear that this first war had helped breed domestic unrest in many of the Arab countries. Soon efforts were being made to get rid of those "to blame."

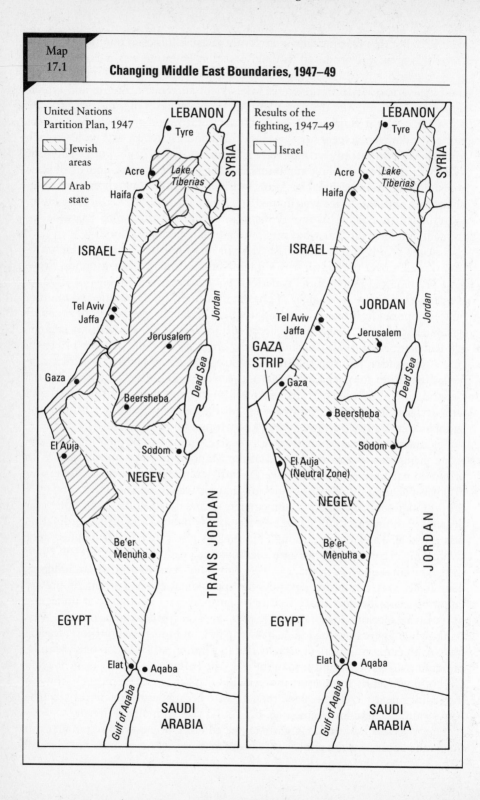

**Map
17.1**

Changing Middle East Boundaries, 1947–49

United Nations
Partition Plan, 1947

Jewish areas

Arab state

LEBANON

Tyre

Acre

Lake Tiberias

SYRIA

Haifa

ISREAL

Tel Aviv
Jaffa

Jerusalem

Gaza

Beersheba

Dead Sea

Jordan

El Auja

Sodom

NEGEV

TRANS JORDAN

Be'er
Menuha

EGYPT

Elat   Aqaba

Gulf of Aqaba

SAUDI
ARABIA

Results of the
fighting, 1947–49

Israel

LEBANON

Tyre

Acre

Lake Tiberias

SYRIA

Haifa

ISRAEL

JORDAN

Tel Aviv
Jaffa

Jerusalem

GAZA
STRIP

Gaza

Beersheba

Dead Sea

Jordan

Sodom

El Auja
(Neutral Zone)

NEGEV

JORDAN

Be'er
Menuha

EGYPT

Elat   Aqaba

Gulf of Aqaba

SAUDI
ARABIA

In March 1949, a coup took place in Syria, in 1951 Jordan's King Abdullah was assassinated by a dissatisfied Palestinian, and in 1952 Egypt's King Farouk was toppled.

The United States had hoped Israel would survive, but despite Israel's victory, the United States gained less from the war than might be imagined. Although it had given strong rhetorical support to the Jewish effort, it had quite deliberately avoided direct involvement. The Israelis took note, concluding that they must be prepared to defend themselves, alone if necessary. Moreover, because the war had not brought peace and the Arabs remained unreconciled to Israel's victory, Israel believed that a strong, self-sufficient military would be necessary. From the Arab perspective, of course, Washington had deliberately decided to be an enemy. Cooperation on some issues might still be possible, but friendly relations were not unless U.S. policies were changed.

The Cold War: What Role?

It was on top of these regional antagonisms that the Cold War was superimposed. Washington, viewing all developments in the Middle East through its Cold War lens, often assumed naively that others held similar views. But, as already indicated, seen through Middle Eastern eyes, the reality of Middle East affairs was quite different. America's effort to entice Egypt in 1951 into an Allied Middle East Command that would include Britain, for example, was rejected within two days. To Egypt, communism was not the problem; Britain and Israel were the enemies. But King Farouk's denunciation of Egypt's treaties with Britain, and his declaration that he was "King of Egypt and the Sudan," did not save Farouk from being overthrown the next summer by a military junta. They were even less sympathetic to Western ties.

Thwarted in the Arab heartland but determined, Washington turned to the nations directly bordering the USSR. In 1954 the United States signed a military assistance agreement with Iraq (then ruled by a king). Iraq and Turkey followed with a bilateral defense treaty (known as the Baghdad Pact),[8] which by fall Britain, Iran, and Pakistan also had joined. Attempting to take regional dynamics into account, America chose to be only closely "associated." It hoped to avoid the Israeli anger that would result from an alliance with an Arab nation. It also was reluctant to be tarred with an "imperialist by association" brush that would come from being allied with Britain and Turkey, states with a long history of imperialism in the region. The third reason was to avoid involvement in inter-Arab rivalries. Nasser bitterly opposed the pact, especially because Iraq was a major rival that now would receive considerable additional support and the new arrangement would also help maintain British influence.

At this juncture, the Arab-Israeli problem again took center stage as Israel launched a surprise assault into the Egyptian-administered Gaza Strip.[9] Nasser responded by intensifying his quest for Western aid. When this failed, he signed the earlier-mentioned arms deal with Czechoslovakia (which was acting as a

Soviet agent). Nasser's aim was to manipulate the superpowers, not vice-versa.

In Chapter 10 we discussed the events triggered by the arms deal, culminating in the Suez crisis. We need not repeat those events here, except to remember that the American role in 1956 necessarily undercut Anglo-French prestige in the area and would soon force the United States to choose between seeing its interests in the area threatened or taking on a more direct and active role.

The question that still must be weighed in Nasser's case is whether American interests would have been better served if Washington had chosen the counterbalancing interest of dealing with Nasser on his terms. Suppose it had. On the negative side, such a deal would not have *permanently* kept Nasser from dealing with the Soviets. Given his positive neutralism and Soviet willingness, cooperating with Nasser would only have postponed the day of reckoning. America's allies would have asked, why be an ally when neutrals are treated so well. And Israel would have been furious. The Tripartite Declaration approach, where Britain, France, and America sought an Arab-Israeli balance (meaning *each* Arab state received much less than Israel), would have been thrown out.

Now look at the positive side. If the deal *had* been made, Washington's action would have altered its image toward greater impartiality in the Arab-Israeli dispute. And it would have given some recognition to Arab independence and nationalism. Given this balance of factors and the Cold Wars lens for viewing the problem, though, we can see why the decision was against a deal.

In the spring of 1957, another regional crisis erupted. Spurred on by Suez, pro-Nasser Jordanians pressured King Hussein to abrogate his ties to the West. Soon a bitter struggle developed. Observers feared it would escalate into full scale civil war, with Egypt and Syria backing the Nasserists and the Iraqis supporting Hussein. Hussein, knowing the American perception of Nasser as an "immoral" neutral who was paving the way for Communist influence, shrewdly claimed he was threatened with a Communist takeover:[10] deteriorating conditions in Jordan were caused by international communism's "efforts to destroy my country."[11] Alarmed, Washington announced that the Sixth Fleet was "returning" to the eastern Mediterranean. The independence and integrity of Jordan were described as "vital" American interests. Hussein soon was triumphant.

Washington believed that a Communist/Nasserist effort to overthrow a pro-Western regime had been thwarted and civil war prevented, that containment was working.[12] But to many Arabs, such "gunboat diplomacy" was a humiliating reminder of the past. Many Arabs believed America had intervened in a totally internal matter, that there was no Cold War issue here.

Scarcely had this turmoil abated when in early August Syria charged there was an American plot to overthrow its regime.[13] Because of Syria's increasingly close relations to the Soviets, "leftist" domestic structure, extreme anti-Israeli attitude, and opposition to Hussein, America had opposed Damascus on many issues. But was there a plot?[14] Washington responded by again ordering the Sixth Fleet to maneuver in the eastern Mediterranean, but this time the tactic backfired. Instead of being cowed, the Syrian policymakers stepped up their anti-American campaign. America's gunboat diplomacy, they said, proved that the United States was the real imperialist in the region, a major enemy of all Arabs.

By early 1958 the preconception of the United States, that all the unrest in the Middle East was the result of Nasserist and/or Communist machinations, was losing to more pragmatic considerations. Thus, when Egypt and Syria formed the United Arab Republic (UAR), Washington reacted very circumspectly. But when a crisis arose in Lebanon, and Lebanon accused the UAR of instigating the trouble, the United States cited the Eisenhower Doctrine and sent marines. Nasser's suspicions increased that Washington's comments were just a pretext for intervention.

To America's surprise and chagrin, the United Nations Observer Group in Lebanon reported the problems were primarily internal. Eisenhower decided not to intervene, but suddenly, on July 14 the pro-Western government in Iraq was deposed by a leftist junta supportive of Nasser. With the most pro-Western government gone, the existing policy framework was in danger of being completely destroyed. Believing Nasser was out to control the entire Arab world, in a classic case of third-party influences the United States responded to Lebanon's plea and landed marines in Beirut, ostensibly to restore order but also to impress Nasser. Almost as soon as they arrived, though, it became evident that the trouble *had* been primarily internal in origin, and soon the troops were withdrawn.

After the Lebanon crisis, for a time the Arab-Israeli and Cold War problems receded in prominence while inter-Arab disputes came to occupy center stage. Egypt and Iraq somewhat surprisingly reverted to their old enmity.[15] Syria seceded from the United Arab Republic, becoming an adversary of both Egypt and Iraq. In a precursor of later events, Iraq laid claim to Kuwait—only to be thwarted by other Arab nations and the British. When civil war broke out in Yemen, Egypt backed the republican government while the Saudis and Jordanians supported the deposed Imam.

Searching for Arab-Israeli Peace 1967–80

In 1966–67, though, the Arab-Israeli conflict reemerged in what many called "the third round." After Syria and the Soviets told Nasser that Israel was planning to attack Syria (with whom Egypt had a defense treaty), Nasser was under enormous Arab pressure to do something. Sending a small force into the Sinai, Egypt asked for a redeployment of United Nations Emergency Force (UNEF) contingents from the Sinai border; other UNEF units were not mentioned. When U.N. Secretary-General U Thant responded that *all* UNEF forces had to move, or none would, Nasser was confronted with a real dilemma.[16] Redeploying *all* UNEF forces (which was *not* what he had asked for) would open Sharm el-Sheikh, the port city at the mouth of the Gulf of Aqaba. That action would place great pressure on him to close the Gulf of Aqaba, an act which Israel had long said would mean war. But largely for reasons of inter-Arab credibility, Nasser, feeling he had no choice, said remove them all. Four days later he closed the Gulf. The die was cast. On June 5 Israel launched a devastating air attack against

Egypt. When the fighting stopped six days later, Israeli forces occupied the Sinai Peninsula, the Golan Heights, the Gaza Strip, and the West Bank, including the old city of Jerusalem (see Map 17.2).

Unlike 1956, the United States did not have a major impact on either the course of events leading to the war or on the war itself. As William Quandt says, almost its entire effort before hostilities "was directed toward restraining Israel and building a multilateral context for diplomatic action."[17] Obviously, it was unsuccessful. Once war began, an America preoccupied with Vietnam was not about to become directly involved.

President Johnson was pleased with the war's outcome. Israel seemed more secure than at any time since 1949. Its primarily opponents had been humiliated, with billions worth of Soviet aid down the drain. Surely, now, Nasser would sue for peace. In this optimistic context Johnson proposed "five great principles of peace."[18] One was that every nation in the area had the right to live and have that right respected by its neighbors, a principle very appealing to Israel.

But Nasser had other ideas. Moscow, eager to regain some of the prestige it lost with the Arabs because of its lack of involvement in the war, provided massive economic and military aid. And Saudi Arabia, Kuwait, and Libya promised $266 million annually, for as long as "the consequences of aggression" remained. At a Khartoum Conference the Arabs said there would be no peace, no negotiations, and no recognition of Israel.

On November 22, 1967, the U.N. Security Council passed the now famous Resolution 242,[19] which recognized the "inadmissibility of the acquisition of territory by war" and the need for a "just and lasting peace in which every state in the area can live in security." The resolution went on to call for "withdrawal of Israeli armed forces from territories occupied in the recent conflict" and "acknowledgment of the sovereignty, territorial integrity, and political independence of every state in the area and their right to live in peace within secure and recognized boundaries. . . ." Interpretations of what 242 meant quickly diverged: To Cairo it was a definite plan for total Israeli withdrawal, but to Israel it was only a set of guidelines for negotiations.

In the next several years, as the Arab-Israeli problem dominated regional concerns, America continued to hope that constructive negotiation based on 242 could begin. Johnson, preoccupied with Vietnam and believing the impetus had to come from the parties, played little active role. Of course, there was no such impetus. Indeed, Nasser was mobilizing Egyptian resources for still another "battle."[20] In 1969 Egypt launched a war of attrition against Israeli positions along the Suez Canal. With violence escalating, the Nixon administration took on a more active role than its predecessor, proposing a standstill cease-fire and the initiation of indirect talks under the U.N. Israel and Egypt both agreed, but Israel soon charged Egypt with cease-fire violations and walked out.

Nixon once said that Vietnam was America's most anguishing problem, but, because of the potential for confrontation with the Soviets, the Middle East was the most dangerous.[21] This too had much to do with his strong response in the 1970 Jordan case, discussed in Chapter 10. And his position was why, once the Jordanian fire was out, Washington again sought to resuscitate Egyptian-

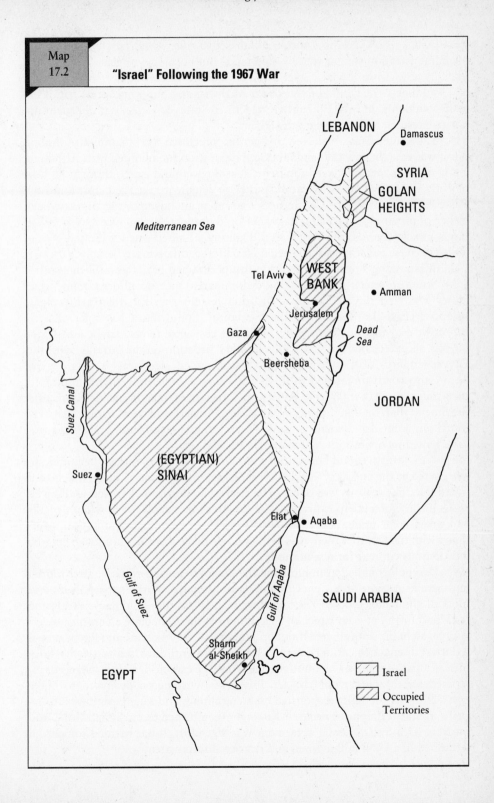

Map 17.2

"Israel" Following the 1967 War

LEBANON

Damascus

SYRIA

GOLAN HEIGHTS

Mediterranean Sea

Tel Aviv

WEST BANK

Amman

Jerusalem

Dead Sea

Gaza

Beersheba

JORDAN

Suez Canal

(EGYPTIAN) SINAI

Suez

Elat   Aqaba

Gulf of Suez

Gulf of Aqaba

SAUDI ARABIA

Sharm al-Sheikh

EGYPT

Israel

Occupied Territories

Israeli talks. The U.N., now too, took an active role. After these efforts failed, the administration sought step-by-step talks. But nothing worked.

By now Anwar Sadat, Egypt's new president, was extremely frustrated. He had said that 1971 would be the "Year of Decision," but no progress had been made. Suddenly, in July 1972, after the United States-Soviet summit brought no positive results, Sadat expelled the Soviets.

The United States believed this action foreclosed Egypt's military option. But it was exactly now that Sadat began preparation for a limited war. Although many of his maneuvers were apparent, Washington (and Israel) thought he was bluffing.[22] After all, Moscow would not want detente jeopardized and would act as a constraint. Even more, with the Soviets gone and given the accumulated evidence of previous wars, Sadat knew he could not win. Yet on October 6, 1973, Egypt attacked across the Suez Canal. Fighting a limited war for limited potential objectives, Sadat aimed at forcing Israel to negotiate more flexibly.

Washington's primary interest in this period had been to establish a stable equilibrium in which no power could dominate. Once hostilities commenced, policy was first directed toward ensuring Israel's survival, then achieving a balanced cease-fire and preventing escalation. Following a Kissinger visit to Moscow, the superpowers jointly proposed cease-fire terms. Egypt and Israel quickly accepted. But the precarious military situation on the ground (with the Egyptian Third Army on the East Bank surrounded, and Israel having cut the Suez-Cairo road) threatened to upset the balance. When the Soviets indicated they might directly intervene, American forces were put on alert. Nixon told Brezhnev "that we could in no event accept [Soviet] unilateral action" and rejected any joint deployment as well.[23] Israel, under significant American pressure, halted its operations, and Moscow backed off.

This "fourth round" produced a paradox. The Arabs, though beginning to lose, acted at the end as if they had won. Israel, the "winner," acted much as if it had lost. The reasons were clear. The Arabs had done much better, and the Israelis much worse, than expected. The "myth of invincibility" in which Israelis had taken great pride, had been destroyed. This psychological situation, combined with the fact that there was neither a full-fledged winner nor loser, created a propitious context for negotiation.

U.S. policy aimed at minimizing the Soviet role. Accordingly, after a brief and formal session of a Geneva conference attended by the superpowers and most of the belligerents,[24] Kissinger began his "shuttle diplomacy," traveling back and forth between Israel and Egypt and Syria to mediate a compromise.[25] As a result of his skillful mediation, on January 18, 1974, Israel and Egypt signed a partial disengagement agreement. Israel would withdraw ten to twenty kilometers into the Sinai, a U.N. buffer zone would be established, and a series of restricted forces zones would be set. Privately, Washington promised to make every effort to be "fully responsive on a continuing and long term basis" to Israel's military equipment needs.[26] Kissinger then turned to the Syrian front, and on May 31 a Syrian-Israeli agreement was signed. It, too, provided for partial withdrawal, a U.N. buffer zone, and restricted forces areas.

More progress came in September 1975, with the signing of the Kissinger-mediated Sinai II Accords. Israel would withdraw from the strategic Sinai mountain passes, returning the oil fields captured in 1973; Egypt would move to the eastern edge of the old U.N. zone. A new U.N. buffer zone would separate them, complete with surveillance stations and American-manned warning facilities. The United States also promised Israel more military aid and guaranteed it would get enough oil to make up for the loss of those oil fields. Finally, Washington promised Israel that it would not negotiate with or recognize the PLO until the PLO recognized Israel's right to exist and accepted Resolutions 242 and 338.[27]

America was pleased. For the first time since 1949 there had been real movement toward Arab-Israeli peace. Moreover, the Soviets, who had wanted a reconvened Geneva Conference, had been shut out of the process. Logically enough, the Soviets strongly opposed the agreement.[28] Many Arabs also opposed, especially the Syrians. They saw such partial agreements as efforts to divide the Arabs and perpetuate "Zionist occupation."

When Carter came to office his initial hope was to reconvene the Geneva Conference and negotiate a comprehensive settlement. Instead of shutting the Soviets out à la Kissinger, he would work *with* them. This also would require some formula for Palestinian participation. Changing course, America now worked with Moscow to produce "mutually acceptable" principles for settlement. By the fall of 1977, to the superpowers' chagrin, these principles were found unacceptable by all parties.

It was in this pessimistic context that Anwar Sadat's stunning initiative and the subsequent Camp David Accords and Egyptian-Israeli peace treaty occurred. With Egypt and Israel at peace, the risk of a Soviet-American confrontation over the Middle East diminished enormously. Israel was more secure, having effectively utilized the conservation of enemies principle to remove Egypt (the strongest Arab power) from its list of enemies. Inter-Arab rivalries were exacerbated, though, with Sadat largely isolated in the Arab world. Under great political pressure at home, a few years later he was assassinated.

With the Camp David Accords and a peace treaty, both superpower and regional tension declined, but overall Arab-Israeli peace was still a long way off.

Oil, Stability, and the Soviets

In the years after the 1967 ("third round") war, American policy, although focused on the Arab-Israeli dispute, also had to consider Gulf oil.

Whereas for most of the post-1945 period America had been a net oil exporter, in the late 1960s and early 1970s things changed significantly. By October 1973 it was importing more than 25 percent of its needs.[29] Recognizing this vulnerability, in the "fourth round" war in 1973 the Arab members of OPEC drastically increased oil prices and instituted an embargo. Long gas lines soon appeared in the United States, causing much consumer bitterness. Fortunately, because of the signing of the Egyptian-Israeli disengagement agreement in early 1974 and evidence of movement in the Syrian negotiations, the Saudis and Egyptians were willing to use their good offices to provide assistance. In March the embargo was lifted. But American vulnerability, so clearly demonstrated, remained.

About this same time, Britain, long the primary external power in the Persian Gulf, was withdrawing all its forces "East of Suez." The United States, bogged down in Vietnam, could not fill the void. But how then to deal with the issue of Gulf stability? Some action seemed imperative. The Soviets, so effectively excluded from the Arab-Israeli peace process, had now decided to exploit Iraq's fears of Iran. Moscow was also maintaining good relations with South Yemen, which made Aden a virtual Soviet base. Given the Kremlin's support of Ethiopia, and Moscow's new "blue water" navy capable of operating in all the oceans of the world, Washington feared a major Soviet effort was in the making to control the region's strategic rimlands and "choke points." Washington's answer was to rely on the two nations (apart from Israel) most attuned to U.S. interests: Iran and Saudi Arabia. These "twin pillars" would be America's surrogates to ensure regional stability.

But more complications appeared. In early 1975, Lebanon, the "Switzerland of the Middle East," descended into what Don Peretz called "The Great Civil War."[30] A country characterized by an incredible diversity of Christian and Muslim religious sects with governmental power delicately distributed along confessional lines, Lebanon long had been ambivalent about its "real" identity. Was it "Arab" or "Western?" When the PLO transferred the bulk of its fighting forces into Lebanon after the unrest in Jordan, the move upset Lebanon's delicate political formula. Lebanon, unable to resist this PLO infiltration, was now brought directly into Arab-Israeli dispute.[31]

Once begun, the civil war soon mushroomed into a full-scale conflagration. Washington tried to restrain both the Lebanese parties and the potential interveners, Syria and Israel. The Soviets also pressured Damascus. But Syria, ignoring these pressures, in mid-1976 invaded in strength. By late fall most of the country, except the area near Israel's northern border, was under Syrian control.[32] There the Lebanon issue rested—temporarily.

Hardly had the Lebanon situation stabilized, when crisis began in Iran (discussed in Chapter 13), knocking out one leg of the twin pillars. Then, as America fumbled its way through the fall of the Shah and the hostage crisis, sporadic fighting broke out between Iran and Iraq. Saddam Hussein's forces attacked, and soon a major war was in progress. More and more now, regional tensions in the Persian Gulf seemed to be escalating out of control. In addition to the war's direct effect on the regional tension level, Iraq's bid for leadership now fragmented an already divided Arab world even further.

The oil problem, too, reemerged. In a clear case of third party influences, the Saudis, angered by America's mediation of Egyptian-Israeli differences and by its unwillingness to intervene to save its ally, the Shah, ceased efforts to moderate OPEC oil prices. Prices, which from 1974 to 1978 had risen only from $10-11 per barrel to $12-13, now went up, reaching the $30-35 range as the 1980s began.

Within hours of the release of the hostages in Iran, Ronald Reagan became president. While he might have despaired at the shifting kaleidoscope of crises and conflicts we have just chronicled, for the most part he ignored it. Reagan's focus was not on regional disputes; it was on the Soviets. The primary exception in this "Cold War II" approach occurred in September 1982. Launching an Arab-Israeli peace initiative, Reagan moved the United States further from Israeli views by proposing that Israel withdraw completely from the West Bank and Gaza Strip, while the Palestinians developed self-government "in association" with Jordan. Israel summarily rejected this plan, while the Arabs, though not rejecting it, pushed their own plan. This plan, developed at an Arab summit in Fez, was "close to the long-standing Soviet peace plan in its emphasis on total withdrawal."[33] But neither plan really made much difference. The reality was that progress on the Arab-Israeli problem could not occur as long as the troubles in Lebanon consumed so much effort. All peace initiatives soon were put on the back burner.

Sporadic Involvement

But hope springs eternal, and inter-Arab initiatives in early 1985 revived optimism. The key was a February 11 agreement between Hussein and PLO Chairman Yasir Arafat. Based on the idea of exchanging territory for peace, the agreement proposed negotiations in an international framework, to include the permanent members of the Security Council. As a critical concession to Israel, the PLO would be part of a *joint* Jordanian/Palestinian delegation.

Washington called this agreement a milestone, but the PLO quickly added that it rejected Resolution 242 and intended to have an independent state. For inter-Arab reasons, Syria opposed any Jordanian-PLO alliance. Israel remained uninterested. After Hussein told Washington in May that the PLO would accept 242, an Arab summit at Casablanca in August showed how little support he had. Syria boycotted the meeting. So did Lebanon, South Yemen, Algeria, Libya, Iraq, even Saudi Arabia. Then the Arab League reaffirmed the Fez Plan, not Hussein's approach. Deadlock again.

The United States had played only a small and reactive role in this process.

Only in the Gulf was the United States more prominent. Though unable to do much to diminish Iranian-Iraqi hostilities, in the spring of 1987 it became involved in another way. Kuwait, perceiving a growing threat from Iran, approached both the Soviets and the Americans for protection for its oil exports. Washington declined initially, but when it became obvious the Soviets *would* increase their role, the United States changed course,[34] agreeing to reflag and escort Kuwaiti tankers. America soon was conducting escort operations. By

October the navy had major forces both in and just outside the Gulf. Interestingly, despite several military incidents in the period, neither the president *nor the Congress* sought to invoke the War Powers Resolution.[35]

In late 1987 and 1988, the Palestinian issue again moved center stage. Spontaneous uprisings broke out in the Israeli occupied territories, first in Gaza and then on the West Bank.[36] Israel, seeking to suppress this *intifada,* tried severe punishments, a policy very controversial both inside and outside the country. Despite this unpromising context, the United States now decided to launch a peace initiative. But by June this "Shultz Plan" was dead, one more well-intentioned effort failed.

A curious series of events now occurred that ultimately resulted in *an American dialogue with the PLO.*[37] After Hussein, increasingly at odds with the PLO and worried that the *intifada* could spread to Jordanian soil, severed Jordan's administrative and judicial links with the West Bank and Gaza, Arafat decided as a tactical move to be more accommodating. In December Arafat renounced terrorism "in all its forms." He announced he was accepting resolutions 242 and 338 as the "basis" for negotiations within the framework of an international conference. To Israel's chagrin, Washington, at the end of the Reagan administration, responded positively to Arafat's comments. Official U.S.-PLO contacts now commenced.

Whether the Reagan legacy to Bush would lead to real progress on the Arab-Israeli problem was unclear in early 1989, but it certainly seemed possible. Though the situation in Lebanon remained unpromising, in the Gulf there was much optimism because the Iran-Iraq war had ended in the preceding summer. Overall there seemed to be a decline in the tension level, fueling hopes for the possibility of a lasting peace. Commentators even speculated that Iraq would join Egypt and Jordan as a moderate on the Israeli issue.[38] But soon things were back to normal. No progress, and the *intifada* continued.

Then came the Gulf War. We have discussed that conflict already. What is important to stress here are two lessons or consequences that went largely unappreciated in the United States as that drama unfolded. First, there was a reaffirmation of two fundamental truths about inter-Arab relations: the fragility of alignments and the importance of third-party influences.[39]

In the 1980s the ever-shifting Jordanian-PLO relationship and Syria's fluctuating relations with Jordan and antagonism toward Iraq over Lebanon had been important power balances. But the Iran-Iraq war was the key axis around which regional alignments had coalesced. Jordan, Egypt, North Yemen, and the members of the Gulf Cooperation Council, including Saudi Arabia, had supported Iraq, while Iran's allies had included Libya and Syria, along with the People's Democratic Republic of Yemen. But after Iraq invaded Kuwait, Egypt and the members of the Gulf Cooperation Council all quit supporting Iraq. Even Syria, despite cool relations with the United States and intense antagonism toward Israel, seeing an opportunity to help deal a severe blow to a bitter rival, joined the anti-Saddam coalition. Jordan found itself in a highly ambivalent position. Because of its ties to the United States and Arab moderates, it was under great pressure to join the anti-Iraqi coalition. But Jordan tilted toward Iraq for both political and economic reasons. These included internal pressures from the large Palestinian population in Jordan, worry about Israel, concern over increased Syrian influence, and a dependence on trade with Baghdad. The PLO, not surprisingly, also supported Iraq.

The second underappreciated result of the Gulf War was the rather ironic shift it caused in the regional balance of power, bringing about new regional alignments and the revival of old problems, like Kurdish nationalism. Obviously, Iraq's influence was decreased, although it was unclear for how long and exactly how much. Whether Saddam remained in power would make a significant difference. And Saudi security was ensured, at least for a time. But a major unintended but natural result was the increase in status of Iraq's two principle rivals, *Syria* and *Iran*. This development was hardly calculated to warm Washington's heart.

As we saw earlier, though, America focused on different lessons from the Gulf War. Washington had "proved" that aggression does not pay, liberated Kuwait, severely reduced Saddam's mischief-making ability, protected an ally and shown it could be counted on when the going gets rough, protected the oil supply, and so on. Moreover, the war's favorable outcome, in Washington's view, created propitious conditions for progress on the Arab-Israeli issue, too. Because of this, in October 1991, President Bush and Mikhail Gorbachev launched a new peace initiative. And, to the surprise of many, multilateral talks soon began at a large international conference in Madrid. This was followed by a number of bilateral talks between Israel and its neighbors. To accompany and supplement the bilateral talks, in January 1992 multilateral negotiations on region-wide issues took place in Moscow. Five subcommittees were established to continue exploring the following topics: (1) the environment, (2) water resources, (3) economic development, (4) refugee problems, and (5) arms control.

But everyone knew that most critical at this point was control of the West Bank and Israeli willingness to trade land for peace. What finally provided some hope of moving this aspect of the problem off dead center was the electoral victory of Yitzhak Rabin's Labor Party in June 1992, displacing the hard-line Likud Party, which had been in power for the previous fifteen years. Rabin immediately gave out signals of stopping additional construction of Jewish settlements in the West Bank, drawing a distinction between strategic settlements on the approach route to Jerusalem and other settlements (except for construction already underway). U.S. Secretary of State Baker immediately hinted that the United States would relax its previous ban on guaranteeing Israeli loans (which it did). Shortly after the election, Rabin was visiting with Egyptian President Hosni Mubarak in Cairo (the first Israeli-Egyptian summit in six years), and Mubarak was planning a visit to Jerusalem. Although it had happened many times before, and although the record was littered with disappointment, once again there was hope.

Then in 1993 truly breathtaking events occurred. In a manner reminiscent of America's "China card" and Anwar Sadat's peace initiative to Israel, Israel and the PLO reappraised their power problems and chose the counterbalancing interest of accommodation. Following months of secret talks mediated by

Norway, in September it was announced that a peace accord providing limited rule for the Palestinians in Gaza and the West Bank city of Jericho had been achieved. An exchange of letters followed with the PLO recognizing the right of Isreal to exist in peace and security and renouncing the use of terrorism, and Isreal recognizing the PLO as the representative of the Palestinian people. Then came the formal signature of a declaration of principles at the White House. While in the proposed five year transition period there would be many problems, there were real grounds for optimism.

Religious Fundamentalism, Hostages, and Terrorists

The Middle East is an area where modern Western modes of thought and action clash with age-old Eastern attitudes and habits. The Shah of Iran's attempt to move his nation into modern times was foreshadowed after World War I by Ataturk's reforms in Turkey, after the overthrow of the Ottoman sultans. But whereas in Turkey secularization took hold, in Iran modernization (and westernization) resulted in a backlash led by the religious leaders who were scandalized by such innovations as modern dress for women. Ataturk had been a very strong-minded man who did not hesitate to eliminate his opponents. He brooked no opposition for very long and insisted on great changes over short periods of time—like Westernizing the alphabet. But the Shah of Iran often hesitated, and despite the (sometimes correct) charges that his secret police were brutal he was unwilling to take decisive action when necessary. Eventually, as his opponents coalesced and America's support was withheld, he was swept away and the religious fundamentalists took over.

The radical change in Iran had several quick and obvious third-party effects. One was the spawning of fear in such nations as Saudi Arabia that the fundamentalist movement would spread to Saudi territory and undermine the monarchy. (After all, Saudi Arabia was modernizing, too.) Another effect was to increase hostage taking, especially by Iran-connected groups resident in politically disintegrated Lebanon. The third effect was to create at least a partial power vacuum in the Gulf, one which Saddam Hussein sought to fill, initially in a war with the now weakened, post-shah Iran, and then in his attempt to take Kuwait. Again, Middle East developments are full of interrelations.

That United States foreign policy was affected by each of these developments is an understatement. Iran, which, under the shah, had been one of the "twin pillars," was transformed into a trouble-maker and perhaps a threat, so far as America was concerned. The hostage issue interacted with American politics in a particularly decisive way, for it was President Reagan's hope to free hostages that led to the arms-for-hostages gambit that mushroomed into the Iran-Contra affair. Washington was going to buy the release of Americans. This was, of course, not only a foolish policy (since new hostages could be taken at least as fast as others were released) but a misguided one (because it conflicted

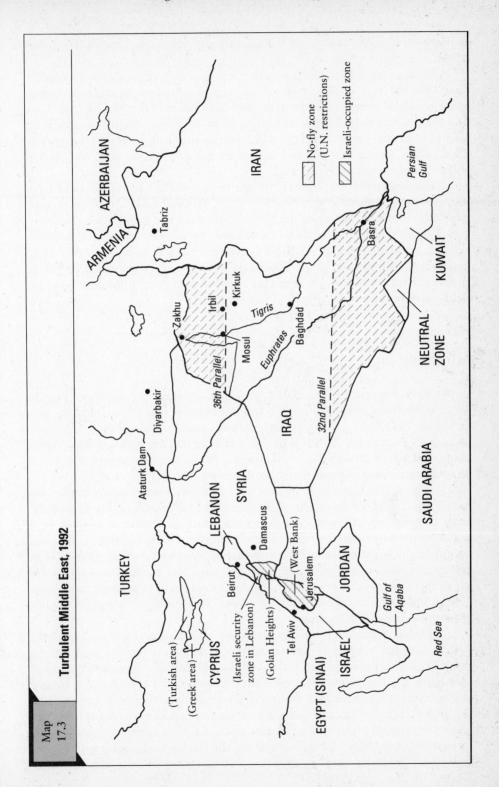

Map
17.3

Turbulent Middle East, 1992

with the oft-repeated pledge not to negotiate with and make concessions to terrorists).

Hostage-taking and terrorism are not a monopoly of groups in the Middle East. But the fact is that most of the several hundred Westerners—many Americans—who have fallen hostage have been taken in the Middle East. That fact also implies that progress in healing some of the running sores of Middle East politics could eliminate a good deal of this problem. Hostage-taking, after all, like the so-frequent car bombing during the Lebanese civil war, is the weapon of the weak and frustrated.

The September 1993 breakthrough in Israeli-PLO relations could have very positive peripheral effects on all the other Middle Eastern problems that we have just described. Religious fundamentalism does not spring from the Arab-Israeli problem, but it certainly is fanned by it. Terrorism and hostage-taking, on the other hand, are directly connected. It was no accident that 1991 ended with the release of all American hostages in Lebanon, at the same time that Israel and the Arabs began the new round of peace negotiations, which culminated in the mutual Israel-PLO recognition.

Summing Up

As we look forward, what guiding principles are there for American policy? What are the fundamental alternatives? Some believed that with its startling success in the Gulf War, the United States was in a position to fundamentally affect or perhaps even direct the future of the Middle East. They believed Washington could deal positively with the major interrelated problems in the region and protect America's vital interests with only moderate risk and cost. Could it?

As we said in Chapter 2, the critical foreign policy decisions are choices between fundamentally divergent alternatives. In logic, America has three basic policy approaches in the Middle East from which to choose: a minor role, a major involvement that emphasizes active intervention and a leading role, and an important but selective involvement that depends on the circumstances. The reality, though, is that the first approach is a non-player and the second and third are simply different degrees of involvement. Because of its superpower status, the United States cannot play only a minor role. "By definition" it *will* be a major player; the choice is in the how.

In terms of guiding principles, the first is that certain characteristics of the Middle East landscape will require continuous attention. Among these are the centrality and enduring reality of the Arab-Israeli problem; the endemic regional instability; the recognition of inter-Arab differences; the role of oil, both as a weapon and as a needed fuel; the fragility and changeability of alignments and the undesirability of banking too much on anyone; and the enormous Arab sensitivity to external pressures (past-future linkages). Even taking into account the differences in the lenses through which the different regional actors view problems, there can be no certainty about the way that many of these nations will respond to various initiatives. Moreover, as the value of various interests fluctuates, and as other nations change their policies, the problems faced automatically alter.

Complicating matters further, in the Middle East as elsewhere the agenda is broadening and new objects of importance are emerging. Water issues, for example, may well play a key economic and political role in the next decade, and beyond. Some believe water is already recognized as the fundamental political weapon in the region.[40] In this semiarid to desert environment, the three major water basins of the Nile, Tigris-Euphrates, and the Jordan and Orontes are shared by unneighborly states. While the region has been blessed with oil and gas, water is another story. Obviously water is a critical resource, and water needs could well serve as either a catalyst for conflict or a foundation for cooperation.

So far, at least, Jordan water has been much more the focus of conflict than cooperation. That is partly because of the hostility of Israel's neighbors, who resent an increasing Israeli drawdown on what is a relatively limited supply. Although the Sea of Galilee, from which the Jordan descends, is a significant body of water, the Jordan stream itself is not one of great volume except in the seasons of rain or melting snow. With the Nile, the military weakness of the Sudan has kept the Egyptians from undue alarm about potential restrictions of its supply.

The situation is different with the Tigris and Euphrates, both of which originate in eastern Turkey. That headwaters area is being systematically developed by the Turkish government, with a view to increasing its habitability and making its abundant water more useful to Turkey. (In back of this move is the need for more farm land to resettle Turks being harassed and deported from Bulgaria.) Called the Eastern Anatolia Project, it affects both the Tigris, which carries 17 billion cubic meters of water directly into Iraq, and the Euphrates, which carries 31 billion meters, first into Syria and then into Iraq. Turkish irrigation plans will cut the flow of the Tigris by at least one fifth (by Turkish estimates) and the Euphrates by even more, once the Ataturk dam is in use. When the dam was being filled early in 1990, for a whole month the Euphrates became a trickle. The Turks have also offered to help create a "peace pipeline," taping two Turkish rivers more to the west, to supply 2.2 billion cubic meters via Syria and Jordan to western Saudi Arabia, and the other via Kuwait to the Gulf sheikdoms. The Arabs were weighing this offer, wanting water but not wanting Israel to participate and also afraid of becoming dependent on the Turkish supply.[41]

Facing such an uncertain regional future, the United States cannot call the tune in all situations. Sometimes it will be wise to try to play a lead role, other times not. In all cases, policy will need to be based solidly on the cardinal principles. Such an approach must ask what America would like to see happen and who might help or hinder in achieving that result, *before* it asks what *America* should do. That is not a recipe implying the United States should not play an active role in a given case. It only says, ask first. Without continual U.S. involvement, for example, sustainable Arab-Israeli peace is very unlikely. Again, among external powers only the United States has the capability to prevent future

Saddam Husseins from capturing major regional assets. But we must also remember that there are some disputes, like the Iran-Iraq war, which can be (and was) settled *without* the United States. And some disputes, settled or not, are not worth worrying about. It is always well to remember that, if the United States does not automatically jump in, others with more at stake may do it instead. The balance of power process may operate much to America's benefit if we will but allow it.

America has valuable assets in this region. It has enormous economic and military power, it really does want regional states to be independent, and it has no territorial ambitions. It also has strong regional friends. Although the list of friends and opponents certainly may change, there is no reason it should not remain of equivalent value. While a "new world order" of peace and harmony may not be in the offing, with a prudent policy of selective leadership the United States really should be able to play a major regional role and effectively protect its interests in this region for years to come.

Notes

1. For an excellent (if pro-Zionist) analysis of Zionism generally, see Walter Laqueur, *A History of Zionism* (New York: Holt, Rinehart and Winston, 1972).

2. For the text, see John Norton Moore, ed., *The Arab-Israeli Conflict, Volume III: Documents* (Princeton, NJ: Princeton University Press, 1974), p. 32. For an excellent and very succinct discussion of the World War I period, see Albert Hourani, *A History of the Arab Peoples* (Cambridge, MA: The Belknap Press of Harvard University Press, 1991), pp. 315-19.

3. Very useful is the classic (pro-Arab) work by George Antonius, *The Arab Awakening: The Story of the Arab National Movement* (New York: Capricorn Books, 1965).

4. For text, see Moore, pp. 24-28.

5. See Joseph B. Schectman, *The United States and the Jewish State Movement* (New York: Herzl Press, 1966), pp. 222-23.

6. As has been accurately stated, "The Israeli-Arab war can properly be said to have begun on 29th November 1947. . . ." Edgar O'Ballance, *The Arab-Israeli War, 1948* (London: Faber and Faber, 1956), p. 31.

7. Both Secretary of Defense Forrestal and the CIA were arguing against partition, as well as Marshall. For Forrestal's views, see Walter Millis, ed., *The Forrestal Diaries* (New York: Viking, 1951), p. 358. The Zionist leader, Chaim Weizmann, always was confident Truman would support partition. Howard Sachar, *A History of Israel: From the Rise of Zionism to Our Time* (New York: Knopf, 1976), p. 303.

8. The Suez Canal Base Agreement getting the British out of Egypt in twenty months had only been signed the preceding October. Now London had its foothold! According to Donald Neff's well-researched analysis, the Baghdad Pact was British Prime Minister "Eden's plan to keep Britain supreme" in the region. Donald Neff, *Warriors at Suez: Eisenhower Takes America into the Middle East* (New York: Linden Press, 1981), p. 75.

9. Nasser called the raid the "turning point" in Egyptian-Israeli relations. See Kenneth Love, *Suez: The Twice-Fought War* (New York: McGraw Hill, 1969), p. 83.

10. See the king's views in King Hussein I of Jordan, *Uneasy Lies the Head: The Autobiography of His Majesty King Hussein I of the Hashemite Kingdom of Jordan* (New York: Bernard Geis and Associates, 1962), p. 161. For a valuable discussion of the crisis and its antecedents see Uriel Dann, *King Hussein and the Challenge of Arab Radicalism: Jordan, 1955-1967* (New York: Oxford University Press, 1989), Chs. 1–4.

11. *New York Times,* April 25, 1957, p. 1.

12. The United States explicitly accused the Soviets of having fomented a revolution to overthrow Hussein. *The New York Times,* May 1, 1957, p. 1.

13. Their case was not harmed when Secretary Dulles said he hoped that "the people of Syria would act to allay the anxiety caused by recent events." This was a thinly disguised invitation for a coup. The quote is from the Department of State, *American Foreign Policy: Current Documents, 1957,* p. 1038.

14. See the discussion in Patrick Seale, *The Struggle for Syria: A Study of Post-war Arab Politics, 1945-1958* (London and New York: Oxford University Press, 1965), Ch. 21.

15. See Malcom Kerr, *The Arab Cold War: A Study of Ideology in Politics,* 2nd ed. (London: Oxford University Press, 1967).

16. U Thant first explained his position to the Egyptian Ambassador to the U.N. He later explained his reasoning publicly. See United Nations, A/6669, 18 May 1967, *Special Report of the Secretary-General of the United Nations, U Thant, to the General Assembly, May 18, 1967, on the United Nations Emergency Force.*

17. William B. Quandt, *Decade of Decisions: American Policy Toward the Arab-Israeli Conflict, 1967–1976* (Berkeley: University of California Press, 1977), p. 40. For a first-rate discussion of Egyptian and Israeli views as the crisis unfolded—including their perceptions of American policy—see Nadav Safran, *From War to War: The Arab-Israeli Confrontation, 1948-1967* (New York: Pegasus, 1969), Ch. 6.

18. See U.S. Department of State, *United States Policy in the Near East Crisis,* Publication 8269, July 1969, pp. 6–8.

19. For the complete text, see United Nations, Security Council, S/RES/242 (1967) (S/8247), November 22, 1967.

20. John K. Cooley, *Green March, Black September: The Story of the Palestinian Arabs* (London: Frank Cass, 1973), p. 103.

21. Richard M. Nixon, "U.S. Foreign Policy for the 1970s: Building for Peace," *A Report to the Congress by Richard Nixon, President of the United States,* February 25, 1971, p. 122.

22. According to the Kalbs, when on October 6 Golda Meir told the American Ambassador that war was coming and the ambassador informed Kissinger, Kissinger did not believe it. Marvin Kalb and Bernard Kalb, *Kissinger* (Boston: Little, Brown, 1974), p. 460. Kissinger, in fact, thought *the Israelis* might attack. He warned them not to.

23. Nixon, *Memoirs,* vol. 2, p. 499.

24. The Geneva Conference, held under U.N. auspices, met only once. The United States and Soviet Union were co-chairs; Egypt, Jordan, and Israel were the other participants. Syria refused to participate.

25. One of the more interesting accounts is Matti Golan, *The Secret Conversations of*

Henry Kissinger: Step-by-Step Diplomacy in the Middle East (New York: Quadrangle/The New York Times Book Co., 1976).

26. See Edward R. F. Sheehan, "How Kissinger Did It: Step by Step in the Middle East," *Foreign Policy,* Spring, 1976, p. 34.

27. Resolution 338 was the cease-fire resolution passed by the U.N. Security Council in the 1973 war.

28. For a discussion of Soviet views in this period, see Robert O. Freedman, *Soviet Policy Toward the Middle East Since 1970,* rev. ed. (New York: Praeger Publishers, 1978), Ch. 6.

29. Western Europe imported more than 60 per cent of its requirements, Japan more than 90.

30. Don Peretz, *The Middle East Today,* 4th ed. (New York: Praeger, 1983), p. 385.

31. For a succinct discussion of the background of this issue and the impact of the Palestinians, see Deborah J. Gerner, *One Land, Two Peoples: The Conflict over Palestine* (Boulder, CO: Westview Press, 1991), pp. 81–85.

32. To their chagrin the superpowers had little operational influence with the Syrians and soon adopted very low profiles. In her *Syrian Intervention in Lebanon,* Naomi Weinberger titles the appropriate chapter "Superpowers on the Sidelines." Naomi Joy Weinberger, *Syrian Intervention in Lebanon: The 1975-76 Civil War* (New York: Oxford University Press, 1986), Ch. 11.

33. Robert O. Freedman, "Soviet Policy in the Middle East," in Robert O. Freedman, ed., *The Middle East Since Camp David* (Boulder, CO: Westview Press, 1984), p. 44.

34. Caspar W. Weinberger, *Fighting for Peace: Seven Critical Years in the Pentagon* (New York: Warner Books, 1990), p. 390.

35. See the excellent discussion in Barry M. Blechman, *The Politics of National Security: Congress and U.S. Defense Policy* (New York: Oxford University Press, 1990), pp. 3–7. One of these incidents—the Iraqi attack on the U.S.S. Stark—resulted in the death of 37 sailors.

36. See F. Robert Hunter, *The Palestinian Uprising: A War by Other Means* (Berkeley: University of California Press, 1991) and Don Peretz, *Intifada* (Boulder, CO: Westview Press, 1990).

37. See the succinct discussion in IISS, *Strategic Survey, 1988-1989* (London: Brassey's, 1989), pp. 156–73.

38. See Laurie A. Mylroie, "After the Guns Fell Silent: Iraq in the Middle East," *Middle East Journal,* Winter 1989, pp. 51–67.

39. For a helpful analysis, see David Garnham, "Explaining Middle Eastern Alignments During the Gulf War," *The Jerusalem Journal of International Relations,* Vol. 13, No. 3, 1991, pp. 63–83.

40. For example, see John F. Kolars and William A. Mitchell, *The Euphrates River and the Southeast Anatolian Development Project* (Carbondale, IL: Southern Illinois University Press, 1991), particularly the preface and Chapter 11. Also see Ewan W. Anderson, "Water: The Next Strategic Resource," in Joyce R. Starr and Daniel C. Stoll, eds., *The Politics of Scarcity: Water in the Middle East* (Boulder, CO: Westview Press, 1988), pp. 1–22.

41. *The Economist,* December 14, 1991 (Turkey Survey).

18

Japan and the Future of Asia

American interest in Asia has fluctuated both in focus and in intensity. In the last half of the nineteenth century interest was moderate. Economic concerns were in the forefront, driven especially by business groups who "clamored for a more spirited Far Eastern policy."[1] But with the Spanish-American War, political-military issues increased in salience. From that watershed conflict (discussed earlier) until the Japanese attack on Pearl Harbor, attention was intermittent. At the same time, there was widespread recognition that Asian affairs and American security were seriously linked. Since World War II, of course, America has considered Asia a region of major interest, having fought two wars on the continent and expended more than 100,000 lives in the struggle against "Communist aggression." In the 1970s things seemed to be coming full circle, economics again emerging as a primary concern. As the United States deals with

413

Asian countries in the years ahead, it may well face a situation that is more complex than ever before, because in the future *both* economic and political-military issues may loom large, simultaneously. Devising policies to deal with these issues will present a daunting challenge.

The Framework

Asia is an enormous region containing more than half the world's people and resources. That, in itself, makes things difficult. As one would expect in so large a region, there is great diversity. Geographically, Asia often is divided into three basic subsystems:[2] East Asia (Japan, China, Taiwan, North and South Korea); Southeast Asia (Vietnam, Cambodia, Laos, Thailand, Malaysia, Indonesia, Singapore, and Brunei); and South Asia (India, Pakistan, and Sri Lanka). But this division leaves out some of the nations of the Pacific Rim such as the Philippines and the South Pacific island chains.

In economic terms one begins with Japan, of course, an economic powerhouse competing for "No. 1" with the United States. There also are the economically dynamic New Industrial Countries (NICs) of South Korea, Taiwan, Singapore, and Hong Kong, also known as the "four little dragons." At the same time, there is great poverty in Asia, from lands of continual disappointment such as India to the gut-wrenching hopelessness of Bangladesh. Widely varying levels of development and great differentiation of both capability and hope are apparent.

There are also great differences in culture, sometimes fed by an almost xenophobic ethnocentrism. Japan's culture (though heavily influenced by the Chinese) is unique. The Japanese have a long history of which they are very proud. The great Chinese civilization was enormously important for hundreds (even thousands) of years and, along with Middle Kingdom concepts, remains so today. There are and have been great religions and philosophies from Buddhism and Confucianism to Hindu, Islam, and Shinto. There is an enormous variety of languages and dialects.

Many more examples exist of Asian diversity, of various "particularisms." But (some would say incongruously) in addition to the nation- and subsystem-particular differences there also is an overlay of widely-shared features. First, war and conflict have been almost constant phenomena in Asia, from time immemorial.

> Japan was plagued by feudal struggles and civil wars until the seventeenth century. China engaged in an endless series of defensive and offensive operations against inland barbarians, as well as many dynastic struggles. India was host to virtually all types of conflict. . . . In Southeast Asia, the lesser states enjoyed brief moments of glory and expansion, only to fall rapidly.[3]

Thus, that there has been much conflict in recent times is not unusual. This long history of conflict and the fact that most of today's governments rose from violent beginnings should not be forgotten. (How different from the American experience discussed in Part Two.)

Second, nearly all of Asia fell under foreign (European) domination in the great pre–twentieth century imperialist expansion.[4] Only Japan escaped (although China was never fully controlled). Since the various nations today are independent, they also thus shared the common experience of achieving that independence, although they certainly took varied paths. The colonization-decolonization process left a permanent mark. Regardless of the many differences that exist and the degree to which other factors may exacerbate or moderate these feelings, Asians are bound to be at least somewhat suspicious of the intentions of foreigners (especially Europeans).

Third, for decades and even centuries Asia was characterized by hierarchical relationships, domestically and internationally. Domestically, individuals had their place, groups had their place, classes had their place, officials had their place, and so on. Internationally, certain nations dominated certain subregions, and in the region as a whole, affairs were largely determined by a few key players. Even in most of the twentieth century there was little doubt about the hierarchy of power in Asia. Many would say that as we look ahead little has changed in this regard. Who doubts that, as it has been for so long, the critical Asian powers are Japan, China, and India, with half-Asian Russia and the United States being primary external actors.

Given the significance of these characteristics, it is probably inevitable that the lenses through which Asians view life bear little relation to those of Americans.

The Changing Environment

Although the foregoing describes the fundamental framework the United States must take into account in formulating its policies, it does not provide the operational context (the trend in current affairs).

At the end of World War II, "the Eurasian heartland was strong, its peripheries weak. . . . [In 1991] the situation is precisely reversed."[5] This geopolitical transformation has been evolving for some time, but the enormous changes of the past few years have greatly accelerated, until today many of the once familiar reference points are scarcely relevant. The demise of the Cold War and general warming of international relationships in the early 1990s have (temporarily?) led to a moderation of regional conflicts. At the same time, a new multipolarity is developing. Many believe that now the key powers in any given situation will vary, depending on the issue and circumstance. We concur in this judgment, but with one caveat: In almost all cases Japan's views will have to be taken into account. Japan is the single most important player in the Asian balance of power.

Box 18.1 Trade with East Asia Soars			
U.S. Trade Turnover with	1967*	1991*	Percentage Increase
East Asia/Pacific	11	316	2,773
Western Europe	18	221	1,128
Latin America	8	118	1,381

*Billions of U.S. Dollars
Source: U.S. Department of State

A second major change may be a shift from geopolitics to geoeconomics, as is illustrated in Box 18.1. Some even believe that an economically trilateral world is developing

[i]n which economic competition (or "geoeconomics") among the European Community, the United States, and an economically resurgent Japan will be the main theme. . . . In this new "geoeconomics," the competition for influence through capital flows rather than troop deployments will be the order of the day.[6]

While only time will show if that statement is too strong (and it may be), there is no doubt that today economic priorities are predominant. Moreover, and quite in contrast to Eastern Europe and the former Soviet Union, much of the ferment in Asia is precisely *because* of economic success and various national expectations for the future. Then-Assistant Secretary of State Richard Solomon even argued that in China it "was the reforms launched in 1978 that fostered a decade of 10% annual growth, an economic expansion which created the social and political pressures that exploded in the spring of last year [1989] at Tiananmen Square."[7]

The third point is that the nature and contours of many of the region's security issues are changing. This is obvious in a broad sense because of the demise of the Cold War. But not only are East-West issues gone, there are other changes. To begin with, the often less noticed East-East concerns such as the Sino-Soviet dispute, too, have largely disappeared. Then, there are regional disputes. It is true that the standdown of the Sino-Soviet dispute, the signature of a peace agreement in Cambodia, and apparently warmer relations between the Koreas are promising harbingers. But many long-standing enmities remain, such as that between India and Pakistan. Lifting superpower dominance will permit national and ethnic rivalries to assert themselves more freely. Nationalism-driven rivalries may well intensify, and minority and religious separatism increase. The political institutions of many nations are already weak, and economic modernization efforts, especially to the extent they cannot meet popular expectations, could lead to disruption. And a number of specific territorial issues remain, such as who should control the Spratly Islands.[8] While the danger of major power war in Asia has decreased significantly, regional conflict is far from eliminated.

With the general framework and operational context complete, we now turn to the major specific problems in American foreign policy. We must begin with the one that colors all others, the Japanese relationship.

Major Decision Area 6: The Japanese Relationship—Background

For most of the twentieth century America's most important relationship in Asia has been with Japan. Much of this period the focus was on security concerns. Even in the 1990s security problems are important and the U.S.-Japan security relationship remains "our strategic anchor in Asia."[9] But today the economic factor is even more crucial. "Japan and the United States together account for 40 percent of the world's economic output and 40 percent of aid to poor countries."[10]

In the early 1990s there was a severe tension in Japanese-American relations. A *New York Times/CBS News/ Tokyo Broadcasting System Poll* reported that 52 percent of Americans thought Japan would "be the No. 1 economic power in the world" in the next century, with only 30% believing America would.[11] Some 63 percent of Japanese believed America was in decline as a world power. Not surprisingly, many Americans believed the trade deficit was in large part due to unfair Japanese trade practices. But 76 percent of Japanese said "the United States is blaming Japan for its own economic problems." One Japanese economist even said the United States was becoming a "vegetable nation" that was suffering from a "kind of degenerative disease which makes it unconscious of its problems and able only to demand to borrow money from Japan and other countries."[12] Many Japanese believed America's decision to drawdown militarily and withdraw some of its forces from the Far East was symptomatic of its decline. Many Americans, meanwhile, were bitter that Japan's contribution to the Persian Gulf War involved treasure (not enough!) but not blood. Paradoxically, though, despite all the foregoing, solid majorities in both countries believed U.S.-Japan relations were friendly and that the mutual security alliance was dependable.

To help us understand this apparent incongruity as well as establish the basis for our later analysis, it is necessary to provide some historical context. Earlier we saw that the American-Japanese relationship after World War I was at first uneasy and then adversarial. In the nineteenth century Japan had been forced out of its policy of national seclusion by the naval mission of United States Commodore Perry (1853–54). But the Meiji Restoration followed, and then a period of rapid economic modernization. Then came expansion, with victories in the Sino-Japanese War and Russo-Japanese War, the annexation of Korea, and the territorial acquisitions in World War I. In the Washington Disarmament

Treaties the United States recognized Tokyo's growing power and sought a *modus vivendi,* while acknowledging Japanese naval supremacy in the Far East. For a while there was some stability, but with Japan's China war, relations with Washington deteriorated severely. Then came Pearl Harbor. In addition to its obvious effects, that attack also showed how the Japanese underestimated American economic strength and misunderstood the American national character.

As a result of World War II Japan was stripped of all its territorial gains. Foreign occupation began. In form it was an Allied venture; in practice it was largely an American operation with real power in the hands of the Supreme Commander of the Allied Powers, General Douglas MacArthur. A liberal democracy was introduced and a new constitution promulgated. Japan renounced armed forces and "war as a sovereign right of the nation."

With the coming of the Cold War, Japan became essential to American defense plans in Asia. Washington's former enemy became an ally. In 1951 a peace treaty was signed, and with it a mutual security treaty. Although termed "mutual," it did not require Japan to defend American territory; rather, it provided that American troops were to be based in Japan until Japan could "assume responsibility for its own defense." During the Korean War, Japan became the main forward American base and the occupation regime was ended.

From the time Japan regained sovereignty, Japanese foreign policy was set largely within the framework of American strategy. Japanese opinion was not entirely favorable, however. As Destler and Nacht write, "There was persistent anti-American sentiment among leftist and extreme rightist Japanese groups in the 1950s and 1960s."[13] By the 1970s there was quite broad support, though, especially with the return of Okinawa in 1972.[14]

But other issues now began to develop. One was the natural result of Japan's increasing power: a belief that it deserved to be treated more equally and consulted on matters of mutual interest. The so-called "twin shocks" of 1971 exemplified the problem. The Japanese, unaware of the secret American negotiations with China, had repeatedly been assured they would be consulted before major policy shifts. When Nixon revealed what had happened (the "China card"), Tokyo was shocked and angry. Clearly, Japan had a major interest in the China question. Then Nixon announced a 10 percent import surcharge and restrictions on the dollar's convertibility into gold. Tokyo had received less than 30 minutes' notice.

About this same time, too, economic issues were emerging. By fiscal 1966 Japan's GNP was over $100 billion. As its rapid growth continued and exports increased, Japan developed a considerable trade surplus with the United States. By 1976 it exceeded $5 billion. America, unaccustomed to foreign economic challenge, was increasingly dismayed. The Carter administration initiated low-key talks to address the trade problem, especially the issue of access to Japanese markets. Despite some reduction in trade barriers, though, by the end of the decade the trade deficit with Japan was $10 billion-plus and growing. All this at a time when Tokyo, although increasing defense spending absolutely, still spent less than 1.0 percent of GNP on the military. Americans grew more and more irritated by what they saw as a Japanese "free ride" while the trade deficit grew.

Reagan's relations with Japan differed little from Carter's: the trade deficit and defense sharing remained the major issues. And little headway was made on either. In 1982 under Prime Minister Yasuhiro Nakasone at first there was much talk about significant defense spending increases. But the reality was different. Not until 1987 did Tokyo spend more than 1 percent of its GNP on defense. Although in 1981 Prime Minister Suzuki had said Japan's policy was to strengthen its capabilities so as to be able to defend its surrounding waters to a distance of several hundred miles and its sea-lanes out to about 1,000 miles, this had not happened. From the American public's perspective, actual capabilities were not the nub of the issue, though. That is why the fact that Japan had the third largest defense expenditure in the world meant so little. The issue was fairness, doing their fair share.

On the economic side, in the early Reagan years there was some optimism. In May 1981 Japan agreed to a "voluntary" reduction in auto exports to the United States. Further negotiations brought reductions in tariff barriers. But Japanese exports continued to flow, and although restrictions on American imports were reduced slightly in selected areas, a vast and pervasive network of nontariff barriers still discriminated against U.S. products (and those of other Western nations). By 1983 the trade deficit was $21 billion, by 1987 it exceeded $56 billion. Americans, confronted with huge U.S. budget deficits and defense expenditures while Japan's enormous economic growth continued, spoke about "unfairness," the need for a "level playing field." The Japanese, believing the United States was primarily at fault, were increasingly resentful. As Nakasone once said, "nothing is more shameful" than to be labeled as unfair.[15]

The Japanese Relationship: Looking Ahead

Washington and Tokyo both recognize the importance of their economic and security relationships, for themselves and for others. And despite all-too-apparent resentments and recriminations, there is a general, if somewhat uneasy, belief that things are better than they may appear.

On the security side, the mutual security treaty remains intact, and the two nations together have unmatched capabilities in the region. While the public and many in Congress focused on the "fairness" issue, in the 1980s "defense cooperation had evolved to include real operational cooperation between U.S. and Japanese forces."[16] By the end of the decade, co-production of certain major systems was in progress, and American aerospace firms were deeply involved in cooperative projects with the Japanese Defense Agency.

There were other grounds for optimism, also. One was common recognition of the widespread concern in Asia about a resurgence of aggressive Japanese militarism. Both nations believed a strong American presence and protective umbrella were useful politically as well as militarily. By 1990, with the demise of the Cold War and the Soviet threat, Americans pushing for a much greater Japanese defense expenditure appeared to have even less of a case. With a defense budget of approximately $30 billion and providing approximately 40 percent of the costs of stationing U.S. forces-in-country, perhaps Japan was doing enough.

Economically, too, there were important trends in the right direction, even if the American public had not really taken them in. By 1990 the trade deficit had narrowed to about $40 billion. In part this was due to further reductions in trade barriers, but the key development was a major exchange rate adjustment. In September 1985, in what was called the Plaza Accord, Japan, the United States, and five other industrialized countries agreed to devalue the dollar against the yen and other leading currencies. The result was to make American goods cheaper, thus increasing U.S. exports and diminishing the now more expensive U.S. imports. In 1989 further efforts to deal with bilateral economics conflicts occurred in the Structural Impediments Initiative (SII). These talks tried to deal with behavior patterns in the two countries that provided some of the foundation for Japan's resistance to American imports (and American non-competitiveness).[17] Under an agreement signed the following year, Tokyo and Washington sought to reduce the deficit and barriers to trade and investment.

Despite the positive trends, the issues of defense sharing and trade deficit were far from resolved. Although the trade deficit had shrunk somewhat, it still was enormous, and in 1992 it began to increase again. In most areas of dispute, SII had had no discernible impact. And there were several other difficulties. First, faced with a stronger yen, Japanese corporations had poured tens of billions of dollars into new technologies, investing more than twice as much as the United States in new plants, equipment, and research. "They turned the country's greatest postwar economic boom into a period of restructuring that left them more competitive than ever."[18] Second, the Japanese had made enormous investments in the Unites States. Indeed, the cross-border capital flows were unparalleled in American history. They helped to finance the U.S. trade and budget deficits.[19] Japanese investments in banking and real estate made Americans especially uncomfortable. Third, Japan and the United States were rivals in precisely the high-technology areas that provide so much of the impetus for modern economic development. There now is a new term in the jargon: technorivals. And finally, the United States was unable to get its own house in order. Budget deficits remained enormous, the personal savings rate was about one-half that of the Japanese, and capital investment was considerably less (although the economy was about twice as large).

It was clear in the early 1990s that American-Japanese relations were in a state of flux. The old premises that had provided the parameters for policy and kept particular disputes subordinated to the larger interests of mutual security had been destroyed. But each nation realized they still had certain common interests. One was regional stability, and the elements of the mutual security treaty remained intact. This was important. Additionally, while they certainly were major competitors economically, their economies also were heavily interdependent. As they looked forward they knew that while future relations would be different, it was important to minimize their enmity (or "conserve enemies"). In Parts One and Two of this book, when we used the term "strategic sensitivity," usually we did so in a political-military context. But strategic sensitivity applies equally to economic issues, and both nations knew only too well how their vital national interests could be harmed if policies led to economic warfare.

One effort to begin to redefine their relationship resulted from a March 1990 meeting between President Bush and Prime Minister Toshiki Kaifu. They spoke of a global partnership.[20] That presumably would mean moving toward greater foreign policy coordination, increased cooperation in international economic assistance, and more equal roles in security relations (at least regionally).

Achieving the cooperation required for such a partnership will not be easy. To begin with, there is the problem of the basic nature of international relations and powerful sovereign nations acting in their own interests in that decentralized anarchy. Then add the erosion of the security-based premises that had brought so much cooperation in the postwar period. With resentments and frustrations fueled by competition, cultural differences, and misperceptions, the trade dispute has significant spillover effects. And, in some cases, national interests just do not coincide.

In looking forward in security matters, Washington has two fundamental alternatives. The first involves a major adjustment of existing policies and obligations to altered circumstances, while retaining their essential thrust. American East Asian security policy has been built on a series of bilateral security relationships designed to contain Communist aggression, the Japan treaty being central but not the only link. Japan, for its part, "spent three decades building a domestic consensus . . . based in large part on the premise of superpower confrontation."[21] But these security relationships, while formed with the Communist menace in mind, also pertain to other threats. Indeed, the United States still has important obligations in Asia. It is largely *because* of the American presence, this argument goes, that Northeast Asia, "a perennial cockpit of great power rivalry and conflict, is today more peaceful and stable . . . than at any time since the beginning of the century. . . ."[22]

According to this view, a significant U.S. drawdown would lead to a lessening of American-Japanese cooperation. That, in turn, would tend to create a power vacuum, a dangerous situation in any era. Because of Japanese concerns about regional powers or developments, such as what might happen in Korea, a power vacuum probably would compel the Japanese to vastly increase their forces. This is not pleasant prospect for Tokyo's neighbors. There also is no guarantee against a resurgence of Chinese militarism, and no one knows what will happen with the forces of the former Soviet Union. For reasons of stability, then, the United States and Japan must continue to cooperate widely in defense matters, although the two countries will have to do so in a more interdependent and equal manner than in the past.

Choosing the counterbalancing interest is much less palatable to American officials: a gradual withdrawal and a largely new relationship. Those who believe that alternative to be likely argue that American domestic economic and political needs, cuts in the defense budget, and an increasingly zero-sum kind of economic rivalry with Japan will place almost unbearable pressures to "bring the boys home." Added to this, as Holbrooke puts it, is the view that because of *regional* factors "the removal of permanent American military facilities and troops from East Asia is probably inevitable."[23]

Perhaps. If this occurred, America would have to decide anew on its policy toward Japan. It is by no means to be taken for granted that Japan would become more militarily assertive. Given the recent tendency toward mutual complaints, too, it is by no means obvious that Japan and the United States under such circumstances will continue to find overriding mutual interests. A largely cooperative and equal relationship might be possible, but the Japanese character adjusts more readily to up or down relationships. And the United States still carries a heavy emotional baggage in remembering Pearl Harbor, as well as resentment over alleged Japanese "ingratitude" for the "free ride" ever since. Crystal balls get cloudy at this point.

One thing is certain: no security policy alternative can be chosen separately from decisions on economic policy. Not only is there a spillover effect, but it may turn out that geoeconomics will so dominate as to largely determine the security aspects.

No matter how bright a face one tries to put on it, the United States-Japanese economic relationship is bound to be strained. The Structural Impediments Initiative, though well-intentioned, is unlikely to have much impact. The bilateral trade relationship—in which the United States has imports of approximately *$100 billion*—shows little prospect for improvement, barring drastic voluntary action by Japan in critical areas such as autos and auto parts (or severe U.S. protectionism). Comparative economic advantage in many areas may continue to move in Japan's direction, financially, industrially, and technologically. In Asia, Japan probably will increasingly displace America, perhaps coming close to creating by economic (instead of military) means a new "Greater East-Asia Co-Prosperity Sphere." American efforts simply to resist Japanese advances or develop a new economic "containment" policy are neither feasible nor prudent.

What is needed, instead, is a policy based on four clear principles. First, no matter what the rhetoric adopted or agreements concluded, the United States simply must put its own economic house in order. The annual budget deficit must be decreased, productive R&D increased, educational problems addressed, and so on. All of this is easier said than done, of course.

Second, although some degree of economic rivalry is inevitable, prudent policy and courteous discourse can do much to alleviate the problem. While Washington surely must continue its efforts to open the Japanese economy, it needs to do so in a way that shows respect for the Japanese culture and its people. It needs to accept that different nations are different. The Japanese are extraordinarily sensitive on this issue. Reciprocally, Japan needs to understand better the American perspective and not think of America primarily as a rapidly deteriorating society unable to help itself and desperately searching for scapegoats.

Third, even if the bilateral economic relationship will have its ups and downs, the two nations can increase their cooperation in multilateral settings. Strengthening GATT, working together on Third World aid and debt, and cooperating within the Group of 7 (G-7) framework on regional and global mat-

ters would be most beneficial. With Japan now the world's largest creditor nation and the United States the largest debtor, there is even more support for this
rationale. While Tokyo already has endorsed "many international programs
with strategic implications—Latin American debt relief, East European recovery, Middle East peacekeeping . . . ,"[24] more can be done.

Finally, as the United States deals with this issue, it needs to restrain its pro-
clivity to "do something even if it's wrong." Because wrong it may be. While
overall national economic statistics can portray increasing comparative doom
and gloom, the average American's lot in life is far better than that of his
Japanese counterpart in terms of living space, automobiles, leisure time, and
many of the other components of what we call the American way of life. Many
Japanese know this only too well. Add to this that Japan is under increasing *regional* challenges from the "four little dragons." Some believe South Korea or
Taiwan or Singapore will be "the Japan" of the twenty-first century. Also,
Japan's economy has been developing problems of its own, as the precipitous fall
in value on the Tokyo stock market in 1992 was signaling.

America has been Japan's consistent and only reliable friend since World
War II. From a coldly rational point of view, even if the security arrangement no
longer mattered, Japan *needs* America both politically and economically. Not
only is the level of their economic interdependence unequaled anywhere else, but
Japan's continued prosperity is probably tied above all to the American market.
And without American political support, Japan would quickly encounter the
still-existing fears of Japanese imperialism that its own past actions earned it.
For all of these reasons, Japan would be ill advised if it chose to alienate the
United States. But rationality does not always prevail in foreign policy or in in-
ternational relations.

Major Decision Area 7: The Chinese Relationship

Part Two of this book showed how the United States, from the turn of the century until World War II, was fond of issuing grand declarations about China and
its future, yet unwilling to make substantive commitments that it would back
with action. In part this reflected American ambivalence about a growing commitment in Asia. That ambivalence masked uncertainty over a more fundamental question: How important was China to the United States?

Before World War II there was no consensus on this issue, although American missionaries returning back home with quaint tales about Chinese customs
(*white* for mourning, firecrackers at funerals) whetted U.S. curiosity. But American do-good efforts in China, even though substantial, were no substitute for an
appreciation among equals of Chinese culture. In those days, too many Americans knew the Chinese in person only as the little laundryman down the street.
As John King Fairbank perceptively wrote, "Out of the mix of past Sino-American relations, Chinese today can stress American imperialism where we see
mainly our philanthropy, exploitation where we see aid to the Chinese people;

and, of course, both views will be true and documentable as far as they go."[25] After all, for centuries China perceived itself to be the center of the civilized world (the "Middle Kingdom") and for hundreds of years exerted dominion over much of Asia. However, most of America's dealings with China before World War II occurred in a period of great weakness and disarray in that country, further hindering productive analysis. Even Japan's recommencing of hostilities in 1937 had not answered the question of China's importance. Pearl Harbor changed all that.[26] But the new perception was not based upon China's value per se, of course. Rather, China was valued for its role in the larger struggle against the Axis.

Paralleling this kind of strategic sensitivity in Washington though, was runaway idealism. There developed an image of a heroic China, personified in Chiang Kai-Shek. Chiang "came to be the apotheosis of the generalissimo . . . , a soldier-saint, and savior of modern China . . . a defender of democracy . . . whose fight was the same as that of America."[27] President Roosevelt was so enamored of China that he included it in his concept of the four postwar policemen, discussed earlier.[28]

Throughout World War II there was a very tenuous and sporadic cooperation against Japan between Chiang's Nationalists and the Communist forces of Mao Zedong. But when hostilities ceased, that cooperation quickly ended. Civil war followed. The United States tried to mediate, but the gulf between the parties was too great, and by late 1949 Chiang's forces had to flee to Taiwan (Formosa). America believed strongly that the "Chi Comms" were hand-in-glove with Moscow, although, as we pointed out earlier, there were clear reasons to think otherwise. The signature of the Sino-Soviet alliance in early 1950 and the Chinese intervention in the Korean War convinced most remaining doubters. From that time until the playing of the "China card" (or China's "American card"), unremitting hostility characterized Sino-American relations, with the deleterious strategic effects we have already examined.

But one should not assume the China card ushered in a period of harmonious relations. Certainly, founded solidly on balance-of-power thinking as it was, it greatly enhanced each nation's security by conserving enemies. But that common interest did not eliminate all other sources of friction (as some Americans had expected), even if it did subordinate them. Indeed, in the Nixon and Ford years there was little movement toward other agreements, and no movement at all toward a convergence of views on Taiwan. The American actions did, however, produce an important and desired shift in another area—normalization of Chinese relations with Japan.[29] In the sequel, Carter continued the effort to enhance cooperation with China, and on January 1, 1979, diplomatic relations were established.[30]

What became increasingly evident, if not entirely welcome, in Washington was that China was determined to chart its own course and not play second fiddle to America's desires. Some of its initiatives were appreciated. In February 1978, Beijing outlined the "four modernizations," a program for major advances in agriculture, industry, science and technology, and defense. This clearly would require help from the West. And it signed a peace and friendship treaty with Japan. But China was worried about the close relationship between Vietnam and the Soviets, and because of that acted quite contrary to American wishes. In late 1978, after Vietnam attacked Kampuchea (Cambodia), Chinese aid to the Khmer Rouge was stepped up. Then in February 1979, China attacked Vietnam. To Beijing's supreme embarrassment, though not defeated, it could not win either, and eventually it withdrew.

The early Reagan years saw a deterioration of Sino-American relations. Reagan, a long time friend of Taiwan, had strongly attacked the Carter agreement on normalization during the presidential campaign. Once in office, he first insisted on selling arms to Taiwan well in excess of Beijing's expectations. But Reagan, recognizing the adverse effects his policies were having, soon adopted some Solomon-like measures in an effort to steer a middle course. As we have pointed out many times, on most important issues the real choice usually is between fundamentally different alternatives, not half-dogs, half-cats. Such was the case here, and Reagan gradually adopted a significantly more pro-Beijing view. Relations gradually warmed, and although China more and more adopted a policy of equidistance between the superpowers, Reagan bequeathed a legacy of cordial Sino-American relations to Bush.

Then in June 1989, Chinese troops brutally crushed pro-democracy demonstrators in the Tiananmen Square massacre. The American public and much of Congress were shocked and angered. The president, too, was upset, but being concerned about the long-run significance of the Chinese relationship, he was hesitant to do more than issue a verbal condemnation. While the strategic significance of China (as a counterbalance to the Soviets) was declining, Bush and the Chinese recognized the important role China would play in the post–Cold War world.[31] Continuous diplomatic engagement would be necessary, not isolation. At the same time, Bush felt some action was necessary, so a variety of sanctions was imposed. Here again one saw that theme so prevalent in American foreign policy: the tension between realism and idealism.

Despite Bush's moves, much of the public and Congress believed he was not doing enough. Human rights concerns required stronger action. Real political reforms would be necessary before there could be business as usual. Another theme, too, was repeating itself: vigorous U.S. legislative-executive struggle, driven primarily by different policy views.

This struggle manifested itself in a dispute over renewing China's most-favored-nation status (MFN). MFN status had been granted in 1980, but under the 1974 Jackson-Vanik amendment the president had to certify annually that an MFN country permits free emigration. Prior to this time extension had been routine. But the renewal effort now became tied up with human rights and political reform issues. As time passed the administration pointed to several "modest steps" taken by Beijing after Tiananmen, arguing they were sufficient for renewal. Much of Congress disagreed.

Although seeking renewal of China's MFN status, the administration simultaneously made clear its dissatisfaction with several of Beijing's policies. Especially frustrating were reports the Chinese intended to sell missiles to Pakistan and Syria and had provided a nuclear reactor to Algeria. In retaliation, Bush canceled the sale of components for Chinese communication satellites. He also initiated potentially punitive actions under the 1988 Omnibus Trade Act (in part because of China's growing trade surplus).[32]

The president's view prevailed on the MFN issue, but that did little to enhance Sino-American relations. Chinese leaders continued to protest interference in their "internal affairs." Their real worry was more fundamental: that America's actions reflected desires for "another era of American global hegemonism and an American design to undermine China's communist regime."[33] There were different points of view in Washington on China's future significance and the degree to which it should be punished for Tiananmen Square, but few voices supported China. Twice in 1992 Congress passes legislation to deny renewal of China's MFN status unless certain improvements were made, but in each case President Bush vetoed and Congress was unable to override. But this issue was far from dead, and when President Clinton extended MFN status for one year in May 1993, he linked future extensions directly to progress on human rights.

Here were two alternatives squarely poised, raising a very old question in American foreign relations: whether (and how) pressures on foreign states could be used to achieve American goals.

Looking forward, the United States needed to consider five overlapping areas in its China policy. In the immediate future the first, inevitably—whether it ought to be or not—would be China's domestic situation. It is a nonstarter to recommend that the United States ought not to concern itself with China's domestic affairs and dispense with ethical judgments. We have pointed out many times that such concerns are ingrained in the American approach. What *is* realistic, though, is an approach that recognizes China's right to be different. While flagrant human rights abuses and dictatorial policies are unacceptable, governmental and social structures, systems, and processes particularly attuned to Chinese tradition and culture are not. The United States ought not to expect China to try to replicate America. The United States needs only to avoid the kind of arrogance that says the American way is the only way.

Second, in the economic arena, most Americans were unaware of what China actually had been doing. They assumed that because China was still Communist the economy was deteriorating and under tight central control. But the fact is that in the last decade China's GNP doubled. As Nichols Kristof wrote:

> It is one of the paradoxes of the 1990s: China, with a hard-line Communist leadership, is booming along at a 6 percent growth rate, with low inflation, foreign investment up, and exports and foreign exchange reserves at record highs.[34]

At the same time, China moved significantly in the direction of a mixed economic system, allowing a variety of private operations with much activity beyond the control of central planners, especially in the southeast region of the country. Most of the economic reforms of the late 1980s stayed in place, even after Tiananmen. Internationally, China's economy opened up considerably. Indeed, as we noted earlier, its trade surplus with the United States had reached the point that it was irritating Congress.

There is no guarantee that China's economic progress will continue, of course, but America must recognize the situation as it is rather than in a way that any preconceptions might suggest. It should adopt a low-key, supportive posture for China's gradual movement away from a centrally planned system, and a moderate and business-like approach to specific trade issues such as textile imports. Because China will need foreign capital, expertise, and technology in its quest for modernization, the United States can evolve closer links on a case-by-case basis. And it should try to help China see the value of further international integration and the realities of economic interdependence. Pushing too hard in any of these areas will be counterproductive, however.

In the political/security area, the changed and changing international environment has made future relationships uncertain. Following the playing of the China card, America had seen Beijing as a major counterweight to the Soviets. Along with the bilateral relationships with Japan and South Korea in support of America's forward deployment policy, China was a key to deterrence and regional stability. China, for its part, had much flexibility as the "swing vote" in the triangular U.S.-USSR-China strategic relationship, maintaining correct but neither too cordial nor adversarial relations with either side. Within this framework it not only sought its own national security. It also pursued economic growth and the recovery of the "lost" territories (including Taiwan).

After Tiananmen Square, China suffered widespread international condemnation, but it very quickly regained much of the lost ground. In the Gulf War it did not use its veto in the U.N. Security Council, enhancing its standing with Washington. At the same time, it criticized the war, preserving its Third World credentials.

> Moreover, since Tiananmen, Beijing has established diplomatic relations with Saudi Arabia and Singapore, restored relations with Indonesia, reduced tensions with Vietnam, and cultivated expanding commercial ties with Taiwan and South Korea. Japan, Australia, and the West European democracies have largely restored their relations to the pre-June 1989 levels.[35]

The fundamental question for the United States in this new era of less dire and clear threats is the same one that puzzled policymakers for so long before the Cold War: How vital is China to American interests? The answer, for the immediate future, is unclear. But if Americans are not sure China is *vital,* that China is important *is* clear. By its size, population base, presence, and potential, China is simply bound to be a major player in the regional balance of power, irrespective of particular inclinations. This is true economically as well as politically.

Fourth, with the end of the Cold War, American policy needs to address China more in a regional context and less in terms of its bilateral fit in the global strategic picture. Other nations, such as the four little dragons, and other entities, such as ASEAN, now will grow in importance. To a great extent, America's China policy needs to be formulated with an eye to China's interests, intentions, and capabilities in that multilateral framework. Specific Sino-American issues, such as assistance in stemming the flow of narcotics from the Golden Triangle to China's coast for shipment to the United States, probably can be productively addressed only in a larger and more amicable context. And cooperation on matters of global interest—preventing the proliferation of nuclear weapons, reducing arms sales, reducing narcotics trafficking, stopping the spread of missile technology—also will only occur if *both* the multilateral and bilateral tension levels can be diminished.

Finally, what about the long run? For more than a century, Americans have talked about China's potential. In January 1988, the high-powered presidential "Commission on Integrated Long-Term Strategy" reported, "By 2010 China may have become the world's second or third largest economy. . . . It may well become a superpower, in military terms. . . ."[36] Only time will tell whether such estimates are close or far off the mark. Either way, though, at a minimum China will be an important player in the regional balance. An American policy of respectful but continuous flexible low-key engagement with a regional and multilateral emphasis seems the way to go.

Regional Interests

America's most important bilateral relationships in the Asian area are first with Japan and then China. These two nations will be serious actors in most important regional (and some global) issues, and their views will have to be taken into account even when they are not directly involved. But Japan and China are not the whole story. From America's perspective there are three other matters that must also be addressed (with the Japanese and Chinese role in each being considered): (1) developments in Southeast Asia, (2) the Korean problem, and (3) the future of South Asia.

For a long time after the Vietnam War, American policy toward Southeast Asia focused on issues still lingering from that conflict (MIAs, for example), and on how to counter the (perceived) Soviet threat. In the late 1970s the major specific question was how to respond to the Vietnamese invasion of Kampuchea (Cambodia) and the Sino-Vietnamese conflict that followed. Washington viewed these developments in the context of the Sino-Soviet dispute and its relation to global issues. Seeing little opportunity to play a positively influential role, the United States wisely did little more than engage in public diplomacy. In the 1980s the Soviet military buildup in the Far East was the major concern. In addition to America's own defense buildup and defense sharing with Japan, in this framework the Philippine bases issue was the prime focus.

The sudden Soviet decline and other regional events combined to push security concerns into second place, however. In 1990 (after Vietnam withdrew its forces in Cambodia), the three parties to the continued civil war in Cambodia accepted (in principle) a U.N. peace plan, and in 1991 the shooting stopped.[37] Helped along by Mother Nature (a massive volcanic eruption that buried much of Clark Air Base), American-Philippine negotiations over military bases culminated in an agreement for American withdrawal.[38]

What occurred in the sequel was the growth of a trend already commenced to some extent, namely, policy with an increasingly multilateral focus, directed more toward ASEAN. While in part due to the relative decline of security concerns, this strategy was also due to the growing importance of economic matters. As Secretary of State Baker pointed out, "ASEAN today is America's fifth largest trading partner, rivaling U.S. commerce with Germany; and America is ASEAN's largest export market."[39] America's simultaneous support for the region-wide Asian Pacific Economic Cooperation process caused some consternation in ASEAN, though, its members seeing a challenge and competition. How this all would work out was not clear, but it was evident that economic matters had replaced security concerns as the focus of attention.

The second major problem was divided Korea and the potential for hostilities. Because of its strategic location, Korea long has been a desirable prize for outside powers. The Sino-Japanese War of 1894 was fought primarily over Korea, for just one example. Ever since the Korean War, the defense of South Korea has been a vital American interest, with major American forces forward-deployed to help achieve this objective. When President Carter in 1979 sought to withdraw ground combat troops, the outburst of opposition at home and in Asia forced him to change his mind.

Even though as 1993 began it was apparent that there would be major U.S. force drawdowns globally, what that meant for Korea was unclear. The United States still considered defense of South Korea a vital interest and believed the North Korean regime was dangerous.

At the same time, though, there was hope for a reduction of tension. After four decades of hostility, North and South Korea had initiated a dialogue to (hopefully) lay the groundwork for better relations. By February 1991 some thirteen meetings had been held. At year's end the two nations signed a nonaggression pact and a "Joint Declaration for a Non-nuclear Korean Peninsula." The latter was particularly significant. South Korea earlier had stipulated that there were no nuclear weapons on its soil. North Korea, however, was widely believed to be moving toward nuclear capability. Although it had signed the Nuclear Nonproliferation Treaty in 1985, it had never permitted the on-site inspection the treaty requires. In early 1992 it signed a nuclear safeguards agreement calling for international inspection, but no one knew if this agreement would actually be implemented. (The fact that none of the major provisions of the nonaggression pact had been put into effect one year after its signature was hardly a promising omen.) The United States, suspicious of North Korea's intentions, worried that South Korea was perhaps moving too fast. Maybe this was only a ploy.[40] When in early 1993 North Korea threatened to withdraw from the NPT, concern increased. Although Pyongyang suspended its decision one day before the withdrawal was to become effective, the problem was far from resolved. Time would tell.

While security concerns were uppermost, America also had economic interests in South Korea. South Korea was one of the four little dragons. Its economic growth had catapulted it into the world's thirteenth largest economy. Its per-capita income had tripled in a single generation. Here the issues were largely single-focus, such as the "excessive" export of "cheap" shoes to America. The United States overall was supportive of South Korea's economic course, its main objectives being to obtain Seoul's support for freer trade.

The third major issue was what to do about South Asia. Some background is necessary here for perspective. American contact with India and Pakistan, the most important nations in South Asia, has essentially all taken place since World War II, since these nations attained their independence. From the end of the Seven Years War (1756–63) until World War II, Britain had controlled the subcontinent (after eliminating all the other European contenders). This long foreign control, quite naturally, left the Indians sensitive to and suspicious of outsiders. With the end of World War II, Britain chose to leave, though it hoped the political unity of India could be preserved and considerable British influence retained. But Hindu-Muslim enmity made unity impossible. Brutal fighting followed, and in August 1947, the separate states of largely Hindu India and largely Muslim Pakistan were born. British relations with both of the new states were fairly good. Indian-Pakistani relations, by contrast, were deeply acrimonious, each nation becoming the other's primary power problem. Hostilities subsequently occurred over Kashmir in 1965, and in 1971 over the establishment of Bangladesh.[41]

Until the late 1980s the United States saw its relations with India and Pakistan (and their relations with each other) through the prism of the Cold War. America would have preferred to sign both up as allies, but given their mutual enmity and India's preference for neutrality, that proved impossible. Pakistan, smaller and more vulnerable, moved fairly close to the United States, joining both SEATO and the Baghdad Pact in the 1950s and receiving considerable economic and military aid. In the Bangladesh crisis, Washington believed the former East Pakistan's rebellion was largely unstoppable by the central government. But Washington worried that India, which was helping the rebellion, also would seek to dismember West Pakistan. By now India had moved closer to the Soviet Union, having signed a friendship treaty with Moscow in August 1971. Washington believed the appropriate response was to "tilt" toward Pakistan and thus thwart the Indian-Soviet designs. Whether it occurred because of American moves or not is controversial, but India soon accepted a cease-fire.

Though subject to the ups and downs of any bilateral relationship whose existence is primarily a derivative of other events (third party influences), American friendship and aid for Pakistan remained fairly steadfast over the next two decades. Even in the 1980s, when it was evident that Pakistan was making progress in developing nuclear capability, things held together fairly well, in part due to Pakistan's support of the mujahadeen in the Afghan war. Throughout most of this period, American relations with India, though, were cool at best, as New Delhi received continuing financial largesse from Moscow, drawing increasingly closer to the Soviets. Because India was bound by a network of political, economic, and military agreements to Moscow, was opposed to the United

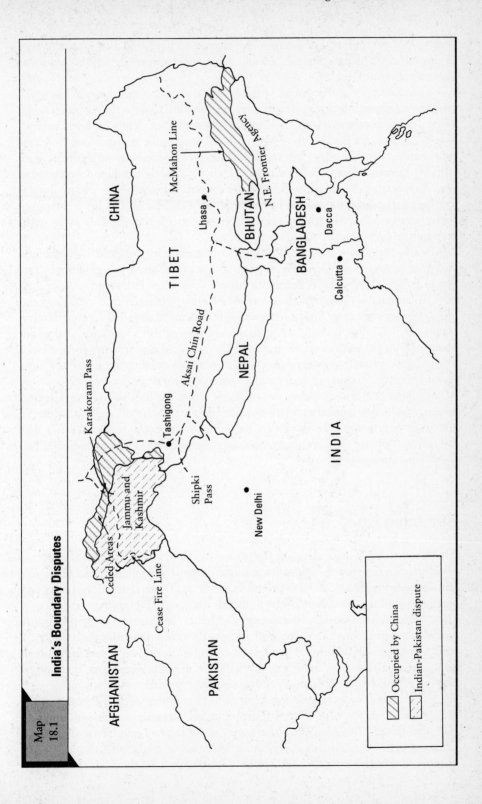

Map 18.1

India's Boundary Disputes

AFGHANISTAN

PAKISTAN

CHINA

TIBET

NEPAL

BHUTAN

BANGLADESH

INDIA

Karakoram Pass

McMahon Line

N.E. Frontier Agency

Lhasa

Dacca

Calcutta

Aksai Chin Road

Tashigong

Shipki Pass

New Delhi

Jammu and Kashmir

Ceded Areas

Cease Fire Line

Occupied by China

Indian-Pakistan dispute

States on many political and economic issues, and harbored a deep and fervent animosity toward Pakistan and China, it is hardly surprising Washington was less than enamored.

Occasionally an American administration sought a more pro-Indian position. Kennedy saw India as the primary Asian alternative to the Chinese model of economic development for the area, a "showcase" of democracy and capitalism in the struggle for the Third World. Even with India unresponsive to American views, from 1946 to 1968 India received more American aid than any state outside Europe, except South Korea. Yet India's foreign policy never became pro-American, or even really neutral. Its economic growth was disappointing. Although its per capita income has gone up since independence, India remains a bitterly poor country with discouraging prospects (in part because of its great population pressures).

Still, as we look forward on the subcontinent, with the Cold War over, the old prism through which all events were seen is gone. There is no big Soviet factor in Indian policy, nor is American friendship toward Pakistan predicated on Cold War criteria. While the past cannot be erased, in each case modified relationships are probable. Pakistan now can be valued in terms of its contribution to regional stability, its willingness to avoid joining the nuclear club, and so on. And literally for the first time in decades, there is an opportunity to develop a constructive relationship with India, free from the debilitating effects of East-West concerns. Because of India and Pakistan's mutual enmity, economic woes, separatist issues, and domestic instability, it would be foolish to think simultaneously close and amicable relations with both are in the offing. But solid and mutually beneficial relationships are indeed possible. In the new post-Cold War atmosphere in late 1993, serious Sino-Indian boundary talks raised hopes of further reductions in tensions.

Summing Up

In Asia as in most other areas of the post–Cold War world, economic concerns have shouldered security issues from center stage. The United States' economic challenge from Japan can be expected to continue. There also will be increasing challenges from others, such as the four little dragons. America cannot deal with these effectively without, to some extent at least, first putting its own house in order. Beyond this, while it needs to address the trade deficit(s), the problem is really broader. Ultimately the problem is economic and societal strength and vitality. What also is required is a policy with a multilateral emphasis, building on the increasing economic interdependence of the international economy.

The preeminence of economics does not mean that security concerns will no longer exist. As with Eastern Europe, many hitherto suppressed enmities, dormant through the Cold War years, may well surface again. What shape such enmities will take, in their interaction, is well nigh unpredictable. What is clear, though, is that the United States, learning its lessons from the past, should exercise great care before being tempted to intervene with military force. If the issue is indeed important, America can also count on the fact that the larger Asian powers will have to take a stance. America's role, if it involves the United States much at all, should be geared to minimize its involvement, and the natural operation of the balance of power process may make that entirely possible.

A further unpredictable joker in the game is the role of religious fundamentalism in Asia, where the Islamic religion, as in the Middle East, has a strong hold.

Perhaps the most important thing of all that should guide U.S. policy is a downplaying of its historic tendencies to sentimentalize the Far East. America, in its self-image, has fought to save China from Japanese imperialism, has assisted the Filipinos ("for whom Christ also died"), has set Japan on a new and democratic path to progress, and has labored (without much success) to teach the Indians better ways to use their post-independence freedom. These past-future linkages essentially reflect a flattering view of American activities, which, although not without historical truth, is only one part of the picture. Regardless of American motivation or past behavior toward Asia, the time has come to reassert American practicality and to deal with Asia on its actual merits—but in a spirit of cooperation rather than condescension, respecting Asian nations as sovereign equals but not yielding, either, where clear American interests are involved. The United States and the American people may not like many things that happen in Asia—such as the Chinese government shooting students—but neither can the United States define the Chinese government's policy. And if the United States attempts to teach the Chinese a lesson, the United States should be prepared for the fact that the Chinese will not wish to be preached at. Insisting on exporting American moral principles of behavior is simply, in the end, another form of sentimentalism. This may be a harsh saying, but it is also realistic.

Notes

1. Davids, *America and the World of Our Time,* 3rd ed. (New York: Random House, 1970), p. 45.

2. Thomas M. Magstadt, *Nations and Governments: Comparative Politics in Regional Perspective* (New York: St. Martin's Press, 1991), Ch. 13.

3. Fred Greene, *The Far East* (New York: Rinehart, 1957), p. 11.

4. Of course, some of the Asian nations have themselves engaged in imperialist behavior.

5. Robert A. Scalapino, "The U.S. and Asia: Future Prospects," *Foreign Affairs,* Winter 1991–92, pp. 19, 20.

6. Chin Kin Wah, "Changing Global Trends and Their Effects on the Asia-Pacific," *Contemporary Southeast Asia,* June 1991, pp. 8–9.

7. Richard H. Solomon, "Asian Security in the 1990s: Integration in Economics, Diversity in Defense," *U.S. Department of State Dispatch,* November 5, 1990, p. 244.

8. Located in the South China Sea, the Spratly Islands have been a potential source of conflict among China, Vietnam, and the Philippines because of the possibility of oil fields nearby.

9. Solomon, p. 245.

10. Steven R. Weisman, *New York Times*, December 3, 1991, p. A6.

11. All data in this paragraph are from that poll. See *New York Times*, December 3, 1991, p. A6.

12. Weisman, p. A6.

13. I.M. Destler and Michael Nacht, "Beyond Mutual Recrimination: Building a Solid U.S.-Japan Relationship in the 1990s," *International Security*, Winter, 1990/91, p. 96.

14. Michael Green argues that in the late 1960s advocates of autonomy and an independent security role were strong in Japan. See Michael J. Green, "Japan in Asia: the American Connection," *Global Affairs*, Summer 1991, pp. 60–63.

15. Quoted in Alan D. Romberg, "New Stirrings in Asia," *Foreign Affairs: America and the World, 1985*, p. 519.

16. Destler and Nacht, p. 97.

17. In his controversial best-seller, Shintaro Ishihara says the talks were just more evidence of an unequal relationship between Japan and the United States, one which ignores distinctive features of Japanese society, especially certain "cultural" aspects. Ishihara believed "racial prejudice" was behind much of the Japan-bashing. The entire book is worth reading. See Ishihara, *The Japan That Can Say No*, English language edition (New York: Simon & Shuster, 1991).

18. James Sterngold, "Intractable Trade Issues With Japan," *New York Times*, December 4, 1991, p. C2.

19. According to Destler and Nacht, Japan literally saved the dollar from collapse in 1987. Japanese investment in the United States, $2.6 billion in 1986, rose to $6.6 billion in 1987, doubled to $12.6 in 1988, rose to $13.6 in 1989, fell to $11.9 in 1990, and sank to $3.8 in 1991.

20. At this meeting also, though, Bush received a promise from Kaifu to take steps to focus Japan's future growth less on exports and more on expanding domestic consumer demand. International Institute for Strategic Studies, *Strategic Survey, 1990–1991* (London: IISS, 1991), p. 108.

21. Green, p. 63.

22. Richard Holbrooke, "Japan and the U.S.: The Unequal Partnership," *Foreign Affairs*, Winter 1991/92, p. 48.

23. Holbrooke, p. 48.

24. Yoichi Funabashi, "Japan and the New World Order," *Foreign Affairs*, Winter 1991/92, p. 61. Japan was the leading donor of aid to the Third World in 1989, the United States in 1990.

25. John King Fairbank, *The United States and China*, 3rd ed. (Cambridge, MA: Harvard University Press, 1971), pp. 402–03.

26. Exemplifying the point that all nations assess events in terms of the impact on their own national interests, Chiang Kai-Shek considered the Japanese attack "a blessing." See Nancy Bernkopf Tucker, "China and America: 1941–1991," *Foreign Affairs*, Winter 1991/92, p. 76.

27. John G. Stoessinger, *Nations in Darkness: China, Russia and America,* 4th ed. (New York: Random House, 1986), p. 33.

28. This was why China, at U.S. insistence, was given a permanent seat on the U.N. Security Council.

29. At the price, for Japan, of worsened Japanese-Soviet relations.

30. Although Washington withdrew recognition from Chiang's government and renounced the 1954 defense treaty, it promised continued military assistance and later set up a variety of mechanisms for continued diplomatic, economic, and military consultation and cooperation.

31. The end of the Cold War and Soviet support for nations such as Vietnam made China's regional role even more important. Vietnam, Japan, and other Asian nations were enhancing relations with Beijing, and America had to be an active player or be left behind.

32. By early 1991 China had the third largest trade surplus with the United States, exceeded only by Japan and Taiwan.

33. Michael Oksenberg, "The China Problem," *Foreign Affairs,* Summer 1991, p. 1.

34. Nicholas D. Kristof, "Hard Line in Beijing Fails to Kill Boom," *New York Times,* December 17, 1991, p. A1. See Barber B. Conable, Jr., and David M. Lampton, "China: The Coming Power," *Foreign Affairs,* Winter 1992/93, pp. 133–149 for a helpful discussion.

35. Oksenberg, p. 9.

36. *Discriminate Deterrence,* Report of the Commission On Integrated Long-Term Strategy (Washington DC: January 1988), p. 6. In 1992 and 1993, China was making far-reaching improvements in its military forces, in part through major equipment purchases from Russia.

37. In February 1992, the U.N. Security Council authorized the establishment of a U.N. peacekeeping operation (United Nations Transitional Authority in Cambodia, or UNTAC), to oversee the country's transition to a new administration after multi-party elections. UNTAC then was the largest, most complex peacekeeping operation in history. There were numerous cease-fire violations, however, and it was not clear that the transition would take place as scheduled. An interesting side point is that with the provision of a 600-man engineering battalion, for the first time since World War II Japanese troops were in Southeast Asia.

38. Some of the naval forces were moved to Singapore.

39. James A. Baker, III, "America in Asia," *Foreign Affairs,* Winter 1991/92, p. 13.

40. Such concerns seriously overrated Seoul's presumed naivete. Demonstrating his grasp of the subtleties of international relations and the cardinal principle of third-party influences, Korea's President Roh Tae Woo said, "The main goal of my 'northern policy' was to open formal relations with North Korea's friends and allies, and through them to influence North Korea itself." He was referring to diplomatic initiatives that had turned China and Russia, once among Seoul's bitterest enemies, into new and growing trading partners. *New York Times,* September 18, 1992, p. A4.

41. John G. Stoessinger writes: "The most savage religious war in history was neither the Christian Crusades against Islam nor the Thirty Years' War that pitted Catholic against Protestant. It was the war of Hindu against Moslem in the twentieth century." *Why Nations Go to War,* 4th ed., p. 115.

19

"New" Problems on the Agenda

As we have made clear throughout this book, decisions concerning conflict and the possible or actual use of force are the most critical ones any government must make. Historically, both during and before the Cold War such decisions were at the top of Washington's priority list, and they will continue to be important. But with the end of the Cold War, other, different kinds of problems began to receive more attention. Energy dependence, the impact of the domestic economy on foreign policy, economic development in the Third World, international trade, exploitation and pollution of the seas, pollution in the atmosphere and space, problems in the ozone layer and global warming, and population growth were among the myriad of problems now regularly appearing on the agenda.

Of course, these problems were not "new" in the sense that they had not existed before, and each had received sporadic attention at one time or another.

But they *were* "new" in terms of their priority and the degree of government attention and resources they received. Each was difficult to handle in and of itself, and because they spanned such a wide gamut, developing any kind of coordinated approach to them collectively was not possible.

In this chapter we can do no more than provide a basic introduction to these varied topics. We will have succeeded if we have alerted the reader to the expanding nature of America's foreign policy agenda and laid out the key facets of some of these new problems.

Major Decision Area 8: Energy Dependence and the American Economy

One fundamental basis of U.S. economic health is the availability at usable prices of adequate energy resources. The United States, which uses much imported oil, could be energy independent if it wished. Given its own oil and natural gas capabilities, there are or could be ample domestic supplementary supplies of alternative fuels such as sunlight, fossil fuel (coal), hot springs, hydroelectric power, nuclear power, gasohol, and the like. From a strictly cost-efficiency point of view, the most promising of these is nuclear power.

In America, nuclear energy is far less developed than it presently is in Europe or Japan. Japanese plans, for example, call for filling 40 percent of Japan's energy needs from nuclear sources. It is ironic that the only nation to suffer from a nuclear attack should be going in this direction while the United States hangs back. It is not that nuclear power plays no role at all in America, of course. In 1990 about 20 percent of electric utility generation of electricity came from nuclear power.[1] It is only that so much less has been done than could have been.

But this condition represents a legitimate political choice by Americans. It stems in part from a natural negative reaction to having dangerous plants in somebody's neighborhood—particularly one's own. It also reflects a lack of confidence that these plants are safe. Standardization of plant design and the government role in operating these plants have been fairly successful in Western Europe and Japan. In the United States the role of the government has been essentially merely regulatory.

But even without an extensive nuclear power program, there are all the other alternatives, not to mention further progress with conservation. Ultimately America's dependence on oil imports for energy is largely a question of political will and political decision.

In the light of these observations, consider the record. Take oil. In 1989 the United States consumed 6,323.6 million barrels of oil. The closest runner up in the world was Japan, with 1,818.1. Then, came West Germany (831.5), Italy (708.1), France (677.4), Canada (643.1), and Britain (634.0). To put the point another way, all the nations listed after the United States consumed together 5,312.2 million barrels, or more than 1,000 *fewer* barrels than the United States alone.[2]

Now consider that 41.6 percent of this consumption was imported, and that since 1973 imports have been at least a quarter of the consumption and more usually a third, rising nearer the half mark in 1990. Every day, in terms of *daily* imports, America was bringing in 7,202,000 barrels of oil, 4,124,000 from OPEC, and of that, 2,128,000 from Arab OPEC sources. Without major policy changes, it is more than likely that the United States will be importing well over half of the oil it consumes by the year 2000.

Even in the best of circumstances, such dependence on foreign sources is risky. If the particular nations involved are unstable, in a volatile area, or willing to use the product manipulatively, the risk increases. In 1991 the primary supplier in the Arab-OPEC category was Saudi Arabia, with Nigeria and Venezuela the leading non-Arab OPEC suppliers, and Mexico the non-OPEC. While because of the volatility of the Middle East the Saudi case is the most obviously risky, in none of these cases can one guarantee that supply will continue in the quantity and at prices that America considers tolerable. (In February 1992 there was a failed military coup in Venezuela, illustrating the risks the United States faces.) And it goes without saying, of course, that this oil has to be paid for.

If we compare the use to which America put its oil in 1970 with 1989, we find that the biggest change is in transportation, where 52.9 percent in 1970 increased to 62.9 percent in 1989.[3] This tremendous use of oil for transportation not only reflects the American love affair with automobiles but also a transportation policy that uses oil for transcontinental trucking while American railroads continue generally to be much inferior to European or Japanese rail transport. Only in very recent years have light-rail networks (and, in some cases, subways) been added to metropolitan districts—and yet less than fifty years ago light-rail systems existed in abundance before they were then supplanted by pollution-causing buses.

It should already be clear how much choices in domestic politics influence the nation's international economic position. We repeat that these are legitimate political choices, whether wise or unwise: the United States can decide to neglect its railroads and use imported oil to maintain road transport, and the American people may continue to prefer this approach. But it is the foreign policy effects that must be taken into account. The United States would not be having a persistently adverse balance of trade if it did not import oil on this scale. That adverse balance of trade, in turn, weakens the dollar and limits what the American government can do to fight the effects of any economic downturn.

The Economic Climate and Effects of Fiscal and Monetary Policies

A nation's fiscal and monetary policies are designed to have domestic economic effects. But such policies also affect the nation's international position. Before we discuss those effects, though, we need to define our terms. *Fiscal policy* is concerned with influencing the economy through changes in government expenditures and revenues. It is concerned with the budget, with taxes, with government spending, with deficits, and with public debt. *Monetary policy,* by contrast, refers to the supply of money in circulation. Obviously, these two kinds of policies have close interrelationships, but they are still distinct subjects.

The impact of public policy on the prevailing economic climate can have telling effects, even apart from the direct results of fiscal or monetary policy. In the 1980s, for example, the rush in the United States to corporate takeovers, along with junk bonds and huge debt service requirements, eventually hobbled businesses that could not keep up with the tremendous cash-flow needs. At the close of 1991, corporate junk bonds (i.e., debts created with very fragile backing of assets) were paying 34.6 percent return on investment (that is, assuming the investment did not go into default!). That may sound very attractive to an investor, but consider the position of the corporate managers who were required to find that kind of money to pay the interest for their borrowings. The defaults and bankruptcies that came along in the wake of these excesses cost jobs by the hundreds of thousands in 1991. The combination of defaults, bankruptcies, and unemployment coincided with a time when the enormous U.S. public debt inhibited federal government stimulation. It is here we come to fiscal policy. In 1991, because it was spending so much more than its taxing policies provided, the government was already borrowing 18 percent of its income. (Compare that to 37 percent of its income received from personal income taxes.) That same year, while 23 percent went to defense and 7 percent to Medicaid, food stamps, and the like, 14 percent went simply to paying interest on the federal debt.[4] It was evident that soon more would be being spent on debt service than on defense.

Meanwhile, the annual federal deficit by now had all the earmarks of a fire out of control. In 1985 Congress, unable to come to grips with growing deficits, had passed the Gramm-Rudman-Hollings Act. Under its terms the president had to submit a budget request that did not exceed legislatively specified deficit levels. And the deficit was to be gradually phased out. Gramm-Rudman-Hollings simply did not work. As a result, the goal of a balanced budget was put off until 1993. But it quickly was clear that that deadline would not be met, either. In 1990 the president and Congress reached another budget compromise, but that, too, proved of little value. When President Bush presented his budget in January 1992, figures showed an estimated federal deficit for fiscal 1992 of $399 *billion,* far above the $269 billion recorded the previous year.[5]

The economic turndown in the United States in the early 1990s coincided with an enormous budget deficit and the savings and loans scandal (and that scandal was, in turn, junk bond-connected). These developments further constrained the U.S. ability to act freely. The government's earlier failure to try at least partially to head off this disaster by disallowing junk bond interest as legitimate income tax deductions (which would have seriously inhibited junk bond investment) was again a legitimate political choice. But in retrospect the failure was hard to explain other than as a manifestation of a rigidly maintained belief in laissez-faire.

The total effect was equivalent to putting the ship of state "in-irons"—caught with no way to move on and, because of the huge public and private debt, unable to increase public spending substantially in order to revive the stalled economy.

Now place this set of problems in an international context. The fluctuating value of the dollar against foreign currencies reflects these public policies.[6] We all know that the dollar can "shrink" domestically as the cost of living goes up. But when it buys less, either at the store down the street or on the Geneva foreign money market, it does so for some specific reasons. One of these, with immediate foreign policy effects, is the prevailing rates of interest on invested money in the United States. Such interest rates are affected within U.S. borders by a variety of supply and demand factors. Because the interest rate (the "price" of money) itself affects supply and demand, and thus affects the amount of money in circulation, the rate is used as a tool by the Federal Reserve Board (or the Fed) and its Federal Reserve Banks. The Federal Reserve Board sets the ratio of deposits that commercial bank members must hold on deposit at their regional Federal Reserve Bank. That in turn affects the amounts that the banks can loan out. As a simple illustration, if the ratio is increased, loaning ability declines, and vice-versa. Another tool the Federal Reserve Board can use to decrease loan ability is to sell bonds on the open market. Whoever purchases these bonds draws down on bank deposits to do so, thus reducing loan capacity. Finally, the Federal Reserve can raise or lower the discount (or rediscount rate, as it often is called) on funds the Fed loans to banks. That particular feature is usually well reported in the newspapers, and it immediately affects the prime rate at which banks offer loans to customers.

In all of these maneuvers, one can see that what is really being controlled is the amount of money in circulation. From the Federal Reserve's point of view, the term "money" and the term "bank deposits" are fairly synonymous. And it is, of course, the Federal Reserve that also issues the bank notes.

When interest rates are pushed lower by the Federal Reserve, as in December 1991, in order to stimulate the economy, we say that the Fed is "making money cheaper." That is to say, it is taking steps that logically will inflate the number of dollars in circulation. Assuming that the figure for goods and services produced remains constant, any increase in the number of dollars will have an inflationary effect. Expressed differently, a greater number of dollars will chase a constant amount of goods to buy. The Federal Reserve hopes, by making dollars cheaper, that business and home-buying will expand. The problem in a weak economy is that monetary policy alone has a limited power to influence it, even apart from the debt and cash-flow features examined above. It is much easier to use the Federal Reserve to brake a too-active economy than to persuade businesses and people faced with large debts to borrow more money.

We normally think of these actions of the Federal Reserve, which put more money or less money into circulation, as they link to the level of domestic inflation. But they also directly affect the value of the dollar in foreign markets.

International Implications of Domestic Economic Policy

The first effect is on investments. Lowering the rediscount rate and U.S. interest rates also discourages the foreign investments that have been of great help in financing U.S. internal debts.[7] Almost simultaneously with the Federal Reserve's action, the German Bundesbank went in the opposite direction, establishing interest rates near ten percent. That is far more than enough spread to cause investment to move from the United States to Germany.

The cheaper dollar at home also affects international trade. Depreciation of the dollar means a comparable appreciation of other currencies. Thus the dollar buys fewer German marks or Japanese yen. That makes imports into the United States more expensive, while making U.S.-made goods more attractive because they are cheaper. Exports tend to increase. By itself, this effect sooner or later will create new jobs in the United States. The greater competition for available goods, with home and foreign demand combined, will gradually raise prices. The dollar will regain value. But that will only happen in a politically neutered world, where economic cause and effect is allowed free rein. In the "real world," governments object to significant increases in imports because they threaten jobs at home and eventually create adverse balances of trade and payments. In the 1930s, when one nation devalued its currency (i.e., made it "cheaper"), usually others followed competitively. Today the situation is much more complicated because of the evolution of such arrangements as the currency stabilization efforts of the European Community. But, then, there are many alternatives open to governments who wish to restrict imports. The Japanese standards for inspecting American automobiles is one example. South Korea manages not to import any American rice. The Australians, meanwhile, complain American regulations keep their agricultural produce out of the United States. The United States, itself, has more than 3,500 quotas.

Ultimately, the value of the dollar[8] and trade policy, let alone investment policy, are all interrelated considerations. American trade policies in the early Reagan years are instructive. The administration's monetary and fiscal policies resulted in record budget deficits and high interest rates. But as Paula Stern has written, the consequences were that

> The high interest rates . . . sent the dollar's exchange rate soaring. While the strong dollar facilitated the financing of the U.S. fiscal deficit and helped to fight inflation, it compounded the trade woes of American industry, making imports cheaper . . . and exports more costly.[9]

Compounding the exchange rate problem in the 1980s were daily capital movements. Indeed, they dwarfed the daily trade in goods.[10] When huge flows of capital cross their borders, national authorities find it extremely hard to control or even significantly affect exchange rates.

The United States, as we observed earlier, has been running a consistent, although more recently reduced, deficit in its balance of trade. The single most

Box 19.1	Major Importing Nations (as of 1990)		
	Billions of Dollars	Per Capita (in dollars)	World Share (in percent)
United States	517	2050	14.3
Germany	356	4460	9.9
Japan	235	1900	6.5
France	234	4150	6.5
Britain	223	3890	6.2
Italy	182	3160	5.0
Holland	126	8460	3.5
Canada	124	4660	3.4
USSR	121	4180	3.3
Belgium-Luxembourg	120	11540	3.3

obvious figure in that balance was the lopsided trade with Japan, accounting for about $40 billion, at least two-thirds of it because of imports of Japanese cars. In 1992, it being an election year in which the American economy was also in bad shape, the political pressure was growing in the U.S. Congress to "retaliate" against the Japanese. (After all, the argument went, the Japanese have been letting the United States carry the defense burden while they have poured those defense-saved resources into outdoing America in manufacturing consumer goods.) The Japanese, for their part, had been sneering at the quality of the American product and blaming America's troubles on what they saw as inferior work habits and a complete lack of fiscal discipline, which both created America's huge internal debt and weakened the dollar. Here, again, we see the close interconnections between economics and politics.

Congress earlier had sought to lay the groundwork for at least partially remedying the problem. Section 301 of the Trade Act of 1974 provided the president with tools to try to force open foreign markets to U.S. products, for example. For political reasons, however, he rarely used them. In 1988, Congress passed the Omnibus Trade and Competitiveness Act of 1988,[11] "the first congressionally initiated major trade bill since the Smoot-Hawley Act half a century earlier."[12] Much of this law was designed to prod the administration into a more assertive trade posture.[13] But little real progress was made.

It was clear that these developments, especially put against the persistent adverse balance of U.S. trade and the proposed creation of a North American Free Trade Agreement with Mexico and Canada,[14] raised the question in national politics of the wisdom of the assumption that the freer the trade, the better. The oldest question in orthodox international economic theory was again raising its head, but in a new setting. The United States had never before had to confront an economically unified Europe, or a Japan whose economy in its major features is essentially directed, financed, and monitored by the government. We shall return to this question in the closing section of this chapter, when we come to the policy alternatives.

Development and Population

So far, much of this book has focused on the "advanced" nations of the world. But as even Americans who have not traveled abroad are becoming aware, courtesy of television news, conditions in many countries around the world are not very promising compared to the United States. Many of the "developing nations" (sometimes called Less Developed Countries, or LDCs) are not developing anything very positive at all. These nations are located primarily in the Third World. They are mainly formerly colonial, largely nonwhite, nations located in Africa, Latin America, and large portions of Asia and the Middle East. All face obstacles to economic development that range from formidable to overwhelming. The list normally would include inadequate capital, insufficient economic infrastructures (marketing, distribution, transportation and communication systems, etc.), low levels of technology, and much too low levels of labor skills, education, and training. Frequently, also, the majority of the labor force is (under)employed in subsistence agriculture. All too often the problems are further compounded by political ineptness and corruption. It is not surprising that so many of today's conflicts are in the Third World and that frustration and instability are widespread.

The relative weakness of the LDCs, and the fact that they so often are dependent in terms of trade and/or capital investment and/or external assistance on the more developed market economies of the United States, Western Europe, or Japan, has given rise to what is called the North-South problem.[15] Perceptual and attitudinal differences exacerbate matters. As John Spanier says:

> These poorer nations have been unified by a set of common attitudes: anger against their former colonial masters, the Western industrial nations, whom they blame for their backwardness and deprivation; a sense that they do not yet control their own political and economic destinies; and a determination to change the status quo as they seek a more equitable distribution of the world's wealth.[16]

Many people in these nations live in very unfortunate natural circumstances that no amount of political wisdom on the part of their governments can do much about. Bangladesh is a prime example. Because of its geography, its people will be the victims of floods and other natural phenomena so long as they live there. But there are other countries that have so many things going for them that, at first glance, their lack of progress is astonishing. Take Iraq. Or Argentina. Or Lebanon. Iraq has oil and fertile land, with two great rivers in an area starved for water. Argentina has fertile land, a secure geostrategic situation, and a skilled population. Even in Biblical times, Lebanon was envied. Psalm 72,

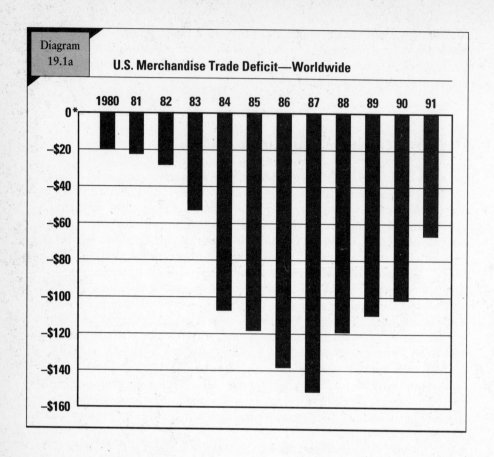

Diagram 19.1a

U.S. Merchandise Trade Deficit—Worldwide

verse 16, striving for a comparison everyone would understand, said "may its fruit flourish like Lebanon." And before civil war devastated the country, it was rich and prosperous, the trading and financial center of the Middle East. Only later was Beirut reduced to ruins, with hundreds of thousands dead.

For many LDCs there is still another problem. Many of the woes and the difficulties they face in overcoming them are complicated further because their population is growing at rates that threaten to outstrip any progress in increasing GNP. Take population growth against GNP in the Middle East, for example. Iran, with an annual average population increase in 1985–89 of 3.2 percent, had negative real GNP growth (–3.6 percent) between 1985 and 1988. Algeria, with 2.7 percent population growth, had a negative GNP (–0.7) for the same years. Egypt's figures were 2.7 and 1.6. Jordan's were 3.3 and 1.9. These nations are all falling behind in the race to keep up with their birthrates. Other countries in the area with the same disparities, like Saudi Arabia (5.6 versus 2.9) or Bahrain (3.9 versus 2.6) do not have the same problem because their oil income is great. And there are bright spots, like Turkey's figures of 2.2 and 5.3 or Morocco's 2.6 and 4.4. But for Jordan and Egypt these statistics are not only very meaningful but also depressing.[17]

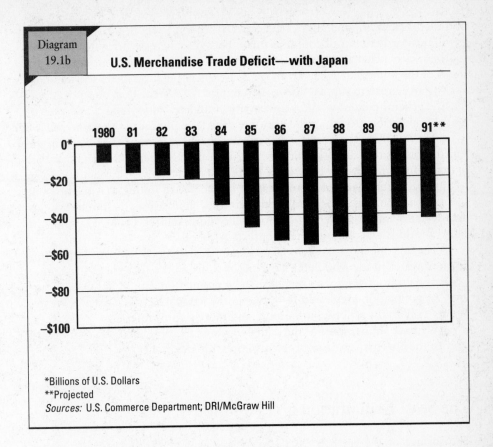

Diagram 19.1b

U.S. Merchandise Trade Deficit—with Japan

1980 81 82 83 84 85 86 87 88 89 90 91**

0*

−$20

−$40

−$60

−$80

−$100

*Billions of U.S. Dollars
**Projected
Sources: U.S. Commerce Department; DRI/McGraw Hill

The population growth figures above represent people already born. Projections that compare potential growth in numbers of people as against population density also provide meaningful comparisons. In the Mediterranean basin, large increases of population by 2025 can be expected in Turkey, Egypt, Algeria, Morocco, Syria, Tunisia, and Lebanon. Of those countries, Syria, Lebanon, Algeria, and Egypt already have a population density of 150 or more people per square kilometer.[18] (For comparison, nations like France, Greece, Turkey, or Morocco have much less density.) Egypt, which is expected to grow the most in the Nile basin, will almost double, Morocco and Algeria will do much the same, and Syria will more than double. But Syria already has more than 250 people per square kilometer, and Egypt, itself over the 150 mark, has very little arable land. Indeed, flying over the Nile, it is perfectly clear where the flooding occurs and cultivation is possible, and where the sharp line of the desert begins. Where are all these people to go, and how are they to survive?

No one has real answers to such questions. Yet the problems are not hypothetical. When we use projections for the year 2025, all those who then will be 35 years or older have already been born by 1990.

Looking at the basin as a whole, and now in terms of population shifts, we find that the urban population is expected to remain at about the same percentage in the northern tier of countries but expected to increase dramatically in the southern tier. (That is probably in part a reflection of the lack of arable land south of the immediate Mediterranean coast. As population increases, it almost has to move north to survive.) If we used figures for Africa, Asia, or Latin America, the general picture would be even worse. Indeed, more than 90 percent of global population growth in the next few decades will occur in those areas.[19]

The one thing the United States can count on for most of the nations of the Third World is that their situations will not get much better in the next decades. In many, in fact, they will get worse. There will predictably be difficulties just in feeding people in many of these areas. It is also worth noting that the amount spent on armaments in Third World countries has been increasing in the last decades at a much greater rate than in the industrialized countries. And, the Third World is where most of the conflicts will be.

There is one more issue. In Chapter 17 we discussed the enormous importance of water in the Middle East. Without water in the first place, life cannot exist; and without water to grow crops, the population cannot in any case survive. As population presses on resources in the Middle East in particular, water and its availability will become a more and more significant issue.

We have shown some of the data and stated the problems. We shall return later to the alternatives these problems imply for U.S. policy.

The Seas: Exploitation and Pollution

The surface of the earth is 70.8 percent salt water. Throughout history humankind has tended to take the seas and oceans for granted, in this century pouring sewage and dumping refuse into them at an ever greater pace while assuming an endless capacity of the water to absorb these pollutants. In the same way, we have thought of quantities so large "as the fish in the sea," without worrying overmuch about the limits to their abundance.

In recent decades all of that has been changing, even if slowly. For one thing, as we saw in Chapter 13, the seas are being "fenced off" by contiguous nations claiming exclusive zones for fisheries and other purposes, sometimes extending as much as 200 miles out from their coasts. Such zones are not "annexed" but simply regulated, and ships simply passing through ("innocent passage") are not interfered with, although those who wish to fish must be licensed. Similarly, nations have expanded their ideas as to actual territorial waters. These areas are treated as part of their territory and therefore completely subject to their jurisdiction. Where even the formerly traditional three-mile limit caused problems between such states as Greece and Turkey, whose territories are sometimes within five miles of each other, the extension of the territorial seas to nine or even twelve miles has caused problems not entirely sorted out at this time.

Ironically, the move by nations to expand their control to sea essentially began with the decision by the United States to proclaim a "neutrality zone" in the Atlantic at the outset of World War II[20]—ironically, because the United States otherwise has been in the forefront of the effort to resist the shrinking of the open seas. In any event, those nations with extensive continental shelves—which is typical, for example, of the east coasts of the Americas—began to see these areas as commercially valuable sources of raw materials. The Latin American nations on South America's *west* coast (which has very little areas of shelving and for the most part has steep descents into relatively deep waters) saw their best hope for resources in restricting fishing. That objective became more pressing as both the Soviet Union and Japan pushed ahead into very large-scale operation of floating fishing factories, utilizing advanced electronics to locate schools of fish and enormous nets to capture the fish by the thousands. Whole species began to be depleted, so the United States, which as we said stood basically for open seas and the free use of such seas, became arrayed on the side of restrictions.

Most of the questions handled by new provisions of the law of the sea had to do with practical issues that already troubled nations. Seabed mining was in a different category, primarily because its real exploitation was still in the future, even though it could be clearly foreseen. Although there are immense deposits of valuable minerals on the seabed at great depths, and especially along the "seam" of the fault lines in the Pacific, there is as yet no commercially cost-effective method for systematic extraction. A major reason is that since many minerals such as gold and manganese are still readily available on the earth's surface, there has been no commercially compelling need to develop such methods.

As restrictions multiplied on fishing, supplies shrank much less. Dolphins and seals came under more efficient protection. But the waters of the earth still presented serious problems in terms of pollution. The casual assumption that the ocean currents would carry toxic wastes away into the vast reaches of the seas proved to be a bit of poetic license. New York City, even as early as the 1960s, found itself confronted with huge masses of floating sewage and debris jettisoned offshore as an easy solution in the face of shrinking landfills. Research on currents began to reveal that choke points around the world, always very important in a strategic sense, had significant effects also on the flow of water. The Mediterranean, closed at both ends except for the narrow gap into it near Gibralter and the man-made exit at Suez, was particularly affected. Earlier we gave figures on population growth in this area. Much of its sewage and toxic waste is still dumped into that essentially inland sea. It takes years for the water to be exchanged from the Mediterranean to the oceans.

Many of the most discouraging trends are relatively recent, unknown 30 years earlier. A *New York Times* report in May 1992 says that "giant tumors on turtles, PCBs in the flesh of fish, amnesic shellfish poisoning of humans by algae blooms" all were unknown earlier. "Autopsies on beluga whales . . . regularly find ulcers, cancers, immune deficiencies and lung infections that may be caused by the mercury, lead, PCBs and other toxins that quietly accumulate in their blubber" as they eat fish from the waters of Europe or America.[21]

The report cites the 40 million gallons of partially untreated sewage New York City empties every day into its rivers. Typhoid is now at least one hundred times more common near the Mediterranean than in Northern Europe, again because of the sewage problem.

The U.S. National Marine Fisheries Service says that 65 out of 153 species are being overfished in U.S. waters; in other words, they are not being replaced as fast as they are being caught. The list includes many fish well known on American tables: Atlantic cod, sea scallops, haddock, flounder, red snapper, bluefin tuna, king mackerel, albacore tuna, abalone, and all salmon except Alaskan.

One area where definite progress had been made is in decreasing intentional oil spills in the open seas. Although most people think that accidental spills are the main source of pollution, that is not actually so.[22] In efforts to control intentional spills, the United States had taken a strong line. As a result, specialized organizations have been created, which have sponsored international agreements. What is most encouraging here is that the decline in spills has occurred even while more oil has been transported at sea. There is, of course, one glaring exception to this otherwise encouraging news: Saddam Hussein's deliberate opening of Kuwaiti oil valves during the Gulf War.

Problems in Air and Space

In air and space, too, problems are multiplying. People-generated pollution fills the skies over many countries. In the 1970s and early 1980s a number of scientific studies even indicated that the ozone layer might be in jeopardy, although there seemed to be some contrary evidence also. Recognizing the global nature of the problem, the United Nations Environment Programme tried to develop a global approach, with only moderate success. But in 1985 the Vienna Convention on Protection of the Ozone Layer was signed. Then in 1987 most doubt was eliminated, and it was "essentially confirmed that the release of man-made chloroflourocarbons into the atmosphere played a major role in creating a 'hole' in the earth's ozone layer over the South Pole."[23]

Also in 1987, the Montreal Protocol on Substances That Deplete the Ozone Layer was signed. This far-reaching agreement provided for a freeze to be instituted in chloroflourocarbons at 1986 levels one year after the treaty entered into force, followed by a 20 percent reduction in 1993–94 and a further 50 percent reduction in 1998–99. Although the Montreal Protocol entered into force in 1989, problems continued, and in early 1992 there were reports of a hole in the ozone layer over the *North* Pole and even some populated areas.

There also are problems "closer" to earth. Acid rain caused by industrial pollution in the United States finds its way north into Canada, damaging lakes, soils, crops, and forests there as well as at home. The sky over Mexico City often is a blanket of brown smog through which airplanes descend. Even "advanced" areas such as Switzerland have had their problems from the use of brown or soft coal for heating in winter where the airflow is restricted. There have been islands of progress. Ankara in Turkey, where in the early 1970s one drove through a smog layer to the apartments of the affluent on the higher hills (and which in those days looked much like Los Angeles in terms of air quality), by the 1990s was in better shape. But in many smog-plagued localities, increases in population are matched by increases in automobile pollution. And, as indicated, these effects can be international. (Many Germans in the 1980s were blaming the slow deterioration of the Black Forest on foreign polluted air.) The Chernobyl nuclear disaster is sufficiently recent to remind everyone of the way in which radiation-contaminated air and soil can drift across frontiers. And many scientists are concerned that the increasing of carbon dioxide and other gases in the atmosphere is creating a "greenhouse effect," a global warming. It does not take a genius to figure where that would lead. All these problems are increasing even for the developed countries, and the newly industrializing nations exacerbate the situation because they spare little time or effort to deal with spin-offs and side effects as they strive for production.

A U.N. report released in May 1992 said that by the year 2000 the ozone layer would likely be depleted by as much as 10 percent during the summer in temperate regions. That would increase most skin cancers by 26 percent. The report documented some gains in pollution reduction in industrialized countries during the last two decades but underlined the fact that the situation in developing countries was getting worse. In negotiations on a new treaty to bring the warming trend under control, the United States took the position that it could not accept precise figure goals for reductions of emissions. Although the European nations were prepared to go to specific goals, given this opposition they had to accept a treaty text that bound no nation to anything very specific. The United States, of course, had the greatest single problem in making progress with emissions, and at a time of recession was unwilling to impose upon itself expensive and mandatory new provisions.

The new treaty was signed at the U.N.-sponsored Earth Summit in June 1992.[24] Whether the document represented progress was bitterly argued. Those who wanted strict standards felt it was inadequate, but those who argued for looser provisions also had a point. In the current state of knowledge about the connection between the emissions and their effects in the atmosphere, rigid provisions might prove counterproductive. Scientists are by no means agreed even on whether a global warming trend is really taking place. On the other hand, complacency about progress in this area may produce really irreversible effects.

One major source of pollution both of the seas and skies has not yet been much mentioned—the now dismantled Soviet empire. Although the world knew decades ago that Czech miners were being exposed to radiation while mining uranium for Soviet nuclear warheads, the full extent to which the Soviet Union and its satellite Communist regimes in Europe wreaked havoc with the environment was hardly suspected until the disaster at Chernobyl. From an ecological and environmental point of view, Eastern Europe is a disaster area. Soviet navy personnel now admit that they dumped spent nuclear fuel into the seas off the Kola Peninsula. The Scandinavian countries are seriously discussing funding a cleanup of polluting plants located within the old Soviet Union but near enough to their own frontiers to cause severe damage. All of Europe remains concerned that the Chernobyl-type nuclear facilities that are still running may have accidents in the future. A significant part of the reason why Germany in 1992 was encountering severe financial strains in coping with reunification stemmed from the environmental damage it must repair to bring the eastern area up to Western standards.

A further sobering thought. Even if the 24 richest industrialized nations should prove able to stabilize carbon dioxide emissions at 1990 levels by the year 2000, which would represent an 11 percent saving over what it would otherwise be by the middle of the next century, the emissions from developing nations—unless something intervenes—will more than cancel out any gains. China's alone is expected to exceed emissions of all 24 nations by the year 2050 as it presses ahead with industrialization.[25]

In the air and atmosphere above the surface of the earth, other developments were causing international repercussions in the last part of the twentieth century. The strategic aspects of these developments are, of course, the most obvious. The advent of ICBMs threatened targets anywhere with instant and unpleasant death. The advent of missiles that transited outer space prompted some consideration of the legal implications. It was quickly realized that, unlike airplanes, which are considered as transiting national territory (and therefore need permission and clearance), objects in space cannot be treated the same way. The distinction is like that which originally governed the width of territorial seas—they were as wide as cannon fire could reach from shore. Similarly, airplanes can be shot down from earth, but objects orbiting far out in outer space cannot. Outer space, therefore, is like the open seas: available to all and controlled exclusively by none.

One other aspect of the strategic use of space should be kept in mind. In the 1980s, as the United States pushed ahead with the Strategic Defense Initiative, the Soviets found themselves potentially seriously outclassed.[26] They tried to limit U.S. development of SDI, but failed. Now that the Soviet Union no longer exists as such and is preoccupied with internal problems, the United States has the opportunity to truly become a world peacemaker by creating defensive systems which could mutually deny any nation an assured victory by launching a surprise missile attack.

Since up to this time the use of outer space has been restricted to only a few nations, primarily the United States and the Soviet Union, the problem of using space without interfering with the rights of other nations has not become as severe as it might be. But the advent of communications satellites has added a commercial as well as strategic advantage to the use of outer space. Such satellites can sample the ocean's parameters—currents, sea states, velocities, discontinuities in the ocean surface. They are extremely useful, too, for weather prediction and important, too, for accurate navigation. The question of use and control of satellites is bound to take its place alongside the seabed mining question as a serious future item in American foreign policy.

The use of space has created still another problem. By 1987 there were approximately six thousand items circulating in their own orbits in space. U.S. Space Command keeps track of all of these, every one of them with its own identifying number, some as small as a hammer.[27] But even a hammer can make far too big a hole in a space suit or the skin of a space vehicle. In short, because there is no easy way to remove articles from space, and since every use of space increases the number of articles in space, casualties are bound ultimately to occur, including damage to satellites.

Implications

Before discussing U.S. policy alternatives in dealing with these problems, a few further words of caution are in order. Foreign policy choices never are (and never were) unlimited. More than once we have emphasized that the really important choices are ones of direction. As the American "recession" deepened and dragged on in 1991 and 1992, a new and rather pessimistic mood was growing in the United States. Although respected publications like the London *Economist* were pointing out that the recessions of the previous decades had, from some statistical standpoints, been more severe—unemployment in 1973–75 hit 9 percent and in 1981–82 rose to 11 percent, as compared to the 7 percent at the end of 1991—there were, this time, important additional changes. Major companies, going through restructuring procedures, were eliminating many thousands of relatively high salaried positions. Those laid off or fired were not finding equally well-paying opportunities opening up elsewhere in the economy. The general salary and wage level in America was being depressed, bit by bit. It was instinctive to blame it on foreign competition, especially as cheap labor in the Far East flooded U.S. markets with goods imported under liberal tariff policies.

It was this mood, rather than the economic facts per se, that was fanning American popular resentment against Japan, a resentment focused in the media on the trade gap and, within that gap, the part caused by Japanese auto imports.[28] The actual trade gap, which reached its peak in recent years in 1987 (about $56 billion), had subsequently declined (although it could turn around again, of course). And it was true that Japanese auto imports alone into the United States accounted for $19.5 billion of the deficit. That made for a figure that had obvious media impact. But if we add up the ten top U.S. exports to Japan in 1990 and compare the total to that of the ten top Japanese exports to the United States, and then leave out the $19.5 figure, the gap shrinks to about $17 billion.[29]

Whether or not the American consumer is going to turn away from the purchase of Japanese automobiles, it would not be hard to shrink that $17 billion figure, assuming convergent U.S. and Japanese policies. The ballyhooed opening of Toys-R-Us in Japan, which coincided with President Bush's visit in January 1992, represented a breakthrough worth noting. Because of special retail certification rules used in the Toys-R-Us case, the more usual decade-long process in Japan was accomplished within 18 months! One can easily see what a loosening of Japanese internal requirements (the kind of non-tariff barriers discussed in Chapter 16) could mean in expanded trade.

Even then, it is well to remember that trade between two nations hardly ever balances, and whether it balances or not is a very minor question so long as a nation's total trade more or less balances. That fact, again, shows that the media concentration on the Japanese trade gap reflects far more than concern over economics. Added to the economic fundamentals is a complex psychological development that shows in Japan as an occasional bluster about technological superiority and that in the United States encourages racially biased assertions about white (or at least Western) superiority. Even a less virulent version of that tension, from an American standpoint, would be rendered as: "They attacked us and we beat them fair and square, and we have been taking care of them ever since while they have not carried their share of the load." This sentiment reflects nascent isolationism in a significant way not seen since the 1930s.

The outside world can be irritating. It can be ungrateful for American efforts. But it cannot, with safety or for prosperity, be ignored. Even in the unlikely event the movement in Europe toward greater economic and financial unity is stalled, the United States can hardly turn its back on the outer world and withdraw. As large as the American GDP is, it would not remain large enough. Today the world, for better or for worse, is really and no doubt permanently interdependent. Much of the material in this chapter shows that from many vantage points.

For a concrete illustration, consider what happened in many nations when in the October 1973 war the Arabs decided to use oil as a political weapon, setting up an embargo on supplies to nations considered friendly to Israel and cutting back production as a part of that move. In less than a year, OPEC had raised prices fourfold, causing a worldwide recession. As a consequence, the price of raw materials such as cocoa or copper plunged. In the many one-crop countries of the Third World, that drop decreased their incomes while raising their energy costs from the previous level of $22 billion a year. Bolivia, dependent more than 50 percent on tin, and Chile on copper, Colombia on coffee, Ethiopia on coffee, Mauritius on sugar, the Sudan on cotton, and Ceylon on tea—all suffered greatly. By coincidence, poor climatic conditions also then lowered food supplies. Inflation then went to double-digit figures in many countries. Using a baseline of 1970 as 100, by mid-1974 Japan's figure was 148, the United Kingdom was 143, Italy was 138, the United States was 123, Chile was 3730, Argentina was 385. In short, although the targeted countries suffered, nations like Japan, which had carefully tried to keep out of Middle Eastern issues, were seriously affected as well. And many of the most seriously affected were nations that had little or nothing to do with the question at all. It is not only not possible to turn away from world affairs and pursue isolationism. Neither is it practical to practice unilateralism, "going it alone," pursuing an active role that ignores the effects on others. For in the end, as we see here, the effects could not be confined, and the whole world, including those who tried this gambit, suffered as a consequence.

We are not arguing, of course, that either isolationism or unilateralism is not a policy option. We are merely pointing out that they are not choices open in a foreign policy that has pretensions to being prudent.

That being so, what are the practical choices?

Alternatives for U.S. Policy

Let us take the economic issues first, especially those flowing from the question of the utility of encouraging free trade.

Among the supposed impediments to free trade, it was popular some years ago to list multinational corporations at or near the top of the list. It was argued that their power was so great as to sideline any efforts of governments to control them. That proved not to be true. Governments *are* sovereign, and they will prevail on issues of control unless they are too inefficient to enforce their own regulations. Some years ago, when a European consortium had agreed to build a natural gas pipeline from Russia to the West, the United States objected and ordered the Dresser Corporation, with headquarters in the United States, not to participate. The French government at the same time ordered Dresser-France, the French subsidiary, to honor its contracts. Both parts of the company obeyed their respective governmental authorities.

There are indeed things governments cannot effectively control, like money, which will flow to where it is either safest or most profitable. But corporations, multinational or not, have to operate where they can be seen.

The real impediments to free trade stem from the decisions of governments. Such decisions are not made at random. In part they reflect domestic pressures from within their territories. In recent years, protectionism of this kind has often been found centered around agriculture, as we saw in Chapter 16. That is probably in part because growing food is so central to existence that, deep in the human psyche, no person wants to see that requirement for life as dependent on some other people. Remember, too, that protecting agriculture can be a legitimate choice. There is nothing in international law or custom that requires that nations subscribe to completely free trade. The argument for free trade is an economic one, not a legal or moral one.

In Chapter 16 we examined briefly the issue of American trade policy, with particular emphasis on Europe. Now a broader discussion is required.

The economic argument for free trade is that, by allowing free passage of goods and services across national frontiers, those who are most efficient in producing any particular good will prevail. If the United States makes the best computer chips, given free trade, the computer chip industry in other nations abroad will wither away. In turn, if beef is grown more efficiently in Argentina, even taking into account transportation, Argentinian beef will supply the market everywhere. Free trade implies *specialization* of function and *division* of labor. By the same token, though, such specialization and division imply vulnerability. When the British went over to free trade in the nineteenth century and their industrial product became preeminent around the world, British agriculture was whittled down because it was comparatively too expensive. In both World War I and World War II, Britain almost starved at certain points because of this vulnerability.

So free trade implies at the very least a relatively stable and peaceful world—which is exactly what people everywhere thought existed between, say, 1871 and 1914. Looked at that way, the great changes in Eastern Europe and the demise of the old Soviet Union, although not necessarily guaranteeing a peaceful world, raise more hopes that such a world will come. One plus for free trade.

But free trade is essentially a capitalist idea in the most fundamental sense, keeping government's role in economics at a minimum. Now, in contemporary times, when government is always intervening in one way or another in economic affairs, whether in the form of taxation or unemployment insurance and the like, it becomes extremely problematical to say in *economic* results what would happen in a modern economy if government had hands off. (We could be sure that unpleasant noneconomic things like pollution would increase!) That is just as true for the United States, the foremost advocate of free trade in the world, as anywhere abroad. So free trade no longer means *really* free trade. Once that fact is recognized, the arguments focus on the degree to which governments permit economic transactions to be determined by market mechanisms. And different peoples with different cultures and different governments have different ideas on this point.

Furthermore, what a people feel is desirable and warranted in terms of controls exercised by business over their own markets varies considerably from nation to nation and even within any nation. In the United States for many years, "fair pricing" laws prevented discounting on many products where the "suggested price" prevailed, because otherwise the supplier would move the product to a different retailer. In Geneva, Switzerland, some years ago—and probably still—if you lived on one side of the street named route de Florissant, you got your milk delivered by Company A. Across the street, Company B delivered. Such competition as there might have been between Company A and Company B was in lining out which districts each would serve as exclusive territories. This kind of cartelism is found everywhere in the world to some degree or other.

But even if governments in capitalistic countries do intervene in economic affairs, it is still true relatively that in the United States business is allowed very extensive control over its own decisions. We as Americans happen to think that is good, even if the economy sometimes goes from boom to bust and less competitive units are forced out of business. But to a people like the Japanese, for example, who have a culture where employment is generally a lifetime commitment, the very idea of eternal ferment and change, forcing companies out of business, is a highly negative concept. It is this feeling that is a fundamental source of the closed Japanese market.

Such cultural differences showed up very clearly in January 1992 on the occasion of President Bush's trip to Japan. After Commerce Secretary Robert Mosbacher rejected one Japanese offer, Japanese officials, led by Trade Minister Koza Watanabe, replied by charging that American officials, in the name of "free trade," were trying to force Tokyo into a "managed" trade system that would guarantee a certain level of Japanese imports of specific American products. That in fact was true, but not because Americans preferred it that way. Given a closed Japanese system due to internal constraints, simply doing away with trade barriers in the form of tariffs would have produced no result.

Enough has been said to indicate what is indeed the truth: the alternatives for U.S. policy on free trade are not so simple as being for it or against it. Complete free trade, to be really complete, would imply the government withdrawing from any controls. On the other hand, moving to an economy sheltered behind high tariff walls, as in the 1930s, would be counterproductive.

So the choice is between doctrinaire free trade, in the sense of removing all governmental restrictions on incoming products and seeking the same from abroad, and a policy that generally fosters free trade while being willing to make exceptions or even exclude certain areas. With such a choice, the latter certainly exceeds the former in possible benefits, always provided America does not get drawn into a retaliation mode rather than making decisions as they affect its own industries.[30]

The ecology issues are, by their very nature, difficult to handle because most of the solutions to pollution require international cooperation and restraints and are costly. In most developed nations there is a continuing struggle between the "production" and "environmentalist" factions. And while developing nations are strongly interested in having the industrialized nations control *their* own pollution, they are not much interested in controlling the pollution they create themselves, given their need for economic development. Consequently, the best policy choice for the United States probably rests with getting consensus among the industrialized nations first, rather than seeking accords in bodies like the United Nations, with well over a hundred interested parties.[31] The pioneer arms agreements for control of nuclear weapons were negotiated in this manner, with those most involved first trying to find agreement among themselves. If this basic strategy can be followed on environmental issues as well, it should then be possible to utilize the United Nations as a fact-spreading body to make pollution control techniques and environmental protection programs easily available worldwide.

On the related population issue, the American people can do little directly about it. Family planning and birth control issues cannot even be resolved at home, and any international initiatives would cause all kinds of complicating reactions abroad. In terms of feasibility, the policy issue here is most likely to become focused on two things: foreign aid and immigration. It seems probable that the population explosion clearly on the horizon in many of the poorer sections of the world will produce unrelieved misery. (Ironically, that very population explosion is in part due to the successful efforts to control many of the diseases that used to sweep over such areas.) Something can be done with technical aid to increase crops and produce a more useful road network and food distribution system. But there are limits.

The pressures on the United States to allow a generous level of immigration are likely to increase. Again, there is an irony here: one successful immigrant then brings his relatives—who also have relatives. It does not take a right-wing skinhead to notice that the culture of the United States is being changed as present immigration patterns continue. Historically, the United States has thrived on immigration, for one thing because it has often been those with initiative and ambition who have sought entrance. And America has been a multiracial society in some senses from the very beginning of its history. There are advantages here and also prices to be paid. What is perhaps most fundamental is that the United States cannot receive people as new citizens simply because they suffer political persecution at home or at least make that claim when seeking admission. Because the United States is one of the most attractive places in the entire world to live (given its political stability and standard of living), in an age when the population explosion is already underway, America simply could not absorb the influx without the most serious kinds of disruption of its own society. Consequently, immigration issues are likely to become very important in future foreign policy. The alternatives for choice here seem almost certain to be focused on degrees of restriction rather than the open doors so characteristic for much of U.S. history. In 1992 serious problems were occurring in Europe because of population migrations in the aftermath of the Soviet demise and the resulting Eastern European instability, demonstrating the disruptive potential of this problem.

Policies on the open seas seem in good shape. America has recognized a standardized twelve-mile limit and taken jurisdiction over fisheries in areas off its coasts that were being depleted. It has cooperated in the development of the law of space. Only in the specific area of seabed mining has the United States differed with the international community. That issue, as we indicated, is more a theoretical problem than a practical one at present, although one day that will change. The argument for multilateral ownership and operation of seabed resources is that all the nations of the world should share in anything of value that is located in what has historically and traditionally been open seas. But tying up such exploitation of resources with a bureaucracy as cumbersome as the United Nations is almost required to invent for such a purpose (with many officials appointed merely to share the honors among all the regions of the world) would not be the best way to go. Those who have the technology for such exploitation ought to do it. What should be done to resolve the argument is to use the United Nations to provide for sharing the proceeds. Indeed, in time those proceeds might actually finance the U.N. and relieve the members from annual expenses to operate it.

In this chapter we have been examining some very complex problems and issues. If there is a common theme to the analysis of U.S. alternatives and the pros and cons of such choices, it is that Americans must not approach any of these questions on a doctrinaire basis. It is because of the very complexity of these issues that we have for the most part refrained from too specific suggestions, preferring to stay with principles capable of adaptation to changing circumstances.

Notes

1. U.S. Department of Energy, *Monthly Energy Review,* November 1991, p. 87.

2. Oil import figures are taken from the U.S. Energy Information Administration, as published in the *World Almanac* for 1991, pp. 182–83.

3. *World Almanac,* pp. 182–83. Interestingly, though, in terms of overall energy use, since 1973 the transportation sector has increased less than residential and commercial.

4. Figures are from 1040 Income Tax Forms and Instructions for 1991, Internal Revenue Service, Department of the Treasury, p. 5.

5. The ratio of federal debt to GNP would, according to this, reach 52.5 percent, a level not seen since the mid-1950s when the government still owed huge amounts from World War II. *New York Times,* January 30, 1992, p. A8.

6. Of course, that value is affected by other factors, also. In the late 1980s daily capital movements assumed great importance, a subject we shall return to later.

7. The counterargument is that that very help has provided foreign nations excessive influence in the United States. Also, see Chapter 18, note 19.

8. Currencies for many reasons do not reflect their "true" exchange value. One amusing attempt at comparisons is the *Economist*'s "Big Mac" chart, compiled since 1986. The idea is to compare the prices of Big Macs against what they "should be," if the price of the dollar implied by the exchange rate is compared with the actual exchange rate. By this standard the range of over (+) or under (–) valuation of the dollar goes, in percent, from +273 (Russia) to Denmark and Sweden at –49. France was –33, Italy was –34, and Germany was –20—a good clue as to why U.S. tourists were groaning at costs in Europe in 1993.

9. Paula Stern, "A Burdensome Legacy: The Reagan Administration's Trade Policy," *The Brookings Review,* Fall, 1991, p. 38.

10. See Peter F. Drucker, "The Changed World Economy," *Foreign Affairs,* Spring 1986, p. 782.

11. As one would expect, within Congress different segments sought various advantages or protections for their constituents in the bill, and a host of legislators "added changes here and there—on everything from cattle and wheat to lead and zinc. . . ." Johnson, *America as a World Power,* p. 361.

12. Stern, p. 42.

13. According to Bill Frenzel, however, "[M]ost GATT member states thought the 1988 act was contrary to the General Agreement." Bill Frenzel, "A Close Call for Free Trade: American Business Returns to the GATT Fold," *The Brookings Review,* Fall 1991, p. 46.

14. The first steps toward North American trade integration occurred with the Canada-U.S. Free Trade Agreement, which took effect on January 1, 1989. The NAFTA agreement was signed in October 1992. Some 2000 pages long and extremely detailed and technical, its ratification was politically controversial at this writing.

15. As John Spanier points out, this phraseology is not entirely accurate geographically, but it is close. And "it has the advantage of emphasizing the frustration of most developing countries over the continued division of the world between the rich and poor nations." John Spanier, *Games Nations Play,* 7th ed. (Washington, D.C.: Congressional Quarterly, 1990), p. 226. For an excellent discussion, see Charles W. Kegley, Jr., and Eugene R. Wittkopf, *World Politics: Trend and Transformation,* 3rd ed. (New York: St. Martin's Press, 1989), Ch. 5. With the end of the Cold War and the disappearance of the Second World (Soviet-led Communist nations), the term "Third World" no longer seemed appropriate. But no one had a better alternative, so the term continued to be used.

16. Spanier, *Games Nations Play*, p. 227.

17. *The Economist*, December 14, 1991, in the article, Survey: Turkey, no page number.

18. *The Economist*, December 21, 1991-January 3, 1992, p. 19.

19. For a first-rate yet succinct discussion of population trends, see Nafis Sadik, "World Population Continues to Rise," reprinted in Jeffrey Elliot, ed., *The Brown and Benchmark Reader in International Relations, 1992* (Dubuque, IA: Wm. C. Brown Publishers, 1992), pp. 291–96. Initially published in *The Futurist*, March/April 1991, pp. 9–14. There are important differences from nation to nation, though. For example, population growth in the LDCs accelerated from an average rate of 2.4 percent in the 1960s to 2.6 percent in the 1980s, while there was a dramatic drop in China and other Asian planned economies. This difference could become even greater in the 1990s. United Nations, *Global Outlook 2000: An Economic, Social and Environmental Perspective* (New York: United Nations Publications, 1990), p. 204. For the argument that rapid population growth in poor countries, "plus the corresponding damage to their ecological base . . . prevents the development that would be their salvation," see Nathan Keyfitz, "Population Growth Can Prevent the Development That Would Slow Population Growth," in Jessica Tuchman Mathews, ed., *Preserving the Global Environment: The Challenge of Shared Leadership* (New York: W.W. Norton, 1991), pp. 39–77.

20. Technically, the hemispheric safety zone was established in consultation and by agreement with the other American republics (except Canada, which was not a member at that time of the Inter-American agreements). In the Declaration of Panama of October 3, 1939, they established a 300-mile zone in both oceans, extending from the southern border of Canada to Cape Horn.

21. *The New York Times*, May 3, 1992, p. E 5.

22. Even with the 35,000 ton spill from the *Exxon Valdez* in 1989, accidents accounted for less than intentional spills.

23. Papp, *Contemporary International Relations*, 2nd ed., p. 499. The Vienna Convention of 1985 created an institutional framework for protecting the ozone layer, followed two years later by the Montreal Protocol. It was hoped that by the year 2000 there would be an outright ban of chemicals that destroy ozone. *New York Times*, June 9, 1992, p. B 8.

24. The history of international treaty efforts to reduce pollution is discussed in a paper prepared for delivery at the International Studies Association 1992 meeting. The paper is by Detlef Sprinz and Tapani Vaahtoranta and is entitled "The Structural Explanation for International Air Pollution Control." A "bio-diversity" treaty also was signed at the Earth Summit, its purpose to preserve diversity and protect ecosystems. America refused to sign on the grounds that the treaty did not do enough to protect intellectual property rights and would make the financing of certain projects mandatory.

25. *The Economist*, May 9–15, 1992, p. 19. There are many sources of information becoming available on these problems. See, for example, Theodore D. Goldfarb, ed., *Taking Sides: Clashing Views on Controversial Environmental Issues*, 4th ed. (Guilford, CT: Dushkin Publishing Group, 1991). See also John L. Allen, ed., *Environment 92/93*, 11th ed. (Guilford, CT: Dushkin Publishing Group, 1992).

26. Now that there is no longer a Soviet Union highly active in military space competition, it is easy to forget statistics such as, in 1986 the Soviets spent $30 billion com-

pared to America's $18 billion and launched 91 times compared to the United States' 9. The Soviets also had the only operational antisatellite system in the world. See Frederick H. Hartmann, *Naval Renaissance: The U.S. Navy in the 1980s*, p. 238. It was well recognized in the U.S. armed forces, if not by the American public generally, that whereas in World War II control of the air was a prerequisite for control of the sea or land, today control means control in space.

27. Each launching of a space flight inevitably adds to the total. Items like hammers represent things inadvertently "dropped."

28. See our discussion in Chapter 18.

29. *New York Times,* January 5, 1992, in the "News of the Week in Review" section.

30. Some who support this alternative generally advocate a tit-for-tat strategy with nations who depart from GATT rules and norms. See Judith L. Goldstein and Stephen D. Krasner, "Unfair Trade Practices: The Case for a Differential Response," in Robert E. Baldwin and J. David Richardson, eds., *International Trade and Finance, Readings,* 3rd ed. (Boston: Little, Brown, 1986), pp. 114–121. The article was initially published in *American Economic Review Papers and Proceedings,* May 1984, pp. 282–87.

31. The problems America encountered at the 1992 Rio Earth Summit, noted earlier, provide a case in point. For the view that there is a need for a "considerable surrender of sovereignty by the major powers [and] more multilateral action and less nationalistic posturing," see Dennis Pirages, *Global Technopolitics: The International Politics of Technology and Resources* (Belmont, CA: Brooks/Cole Publishing Company, 1989), p. 213.

20

Guidelines for American Foreign Policy in a Complex World

There is a built-in handicap for anyone who tries to judge accurately what any contemporary problem in American foreign policy really involves. What will later seem to be the core facts and conditions will almost always be obscure at the time in a cloud of miscellaneous clutter. It is only in retrospect that full clarity emerges.

Some very weird notions can be introduced into the discussion of the problem by those who either do not understand what they are observing or who have some kind of axe to grind. In the last 50 years or so it has been seriously and repeatedly proclaimed by would-be pundits that a number of things would not happen that did, and that another set of things that did not happen would.

High on this list is the proposition that Germany, divided into two states by the Cold War, would never again be unified. It was even claimed that East

Germans—despite the Wall—liked being separated! In Germany, it was argued, even two separate vocabularies had grown up, and whole generations were accustomed not to think of the people *drüben* ("over there") as kinfolk. That argument flew in the face of nationalism. And not just anybody's nationalism but German nationalism—the nationalism of a people where the Bundestag library's first entry under "the reunification question" dates back to Napoleonic times. A few decades were not going to eliminate this national feeling.

The second argument for why Germany would not be reunited was that the Soviet Union would never permit it. That argument, too, was repeated ad nauseum in print. Yet that was not correct.

In discussing the Korean War and why and how it began, we showed U.S. officials unanimously agreeing that it was ordered by Moscow. But in fact Moscow endorsed an action initiated by the North Korean leader. That distinction makes a difference—especially because the conviction of a worldwide Communist aggressive movement seeking all opportunities for aggression led to important U.S. commitments and judgments in the decades that followed. Evidence of fissures in the Communist group of states was ignored—such as the earlier dissolution of the Comintern announcement, or later, the open diatribe between the Communist Chinese and the Soviets—clear evidence of dissension publicly known in the years before the United States went into the Vietnam War believing that it was blunting a new attack by a united world Communist movement. In fact, instead, the United States was delaying the breakup of the Communist bloc!

Then there was the misjudgment of the former Soviet Union itself, of its strength and ability to compete with the United States on a worldwide basis. Here the record is more comforting, because many Americans were sure the whole time that the Soviets would eventually take a tumble if they were contained, like George Kennan predicted.

We could go on with the illustrations. But the point is probably made. Many things that are not so are nonetheless believed and believed implicitly, and then acted on, often at great cost. Since Americans know comparatively little history, and since the "documentaries" shown on television are written in many cases by individuals whose adult memory does not include the period "documented," distortions—often subtle—easily creep in. So we know how the problem tends to become cluttered with misimpressions. But what can be done about it? After all, to err is human.

We have tried very consistently in this book to show how the situation can be improved. There is, of course, no substitute for serious study of the American past as the point of departure. Therefore, we have gone to pains to sketch in many of the events of our past, often as they were understood at the time as well as how they appear today. Historical knowledge is a must as a beginning. Colin S. Gray, in a 1992 presentation, cited Arnold J. Toynbee's observation about Thucydides.[1] Toynbee, the famous historian of the rise and fall of civilizations, looking back on his life, tells how he was teaching Thucydides when World War I broke out in 1914. Thucydides took on a new meaning for Toynbee because Toynbee had now encountered a similar historical crisis in his own time:

"his present had been my future. But this made nonsense of the chronological notation which registered my world as 'modern' and Thucydides' world as 'ancient.' Whatever chronology might say, Thucydides' world and my world had now proved to be philosophically contemporary." Toynbee is doing no more than recognizing the truth of Thucydides' own assertion, that he was sure, given the nature of humans, that the kind of events he was describing would reappear in much the same way at a later time. Gray's point is that it is highly dangerous to assume at any point that the world has fundamentally changed in geopolitical terms—even if the end of the Cold War ends one form of tension in the world.

But historical knowledge without some sort of organizing principles is merely a welter of facts, leading only to confusion. The wrong set of principles, as we saw, can lead to expensive policy mistakes, but one must have some set of principles or it will be impossible to make judgments. Such an analytical framework must be simple enough to use but accurate in its guidance. It is for that reason we provided the four cardinal principles. They open the door to understanding not only policy positions toward international problems. They also enable us to understand the international context. We shall come back to the cardinal principles as guidelines in more detail a bit later. But here one comment must be made, for one of the most important reasons why evaluations of events can go astray is that people fail to look at all four values of any problem—the plus and the minus of each of the two alternatives for any serious major question. If we instead cultivated the intellectual habit of looking at problems consistently through the discipline of counterbalancing national interests we would not make such mistakes as assuming that the Germans had become indifferent to reunification, or that the Soviets would never agree to evacuate Eastern Europe, or that the Chinese and Soviets would get along well indefinitely. Such assumptions typically leave out the opposing values in the equation. To each argument that something is so, we need to posit a counter question as to why that might not really be true. What in the history of each relationship would lead to an opposite conclusion? What might undermine what at any given moment might appear solid? What might induce any player to change his play? A serious student of American foreign policy could hardly err by cultivating the habit of asking about why something might be true or not true "forever." The advantages of any choice never exist without disadvantages, and the rejection of one alternative is never without lingering thoughts about the conceivable advantages if one had chosen otherwise.

A student of American foreign policy, at the end of a course, will go away remembering relatively little about events or facts or dates. But if he or she closes this book without taking away a standard or judgment of policy, we have all wasted our time.

James Reston in his memoirs tells how Henry Kissinger once explained to Tony Day of the *Los Angeles Times* his approach to difficult problems in a difficult time. "What a national leader has to do at such a time is to take his society and the world, insofar as the issues are international, from where it is to where it has never been." What made that a real test of leadership was that the leader "cannot prove the destination is desirable until the society or the world gets there."[2] Kissinger thought that Churchill, de Gaulle, Lincoln, and Roosevelt all shared that sort of vision.

From the beginning of this book we have pointed out that decisions on foreign policy questions, made in the here and now, are directed at a foreseen future, and that the vision of that future is greatly influenced by the past experience of the nation. That perspective is inevitable and built-in because only one's view of the past can provide any way of projecting the potential future. If a foreign policy analysis does not take care to show how American attitudes and judgments can be traced back to U.S. historical experience, that policy stands on weak ground.

In America's own case it was extremely fortunate in its historical experience, benefiting more than most by several happy coincidences. It was geographically remote from the quarreling great powers of Europe, whose jealousies and quarrels effectively barred them from intervening in American affairs during the initial and vulnerable decades of weakness. Only the British were really in a position to do America great harm, because they controlled the sea-lanes in those early decades, and the British had more than half their mind on Napoleon and France, so their effort against the United States in the War of 1812 was not wholehearted. Nor was that war pursued to the end. Revolutions swept Europe in 1830 and 1848, and by the 1860s the powers were concentrating on the changes in the balance of power being wrought by the unification of Italy and, particularly, Germany. By the end of the Franco-Prussian War in 1871, the United States had already passed through its second vulnerable period, the Civil War. As we quoted General Sherman, after that it was simply not feasible for any European great power to bring meaningful war to the U.S. shores. Nor did the prolonged great power peace make it likely that anyone would try. Then came World War I. America's past experience with the great powers made Americans highly reluctant to become involved, or even to choose sides. The population, including so many recent immigrants from nations now on both sides of the fighting, reinforced U.S. clinging to precarious neutrality. Only when the Germans showed their contempt for U.S. protests by resuming unrestricted submarine warfare did America reluctantly enter the war. When it did, it astounded the powers by the scope and rapidity of its response. The motto on American victory medals showed—not for the first time—the habit of intertwining practical considerations like preserving American rights at sea with idealistic slogans proclaiming a wider context for U.S. efforts.

But the euphoria over the victory of World War I soon ended. And once there was no threat on the horizon, the fact of a threat was soon forgotten. America turned its back on international cooperation to maintain peace, only to find that war again threatened at the end of the terrible thirties. The difference this time was that, once Hitler was defeated, Stalin gave America no time for any nascent tendency to retreat into an isolationist or unilateralist shell before he made the Soviet challenge clear. The United States was soon caught up with decades of Cold War and resistance to what American policymakers considered an organized Communist conspiracy to subvert the Free World.

Where America's early experience had taught the value of staying out of foreign affairs as much as possible, especially where the great powers were concerned, America's experience in the twentieth century has taught the American people not to expect to retire from a frontline role. Indeed, it has created a tendency for the United States to accept the lead role in some respects in whatever is going on anywhere. To some extent, that position is, of course, inevitable, simply because America is a superpower, but the tendency needs watching.

How Well Does Our Past Prepare Us for Now?

But the world is changing again, and drastically so, before our very eyes. How well does that past prepare Americans for what they face now? The answer in one respect is very positive and reassuring: history has taught Americans, above all else, to be flexible.

In these days, when the old dramas of the settlement of the West are much more rarely seen, their place being taken on TV by urban shootings, Americans may tend to forget the self-reliance bred into generations of their forebears, beginning on the East Coast and continuing ever westward for two hundred years. In terms of Western civilization, what is in the United States today Americans created—all of it within a relatively small amount of time. Nothing was here in the early 1600s when the first settlers arrived. They had to create everything, including churches, schoolhouses, factories, laws, and regulations. They learned self-reliance, and they learned flexibility. They had to, to survive. They also learned the trick, hardly known outside U.S. frontiers, of spontaneous organization among people to provide a response to a problem. Therefore, if there is any trait in which Americans excel, it is the ability to adjust. That will stand the United States in great stead now.

The one important weakness Americans have is, not surprisingly, the obverse side of this strength. America is a pendulum country. Being pragmatic as well as idealistic, it tends to find solutions by trying different things, moving by increments to find a consensus. This pendulum swing has been demonstrated many times in U.S. history, the ability to reverse course entirely—as in the transformation from isolationism to involved superpower. America's very flexibility allows people to make these changes very fast. The weakness is in the tendency to go too far each time.

When Dean Acheson tried to soothe congressional fears that the Truman Doctrine was the harbinger of perpetual tinkering in other peoples' affairs, he said—as we quoted him—that each situation would be judged on its own merits. That the United States did not intend to follow aid to and defense of Greece and Turkey with aid to and defense of everybody else who might be threatened by world communism. And yet that Truman Doctrine was then followed by an Eisenhower Doctrine superimposed upon a Middle East hardly put to that kind of pattern. It was a Middle East to whom a Soviet threat seemed very far-fetched. The United States followed that under Johnson with the Vietnam War, surely the example above all examples of just what Acheson said would not be done.

Now that the Soviet Union as such no longer exists, now that the Warsaw Pact is no more, there are many voices arguing for severe reductions in defense spending. They are not wrong to do so, because the threat has at this point been very drastically reduced. The problem is that armed forces are easier to reduce than to increase, easier to take apart than to rebuild. A force which becomes ineffective because it is starved for spare parts or loses incentives to keep qualified petty officers and sergeants takes years to restore. America's last experience with such a problem indicates that five years is a minimum and seven years is probably more accurate. So when the United States makes changes in its military to adjust those forces to the requirements of a new foreign policy, Americans should remember that the timescale, for example, for Eastern Europe to become free, or for Germany to be reunified, or for the Soviet Union to be transformed from a monolith to a so-called commonwealth of independent states is very much smaller than the timescale for improving seriously impaired armed forces. Threats can increase or reduce faster than the forces needed to cope with them.

The point here, although made about armed forces, is really a generic one, applying to the whole spectrum of policy: change occurs in different arenas or for different problems at nonuniform rates. It does not pay to let one aspect govern the whole.

Kissinger is right about farseeing statesmen. With everything in flux, they see what is critical and how the important pieces are related. Often the future is fairly predictable in its larger outlines, but how it comes about makes a difference too. Despite the fact that many people and even experts thought otherwise, it was always unlikely that the Soviet Union would be able permanently to maintain its grip on Eastern Europe. Or that Germany would permanently be divided. What was unforseeable was just how the change would come about, the actual circumstances. We could see that the Soviet Union could not stand the strain, once it began, after 1955, to give aid and support to widely scattered movements around the world, Communist or not, so long as they served to harass the West. The Soviets could not aid those movements, keep Germany divided and East Europe subordinated, and at the same time improve their standard of living at home. But the breaking point came very suddenly.

Breaking points, dramatic change points, always do. The Nazi-Soviet Pact of 1939, the Japanese attack on Pearl Harbor in 1941, the collapse of the Soviet Union in 1991—all of these came from long roots but with startling suddenness. And the next problems that America will confront will have been both long roots and may also create crises without much or any advance notice. The very flexibility of Americans *could* keep the United States ready to adjust as need be, rather than to pendulum-swing too far from a pragmatic approach.

The Cardinal Principles as Guidelines

We have presented four cardinal principles as guidelines to deciding foreign policy choices. Because the world environment can and does change very abruptly from time to time, not all of these four principles seem equally relevant at any one time. The conservation of enemies, for instance, was particularly apropos when U.S. military planning was assuming America might fight both China and the Soviet Union simultaneously—an almost suicidal choice. That stark reality eventually led to the China card. Serving equally well the national interests of Communist China and the United States, the China card relieved serious strategic pressures on America. But now that the Soviet Union has collapsed, there may be temptation to dismiss conservation of enemies. After all, there is hardly a meaningful enemy in sight. But the principle is still valid. It helps to explain international behavior, because few states are so irrational as to take on gratuitously and continue with a whole host of enemies. As we have pointed out, the amount of enmity one encounters is substantially influenced by the alternatives one chooses. If for the moment this principle seems unnecessary to Americans, we need only wait. Sooner or later serious security problems will reemerge. It is the way of the world. This reality is what the idea of the balance of power, so long derided by Americans, was always meant to convey. When one power declines, others automatically are enhanced. When the danger recedes on some nation's frontiers, others will be tempted to make a greater nuisance of themselves.

We have already discussed past-future linkages. The utility of the remaining two cardinal principles is obvious, regardless of a Soviet decline or a changing world. Third-party influences are always operative in a multinational world. No foreign policy decision is ever truly bilateral, since third parties are affected, and their reactions must be taken into account. The argument in 1991 between the United States and the EC over agricultural subsidies in the Uruguay Round of GATT has far-reaching implications for the Japanese restriction of their rice market. Each nation, talking to another, is always also talking to the rest.

Counterbalancing national interests is the most useful principle of all, because it continually reminds us about choices. Making foreign policy *means* choosing between alternatives. The significance of the choices in terms of their results is by no means uniform, but the major choices are always about whether to go in or stay out, to become more involved or less involved. Major choices set directions, like an arrow on a map. Because they set directions, increasing or decreasing involvement or commitment, they normally can best be understood as pairs of opposites, each with a plus and minus value. For example, as American public irritation with Japan's trade policies grew in 1992, sentiment was increasing for some retaliation. There was an argument that could be made for that policy. The most obvious drawback was that Japan could retaliate to the retaliation. But if nothing were done and the trade imbalance continued, the continuing American irritation would gradually undermine U.S. postwar policy toward Japan, although avoiding an outright trade war. These are four different values, and all of them have to be weighed before a decision is made.

If we picture the world's nations as aware of the rest while dealing each with another, as considering alternatives while gauging the future through the lenses of their past, we shall have a fairly accurate model of reality—especially if we add that the general prudential rule within which most serious decisions will be made is to avoid unnecessary enmity.

The Outlook for the Future

By our very emphasis in Part Five, as we examined major decision areas, it is apparent which choices we believe will be important for U.S. foreign policy in the years just ahead. Before summarizing our conclusions in these chapters, though, five points require special emphasis, some of which do not readily fall into decision area categories at all, but all of which will unquestionably be very significant in the next decade.

We have devoted much space to arms control. But despite undoubted progress, there remains a very serious danger of nuclear proliferation. Today, only the United States, China, Russia (and at this writing three other USSR-successor states: Ukraine, Belarus, and Kazakhstan), France, and the United Kingdom officially have nuclear weapons, but most observers are convinced that Israel does, and maybe Pakistan. It is apparent that Libya, Iran, Algeria, and North Korea are moving toward nuclear capability also, and only the 1991 Gulf War halted Iraq's efforts. And many other nations (including Germany and Japan) have the ability to join the nuclear club if they should choose.[3]

The most important multilateral mechanism whose purpose is to inhibit the spread of nuclear weapons is the 1970 NonProliferation Treaty.[4] With China's accession in 1992, all five of the declared weapons countries are members. But Pakistan, Israel, and India (which detonated a nuclear device in 1974) are not. Moreover, since Iraq had been a member and still was covertly building weapons, it's clear that mere membership is no guarantee of nonproliferation. While the inspection efforts of the International Atomic Energy Agency (IAEA) are designed to help control proliferation, they cannot detect *covert* programs. And although the 27-member London Nuclear Suppliers Group's efforts to establish export control guidelines for nuclear transfers have some utility, they regulate only the members (and even in that regard success has been moderate). A similar effort to control the export of missile technology is the eight-nation Missile Technology Control Regime (MTCR).[5] It could contribute to nonproliferation, but the MTCR has been largely ineffective and today as many as 15 or more *Third World* countries are developing or deploying ballistic missiles.

With the spread of technology and "know-how," nuclear weapons and advanced delivery systems are within the reach of scores of nations. Indeed, most of the equipment and material needed to develop the first generation of atomic weapons is available even to *research* establishments and universities, worldwide.[6] Another key factor in the mix is the enormous cadre of Ph.D.'s in science and engineering returning to the Third World with First World degrees, as well as the problem of now-unemployed former Soviet scientists.

It is not only that proliferation is probable. It also is that even though the direct threat to American security has receded, few other nations' power problems have been diminished equally. Indeed, in many instances quite the contrary is true. India and Pakistan, for example, have not relaxed their antagonism, any more than have Turkey and Greece. Iran, frustrated over its lost war with Iraq, makes plans for new military power while pushing ahead to acquire nuclear devices and a potent missile capability. Israel's possession of nuclear weapons is not doubted by any of its neighbors and remains a classic temptation for those nations to go and do likewise. Iraq can in time rebuild and increase its arsenal, once international controls relax. The history of enforced disarmament clearly indicates that the determination of a disarmed nation to rearm has again and again been greater in the long run than the will of those who disarmed it.

The list could continue but the point is made. If the United States no longer directly confronts a formidable enemy such as the Soviet Union once was, there is still the potential for involvement in many other potential conflicts, especially in, but not confined to, the Middle East. And these particular conflicts include a great danger to become nuclear. The United States clearly must continue to exert itself to inhibit and prevent such nuclear proliferation. But it is apparent that success will not be easy to achieve.

A second set of problems we have discussed deserves additional mention. They focus on the world economy. Not since the Great Depression of the 1930s has the world confronted the kind of situation that existed in the early 1990s. Even with all the media reporting available to Americans, very few were getting the kind of information they needed to understand what they were seeing. Very few, for example, even knew that Canada had an unemployment rate greater than America's own; that the United Kingdom's economy was also in recession; that the Tokyo stock market had declined very significantly. The economic difficulties were indeed spread throughout the industrial world, with serious spinoffs to the unindustrialized.

The one international commodity support organization with a fairly successful track record, the International Rubber Agreement, was in difficulty as the price of natural rubber dipped below the support level for only the second time since 1985. In early 1992, commodity price levels in general were at a very low mark in real terms. The all-items index had fallen by 10 percent in 1991 alone, and was 38 percent below its peak at the beginning of 1989. Metal prices had dropped by 20 percent from the April 1991 peak. Aluminum prices fell to where most aluminum producers had to run at a loss. Copper prices slumped; wool reserves expanded. Cotton prices fell. The statistics could be quoted almost endlessly, but all to the same effect. The economy of the whole world had slowed drastically. In this gloomy set of statistics, of course, was also promise of a kind—low prices might in the end increase sales and act as a stimulus to new production.

Much in the economy depended on other factors. Americans were aware of junk bonds used to finance acquisitions. This device produced "high-leveraged" corporations: meaning that they had a very high debt to finance. Americans knew, too, about the "collapse" of real estate values connected to the savings and loans scandals. But this "collapse" was as nothing compared to what was happening in Japan. There, the continuing decline of real estate values was potentially much more serious. The supposed values of such properties (inflated out of sight of their real values for this specific purpose) were the security for much bank-loaned money. The collapse could be drastic. The crux of the problem here was that fiscal policy is the last reserve of national sovereignty, and interference from abroad is usually both resented and ineffective. In early 1992 the Japanese were so busy pointing with scorn to American industrial inefficiency and over-spending that they did not notice the potential abyss opening at their own feet. The problem here is that the world's economy is now highly intertwined, and decisions in any one of the major industrial states affect everyone else. But everyone else has limited say in how things should be handled *there*.

Only the oldest Americans remembered the Depression. It did not begin, of course, with the Wall street crash in October 1929. What began then was a contraction in credit caused on Wall Street when margin was called in to cover falling prices. That soon caused an overall credit constriction, which spread to the German use of short-term borrowed money to pay war reparations for World War I. As money flow stagnated, businesses were unable to pay their debts, and the problem spread to suppliers and to employees, who had to be fired when profits evaporated. Much of this same chain of events was happening in 1991 and 1992, and the likelihood of a light-hearted early recovery was small until a debt-laden world could dig itself out bit by bit. The economic stringency, worldwide, set real limits to what the United States could choose to do if that choice cost money. It would be difficult, for example, in a continuing economic stagnation, to give Russia substantial financial support while Americans were clamoring for the government to do something at home. In short, while this situation continued, the government's foreign policy alternatives would be correspondingly restricted.

A third set of problems we have noted but which needs further underlining is the pressure of population on resources. As always, it is in the countries least able to support population increases that the increases are most marked. In the present economic circumstances, it is highly doubtful that the United States will be able to maintain the flow of humanitarian aid on its previously generous scale. There is the connected problem of disease, once assumed to be well in hand by virtue of worldwide programs under the direction of the World Health Organization. Africa now accounts for half the active AIDS cases in the world; even larger numbers of people there are starving. There are simply no easy solutions here.

A fourth item that needs specific underlining is the now marked decline of socialism throughout the world, and the almost equally marked increase of democratic institutions. Socialism's decline, especially in the defunct Soviet Union, has spilled over into many changes elsewhere. Only a few doctrinaire holdouts remain, such as Castro's Cuba or the North Korean dictatorship. That change is not only good ideologically for the United States but it is good for the people whose situation has changed. If the twentieth century showed anything clearly, it was that, apart from defense, highways, and a few other areas, state-run institutions should be a preferred last resort if people want abundant supplies at reasonable costs.

Even so, the collapse of communism and the spread of democracy should not lull us into thinking that these changes will usher in a time of ever-decreasing tensions. There was a time, before Karl Marx, when communism did not exist. But the world was not warless. Nor will the spread of democracy ensure peace; what it ensures is that the will of a people, rather than that of the few in power, will prevail. Israel is a democracy and seriously split between those who want peace with their neighbors by trading the occupied areas and those who want to colonize these areas and maintain Israel's security by force. France was a democracy in the last decades of the nineteenth century when it took colonies around the world. Democracy and peace are not synonyms because nationalism's main trait is to encourage an emotional identification of "us" against "them." Since nationalism is required for the unity of a nation, we cannot expect that this reality will change greatly.

The final set of problems concerns how to deal with the expanding post–Cold War role of the United Nations, especially in what are generally (and often somewhat inaccurately) called "peacekeeping" operations. As Secretary General Boutros Boutros-Ghali wrote in 1992: "Since 1988 14 new operations have been established. . . . In the first half of 1992 the number of U.N. soldiers and police officers increased fourfold. . . ."[7]

U.N. peacekeeping has a long history. Although there were some exceptions, for the most part prior to the end of the Cold War, peacekeeping operations involved a physical presence interposed between disputants, with the general goal of helping to control unresolved conflicts. In some cases the mandate was simply to observe, supervise, and report on compliance with or violations of a cease-fire. Sometimes the mission was largely fact-finding. Occasionally the mandate was broader. Following the 1956 Suez Crisis, the United Nations Emergency Force was created to direct and administer the cessation of hostilities, bring about and supervise the withdrawal of forces, and then seek observance of, and report on, the cease-fire. Nearly all these cases met four criteria. First, the issues were not central to the U.S.-Soviet relationship. Second, the operations involved the minimum use of force or none at all. Third, the operations occurred only with the consent of the parties. And fourth, the troops came from non–Cold War states (at least usually) and served under the command of the Secretary General.

But in the new era much appeared changed. Many of the new operations were set up to *help implement* negotiated settlements of long conflicts, such as in El Salvador and Namibia. Protecting the delivery of humanitarian supplies became a new task, in Cambodia and Somalia. In 1993 terms like "peace enforcement" were in vogue, as the United States, Britain, and France sought to enforce U.N. resolutions concerning no-fly zones in Iraq, and U.N. members debated whether to authorize the use of force in the former Yugoslavia. In some of these operations, the use of force was evident, superpower forces were involved, there was a national chain of command, and the operation did not have the consent of all of the parties. The cardinal principle of past-future linkages at work here was because nations were still basking in the afterglow of successfully enforcing U.N. resolutions in the Persian Gulf War.

But the Persian Gulf scenario is most unlikely to be repeated, and new situations may bear little or no similarity. One must be careful of drawing lessons from what probably was relatively unique.

America must keep two things clearly in mind in this area. First, it must not lose sight of the fundamental fact that the United Nations is largely what the member states have made it. The U.N. is state controlled, and as such is *more a reflector than a determiner of* policies. Thus, where relationships among key nations generally are cooperative, they can utilize the U.N. effectively to achieve or protect their interests. But if those relationships change for the worse, "the U.N." will be less effective. Second, even without Cold War problems to hinder effective action, the U.N. will be limited in what it can accomplish. The dispatch in 1992 of thousands of troops to Yugoslavia (UNPROFOR), for example, did not resolve that problem.

The United States needs to think about the role of the U.N. and America's participation in its various operations in the same way the United States thinks about other American policy choices. America will always be influenced by ethical concerns. Moral, ethical, and emotional factors should, of course, play a role in its decisions. But those factors should not predominate. America must be strategically sensitive and must ask how each situation and suggested policy alternative will affect its vital interests and the global tension level. It should use the cardinal principles to help determine whether a serious involvement ultimately will be beneficial. And it has to be prudent and ask the following questions *in the right order:* (1) What is the desired possible outcome? (2) What will other nations, acting in their own interests, tend to do that will influence that outcome? (3) What *then,* if anything, should the United States do, either cooperatively or unilaterally?

Finally, policymakers must recognize that any coalition military operation, let alone one involving a host of very different nations, is intrinsically difficult. Nations have their own individual command, control, and communicatio structures and processes, logistic supply organizations, strategies, military doctrines, training bases, technologies, political constraints, rules of engagement, and so on, and bringing these factors together and developing a smoothly functioning military machine is a task of momentous proportions. Individuals without military expertise very often fail to recognize or adequately take this into account, apparently just assuming that once the political decision is made all things military can be worked out easily. But life is not so simple. Thus while in certain cases there may be sound *political* reasons to undertake action, it is almost inevitable that if that action is done there will be at least some degree of *military* inefficiency. That is not to say a military action should not be done, only that the complexities need to be understood up front, with decisions made accordingly.

A Sense of the Possible

Part Five examined eight major decision areas for U.S. foreign policy; in each discussion we examined the leading alternatives. Let us summarize our judgments here. The decisions being made to deal with area 1, the former Soviet Union, are on the right track. Russia must be helped, but only where the help will not be dissipated by a lack of serious effort at economic reform. It is also highly desirable to offer aid for the specific purpose of accelerating nuclear disarmament. In area 2, policy toward Eastern Europe, the United States has the advantage that these states (in most cases) had a history of association with Western culture before they were confined to the Soviet orbit, so they may take more readily to economic transformation. On the other hand, the nationalist mishmash and ethnic conflict that has historically existed in the region is not an easy thing to handle. The United States should be very hesitant about becoming enmeshed in the civil strife in this area.

Policy toward the European Community remains on track. America, which encouraged the movement toward European unity, would be ill-advised to try to turn the clock back. But America is correct to insist that its interests also be observed as the EC moves forward with its plans. Without continuing pressure by the United States, no reforms would occur in Western European agricultural subsidies. At the same time, the United States must not forget its own extensive subsidy programs. America cannot have its cake and eat it too.

Middle Eastern policy has had its ups and downs. Ever since the Israelis began to be a West Bank occupying force, U.S. sympathies for the former underdog could be expected to diminish. In principle, the pressures finally exerted by the Bush administration were well overdue, even if they could not be used until the Gulf War had transformed political conditions in the area. The U.S. pressures, correctly understood, are not at all anti-Israel, for if Israel does not settle its problems, it cannot ultimately survive. That may have sunk in.

Japanese policy has wobbled in the past years, although its main emphasis is on working out the frictions that have grown in American-Japanese relations. That task has not been easy, partly because there is a tendency for Japan to look down on the United States as a sort of economic has-been. This attitude tries American patience, particularly because Americans used to make the same assumptions in reverse about Japanese inferiority. There are serious problems in the relations between the two countries. It is not that U.S. policy is incorrect but rather that there may be little that can be done effectively to head off further friction—especially since Japan is less worried about its security since the breakup of the USSR.

The policy toward China, the seventh area we looked at, almost went astray during Reagan's early years, but his administration finally came to a much more practical point of view. The United States cannot effectively pressure China, whatever Americans may think about China's human rights violations. There are just too many Chinese to pressure, and their government is not doing everything wrong: The move toward a market economy is now more advanced in southeast China. Adapting a more militant stance toward China also violates the principle of the conservation of enemies at a time when relations with Japan are so unsettled and unpromising.

The final area is one in which the United States has been severely criticized by the Third World and even by its Western European allies: policy on the environment and natural resources. The question here is more complicated than often reported. For one thing, since the United States is *the* great consumer nation in the world and also the single greatest polluter, etc., because of the sheer magnitude of U.S. environmental challenges, it is only misleading if the United States pledges to do more than it probably can accomplish in any short span of time. Where the policy has been very mistaken, however, is in allowing the impression to gain credence that the United States is preparing to ignore the rest of the world on these issues. That impression began when the Reagan administration refused to sign the new Law of the Sea agreement, and it was reinforced by events before and during the 1992 Earth Summit. The appearance and the reality are farther apart than many foreigners think, and it is ill-advised to allow the wrong appearance to become well established.

But there is, as we hope we have shown, much more to a prudent foreign policy than a carefully assembled list of alternatives, however useful that may be. Behind any set of choices is always a set of philosophical assumptions. As Kissinger puts it, to get where we have never been takes a sense of direction. The besetting sin of any State Department or foreign office is to become lost in the trivia of the day, to sink back into a reactive mode as the cables pour in and require decisions on issues posed by others. To overcome the built-in inertia that condition produces takes determination, takes effort. That effort must, above all else, be intellectual. Anyone reading this book will easily forget much of its detailed discussions not long after closing its covers. What hopefully will remain in mind are those passages where we have attempted to describe the international *context* in which decisions have been made, America's degree of understanding of that context, and how that in turn affected U.S. choices of policy *direction*.

In facing such problems as crop up in the coming decade, the United States must keep a sense of the possible. America cannot eliminate all problems. Nor is it going to arrive at a peaceful and prosperous world that maintains itself simply by the kindness implicit in human nature. That unfortunate limitation on progress arises out of the very context of the international scene. The world is fragmented into sovereignties, and nothing is likely to change that situation, except on the fringes. It is probably good that the EC has been formed and that many other European nations want to become members. It is certainly good for the world to confront its trade questions through the GATT series, and hopefully continue to reach mutually useful agreements. It is very good that the world is giving increasing attention to the pollution of the seas and conserving the earth's environment. These are all measures of cooperation, and all are good. But one must not forget that it is cooperation by states, by sovereign entities, by units who can opt out or obstruct. With about 180 or so such entities, universal agreement is hard to achieve. Theoretically and, of course, logically, nations could do away with this problem by all agreeing to a world government. That will not happen. And if it did, it would bring such culturally diverse peoples as Americans and Japanese into a much more intimate context that, almost without question, would exacerbate the problems we have now. But the fact that sovereignty will continue ultimately means that some of these units will decide to go their own way, to the disadvantage of others. That is the ultimate reason why we cannot expect to arrive at a condition of perfect world accord.

A sense of direction is important in a people confronted by foreign policy problems—a sense of agreed direction. Nothing vitiates results faster than an inability to agree on the goals. Hitler might have been stopped before he caused so much tragedy if there had been sufficient consensus on stopping him.

A sense of direction is even more important in the nation's leadership, a sense of direction and an instinct for knowing how to move the ponderous ship of state in the right direction. Ronald Reagan used to be criticized when he was president for not knowing the detail of policy. That became quite obvious from time to time. On the other hand, Jimmy Carter immersed himself in the detail of policy. Hardly a greater contrast in style could be found in the history of the last decades. Reagan's foreign policy was generally successful, though, and Carter's quite unsuccessful. Even if we wanted to explain the difference by saying that they faced quite diverse foreign policy situations, and that their success or failure can be attributed to that, we would have a hard time making that argument stick. They faced much the same problems. And Carter's policies were not all unsuccessful—take the Camp David Accords—and neither were all of Reagan's policies a success. But, for all that Reagan ignored detail and Carter absorbed it, the real difference that stands out in their approach to foreign policy is that Reagan knew the direction he wanted to influence things toward and knew how to get the government to go in that direction. Whatever one thinks of the merits of SDI, once Reagan was informed that a defense might be possible, he moved quickly and decisively to orient a major aspect of the government's defense efforts in that direction. Carter had far less of a strategic sense and only a limited practical grasp on how to get where he wanted to go. His intimates often complained that *he* was the program.

The consideration of foreign policy alternatives takes place not in quiet but in a very busy world that keeps thrusting side issues upon us while we are trying to think. We saw how President Bush, in setting policy and commitment during the Gulf crisis, also had to juggle domestic considerations (especially the Congress), along with creating a workable allied coalition, working both sides of the problem simultaneously. Even when the issue is not war or peace, the same problem exists. As Gorbachev moved increasingly to a commitment to withdraw from Eastern Europe and to lower Soviet defenses, he, too, repeatedly had to satisfy his internal constituencies that the United States would not simply take advantage of these moves. Correspondingly, President Bush, as he saw how vulnerable that made Gorbachev and, therefore, how much Gorbachev had to rely upon a proper response from the United States, had to deal with elements in his staff who saw what was occurring as an opportunity to weaken the Soviet Union. What did occur, with the policies of both "superpowers" moving more or less in tandem toward cooperation, took nice judgment on both sides, especially by the leaders. As Bush correctly replied to UPI correspondent Helen Thomas, when she asked who NATO's enemy was, now that the Soviets were less and less of a problem, the new enemy "is *unpredictability*. The enemy is *instability*."[8]

It takes determination, therefore, to concentrate attention on those issues of preeminent value. There is only so much energy and time available to an administration, and the media often tempt the leaders off into sidepaths. The good chief executive in a nation like America will be one who, like a general under attack in the field, can still concentrate his attention on the assault he means to make rather than to be drawn off into reacting to his enemy's initiatives. And the same thing is true of a people. They cannot do everything, and certainly not all at once. So they must learn to choose efficiently and effectively by identifying those most critical problems and the foreign policy direction implied by the alternatives. They must learn to weigh the merits of these alternatives, while not forgetting that, in an ever-changing world, the calculus of advantage for anything done or not done can and will change.

Notes

1. Colin S. Gray, "The Changing Nature of Global Power?" a paper prepared for the Fifteenth Annual Aerospace Wargaming Symposium, Air University, March 3–6, 1992.

2. James Reston, *Deadline: A Memoir* (New York: Random House, 1991), p. 419.

3. South Africa acceded to the NPT in 1991, thus agreeing not to be a nuclear weapon state. In early 1993 it stated that it had assembled six nuclear weapons before 1990, when it ended its weapons program and dismantled the weapons. For an interesting discussion of South Africa and other "repentant" states, see Leonard S. Spector, "Repentant Nuclear Proliferants," *Foreign Policy*, Fall 1992, pp. 21–37.

4. For a useful discussion of the NonProliferation Treaty, International Atomic Energy Agency inspection capability, and the Missile Technology Control Regime, see John M. Deutch, "The New Nuclear Threat," *Foreign Affairs*, Fall 1992, pp. 120–34.

5. Members of the MTCR are the United States, Britain, Canada, Japan, Germany, Italy, Spain, and France.

6. On this and the following point, see the provocative article by Tom Clancy and Russell Seitz, "Five Minutes Past Midnight—and Welcome to the Age of Proliferation," *The National Interest*, Winter 1991/1992, pp. 3–12.

7. The total number of operations between 1948 and 1978 was 13. The quote is from Boutros Boutros-Ghali, "Empowering the United Nations," *Foreign Affairs*, Winter 1992/1993, p. 90.

8. In *At the Highest Levels: The Inside Story of the End of the Cold War* (Boston: Little, Brown, 1993), Michael R. Beschloss and Strobe Talbott devote a considerable part of their book to detailing these points. The quote is from p. 192.

Index